THE BASIC WRITINGS OF COMMUNISM

THE COMMUNIST MANIFESTO, the momentous proclamation of 1848 by Marx and Engels.

SOCIALISM: UTOPIAN AND SCIENTIFIC, the classic Marxist attack on competing theories of socialism.

STATE AND REVOLUTION, Lenin's application of Marxist teachings to the Russian Revolution.

THE FOUNDATIONS OF LENINISM, in which Stalin writes of the consolidation of Russian communism.

A selection from THE NEW CLASS, Djilas' statement of the revisionist position.

COMBAT LIBERALISM and ON PRACTICE by Mao Tse-tung, expressing the new orthodoxy.

And, finally, THE NEW PROGRAM OF THE COMMUNIST PARTY OF THE SOVIET UNION, announced by Khrushchev in 1961, which appears here in its entirety—a comprehensive statement of the aims and ideals of the Communist Party.

BANTAM POLITICAL SCIENCE

ESSENTIAL WORKS OF
MARXISM

edited by Arthur P. Mendel

ESSENTIAL WORKS OF MARXISM

A Bantam Classic / published December 1961
2nd printing .... August 1962
3rd printing ...... April 1963
Bantam Matrix edition published January 1965

5th printing ..... January 1965	9th printing .... May 1968
6th printing .... February 1966	10th printing ...... April 1969
7th printing .... October 1966	11th printing .... January 1970
8th printing .... July 1967	12th printing .. November 1970

Bantam edition published September 1971
14th printing
15th printing

ACKNOWLEDGMENTS

"The New Class," from THE NEW CLASS by Milovan Djilas, is included with the permission of Frederick A. Praeger, Inc.

"The Conspiracy of Ivory Tower Intellectuals," from RESPONSIBILITY AND HISTORY by Laszek Kolakowski, is included with the permission of the publishers and editors of EAST EUROPE.

Bantam Books are published by Bantam Books, Inc., a National General company. Its trade-mark, consisting of the words "Bantam Books" and the portrayal of a bantam, is registered in the United States Patent Office and in other countries. Marca Registrada. Bantam Books, Inc., 666 Fifth Avenue, New York, N.Y. 10019.

PRINTED IN THE UNITED STATES OF AMERICA

CONTENTS

INTRODUCTION

"A specter is haunting Europe—the specter of communism." This famous pronouncement made by Marx and Engels over a century ago no longer adequately describes the movement they began. Communism no longer merely haunts: it has conquered an area vastly greater than the Europe of Marx's time and it is daily expanding its influence.

Marxism has won the devoted allegiance of people of various backgrounds the world over. It has had particular success among the educated and idealistic youth that has so often served as the "vanguard" of successful political revolutions of diverse ideological complexions. Why has the movement been able to inspire such intense devotion among many young men and women of good will and high ideals? It would do us no good to deny this devotion; to argue, for example, that brute external military force or unscrupulous internal subversion are alone responsible for the success of international communism. It is far simpler to defend ourselves against force than against ideals and ideas. But it should be abundantly clear by now that this easy way out can only do us immeasurable harm by misdirecting our response to the great challenge.

Efforts to explain the success of Marxism have concentrated on two sets of factors: the main themes in the Marxist ideology and the prevailing social, economic, and political conditions under which they make their appeal. While giving due emphasis to the significance of these latter factors, this collection of readings and the accompanying commentaries will focus attention on the ideology itself. The basic rationale for this is the belief that if carefully read, the Marxist publications will enable the reader to reconstruct the essentials of the Marxist world view and, thereby, to understand its appeal, particularly to the youth of the underdeveloped economies.

This underlying purpose has determined several other aspects of the book. Any collection of this sort presents the editor with a number of choices. What authors should be represented? Which works of these authors should be used? Should entire publications be included or only short excerpts? What should the commentaries attempt to do? Since the "Marxism" that concerns us today is mainly that of Russia, Eastern Europe, and China, where Marxist parties are in power and on the basis of this power are rapidly extending their ideological influence, the collection will concentrate primarily on what might be called "eastern Marxism." The choice of publications is based on a desire to present works that reflect different sides of Marxism, that are associated with different periods of Marxist history and, finally, that are short enough to be presented without editorial deletions. This last requirement is especially important: only by reading entire works or complete, unedited sections can one follow the logic of the argument, grasp the theme as a whole as it is grasped by those who accept it, and, finally, avoid the probably inevitable distortion that results when editors of controversial material select and gather a large number of brief excerpts. Since the purpose of the collection is to enable the reader to understand the appeal of Marxism under certain conditions, the commentaries will be primarily concerned with setting the stage, describing the prevailing background conditions and summarizing essential aspects of the ideology not covered in the selections. The commentaries are not intended to serve as an accompanying critique, disclosing factual errors, logical inconsistencies, and politically motivated distortions.

The collection is divided into five sections. The first section contains works by Marx and Engels, summarizing the foundations of "scientific socialism." Publications by Lenin and Stalin comprise the following two sections, and together they trace the evolution of Russian Marxism, showing the dramatic and fateful molding of West European Marxism to fit the conditions of an economically underdeveloped country. A central theme in this analysis of Russian Marxism concerns the reasons for and the consequences of a premature socialist revolution in a society lacking the economic, political, and cultural conditions that most western Marxists considered indispensable for a successful socialist society.

The fourth section deals with the problem facing the Soviet Communist Party in a society that is rapidly acquiring an urban character and is, consequently, promoting among

Soviet citizens attitudes and desires similar to those prevailing in the "bourgeois" West. The selections and the commentary in this section concern expressions of these new tendencies and the Party's ambiguous response to them, its vacillation between concession and repression. To illustrate this ambiguous response and to present the present goals of the Party, the new program of the Soviet Communist Party, published in July 1961, is reprinted in its entirety.

The closing section of the collection contains two writings by Mao Tse-tung, and a recent (1959) statement summarizing the present official Chinese Communist views and revealing the fundamentalist, doctrinaire impatience with what are considered signs of a decline in Russian revolutionary zeal.

Where existing Soviet translations have been used they have been checked with the Russian originals and when necessary modified to bring them closer to the original or to modernize syntax and spelling. In the case of the two selections by Marx and Engels a similar attempt has been made to bring the spelling, syntax, and, on several occasions, the terminology of the translations up to date.

I would like to express here my gratitude to the Praeger Publishing Company for their kind permission to use the chapter "The New Class" from *The New Class* by Milovan Djilas; to the publishers and editors of *East Europe* for allowing me to use their translation of the essay from Laszek Kolakowski's *History and Responsibility*, which appears in complete translation for the first time in the present collection; and to *The New York Times* for permission to reprint the draft program of the Soviet Communist Party.

I.
THE FORMATION AND APPEAL OF "SCIENTIFIC SOCIALISM"

The essential features of Marxism, as well as its appeal, should be more readily understandable to the Western reader than they seem to be; since, as has often been said, Marxism is a quite legitimate offspring of Western culture and civilization. Moreover, this is true for "eastern" Marxism as well as West European Marxism, notwithstanding major modifications of the ideology to fit conditions in Russia and in the underdeveloped areas of the world. So much is this the case that one might even consider contemporary Marxism as a vehicle for expanding Western culture eastward.

The foundations of Marxism include secularism, empiricism, rationalism, materialism, and an optimistic faith in progress—themes that have largely dominated European cultural history from the Renaissance until our own day, in spite of recurrent attacks from powerful opposing intellectual currents. Karl Marx has himself been called the "last *philosophe*," the last advocate of the eighteenth-century Enlightenment; and while one might well question his being the last, everything he wrote justifies the classification itself. Following his father's footsteps, Marx was a devoted disciple of the French rationalists. He believed firmly in man's inherent rationalism and virtue, however much both might be crushed and distorted by the evils and irrationalities of society. He was convinced that social and historical processes followed laws no less universal than those of physics and chemistry, that these laws were accessible to rational men, and that guided by them mankind could create the good society. In fact, he regarded all human history as a step-by-step advance in the direction of such a society, free of ignorance, injustice, and cruelty and enjoying the abundant material fruits of man's scientific genius. Any theory that even verged on the supernatural or the irrational or that seemed willing to tolerate social evil met from him as

1

bitter an attack as any eighteenth-century rationalist unleashed.

The rationalistic Enlightenment, however, was only one of a number of Western intellectual tendencies that were synthesized in Marxism. Another, of far longer duration though obviously related to the Enlightenment, was the Judeo-Christian demand for social justice. If Marx's father was a deist, his grandfathers on both sides were rabbis. This may or may not have been a source of Marx's deep sympathy for the "injured and the insulted" laboring masses; but whatever the source no one who reads Marx can fail to sense this intensely passionate sympathy. Attempts to ignore this aspect of Marxism, for whatever reason, are not only an injustice to Marx, but also a powerful barrier in the way of understanding one reason for his appeal.

There was, of course, nothing unique in Marx's denunciation of the social evils that accompanied the industrial revolution. A host of social critics of all countries incessantly decried the abuses fostered by the emerging urban-industrial civilization—Robert Southey, Thomas Carlyle, Samuel Coleridge, Charles Dickens, Charles Reade, John Ruskin, Matthew Arnold, George Sand, Ralph Waldo Emerson, the "Christian Socialists" (de Lamennais, Maurice, and Kingsley), the "Utopian Socialists" (Owen, Fourier, and Saint-Simon), and many others. After reading what these writers had to say about the shortcomings of industrial "capitalism," it would be difficult to believe that anything a modern eastern Marxist could say had not been said with equal passion a century ago in the West.

But if both the rationalism and "scientism" of the Enlightenment and the ethically based social protest against industrialism prevailed quite apart from Marx, what then did Marx add? His fateful achievement was to unite both tendencies, to weave a fabric of science and ethics, and thereby satisfy perfectly the need of the age for "preaching in the garb of science." Passionate social criticism and ethically grounded appeals for support of utopian blueprints were inadequate to stir, mobilize, and direct revolutionary sentiment. They were too inconsistent with the mood of the times and with the prevailing intellectual tendencies. The rationalism, skepticism, and empiricism inherited from the Enlightenment and the compelling influence of the hard, brute facts of urban-industrial life furnished poor soil for what seemed sentimental idealism.

It was between 1830 and 1842, which included Marx's university years, that Auguste Comte published his *Cours de philosophie positive,* the foundations of modern sociology. During this same period, 1831-1836, Charles Darwin toured the world on the *Beagle,* gathering the insights and the information that were later to appear in his theories of evolution. Ludwig Andreas Feuerbach published his *Geschichte der neureren Philosophie* in the years 1833-1837 and his *Das Wesen des Christentums* in 1841, thereby paving the way later followed by Marx from Hegelian idealism to naturalism and materialism. In the fifties, one meets the works of the extreme materialists, Büchner, Moleschott, and Vogt, and the first compositions of the great positivist, Herbert Spencer. With works like these setting the tone for the young intellectuals there was little patience for bare ethical appeals. Then, as now, however they might be moved by a call for social justice, few intellectuals could respond unless the appeal was somehow associated with the latest truths of science and sociology. The synthesis of science and ethics is, thus, a primary reason for the success of Marxism, both in Marx's time and our own.

But in Marxism, the socially conscious intellectual finds more than scientific sanction for his ethically motivated sympathies. He finds as well, because of the particular character of Marx's "scientific" theories, absolute certainty that his ideals will be realized. It was this feature of inevitability that made Marxism then, and continues to make it now, so appealing to young idealists willing enough to run risks in the name of social justice, but eager for assurance that the risks, deprivations, and sacrifices will not be made in vain.

It would not be an exaggeration to say that virtually all of Marxism is directed toward demonstrating this inevitability in a rigorously "scientific" manner, toward proving beyond any doubt that social justice must come. The basis of both Marx's merger of science and ethics and his proof of the ineluctable victory of socialism can be found in Hegel's philosophy of history. While a student at the University of Berlin, Marx was drawn into the incessant quarrels over what Hegel "really meant." Although Marx was later to attack Hegel's idealistic or transcendental views, he retained the Hegelian pattern of historical evolution. According to Hegel, history represented an unfolding, a gradual emergence of a metaphysical World Spirit or Universal Reason. Each age was dominated by a particular "spirit of

the times" that placed its stamp on all aspects of the period.
As a natural response to these dominant features, there
gradually appeared opposing tendencies. These tendencies
matured, quantitatively accumulating until they produced a
great qualitative transformation. From this transformation
there emerged a new society, representing a "synthesis" of
the positive, durable features of the old society (the thesis)
and the successful new tendencies (the anti-thesis). Thus,
from the ancient Middle Eastern civilization through the
classical civilization of Greece and Rome, to nineteenth-century Teutonic Europe, humanity progressed dialectically
from thesis, through anti-thesis, to synthesis, which in turn
became the thesis for the next cycle. No matter how unjust,
evil, or irrational any institution appeared to be, its very
existence, its "reality" proved it was rational and even desirable, for somehow it played a necessary part in the unfolding drama of human progress.

While ruthlessly purging the supernatural elements from
this conception of history, Marx retained the form. For
Marx, no less than for Hegel, history followed a lawful and
necessary pattern that advanced inevitably from phase to
phase. For Marx, also, there was a central theme in each
period that gave it a special character. Finally, the Marxist
evolution is similarly a dialectical one, each period creating
the "germs of its own destruction," and all seemingly negative features in history both justified and required by the
thesis-anti-thesis-synthesis pattern. The essential difference
between the Hegelian and the Marxist philosophy of history
involves the occupant of the driver's seat. In place of the
traditional God of Western Christendom, Hegel had set
Universal Reason or Spirit. Marx further depersonalized the
"first cause" by giving the reins to an inanimate economic
process, formulating thereby a philosophy of history strangely
similar to the animistic myths of primitive man. Marx took
this crucial step under the guidance of the "left Hegelians"
who rejected both Hegel's metaphysics and religion in general. The writer exerting the most influence on Marx in
this direction was probably Feuerbach, who completely
reversed Hegelian relationship of spirit to matter by arguing
that the mind and its creations merely reflected man's
prosaic, essentially economic requirements and functions.

Marx's economic determinism was one result of this merger
of Hegel with Feuerbach. According to this theory, the character of every age is determined by the "mode of produc-

tion" of that age; that is, by the way people satisfy their material needs. The "mode of production" in turn contains two components: the "productive forces," which include such things as available technology, skills, material resources, and sources of power (manual, steam, electricity, and the like) and the "productive relations," that is the relationships between people engaged in producing material goods. The most important "productive relation" is that between those owning the "means of production" (i.e., land and machinery) and the laboring masses who use these means under the direction of the owners to satisfy society's economic needs. It is this relationship that divides all known human societies throughout human history into "classes"—slave and slave owner, serf and lord, proletarian and capitalist.

The mode of production, particularly the class relationship of production, represents the economic "substructure" which gives form and character to the social, political, and ideological "superstructure" of society at each stage in human history. In effect, this means that the prevailing intellectual ideas and ethical ideals, the artistic tastes and political institutions, and everything else that comprises the culture and civilization of the period are consistent with and reflect the interests of the dominant class, the class in control of the means of production. Resting on such theories, economic determinism can be summarized by the famous statement that "it is not the consciousness of men that determines their existence, but rather it is their social existence that determines their consciousness."

Economic determinism provides most of the Marxist "scientific" sociology. With it the Marxist possesses an absolute confidence in his ability to give simple, clear, rational, and thoroughly objective explanations for virtually everything that happens in man's personal and social existence. However, even though this social theory can be applied to all past historical periods, it does not in itself explain the historical process that leads humanity out of one phase of its evolution into and through another. And while the comprehensiveness of Marxism as a system for explaining social events at any given time is unquestionably an important part of its success among intellectuals, the principal reason for its appeal to revolutionaries is its theory of historical determinism which assures them of victory.

Marx attempted to provide this necessary proof, to give specific content to the Hegelian dialectical form, by his economic analysis of the rise and the predicted fall of the capitalist society. If the idea of progress and the Hegelian dialectic provided, respectively, the inspiration and the formal framework of Marx's historical inevitability, the painstakingly detailed analysis published in *Capital* demonstrated precisely how the dialectic worked in practice, how one economic system created "the germs of its own destruction" and the foundations for the next society that must follow. As an additional attraction it provided this demonstration for the one specific transition that really mattered, at least in the West—that from capitalism to socialism. This almost revered, but largely unread, treatise not only became the bedrock on which the Marxist bases his views of the past, present, and future of capitalist societies; it also served as proof for Marx's historical philosophy as a whole, for his theories of the dynamics driving mankind from any past society to its immediate successor.

The entire argument in *Capital* rests on the labor theory of value. As was the case with virtually all the parts that Marx fused into his system, this concept was borrowed from other writers, in this case from the "classical" economists such as Adam Smith and, especially, David Ricardo. It is primarily a price theory, according to which "commodities" should exchange on the basis of the "socially necessary" labor time devoted to their production. In other words, the amount of time a laborer works to produce a particular item determines its "exchange value": two products of equal labor value would thus be exchanged for one another.

Having incorporated the labor theory of value, Marx derived from it a second step in his demonstration: the theory of "surplus" labor value. According to this theory, the worker does not receive in wages an amount equal to the value of the goods he produces. We must keep in mind that the influence of the "pessimistic economists" still prevailed, as did the conditions promoting their pessimism. Drawing their conclusions from their own observations and from official government reports on working-class conditions in England during the industrial revolution, economists like Malthus and Ricardo argued that an "iron law of wages" existed that would keep wages down to a minimum necessary to meet the workers' basic needs. Marx accepted this and drew the conclusions he desired: on the one hand, the labor theory of value argued that labor created all the value of the goods sold by the capitalist; on the other hand, an "iron law of wages" kept the laborer's income down to a subsistence minimum; consequently, it must follow that the workers were not receiving the full value of their labor, that there was a large "surplus" kept by the capitalist owner of the means of production.

Now this alone could evoke indignation among those sympathetic with the plight of the working class. But moral condemnation did not constitute a scientific proof of the inevitable demise of the immoral exploiter. We come closer to this desired proof when we see what, according to Marx, the capitalists did with their exploited surplus value. It would not do merely to draw up lists of capitalists' luxuries; for this, too, would carry one no further than moral indignation. In fact, Marx was actually more lenient with the capitalists on this score than were other socialists, but it was only because this leniency would allow him to undermine more thoroughly and irremediably the foundations of capitalism itself. Marx argued that the capitalist could not spend most of his profits on personal luxuries even if he had wanted to do so. He was surrounded by competitors who tried to increase their share of the market by lowering the costs through increased productivity, that is, by using more machinery. In order to stay in business the capitalist had to keep up technologically, to invest his profits in the purchase of machinery.

When we add this process to the labor theory of value we can begin to see the tensions that Marx believed must one day destroy the capitalist system. The capitalist is forced by competitors (who are similarly forced by other competitors, and so on) to purchase machinery. This involves the displacement of workers. According to the labor theory of value, however, only workers produce value and surplus value (profit). Therefore, the result of more machinery is a lower rate of profit! To compensate, the capitalist lowers wages and buys more price-cutting machinery. Two completely opposing tendencies evolve. As a consequence of the labor displacement, the "industrial reserve army" increases and its pressure forces further reductions in wages. This means that the mass purchasing power provided by the working class continually declines. The market for goods contracts. But the struggle for markets forces the competing capitalists to introduce more and more machinery and thereby produce more and more commodities. The supply of goods expands. There is only one possible outcome: overproduction crisis accompanied by intolerable misery for the working classes and a deepening in their hatred of the system.

Every such crisis brings the revolution nearer. During each crisis the smaller capitalists go under. Their factories are absorbed by the sturdier, bigger enterprises, and they themselves fall into the ranks of the proletariat. In the wake of each crisis, ever-increasing numbers of workers find themselves more concentrated in these continually expanding industrial centers, more ruthlessly exploited and more passionately opposed to the exploiters. At a certain phase of this process, intellectuals of bourgeois origins, who sympathize with the distress of the working class and who are able to foresee the inevitable doom of the bourgeois system, defect from their own class and take the side of the workers, enlightening them and molding them into a powerful revolutionary force. While all this is taking its natural course, the indispensable prerequisites of a properly functioning socialist economy are being prepared by a continual advance of science and technology, a growing interdependence between the various parts of the economy, and a maturation of the "consciousness" of the working class. When these tendencies have "quantitatively" increased to the necessary point, they will merge to produce the desired "qualitative" transformation of the economy and the society. Once, in other words, the economic "substructure" has developed to a point that it can furnish both the necessary conditions for the overthrow of the capitalist state and the economic prerequisites for socialist society, then the socialist revolution will occur.

The Marxist had unqualified faith that with the establishment of socialism the history of humanity would enter a new phase. The era of classes would be at an end. Man would no longer exploit man, but each would freely join with others to better the lives of all. Marxists envisioned a society and economy that fully, rationally, and harmoniously utilized man's labor and genius for the ever greater satisfaction of human needs. The core of their utopia was the belief that "the free development of each is the condition for the free development of all."

Here was a vision and a way for many intellectuals alienated for various reasons from their society. There was nothing lacking. The goal combined Judeo-Christian love, justice, and charity and the economic hedonism of the post-Renaissance materialistic civilization. Moreover, the explicit appeal was to the mind, as it must be in an age of science and skepticism. Also, since most intellectuals, then as now, were products of urban society and reflected urban preferences, they were more receptive to Marxism than to competing socialist theories that often criticized industrialization and urbanism as such and explicitly or implicitly yearned for an idealized, rural life. Marx, on the contrary, lauded the industrial and technical achievements of capitalism, attacked only the bourgeois system that he considered responsible for their misuse, and scoffed at the defenders of the "idiocy of the countryside." The principal appeal, however, as this introductory commentary has emphasized, was the "scientifically" grounded assurance of ultimate victory. And along with this went the protection that the dialectic provided against the disillusionment usually resulting from short-run defeats. Since they expected historical evolution to follow a dialectical pattern, the Marxists believed that things must get worse before they got better and that failures simply meant that conditions for success were not yet ready. Defeats in no way disproved the theory itself. While waiting for the proper circumstances, finally, the Marxists were spared the frustrations experienced by those who urged the capitalists or "their governments" to be more charitable or who drafted reform programs and appealed vainly for support.

The Marxists, thus, possessed a credo that in their eyes allowed them to give objective, scientific answers to virtually all questions; that inspired in them an absolute faith in victory and safeguarded them from disillusioning defeats; and that gave them a sense of fighting for a way of life that at last would satisfy simultaneously all human and social needs. But, as the later history of some Marxist parties was to show, there lay many dangers in this inspiring and encouraging credo. By basing the goal and the movement on what were claimed to be objective, scientific facts and laws, Marxism fostered more than a sense of self-confidence. The emphasis on science and its role in the revolutionary movement provided a powerful support for the emergence of a guiding elite, an intellectual vanguard who alone knew these laws and who therefore must direct the movement.

Perhaps the most distressing consequence of this dependency on science as the ultimate justification for values was the opportunity it allowed the Marxists to escape the burden of responsibility for their actions. According to them they are merely carrying out the demands of the historical situation and are in no way personally to blame for the unpleasantness required by history. The effects of this historical justification were even worse in Marxism than they were in other similar credos because of the "dialectic" which not only tolerated evil and distress, but actually expected them and, in fact, depended on them for the historical dynamics that must in time bring victory.

A similarly unfortunate attitude was fostered by the class theory that played so great a role in Marxist social and revolutionary theory. What room was there for honest co-operation and compromise between the Marxists and their opponents when these opponents and their programs and actions were explained away by the class theory? Also, what hopes were there for gradual reform within the existing system when class theory defined the existing state as a bourgeois state completely unable to legislate in the interests of the oppressed masses? A powerful tendency toward elitism, an inability to reach a serious and sincere understanding with the "class enemy," and an expectancy of revolutionary violence required by both the class theory and the Hegelian dialectic—these are a few of the components that comprise the Marxist heritage.

The two selections that have been chosen to represent the "classical" works of Marx and Engels are *The Communist Manifesto* and *Socialism: Scientific and Utopian*. From the time of their appearance, in 1848 and 1880 respectively, these two works have been the most widely read of all Marxist publications. Together they provide the reader with an excellent statement of the principal themes of both the communist ideology and the communist program, as outlined by the founders of Marxist socialism.

Karl Marx / Friedrich Engels

THE COMMUNIST MANIFESTO

Friedrich Engels

SOCIALISM:
UTOPIAN AND SCIENTIFIC

Karl Marx / Friedrich Engels

THE COMMUNIST MANIFESTO

A specter is haunting Europe—the specter of communism. All the powers of old Europe have entered into a holy alliance to exorcise this specter: Pope and Czar, Metternich and Guizot, French Radicals [1] and German police-spies.

Where is the party in opposition that has not been decried as communistic by its opponents in power? Where the opposition that has not hurled the branding reproach of communism, against the more advanced opposition parties, as well as against its reactionary adversaries?

Two things result from this fact.

I. Communism is already acknowledged by all European powers to be itself a power.

II. It is high time that Communists should openly, in the face of the whole world, publish their views, their aims, their tendencies, and meet this nursery tale of the specter of communism with a Manifesto of the party itself.

To this end, Communists of various nationalities have assembled in London, and sketched the following Manifesto, to be published in the English, French, German, Italian, Flemish, and Danish languages.

I. BOURGEOISIE AND PROLETARIANS [2]

The history of all hitherto existing society [3] is the history of class struggles.

Freeman and slave, patrician and plebeian, lord and serf, guild-master [4] and journeyman, in a word, oppressor and oppressed, stood in constant opposition to one another, carried on an uninterrupted, now hidden, now open fight, a fight that each time ended, either in a revolutionary reconstitution of society at large, or in the common ruin of the contending classes.

In the earlier epochs of history, we find almost everywhere a complicated arrangement of society into various orders, a manifold gradation of social rank. In ancient Rome

13

we have patricians, knights, plebeians, slaves; in the Middle Ages, feudal lords, vassals, guild-masters, journeymen, apprentices, serfs; in almost all of these classes, again, subordinate gradations.

The modern bourgeois society that has sprouted from the ruins of feudal society has not done away with class antagonisms. It has but established new classes, new conditions of oppression, new forms of struggle in place of the old ones.

Our epoch, the epoch of the bourgeoisie, possesses, however, this distinctive feature: it has simplified the class antagonisms. Society as a whole is more and more splitting up into two great hostile camps, into two great classes directly facing each other: bourgeoisie and proletariat.

From the serfs of the Middle Ages sprang the chartered burghers of the earliest towns. From these burgesses the first elements of the bourgeoisie were developed.

The discovery of America, the rounding of the Cape, opened up fresh ground for the rising bourgeoisie. The East-Indian and Chinese markets, the colonization of America, trade with the colonies, the increase in the means of exchange and in commodities generally, gave to commerce, to navigation, to industry, an impulse never before known, and, thereby, a rapid development to the revolutionary element in the tottering feudal society.

The feudal system of industry, under which industrial production was monopolized by closed guilds, now no longer sufficed for the growing wants of the new markets. The manufacturing system took its place. The guild-masters were pushed to one side by the manufacturing middle class; division of labor between the different corporate guilds vanished in the face of division of labor in each single workshop.

Meantime the markets kept ever growing, the demand ever rising. Even manufacture no longer sufficed.[5] Thereupon, steam and machinery revolutionized industrial production. The place of manufacture was taken by the giant, modern industry, the place of the industrial middle class, by industrial millionaires, the leaders of whole industrial armies, the modern bourgeois.

Modern industry has established the world market, for which the discovery of America paved the way. This market has given an immense development to commerce, to navigation, to communication by land. This development has, in its turn, reacted on the extension of industry; and in proportion as industry, commerce, navigation, railways extended, in the same proportion the bourgeoisie developed, increased its capital, and pushed into the background every class handed down from the Middle Ages.

We see, therefore, how the modern bourgeoisie is itself the product of a long development, of a series of revolutions in the modes of production and exchange.

Each step in the development of the bourgeoisie was accompanied by a corresponding political advance of that class. An oppressed class under the sway of the feudal nobility, an armed and self-governing association in the medieval commune.[6] At first, an independent urban republic (as in Italy and Germany) or a taxable "third estate" of the monarchy (as in France), afterwards, in the period of manufacture proper, serving either the semi-feudal or the absolute monarchy as a counterpoise against the nobility, and, in fact, cornerstone of the great monarchies in general, the bourgeoisie has at last, since the establishment of modern industry and of the world market, conquered for itself, in the modern representative State, exclusive political sway. The executive of the modern State is but a committee for managing the common affairs of the whole bourgeoisie.

The bourgeoisie, historically, has played a most revolutionary part.

The bourgeoisie, wherever it has got the upper hand, has put an end to all feudal, patriarchal, idyllic relations. It has pitilessly torn asunder the motley feudal ties that bound man to his "natural superiors," and has left remaining no other nexus between man and man than naked self-interest, than callous "cash payment." It has drowned the most heavenly ecstasies of religious fervor, of chivalrous enthusiasm, of philistine sentimentalism, in the icy water of egotistical calculation. It has resolved personal worth into exchange value, and in place of the numberless indefeasible chartered freedoms, has set up that single, unconscionable freedom—Free Trade. In a word, for exploitation, veiled by religious and political illusions, it has substituted naked, shameless, direct, brutal exploitation.

The bourgeoisie has stripped of its halo every occupation hitherto honored and looked up to with reverent awe. It has converted the physician, the lawyer, the priest, the poet, and the man of science into its paid wage-laborers.

The bourgeoisie has torn away from the family its senti-mental veil and has reduced the family relation to a mere money relation.

The bourgeoisie has disclosed how it came to pass that the brutal display of vigor in the Middle Ages, which reactionaries so much admire, found its fitting complement in the most slothful indolence. It has been the first to show what man's activity can bring about. It has accomplished wonders far surpassing Egyptian pyramids, Roman aque-ducts, and Gothic cathedrals. It has conducted expeditions that put in the shade all former Exoduses of nations and crusades.

The bourgeoisie cannot exist without constantly revolu-tionizing the instruments of production, and thereby the re-lations of production, and with them all social relations. Conservation of the old modes of production in unaltered form, was, on the contrary, the first condition of existence for all earlier industrial classes. Constant revolutionizing of production, uninterrupted disturbance of all social condi-tions, everlasting uncertainty and agitation distinguish the bourgeois epoch from all earlier ones. All fixed, fast-frozen relations, with their train of ancient and venerable prejudices and opinions are swept away, all newly formed ones become antiquated before they can ossify. All that is solid melts into air, all that is holy is profaned, and man is at last com-pelled to face with sober senses, his real conditions of life, and his relations with his kind.

The need of a constantly expanding market for its products chases the bourgeoisie over the whole face of the globe. It must nestle everywhere, settle everywhere, establish con-nections everywhere.

The bourgeoisie has through its exploitation of the world market given a cosmopolitan character to production and consumption in every country. To the great chagrin of re-actionaries, it has drawn from under the feet of industry the national ground on which it stood. All old, established na-tional industries have been destroyed or are daily being de-stroyed. They are dislodged by new industries, whose in-troduction becomes a life and death question for all civilized nations, industries that no longer work with indigenous raw material, but raw material drawn from the remotest regions, industries whose products are consumed, not only at home, but in every quarter of the globe. In place of the old wants, satisfied by the productions of the country, we find new wants, requiring for their satisfaction the products of distant lands and climes. In place of the old local and national seclusion and self-sufficiency, we have intercourse in every direction, a universal interdependence of nations. And as in material, so also in intellectual production. The intellectual creations of individual nations become common property. National one-sidedness and narrow-mindedness become more and more impossible, and from the numerous national and local literatures, there arises a world literature.

The bourgeoisie, by the rapid improvement of all instruments of production, by the immensely facilitated means of communication, draws all, even the most barbarian, nations into civilization. The cheap prices of its commodities are the heavy artillery with which it batters down all Chinese walls, with which it forces the barbarians' intensely obstinate hatred of foreigners to capitulate. It compels all nations, on pain of extinction, to adopt the bourgeois mode of production; it compels them to introduce what it calls civilization into their midst, *i.e.*, to become bourgeois themselves. In one word, it creates a world after its own image.

The bourgeoisie has subjected the country to the rule of the towns. It has created enormous cities, greatly increased the urban population as compared with the rural, and thus rescued a considerable part of the population from the idiocy of rural life. Just as it has made the country dependent on the towns, so it has made barbarian and semi-barbarian countries dependent on the civilized ones, nations of peasants on nations of bourgeoisie, the East on the West. More and more the bourgeoisie continues to do away with the scattered state of population, means of production, and property. It has agglomerated population, centralized means of production, and concentrated property in a few hands. The necessary consequence of this was political centralization. Independent, or but loosely connected, provinces with separate interests, laws, governments and systems of taxation, became lumped together into one nation, with one government, one code of laws, one national class-interest, one frontier and one customs-tariff.

The bourgeoisie, during its rule of scarcely one hundred years, has created more massive and more colossal productive forces than have all preceding generations together. The subjection of nature's forces to man and machinery; the application of chemistry to industry and agriculture; [the development of] steam-navigation, railways and electric telegraphs; the clearing of whole continents for cultivation; the canalization of rivers and the conjuring of whole populations out of the ground—what earlier century had even a presentiment that such productive forces slumbered in the lap of social labor?

We see then: the means of production and exchange, on whose foundation the bourgeoisie built itself up, were generated in feudal society. At a certain stage in the development of these means of production and exchange, the conditions under which feudal society produced and exchanged, the feudal organization of agriculture and manufacturing industry, in one word, the feudal relations of property became no longer compatible with the already developed productive forces; they became so many fetters. They had to be burst asunder. They were burst asunder.

Into their place stepped free competition, accompanied by a social and political constitution adapted to it and by the economical and political sway of the bourgeois class.

A similar movement is going on before our own eyes. Modern bourgeois society with its relations of production, exchange and property, a society that has conjured up such gigantic means of production and exchange, is like the sorcerer, who is no longer able to control the powers of the nether world whom he has called up by his spells. For many decades the history of industry and commerce has been but the history of the revolt of modern productive forces against modern conditions of production, against the property relations that are the conditions for the existence of the bourgeoisie and of its rule. It is enough to mention the commercial crises that by their periodic return put on its trial, each time more threateningly, the existence of the entire bourgeois society. In these crises a great part not only of the existing products, but also of the previously created productive forces are periodically destroyed. In these crises there breaks out an epidemic that in all earlier epochs would have seemed an absurdity—the epidemic of overproduction. Society suddenly finds itself put back into a state of momentary barbarism. It appears as if a famine or a universal war of devastation had cut off the supply of every means of subsistence. Industry and commerce seem to be destroyed. And why? Because there is too much civilization, too much means of subsistence, too much industry, too much commerce. The productive forces at the disposal of society no

longer tend to further the development of the conditions
of bourgeois property. On the contrary, they have become
too powerful for these conditions, by which they are fettered,
and so soon as they overcome these fetters, they bring disorder into the whole of bourgeois society, endanger the existence of bourgeois property. The conditions of bourgeois society are too narrow to encompass the wealth created by
them. And how does the bourgeoisie get over these crises?
On the one hand by enforced destruction of a mass of
productive forces; on the other, by the conquest of new
markets, and by the more thorough exploitation of the old
ones. That is to say, by paving the way for more extensive
and more destructive crises, and by diminishing the means
whereby crises are prevented.

The weapons with which the bourgeoisie brought feudalism to the ground are now turned against the bourgeoisie itself.

But not only has the bourgeoisie forged the weapons that
bring death to itself; it has also called into existence the
men who are to wield those weapons—the modern working
class—the proletariat.

In proportion as the bourgeoisie, *i.e.*, capital, develops,
in the same proportion the proletariat, the modern working
class, develops—a class of laborers, who live only so long as
they find work, and who find work only so long as their
labor increases capital. These laborers, who must sell themselves piecemeal, are a commodity, like every other article
of commerce, and are consequently exposed to all the vicis-
situdes of competition, to all the fluctuations of the market.

Owing to the extensive use of machinery and to the division of labor, work for the proletarians has lost all individual character, and, consequently, all charm for the
workman. He becomes an appendage of the machine, and it
is only the simplest, most monotonous, and most easily acquired knack that is required of him. Hence, the cost of
production of a workman is restricted, almost entirely, to the
means of subsistence that he requires for his maintenance
and for the propagation of his race. But the price of a
commodity, and therefore also of labor, is equal to its cost of
production. In proportion, therefore, as the repulsiveness of
the work increases, the wage decreases. Nay more, to the
extent that the use of machinery and the division of labor
increases, to the same extent the burden of toil also in-

creases, whether by the prolongation of working hours, the increase of the work exacted in a given time or the increased speed of the machinery, etc.

Modern industry has converted the little workshop of the patriarchal master into the great factory of the industrial capitalist. Masses of laborers crowded into the factory are organized like soldiers. As privates of the industrial army they are placed under the command of a perfect hierarchy of officers and sergeants. Not only are they slaves of the bourgeois class and the bourgeois state; they are daily and hourly enslaved by the machine, by the supervisor, and, above all, by the individual bourgeois manufacturer himself. The more openly this despotism proclaims gain to be its end and aim, the more petty, the more hateful and the more embittering it is.

The less the skill and exertion of strength involved in manual labor (in other words, the more modern industry becomes developed), the more the labor of men is replaced by that of women. Differences of age and sex have no longer any distinctive social validity for the working class. All are instruments of labor, more or less expensive to use, according to their age and sex.

No sooner is the exploitation of the laborer by the manufacturer, so far, at an end, that he receives his wages in cash, than he is set upon by the other portions of the bourgeoisie, the landlord, the shopkeeper, the pawnbroker, etc.

The lower strata of the middle class—small tradespeople, shopkeepers, retired tradesmen,[7] handicraftsmen and peasants—all these sink gradually into the proletariat, partly because their diminutive capital does not suffice for the scale on which modern industry is carried on and is swamped in the competition with the large capitalists, partly because their specialized skill is rendered worthless by new methods of production. Thus, the proletariat is recruited from all classes of the population.

The proletariat goes through various stages of development. With its birth begins its struggle with the bourgeoisie. At first the contest is carried on by individual laborers, then by the workers of a factory, then by the laborers of one trade in one locality, against the individual bourgeois who directly exploits them. They direct their attacks not against the bourgeois conditions of production, but against the instruments of production themselves; they destroy imported wares that compete with their labor, they smash to pieces machinery, they set factories ablaze, they seek to restore by force the vanished status of the workman of the Middle Ages.

At this stage the laborers still form an incoherent mass scattered over the whole country, and divided by their mutual competition. If they unite anywhere to form more compact bodies, this is not yet the consequence of their own active union, but of the union of the bourgeoisie, which, in order to attain its own political ends, is compelled to set the whole proletariat in motion, and is moreover yet, for a time, able to do so. At this stage, therefore, the proletarians do not fight their enemies, but the enemies of their enemies, the remnants of absolute monarchy, the landowners, the non-industrial bourgeois, the petty bourgeoisie. Thus the whole historical movement is concentrated in the hands of the bourgeoisie; every victory so obtained is a victory for the bourgeoisie.

But with the development of industry the proletariat not only increases in number; it becomes concentrated in greater masses, its strength grows, and it becomes more aware of that strength. The various interests and conditions of life within the ranks of the proletariat are more and more equalized, in proportion as machinery obliterates all distinctions of labor, and nearly everywhere reduces wages to the same low level. The growing competition among the bourgeoisie and the resulting commercial crises, make the wages of the workers ever more fluctuating. The unceasing improvement of machinery, ever more rapidly developing, makes their livelihood more and more precarious. The collisions between individual workmen and individual bourgeois take more and more the character of collisions between two classes. Thereupon the workers begin to form combinations (trade unions) against the bourgeois; they join together in order to keep up the rate of wages; they form permanent associations in order to make provision beforehand for these occasional revolts. Here and there the contest breaks out into riots.

Now and then the workers are victorious, but only for a time. The real fruit of their battles lies, not in the immediate result, but in the ever-expanding union of the workers. This union is helped on by the improved means of communication that are created by modern industry and that place the workers of different localities in contact with one another.

It was just this contact that was needed to centralize the numerous local struggles, all of the same character, into one national struggle between classes. But every class struggle is a political struggle. And that union, which took the burghers of the Middle Ages, with their miserable highways, centuries to acquire, the modern proletarians, thanks to railways, achieve in a few years.

This organization of the proletarians into a class, and consequently into a political party, is continually being upset again by the competition between the workers themselves. But it continually re-emerges, stronger, firmer, mightier. It compels legislative recognition of particular interests of the workers, by taking advantage of the divisions among the bourgeoisie itself. Thus the ten-hours' bill in England was carried.[8]

The sum of these collisions between the classes of the old society further, in many ways, the development of the proletariat. The bourgeoisie finds itself involved in a constant battle. At first with the aristocracy; later, with those portions of the bourgeoisie itself, whose interests have become antagonistic to the progress of industry; at all times, with the bourgeoisie of foreign countries. In all these battles it sees itself compelled to appeal to the proletariat, to ask for its help, and thus, to drag it into the political arena. The bourgeoisie itself, therefore, supplies the proletariat with its own elements of political and general education, in other words, it furnishes the proletariat with weapons for fighting the bourgeoisie.

Further, as we have already seen, entire sections of the ruling classes are, by the advance of industry, precipitated into the proletariat, or are at least threatened in their conditions of existence. These also supply the proletariat with fresh elements of enlightenment and progress.

Finally, in times when the class struggle nears the decisive hour, the process of dissolution going on within the ruling class (in fact, within the whole range of old society) assumes such a violent, glaring character, that a small section of the ruling class cuts itself adrift, and joins the revolutionary class, the class that holds the future in its hands. Just as, therefore, at an earlier period, a section of the nobility went over to the bourgeoisie, so now a portion of the bourgeoisie goes over to the proletariat, and in particular, a portion of the bourgeois ideologists, who have raised themselves to • the level of comprehending theoretically the historical movement as a whole.

Of all the classes that stand face to face with the bourgeoisie today, the proletariat alone is a really revolutionary class. The other classes decay and finally disappear in the face of modern industry; the proletariat is its special and essential product.

The lower middle class, the small manufacturer, the shopkeeper, the artisan, the peasant—all these fight against the bourgeoisie, to save from extinction their existence as fractions of the middle class. They are therefore not revolutionary, but conservative. Nay more, they are reactionary, for they try to roll back the wheel of history. If by chance they are revolutionary, they are so only in view of their impending transfer into the proletariat, they thus defend not their present, but their future interests, they desert their own standpoint to place themselves at that of the proletariat.

The "dangerous class," the social scum, that passively rotting mass thrown off by the lowest layers of the old society, may, here and there, be swept into the movement by a proletarian revolution; its conditions of life, however, prepare it far more for the part of a bribed tool of reactionary intrigue.

For the proletariat, the conditions of the old society are already virtually swamped. The proletarian is without property; his relation to his wife and children has no longer anything in common with the bourgeois family relations; modern industrial labor, modern subjection to capital, the same in England as in France, in America as in Germany, has stripped him of every trace of national character. Law, morality, religion, are to him so many bourgeois prejudices, behind which lurk in ambush just as many bourgeois interests.

All the preceding classes that got the upper hand sought to fortify their already acquired status by subjecting society at large to their conditions of appropriation. The proletarians cannot become masters of the productive forces of society, except by abolishing their own previous mode of appropriation, and thereby also every other previous mode of appropriation. They have nothing of their own to secure and to fortify; their mission is to destroy all previous securities for, and insurances of, individual property.

All previous historical movements were movements of

minorities, or in the interest of minorities. The proletarian movement is the self-conscious, independent movement of the immense majority, in the interest of the immense majority. The proletariat, the lowest stratum of our present society, cannot stir, cannot raise itself, without the whole overlying strata of official society being sprung into the air.

Though not in substance, yet in form, the struggle of the proletariat with the bourgeoisie is at first a national struggle. The proletariat of each country must, of course, first of all settle matters with its own bourgeoisie.

In depicting the most general phases of the development of the proletariat, we traced the more or less veiled civil war raging within existing society, up to the point where that war breaks out into open revolution, and where the violent overthrow of the bourgeoisie lays the foundation for the sway of the proletariat.

Hitherto, every form of society has been based, as we have already seen, on the antagonism between oppressing and oppressed classes. But in order to oppress a class, certain conditions must be assured to it under which it can, at least, continue its slavish existence. The serf, in the period of serfdom, raised himself to membership in the commune, just as the petty bourgeois, under the yoke of feudal absolutism, managed to develop into a bourgeois. The modern laborer, on the contrary, instead of rising with the progress of industry, sinks deeper and deeper below the conditions of existence of his own class. He becomes a pauper, and pauperism develops more rapidly than population and wealth. And here it becomes evident that the bourgeoisie is unfit any longer to be the ruling class in society and to impose on society its own conditions of existence as an overriding law. It is unfit to rule because it is incompetent to assure an existence to its slave within his slavery, because it cannot help letting him sink into such a state that it has to feed him, instead of being fed by him. Society can no longer live under this bourgeoisie. In other words, its existence is no longer compatible with society.

The essential condition for the existence, and for the sway of the bourgeois class is the formation and augmentation of capital; the condition for capital is wage labor. Wage labor rests exclusively on competition between the laborers. The advance of industry, that the bourgeoisie involuntarily promotes, replaces the isolation of the laborers, due to competition, by their revolutionary combination, due to association. The development of modern industry, therefore, cuts from under its feet the very foundation on which the bourgeoisie produces and appropriates products. What the bourgeoisie, therefore, produces, above all, is its own gravediggers. Its fall and the victory of the proletariat are equally inevitable.

II. PROLETARIANS AND COMMUNISTS

In what relation do the Communists stand to the proletarians as a whole?

The Communists do not form a separate party opposed to other working-class parties.

They have no interests separate and apart from those of the proletariat as a whole.

They do not set up any sectarian principles of their own, by which to shape and mold the proletarian movement.

The Communists are distinguished from the other working-class parties by this only: 1. In the national struggles of the proletarians of the different countries, they point out and bring to the fore the common interests of the entire proletariat, independent of all nationality. 2. In the various stages of development through which the struggle of the working class against the bourgeoisie has to pass, they always and everywhere represent the interests of the movement as a whole.

The Communists, therefore, are on the one hand, in the sphere of practice, the most advanced and resolute section of the working-class parties of every country, that section which pushes forward all others; and on the other hand, in the realm of theory, they have over the great mass of the proletariat the advantage of clearly understanding the line of march, the conditions, and the ultimate general results of the proletarian movement.

The immediate aim of the Communists is the same as that of all the other proletarian parties: the formation of the proletariat into a class; the overthrow of the bourgeois supremacy; and the conquest of political power by the proletariat.

The theoretical conclusions of the Communists are in no way based on ideas or principles that have been invented or discovered by this or that would-be universal reformer.

They merely express, in general terms, actual relations

springing from an existing class struggle, from a historical movement going on under our very eyes. The abolition of existing property relations is not at all a distinctive feature of Communism.

All property relations in the past have continually been subject to historical change resulting from the change in historical conditions.

The French Revolution, for example, abolished feudal property in favor of bourgeois property.

The distinguishing feature of Communism is not the abolition of property generally, but the abolition of bourgeois property. But modern bourgeois private property is the final and most complete expression of the system of .producing and appropriating products, that is based on class antagonisms, on the exploitation of the many by the few.

In this sense, the theory of the Communists may be summed up in the single sentence: the abolition of private property.

We Communists have been reproached with the desire of abolishing the right of personally acquiring property as the fruit of a man's own labor, the property that is alleged to be the foundation of all personal freedom, activity and independence.

Hard-won, self-acquired, self-earned property! Do you mean the property of the petty artisan and of the small peasant, a form of property that preceded the bourgeois form? There is no need to abolish that: the development of industry has to a great extent already destroyed it and is still destroying it daily.

Or do you mean modern bourgeois private property?

But does wage labor create any property for the laborer? Not a bit. It creates capital, *i.e.*, that kind of property which exploits wage labor, and which cannot increase except upon condition of begetting a new supply of wage labor for fresh exploitation. Property, in its present form, is based on the antagonism of capital and wage labor. Let us examine both sides of this antagonism.

To be a capitalist, is to have not only a purely personal, but also a social *status* in production. Capital is a collective product, and only by the united action of many members, nay, in the last resort, only by the united action of all members of society, can it be set in motion.

Capital is, therefore, not a personal but a social power. When, therefore, capital is converted into common prop-

erty, into the property of all members of society, personal
property is not thereby transformed into social property. It
is only the social character of the property that is changed.
It loses its class character.

Let us now take wage labor.

The average price of wage labor is the minimum wage,
i.e., that quantity of the means of subsistence, which is absolutely requisite to keep the laborer in bare existence as a
laborer. What, therefore, the wage-laborer appropriates by
means of his labor, merely suffices to prolong and reproduce
a bare existence. We by no means intend to abolish this personal appropriation of the products of labor, an appropriation that is made for the maintenance and reproduction of
human life and that leaves no surplus wherewith to command the labor of others. All that we want to do away with
is the miserable character of this appropriation, under which
the laborer lives merely to increase capital and is allowed
to live only in so far as the interest of the ruling class requires it.

In bourgeois society, living labor is but a means to increase accumulated labor. In Communist society, accumulated labor is but a means to widen, to enrich, to promote
the existence of the laborer.

In bourgeois society, therefore, the past dominates the
present; in Communist society, the present dominates the
past. In bourgeois society capital is independent and has individuality, while the living person is dependent and has no
individuality.

And the abolition of this state of things is called by the
bourgeois abolition of individuality and freedom! And rightly
so. The abolition of bourgeois individuality, bourgeois independence, and bourgeois freedom is undoubtedly aimed
at.

By freedom is meant, under the present bourgeois conditions of production, free trade, free selling and buying.

But if selling and buying disappears, free selling and
buying disappears also. This talk about free selling and
buying, and all the other "brave words" of our bourgeoisie
about freedom in general, have a meaning, if any, only in
contrast with restricted selling and buying, with the fettered traders of the Middle Ages, but have no meaning
when opposed to the Communistic abolition of buying and
selling, of the bourgeois conditions of production, and of the
bourgeoisie itself.

You are horrified at our intending to do away with private property. But in your existing society, private property is already done away with for nine tenths of the population; its existence for the few is solely due to its nonexistence in the hands of those nine tenths. You reproach us, therefore, with intending to do away with a form of property, the necessary condition for whose existence is, the nonexistence of any property for the immense majority of society.

In one word, you reproach us with intending to do away with your property. Precisely so; that is just what we intend.

From the moment when labor can no longer be converted into capital, money, or rent, into a social power capable of being monopolized, *i.e.*, from the moment when individual property can no longer be transformed into bourgeois property, into capital, from that moment, you say, individuality vanishes.

You must, therefore, confess that by "individual" you mean no other person than the bourgeois, than the middle-class owner of property. This person must, indeed, be swept out of the way, and made impossible.

Communism deprives no man of the power to appropriate the products of society; all that it does is to deprive him of the power to subjugate the labor of others by means of such appropriation.

It has been objected that upon the abolition of private property all work will cease, and universal laziness will overtake us.

According to this, bourgeois society ought long ago to have gone to the dogs through sheer idleness; for those of its members who work, acquire nothing, and those who acquire anything, do not work. The whole of this objection is but another expression of the tautology: that there can no longer be any wage labor when there is no longer any capital.

All objections urged against the Communistic mode of producing and appropriating material products, have, in the same way, been urged against the Communistic modes of producing and appropriating intellectual products. Just as, to the bourgeois, the disappearance of class property is the disappearance of production itself, so the disappearance of class culture is to him identical with the disappearance of all culture.

That culture, the loss of which he laments, is for the enormous majority a mere training to act as a machine.

But don't wrangle with us so long as you apply to our intended abolition of bourgeois property the standard of your bourgeois notions of freedom, culture, law, etc. Your very ideas are but the outgrowth of the conditions of your bourgeois production and bourgeois property, just as your jurisprudence is but the will of your class made into a law for all, a will, whose essential character and direction are determined by the economic conditions of existence of your class.

The selfish misconception that induces you to transform into eternal laws of nature and of reason, the social forms springing from your present mode of production and form of property—historical relations that rise and disappear in the progress of production—this misconception you share with every ruling class that has preceded you. What you see clearly in the case of ancient property, what you admit in the case of feudal property, you are of course forbidden to admit in the case of your own bourgeois form of property.

Abolition of the family! Even the most radical flare up at this infamous proposal of the Communists.

On what foundation is the present family, the bourgeois family, based? On capital, on private gain. In its completely developed form this family exists only among the bourgeoisie. But this state of things finds its complement in the practical absence of the family among the proletarians and in public prostitution.

The bourgeois family will vanish as a matter of course when its complement vanishes, and both will vanish with the vanishing of capital.

Do you charge us with wanting to stop the exploitation of children by their parents? To this crime we plead guilty.

But, you will say, we destroy the most hallowed of relations when we replace home education by social.

And your education! Is not that also social and determined by the social conditions under which you educate, by the intervention, direct or indirect, of society, by means of schools, etc.? The Communists have not invented the intervention of society in education; they only seek to alter the character of that intervention and to rescue education from the influence of the ruling class.

The bourgeois claptrap about the family and education, about the hallowed relationship between parent and child, becomes all the more disgusting, the more that, as a result of modern industry, all family ties among the proletarians are torn asunder and their children transformed into simple articles of commerce and instruments of labor.

But you Communists would introduce community of women, screams the whole bourgeoisie in chorus.

The bourgeois sees in his wife a mere instrument of production. He hears that the instruments of production are to be exploited in common, and, naturally, can come to no other conclusion than that the lot of being common to all will likewise fall to the women.

He has not even a suspicion that the real point aimed at is to do away with the status of women as mere instruments of production.

For the rest, nothing is more ridiculous than the virtuous indignation of our bourgeois at the community of women which, they pretend, is to be openly and officially established by the Communists. The Communists have no need to introduce community of women; it has existed almost from time immemorial.

Our bourgeois, not content with having the wives and daughters of their proletarians at their disposal, not to speak of common prostitutes, take the greatest pleasure in seducing each others' wives.

Bourgeois marriage is in reality a system of wives in common and thus, at the most, what the Communists might possibly be reproached with is that they desire to introduce, in place of a hypocritically concealed community of women, an openly legalized one. For the rest, it is self-evident that the abolition of the present system of production must bring with it the abolition of the community of women springing from that system, *i.e.*, of prostitution both public and private.

The Communists are further reproached with desiring to abolish countries and nationality.

The woking men have no country. We cannot take from them what they have not got. Since the proletariat must first of all acquire political supremacy, must rise to be the leading class of the nation, must constitute itself *the* nation, it is to this extent itself national, though not in the bourgeois sense of the word.

National differences and antagonisms between peoples are daily more and more vanishing, owing to the development of the bourgeoisie, to freedom of commerce, to the world market, to uniformity in the mode of production and in the conditions of life corresponding thereto.

The supremacy of the proletariat will cause them to vanish still faster. United action, at least of the leading civilized countries, is one of the first conditions for the emancipation of the proletariat.

To the extent that the exploitation of one individual by another is put to an end, the exploitation of one nation by another will also be put to an end. To the extent that the antagonism between classes within the nation vanishes, the hostility of one nation to another will come to an end.

The charges against Communism made from a religious, a philosophical, and, generally, from an ideological standpoint, are not deserving of serious examination.

Does it require deep intuition to comprehend that man's ideas, views and conceptions, in one word, man's consciousness, changes with every change in the conditions of his material existence, in his social relations and in his social life?

What else does the history of ideas prove than that intellectual production changes its character to the extent that material production is changed? The ruling ideas of each age have always been the ideas of its ruling class.

When people speak of ideas that revolutionize society, they only express the fact, that within the old society, the elements of a new one have been created, and that the dissolution of the old ideas keeps pace with the dissolution of the old conditions of existence.

When the ancient world was in its last throes, the ancient religions were overcome by Christianity. When Christian ideas succumbed in the eighteenth century to rationalist ideas, feudal society fought its death battle with the then revolutionary bourgeoisie. The ideas of religious liberty and freedom of conscience merely gave expression to the sway of free competition within the domain of knowledge.

"Undoubtedly," it will be said, "religious, moral, philosophical and juridical ideas have been modified in the course of historical development. But religion, morality, philosophy, political science, and law constantly survived this change."

"There are, besides, eternal truths, such as Freedom, Justice, etc., that are common to all states of society. But Communism abolishes eternal truths; it abolishes all religion, and all morality, instead of constituting them on a new basis; it therefore acts in contradiction to all past historical experience."

To what does this accusation reduce itself? The history of

all past society has consisted in the development of class antagonisms, antagonisms that assumed different forms at different epochs.

But whatever form they may have taken, one fact is common to all past ages, *viz.*, the exploitation of one part of society by the other. No wonder, then, that the social consciousness of past ages, despite all the multiplicity and variety it displays, moves within certain common forms, or general ideas, which cannot completely vanish except with the total disappearance of class antagonisms.

The Communist revolution is the most radical rupture with traditional property relations; no wonder that its development involves the most radical rupture with traditional ideas.

But let us be done with the bourgeois objections to Communism.

We have seen above that the first step in the revolution by the working class is to raise the proletariat to the position of ruling class, to win the battle of democracy.

The proletariat will use its political supremacy to wrest, by degrees, all capital from the bourgeoisie, to centralize all instruments of production in the hands of the State (*i.e.*, the proletariat organized as the ruling class), and to increase the total of productive forces as rapidly as possible.

Of course, in the beginning, this cannot be effected except by means of despotic inroads on the rights of property and on the conditions of bourgeois production; by means of measures, therefore, which appear economically insufficient and untenable, but which, in the course of the movement, outstrip themselves, necessitate further inroads upon the old social order, and are unavoidable as a means of entirely revolutionizing the mode of production.

These measures will of course be different in different countries.

Nevertheless in the most advanced countries, the following will be pretty generally applicable.

1. Abolition of property in land and application of all rents of land to public purposes.

2. A heavy progressive or graduated income tax.

3. Abolition of all right of inheritance.

4. Confiscation of the property of all emigrants and rebels.

5. Centralization of credit in the hands of the State, by means of a national bank with State capital and an exclusive monopoly.

6. Centralization of the means of communication and transport in the hands of the State.

7. Extension of factories and instruments of production owned by the State; cultivation of waste-lands; and improvement of the soil generally in accordance with a common plan.

8. Equal liability of all to labor. Establishment of industrial armies, especially for agriculture.

9. Combination of agriculture with manufacturing industries; and gradual abolition of the distinction between town and country by a more equable distribution of the population over the country.

10. Free education for all children in public schools. Abolition of children's factory labor in its present form. Combination of education with industrial production, etc.

When, in the course of development, class distinctions have disappeared and all production has been concentrated in the hands of a vast association of the whole nation, the public power will lose its political character. Political power, properly so called, is merely the organized power of one class for oppressing another. If the proletariat during its contest with the bourgeoisie is compelled, by the force of circumstances, to organize itself as a class, if, by means of a revolution, it makes itself the ruling class and as such sweeps away by force the old conditions of production, then it will have swept away, along with these conditions, the conditions for the existence of class antagonisms and classes generally and will thereby have abolished its own supremacy as a class.

In place of the old bourgeois society, with its classes and class antagonisms, we shall have an association in which the free development of each is the condition for the free development of all.

III. SOCIALIST AND COMMUNIST LITERATURE

1. REACTIONARY SOCIALISM

a. Feudal Socialism

Owing to their historical position, it became the vocation of the aristocracies of France and England to write pamphlets against modern bourgeois society. In the French revo-

lution of July 1830 [9] and in the English reform agitation,
these aristocracies again succumbed to the hateful upstart.
Thenceforth, a serious political contest was altogether out
of the question. A literary battle alone remained possible.
But even in the domain of literature the old cries of the restoration period [10] had become impossible.

In order to arouse sympathy, the aristocracy were obliged
to lose sight, apparently, of their own interests and to formulate their indictment against the bourgeoisie in the interest
of the exploited working class alone. Thus the aristocracy
took their revenge by singing lampoons on their new master
and whispering in his ears sinister prophecies of coming
catastrophe.

In this way arose feudal Socialism: half lamentation, half
lampoon; half echo of the past, half menace of the future;
at times, by its bitter, witty and incisive criticism, striking
at the very heart of the bourgeoisie; but always ludicrous in
its effect, because of its total incapacity to comprehend the
march of modern history.

The aristocracy, in order to rally the people, waved the
proletarian alms-bag in front as a banner. But the people,
so often as it joined them, saw on their hindquarters the old
feudal coats of arms and deserted with loud and irreverent
laughter.

One section of the French Legitimists [11] and "Young England" [12] exhibited this spectacle.

In pointing out that their mode of exploitation was different from that of the bourgeoisie, the feudalists forget
that they exploited under circumstances and conditions that
were quite different and that are now antiquated. In showing that, under their rule, the modern proletariat never existed, they forget that the modern bourgeoisie is the necessary offspring of their own form of society.

For the rest, so little do they conceal the reactionary character of their criticism that their chief accusation against the
bourgeoisie amounts to this, that under the bourgeois *régime*
a class is being developed, which is destined to cut up root
and branch the old order of society.

What they upbraid the bourgeoisie with is not so much
that it creates a proletariat, as that it creates a *revolutionary*
proletariat.

In political practice, therefore, they join in all coercive
measures against the working class; and in ordinary life,
despite their high-falutin phrases, they stoop to pick up the

golden apples dropped from the tree of industry, and to barter truth, love, and honor for traffic in wool, beetroot-sugar, and potato spirits.[13]

As the parson has always gone hand in hand with the landlord, so has Clerical Socialism with Feudal Socialism.

Nothing is easier than to give Christian asceticism a Socialist tinge. Has not Christianity declaimed against private property, against marriage, against the State? Has it not preached in the place of these, charity and poverty, celibacy and mortification of the flesh, monastic life and Mother Church? Christian Socialism is but the holy water with which the priest consecrates the heart-burnings of the aristocrat.[14]

b. Petty-Bourgeois Socialism

The feudal aristocracy was not the only class that was ruined by the bourgeoisie, not the only class whose conditions of existence pined and perished in the atmosphere of modern bourgeois society. The medieval townspeople and the small peasant proprietors were the precursors of the modern bourgeoisie. In those countries which are but little developed, industrially and commercially, these two classes still vegetate side by side with the rising bourgeoisie.

In countries where modern civilization has become fully developed, a new class of petty bourgeois has been formed, fluctuating between proletariat and bourgeoisie and ever renewing itself as a supplementary part of bourgeois society. The individual members of this class, however, are being constantly hurled down into the proletariat by the action of competition, and, as modern industry develops, they even see the moment approaching when they will completely disappear as an independent section of modern society, to be replaced, in manufactures, agriculture and commerce, by supervisors, bailiffs and foremen.

In countries like France, where the peasants constitute far more than half of the population, it was natural that writers who sided with the proletariat against the bourgeoisie, should use, in their criticism of the bourgeois *régime,* the standard of the peasant and petty bourgeois, and from the standpoint of these intermediate classes should take up the cudgels for the working class. Thus arose petty-bourgeois socialism. Sismondi was the head of this school, not only in France but also in England.

This school of socialism dissected with great acuteness the contradictions in the conditions of modern production. It laid bare the hypocritical apologies of economists. It proved, irrefutably, the disastrous effects of machinery and the division of labor; the concentration of capital and land in a few hands; overproduction and crises; it pointed out the inevitable ruin of the petty bourgeois and peasant, the misery of the proletariat, the anarchy in production, the crying inequalities in the distribution of wealth, the industrial war of extermination between nations, the dissolution of old moral bonds, of the old family relations, of the old nationalities.

In its positive aims, however, this form of socialism hopes either to restore the old means of production and exchange, and with them the old property relations and the old society, or to cramp the modern means of production and exchange, within the framework of the old property relations that have been, and were bound to be, exploded by those means. In either case, it is both reactionary and utopian.

Its last words are: corporate guilds for manufacture and patriarchal relations in agriculture.

Ultimately, when stubborn historical facts had dispersed all intoxicating effects of self-deception, this form of socialism ended in a miserable fit of the blues.

c. German, or "True," Socialism

The socialist and communist literature of France, a literature that originated under the pressure of a bourgeoisie in power and that expressed the struggle against this power, was introduced into Germany at a time when the bourgeoisie in that country had just begun its contest with feudal absolutism.

German philosophers, would-be philosophers, and *beaux esprits*, eagerly seized on this literature, forgetting, that when these writings immigrated from France into Germany, French social conditions had not immigrated along with them. In contact with German social conditions, this French literature lost all its immediate practical significance and assumed a purely literary aspect. Thus, to the German philosophers of the eighteenth century, the demands of the first French Revolution were nothing more than the demands of "Practical Reason" [15] in general, and the expression of the will of the revolutionary French bourgeoisie signified in their eyes the laws of pure will, will as it was bound to be, true human will generally.

The work of the German *literati* consisted solely in bringing the new French ideas into harmony with their ancient philosophical conscience, or rather, in annexing the French ideas without deserting their own philosophic point of view.

This annexation took place in the same way in which a foreign language is appropriated, namely, by translation.

It is well known how the monks wrote silly lives of Catholic saints *over* the manuscripts on which the classical works of ancient heathendom had been written. The German *literati* reversed this process with the profane French literature. They wrote their philosophical nonsense beneath the French original. For instance, beneath the French criticism of the economic functions of money, they wrote "alienation of humanity," and beneath the French criticism of the bourgeois state they wrote, "dethronement of the category of the general," and so forth.[16]

The introduction of these philosophical phrases at the back of the French historical criticisms they dubbed "philosophy of action," "true socialism," "German science of socialism," "philosophical foundation of socialism," and so on.

The French socialist and communist literature was thus completely emasculated. And, since it ceased in the hands of the German to express the struggle of one class with the other, he felt conscious of having overcome "French onesidedness" and of representing, not true requirements, but the requirements of Truth; not the interests of the proletariat, but the interests of Human Nature, of Man in general, who belongs to no class, has no reality, and exists only in the misty realm of philosophical fantasy.

Meanwhile, this German socialism, which took its schoolboy task so seriously and solemnly and extolled its poor stock-in-trade in such mountebank fashion, gradually lost its pedantic innocence.

The fight of the German, and, especially, of the Prussian bourgeoisie, against feudal aristocracy and absolute monarchy, in other words, the liberal movement, became more earnest.

By this, the long wished-for opportunity was offered to "True" socialism of confronting the political movement with the socialist demands, of hurling the traditional anathemas against liberalism, representative government, bourgeois competition, bourgeois freedom of the press, bourgeois legislation, bourgeois liberty and equality, and of preaching to the masses that they had nothing to gain, and everything to lose, by this bourgeois movement. German socialism forgot, in the nick of time, that the French criticism, whose silly echo it was, presupposed the existence of modern bourgeois society with its corresponding economic conditions of existence and the political constitution adapted thereto—the very things whose attainment was the object of the pending struggle in Germany.

To the absolute governments, with their following of parsons, professors, country squires and officials, it served as a welcome scarecrow against the threatening bourgeoisie.

It was a sweet finish after the bitter pills of floggings and bullets with which these same governments, just at that time, dosed the German working-class risings.

While this "True" socialism thus served the governments as a weapon for fighting the German bourgeoisie, it, at the same time, directly represented a reactionary interest, the interest of the German philistines. In Germany the *pettybourgeois* class, a relic of the sixteenth century and since then constantly cropping up again under various forms, is the real social basis of the existing state of things.

To preserve this class is to preserve the existing state of things in Germany. The industrial and political supremacy of the bourgeoisie threatens it with certain destruction; on the one hand, from the concentration of capital; on the other, from the rise of a revolutionary proletariat. "True" socialism appeared to kill these two birds with one stone. It spread like an epidemic.

The robe of speculative cobwebs, embroidered with flowers of rhetoric and steeped in the dew of sickly sentiment, this transcendental robe in which the German socialists wrapped their sorry, skin-and-bones "eternal truths" served wonderfully to increase the sale of their goods to such a public.

And on its part, German socialism recognized, more and more, its own calling as the bombastic representative of the petty-bourgeois philistine.

It proclaimed the German nation to be the model nation and the German petty philistine to be the typical man. To every villainous meanness of this model man it gave a hidden, higher, socialistic interpretation, the exact contrary of its real character. It went to the extreme length of directly opposing the "brutally destructive" tendency of communism and of proclaiming its supreme and impartial contempt of all class struggles. With very few exceptions, all the so-called socialist and communist publications that now (1847) circulate in Germany belong to the domain of this foul and enervating literature.

2. CONSERVATIVE, OR BOURGEOIS, SOCIALISM

A part of the bourgeoisie is desirous of redressing social grievances, in order to secure the continued existence of bourgeois society.

To this section belong economists, philanthropists, human-itarians, improvers of the condition of the working class, or-ganizers of charity, members of societies for the prevention of cruelty to animals, temperance fanatics, hole-and-corner reformers of every imaginable kind. This form of socialism has, moreover, been worked out into complete systems.

We may cite Proudhon's *Philosophie de la Misère* as an example of this form.

The socialistic bourgeois want all the advantages of mod-ern social conditions without the struggles and dangers nec-essarily resulting from them. They desire the existing state of society minus its revolutionary and disintegrating ele-ments. They wish for a bourgeoisie without a proletariat. The bourgeoisie naturally conceives the world in which it is supreme to be the best; and bourgeois socialism develops this comfortable conception into various more or less com-plete systems. In requiring the proletariat to carry out such a system, and thereby to march right into the social New Jerusalem, it is only really requiring that the proletariat should remain within the bounds of existing society, but should cast away all its hateful ideas concerning the bour-geoisie.

A second and more practical, but less systematic, form of this socialism sought to depreciate every revolutionary move-ment in the eyes of the working class, by showing that no mere political reform, but only a change in the material con-ditions of existence, in economic relations, could be of any advantage to them. However, by changes in the ma-terial conditions of existence, this form of socialism by no means understands abolition of the bourgeois relations of production, an abolition that can be effected only by a revolution, but administrative reforms, based on the continued existence of these relations; reforms, therefore, that in no respect affect the relations between capital and labor, but, at the best, lessen the cost, and simplify the administrative work, of bourgeois government.

Bourgeois socialism attains adequate expression, when, and only when, it becomes a mere figure of speech.

Free trade—for the benefit of the working class. Protective duties—for the benefit of the working class. Prison Reform—for the benefit of the working class. This is the last word and the only seriously meant word of bourgeois socialism.

It is summed up in the phrase: the bourgeois is a bourgeois—for the benefit of the working class.

3. CRITICAL-UTOPIAN SOCIALISM AND COMMUNISM

We do not here refer to that literature which, in every great modern revolution, has always given voice to the demands of the proletariat, such as the writings of Babeuf and others.

The first direct attempts of the proletariat to attain its own ends, made in times of universal excitement, when feudal society was being overthrown, these attempts necessarily failed, owing to the then undeveloped state of the proletariat, as well as to the absence of the economic conditions for its emancipation, conditions that had yet to be produced, and that could be produced only by the impending bourgeois epoch. The revolutionary literature that accompanied these first movements of the proletariat had necessarily a reactionary character. It inculcated universal asceticism and social leveling in its crudest form.

The socialist and communist systems properly so called, those of Saint Simon, Fourier, Owen and others, spring into existence in the early undeveloped period, described above, of the struggle between proletariat and bourgeoisie (*see* Section I. Bourgeoisie and Proletariat).

The founders of these systems see, indeed, the class antagonisms as well as the action of the decomposing elements in the prevailing form of society. But the proletariat, as yet in its infancy, offers to them the spectacle of a class without any historical initiative or any independent political movement.

Since the development of class antagonism keeps even

pace with the development of industry, the economic situation, as such socialists find it, does not as yet offer to them the material conditions for the emancipation of the proletariat. They therefore search after a new social science, after new social laws, that are to create these conditions.

Historical action is to yield to their personal inventive action, historically created conditions of emancipation to fantastic ones, and the gradual, spontaneous class organization of the proletariat to an organization of society specially contrived by these inventors. Future history resolves itself, in their eyes, into the propaganda and the practical carrying out of their social plans.

In the formation of their plans they are conscious of caring chiefly for the interests of the working class, as the most suffering class. Only from the point of view of being the most suffering class does the proletariat exist for them.

The undeveloped state of the class struggle, as well as their own surroundings, causes socialists of this kind to consider themselves far superior to all class antagonisms. They want to improve the condition of every member of society, even that of the most favored. Hence, they habitually appeal to society at large, without distinction of class; nay, by preference, to the ruling class. For how can people, when once they understand their system, fail to see in it the best possible plan of the best possible state of society?

Hence, they reject all political, and especially all revolutionary, action; they wish to attain their ends by peaceful means and endeavor by small experiments, necessarily doomed to failure, and by the force of example, to pave the way for the new social gospel.

Such fantastic pictures of future society, painted at a time when the proletariat is still in a very undeveloped state and has but a fantastic conception of its own position, correspond with the first instinctive yearnings of that class for a general reconstruction of society.

But these socialist and communist publications contain also a critical element. They attack every principle of existing society. Hence they are full of the most valuable materials for the enlightenment of the working class. The practical measures proposed in them—such as the abolition of the distinction between town and country; the abolition of the family, private gain, and the wage system; the proclamation of social harmony; the conversion of the functions of the state into a mere superintendence of production—all

these proposals point solely to the disappearance of class
antagonisms which were, at that time, only just cropping up,
and which, in these publications, are recognized only in
their earliest indistinct and undefined forms. These proposals, therefore, are of a purely utopian character.

The significance of critical-utopian socialism and communism bears an inverse relation to historical development. In
proportion as the modern class struggle develops and takes
definite shape, this fantastic standing apart from the contest, these fantastic attacks on it, lose all practical value and
all theoretical justification. Therefore, although the originators of these systems were, in many respects, revolutionary,
their disciples have, in every case, formed mere reactionary
sects. They hold fast by the original views of their masters,
in opposition to the progressive historical development of the
proletariat. They, therefore, endeavor, and that consistently,
to deaden the class struggle and reconcile the class antagonisms. They still dream of experimental realization of their
social utopias, of founding isolated *"phalanstères,"* establishing "home colonies," of setting up a "Little Icaria" [17]
—pocket editions of the New Jerusalem. To realize all these
castles in the air, they are compelled to appeal to the feelings and purses of the bourgeoisie. By degrees they sink into
the category of the reactionary conservative socialists depicted above, differing from these only by more systematic
pedantry and by their fanatical and superstitious belief in
the miraculous effects of their social science.

They, therefore, violently oppose all political action on
the part of the working class; such action, according to them,
can only result from blind unbelief in the new gospel.

The Owenites in England, and the Fourierists in France,
respectively oppose the Chartists [18] and the *Réformistes.* [19]

IV. POSITION OF THE COMMUNISTS IN RELATION
TO THE VARIOUS EXISTING OPPOSITION PARTIES

Section II has made clear the relations of the Communists to the existing working-class parties, such as the Chartists in England and the Agrarian Reformers in America. [20]

The Communists fight for the attainment of the immediate aims, for the enforcement of the momentary interests of
the working class; but in the movement of the present, they
also represent and take care of the future of that movement.

In France the Communists ally themselves with the Social Democrats [21] against the conservative and radical bourgeoisie, reserving, however, the right to take up a critical position in regard to phrases and illusions traditionally handed down from the great Revolution.

In Switzerland they support the Radicals, without losing sight of the fact that this party consists of antagonistic elements, partly of Democratic Socialists, in the French sense, partly of radical bourgeois.

In Poland they support the party that insists on an agrarian revolution as the prime condition for national emancipation, that party which fomented the insurrection of Cracow in 1846.

In Germany they fight with the bourgeoisie whenever it acts in a revolutionary way against the absolute monarchy, the feudal squirearchy, and the petty bourgeoisie.

But they never cease for a single instant to instill into the working class the clearest possible recognition of the hostile antagonism between bourgeoisie and proletariat, in order that the German workers may use as so many weapons against the bourgeoisie the social and political conditions that the bourgeoisie must necessarily introduce along with its supremacy, and in order that, after the fall of the reactionary classes in Germany, the fight against the bourgeoisie itself may immediately begin.

The Communists turn their attention chiefly to Germany, because that country is on the eve of a bourgeois revolution that is bound to be carried out under more advanced conditions of European civilization, and with a much more developed proletariat, than that of England was in the seventeenth, and of France in the eighteenth century, and because the bourgeois revolution in Germany will be but the prelude to an immediately following proletarian revolution.

In short, the Communists everywhere support every revolutionary movement against the existing social and political order of things.

In all these movements they bring to the fore, as the leading question in each, the property question, no matter what its degree of development at the time.

Finally, they labor everywhere for the union and agreement of the democratic parties of all countries.

The Communists disdain to conceal their views and aims. They openly declare that their ends can be attained only by the forcible overthrow of all existing social conditions. Let the ruling classes tremble at a Communistic revolution. The proletarians have nothing to lose but their chains. They have a world to win.

WORKING MEN OF ALL COUNTRIES, UNITE!

Friedrich Engels

SOCIALISM: UTOPIAN AND SCIENTIFIC

I

Modern socialism is, in its essence, the direct product of
the recognition, on the one hand, of the class antagonisms
existing in the society of today between proprietors and non-
proprietors, between capitalists and wage-workers; on the
other hand, of the anarchy existing in production. But, in its
theoretical form, modern socialism originally appears ostensibly as a more logical extension of the principles laid down
by the great French philosophers of the eighteenth century.
Like every new theory, modern socialism at first had to connect itself with the intellectual stock-in-trade ready at hand,
however deeply its roots lay in material economic facts.

The great men, who in France prepared men's minds for
the coming revolution, were themselves extreme revolution-
ists. They recognized no external authority of any kind whatever. Religion, natural science, society, political institutions
—everything was subjected to the most unsparing criticism:
everything must justify its existence before the judgment of
reason or give up existence. Reason became the sole measure of everything. It was the time when, as Hegel says, the
world stood upon its head; [22] first in the sense that the human head, and the principles arrived at by its thought,
claimed to be the basis of all human action and association;
but by and by, also, in the wider sense that the reality which
was in contradiction to these principles had, in fact, to be
turned upside down. Every form of society and government
then existing, every old traditional notion was flung into the
lumber-room as irrational; the world had hitherto allowed
itself to be led solely by prejudices; everything in the past
deserved only pity and contempt. Now, for the first time, appeared the light of day, the kingdom of reason; henceforth
superstition, injustice, privilege, oppression, were to be superseded by eternal truth, eternal Right, equality based on
Nature and the inalienable rights of man.

We know today that this kingdom of reason was nothing

more than the idealized kingdom of the bourgeoisie; that this eternal Right found its realization in bourgeois justice; that this equality reduced itself to bourgeois equality before the law; that bourgeois property was proclaimed as one of the essential rights of man; and that the government of reason, the Social Contract [23] of Rousseau, came into being, and only could come into being, as a democratic bourgeois republic. The great thinkers of the eighteenth century could, no more than their predecessors, go beyond the limits imposed upon them by their epoch.

But, side by side with the antagonism of the feudal nobility and the burghers, who claimed to represent all the rest of society, was the general antagonism of exploiters and exploited, of rich idlers and poor workers. It was this very circumstance that made it possible for the representatives of the bourgeoisie to put themselves forward as representing not one special class, but the whole of suffering humanity. Still further. From its origin the bourgeoisie was saddled with its antithesis: capitalists cannot exist without wage-workers, and, in the same proportion as the medieval burgher of the guild developed into the modern bourgeois, the guild journeyman and the day-laborer, outside the guilds, developed into the proletarian. And although, upon the whole, the bourgeoisie, in their struggle with the nobility, could claim to represent at the same time the interests of the different working classes of that period, yet in every great bourgeois movement there were independent outbursts of that class which was the forerunner, more or less developed, of the modern proletariat. For example, at the time of the German Reformation and the Peasants' War, the Anabaptists and Thomas Münzer; in the great English Revolution, the Levellers; [24] in the great French Revolution, Babeuf.

There were theoretical enunciations corresponding to these revolutionary uprisings of a class not yet developed; in the sixteenth and seventeenth centuries, utopian pictures of ideal social conditions; [25] in the eighteenth, actual communistic theories (Morelly and Mably). The demand for equality was no longer limited to political rights; it was extended also to the social conditions of individuals. It was not simply class privileges that were to be abolished, but class distinctions themselves. A communism, ascetic, denouncing all the pleasures of life, Spartan, was the first form of the new teaching. Then came the three great Utopians: Saint-Simon, to whom the middle-class movement, side by side with the proletarian, still had a certain significance; Fourier; and Owen, who in the country where capitalist production was most developed, and under the influence of the antagonisms derived from this, worked out his proposals for the removal of class distinction systematically and in direct relation to French materialism.

One thing is common to all three. Not one of them appears as a representative of the interests of that proletariat which historical development had, in the meantime, produced. Like the French philosophers, they do not claim to emancipate a particular class to begin with, but all humanity at once. Like them, they wish to bring in the kingdom of reason and eternal justice, but this kingdom, as they see it, is as far as heaven from earth, from that of the French philosophers.

For, to our three social reformers, the bourgeois world, based upon the principles of these philosophers, is quite as irrational and unjust, and, therefore, finds its way to the dust-hole quite as readily as feudalism and all the earlier stages of society. If pure reason and justice have not, hitherto, ruled the world, this has been the case only because men have not rightly understood them. What was needed was the individual man of genius, who has now arisen and who understands the truth. That he has now arisen, that the truth has now been clearly understood, is not an inevitable event, following of necessity in the chain of historical development, but a mere happy accident. He might just as well have been born 500 years earlier, and might then have spared humanity 500 years of error, strife, and suffering.

We saw how the French philosophers of the eighteenth century, the forerunners of the Revolution, appealed to reason as the sole judge of all that is. A rational government, rational society, were to be founded; everything that ran counter to eternal reason was to be remorselessly done away with. We saw also that this eternal reason was in reality nothing but the idealized understanding of the eighteenth-century citizen, just then evolving into the bourgeois. The French Revolution had realized this rational society and government.

But the new order of things, rational enough as compared with earlier conditions, turned out to be by no means absolutely rational. The state based upon reason completely collapsed. Rousseau's Social Contract had found its realization in the Reign of Terror, from which the bourgeoisie, who had lost confidence in their own political capacity, had taken refuge first in the corruption of the Directorate,[26] and, finally, under the wing of the Napoleonic despotism. The promised eternal peace was turned into an endless war of conquest. The society based upon reason had fared no better. The antagonism between rich and poor, instead of dissolving into general prosperity, had become intensified by the removal of the guild and other privileges, which had to some extent bridged it over, and by the removal of the charitable institutions of the Church. The "freedom of property" from feudal fetters, now veritably accomplished, turned out to be, for the small capitalists and small proprietors, the freedom to sell their small property, crushed under the overwhelming competition of the large capitalists and landlords, to these great lords, and thus, as far as the small capitalists and peasant proprietors were concerned, became "freedom *from* property." The development of industry upon a capitalistic basis brought poverty and misery to the working masses' conditions of social existence. Cash payment became more and more, in Carlyle's phrase, the sole nexus between man and man. The number of crimes increased from year to year. Formerly, the feudal vices had openly stalked about in broad daylight; though not eradicated, they were now at any rate thrust into the background. In their place, the bourgeois vices, hitherto practiced in secret, began to blossom all the more luxuriantly. Trade became to a greater and greater extent cheating. The "fraternity" of the revolutionary motto was realized in the chicanery and rivalries of the battle of competition. Oppression by force was replaced by corruption; the sword, as the first social lever, by gold. The right of the first night was transferred from the feudal lords to the bourgeois manufacturers. Prostitution increased to an unheard-of extent. Marriage itself remained, as before, the legally recognized form, the official cloak of prostitution, and, moreover, was supplemented by rich crops of adultery.

In a word, compared with the splendid promises of the philosophers, the social and political institutions born of the "triumph of reason" were bitterly disappointing caricatures. All that was wanting was the men to formulate this disappointment, and they came with the turn of the century. In 1802 Saint-Simon's Geneva letters appeared; in 1808 appeared Fourier's first work, although the groundwork of his theory dated from 1799; on January 1, 1800, Robert Owen undertook the direction of New Lanark.

At this time, however, the capitalist mode of production, and with it the antagonism between the bourgeoisie and the proletariat, was still very incompletely developed. Modern industry, which had just arisen in England, was still unknown in France. But modern industry develops, on the one hand, the conflicts which make absolutely necessary a revolution in the mode of production, and the abolition of its capitalistic character—conflicts not only between the classes derived from it, but also between the very productive forces and the forms of exchange created by it. And, on the other hand, it develops, in these very gigantic productive forces, the means of ending these conflicts. If, therefore, about the year 1800, the conflicts arising from the new social order were only just beginning to take shape, this holds still more fully as to the means of ending them. The "have-nothing" masses of Paris, during the Reign of Terror, were able for a moment to gain the mastery, and thus to lead the bourgeois revolution to victory in spite of the bourgeoisie themselves. But, in doing so, they only proved how impossible it was for their domination to last under the conditions then prevailing. The proletariat, which then for the first time evolved itself from these "have-nothing" masses as the nucleus of a new class, as yet quite incapable of independent political action, appeared as an oppressed, suffering order, to whom, because of incapacity to help itself, help could at best be brought from without or from above.

This historical situation also dominated the founders of socialism. To the crude conditions of capitalistic production and the crude class conditions corresponded crude theories. The solution of the social problems, which as yet lay hidden in undeveloped economic conditions, the Utopians attempted to evolve out of the human brain. Society presented nothing but wrongs; to remove these was the task of reason. It was necessary, then, to discover a new and more perfect system of social order and to impose this upon society from without by propaganda, and, wherever it was possible, by the example of model experiments. These new social systems were foredoomed as utopian; the more completely they were worked out in detail, the more they could not avoid drifting off into pure fantasies.

These facts once established, we need not dwell a moment longer upon this aspect of the question, now wholly belonging to the past. We can leave it to the literary small fry to solemnly quibble over these fantasies, which today only

make us smile, and to crow over the superiority of their own
bald reasoning, as compared with such "insanity." For ourselves, we delight in the stupendously grand thoughts and
germs of thought that everywhere break out through their
fantastic covering, and to which these philistines are blind.

Saint-Simon was a son of the great French Revolution,
at the outbreak of which he was not yet thirty. The Revolution
was the victory of the third estate, *i.e.*, of the great masses
of the nation, *working* in production and in trade, over the
privileged *idle* classes, the nobles and the priests. But the
victory of the third estate soon revealed itself as exclusively
the victory of a small part of this "estate," as the conquest
of political power by the socially privileged section of it,
i.e., the propertied bourgeoisie. And the bourgeoisie had
certainly developed rapidly during the Revolution, partly by
speculation in the lands of the nobility and of the Church,
confiscated and afterwards put up for sale, and partly by
frauds upon the nation by means of army contracts. It was
the domination of these swindlers that, under the Directorate, brought France to the verge of ruin, and thus gave
Napoleon the pretext for his *coup d'état*.

Hence, to Saint-Simon the antagonism between the third
estate and the privileged classes took the form of an antagonism between "workers" and "idlers." The idlers were not
merely the old privileged classes, but also all who, without
taking any part in production or distribution, lived on their
incomes. And the workers were not only the wage-workers,
but also the manufacturers, the merchants, the bankers. That
the idlers had lost the capacity for intellectual leadership
and political supremacy had been proved, and was finally
settled by the Revolution. That the propertyless classes did
not have this capacity seemed to Saint-Simon proved by the
experiences of the Reign of Terror. Then, who was to lead
and command? According to Saint-Simon, science and industry, united by a new religious bond, destined to restore that
unity of religious ideas which had been lost since the time
of the Reformation—a necessarily mystical and rigidly hierarchical "new Christianity." Now science meant the scholars;
and industry meant, in the first place, the working bourgeoisie,
manufacturers, merchants, bankers. These bourgeoisie were,
certainly, intended by Saint-Simon to transform themselves into
some kind of public officials, of social trustees; but they were
still to hold, *vis-à-vis* the workers, a commanding and
economically privileged position. The bankers especially were

to be called upon to direct the whole of social production by the regulation of credit. This conception was in exact keeping with a time in which modern industry in France and, with it, the chasm between bourgeoisie and proletariat was only just coming into existence. But what Saint-Simon especially lays stress upon is this: what interests him first, and above all other things, is the lot of the class that is the most numerous and the poorest (*"la classe la plus nombreuse et la plus pauvre"*).

Already in his Geneva letters, Saint-Simon lays down the proposition that "all men ought to work." In the same work he recognizes also that the Reign of Terror was the reign of the propertyless masses. "See," he says to them, "what happened in France at the time when your comrades held sway there: they brought about a famine." But to recognize the French Revolution as a class war, not simply one between nobility and bourgeoisie, but between nobility, bourgeoisie, and the propertyless, was, in the year 1802, a most pregnant discovery. In 1816, he declares that politics is the science of production, and foretells the complete absorption of politics by economics. The knowledge that economic conditions are the basis of political institutions appears here only in embryo. Yet what is here already very plainly expressed is the idea of the future conversion of political rule over men into an administration of things and a direction of processes of production—that is to say, the "abolition of the state," about which there has been so much noise recently.

Saint-Simon shows the same superiority over his contemporaries when, in 1814, immediately after the entry of the allies into Paris, and again in 1815, during the Hundred Days' War, he proclaims the alliance of France with England, and then of both these countries with Germany, as the only guarantee for the prosperous development and peace of Europe. To preach to the French in 1815 an alliance with the victors of Waterloo required as much courage as historical foresight.

If in Saint-Simon we find a comprehensive breadth of view, by virtue of which almost all the ideas of later socialists that are not strictly economic are found in him in embryo, we find in Fourier a criticism of the existing conditions of society, genuinely French and witty, but not upon that account any the less thorough. Fourier takes the bourgeoisie, their inspired prophets before the Revolution, and their interested eulogists after it, at their own word. He remorselessly lays bare the material and moral misery of the bourgeois world. He confronts it with the earlier philosophers' dazzling promises of a society in which reason alone would reign, a civilization in which happiness would be universal, a limitless human perfectibility, and he does this with the rose-colored phraseology of the bourgeois ideologists of his time. He points out how everywhere the most pitiful reality compares to the most high-sounding phrases, and he overwhelms this hopeless fiasco of phrases with his mordant sarcasm.

Fourier is not only a critic; his imperturbably serene nature makes him a satirist, and assuredly one of the greatest satirists of all time. He depicts, with equal power and charm, the swindling speculations that blossomed out upon the downfall of the Revolution, and the shopkeeping spirit prevalent in, and characteristic of, French commerce at that time. Still more masterly is his criticism of the bourgeois form of the relations between the sexes, and the position of woman in bourgeois society. He was the first to declare that in any given society the degree of woman's emancipation is the natural measure of the general emancipation.

But Fourier is at his greatest in his conception of the history of society. He divides its whole course, thus far, into four stages of evolution—savagery, barbarism, the patriarchate, civilization. This last is identical with the so-called civil, or bourgeois, society of today—*i.e.*, with the social order that came in with the sixteenth century. He proves "that the civilized stage raises every vice practised by barbarism in a simple fashion to a form of existence that is complex, ambiguous, equivocal, hypocritical"—that civilization moves in "a vicious circle," in contradictions which it constantly reproduces without being able to solve them; hence, it constantly arrives at the very opposite of that which it wants to attain, or pretends to want to attain, so that, *e.g.*, "under civilization poverty is born of superabundance itself."

Fourier, as we see, uses the dialectic method in the same masterly way as his contemporary, Hegel. Using these same dialectics, he argues against the talk about limitless human perfectibility, that every historical phase has its period of ascent and also its period of descent, and he applies this observation to the future of the whole human race. As Kant introduced into natural science the idea of the ultimate destruction of the earth, Fourier introduced into historical science that of the ultimate destruction of the human race.

While in France the hurricane of the Revolution swept over the land, in England a quieter, but not on that account less tremendous, revolution was going on. Steam and the new tool-making machinery were transforming manufacturing into modern industry, and thus revolutionizing the whole foundation of bourgeois society. The sluggish march of development in the manufacturing period changed into a veritable storm-and-stress period of production. With constantly increasing swiftness the division of society into large capitalists and propertyless proletarians went on. Between these, instead of the former stable middle class, an unstable mass of artisans and small shopkeepers, the most fluctuating portion of the population, now led a precarious existence.

The new mode of production was, as yet, only at the beginning of its period of ascent; as yet it was the normal, regular method of production—the only one possible under existing conditions. Nevertheless, even then it was producing crying social abuses—the herding together of a homeless population in the worst quarters of the large towns; the loosening of all traditional moral bonds, patriarchal subordination, family relations; overwork, especially of women and children, to a frightful extent; complete demoralization of the working class, suddenly flung into altogether new conditions, from the country into the town, from agriculture into modern industry, from stable conditions of existence into insecure ones that changed from day to day.

At this juncture there came forward as a reformer a manufacturer 29 years old—a man of almost sublime, childlike simplicity of character, and at the same time one of the few born leaders of men. Robert Owen had adopted the teaching of the materialistic philosophers: that man's character is the product, on the one hand, of heredity; on the other, of the environment of the individual during his lifetime, and especially during his period of development. In the industrial revolution most of his class saw only chaos and confusion, and the opportunity of fishing in these troubled waters and quickly making large fortunes. He saw in it the opportunity of putting into practice his favorite theory, and so of bringing order out of chaos. He had already tried it with success, as superintendent of more than five hundred men in a Manchester factory. From 1800 to 1829, he directed the great cotton mill at New Lanark, Scotland, as managing partner, along the same lines, but with greater freedom of action and with a success that made him a European rep-

utation. A population, originally consisting of the most
diverse and, for the most part, very demoralized elements,
a population that gradually grew to 2,500, he turned into a
model colony, in which drunkenness, police, magistrates,
lawsuits, poor laws, and charity were unknown. And all
this simply by placing the people in conditions worthy of
human beings and especially by carefully bringing up the
rising generation. He was the founder of infant schools and
introduced them first at New Lanark. At the age of two the
children came to school, where they enjoyed themselves so
much that they could scarcely be gotten home again. While
his competitors worked their people thirteen or fourteen
hours a day, in New Lanark the working day was only ten
and a half hours. When a crisis in cotton stopped work for
four months, his workers received their full wages all the
time. And with all this the business more than doubled in
value and to the last yielded large profits to its proprietors.

In spite of all this, Owen was not content. The existence
which he secured for his workers was, in his eyes, still far
from being worthy of human beings. "The people were slaves
at my mercy." The relatively favorable conditions in which he
had placed them were still far from allowing a rational development of the character and intellect in all directions,
much less of the free exercise of all their faculties. "And yet,
the working part of this population of 2,500 persons was
daily producing as much real wealth for society as, less than
half a century before, it would have required the working
part of a population of 600,000 to create. I asked myself,
what became of the difference between the wealth consumed by 2,500 persons and that which would have been
consumed by 600,000?" [27]

The answer was clear. It had been used to pay the proprietors of the establishment five percent on the capital they
had laid out, in addition to over £300,000 clear profit. And
that which held for New Lanark held to a still greater extent
for all the factories in England. "If this new wealth had not
been created by machinery, imperfectly as it has been applied, the wars of Europe against Napoleon and in support
of the aristocratic principles of society, could not have been
maintained. And yet this new power was the creation of the
working class." [28] To them, therefore, the fruits of this new
power belonged. The newly created gigantic productive
forces, hitherto used only to enrich individuals and to en-
slave the masses, offered to Owen the foundations for a recon-

struction of society; they were destined, as the common property of all, to be worked for the common good of all.

Owen's communism was based upon this purely business foundation, the outcome, so to say, of commercial calculation. Throughout, it maintained this practical character. Thus, in 1823, Owen proposed the relief of the distress in Ireland by communist colonies and drew up complete estimates of the costs of founding them, yearly expenditure, and probable revenue. And in his definite plan for the future, the technical working out of details is managed with such practical knowledge—ground plan, front, side and bird's-eye views all included—that the Owen method of social reform once accepted, there is from the practical point of view little to be said against the acutal arrangement of details.

His advance in the direction of communism was the turning-point in Owen's life. As long as he was simply a philanthropist, he was rewarded with nothing but wealth, applause, honor, and glory. He was the most popular man in Europe. Not only men of his own class, but statesmen and princes listened to him approvingly. But when he came out with his communist theories, that was quite another thing. Three great obstacles seemed to him especially to block the path to social reform: private property, religion, and the present form of marriage. He knew what confronted him if he attacked these—outlawry, excommunication from official society, the loss of his entire social position. But nothing of this prevented him from attacking them without fear of consequences, and what he had foreseen happened. Banished from official society, with a conspiracy of silence against him in the press, ruined by his unsuccessful communist experiments in America, in which he sacrificed all his fortune, he turned directly to the working class and continued working in their midst for thirty years. Every social movement, every real advance in England on behalf of the workers links itself to the name of Robert Owen. He forced through in 1819, after five years' fighting, the first law limiting the hours of labor of women and children in factories. He was president of the first Congress at which all the Trade Unions of England united in a single great trade association. He introduced as transition measures to the complete communistic organization of society, on the one hand, co-operative societies for retail trade and production. These have since that time, at least, given practical proof that the merchant and the manufacturer are socially quite unnecessary. On the other hand, he intro-

duced labor bazaars for the exchange of the products of
labor through the medium of labor-notes, whose unit was a
single hour of work; institutions necessarily doomed to failure,
but completely anticipating Proudhon's bank of exchange of
a much later period, and differing entirely from this in that it
did not claim to be the panacea for all social ills, but only
a first step towards a much more radical revolution of society.

The Utopians' mode of thought for a long time governed the
socialist ideas of the nineteenth century, and still governs
some of them. Until very recently all French and English
socialists did homage to it. The earlier German communism,
including that of Weitling, was of the same school. To all
these, socialism is the expression of absolute truth, reason
and justice, and has only to be discovered to conquer all the
world by virtue of its own power. And as absolute truth is
independent of time, space, and of the historical development of man, it is a mere accident when and where it is
discovered. With all this, absolute truth, reason, and justice
are different with the founder of each different school. And
as each one's special kind of absolute truth, reason, and
justice is again conditioned by his subjective understanding,
his conditions of existence, the measure of his knowledge and
his intellectual training, there is no other ending possible in
this conflict of absolute truths than that they shall be mutually
exclusive one of the other. Hence, from this nothing could
come but a kind of eclectic, average socialism, which, as
a matter of fact, has up to the present time dominated the
minds of most of the socialist workers in France and England.
Hence, a mish-mash allowing of the most manifold shades of
opinion; a mish-mash of such critical statements, economic
theories, pictures of future society by the founders of different
sects, as excite a minimum of opposition; a mish-mash which
is the more easily brewed the more the definite sharp
edges of the individual constituents are rubbed down in the
stream of debate, like rounded pebbles in a brook.

To make a science of socialism, it had first to be placed
upon a real basis.

II

In the meantime, along with and after the French philosophy of the eighteenth century there had arisen the new
German philosophy, culminating in Hegel. Its greatest
merit was the resumption of dialectics as the highest form of

reasoning. The old Greek philosophers were all born dialecticians, and Aristotle, the most encyclopedic intellect among them, had already analyzed the most essential forms of dialectic thought. The newer philosophy, on the other hand, although it also included brilliant exponents of dialectics (*e.g.*, Descartes and Spinoza), had, especially through English influence, become more and more rigidly fixed in the so-called metaphysical mode of reasoning, by which the French of the eighteenth century were also almost wholly dominated, at all events in their special philosophical work. Outside philosophy in the restricted sense, the French nevertheless produced masterpieces of dialectics. We need only call to mind Diderot's *Le Neveu de Rameau* and Rousseau's *Discours sur l'origine et les fondements de l'inégalité parmi les hommes*. We give here, in brief, the essential character of these two modes of thought.

When we consider and reflect upon Nature at large or the history of mankind or our own intellectual activity, at first we see the picture of an endless entanglement of relations and reactions, permutations and combinations, in which nothing remains what, where and as it was, but everything moves, changes, comes into being and passes away. We see, therefore, at first the picture as a whole, with its individual parts still more or less kept in the background; we observe the movements, transitions, connections, rather than the things that move, combine and are connected. This primitive, naïve but intrinsically correct conception of the world is that of ancient Greek philosophy, and was first clearly formulated by Heraclitus: everything is and is not, for everything is fluid, constantly changing, constantly coming into being and passing away.

But this conception, correctly as it expresses the general character of the picture of appearances as a whole, does not suffice to explain the details that make up this picture, and so long as we do not understand these, we do not have a clear idea of the whole picture. In order to understand these details we must detach them from their natural or historical connection and examine each one separately, its nature, special causes, effects, etc. This is, primarily, the task of natural science and historical research: branches of science which the Greeks of classical times, on very good grounds, relegated to a subordinate position, because they had first of all to collect materials for these sciences to work upon. A certain amount of natural and historical material must be collected before there can be any critical analysis, comparison, and arrangement in classes, orders, and species. The foundations of the exact natural sciences were, therefore, first worked out by the Greeks of the Alexandrian period,[29] and later on, in the Middle Ages, by the Arabs. Real natural science dates from the second half of the fifteenth century, and thence onward it has advanced with constantly increasing rapidity. The analysis of Nature into its individual parts, the grouping of the different natural processes and objects in definite classes, the study of the internal anatomy of organic bodies in their manifold forms—these were the fundamental conditions of the gigantic strides in our knowledge of Nature that have been made during the last four hundred years. But this method of work has also left us as a legacy the habit of observing natural objects and processes in isolation, apart from their connection with the vast whole; of observing them in repose, not in motion; as constants, not as essentially variables; in their death, not in their life. And when this way of looking at things was transferred by Bacon and Locke from natural science to philosophy, it produced the narrow, metaphysical mode of thought peculiar to the last century.

To the metaphysician, things and their mental reflexes, ideas, are isolated, are to be considered one after the other and apart from each other, are objects of investigation fixed, rigid, given once for all. He thinks in absolutely irreconcilable antitheses. "His communication is 'yea, yea; nay, nay'; for whatsoever is more than these cometh of evil." For him a thing either exists or does not exist; a thing cannot at the same time be itself and something else. Positive and negative absolutely exclude one another; cause and effect stand in a rigid antithesis one to the other.

At first sight this mode of thinking seems to us very luminous, because it is that of so-called sound common sense. But sound common sense, respectable fellow that he is in the homely realm of his own four walls, has very wonderful adventures as soon as he ventures out into the wide world of research. And the metaphysical mode of thought, justifiable and necessary as it is in a number of domains whose extent varies according to the nature of the particular object of investigation, sooner or later reaches a limit, beyond which it becomes one-sided, restricted, abstract, lost in insoluble contradictions. In the contemplation of individual things, it forgets the connection between them; in the contemplation of their existence, it forgets the beginning and end of that existence; of their repose, it forgets their motion. It cannot see the wood for the trees.

For everyday purposes we know and can say, *e.g.*, whether an animal is alive or not. But, upon closer inquiry, we find that this is, in many cases, a very complex question, as the jurists know very well. They have racked their brains in vain to discover a rational limit beyond which the killing of the child in its mother's womb is murder. It is just as impossible to determine absolutely the moment of death, for physiology proves that death is not an instantaneous, momentary phenomenon, but a very protracted process.

In like manner, every organic being is every moment the same and not the same; every moment it assimilates matter supplied from without, and gets rid of other matter; every moment some cells of its body die and others build themselves anew; in a longer or shorter time the matter of its body is completely renewed, and is replaced by other molecules of matter, so that every organic being is always itself, and yet something other than itself.

Further, we find upon closer investigation that the two poles of antithesis, positive and negative, *e.g.*, are as inseparable as they are opposed, and that despite all their opposition, they mutually interpenetrate. And we find, in like manner, that cause and effect are conceptions which only hold good in their application to individual cases; but as soon as we consider the individual cases in their general connection with the universe as a whole, they run into each other, and they become confounded when we contemplate that universal action and reaction in which causes and effects are eternally changing places, so that what is effect here and now will be cause there and then, and vice versa.

None of these processes and modes of thought enters into the framework of metaphysical reasoning. Dialectics, on the other hand, comprehends things and their representations, ideas, in their essential connection, concatenation, motion, origin, and ending. Such processes as those mentioned above are, therefore, so many corroborations of its own method of procedure.

Nature is the proof of dialectics, and it must be said for modern science that it has furnished this proof with very rich materials increasing daily, and thus has shown that, in the last resort, Nature works dialectically and not metaphysically; that she does not move in the eternal oneness of a perpetually recurring circle; but goes through a real historical evolution. In this connection Darwin must be named before all others. He dealt the metaphysical conception of Nature the heaviest blow by his proof that all organic beings, plants, animals, and man himself, are the products of a process of evolution going on through millions of years. But the naturalists who have learned to think dialectically are few and far between, and this conflict between the results of discovery and preconceived modes of thinking explains the endless confusion now reigning in theoretical natural science, the despair of teachers as well as students, of authors and readers alike.

An exact representation of the universe, its evolution, the development of mankind, and the reflection of this evolution in the minds of men, can therefore only be obtained by the methods of dialectics with its constant regard to the innumerable actions and reactions of life and death, of progressive or retrogressive changes. And in this spirit the new German philosophy has worked. Kant began his career by resolving the stable solar system of Newton and its eternal duration, after the famous initial impulse had once been given, into the result of a historic process, the formation of the sun and all the planets out of a rotating nebulous mass. From this he at the same time drew the conclusion that, given this origin of the solar system, its future death followed of necessity. His theory half a century later was established mathematically by Laplace, and half a century after that the spectroscope proved the existence in space of such incandescent masses of gas in various stages of condensation.

This new German philosophy culminated in the Hegelian system. In this system—and herein is its great merit—for the first time the whole world, natural, historical, intellectual, is represented as a process, *i.e.*, as in constant motion, change, transformation, development; and the attempt is made to trace out the internal connection that makes a continuous whole of all this movement and development. From this point of view the history of mankind no longer appeared as a wild whirl of senseless deeds of violence, all equally condemnable by the judgment of mature philosophic reason and best forgotten as quickly as possible, but as the process of evolution of man himself. It was now the task of the intellect to follow the gradual march of this process through all its devious ways, and to trace out the inner law running through all its apparently accidental phenomena.

That the Hegelian system did not solve the problem it propounded is here immaterial. Its epoch-making merit was that it propounded the problem. This problem is one that no single individual will ever be able to solve. Although Hegel was—with Saint-Simon—the most encyclopedic mind of his time, yet he was limited, first, by the necessarily limited extent of his own knowledge and, second, by the limited extent and depth of the knowledge and conceptions of his age. To these limits a third must be added. Hegel was an idealist. To him the thoughts within his brain were not the more or less abstract pictures of actual things and processes, but, conversely, things and their evolution were only the realized pictures of the "Idea," existing somewhere from eternity before the world was. This way of thinking turned everything upside down, and completely reversed the actual connection of things in the world. Correctly and ingeniously as many individual groups of facts were grasped by Hegel, yet, for the reasons just given, there is much that is botched, artificial, labored, in a word, wrong in point of detail. The Hegelian system, in itself, was a colossal miscarriage—but it was also the last of its kind. It was suffering, in fact, from an internal and incurable contradiction. On the one hand, its essential proposition was the conception that human history is a process of evolution, which, by its very nature, cannot find its intellectual final term in the discovery of any so-called absolute truth. But, on the other hand, it laid claim to being the very essence of this absolute truth. A system of natural and historical knowledge, embracing everything, and final for all time, is a contradiction of the fundamental law of dialectic reasoning. This law, indeed, by no means excludes, but, on the contrary, includes the idea that the systematic knowledge of the external universe can make giant strides from age to age.

The perception of the fundamental contradiction in German idealism led necessarily back to materialism, but, *nota bene,* not to the simply metaphysical, exclusively mechanical materialism of the eighteenth century. Old materialism looked upon all previous history as a crude heap of irrationality and violence; modern materialism sees in it the process of evolution of humanity, and aims at discovering the laws thereof. With the French of the eighteenth century, and even with Hegel, the prevailing conception was one of Nature as a whole, moving in narrow circles, and for ever immutable, with its eternal celestial bodies, as New-

ton taught, and unalterable organic species, as Linnaeus
taught. Modern materialism embraces the more recent discoveries of natural science, according to which Nature also
has its history in time, the celestial bodies, like the organic
species that, under favorable conditions, people them, being
born and perishing. And even if Nature, as a whole, must
still be said to move in recurrent cycles, these cycles assume
infinitely larger dimensions. In both aspects, modern materialism is essentially dialectic, and no longer requires the
assistance of that sort of philosophy which, queenlike, pre-
tended to rule the remaining mob of sciences. As soon as
each special science makes clear its position in the great
totality of things and our knowledge of things, a special
science dealing with this totality is superfluous or unnecessary. That which still survives of all earlier philosophy is
the science of thought and its laws—formal logic and dialectics. Everything else is subsumed in the positive science
of Nature and history.

While, however, the revolution in the conception of Nature could only be made in proportion to the corresponding
positive materials furnished by research, already much earlier certain historical facts had occurred which led to a decisive change in the conception of history. In 1831, the first
working-class rising took place in Lyons; between 1838 and
1842, the first national working-class movement, that of the
English Chartists, reached its height. The class struggle between proletariat and bourgeoisie came to the fore in the
history of the most advanced countries in Europe, in proportion to the development, on the one hand, of modern
industry, and on the other, of the newly acquired political
supremacy of the bourgeoisie. Facts more and more forcefully gave the lie to the teachings of bourgeois economy as
to the identity of the interests of capital and labor, as to the
universal harmony and universal prosperity that would be the
consequence of unbridled competition. All these things could
no longer be ignored, any more than the French and English
socialism, which, though very imperfect, was their theoretical
expression. But the old idealist conception of history, which
was not yet dislodged, knew nothing of class struggles
based upon economic interests, knew nothing of economic
interests; production and all economic relations appeared in
it only as incidental, subordinate elements in the "history
of civilization."

The new facts made imperative a new examination of all

past history. Then it was seen that *all* past history, with the exception of its primitive stages, was the history of class struggles; that these warring classes of society are always the products of the modes of production and of exchange—in a word, of the *economic* conditions of their time; that the economic structure of society always furnishes the real basis, starting from which we can alone work out the ultimate explanation of the whole superstructure of juridical and political institutions as well as of the religious, philosophical, and other ideas of a given historical period. Hegel had freed history from metaphysics—he had made it dialectic; but his conception of history was essentially idealistic. But now idealism was driven from its last refuge, the philosophy of history; now a materialistic treatment of history was propounded, and a method found of explaining man's "knowing" by his "being," instead of, as heretofore, his "being" by his "knowing."

From that time forward socialism was no longer an accidental discovery of this or that ingenious brain, but the necessary outcome of the struggle between two historically developed classes—the proletariat and the bourgeoisie. Its task was no longer to manufacture a system of society as perfect as possible, but to examine the historico-economic succession of events from which these classes and their antagonism had of necessity sprung, and to discover in the economic conditions thus created the means of ending the conflict. But the socialism of earlier days was as incompatible with this materialistic conception as the conception of Nature of the French materialists was with dialectics and modern natural science. The socialism of earlier days certainly criticized the existing capitalistic mode of production and its consequences. But it could not explain them, and, therefore, could not master them. It could only simply reject them as bad. The more strongly this earlier socialism denounced the exploitation of the working class, inevitable under capitalism, the less able was it clearly to show in what this exploitation consisted and how it arose. But for this it was necessary—(1) to present the capitalistic method of production in its historical connection and its inevitableness during a particular historical period, and therefore, also, to present its inevitable downfall; and (2) to lay bare its essential character, which was still a secret. This was done by the discovery of *surplus value*. It was shown that the appropriation of unpaid labor is the basis of the capitalist mode of production and of the exploitation of the worker that occurs under it; that even if the capitalist buys the labor power of his laborer at its full value as a commodity on the market, he yet extracts more value from it than he paid for; and that in the ultimate analysis this surplus value forms those sums of value from which are heaped up the constantly increasing masses of capital in the hands of the possessing classes. The genesis of capitalist production and the production of capital were both explained.

These two great discoveries, the materialistic conception of history and the revelation of the secret of capitalistic production through surplus value, we owe to Marx. With these discoveries socialism became a science. The next thing was to work out all its details and relations.

III

The materialist conception of history starts from the proposition that the production of the means to support human life and, next to production, the exchange of things produced, is the basis of all social structure; that in every society that has appeared in history, the manner in which wealth is distributed and society divided into classes or orders is dependent upon what is produced, how it is produced, and how the products are exchanged. From this point of view the final causes of all social changes and political revolutions are to be sought, not in men's brains, not in man's better insight into eternal truth and justice, but in changes in the modes of production and exchange. They are to be sought not in the *philosophy*, but in the *economics* of each particular epoch. The growing perception that existing social institutions are unreasonable and unjust, that reason has become unreason and right wrong, is only proof that in the modes of production and exchange changes have silently taken place with which the social order, adapted to earlier economic conditions, is no longer in keeping. From this it also follows that the means of getting rid of the incongruities that have been brought to light must also be present, in a more or less developed condition, within the changed modes of production themselves. These means are not to be invented by deduction from fundamental principles, but are to be discovered in the stubborn facts of the existing system of production.

What is, then, the position of modern socialism in this connection?

The present structure of society—this is now pretty generally conceded—is the creation of the ruling class of today, of the bourgeoisie. The mode of production peculiar to the bourgeoisie, known, since Marx, as the capitalist mode of production, was incompatible with the feudal system, with the privileges it conferred upon individuals, entire social ranks and local corporations, as well as with the hereditary ties of subordination which constituted the framework of its social organization. The bourgeoisie broke up the feudal system and built upon its ruins the capitalist order of society, the kingdom of free competition, personal liberty, the equality, before the law, of all commodity owners, and all the rest of the capitalist blessings. Thenceforth the capitalist mode of production could develop in freedom. Since steam, machinery, and the making of machines by machinery transformed the older manufacturing into modern industry, the productive forces evolved under the guidance of the bourgeoisie developed with a rapidity and to a degree unheard of before. But just as the older manufacturing, in its time, and handicraft, further developing under its influence, had come into collision with the feudal trammels of the guilds, so now modern industry, in its more complete development, comes into collision with the bounds within which the capitalistic mode of production confines it. The new productive forces have already outgrown the capitalistic mode of using them. And this conflict between productive forces and modes of production is not a conflict engendered in the mind of man, like that between original sin and divine justice. It exists, in fact, objectively, outside us, independently of the will and actions even of the men that have brought it on. Modern socialism is nothing but the reflex, in thought, of this conflict in fact; its ideal reflection in the minds, first, of the class directly suffering under it, the working class.

Now, in what does this conflict consist?

Before capitalistic production, i.e., in the Middle Ages, the system of petty industry generally prevailed, based upon the private property of the laborers in their means of production; in the country, the agriculture of the small peasant, freeman or serf; in the towns, the handicrafts organized in guilds. The instruments of labor—land, agricultural implements, the workshop, the tool—were the instruments of labor of single individuals, adapted for the use of one worker, and, therefore, of necessity, small, dwarfish, circumscribed. But, for this very reason they belonged, as a rule, to the producer himself. To concentrate these scattered, limited means of production, to enlarge them, to turn them into the powerful levers of production of the present day—this was precisely the historic role of capitalist production and of its upholder, the bourgeoisie. In the fourth section of *Capital* Marx has explained in detail, how since the fifteenth century this has been historically worked out through the three phases of simple co-operation, manufacturing and modern industry. But the bourgeoisie, as is also shown there, could not transform these puny means of production into mighty productive forces without transforming them, at the same time, from means of production of the individual into *social* means of production only workable by a collectivity of men. The spinning-wheel, the hand-loom, the blacksmith's hammer were replaced by the spinning-machine, the power-loom, the steam-hammer; the individual workshop, by the factory involving the co-operation of hundreds and thousands of workmen. In like manner, production itself changed from a series of individual into a series of social acts, and the products from individual to social products. The yarn, the cloth, the metal articles that now came out of the factory, were the joint product of many workers, through whose hands they had successively to pass before they were ready. No one person could say of them: "I made that; this is *my* product."

But where, in a given society, the fundamental form of production is that spontaneous division of labor which creeps in gradually and not upon any preconceived plan, there the products take on the form of *commodities*, whose mutual exchange, buying and selling, enable the individual producers to satisfy their manifold wants. And this was the case in the Middle Ages. The peasant, *e.g.*, sold to the artisan agricultural products and bought from him the products of handicraft. Into this society of individual producers, of commodity producers, the new mode of production thrust itself. In the midst of the old division of labor, grown up spontaneously and upon *no definite plan*, which had governed the whole of society, now arose division of labor upon a *definite plan*, as organized in the factory; side by side with *individual* production appeared *social* production.

The products of both were sold in the same market, and, therefore, at prices at least approximately equal. But organization upon a definite plan was stronger than spontaneous division of labor. The factories working with the combined social forces of a collectivity of individuals produced their commodities far more cheaply than the individual small producers. Individual production succumbed in one department after another. Socialized production revolutionized all the old methods of production. But its revolutionary character was, at the same time, so little recognized that it was, on the contrary, introduced as a means of increasing and developing the production of commodities. When it arose, it found ready-made, and made liberal use of, certain machinery for the production and exchange of commodities: merchants' capital, handicraft, wage-labor. Socialized production thus introducing itself as a new form of the production of commodities, it was a matter of course that under it the old forms of appropriation remained in full swing and were applied to its products as well.

In the medieval stage of the evolution of commodity production, the question as to the owner of the product of labor could not arise. The individual producer, as a rule, had, from raw material belonging to himself and generally his own handiwork, produced it with his own tools, by the labor of his own hands or of his family. There was no need for him to appropriate the new product. It belonged wholly to him, as a matter of course. His property in the product was, therefore, based *upon his own labor*. Even where external help was used, this was, as a rule, of little importance, and very generally was compensated by something other than wages. The apprentices and journeymen of the guilds worked less for board and wages than for education, in order that they might become master craftsmen themselves.

Then came the concentration of the means of production and of the producers in large workshops and manufactories, their transformation into actual socialized means of production and socialized producers. But the socialized producers and means of production and their products were still treated, after this change, just as they had been before, *i.e.*, as the means of production and the products of individuals. Hitherto, the owner of the instruments of labor had himself appropriated the product, because, as a rule, it was his own product and the assistance of others was the exception. Now the owner of the instruments of labor always appropriated to himself the product, although it was no longer *his* product but exclusively the product of the *labor of others*. Thus, the products now produced socially were not appropriated by those who had actually set in motion the means of production and actually produced the commodities, but by the *capitalists*. The means of production, and production itself, had become in essence socialized. But they were subjected to a form of appropriation which presupposes the private production of individuals, under which, therefore, everyone owns his own product and brings it to market. The mode of production is subjected to this form of appropriation, although it abolishes the conditions upon which the latter rests.

This contradiction, which gives to the new mode of production its capitalistic character, *contains the germ of all the social antagonisms of today*. The greater the mastery obtained by the new mode of production over all important fields of production and in all manufacturing countries, the more it reduced individual production to an insignificant residuum, *the more clearly was brought out the incompatibility of socialized production with capitalistic appropriation*.

The first capitalists found, as we have said, alongside other forms of labor, wage-labor ready-made for them on the market. But it was exceptional, complementary, accessory, transitory wage-labor. The agricultural laborer, though upon occasion hiring himself out by the day, had a few acres of his own land on which he could at all events live in a pinch. The guilds were so organized that the journeyman of today became the master of tomorrow. But all this changed, as soon as the means of production became socialized and concentrated in the hands of capitalists. The means of production, as well as the product, of the individual producer became more and more worthless; there was nothing left for him but to turn wage-worker under the capitalist. Wage-labor, heretofore the exception and accessory, now became the rule and basis of all production; heretofore complementary, it now became the sole remaining function of the worker. The wage-worker for a time became a wage-worker for life. The number of these permanent wage-workers was further enormously increased by the breaking-up of the feudal system that occurred at the same time, by the disbanding of the retainers of the feudal lords, the eviction of the peasants from their homesteads, etc. The separation was made complete between the means of production concentrated in the hands of the capitalists, on the one side, and the producers, possessing nothing but their labor-power, on the other. *The contradiction between socialized production and capitalistic appropriation manifested itself as the antagonism between proletariat and bourgeoisie.*

We have seen that the capitalistic mode of production thrust its way into a society of commodity producers, of individual producers, whose social bond was the exchange of their products. But every society based upon the production of commodities has this peculiarity: the producers have lost control over their own social interrelations. Each man produces for himself with such means of production as he may happen to have, and for such exchange as he may require to satisfy his remaining wants. No one knows how much of his particular article is coming on the market, nor how much of it will be wanted. No one knows whether his individual product will meet an actual demand, whether he will be able to make good his costs of production or even to sell his commodity at all. Anarchy reigns in socialized production.

But the production of commodities, like every other form of production, has its peculiar, inherent laws inseparable from it; and these laws work, despite anarchy, in and through anarchy. They reveal themselves in the only persistent form of social interrelations, *i.e.*, in exchange, and here they affect the individual producers as compulsory laws of competition. They are, at first, unknown to these producers themselves, and have to be discovered by them gradually and as the result of experience. They work themselves out, therefore, independently of the producers, and in antagonism to them, as inexorable natural laws of their particular form of production. The product governs the producers.

In medieval society, especially in the earlier centuries, production was essentially directed towards satisfying the wants of the individual. It satisfied, in the main, only the wants of the producer and his family. Where relations of personal dependence existed, as in the country, it also helped to satisfy the wants of the feudal lord. In all this there was, therefore, no exchange; the products, consequently, did not assume the character of commodities. The family of the peasant produced almost everything they wanted: clothes and furniture, as well as means of subsistence. Only when it began to produce more than was sufficient to supply its own wants and the payments in kind to the feudal lord, only then did it

also produce commodities. This surplus, thrown into socialized exchange and offered for sale, became commodities.

The artisans of the towns, it is true, had from the first to
produce for exchange. But they, also, themselves supplied
the greatest part of their own individual wants. They had
gardens and plots of land. They turned their cattle out into
the communal forest, which also yielded them timber and
firing. The women spun flax, wool, and so forth. Production
for the purpose of exchange, production of commodities,
was only in its infancy. Hence, exchange was restricted, the
market narrow, the methods of production stable; there was
local exclusiveness toward the outside, local unity within;
the Mark ³⁰ in the country; in the town, the guild.

But with the extension of the production of commodities
and especially with the introduction of the capitalist mode of
production, the laws of commodity production, hitherto latent, came into action more openly and with greater force.
The old bonds were loosened, the old exclusive limits broken
through, the producers were more and more turned into
independent, isolated producers of commodities. It became
apparent that the production of society at large was ruled
by absence of plan, by accident, by anarchy; and this anarchy
grew to greater and greater height. But the chief means by aid
of which the capitalist mode of production intensified this
anarchy of socialized production was the exact opposite of
anarchy. It was the increasing organization of production,
upon a social basis, in every individual productive establishment. By this, the old, peaceful, stable condition of things
was ended. Wherever this organization of production was
introduced into a branch of industry, it brooked no other
method of production by its side. The field of labor became
a battleground. The great geographical discoveries and the
colonization following upon them, multiplied markets and
quickened the transformation of handicraft into manufacturing. The war did not simply break out between the individual producers of particular localities. The local struggles
produced in their turn national conflicts, the commercial wars
of the seventeenth and the eighteenth centuries.

Finally, modern industry and the opening of the world
market made the struggle universal and at the same time
gave it an unheard-of virulence. Advantages in natural or
artificial conditions of production now decide the existence
or nonexistence of individual capitalists, as well as of whole
industries and countries. He that falls is remorselessly cast

aside. It is the Darwinian struggle of the individual for
existence transferred from Nature to society with intensified
violence. The conditions of existence natural to the animal
appear as the final term of human development. The contradiction between socialized production and capitalistic appropriation now presents itself as *an antagonism between
the organization of production in the individual workshop
and the anarchy of production in society generally.*

The capitalistic mode of production moves in these two
forms of the antagonism immanent to it from its very origin.
It is never able to get out of that "vicious circle" which Fourier had already discovered. What Fourier could not, indeed,
see in his time is that this circle is gradually narrowing; that
the movement becomes more and more a spiral and must
come to an end, like the movement of the planets, by collision with the center. It is the compelling force of anarchy in
the production of society at large that more and more completely turns the great majority of men into proletarians;
and it is the masses of the proletariat again who will finally
put an end to anarchy in production. It is the compelling force
of anarchy in social production that turns the limitless perfectibility of machinery under modern industry into a compulsory law by which every individual industrial capitalist
must perfect his machinery more and more, under penalty
of ruin.

But the perfecting of machinery is making human labor
superfluous. If the introduction and increase of machinery
means the displacement of millions of manual workers by a
few machine-workers, improvement in machinery means the
displacement of more and more of the machine-workers
themselves. It means, in the last analysis, the production of
a number of available wage-workers in excess of the average
needs of capital, the formation of a complete industrial reserve army, as I called it in 1845,[31] available at the times
when industry is working at high pressure, to be cast out
on the street when the inevitable crash comes, a constant
dead weight upon the limbs of the working class in its
struggle for existence with capital, a regulator for keeping
wages down to the low level that suits the interests of capital.
Thus it comes about, to quote Marx, that machinery becomes the most powerful weapon in the war of capital against
the working class; that the instruments of labor constantly
tear the means of subsistence out of the hands of the laborer;
that the very product of the worker is turned into an instru-

ment for his subjugation. Thus it comes about that the
economizing of the instruments of labor becómes at the
same time, from the outset, the most reckless waste of
labor power, and robbery based upon the normal conditions
under which labor functions; that machinery, "the most
powerful instrument for shortening labor time, becomes the
most unfailing means for placing every moment of the
laborer's time and that of his family at the disposal of the
capitalist for the purpose of expanding the value of his
capital." (*Capital,* English edition, p. 406.) Thus it comes
about that the overwork of some becomes the preliminary
condition for the idleness of others, and that modern industry, which hunts after new consumers over the whole
world, forces the consumption of the masses at home down
to a starvation minimum, and in doing this destroys its own
home market. "The law that always equilibrates the relative
surplus population, or industrial reserve army, to the extent
and energy of accumulation, this law rivets the laborer to
capital more firmly than the wedges of Vulcan did Prome-
theus to the rock. It establishes an accumulation of misery,
corresponding to the accumulation of capital. Accumulation
of wealth at one pole is, therefore, at the same time, accumulation of misery, agony of toil, slavery, ignorance, bru-
tality, mental degradation, at the opposite pole, *i.e.,* on the
side of the class that produces *its own product in the form
of capital."* (Marx's *Capital,* p. 661.) And to expect any
other division of the products from the capitalistic mode of
production is the same as expecting the electrodes of a battery not to decompose acidulated water, not to liberate oxygen
at the positive, hydrogen at the negative pole, so long as they
are connected with the battery.

We have seen that the ever-increasing perfectibility of
modern machinery is, by the anarchy of social production,
turned into a compulsory law that forces the individual industrial capitalist always to improve his machinery, always
to increase its productive force. The bare possibility of extending the field of production is transformed for him into
a similar compulsory law. The enormous expansive force
of modern industry, compared with which that of gases is
mere child's play, appears to us now as a *necessity* for expansion, both qualitative and quantitative, that laughs at
all resistance. Such resistance is offered by consumption, by
sales, by the markets for the products of modern industry.
But the capacity for extension, extensive and intensive, of

the markets is primarily governed by quite different laws that work much less energetically. The extension of the markets cannot keep pace with the extension of production. The collision becomes inevitable, and as this cannot produce any real solution so long as it does not break in pieces the capitalist mode of production, the collisions become periodic. Capitalist production has produced another "vicious circle."

As a matter of fact, since 1825, when the first general crisis broke out, the whole industrial and commercial world, production and exchange among all civilized peoples and their more or less barbaric hangers-on, are thrown out of joint about once every ten years. Commerce is at a standstill, the markets are glutted, products accumulate, as multitudinous as they are unsaleable, hard cash disappears, credit vanishes, factories are closed, the mass of the workers are in want of the means of subsistence, because they have produced too much of the means of subsistence; bankruptcy follows upon bankruptcy, execution follows execution. The stagnation lasts for years; productive forces and products are wasted and destroyed wholesale, until the accumulated mass of commodities finally filters off, more or less depreciated in value, until production and exchange gradually begin to move again. Little by little the pace quickens. It becomes a trot. The industrial trot breaks into a canter, the canter in turn grows into the headlong gallop of a perfect steeplechase of industry, commercial credit, and speculation which finally, after breakneck leaps, ends where it began—in the ditch of a crisis. And so over and over again. We have now, since the year 1825, gone through this five times, and at the present moment (1877) we are going through it for the sixth time. And the character of these crises is so clearly defined that Fourier hit all of them off when he described the first as *"crise pléthorique,"* a crisis from plethora.

In these crises, the contradiction between socialized production and capitalist appropriation ends in a violent explosion. The circulation of commodities is, for the time being, stopped. Money, the means of circulation, becomes a hindrance to circulation. All the laws of production and circulation of commodities are turned upside down. The economic collision has reached its apogee. *The mode of production is in rebellion against the mode of exchange.*

The fact that the socialized organization of production within the factory has developed so far that it has become incompatible with the anarchy of production in society, which exists side by side with and dominates it, is brought home to the capitalists themselves by the violent concentration of capital that occurs during crises, through the ruin of many large, and a still greater number of small, capitalists. The whole mechanism of the capitalist mode of production breaks down under the pressure of the productive forces, its own creations. It is no longer able to turn all this mass of means of production into capital. They lie fallow, and for that very reason the industrial reserve army must also lie fallow. Means of production, means of subsistence, available laborers, all the elements of production and of general wealth, are present in abundance. But "abundance becomes the source of distress and want" (Fourier), because it is the very thing that prevents the transformation of the means of production and subsistence into capital. For in capitalistic society the means of production can only function when they have undergone a preliminary transformation into capital, into the means of exploiting human labor power. The necessity of this transformation into capital of the means of production and subsistence stands like a ghost between these and the workers. It alone prevents the coming together of the material and personal levers of production; it alone forbids the means of production to function, the workers to work and live. On the one hand, therefore, the capitalistic mode of production stands convicted of its own incapacity to further direct these productive forces. On the other, these productive forces themselves, with increasing energy, press forward to the removal of the existing contradiction, to the abolition of their quality as capital, to the *practical recognition of their character as social productive forces.*

This rebellion of the productive forces, as they grow more and more powerful, against their quality as capital, this stronger and stronger command that their social character shall be recognized, forces the capitalist class itself to treat them more and more as social productive forces, so far as this is possible under capitalist conditions. The period of industrial high pressure, with its unbounded inflation of credit, not less than the crash itself, by the collapse of great capitalist establishments, tends to bring about that form of socialization of the great masses of means of production which we meet within the different kinds of joint-stock companies. Many of these means of production and distribution are, from the outset, so colossal that, like the railways, they exclude all other forms of capitalistic exploitation. At a further stage of evolution this form also becomes insufficient. The producers on a large scale in a particular branch of industry in a particular country unite in a trust, a union for the purpose of regulating production. They determine the total amount to be produced, parcel it out among themselves, and thus enforce the selling price fixed beforehand. But trusts of this kind, as soon as business becomes bad, are generally liable to break up, and on this very account compel a yet greater concentration of association. The whole of the particular industry is turned into one gigantic joint-stock company; internal competition gives place to the internal monopoly of this one company. This has happened in 1890 with the English alkali production, which is now, after the fusion of 48 large works, in the hands of one company, conducted upon a single plan, and with a capital of £6,000,000.

In the trusts, freedom of competition changes into its very opposite—into monopoly; and production without any definite plan of capitalistic society capitulates to production upon a definite plan of the invading socialistic society. Certainly this is so far still to the benefit and advantage of the capitalists. But in this case the exploitation is so palpable that it must break down. No nation will put up with production conducted by trusts, with so barefaced an exploitation of the community by a small band of dividend-mongers.

In any case, with trusts or without, the official representative of capitalist society—the state—will ultimately have to undertake the direction of production.[32] This necessity for conversion into state property is felt first in the great institutions for intercourse and communication—the post office, the telegraphs, the railways.

If the crises demonstrate the incapacity of the bourgeoisie for managing any longer modern productive forces, the transformation of the great establishments for production and distribution into joint-stock companies, trusts and state property shows how unnecessary the bourgeoisie are for that purpose. All the social functions of the capitalist are now performed by salaried employees. The capitalist has no further social function than that of pocketing dividends, tearing off coupons, and gambling on the Stock Exchange, where the different capitalists despoil one another of their capital. At first the capitalistic mode of production forces out the workers. Now it forces out the capitalists, and reduces them, just as it reduced the workers, to the ranks of the surplus population, although not immediately into those of the industrial reserve army.

But the transformation, either into joint-stock companies and trusts, or into state ownership, does not do away with the capitalistic nature of the productive forces. In the joint-stock companies and trusts this is obvious. And the modern state, again, is only the organization that bourgeois society takes on in order to support the external conditions of the capitalist mode of production against the encroachments as well of the workers as of individual capitalists. The modern state, no matter what its form, is essentially a capitalist machine, the state of the capitalists, the ideal personification of the total national capital. The more it proceeds to the taking over of productive forces, the more does it actually become the national capitalist, the more citizens does it exploit. The workers remain wage-workers—proletarians. The capitalist relation is not done away with. It is rather brought to a head. But, brought to a head, it topples over. State ownership of the productive forces is not the solution of the conflict, but concealed within it are the technical conditions that form the elements of that solution.

This solution can only consist in the practical recognition of the social nature of the modern forces of production, and therefore in harmonizing the modes of production, appropriation, and exchange with the socialized character of the means of production. And this can only come about by society openly and directly taking possession of the productive forces which have outgrown all control except that of society as a whole. The social character of the means of production and of the products today reacts against the producers, periodically disrupts all production and exchange, and acts only like a law of Nature, working blindly, forcibly, destructively. But with the assumption by society of the productive forces, the social character of the means of production and of the products will be utilized by the producers with a perfect understanding of its nature, and instead of being a source of disturbance and periodic collapse, will become the most powerful lever of production itself.

Active social forces work exactly like natural forces: blindly, forcibly, destructively, so long as we do not understand and reckon with them. But once we understand them, once we grasp their action, their direction, their effects, it depends only upon ourselves to subject them more and more to our own will, and by means of them to reach our own ends.

And this holds especially for the mighty productive forces of today. As long as we obstinately refuse to understand the nature and the character of these social means of action—and this understanding goes against the grain of the capitalist mode of production and its defenders—so long will these forces work in spite of us, in opposition to us, so long will they master us, as we have shown above in detail.

But once their nature is understood, they can, in the hands of the producers working together, be transformed from master demons into willing servants. The difference is as that between the destructive force of electricity in the lightning of a storm, and electricity under command in a telegraph and a voltaic arc; the difference between a conflagration, and fire working in the service of man. With this recognition, at last, of the real nature of the productive forces of today, the social anarchy of production gives place to a social regulation of production upon a definite plan, according to the needs of the community and of each individual. Then the capitalist mode of appropriation, in which the product enslaves first the producer and then the appropriator, is replaced by the mode of appropriation of the products that is based upon the nature of the modern means of production: on the one hand, direct social appropriation, as means for the maintenance and extension of production; on the other, direct individual appropriation, as means of subsistence and enjoyment.

While the capitalist mode of production more and more completely transforms the great majority of the population into proletarians, it creates the power which, under penalty of its own destruction, is forced to accomplish this revolution. While it forces on more and more the transformation of the vast means of production, already socialized, into state property, it shows itself the way to accomplish this revolution. *The proletariat seizes political power and turns the means of production into state property.*

But, in doing this, it abolishes itself as proletariat, abolishes all class distinctions and class antagonisms, abolishes also the state as state. Society thus far, based upon class antagonisms, had need of the state; that is, of an organization of the particular class which was *pro tempore* the exploiting class, an organization for the purpose of preventing any interference with the existing conditions of production, and, therefore, especially, for the purpose of forcibly keeping the exploited classes in the condition of oppression corresponding with the given mode of production (slavery, serfdom, wage-labor). The state was the official representative of society as a whole, the gathering of it into a visible embodiment. But it was this only in so far as it was the state of that class which itself represented, for the time being, society as a whole: in ancient times, the state of slaveowning citizens; in the Middle Ages, the feudal lords; in our own time, the bourgeoisie. When at last it becomes the real representative of the whole of society, it renders itself unnecessary. As soon as there is no longer any social class to be held in subjection; as soon as class rule, and the individual struggle for existence based upon our present anarchy in production, with the collisions and excesses arising from these, are removed, nothing more·remains to be repressed, and a special repressive force, a state, is no longer necessary. The first act by virtue of which the state really constitutes itself the representative of the whole of society— the taking possession of the means of production in the name of society—this is, at the same time, its last independent act as a state. State interference in social relations becomes, in one domain after another, superfluous, and then dies out by itself; the government of persons is replaced by the administration of things and by the conduct of the processes of production. The state is not "abolished." *It dies out.* This gives the measure of the value of the phrase *"a free state,"* both as to its justifiable use at times by agitators and as to its ultimate scientific insufficiency; and also of the demands of the so-called anarchists for the abolition of the state out of hand.

Since the historical appearance of the capitalist mode of production, the appropriation by society of all the means of production has often been dreamed of, more or less vaguely, by individuals, as well as by sects, as the ideal of the future. But it could become possible, could become a historical necessity, only when the actual conditions for its realization were there. Like every other social advance, it becomes practicable, not by men understanding that the existence of classes is in contradiction to justice, equality, etc., not by the mere willingness to abolish these classes, but by virtue of certain new economic conditions. The separation of society into an exploiting and an exploited class, a ruling and an oppressed class, was the necessary consequence of the deficient and restricted development of production in former times. So long as the total social labor only yields a produce which but slightly exceeds that barely necessary for the existence of all; so long, therefore, as labor engages all or almost all the time of the great majority of the members of society—so long, of necessity, is this society divided into classes. Side by side with the great majority, exclusively bond slaves to labor, arises a class freed from direct productive labor, which looks after the general affairs of society: the direction of labor, state business, law, science, art, etc. It is, therefore, the law of division of labor that lies at the basis of the division into classes. But this does not prevent the division into classes from being carried out by means of violence and robbery, trickery and fraud. It does not prevent the ruling class, once having the upper hand, from consolidating its power at the expense of the working class, from turning its social leadership into an intensified exploitation of the masses.

But if, upon this showing, division into classes has a certain historical justification, it has this only for a given period, only under given social conditions. It was based upon the insufficiency of production. It will be swept away by the complete development of modern productive forces. And, in fact, the abolition of classes in society presupposes a degree of historical evolution at which the existence, not simply of this or that particular ruling class, but of any ruling class at all, and, therefore, the existence of class distinction itself has become an obsolete anachronism. It presupposes, therefore, the development of production carried out to a degree at which appropriation of the means of production and of the products, and, with this, of political domination, of the monopoly of culture, and of intellectual leadership by a particular class of society, has become not only superfluous but economically, politically and intellectually, a hindrance to development.

This point is now reached. Their political and intellectual bankruptcy is scarcely any longer a secret to the bourgeoisie themselves. Their economic bankruptcy recurs regularly every ten years. In every crisis, society is suffocated beneath the weight of its own productive forces and products, which it cannot use, and stands helpless, face to face with the absurd contradiction that the producers have nothing to consume, because consumers are wanting. The expansive force of the means of production bursts the bonds that the capitalist mode of production had imposed upon them. Their deliverance from these bonds is the one precondition for

an unbroken, constantly accelerated development of the productive forces, and therewith for a practically unlimited increase of production itself. Nor is this all. The socialized
appropriation of the means of production does away, not
only with the present artificial restrictions upon production,
but also with the positive waste and devastation of productive forces and products that are at the present time the
inevitable concomitants of production and that reach their
height in the crises. Further, it sets free for the community at
large a mass of means of production and of products by
doing away with the senseless extravagance of the ruling
classes of today and their political representatives. The possibility of securing for every member of society, by means of
socialized production, an existence not only sufficient materially, and becoming day by day more fully so, but an
existence guaranteeing to all the free development and exercise of their physical and mental faculties—this possibility is
now for the first time here, but *it is here*.[33]

With the seizing of the means of production by society,
production of commodities and, simultaneously, the mastery of the product over the producer are abolished. Anarchy
in social production is replaced by systematic, definite organization. The struggle for individual existence disappears.
Then for the first time man, in a certain sense, is finally
marked off from the rest of the animal kingdom and emerges
from mere animal conditions of existence into really human
ones. The whole sphere of the conditions of life which surround man, and which have hitherto ruled man, now comes
under the dominion and control of man, who for the first
time becomes the real, conscious lord of Nature, because he
has now become master of his own social organization. The
laws of his own social action, hitherto standing face to face
with man as laws of Nature foreign to and dominating him,
will then be used with full understanding and thereby
mastered by him. Man's own social organization, hitherto
confronting him as a necessity imposed by Nature and history,
now becomes the result of his own free action. The extra-
neous objective forces that have hitherto governed history
pass under the control of man himself. Only from that time
will man himself, more and more consciously, make his own
history—only from that time will the social causes set in
motion by him have, in the main and in a constantly
growing measure, the results intended by him. It is the ascent

of man from the kingdom of necessity to the kingdom of freedom.

Let us us briefly sum up our sketch of historical evolution.

I. *Medieval Society*—Individual production on a small scale. Means of production adapted for individual use; hence primitive, ungainly, petty, dwarfed in action. Production for immediate consumption, either of the producer himself or of his feudal lord. Only where an excess of production over this consumption occurs is such excess offered for sale, enters into exchange. Production of commodities, therefore, only in its infancy. But already it contains within itself, in embryo, *anarchy in the production of society at large.*

II. *Capitalist Revolution*—Transformation of industry, at first by means of simple co-operation and manufacturing. Concentration of the means of production, hitherto scattered, into great workshops. As a consequence, their transformation from individual to social means of production—a transformation which does not, on the whole, affect the form of exchange. The old forms of appropriation remain in force. The capitalist appears. In his capacity as owner of the means of production, he also appropriates the products and turns them into commodities. Production has become a *social* act. Exchange and appropriation continue to be *individual* acts, the acts of individuals. *The social product is appropriated by the individual capitalist.* Fundamental contradiction, whence arise all the contradictions in which our present-day society moves and which modern industry brings to light.

A. Severance of the producer from the means of production. Condemnation of the worker to wage-labor for life. *Antagonism between the proletariat and the bourgeoisie.*

B. Growing predominance and increasing effectiveness of the laws governing the production of commodities. Unbridled competition. *Contradiction between socialized organization in the individual factory and social anarchy in production as a whole.*

C. On the one hand, the perfecting of machinery made by competition compulsory for each individual manufacturer and complemented by a constantly growing displacement of laborers. *Industrial reserve army.* On the other hand, unlimited extension of production, also compulsory under competition for every manufacturer. On both sides, unheard-of development of productive forces, excess of supply over demand, overproduction, glutting of the markets, crises every

ten years, the vicious circle: excess here, of means of production and products—excess there, of laborers, without
employment and without means of existence. But these
two levers of production and of social well-being are unable
to work together, because the capitalist form of production
prevents the productive forces from working and the products
from circulating, unless they are first turned into capital—
which their very superabundance prevents. The contradiction
has grown into an absurdity. *The mode of production rises in
rebellion against the form of exchange.* The bourgeoisie are
convicted of incapacity further to manage their own social
productive forces.

D. Partial recognition of the social character of the productive forces forced upon the capitalists themselves. Taking
over of the great institutions for production and communication, first by joint-stock companies, later on by trusts,
then by the state. The bourgeoisie demonstrated to be a superfluous class. All its social functions are now performed by
salaried employees.

III. *Proletarian Revolution*—Solution of the contradictions.
The proletariat seizes the public power, and by means of
this transforms the socialized means of production, slipping
from the hands of the bourgeoisie, into public property. By
this act, the proletariat frees the means of production from
the character of capital they have thus far borne, and
gives their socialized character complete freedom to work
itself out. Socialized production upon a predetermined plan
becomes henceforth possible. The development of production makes the existence of different classes of society thenceforth an anachronism. In proportion as anarchy in social production vanishes, the political authority of the state dies out.
Man, at last the master of his own form of social organization, becomes at the same time the lord over Nature, his
own master—free.

To accomplish this act of universal emancipation is the
historical mission of the modern proletariat. To comprehend
thoroughly the historical conditions and thus the very nature of this act, to impart to the now oppressed proletarian
class a full knowledge of the conditions and of the meaning
of the momentous act it is called upon to accomplish, this
is the task of the theoretical expression of the proletarian
movement, scientific socialism.

II.

~ LENIN AND THE
PREMATURE SOCIALIST REVOLUTION

The most fateful event for the world Marxist movement and perhaps for contemporary history as well was the adoption of Marxism by nineteenth-century Russian socialists and their adjustment of western Marxism to fit conditions of an economically underdeveloped, rural society.

Western Marxism came to Russia in two waves. The first wave, led by George Plekhanov in the 1880's, carried a number of former Russian "populists" to Western Europe where they formulated the theory and outlined the practice of their new credo. In the 1890's the second wave occurred, but this time the new adherents remained in Russia, and in a remarkably short time won the allegiance of the young intellectuals that had for so long been the pride of Russian populism.

Much of the explanation for this remarkable success lies in the character of the preceding decade. It was a period of extreme reaction in government policy and timid retreat in the mood of the public. Throughout the 1880's, Tsar Alexander III attempted to undo what was left of the "great reforms" of Alexander II. The powers of the local self-government bodies were sharply curtailed, the universities lost their autonomous rights, the independence of the judiciary was abridged, and the activities of the censor and the secret police became again what they had been in the reign of Nicholas I. What was particularly unusual in this decade, however, was the popular mood. In place of the dramatic boldness of "heroic" populism and the usual insistence on socially conscious art and literature, there appeared a variety of tendencies that seemed to the few remaining radicals to reflect conservatism, escapism or simple cowardice: Tolstoyan nonresistance to evil, an art-for-art's-sake vogue and a concern with moderate achievements or, as they were called, "small deeds." The sharp contrast of Marxism to this moderation and apparent escapism made the new revolutionary theory and practice particularly attractive to those with more radical temperaments.

But this was only one of many appeals. Another, and a more immediate cause for the shift to Marxism beginning when it did in the early 1890's, was the disastrous famine of 1891-1892. Here, at last, the remaining populists thought was the stimulus for the long-awaited peasant rising. Once again, however, the peasants disillusioned the revolutionaries: instead of attacking the landlords and government officials, they turned against the doctors who had come to check the epidemic that accompanied the famine. Even populist groups now gave up hope in the peasantry and turned virtually all their attention to agitation among the nascent urban proletariat. So much was this the case that it was often impossible for the police to distinguish between them and the Marxists.

The greater the populist failures, the greater the attraction of a doctrine that seemed to demonstrate with complete scientific objectivity the inevitability of victory. An exhilarating tone of proud self-confidence marks the writings of the young Marxists of that time. As one contemporary wrote, the young Marxists were an entirely new people, "militant, energetic, with burning eyes and flaming heart," people who saw their "happiness . . . in struggle—in the struggle for something in which they firmly believed" and who knew neither doubts nor hesitation.

Even with this, however, we have only begun to list the appeals of Marxism to young Russians. A major attraction, perhaps the main reason for the success of Marxism in the 1890's, was its acceptance of the policies of rapid industrialization pursued by Nicholas II and his Finance Minister von Witte. Populists had persistently opposed such "capitalistic" industrialization, but all their efforts had been in vain, providing yet another source of disappointment for them. Marxists, on the contrary, eagerly welcomed all measures that promoted capitalism and urbanization. They did so for a number of reasons. For one thing, the Russian intelligentsia were largely "westerners"; that is, they were well aware of the cultural and economic benefits associated with the urban civilization of the West, and they usually traveled extensively in the West. Actually this was no less true for the populists than it was for the Marxists. A leading populist author, Vorontsov, gave graphic expression to this "westerner" sentiment when he wrote:

Russia belongs to the family of civilized nations and, moreover, has entered the twentieth century of our era. This means that its needs and the forms of their satisfaction must be commensurate not with the cultural level on which it finds itself, but with those forms that have been devised and applied by Western Europe. . . . We want to eat, dress, entertain ourselves, and construct our homes, streets, and urban buildings on the model of what is being done in these areas by modern Europe, not by the Europe of the Middle Ages. . . .

Expressing a similar attitude, the Marxist Serge Bulgakov extolled the emergence of a westernized economy in Russia, since with every step in this direction "Russia rapidly approximates West European culture and loses its former characteristics of an exclusively peasant and crude country. . . . Every new factory, every new industrial enterprise carries us forward, increasing the numbers of people capable of intellectual Europeanization." To oppose this process, he wrote, was to oppose "all the benefits of European culture which alone give beauty to our lives."

What had kept many earlier intellectuals, particularly the populists, from supporting the development of a western urban society was the fact that in their minds such a society required capitalism and rapid industrialization. Both, in their eyes, meant destructive burdens on the already impoverished peasantry, the end of the peasant commune on which the populists based their socialist hopes, and the establishment of that very exploitative system that they had learned (in part from western Marxism) to detest. All this considered, it was difficult for those dedicating their lives to the defense of the peasant masses to accept a western economic development, however much they might envy the cultural benefits that were associated with it.

Marxism removed this dilemma completely. The westernized intellectual who accepted Marxism need not feel any conflict between his own western, urban preferences and his socialist concern for mass welfare; for only by means of establishing a technologically advanced, industrialized economy could society gain the necessary conditions for socialism, the only way to true social justice.

In addition to the much-desired material and "cultural"

benefits of a western urban society there were the gains of political freedom, civil liberties that, according to Marx, were parts of the "superstructure" that emerged from the bourgeois economic substructure. The importance of this link between constitutional democracy and economic capitalism in the minds of many young Russian Marxists is often missed by those who view Marxism through Leninist eyes, whether in Soviet Russia or in the West. Some appreciation of this aspect of the subject can be gained from the following statement by a leading Marxist, Peter Struve:

I was . . . a constitutionalist and a political Liberal before the problem of socialism arose before my mind. . . . Socialism was an abstract and remote ideal, while the struggle for civil and political liberties was a vital task. . . . I was interested in socialism chiefly as an ideological force, which, according to the adoption of this or that sociological conception of Russia's development, could be turned either for or against the conquest of civil and political liberties.

To a certain extent this was a continuation of Plekhanov's general approach to the bourgeois constitutional phase of the historical process leading from feudalism to socialism. Consistent with his view of Marxism, Plekhanov expected socialism to result from political power gradually won by socialists through parliamentary institutions. As he wrote in 1884:

They [the workers], of course, will not suddenly achieve this dominant position. . . . For a long time, they will obtain only concessions [and] will demand merely those reforms that would give them not dominance, but only the possibility of growing and maturing toward future dominance; reforms that would satisfy only their most essential, most immediate needs and, if only slightly, extend the sphere of their influence in the social life of the country.

"The so-called revolution," he concluded, "is only the last act in a long drama."

In a bitter and far-ranging debate, the populists attacked all aspects of the Marxists' theories and programs. They denied the validity of historical determinism according to which all nations must inevitably follow the same path, and they were particularly ardent in their attack on what seemed to them the Marxists' cold-blooded willingness to stand by and watch the existing mass Russian population, the peasantry, suffer as a result of the government's policy of rapid industrialization. In reply, the Marxists emphasized the long failure of the populists, the political backwardness of the peasants and, above all, the objectively valid, scientific character of Marxism. The theme in Marxism that gave particular support to its adherents in Russia at this time was the dialectic, since it completely explained and thereby justified the need of short-run distress, such as that suffered by the peasantry during Tsarist industrialization. Why should the Marxist feel responsible for this inevitable distress? Why should it clash with his socialist conviction? On the contrary, he argued, since only the rapid industrialization and the Russian bourgeois society Marxism predicted could pave the way for a later socialism, the populists should feel guilty for standing in the way of ultimate social justice. In the words of the Russian Marxists writing in the nineties, they were social scientists who look "bravely into the eyes of reality" and who do not "give way to the impulse of moral feeling"; who "idealize nothing, but only outline completely objectively a certain pattern of development . . . without ever shedding tears over the 'painful paths' of economic development"; and who are able to accept "the pitiless laws" of history. As for the populists, they were simply "weeping ideologists" who attacked this inevitable development with "melancholic lamentations and ethical accusations."

In addition to the contrast it made with the unsuccessful populist movement, a contrast re-emphasized as a result of the famine of 1891, Marxism thus won critically important advantages because of its association with economic progress, the emergence of a strong constitutional movement and the obvious desire of intellectuals—even those with socialist sentiments—to feel part of this exciting advance toward a modern, progressive and culturally advanced society on the model of Western Europe.

For some Marxists, however, their cause was simply too successful in this decade. Science, technology, western urbanism, welfare legislation for the workers, the establishment of a bourgeois parliamentary democracy and bourgeois civil liberties—all this was certainly important. But what if one or another of these became the principal goal, to the neglect of the class struggle and a socialist revolution? Here we see one of a series of difficult dilemmas facing the Marxist in an underdeveloped economy. It was one thing to be a Marxist in Western Europe where, in the eyes of Marxists, capitalism was already developed and moving toward a socialist society. In Russia, however, the development of capitalism had hardly begun, and the Russian Marxist was faced with the prospect not merely of waiting for Russia to pass through the entire phase of capitalism, but, if he wanted to be consistent, of actually promoting the establishment of a West European, bourgeois, capitalist society in Russia. The basis error of the populist socialists, according to the Marxists, was their belief in the possibility of skipping this intermediary phase. But in striving to promote these intermediary, bourgeois institutions, the Marxists might forget that they were only temporary means toward the great goal of socialist revolution.

This is what seemed to be happening in the 1890's. Russian Marxism in that decade can be divided into two groups: the so-called Legal Marxists who defended Marxism publicly, in articles and lectures; and those, usually referred to as the Economists, who were more directly associated with the emerging labor movement. The focus of the first was on achieving rapid industrialization, urbanization and the social, political and psychological benefits that, on the basis of Marxist theory and West European history, they associated with this economic progress. Consequently, relatively little is said about class struggle or socialist revolution in their writings. As for the Economists, they seemed almost exclusively concerned with gaining better conditions for the workers, leaving politics to the bourgeoisie and intentionally ignoring questions of the future socialist revolution and socialist society. They argued that the workers were not ready for such political or socialist propaganda, since Russia was only at the beginning of its industrial, urban development, and that if they insisted on such propaganda, they would lose contact with the workers' real desires and thereby lose the leadership of the nascent working-class movement.

What Marxism seemed to be promoting in Russia in the nineties, therefore, was not a struggle for socialism, but a struggle for a bourgeois society with a parliamentary government, an urban culture, and a highly productive, well-organized working class utilizing relatively peaceful political and economic means to improve its conditions of life and work. There is nothing, of course, wrong with this from the West European Marxist point of view: it quite properly reflected historical determinism and the pattern of historical stages.

There were some revolutionary Russian Marxists, however, who simply could not support a system that they ardently opposed or wait patiently while History turned Russia into a fully bourgeois, capitalistic society. Moreover, during the 1890's "revisionism" was gathering strength in Western Europe, and those in Russia unwilling to tolerate a bourgeois Russia could make good use of the arguments directed against the Revisionists by the so-called Orthodox Marxists. According to the "revisionists," socialism would gradually evolve as a result of improvements in working-class economic and political conditions. If the revisionist interpretation were correct, the Orthodox maintained, then it was doubtful that socialism would ever arrive. With constant improvements in living conditions, the workers were becoming essentially bourgeois in their interests and desires and more or less satisfied with the existing bourgeois system, as long as it continued to meet the economic needs of labor. Every step in the direction of better living conditions meant one step away from socialist revolution. From the point of view of Russian revolutionary history this meant that the workers were losing precisely the revolutionary fervor that the Russian Marxists had long believed distinguished them from the peasantry. The old guard of Russian Marxism, Plekhanov and his followers, were well aware of these dangers and bitterly attacked the "revisionist" attitudes expressed in the policies of the Legal Marxists and the Economists. However, they were too strongly bound to Marxist historical determinism with which these policies seemed consistent, at least in Russia at the time, and were, therefore, unable to recommend radical measures against them. Lenin was willing and able to do so.

In Lenin's Marxism, or Leninism, one sees an intensification of the dilemma of Marxism in an underdeveloped economy. Marxism in an underdeveloped economy required revolutionaries with an extremely rare combination of attitudes. They must be devoted revolutionaries willing to give up the usual benefits available to the more educated members of society and to risk prison, exile or worse in the name of their cause. Yet, at the same time, they must be extraordinarily patient and not only wait until history has brought the country through capitalism, but actually help establish this system, however hateful it was to them as Marxist socialists. As Marxists, they must denounce bourgeois political and economic institutions and promote class struggle at every turn.

Yet, since this was feudal Russia and not the bourgeois West, they must support the bourgeois constitutional movement and promote the exploitative capitalist system. One can easily imagine the frustrating and embarrassing position in which this dilemma placed Russian Marxists on virtually every issue arising from day-to-day political and economic events, especially in their relations with other non-Marxist socialists. There were two ways of escaping this situation: one could ignore the goal and stress the intermediary phases, as the Legal Marxists and the Economists seemed to do; or one could shorten or even completely skip the intermediary phases in order to strive for an immediate socialist revolution. The pressure toward the latter response was intensified by concurrent tendencies in the West where, as mentioned above, some socialists were arguing that the established bourgeois system promoted not revolutionary socialism but cowardly, opportunistic reformism that only sought further benefits within the capitalist system and not the overthrow of the system itself.

The essential achievement of Leninism was to justify in theory and express in practice the program of skipping the stage of bourgeois capitalism. In this Lenin made his basic retreat to populism. Plekhanov's anti-populist Marxism of the 1880's was based on his insistence that Russia must pass through a westernized, bourgeois stage with its appropriate bourgeois parliamentary government before there could be any thought of a socialist revolution. One of the characteristics that distinguished Lenin from Plekhanov's group even at the first meeting of the two in 1895 was Lenin's intense hatred of the constitutional liberals and his reluctance to support or even to tolerate their playing the role that Marxism assigned them in a country that, like Russia, was just emerging from feudalism.

In 1887, Lenin's brother was hanged together with two others for planning the assassination of Tsar Alexander III. In recalling his response to this tragedy some years later, Lenin referred with particular venom to the way in which the local liberals had treated his family at the time. "From the age of seventeen," he wrote, "I began to despise the liberals . . '. not a single liberal 'canaille' in Simbirsk came forward with the slightest word of sympathy for my mother after my brother's execution. In order not to run into her, they would cross to the other side of the street." To appreciate this experience, one should realize that Lenin's family had been highly respected: his father had risen high enough in the government service, as inspector of schools, to receive the title of nobility.

From the time of his brother's execution until about 1892, Lenin, following his brother's example, was a revolutionary populist. He then experienced the conversion from populism to Marxism that was becoming a common event among young Russian socialists. By the end of 1893 he was in St. Petersburg, a devoted Marxist participating in public debates with the populists. The following year he made his debut as a leading Marxist theorist in his book *What Are the Friends of the People?* This was soon followed by a long essay that he read before a group of Marxists and that clearly revealed his divergence from the position of other Russian Marxists. The essay, entitled *The Reflection of Marxism in Bourgeois Literature*, contained a full-scale attack against the moderate "reformist" tendencies of the Legal Marxists. In the spring of 1895 Lenin went to Switzerland where he debated the whole issue of the role of the liberals with Plekhanov and his followers. "By your tactics," Plekhanov is said to have told him, "you are isolating the workers from liberal democratic society and weakening, thereby, the general blow against absolutism."

Having shown his disagreement with the Plekhanov group over the role of the liberals, Lenin returned to Russia to express his opposition against the second of the two gradual "reformist" groups in Russian Marxism, the Economists, who argued that workers should leave politics to the bourgeoisie and concern themselves with day-to-day improvements in working conditions. In 1895, Lenin was arrested and sentenced to exile. For five years he remained in exile, drawing conclusions from his contacts with Plekhanov in the West and his disagreements with the Legal Marxists and the Economists in Russia. Whan he left Siberia in 1900 he was a confirmed "Leninist," and in debates, articles in the party newspaper, *Iskra*, and above all, in his book *What Is To Be Done?* (1902), he argued the views that were to serve as the basis of Bolshevism and Soviet power.

The foundation of Leninism is an unwillingness to wait patiently for history to carry a feudal underdeveloped economy with an autocratic government through a prolonged period of bourgeois capitalism and parliamentary government. Russian Marxists before Lenin had often expressed doubts over the ability of the Russian bourgeoisie to carry out their revolution successfully, and they had, consequently, assigned to the workers an unusually large role in the bourgeois struggle against Tsarism and feudalism. Plekhanov himself had taken the first step toward Leninism when he wrote: "The real peculiarity of the Russian historical development . . . is that the socialist movement begins when capitalism is still in its embryonic stage." But Lenin went much further than this. In 1898, for example, in describing the proper relationship between the proletariat and the liberals, Lenin said that "the term 'utilization' is a more precise and suitable word than the phrase 'support and alliance.'" Utilize for what? For the bourgeois revolution or for something else? In *What Is To Be Done?* we see more clearly that Lenin is not at all concerned with helping the bourgeoisie succeed in its own revolution, but with bringing Russian socialists to power at the first opportunity.

But what forces were available for such a premature socialist revolution? It was all well and good to talk about the workers struggling toward socialism; but workers in the early stages of capitalism were far from the mature, politically conscious and numerically overwhelming socialist force that Marxists assumed would emerge in a mature capitalist society. Lenin himself called repeated attention to the backwardness of the Russian working class, their concern with relatively insignificant economic gains and their inability to understand the whole pattern of history and society carrying Russia toward socialism. Perhaps, given time, Russian workers would have developed as Marxism predicted they must: since one's economic conditions supposedly determines one's consciousness, it would follow that the conditions of the working class should foster in them a socialist consciousness. But either because he was too impatient to wait, or because of what he observed in the western "revisionist" labor movement, Lenin refused to give History or Marxism a chance. The workers themselves, he concluded, would never become socialists.

We have said that *there could not yet be* social-democratic consciousness among the workers. It could only be brought to them from without. The history of all countries shows that the working class, exclusively by its own effort, is able to develop only trade-union consciousness, *i.e.*, the conviction that it is necessary to combine in unions, fight the employers and strive to compel the government to pass necessary labor legislation, etc. The theory of socialism, however, grew out of the philosophic, historical and economic theories that were elaborated by the educated representatives of the propertied classes, the intellectuals. According to their social status, the founders of modern scientific socialism, Marx and Engels, themselves belonged to the bourgeois intelligentsia. In the very same way, in Russia, the theoretical doctrine of social-democracy arose quite independently of the spontaneous growth of the working-class movement; it arose as a natural and inevitable outcome of the development of ideas among the revolutionary socialist intelligentsia.

Having replaced the liberals, the proletariat was in turn replaced by the "revolutionary socialist intelligentsia," because at this early stage of Russian capitalism the workers were not ready for the tasks Lenin assigned them. In other words, by reviving the populists' plans to move as quickly as possible to socialism, Lenin was forced to echo the populists' stress on the intellectual elite. There was another reason for this stress on leadership and for sharply distinguishing the socialist leadership from the laboring masses, a reason that also derived from Lenin's impatience to achieve Russian socialism. A socialist party functioning in a bourgeois parliamentary society enjoys freedoms that allow it to exist as an open, democratic, mass party. Unwilling to wait for these benefits of a bourgeois society, Lenin was forced to organize his socialist party under repressive Tsarist conditions; and to survive such conditions the party had to be tightly organized, well disciplined and united by common doctrines and strategy. The militant, professional party organization resulting from Lenin's revolutionary impatience can be seen in the following statements made by Lenin in the early 1900's.

Pray tell me: when bricklayers lay bricks in various parts of an enormous structure the like of which has never been seen before, is it "paper" work to use a line to help them find the correct place in which to put each brick, to indicate to them the ultimate purpose of the work as a whole, enable them to use not only every brick but even every piece of brick which, joining with the bricks placed before and after it, forms a complete and all-embracing line? And are we not now passing through just such a period in our Party life when we have bricks and bricklayers, but lack the guiding line which all could see and follow?

Not a single class in history has reached power without thrusting forward its political leaders, without advancing leading representatives capable of directing and organizing the movement. We

must train people who will dedicate to the revolution not a free
evening but the whole of their lives; we must prepare an organization so strong that we can enforce a firm division of labor in the
various aspects of our work. . . .

The section of the Organization Committee abroad should be a
section of the Russian Organization Committee—which should
adopt an arch-important and an arch-severe attitude . . . either
recognition of the Organization Committee and subjection to it,
or war.

Bureaucratism versus democratism, *i.e.*, precisely centralism
versus autonomy, such is the organization principle of revolutionary social democracy as against that of the opportunists. The latter
principle strives to go from below upward, and therefore defends,
as far as possible and wherever possible, autonomy and democracy. . . . But the organization principle of revolutionary social
democracy strives to go from the top downward, and defends the
enlargement of the rights and plenary powers of the central body
against the parts.

After returning to two basic principles of the populists, an
unwillingness to see a bourgeois society emerge in Russia
and a strong emphasis on leadership, Lenin was virtually
compelled to take a final step and revive hopes in the peasantry. He distrusted the liberals; he was well aware that
the proletariat were relatively few in number and far from
socialist in ideology; and he was too realistic to consider a
coup d'état by the party elite, no matter how well organized or ideologically orthodox. Moreover, partly as a result
of an economic crisis beginning in Russia at the turn of the
century, the Russian peasantry were at long last giving vent
to their dissatisfaction by acts of violence against landlords
and officials and even by some scattered village risings. Why
not recruit this peasant force for the proletarian revolution?
One very compelling reason for doing so was the fact that in
response to this new revolutionary sentiment among the peasantry, a populist-type party had emerged in the form of the
Socialist Revolutionary Party and was showing remarkable
success among the peasantry and the more radical elements
of the intelligentsia. What a disturbing situation for a revolutionary Marxist like Lenin! On the one hand, the Russian
Marxists were more or less patiently allowing the bourgeois
society to take its historically rightful place: they were, in
effect, turning into constitutional democrats or trade union
reformers. On the other hand, the Socialist Revolutionaries,

who saw no reason to let the western capitalist economy and government establish themselves in Russia, were gaining the support of the truly revolutionary elements among the intelligentsia.

In his book *Two Tactics* Lenin made the necessary modifications in Marxism to take account of this situation. There would indeed be two revolutions as Marx had predicted. But the participants in each were hardly those anticipated by Marx. The first revolution would be led by the urban proletariat but supported by the wealthier, petty-bourgeois peasantry against the feudal landlords and the autocratic state. This would be the "bourgeois" revolution. The second, to begin soon afterwards, would also be led by the urban proletariat but would be supported by the rural proletariat, the poor peasantry in opposition to the private-propertied wealthier peasantry. This would be the proletarian revolution.

Whatever Lenin's temporary, tactical shifts in policy during the fifteen years between the development of these views and the Bolshevik revolution, he retained these concepts and the long-range strategy they implied. Rejection of bourgeois capitalism and bourgeois parliamentary liberalism, distrust of the "spontaneous" mass labor movement, a tightly knit, highly disciplined party of professional revolutionaries, and a realization that no revolution could succeed in an underdeveloped rural country without the support of the peasantry—these are among the essentials of Leninism and they are all part of Lenin's retreat from western Marxism to Russian revolutionary populism, a retreat that clearly reflects the dilemmas of Marxism in an economically underdeveloped society.

The severe dislocations, burdens and deprivations imposed on Russia during the First World War provided a situation admirably suited for the Leninist combination of populism and Marxism. But the power won by the Bolsheviks in October 1917 was power won at the wrong time in the wrong place. There were none of the economic, political or cultural prerequisites that Marx had considered indispensable for both the establishment and the successful functioning of socialism. In fact, it was almost as though a populist party had won power.

Almost, but not quite the same. For although the Bolsheviks won power as revolutionary, "voluntaristic" populists, their attitude toward the use of power revealed the Marxist heritage. The Bolsheviks may not have waited for the proper economic conditions to have developed before leading the "proletarian" revolution, but they were absolutely convinced that only on the basis of such advanced economic conditions could a socialist society be established. Whether utopian or not, the traditional Russian populists felt that socialism could be built on the foundations of the existing rural commune. They further believed that by gaining power and establishing socialism on this basis, the mass laboring population of Russia, the peasantry, would be liberated from poverty and oppression. Their principal goal, therefore, was to serve the needs of the *existing* mass population. Since the Marxists believed that only a fully industrialized, urbanized economy could give birth to socialism, they had supported Tsarist efforts to industrialize Russia at the cost of undermining traditional rural institutions and intensifying the burdens on the existing Russian laboring class, the peasantry. Once in power, how could they avoid continuing these Tsarist policies? Russia must still be industrialized, and by what other means could this be done than by imposing "forced savings" on the mass peasantry? There seemed to the Marxists only one way in which this terrible situation might be avoided: if the premature Russian socialist revolution "sparked" a socialist revolution in an economically advanced country like Germany, then this advanced socialist neighbor would be able to support the underdeveloped socialist economy.

With this hope in international revolution to sustain them, the Bolsheviks approached the enormous tasks of power. With fervent optimism, the Bolsheviks attempted to put their idealistic program into effect: factories were turned over to the workers for administration and control, salaries for managers, specialists and state officials were sharply reduced to working-class levels, a decentralized system of self-governing Soviets was established, the army was transformed into a citizen militia with elected officers and without the embellishments of decorations, ranks or high salaries. But all this was justifiable, if at all, only in a society that possessed the prerequisites for socialism or, as the Bolsheviks now argued, if the young Russian socialist state received aid soon from an economically advanced socialist country.

Revolution seemed most promising in Germany, partly because of the economic distress resulting from the burdensome two-front war. To promote a German revolution, therefore, Russia should make the war situation as difficult as possible for the German government. But this need of a German revolution as a means of allowing rural Russia to establish socialism was in complete contradiction with another compelling requirement: the Bolsheviks must end the war or risk being overthrown. They were well aware of the fact that the most important single reason for the fall of both Tsarism and the Provisional Government was the war, and that the most attractive part of their prerevolutionary program had been its promise to leave the war. Failure to do so now might turn the masses to other parties who would use the war issue against the Bolsheviks as the Bolsheviks had used it against their own predecessors. The choice was clear: either sacrifice, at least for the time, socialism in Russia or risk losing power altogether by provoking an antiwar revolution in Russia. Lenin chose to preserve the Bolshevik power at all costs, and, in opposition to the "international" Bolsheviks who were willing to risk the loss of power in Russia in the interests of a revolution in industrialized Western Europe, he took Russia out of the war.

Although there were to be other times when revolutions in the West raised Bolshevik hopes, Lenin's party after 1918 was faced with that very situation that Plekhanov had warned against in his debates with the populists: a minority socialist party ruling a non-socialist peasant land. To make matters worse, the party was, until 1920, taxed with civil war and foreign intervention. Faced with both sets of circumstances, the absence of support from an advanced, socialist state in the West and the demands of civil war, the party had to abandon all the hopeful, idealistic measures it had promulgated during the first months of power. The citizen army gave way to a highly organized and centrally controlled regular army. The inefficient and unproductive system of workers' control was replaced by a rapidly established centralized economy and the familiar staff of managers and specialists. Instead of diminishing to the envisioned point of total disappearance, the state bureaucracy increased steadily along with the salaries for its officials. On the eve of the revolution, Lenin had written that the workers would be able to manage the banks and the factories "since capitalism has simplified the functions of accounting and control, reduced them to comparatively straightforward entries comprehensible to every literate person." In April 1918, he thought differently:

Our work of organizing proletarian accounting and control has obviously . . . lagged behind the work of directly expropriating the expropriators. . . . The art of administration is not an art that one is born to, it is acquired by experience. . . . Without the guidance of *specialists* in the various fields of knowledge, technology and experience, the transition to socialism will be impossible. . . . Because of the indispensability of the specialists we have had to resort to the old bourgeois method and to agree to pay a very high price for the 'services' of the biggest bourgeois specialists. . . . Clearly, such a measure is a compromise, a departure from the principles of the Paris Commune. . . . A step backward on the part of our Socialist Soviet state power, which from the very outset proclaimed and pursued the policy of reducing high level salaries to the level of the wages of the average worker."

In summarizing the whole unfortunate experience, he wrote in 1921, on the fourth anniversary of the Revolution:

Borne along on the crest of the wave of enthusiasm . . . we reckoned . . . on being able to organize the state production and the state distribution of products on communist lines in a small-peasant country by order of the proletarian state. Experience has proved that we were wrong. It transpires that a number of transitional stages are necessary—state capitalism and socialism—in order to prepare by many years of effort for the transition to communism. . . . We must first set to work in this small-peasant country to build solid little gangways to socialism by way of state capitalism. Otherwise we shall never get to communism: we shall never bring these scores of millions of people to communism. That is what experience, what the objective course of development of the revolution has taught us.

In short, the Bolshevik Party was faced with the task of industrializing a basically rural economy. It was impossible to undertake this vast enterprise in 1921, when he so frankly described the dilemma. The burdens of the civil war, particularly the drastic decline in consumer goods production, and the confiscation of peasant production had led to increasing hostility among the masses as well as among important military units filled by soldiers and sailors from the working classes. While the civil war was in progress these burdens could be justified. But it would have been impossible to continue and intensify them after the civil war in order to meet the costs of rapid industrialization. A temporary retreat was necessary and Lenin made it in his famous New Economic Policy (NEP) of 1921. The intent of NEP was to allow the peasants to produce and sell their goods freely, and to return the bulk of light industries to private ownership in order to get more consumers' goods into the market and thereby satisfy the peasants and stimulate agriculture production. "Only an agreement with the peasantry can save the socialist revolution in Russia," Lenin wrote, "until the revolution has occurred in other countries." Expressing the same conclusion, he conceded that the "proletariat directs the peasantry, but this class cannot be driven out of existence as the landlords and capitalists were driven out of existence. It must be re-fashioned over a long period, with great effort and privations." There was no doubt, however, that this was only a temporary halt. The year after beginning NEP, for example, Lenin wrote:

The salvation of Russia lies not only in a good harvest on the peasant farms, that is not enough; and not only in the good condition of light industry which provides the peasantry with consumers' goods—this too is not enough; we also need heavy industry. . . . Unless we save heavy industry, unless we restore it, we shall not be able to build any industry; and without heavy industry we shall be doomed as an independent country.

In the meantime, the proletariat party must hold firmly to power. Within the country there were the petty-bourgeois peasantry and middle-class "nepmen" who were benefiting from the retreat, and who might advance political claims on the basis of their economic gains. Outside the country there was the vast, rich, powerful capitalist world, which, the Bolsheviks were convinced, would attempt to destroy the new socialist state at the first opportunity. Once again, the Bolsheviks found themselves in a hostile, alien environment, much like the one that surrounded them before the Revolution. And once again their response was to enforce discipline and centralization in their party ranks. Having already excluded all other socialist parties from participation in the Bolshevik government, Lenin went on to lay the foundations for the monolithic party. Significantly, he did so at the same Congress at which he announced his economic retreat.

We do not need any opposition now, comrades, it's not the time for it. Either here, or over there, with a rifle, but not with the opposition (*i.e.*, either all for the leadership or completely against it, on the side of the Whites). It is no good reproaching me: it follows from the state of affairs. No more opposition now, comrades. And, in my view, the Congress will have to draw the conclusion that the time has come to put an end to opposition, to put the lid on it. We have had enough opposition.

The way was ready for the next phase of this sad history. At the time of his death in 1924, Lenin had accumulated a powerful heritage, a heritage ultimately derived from his premature revolution. The country was controlled by a single party that was already assuming the form of a disciplined, monolithic structure. The party was completely committed by Marxist theory and some would argue, by both international and purely economic necessities, to rapid industrialization. By the early twenties most of the leaders realized that this transformation would have to be paid for by Russia's own, limited, and underdeveloped resources, since the expected revolution in the industrialized West had failed to materialize. And, finally, few doubted that the immense burdens of this indispensable economic advance would have to fall on the mass Russian peasantry.

State and Revolution, written during the months immediately preceding the Bolshevik Revolution, clearly reveals the dilemmas of Marxism in an underdeveloped economy. Throughout this work, probably his most famous publication, Lenin attempts to retain Marx's virtually anarchistic political ideals that had relevance, if at all, only to a society possessing the political, economic and cultural heritage of mature capitalism. At the same time, however, he tries to justify a political system powerful enough to meet the challenges that would face any government in a backward rural economy and that would be particularly severe for a party committed to industrialization.

Vladimir Lenin

STATE AND REVOLUTION

THE MARXIST TEACHING ON THE STATE AND THE
TASKS OF THE PROLETARIAT IN THE REVOLUTION

I. CLASS SOCIETY AND THE STATE

1. The State as the Product of the Irreconcilability of Class Antagonisms

What is now happening to Marx's teaching has, in the course of history, happened repeatedly to the teachings of revolutionary thinkers and leaders of oppressed classes struggling for emancipation. During the lifetime of great revolutionaries, the oppressing classes constantly hounded them, received their teachings with the most savage malice, the most furious hatred and the most reckless campaigns of lies and slander. After their death, attempts are made to convert them into harmless icons, to canonize them, so to say, and to surround their *names* with a certain halo for the "consolation" of the oppressed classes and for the purpose of duping them, while at the same time emasculating the *content* of the revolutionary teaching, blunting its revolutionary edge and vulgarizing it. At the present time, the bourgeoisie and the opportunists within the working-class movement concur in this "doctoring" of Marxism. They omit, obliterate and distort the revolutionary side of this teaching, its revolutionary soul. They push to the foreground and extol what is or seems acceptable to the bourgeoisie. All the social-chauvinists are now "Marxists" (don't laugh!). And more and more frequently, German bourgeois scholars, only yesterday specialists in the annihilation of Marxism, are speaking of the "national-German" Marx, who, they aver, educated the workers' unions which are so splendidly organized for the purpose of conducting a predatory war!

In such circumstances, in view of the unprecedentedly widespread distortion of Marxism, our prime task is to *re-establish* what Marx really taught on the subject of the state. For this purpose it will be necessary to quote at length from the works of Marx and Engels themselves. Of course, long quotations will render the text cumbersome and will not help at all to make it popular reading, but we cannot possibly avoid them. All, or at any rate, all the most essential passages in the works of Marx and Engels on the subject of the state must without fail be quoted as fully as possible, in order that the reader may form an independent opinion of the

totality of the views of the founders of scientific socialism
and of the development of those views, and in order that
their distortion by the now prevailing "Kautskyism" may be
documentarily proved and clearly demonstrated.

Let us begin with the most popular of Engels' works, *The
Origin of the Family, Private Property, and the State*, the
sixth edition of which was published in Stuttgart as far back
as 1894. We shall have to translate the quotations from the
German originals, as the Russian translations, although very
numerous, are for the most part either incomplete or very
unsatisfactory.

Summing up his historical analysis, Engels says:

The state is by no means a power forced on society from without.
Neither as little is it 'the reality of the ethical idea,' 'the image
and reality of reason,' as Hegel maintains. The state is a product
of society at a certain stage of development; it is the admission
that this society has become entangled in an insoluble contradiction with itself, that it is cleft into irreconcilable antagonisms
which it is powerless to dispel. But in order that these antagonisms, classes with conflicting economic interests, might not
consume themselves and society in sterile struggle, a power seemingly standing above society became necessary for the purpose of
moderating the conflict, of keeping it within the bounds of 'order'.
And this power, arisen out of society, but placing itself above it,
and increasingly alienating itself from it, is the state. (pp. 177-78,
sixth German edition.)

This expresses with perfect clarity the basic idea of Marxism on the question of the historical role and the meaning of
the state. The state is the product and the manifestation of
the *irreconcilability* of class antagonisms. The state arises
when, where and to the extent that class antagonisms objectively *cannot* be reconciled. And, conversely, the existence
of the state proves that the class antagonisms are irreconcilable.

It is precisely on this most important and fundamental
point that the distortion of Marxism, proceeding along two
main lines, begins.

On the one hand, the bourgeois and particularly the petty-
bourgeois ideologists, compelled under the weight of indisputable historical facts to admit that the state only exists
where there are class antagonisms and the class struggle,
"correct" Marx in such a way as to make it appear that the
state is an organ for the *reconciliation* of classes. According

to Marx, the state could neither arise nor maintain itself if it were possible to reconcile classes. According to the petty-bourgeois and philistine professors and publicists it appears —very frequently with benevolent references to Marx—that the state does in fact reconcile classes. According to Marx, the state is an organ of class *rule*, an organ for the *oppression* of one class by another; it is the creation of "order," which legalizes and strengthens this oppression by moderating the conflict between the classes. In the opinion of the petty-bourgeois politicians, order means precisely the reconciliation of classes, and not the oppression of one class by another; to moderate the conflict means reconciling classes and not depriving the oppressed classes of definite means and methods of struggle to overthrow the oppressors.

For instance, when, in the Revolution of 1917, the question of the significance and role of the state arose in all its magnitude as a practical question demanding immediate action on a mass scale, all the Socialist-Revolutionaries and Mensheviks immediately and completely sank to the petty-bourgeois theory that the "state" "reconciles" classes. Innumerable resolutions and articles by politicians of both these parties are thoroughly saturated with this petty-bourgeois and philistine "reconciliation" theory. That the state is an organ of the rule of a definite class which *cannot* be reconciled with its antipode (the class opposite to it), is something the petty-bourgeois democrats will never be able to understand. Their attitude towards the state is one of the most striking manifestations of the fact that our Socialist-Revolutionaries and Mensheviks are not socialists at all (a point that we Bolsheviks have always maintained), but petty-bourgeois democrats with near-socialist phraseology.

On the other hand, the "Kautskyite" distortion of Marxism is far more subtle. "Theoretically," it is not denied that the state is an organ of class rule, or that class antagonisms are irreconcilable. But what is lost sight of or glossed over is this: if the state is the product of the irreconcilability of class antagonisms, if it is a power standing *above* society and *"increasingly alienating"* itself from it," then it is obvious that the liberation of the oppressed class is impossible not only without a violent revolution, *but also without the destruction* of the apparatus of state power which was created by the ruling class and which is the embodiment of this "alienation." As we shall see later, Marx very definitely drew this theoretically self-evident conclusion as a result of a concrete historical analysis of the tasks of the revolution. And—as we shall show in detail further on—it is precisely this conclusion which Kautsky . . . has "forgotten" and distorted.

2. SPECIAL DETACHMENTS OF ARMED MEN, PRISONS, ETC.

Engels continues:

> . . . In contrast to the old gentile (tribal or clan) organization, the state is distinguished, first, by the division of its subjects according to territory. . . .
> Such a division seems "natural" to us, but it cost a prolonged struggle against the old form of tribal or clan society.
> . . . The second distinguishing feature is the establishment of a public power which no longer directly coincided with the population organized as an armed force. This special public power is necessary, because a self-activating armed organization of the population has become impossible since the cleavage of society into classes. . . . This public power exists in every state. It consists not merely of armed people, but also of material adjuncts, prisons and coercive institutions of all kinds, of which tribal (clan) society knew nothing. . . .

Engels further elucidates the concept of that "power" which is termed the state—a power which arose from society, but places itself above it and alienates itself more and more from it. Of what does this power mainly consist? It consists of special detachments of armed men, having at their command prisons, etc.

We are justified in speaking of special detachments of armed men, because the public power which is an attribute of every state "does not directly coincide" with the armed population, with its "self-activating armed organization."

Like all great revolutionary thinkers, Engels tries to draw the attention of the class-conscious workers to the very fact which prevailing philistinism regards as least worthy of attention, as the most habitual, sanctified not only by firmly rooted, but, one might say, by petrified prejudices. A standing army and police are the chief instruments of state power. But can it be otherwise?

From the viewpoint of the vast majority of Europeans of the end of the nineteenth century whom Engels was addressing, and who had not lived through or closely observed a single great revolution, it could not be otherwise. They completely failed to understand what a "self-activating armed organization of the population" was. To the question, why did there arise a need for special detachments of armed men, placed above society and alienating themselves from it (police and standing army), the West-European and Russian philistines are inclined to answer with a few phrases borrowed from Spencer or Mikhailovsky, with references to the growing complexity of social life, to the differentiation of functions, and so forth.

Such a reference seems "scientific" and effectively dulls the senses of the philistine by obscuring the most important and basic fact, namely, the cleavage of society into irreconcilably antagonistic classes.

Were it not for this cleavage, the "self-activating armed organization of the population" would differ from the primitive organization of a stick-wielding herd of monkeys, or of primitive man, or of men united in clans, by its complexity, its high technique, and so forth; but such an organization would still be possible.

It is impossible, because civilized society is split into antagonistic and, moreover, irreconcilably antagonistic classes, and their self-activating arming would lead to an armed struggle between them. A state arises, a special power is created (special detachments of armed men) and every revolution, by destroying the state apparatus, clearly demonstrates to us how the ruling class strives to restore the special detachments of armed men which serve *it*, and how the oppressed class strives to create a new organization of this kind, capable of serving not the exploiters but the exploited.

In the above argument, Engels raises theoretically the very same question which every great revolution raises before us in practice, palpably and, what is more, on a scale of mass action, namely, the question of the relation between "special" detachments of armed men and the "self-activating armed organization of the population." We shall see how this question is concretely illustrated by the experience of the European and Russian revolutions.

But let us return to Engels' exposition.

He points out that sometimes, for example, in certain parts of North America, this public power is weak (he has in mind a rare exception in capitalist society, those parts of North America in its pre-imperialist days where the free colonist predominated), but that, generally speaking, it grows stronger:

. . . The public power grows stronger, however, in proportion as class antagonisms within the state become more acute, and as adjacent states become larger and more populated. We have only to look at our present-day Europe, where class struggle and rivalry in conquest have elevated the public power to such a height that it threatens to devour the whole of society and even the state. . . .

This was written not later than the beginning of the nineties of the last century, Engels' last preface being dated June 16, 1891. The turn towards imperialism—meaning the complete domination of the trusts, the omnipotence of the big banks, a grand-scale colonial policy, and so forth—was only just beginning in France and was even weaker in North America and in Germany. Since then "rivalry in conquest" has made gigantic strides—especially since by the beginning of the second decade of the twentieth century, the whole world had been finally divided up among these "rivals in conquest," *i.e.*, among the great predatory powers. Since then, military and naval armaments have grown incredibly to monstrous proportions, and the predatory war of 1914-1917 for the domination of the world by England or Germany, for the division of the spoils, has brought the "devouring" of all the forces of society by the rapacious state power to the verge of complete catastrophe.

As early as 1891 Engels was able to point to "rivalry in conquest" as one of the most important distinguishing features of the foreign policy of the Great Powers, but in 1914-1917, when this rivalry, many times intensified, has given rise to an imperialist war, the social-chauvinist scoundrels cover up the defence of the predatory interests of "their own" bourgeoisie with phrases about "defence of the fatherland," "defence of the republic and the revolution," etc.l

3. The State—the Instrument for the Exploitation of the Oppressed Class

For the maintenance of the special public power standing above society, taxes and state loans are needed.

"Possessing of the public power and the right to levy taxes, the officials," Engels writes, "as organs of society, now stand *above* society. The free, voluntary respect that was accorded to the organs of the tribal (clan) society does not satisfy them, even if they could gain it. . . ." Special laws are enacted proclaiming the sanctity and immunity of the officials. "The shabbiest police servant" has more "authority" than the representatives of the clan, but even the head of the military power of a civilized state may well envy an elder of a clan who enjoys "uncoerced respect" of society.

Here the problem of the privileged position of the officials as organs of state power is raised. The main question indicated is: what is it that places them *above* society? We shall see how this theoretical question was answered in practice by the Paris Commune in 1871 and how it was blurred in a reactionary manner by Kautsky in 1912.

". . . As the state arose from the need to hold class antagonisms in check, but as it arose, at the same time, in the midst of the conflict of these classes, it is, as a rule, the state of the most powerful, economically dominant class, which, through the medium of the state, becomes also the politically dominant class and thus acquires new means of holding down and exploiting the oppressed class. . . ." Not only were the ancient and feudal states organs for the exploitation of the slaves and serfs but "the modern representative state is an instrument of exploitation of wage labor by capital. By way of exception, however, periods occur in which the warring classes balance each other so nearly that the state power, as ostensible mediator, acquires, for the moment, a certain degree of independence of both. . . ." Such were the absolute monarchies of the seventeenth and eighteenth centuries, the Bonapartism of the First and Second Empires in France, and Bismarck in Germany.

Such, we may add, is the Kerensky government in republican Russia since it began to persecute the revolutionary proletariat at a moment when, owing to the leadership of the petty-bourgeois democrats, the Soviets have *already* become impotent, while the bourgeoisie is not *yet* strong enough simply to disperse them.

"In a democratic republic," Engels continues, "wealth exercises its power indirectly, but all the more surely," first, by means of the "direct corruption of officials" (America); second, by means of "an alliance between the government and Stock Exchange" (France and America).

At the present time, imperialism and the domination of the banks have "developed" both these methods of upholding and giving effect to the omnipotence of wealth in democratic republics of all descriptions into an unusually fine art. If, for instance, in the very first months of the Russian democratic republic, one might say during the honeymoon of the "Socialist" S.-R.'s [Socialist-Revolutionaries] and the Mensheviks joined in wedlock to the bourgeoisie, Mr. Palchinsky, in the coalition government, obstructed every measure intended for curbing the capitalists and their marauding practices, their plundering of the treasury by means of war contracts; and if later on Mr. Palchinsky resigned (and, of course, was replaced by another exactly such Palchinsky), and the capitalists "rewarded" him with a soft job at a salary of 120,000 rubles per annum—what would you call this—direct or indirect bribery? An alliance between the government and the directors of syndicates, or "merely" friendly relations? What role do the Chernovs, Tseretelis, Avksentyevs and Skobelevs play? Are they the "direct" or only the indirect allies of the millionaire treasury-looters?

The reason why the omnipotence of "wealth" is better *secured* in a democratic republic is that it does not depend on the individual defects of the political mechanism. A democratic republic is the best possible political shell for capitalism, and, therefore, once capital has gained control of this very best shell (through the Palchinskys, Chernovs, Tseretelis and Co.), it establishes its power so securely, so firmly, that *no* change, whether of persons, of institutions, or of parties in the bourgeois-democratic republic, can shake it.

We must also note that Engels is most definite in calling universal suffrage an instrument of bourgeois rule. Universal suffrage, he says, obviously summing up the long experience of German Social Democracy, is

the gauge of the maturity of the working class. It cannot and never will be anything more in the present-day state.

The petty-bourgeois democrats, such as our Socialist-Revolutionaries and Mensheviks, and also their twin brothers, all the social-chauvinists and opportunists of Western Europe, expect precisely this "more" from universal suffrage. They themselves share and instill into the minds of the people the false notion that universal suffrage "in the present-day state" is really capable of ascertaining the will of the majority of the laborers and of securing its realization.

Here we can only indicate this false notion, only point

out that Engels' perfectly clear, precise and concrete statement is distorted at every step in the propaganda and agitation of the "official" (*i.e.*, opportunist) socialist parties. A detailed exposure of the utter falsity of this notion which Engels brushes aside here is given in our further account of the views of Marx and Engels on the *"present-day"* state.

Engels gives a general summary of his views in the most popular of his works in the following words:

The state, then, has not existed from all eternity. There have been societies that did without it, that had no conception of the state and state power. At a certain stage of economic development, which was necessarily bound up with the cleavage of society into classes, the state became a necessity owing to this cleavage. We are now rapidly approaching a stage in the development of production at which the existence of these classes not only will have ceased to be a necessity, but will become a positive hindrance to production. They will vanish as inevitably as they arose at an earlier stage. Along with them the state will inevitably vanish. The society that will organize production on the basis of a free and equal association of the producers will put the whole machinery of state where it will then belong: into the Museum of Antiquities, by the side of the spinning wheel and the bronze axe.

We do not often come across this passage in the propagandist and agitational literature of present-day Social Democracy. But even when we do come across it, it is mostly quoted in the same manner as one bows before an icon, *i.e.*, it is done to show official respect for Engels, and no attempt is made to gauge the breadth and depth of the revolution that this relegating of "the whole state machine to the Museum of Antiquities" presupposes. In most cases we do not even find an understanding of what Engels calls the state machine.

4. The "Withering Away" of the State and Violent Revolution

Engels' words regarding the "withering away" of the state are so widely known, so often quoted, and so clearly reveal the essence of the customary adulteration of Marxism into opportunism that we must deal with them in detail. We shall quote the whole argument from which they are taken.

The proletariat takes political power and turns the means of production in the first instance into state property. But, in doing this, it abolishes itself as proletariat, abolishes all class distinctions and class antagonisms, and abolishes also the state as state. Society thus far, based upon class antagonisms, had need of the state, that is, of an organization of the exploiting class, for the maintenance of its external conditions of production; which means especially for the purpose of forcibly keeping the exploited classes in the condition of oppression corresponding with the given mode of production (slavery, serfdom, wage labor). The state was the official representative of society as a whole; the gathering of it together into a visible embodiment. But it was this only in so far as it was the state of that class which itself represented, for the time being, society as a whole: in ancient times, the state of slave-owning citizens; in the Middle Ages, the feudal lords; in our own time, the bourgeoisie. When at last it becomes the real representative of the whole of society, it renders itself unnecessary. As soon as there is no longer any social class to be held in subjection; as soon as class rule, and the individual struggle for existence based upon our present anarchy in production, with the collisions and excesses arising from these, are removed, nothing more remains to be repressed, and a special repressive force, a state, is no longer necessary. The first act by virtue of which the state really constitutes itself the representative of the whole of society—the taking possession of the means of production in the name of society—this is, at the same time, its last independent act as a state. State interference in social relations becomes, in one domain after another, superfluous, and then withers away of itself. The government of persons is replaced by the administration of things and by the management of the processes of production. The state is not "abolished." *It withers away.* This gives the measure of the value of the phrase "a free people's state," which can justifiably be used at times by agitators, but which is, in the final analysis, scientifically inadequate. It is on this basis that we should also evaluate the demands of the so-called anarchists for the immediate abolition of the state. (*Herr Eugen Dühring's Revolution in Science [Anti-Dühring]*, pp. 301-03, third German edition.)

It may be said without fear of error that of this argument of Engels' which is so remarkably rich in ideas, only one point has become an integral part of socialist thought among modern socialist parties, namely, that according to Marx the state "withers away"—as distinct from the anarchist doctrine of the "abolition" of the state. To prune Marxism in such a manner is to reduce it to opportunism, for such an "interpretation" only leaves a vague notion of a slow, even, gradual change, of absence of leaps and storms, of absence of revolution. The current, widespread, mass, if one may say so, conception of the "withering away" of the state undoubtedly means toning down, if not repudiating, revolution.

Such an "interpretation," however, is the crudest distortion of Marxism, advantageous only to the bourgeoisie; in point of theory, it is based on a disregard for the most important circumstances and considerations indicated, even in Engels' "summary" argument we have just quoted in full.

In the first place, at the very outset of his argument Engels says that, in taking state power, the proletariat thereby "abolishes the state as state." It is not "good form" to ponder over the meaning of this. Generally, it is either ignored altogether, or is considered to be something in the nature of an "Hegelian weakness" on Engels' part. As a matter of fact, however, these words briefly express the experience of one of the greatest proletarian revolutions, the Paris Commune of 1871, of which we shall speak in greater detail in its proper place. As a matter of fact, Engels speaks here of the proletarian revolution "abolishing" the *bourgeois* state, while the words about the state withering away refer to the remnants of the *proletarian* state *after* the socialist revolution. According to Engels the bourgeois state does not "wither away," but is "*abolished*" by the proletariat in the course of the revolution. What withers away after this revolution is the proletarian state or semi-state.

Secondly, the state is a "special repressive force." Engels gives this splendid and extremely profound definition here with the utmost lucidity. And from it follows that the "special repressive force" for the suppression of the proletariat by the bourgeoisie, of millions of laborers by handfuls of the rich, must be replaced by a "special repressive force" for the suppression of the bourgeoisie by the proletariat (the dictatorship of the proletariat). This is precisely what is meant by "the abolition of the state as state." This is precisely the "act" of taking possession of the means of production in the name of society. And it is self-evident that *such* a replacement of one (bourgeois) "special force" by another (proletarian) "special force" cannot possibly take place in the form of "withering away."

Thirdly, in speaking of the state "withering away," and the even more graphic and colorful "ceasing of itself," Engels refers quite clearly and definitely to the period *after* "the state has taken possession of the means of production in the name of the whole of society," that is, *after* the socialist revolution. We all know that the political form of the "state" at that time is the most complete democracy. But it never enters the head of any of the opportunists who shamelessly distort Marxism that Engels is consequently speaking here of *democracy* "ceasing of itself," or "withering away." This seems very strange at first sight. But it is "incomprehensible" only to those who have not pondered over the fact that democracy is *also* a state and that, consequently, democracy will also disappear when the state disappears. Revolution alone can "abolish" the bourgeois state. The state in general, *i.e.*, the most complete democracy, can only "wither away."

Fourthly, after formulating his famous proposition that "the state withers away," Engels at once explains specifically that this proposition is directed against both the opportunists and the anarchists. In doing this Engels puts in the forefront that conclusion drawn from the proposition that "the state withers away" which is directed against the opportunists.

One can wager that out of every 10,000 persons who have read or heard about the "withering away" of the state, 9,990 are completely unaware, or do not remember, that Engels directed his conclusions from this proposition *not only* against the anarchists. And of the remaining ten, probably nine do not know the meaning of "free people's state" or why an attack on this slogan means an attack on the opportunists. This is how history is written! This is how a great revolutionary teaching is imperceptibly falsified and adapted to prevailing philistinism! The conclusion directed against the anarchists has been repeated thousands of times, vulgarized, dinned into people's heads in the shallowest form and has acquired the strength of a prejudice. But the conclusion directed against the opportunists has been slurred over and "forgotten"!

The "free people's state" was a program demand and a widely current slogan of the German Social Democrats in the seventies. This slogan is devoid of all political content except for the fact that it describes the concept of democracy in the pompous philistine fashion. In so far as it hinted in a legally permissible manner at a democratic republic, Engels was prepared to "justify" its use "for a time" from an agitational point of view. But it was an opportunist slogan, for it expressed not only an embellishment of bourgeois democracy, but also failure to understand the socialist criticism of the state in general. We are in favor of a democratic republic as the best form of the state for the proletariat under capitalism; but we have no right to forget that wage slavery is the lot of the people even in the most democratic bourgeois republic. Furthermore, every state is a "special force for the suppression" of the oppressed class. Consequently, no state is *free* or is a *people's state*. Marx and Engels explained this repeatedly to their party comrades in the seventies.

Fifthly, this very same work of Engels', of which everyone remembers the argument about the withering away of the state, also contains an argument of the significance of violent revolution. Engels' historical analysis of its role becomes a veritable panegyric on violent revolution. This "no one remembers." It is not good form in modern socialist parties to talk or even think about the significance of this idea, and it plays no part whatever in their daily propaganda and agitation among the masses. And yet, it is inseparably bound with the "withering away" of the state into one harmonious whole.

Here is Engels' argument:

. . . Force, however, plays also another role in history (other than that of a diabolical power), namely, a revolutionary role. In the words of Marx, it is the midwife of every old society which is pregnant with a new one; it is the instrument with the aid of which social movement forces its way through and shatters the dead, fossilized political forms—of this there is not a word in Herr Dühring. It is only with sighs and groans that he admits the possibility that force will perhaps be necessary for the overthrow of the economic system of exploitation—unfortunately, because all use of force, forsooth, demoralizes the person who uses it. And this in spite of the immense moral and spiritual impetus which has been given by every victorious revolution! And this in Germany, where a violent collision—which indeed may be forced on the people— would at least have the advantage of wiping out the servility which has permeated the national consciousness as a result of the humiliation of the Thirty Years' War. And this parson's mode of thought—lifeless, insipid and impotent—claims the right to impose itself on the most revolutionary party that history has known! (p. 193, third German edition, part II, end of chap. IV.)

How can this panegyric on violent revolution, which Engels insistently brought to the attention of the German Social Democrats between 1878 and 1894, *i.e.*, right up to the time of his death, be combined with the theory of the "withering away" of the state to form a single doctrine?

Usually the two are combined by means of eclecticism, by an unprincipled, or sophistic selection made arbitrarily (or to please the powers that be) of now one, now another argument, and in ninety-nine cases out of a hundred, if not more often, it is the idea of the "withering away" that is placed in the forefront. Dialectics are replaced by eclecticism—this is the most usual, the most widespread phenomenon to be met with in present-day official Social-Democratic literature in relation to Marxism. This sort of substitution is, of course, no new thing, it was observed even in the history of classic Greek philosophy. In falsifying Marxism in opportunist fashion, the substitution of eclecticism for dialectics is the easiest way of deceiving the masses; it gives an illusory satisfaction; it seems to take into account all sides of the process, all tendencies of development, all the conflicting influences, and so forth, whereas in reality it presents no integral and revolutionary conception of the process of social development at all.

We have already said above, and shall show more fully later, that the teaching of Marx and Engels concerning the inevitability of a violent revolution refers to the bourgeois state. The latter *cannot* be superseded by the proletarian state (the dictatorship of the proletariat) through the process of "withering away," but, as a general rule, only through a violent revolution. The panegyric Engels sang in its honor, and which fully corresponds to Marx's repeated declarations (recall the concluding passages of *The Poverty of Philosophy* and the *Communist Manifesto,* with their proud and open proclamation of the inevitability of a violent revolution; recall what Marx wrote nearly thirty years later, in criticizing the Gotha Program of 1875,[1] when he mercilessly castigated the opportunist character of that program)—this panegyric is by no means a mere "impulse," a mere declamation or a polemical sally. The necessity of systematically imbuing the masses with *this* and precisely this view of violent revolution lies at the root of *all* the teachings of Marx and Engels. The betrayal of their teaching by the now predominant social-chauvinist and Kautskyite trends is expressed in striking relief by the neglect of *such* propaganda and agitation by both these trends.

The replacement of the bourgeois state by the proletarian state is impossible without a violent revolution. The abolition of the proletarian state, *i.e.,* of the state in general, is impossible except through the process of "withering away."

A detailed and concrete elaboration of these views was given by Marx and Engels when they studied each separate revolutionary situation, when they analyzed the lessons of the experience of each individual revolution. We shall now pass to this, undoubtedly the most important part of their teaching.

II. THE EXPERIENCE OF 1848–1851

1. THE EVE OF THE REVOLUTION

The first works of mature Marxism—*The Poverty of Philosophy* and the *Communist Manifesto*—appeared just on the eve of the Revolution of 1848. For this reason, in addition to presenting the general principles of Marxism, they reflect to a certain degree the concrete revolutionary situation of the time. Hence, it will be more expedient, perhaps, to examine what the authors of these works said about the state immediately before they drew conclusions from the experience of the years 1848-1851.

In *The Poverty of Philosophy* Marx wrote:

. . . The working class, in the course of its development, will substitute for the old bourgeois society an association which will exclude classes and their antagonism, and there will be no more political power properly so-called, since political power is precisely the official expression of antagonism in bourgeois society. (p. 182, German edition, 1885.)

It is instructive to compare this general exposition of the idea of the state disappearing after the abolition of classes with the exposition contained in the *Communist Manifesto,* written by Marx and Engels a few months later—to be exact, in November 1847:

. . . In depicting the most general phases of the development of the proletariat, we traced the more or less veiled civil war, raging within existing society, up to the point where that war breaks out into open revolution, and where the violent overthrow of the bourgeoisie lays the foundation for the sway of the proletariat. . . .

. . . We have seen above, that the first step in the revolution by the working class, is to raise the proletariat to the position of ruling class, to win the battle of democracy.

The proletariat will use its political supremacy to wrest, by degrees, all capital from the bourgeoisie, to centralize all instruments of production in the hands of the state, *i.e.*, of the proletariat organized as the ruling class; and to increase the total of productive forces as rapidly as possible. (pp. 31 and 37, seventh German edition, 1906.)

Here we have a formulation of one of the most remarkable and most important ideas of Marxism on the subject of the state, namely, the idea of the "dictatorship of the proletariat" (as Marx and Engels began to call it after the Paris Commune); and also a supremely interesting definition of the state which is also one of the "forgotten words" of Marxism: *"the state, i.e., the proletariat organized as the ruling class."*

This definition of the state has never been explained in the prevailing propaganda and agitation literature of the official Social-Democratic parties. More than that, it has been quite forgotten, for it is absolutely irreconcilable with reformism, and is a slap in the face of the common opportunist prejudices and philistine illusions about the "peaceful development of democracy."

The proletariat needs the state—this is repeated by all the opportunists, social-chauvinists and Kautskyites, who assure us that this is what Marx taught. But they *"forget"* to add that, in the first place, according to Marx, the proletariat needs only a state which is withering away, *i.e.*, a state so constituted that it begins to wither away immediately, and cannot but wither away. And, secondly, the toilers need a "state, *i.e.*, the proletariat organized as the ruling class."

The state is a special organization of force: it is an organization of violence for the suppression of some class. What class must the proletariat suppress? Naturally, only the exploiting class, *i.e.*, the bourgeoisie. The toilers need a state only to suppress the resistance of the exploiters, and only the proletariat is in a position to direct this suppression, carry it out; for the proletariat is the only class that is consistently revolutionary, the only class that can unite all the toilers and the exploited in the struggle against the bourgeoisie, in completely displacing it.

The exploiting classes need political rule in order to maintain exploitation, *i.e.*, in the selfish interests of an insignificant minority against the vast majority of the people. The exploited classes need political rule in order completely to abolish all exploitation, *i.e.*, in the interests of the vast majority of the

people, and against the insignificant minority consisting of
the modern slaveowners—the landlords and the capitalists.

The petty-bourgeois democrats, those sham socialists who
have replaced class struggle by dreams of class harmony,
even pictured the socialist transformation in a dreamy fashion
—not as the overthrow of the rule of the exploiting class,
but as the peaceful submission of the minority to the majority which has become conscious of its aims. This petty-
bourgeois utopia, which is inseparably connected with the
idea of the state being above classes, led in practice to the
betrayal of the interests of the laboring classes, as was
shown, for example, by the history of the French revolutions
of 1848 and 1871, and by the experience of "socialist" participation in bourgeois cabinets in England, France, Italy
and other countries at the end of the nineteenth and the
beginning of the twentieth centuries.

Marx fought all his life against this petty-bourgeois socialism—now resurrected in Russia by the Socialist-Revolutionary
and Menshevik parties. He applied his teaching on the class
struggle consistently, down to the teaching on political power,
on the state.

The overthrow of bourgeois rule can be accomplished only
by the proletariat, as the particular class whose economic
conditions of existence prepare it for this task and provide
it with the possibility and the power to perform it. While
the bourgeoisie breaks up and disintegrates the peasantry
and all the petty-bourgeois strata, it welds together, unites
and organizes the proletariat. Only the proletariat—by virtue
of the economic role it plays in large-scale production—is
capable of being the leader of *all* the laboring and exploited
masses, whom the bourgeoisie exploits, oppresses and crushes
often not less, but more, than it does the proletariat, but
who are incapable of waging an *independent* struggle for
their emancipation.

The teaching on the class struggle, when applied by Marx
to the question of the state and of the socialist revolution,
leads of necessity to the recognition of the *political rule* of
the proletariat, of its dictatorship, *i.e.*, of power shared with
none and relying directly upon the armed force of the
masses. The overthrow of the bourgeoisie can be achieved
only by the proletariat becoming transformed into the *ruling
class*, capable of crushing the inevitable and desperate resistance of the bourgeoisie, and of organizing *all* the laboring
and exploited masses for the new economic order.

The proletariat needs state power, the centralized organization of force, the organization of violence, both to crush the resistance of the exploiters and to *lead* the enormous mass of the population—the peasantry, the petty bourgeoisie, the semi-proletarians—in the work of organizing socialist economy.

By educating the workers' party, Marxism educates the vanguard of the proletariat which is capable of assuming power and *of leading the whole people* to socialism, of directing and organizing the new order, of being the teacher, the guide, the leader of all the laborers and exploited in the task of building up their social life without the bourgeoisie and against the bourgeoisie. As against this, the opportunism which now holds sway trains the membership of the workers' party to be the representatives of the better-paid workers, who lose touch with the rank and file, "get along" fairly well under capitalism, and sell their birthright for a mess of pottage, *i.e.*, renounce their role of revolutionary leaders of the people against the bourgeoisie.

"The state, *i.e.*, the proletariat organized as the ruling class"—this theory of Marx is inseparably bound with all he taught on the revolutionary role of the proletariat in history. The culmination of this role is the proletarian dictatorship, the political rule of the proletariat.

But if the proletariat needs a state as a *special* form of organization of violence *against* the bourgeoisie, the following conclusion suggests itself: is it conceivable that such an organization can be created without first abolishing, destroying the state machine created by the bourgeoisie *for itself?* The *Communist Manifesto* leads straight to this conclusion, and it is of this conclusion that Marx speaks when summing up the experience of the Revolution of 1848-1851.

2. THE REVOLUTION SUMMED UP

Regarding the question of the state with which we are concerned here, Marx reviews the Revolution of 1848-1851 in the following argument, contained in *The Eighteenth Brumaire of Louis Bonaparte:*

. . . But the revolution is thoroughgoing. It is still journeying through purgatory. It does its work methodically. By December 2, 1851 (the day of Louis Bonaparte's *coup d'état*), it had completed one half of its preparatory work; it is now completing the other half. First it perfected the parliamentary power, in order to be able to overthrow it. Now that it has attained this, it perfects the *executive power*, reduces it to its purest expression, isolates it, sets it up against itself as the sole target, *in order to concentrate all its forces of destruction against it* (italics ours). And when it has done this second half of its preliminary work, Europe will leap from its seat and exultantly exclaim: well grubbed, old mole!

This executive power with its enormous bureaucratic and military organization, with its complex and artificial state machinery, with a host of officials numbering half a million, besides an army of another half million, this appalling parasitic organism, which enmeshes the body of French society like a net and chokes all its pores, sprang up in the days of the absolute monarchy, when the feudal system was decaying, a decay that this organism helped to hasten. The first French Revolution developed centralization, "but at the same time it increased the extent, the attributes and the number of agents of governmental power. Napoleon perfected this state machinery." The legitimatist monarchy and the July monarchy[2] "added nothing but a greater division of labor. . . ."

. . . Finally, in its struggle against the revolution, the parliamentary republic found itself compelled to strengthen, along with the repressive measures, the resources and centralization of governmental power. *All revolutions perfected this machine instead of smashing it* (italics ours). The parties that contended in turn for domination regarded the possession of this huge state edifice as the principal spoils of the victor. (*The Eighteenth Brumaire of Louis Bonaparte*, pp. 98-99, fourth edition, Hamburg, 1907.)

In this remarkable argument Marxism takes a tremendous step forward compared with the *Communist Manifesto*. In the latter, the question of the state is still treated in an extremely abstract manner, in the most general terms and expressions. In the above-quoted passage, the question is treated in a concrete manner, and the conclusion is extremely precise, definite, practical and tangible: all the revolutions which have occurred up to now perfected the state machine, whereas it must be broken, smashed.

This is the chief and fundamental conclusion concerning the state in Marxism. And it is precisely this fundamental point which has been not only completely *forgotten* by the dominant official Social-Democratic parties, but simply *distorted* (as we shall see later) by the foremost theoretician of the Second International, K. Kautsky.

The *Communist Manifesto* gives a general summary of history, which compels us to regard the state as the organ of class rule and leads us to the inevitable conclusion that the proletariat cannot overthrow the bourgeoisie without first capturing political power, without attaining political supremacy, without transforming the state into the "proletariat organized as the ruling class"; and that this proletarian state will begin to wither away immediately after its victory, because the state is unnecessary and cannot exist in a society in which there are no class antagonisms. The question as to how, from the point of view of historical development, the replacement of the bourgeois state by the proletarian state is to take place is not raised here.

This is the question Marx raises and answers in 1852. True to his philosophy of dialectical materialism, Marx takes as his basis the historical experience of the great years of revolution, 1848 to 1851. Here, as everywhere, his teaching is the *summing up of experience*, illuminated by a profound philosophical world view and a rich knowledge of history.

The problem of the state is put concretely: how did the bourgeois state, the state machine necessary for the rule of the bourgeoisie, come into being historically? What changes did it undergo, what evolution did it experience in the course of the bourgeois revolutions and in the face of the independent actions of the oppressed classes? What are the tasks of the proletariat in relation to this state machine?

The centralized state power that is peculiar to bourgeois society came into being in the period of the fall of absolutism. Two institutions are most characteristic of this state machine: the bureaucracy and the standing army. In their works, Marx and Engels repeatedly show that it is the bourgeoisie with whom these institutions are connected by thousands of threads. The experience of every worker illustrates this connection in an extremely graphic and impressive manner. From its own bitter experience, the working class learns to recognize this connection. That is why it so easily grasps and so firmly learns the doctrine which shows the inevitability of this connection, a doctrine which the petty-bourgeois democrats either ignorantly and flippantly deny, or still more flippantly admit "in general," while forgetting to draw the corresponding practical conclusions.

The bureaucracy and the standing army are a "parasite" on the body of bourgeois society—a parasite created by the internal antagonisms which rend that society, but still a parasite, "choking" all its vital pores. The Kautskyite opportunism now dominating official Social Democracy considers the view that the state is a *parasitic organism* to be the peculiar and exclusive attribute of anarchism. It goes without saying that this distortion of Marxism is of extreme advantage to those philistines who have reduced socialism to the unprecedented disgrace of justifying and embellishing the imperialist war by applying to it the concept of "defense of the fatherland." But it is unquestionably a distortion, nevertheless.

The development, perfection and strengthening of the bureaucratic and military apparatus proceeded during all the numerous bourgeois revolutions which Europe has witnessed since the fall of feudalism. In particular, it is precisely the petty bourgeoisie that is attracted to the side of the big bourgeoisie and is subordinated to it to a large extent by means of this apparatus, which provides the upper strata of the peasantry, small artisans, tradesmen and the like with comparatively comfortable, quiet and respectable jobs, raising their holders *above* the people. Consider what happened in Russia during the six months following February 27, 1917.[3] The official posts which formerly were given by preference to members of the Black Hundreds [4] became the spoils of the Cadets,[5] Mensheviks and Socialist-Revolutionaries. Nobody has really thought of introducing any serious reforms. Every effort has been made to put them off "until the Constituent Assembly [6] meets," and to put off little by little the convocation of the Constituent Assembly until the end of the war! But there has been no delay, no waiting for the Constituent Assembly in the matter of dividing the spoils, of getting the soft jobs of ministers, vice-ministers, governors-general, etc., etc.! The game of combinations that has been played in forming the government has been, in essence, only an expression of this division and redivision of the "spoils" which has been going on high and low, throughout the country, in every department of central and local government. The six months between February 27 and August 27, 1917,[7] can be summed up, objectively summed up beyond all dispute, as follows: reforms shelved, distribution of official jobs accomplished and "mistakes" in the distribution corrected by a few redistributions.

But the more the bureaucratic apparatus is "redistributed" among the various bourgeois and petty-bourgeois parties (among the Cadets, Socialist-Revolutionaries and Mensheviks in the case of Russia), the more clearly the oppressed classes, and the proletariat at their head, become conscious of their irreconcilable hostility to the *whole* of bourgeois society. That is why it becomes necessary for all bourgeois parties, even for the most democratic and "revolutionary-democratic" among them, to intensify repressive measures against the revolutionary proletariat, to strengthen the apparatus of repression, *i.e.*, that very state machine. This course of events compels the revolution "*to concentrate all its forces of destruction*" against the state power, to set itself the aim, not of perfecting the state machine, but of *smashing and destroying* it.

It was not logical reasoning, but the actual development of events, the living experience of 1848-1851, that led to the problem being presented in this way. The extent to which Marx held strictly to the solid ground of historical experience can be seen from the fact that, in 1852, he did not yet concretely raise the question of *what* would replace the state machine that was to be destroyed. Experience had not yet provided material for the solution of this problem which history placed on the order of the day later on, in 1871. In 1852 all that it was possible to establish with the accuracy of scientific-historical observation was that the proletarian revolution *had approached* the task of "concentrating all its forces of destruction" against the state power, of "smashing" the state machine.

Here the question may arise: is it correct to generalize the experience, observations and conclusions of Marx, to apply them to a field that is wider than the history of France during the three years 1848-1851? In dealing with this question let us first recall a remark made by Engels, and then examine the facts. In his introduction to the third edition of *The Eighteenth Brumaire* Engels wrote:

. . . France is the land where, more than anywhere else, the historical class struggles were each time fought out to a decision. In France, consequently, the changing political forms within which the class struggles advanced and in which their results are summarized have been stamped in the sharpest outlines. The center of feudalism in the Middle Ages, the model since the Renaissance of a unified monarchy resting on estates, France demolished feudalism in the Great Revolution and established the pure rule of the bourgeoisie in a classical clarity unequaled by any other European country. And the struggle of the emerging proletariat against the ruling bourgeoisie appeared here in an acute form unknown elsewhere. (p. 4, 1907 edition.)

The last sentence is out of date, inasmuch as since 1871 the revolutionary struggle of the French proletariat has been interrupted, although, long as this interruption may be, it does not at all preclude the possibility that, in the coming proletarian revolution, France may show herself to be the classic land of the class struggle to a finish.

Let us, however, cast a general glance over the history of the advanced countries at the end of the nineteenth and beginning of the twentieth centuries. We shall see that the same process has been going on more slowly, in more varied forms, on a much wider field: on the one hand, the development of "parliamentary power" both in the republican countries (France, America, Switzerland) and in the monarchies (England, Germany to a certain extent, Italy, the Scandinavian countries, etc.); on the other hand, a struggle for power among the various bourgeois and petty-bourgeois parties which distributed and redistributed the "spoils" of office, while the foundations of bourgeois society remained unchanged; and, finally, the perfection and consolidation of the "executive power," its bureaucratic and military apparatus.

There is not the slightest doubt that these features are common to the whole of the modern evolution of capitalist states in general. In the three years 1848-1851, France displayed, in a swift, sharp, concentrated form, the very same processes of development which are peculiar to the whole capitalist world.

Imperialism—the era of bank capital, the era of gigantic capitalist monopolies, the era of the development of monopoly capitalism into state-monopoly capitalism—has demonstrated with particular force the extraordinary strengthening of the "state machine" and the unprecedented growth of its bureaucratic and military apparatus, in connection with an intensification of repressive measures against the proletariat both in the monarchical and in the freest, republican countries.

On an incomparably larger scale than in 1852 world history is now undoubtedly leading to the "concentration of all the forces" of the proletarian revolution for the "destruction" of the state machine.

What the proletariat will put in its place is indicated by the extremely instructive material furnished by the Paris Commune.

3. The Presentation of the Question by Marx in 1852

In 1907, Mehring published in the magazine *Neue Zeit* [8] (Vol. XXV, 2, p. 164) extracts from a letter written by Marx to Weydemeyer on March 5, 1852. This letter, among other things, contains the following remarkable observations:

And now as to myself, no credit is due me for discovering the existence of classes in modern society or the struggle between them. Long before me bourgeois historians had described the historical development of this class struggle and bourgeois economists, the economic anatomy of the classes. What I did that was new was to prove: 1) that the existence of classes is only bound up with particular historical phases in the development of production (*historische Entwicklungsphasen der Produktion*); 2) that the class struggle necessarily leads to the dictatorship of the proletariat; 3) that this dictatorship itself only constitutes the transition to the abolition of all classes and to a classless society. . . .

In these words Marx succeeded in expressing with striking clarity, firstly, the chief and radical difference between his teaching and that of the foremost and most profound thinkers of the bourgeoisie; and, secondly, the essence of his teaching on the state.

It is often said and written that the main point in Marx's teachings is the class struggle. But this is not true. And from this untruth very often springs the opportunist distortion of Marxism, its falsification in such a way as to make it acceptable to the bourgeoisie. For the doctrine of the class struggle was created *not* by Marx, *but* by the bourgeoisie *before* Marx, and generally speaking it is *acceptable* to the bourgeoisie. Those who recognize *only* the class struggle are not yet Marxists; they may be found to be still within the boundaries of bourgeois thinking and bourgeois politics. To confine Marxism to the doctrine of the class struggle means curtailing Marxism, distorting it, reducing it to something which is acceptable to the bourgeoisie. Only he is a Marxist who *extends* the recognition of the class struggle to the recognition of the *dictatorship of the proletariat*. This is what constitutes the most profound difference between the Marxist and the ordinary petty (as well as big) bourgeois. This is the touchstone on which the *real* understanding and recognition of Marxism is to be tested. And it is not surprising that when the history of Europe brought the working class face to face with this question as a *practical* issue, not only all the opportunists and reformists, but all the "Kautsky-ites" (people who vacillate between reformism and Marxism) proved to be miserable philistines and petty-bourgeois democrats who *repudiate* the dictatorship of the proletariat. Kautsky's pamphlet, *The Dictatorship of the Proletariat*, published in August 1918, *i.e.*, long after the first edition of the present book, is a perfect example of petty-bourgeois distortion of Marxism and base renunciation of it *in practice*, while hypocritically recognizing it *in words* (see my pamphlet, *The Proletarian Revolution and the Renegade Kautsky*, Petrograd and Moscow, 1918).

Present-day opportunism in the person of its principal representative, the ex-Marxist, K. Kautsky, fits in completely with Marx's characterization of the *bourgeois* position quoted above, for this opportunism limits the recognition of the class struggle to the sphere of bourgeois relationships. (Within this sphere, within its framework, not a single educated liberal will refuse to recognize the class struggle "in principle"! (Opportunism *does not extend* the recognition of class struggle to what is the cardinal point, to the period of the *overthrow* and the complete *destruction* of the bourgeoisie. In reality, this period is inevitably a period of unprecedentedly violent class struggle in unprecedentedly acute forms and, consequently, during this period the state must inevitably be a state that is democratic *in a new way* (for the proletariat and the propertyless in general) and dictatorial *in a new way* (against the bourgeoisie).

To proceed. The essence of Marx's teaching on the state has been mastered only by those who understand that the dictatorship of a *single* class is necessary not only for every class society in general, not only for the *proletariat* which has overthrown the bourgeoisie, but also for the entire *historical period* which separates capitalism from "classless society," from communism. The forms of bourgeois states are extremely varied, but their essence is the same: all these states, whatever their form, in the final analysis are inevitably *the dictatorship of the bourgeoisie*. The transition from capitalism to communism certainly cannot but yield a tremendous abundance and variety of political forms, but the essence will inevitably be the same: *the dictatorship of the proletariat*.

III. THE EXPERIENCE OF THE PARIS COMMUNE OF 1871. MARX'S ANALYSIS

1. WHEREIN LAY THE HEROISM OF THE COMMUNARDS' ATTEMPT?

It is well known that in the autumn of 1870, a few months before the Commune, Marx warned the Paris workers that any attempt to overthrow the government would be the folly of despair. But when, in March 1871, a decisive battle was *forced* upon the workers and they accepted it, when the uprising had become a fact, Marx greeted the proletarian revolution with the greatest enthusiasm, in spite of unfavorable auguries. Marx did not assume the rigidly pedantic attitude of condemning an "untimely" movement as did the ill-famed Russian renegade from Marxism, Plekhanov, who, in November 1905, wrote encouragingly about the workers' and peasants' struggle, but, after December 1905, cried, liberal fashion: "They should not have taken to arms."

Marx, however, was not only enthusiastic about the heroism of the Communards who, as he expressed it, "stormed Heaven." Although the mass revolutionary movement did not achieve its aim, he regarded it as a historic experience of enormous importance, as a certain advance of the world proletarian revolution, as a practical step that was more important than hundreds of programs and arguments. To analyze this experiment, to draw tactical lessons from it, to re-examine his theory in the light of it—that was the task that Marx set himself.

The only "correction" Marx thought it necessary to make in the *Communist Manifesto*, he made on the basis of the revolutionary experience of the Paris Communards.

The last preface to the new German edition of the *Communist Manifesto*, signed by both its authors, is dated June 24, 1872. In this preface the authors, Karl Marx and Frederick Engels, say that the program of the *Communist Manifesto* "has in some details become antiquated," and they go on to say:

. . . In particular, the Commune proved that 'the working class cannot simply take control of the ready-made state machinery and use it for its own purposes'. . . .

The authors took the words that are in quotation marks in this passage from Marx's book, *The Civil War in France*.

Thus, Marx and Engels regarded one principal and fundamental lesson of the Paris Commune as being of such enormous importance that they introduced it as a substantial correction into the *Communist Manifesto*.

It is extremely characteristic that it is precisely this substantial correction that has been distorted by the opportunists, and its meaning probably is not known to nine tenths, if not ninety-nine hundredths, of the readers of the *Communist Manifesto*. We shall deal with this distortion more fully further on, in a chapter devoted specially to distortions. Here it will be sufficient to note that the current, vulgar "interpretation" of Marx's famous utterance just quoted is that Marx here allegedly emphasizes the idea of slow development in contradistinction to the seizure of power, and so on.

As a matter of fact, *exactly the opposite is the case.* Marx's idea is that the working class must *break up, smash* the "ready-made state machinery," and not confine itself merely to taking control of it.

On April 12, 1871, *i.e.*, just at the time of the Commune, Marx wrote to Kugelmann:

. . . If you look at the last chapter of my *Eighteenth Brumaire,* you will find that I declare that the next attempt of the French Revolution will be no longer, as before, to transfer the bureaucratic-military machine from one hand to another, but *to smash* it [Marx's italics—the original is *zerbrechen*], and this is the preliminary condition for every real people's revolution on the Continent. This is exactly what our heroic party comrades in Paris are attempting. (*Neue Zeit,* Vol. XX, 1, 1901-02, p. 709.) (The letters of Marx to Kugelmann have appeared in Russian in no less than two editions, one of which I edited and supplied with a preface.)

The words "to smash the bureaucratic-military machine" briefly express the principal lesson of Marxism regarding the tasks of the proletariat during a revolution in relation to the state. And it is precisely this lesson that has been not only completely forgotten, but positively distorted by the prevailing, Kautskyite "interpretation" of Marxism!

As for Marx's reference to *The Eighteenth Brumaire,* we have quoted the corresponding passage in full above.

It is interesting to note, in particular, two points in the above-quoted argument of Marx. First, he restricts his conclusion to the Continent. This was understandable in 1871, when England was still the model of a purely capitalist country, but without a militarist clique and, to a considerable degree, without a bureaucracy. Hence, Marx excluded England, where a revolution, even a people's revolution, then seemed possible, and indeed was possible, *without* the preliminary condition of destroying the "ready-made state machinery."

Today, in 1917, in the epoch of the first great imperialist war, this restriction made by Marx is no longer valid. Both England and America, the biggest and the last representatives —in the whole world—of Anglo-Saxon "liberty," in the sense that they had no militarist cliques and bureaucracy, have completely sunk into the all-European filthy, bloody morass of bureaucratic-military institutions which subordinate everything to themselves, trample everything underfoot. Today, both in England and in America, "the preliminary condition for every real people's revolution" is the *smashing*, the *destruction* of the "ready-made state machinery" brought in those countries to "European," general imperialist, perfection in the years 1914-17.

Secondly, particular attention should be paid to Marx's remarkably profound observation that the destruction of the bureaucratic-military state machine is "the preliminary condition for every real *people's* revolution." This idea of a "people's" revolution seems strange coming from Marx, and the Russian Plekhanovites and Mensheviks, those followers of Struve who wish to be regarded as Marxists, might possibly declare such an expression to be a "slip of the pen" on Marx's part. They have reduced Marxism to such a state of wretchedly liberal distortion that nothing exists for them beyond the antithesis between bourgeois revolution and proletarian revolution—and even this antithesis they interpret in a completely lifeless way.

If we take the revolutions of the twentieth century as examples we shall, of course, have to admit that the Portuguese and the Turkish revolutions are both bourgeois revolutions. Neither of them, however, is a "people's" revolution, inasmuch as in neither does the mass of the people, its enormous majority, come out actively, independently, with its own economic and political demands to any noticeable degree. In contrast to this, although the Russian bourgeois revolution of 1905-1907 displayed no such "brilliant" successes as at times fell to the lot of the Portuguese and Turkish revolutions, it was undoubtedly a "real people's" revolution, since the mass of the people, its majority, the very lowest social strata, crushed by oppression and exploitation, rose independently and placed on the entire course of the revolution the impress of *their* own demands, of *their* attempts to build in their own way a new society in place of the old society that was being destroyed.

In Europe, in 1871, there was not a single country on the Continent in which the proletariat constituted the majority of the people. A "people's" revolution, one that actually swept the majority into its stream, could be such only if it embraced both the proletariat and the peasantry. These two classes then constituted the "people." These two classes are united by the fact that the "bureaucratic-military state machine" oppresses, crushes, exploits them. *To smash* this machine, *to break it up*—this is truly in the interest of the "people," of their majority, the workers and most of the peasants, this is "the preliminary condition" for a free alliance between the poorest peasants and the proletarians, whereas without such an alliance democracy is unstable and a socialist transformation is impossible.

As is well known, the Paris Commune was indeed working its way toward such an alliance, although it did not reach its goal owing to a number of circumstances, internal and external.

Consequently, in speaking of a "real people's revolution," Marx, without in the least forgetting the peculiar characteristics of the petty bourgeoisie (he spoke a great deal about them and often), took strict account of the actual balance of class forces in the majority of continental countries in Europe in 1871. On the other hand, he stated that the "smashing" of the state machine was required by the interests of both the workers and the peasants, that it unites them, that it places before them the common task of removing the "parasite" and replacing it by something new.

By what exactly?

2. WHAT WILL REPLACE THE SMASHED STATE MACHINE?

In 1847, in the *Communist Manifesto,* Marx's answer to this question was as yet a purely abstract one, or, to speak more correctly, it was an answer that indicated the tasks, but not the ways of accomplishing them. The answer given in the *Communist Manifesto* was that this machine was to be replaced by "the proletariat organized as the ruling class," by the "victory of democracy."

Not indulging in utopias, Marx expected the *experience* of the mass movement to provide the reply to the question as to what specific forms this organization of the proletariat as the ruling class will assume and as to the exact manner in which this organization will be combined with the most complete and consistent "victory of democracy."

Marx subjected the experience of the Commune, meager as it was, to the most careful analysis in *The Civil War in France*. Let us quote the most important passages of this work.

Originating from the Middle Ages, there developed in the nineteenth century "the centralized state power, with its ubiquitous organs of standing army, police, bureaucracy, clergy, and judicature." With the development of class antagonisms between capital and labor, ". . . the state power assumed more and more the character of a public force for the oppression of labor, an engine of class rule. After every revolution marking a progressive phase in the class struggle, the purely repressive character of the state power stands out in bolder and bolder relief." After the Revolution of 1848-1849, the state power became "the national war weapon of capital against labor." The Second Empire consolidated this.

The direct antithesis to the empire was the Commune. "It was the positive form" of "a republic that was not only to supersede the monarchical form of class-rule, but class-rule itself. . . ."

What was this "positive" form of the proletarian, the socialist republic? What was the state it began to create?

. . . The first decree of the Commune . . . was the suppression of the standing army and its replacement by the armed people. . . .

This demand now figures in the program of every party claiming the name of socialist. But the real worth of their programs is best shown by the behavior of our Socialist-Revolutionaries and Mensheviks, who, right after the revolution of February 27, actually refused to carry out this demand!

. . . The Commune was formed of the municipal councillors, chosen by universal suffrage in the various wards of the town, responsible and removable at any time. The majority of its members were naturally working men, or acknowledged representatives of the working class. . . .

Instead of continuing to be the agent of the central government, the police was at once stripped of its political attributes, and turned into the responsible and at all times revocable organ of the Commune. The same was true for the officials of all other branches of the Administration. From the members of the Commune downwards, public service had to be done at *workmen's wages*. All privileges and the representation allowances of the high dignitaries of state disappeared along with the high dignitaries themselves. . . . Having once got rid of the standing army and the police, the instruments of physical force of the old government, the Commune was anxious to break the spiritual force of repression, the power of the priests. . . . The judicial functionaries were to be divested of that sham independence . . . they were to be elective, responsible, and revocable. . . .

Thus the Commune appears to have replaced the smashed state machine "only" by fuller democracy. The standing army was abolished, and all officials were to be elected and subject to recall. But as a matter of fact this "only" signifies a gigantic replacement of certain institutions by other institutions of a fundamentally different order. This is, in fact, a case of "the transformation of quantity into quality": democracy, introduced as fully and consistently as is at all conceivable, transformed from bourgeois democracy into proletarian democracy, from the state (= a special force for the suppression of a particular class) into something which is no longer really the state.

It is still necessary to suppress the bourgeoisie and crush its resistance. This was particularly necessary for the Commune, and one of the reasons for its defeat was that it did not do this with sufficient determination. But the organ of suppression is now the majority of the population, and not a minority, as was always the case under slavery, serfdom and wage slavery. And since the majority of the people *itself* suppresses its oppressors, a "special force" for suppression is *no longer necessary!* In this sense the state *begins to wither away*. Instead of the special institutions of a privileged minority (privileged officialdom, the chiefs of the standing army), the majority itself can directly fulfill all these functions, and the more the functions of state power devolve upon the people as a whole the less need is there for the existence of this power.

In this connection the following measures of the Commune emphasized by Marx are particularly noteworthy: the abolition of all representation allowances and of all monetary privileges for officials; the reduction of the remuneration of *all* servants of the state to the level of *"workmen's wages."* This shows more clearly than anything else the *sudden change* from bourgeois democracy to proletarian democracy, from the democracy of the oppressors to the democracy of the oppressed classes, from the state as a *"special force"* for the suppression of a particular class to the suppression of the oppressors by the *general force* of the majority of the people—the workers and the peasants. And it is precisely on this particularly striking point, perhaps the most important as far as the problem of the state is concerned, that the teachings of Marx have been most completely forgotten! In popular commentaries, the number of which is legion, this is not mentioned. It is "good form" to keep silent about it as if it were a piece of old-fashioned "naïveté," just as the Christians, after their religion had been given the status of a state religion, "forgot" the "naïveté" of primitive Christianity with its democratic revolutionary spirit.

The reduction of the remuneration of the highest state officials seems to be "simply" a demand of naïve, primitive democracy. One of the "founders" of modern opportunism, the ex-Social Democrat, Eduard Bernstein, has more than once indulged in repeating the vulgar bourgeois jeers at "primitive" democracy. Like all opportunists, and like the present Kautskyites, he utterly failed to understand that, first of all, the transition from capitalism to socialism is *impossible* without a certain "reversion" to "primitive" democracy (for how else can the majority, and then the whole population without exception, proceed to discharge state functions?); and, secondly, that "primitive democracy" based on capitalism and capitalist culture is not the same as primitive democracy in prehistoric or precapitalist times. Capitalist culture has *created* large-scale production, factories, railways, the postal service, telephones, etc., and *on this basis* the great majority of the functions of the old "state power" have become so simplified and can be reduced to such exceedingly simple operations of registration, filing and checking that they can be easily performed by every literate person, that they can quite easily be performed for ordinary "workmen's wages," and that these functions can (and must) be stripped of every shadow of privilege, of every semblance of "official grandeur."

All officials, without exception, elected and subject to recall *at any time*, their salaries reduced to the level of ordinary "workmen's wages"—these simple and "self-evident" democratic measures, while completely uniting the interests of the workers and the majority of the peasants, at the same time serve as a bridge leading from capitalism to socialism. These measures concern the state, the purely political reconstruction of society; but, of course, they acquire their full meaning and significance only in connection with the "expropriation of the expropriators" either being accomplished or in preparation, *i.e.*, with the transformation of capitalist private ownership of the means of production into social ownership.

"The Commune," Marx wrote, "made that catchword of bourgeois revolutions, cheap government, a reality, by destroying the two greatest sources of expenditure—the standing army and state bureaucracy."

From the peasantry, as from other sections of the petty bourgeoisie, only an insignificant few "rise to the top," "get on in the world" in the bourgeois sense, *i.e.*, become either well-to-do people, bourgeois, or officials in secure and privileged positions. In every capitalist country where there is a peasantry (as there is in most capitalist countries), the vast majority of the peasants are oppressed by the government and long for its overthrow, long for "cheap" government. This can be achieved *only* by the proletariat; and by achieving it, the proletariat at the same time takes a step towards the socialist reconstruction of the state.

3. ABOLITION OF PARLIAMENTARISM

"The Commune," Marx wrote, "was to be a working, not a parliamentary, body, executive and legislative at the same time. . . ."

". . . Instead of deciding once in three or six years which member of the ruling class was to represent and repress (*ver- und zertreten*) the people in Parliament, universal suffrage was to serve the people, constituted in Communes, as individual suffrage serves every other employer in search of workers, foremen and bookkeepers for his enterprises.

Owing to the prevalence of social-chauvinism and opportunism, this remarkable criticism of parliamentarism made in 1871 also belongs now to the "forgotten words" of Marxism. The professional cabinet ministers and parliamentarians, the traitors to the proletariat and the "practical" socialists of our day, have left all criticism of parliamentarism to the anarchists, and on this wonderfully reasonable ground, they denounce *all* criticism of parliamentarism as "anarchism"!! It is not surprising that the proletariat of the "advanced" parliamentary countries, disgusted with such "socialists" as the Scheidemanns, Davids, Legiens, Sembats, Renaudels, Hendersons, Vanderveldes, Staunings, Brantings, Bissolatis and Co., has been with increasing frequency giving its sympathies to anarchosyndicalism, in spite of the fact that the latter is but the twin brother of opportunism.

For Marx however revolutionary dialectics was never the empty fashionable phrase, the toy rattle, which Plekhanov, Kautsky and the others have made of it. Marx knew how to break with anarchism ruthlessly for its inability to make use even of the "pig-sty" of bourgeois parliamentarism, especially when the situation is obviously not revolutionary; but at the same time he knew how to subject parliamentarism to genuine revolutionary-proletarian criticism.

To decide once every few years which member of the ruling class is to repress and crush the people through parliament—such is the real essence of bourgeois parliamentarism, not only in parliamentary-constitutional monarchies, but also in the most democratic republics.

But if we deal with the question of the state, and if we consider parliamentarism as one of the institutions of the state, from the point of view of the tasks of the proletariat in *this* field, what is the way out of parliamentarism? How can it be dispensed with?

Again and again we have to repeat: the lessons of Marx, based on the study of the Commune, have been so completely forgotten that the present-day "Social Democrat" (read present-day traitor to socialism) really cannot understand any criticism of parliamentarism other than anarchist or reactionary criticism.

The way out of parliamentarism is not, of course, the abolition of representative institutions and the electoral principle, but the conversion of the representative institutions from talking shops into "working" bodies. "The Commune was to be a working, not a parliamentary body, executive and legislative at the same time."

"A working, not a parliamentary body"—this hits straight from the shoulder at the present-day parliamentarians and parliamentary "house-broken dogs" of Social Democracy! Take any parliamentary country, from America to Switzerland, from France to England, Norway and so forth—in these countries the real business of "state" is performed behind the scenes and is carried on by the departments, chancelleries and general staffs. Parliament itself is given up to talk for the special purpose of fooling the "common people." This is so true that even in the Russian republic, a bourgeois-democratic republic, all these sins of parliamentarism were immediately revealed, even before it managed to set up a real parliament. The heroes of rotten philistinism, such as the Skobelevs and Tseretelis, the Chernovs and Avksentyevs, have even succeeded in polluting the Soviets after the fashion of a most disgusting bourgeois parliamentarism and have converted them into mere talking shops. In the Soviets, the "socialist" Ministers are duping the credulous rustics with phrasemongering and resolutions. In the government itself a sort of permanent quadrille is going on in order that, on the one hand, as many Socialist-Revolutionaries and Mensheviks as possible may in turn get near the "pie," the lucrative and honorable posts, and that, on the other hand, the "attention of the people" may be engaged. Meanwhile, it is in the chancelleries and staffs that they "work" at the business of "state."

Delo Naroda,[9] the organ of the ruling "Socialist-Revolutionary" Party, recently admitted in an editorial article—with the matchless candor of people of "good society," in which "all" are engaged in political prostitution—that even in the ministries headed by the "socialists" (excuse the expression!), the whole bureaucratic apparatus has in fact remained as of old, working in the old way and quite "freely" sabotaging revolutionary measures! Even without this admission, does not the actual history of the participation of the Socialist-Revolutionaries and Mensheviks in the government prove this? What is noteworthy about it is only the fact that, in the ministerial company of the Cadets, Messrs. Chernovs, Rusanovs, Zenzinovs and the other editors of *Delo Naroda* have so completely lost all sense of shame as to unblushingly proclaim, as if it were a trivial matter, that in "their" ministries everything has remained

as of old!! Revolutionary-democratic phrases to fool the rural
Simple Simons; bureaucracy and red tape to "gladden the
heart" of the capitalists—that is the *essence* of the "honest"
coalition.

The Commune substitutes for the venal and rotten parliamentarism of bourgeois society institutions in which freedom of opinion and of discussion does not degenerate into
deception, for the parliamentarians themselves have to work,
have to execute their own laws, have themselves to test
their results in real life, and to render account directly to
their constituents. Representative institutions remain, but
there is *no* parliamentarism here as a special system, as the
division of labor between the legislative and the executive,
as a privileged position for the representatives. We cannot
imagine democracy, even proletarian democracy, without
representative institutions, but we can and *must* imagine
democracy without parliamentarism, if criticism of bourgeois society is not mere empty words for us, if the desire
to overthrow the rule of the bourgeoisie is our earnest and
sincere aim, and not a mere "campaign issue" for catching
workers' votes, as it is with the Mensheviks and Socialist-
Revolutionaries, the Scheidemanns and Legiens, the Sembats
and Vandeveldes.

It is extremely instructive to note that, in speaking of the
functions of *those* officials who are necessary for the Commune and for proletarian democracy, Marx compares them
to the workers of "every other employer," that is, of the
ordinary capitalist enterprise, with its "workers, foremen and
bookkeepers."

There is no trace of utopianism in Marx, in the sense
that he made up or invented a "new" society. No, he studied
the *birth* of the new society *out of* the old, the forms of
transition from the latter to the former as a natural-historical
process. He examined the actual experience of a mass proletarian movement and tried to draw practical lessons from
it. He "learned" from the Commune, just as all the great
revolutionary thinkers were not afraid to learn from the experience of the great movements of the oppressed classes,
and never addressed them with pedantic "homilies" (such
as Plekhanov's: "they should not have taken to arms" or
Tsereteli's: "a class must limit itself").

There can be no thought of abolishing the bureaucracy at
once, everywhere and completely. That is utopia. But *to
smash* the old bureaucratic machine at once and to begin

immediately to construct a new one that will permit the gradual abolition of all bureaucracy—this is *not* utopia, this is the experience of the Commune, this is the direct and immediate task of the revolutionary proletariat.

Capitalism simplifies the functions of "state" administration; it makes it possible to cast "bossing" aside and to confine the whole matter to the organization of the proletarians (as the ruling class), which will hire "workers, foremen and bookkeepers" in the name of the whole of society.

We are not utopians, we do not indulge in "dreams" of dispensing *at once* with all administration, with all subordination. These anarchist dreams, based upon a lack of understanding of the tasks of the proletarian dictatorship, are totally alien to Marxism, and, as a matter of fact, serve only to postpone the socialist revolution until people are different. No, we want the socialist revolution with people as they are now, with people who cannot dispense with subordination, control and "foremen and bookkeepers."

But the subordination must be to the armed vanguard of all the exploited and laboring people, *i.e.*, to the proletariat. A beginning can and must be made at once, overnight, of replacing the specific "bossing" of state officials by the simple functions of "foremen and bookkeepers," functions which are already fully within the capacity of the average city dweller and can well be performed for "workmen's wages."

We ourselves, the workers, will organize large-scale production on the basis of what capitalism has already created, relying on our own experience as workers, establishing strict, iron discipline supported by the state power of the armed workers. We will reduce the role of the state officials to that of simply carrying out our instructions as responsible, revocable, modestly paid "foremen and bookkeepers" (of course, with the aid of technicians of all sorts, types and degrees). This is *our* proletarian task, this is what we can and must *start* with in accomplishing the proletarian revolution. Such a beginning, on the basis of large-scale production, will of itself lead to the gradual "withering away" of all bureaucracy, to the gradual creation of an order, an order without quotation marks, an order bearing no similarity to wage slavery, an order in which the functions of control and accounting—becoming more and more simple—will be performed by each in turn, will then become a habit and will finally die out as the *special* functions of a special section of the population.

A witty German Social Democrat of the seventies of the last century called the *postal service* an example of the socialist economic system. This is very true. At present the postal service is a business organized on the lines of a state-*capitalist* monopoly. Imperialism is gradually transforming all trusts into organizations of a similar type, in which, standing over the "common" laborers, who are overworked and starved, is the same bourgeois bureaucracy. But the mechanism of social management is here already at hand. We have but to overthrow the capitalists, to crush the resistance of these exploiters with the iron hand of the armed workers, to smash the bureaucratic machine of the modern state—and we shall have a splendidly equipped mechanism, freed from the "parasite," a mechanism which can very well be set going by the united workers themselves, who will hire technicians, foremen and bookkeepers, and pay them *all*, as, indeed *all* "state" officials in general, a workman's wage. Here is a concrete, practical task, immediately possible of fulfillment in relation to all trusts, a task that will rid the laborers of exploitation and take account of what the Commune had already begun to practice (particularly in building up the state).

To organize the *whole* national economy on the lines of the postal service, so that the technicians, foremen, bookkeepers, as well as *all* officials, shall receive salaries no higher than "a workman's wage," all under the control and leadership of the armed proletariat—this is our immediate aim. It is such a state, standing on such an economic foundation, that we need. This is what will bring about the abolition of parliamentarism and the preservation of representative institutions. This is what will rid the laboring classes of the prostitution of these institutions by the bourgeoisie.

4. The Organization of National Unity

". . . In a rough sketch of national organization which the Commune had no time to develop, it states clearly that the Commune was to be . . . the political form of even the smallest country hamlet. . . ." The Communes were to elect the "National Delegation" in Paris.

". . . The few but important functions which still would remain for a central government were not to be suppressed, as has been intentionally misstated, but were to be discharged by Communal, and therefore strictly responsible, officials.

". . . The unity of the nation was not to be broken, but, on the contrary, to be organized by the Communal organization. It was to become a reality by the destruction of the state power which claimed to be the embodiment of that unity but which wanted to be independent of, and superior to, the nation itself. In fact, this state power was but a parasitic growth on the body of the nation. . . . While the merely repressive organs of the old governmental power were to be amputated, its legitimate functions were to be wrested from an authority claiming to stand over society and restored to the responsible servants of society."

To what extent the opportunists of present-day Social Democracy have failed to understand—or perhaps it would be more true to say did not want to understand—these observations of Marx is best shown by that book of Herostratean fame of the renegade Bernstein, *The Premises of Socialism and the Tasks of Social Democracy*. It is precisely in connection with the above passage from Marx that Bernstein wrote that this program ". . . in its political content, displays in all its essential features the greatest similarity to the federalism of Proudhon. . . . In spite of all the other points of difference between Marx and the 'petty-bourgeois' Proudhon (Bernstein places the words "petty-bourgeois" in quotation marks in order to make it sound ironical) on these points their lines of reasoning run as close as could be." Of course, Bernstein continues, the importance of the municipalities is growing, but "it seems doubtful to me whether the first task of democracy would be such a dissolution (*Auflösung*) of the modern states and such a complete transformation (*Umwandlung*) of their organization as is visualized by Marx and Proudhon (the formation of a National Assembly from delegates of the provincial or district assemblies, which, in their turn, would consist of delegates from the Communes), so that the whole previous mode of national representation would vanish completely." (Bernstein, *Premises*, German edition, 1899, pp. 134 and 136.)

To confuse Marx's views on the "destruction of the state power—the parasite"—with Proudhon's federalism is positively monstrous! But it is no accident, for it never occurs to the opportunist that Marx does not speak here at all about federalism as opposed to centralism, but about smashing the old, bourgeois state machine which exists in all bourgeois countries.

The only thing that penetrates the opportunist's mind is what he sees around him, in a society of petty-bourgeois philistinism and "reformist" stagnation, namely, only "municipalities"! The opportunist has even forgotten how to think about proletarian revolution.

It is ridiculous. But the remarkable thing is that nobody argued with Bernstein on this point. Bernstein has been refuted by many, especially by Plekhanov in Russian literature and by Kautsky in European literature, but neither of them said *anything* about *this* distortion of Marx by Bernstein.

To such an extent has the opportunist forgotten how to think in a revolutionary way and to ponder over revolution that he attributes "federalism" to Marx and confuses him with the founder of anarchism, Proudhon. And Kautsky and Plekhanov, who claim to be orthodox Marxists and defenders of the doctrine of revolutionary Marxism, are silent on this point! Herein lies one of the roots of the extreme vulgarization of the views concerning the difference between Marxism and anarchism, which is characteristic of the Kautskyites and of the opportunists and which we shall discuss later.

Marx's above-quoted observations on the experience of the Commune contain not a trace of federalism. Marx agreed with Proudhon on the very point that the opportunist Bernstein failed to see. Marx disagreed with Proudhon on the very point on which Bernstein found a similarity between them.

Marx agreed with Proudhon in that they both stood for the "smashing" of the present state machine. The similarity of views on this point between Marxism and anarchism (both Proudhon and Bakunin) neither the opportunists nor the Kautskyites wish to see because on this point they have departed from Marxism.

Marx disagreed both with Proudhon and with Bakunin precisely on the question of federalism (not to mention the dictatorship of the proletariat). Federalism as a principle follows logically from the petty-bourgeois views of anarchism. Marx was a centralist. There is no departure whatever from centralism in his observations just quoted. Only those who are imbued with the philistine "superstitious belief" in the state can mistake the destruction of the bourgeois state machine for the destruction of centralism!

But if the proletariat and the poorest peasantry take state power into their own hands, organize themselves quite freely in communes, and *unite* the action of all the communes in striking at capital, in crushing the resistance of the capitalists, and in transferring the privately owned railways, factories, land and so forth to the *entire* nation, to the whole of society—will that not be centralism? Will that not be the most consistent democratic centralism? And proletarian centralism at that?

Bernstein simply cannot conceive of the possibility of voluntary centralism, of the voluntary amalgamation of the communes into a nation, of the voluntary fusion of the proletarian communes, for the purpose of destroying bourgeois rule and the bourgeois state machine. Like all philistines, Bernstein can imagine centralism only as something from above, to be imposed and maintained solely by the bureaucracy and the military clique.

Marx, as though foreseeing the possibility of his views being distorted, purposely emphasized the fact that the charge that the Commune wanted to destroy the unity of the nation, to abolish the central authority, was a deliberate fake. Marx purposely used the words: "The unity of the nation was . . . to be organized," so as to oppose conscious, democratic, proletarian centralism to bourgeois, military, bureaucratic centralism.

But . . . there are none so deaf as those who will not hear. And the very thing the opportunists of present-day Social Democracy do not want to hear about is the destruction of the state power, the amputation of the parasite.

5. The Abolition of the Parasitic State

We have already quoted Marx's statements on this subject, and we must now supplement them.

". . . It is generally the fate of new historical creations," he wrote, "to be mistakenly considered as similar to older and even defunct forms of social life, to which they may bear a certain likeness. Thus, this new Commune, which breaks the modern state power, has been mistaken for a reproduction of the mediaeval Communes . . . for a federation of small states (Montesquieu, the Girondins)[10] . . . for an exaggerated form of the ancient struggle against overcentralization. . . .

"The Communal organization would have restored to the social body all the forces hitherto absorbed by the state parasite feeding upon and hampering the free movement of society. By this one act it would have promoted the regeneration of France. . . .

"The Communal organization would have brought the rural producers under the intellectual lead of the central towns of their districts, and there secured to them, in the working men, the natural trustees of their interests. The very existence of the Commune involved, as a matter of course, local municipal liberty, but no longer as a check upon state power, which would then have become superfluous."

"The destruction of the state power," which was a "parasitic growth"; its "amputation," its "smashing"; "the state power, which would then have become superfluous"—these are the expressions Marx used in regard to the state when appraising and analyzing the experience of the Commune.

All this was written a little less than half a century ago, and now one has to engage in excavations, as it were, in order to bring undistorted Marxism to the knowledge of the masses. The conclusions drawn from the observation of the last great revolution which Marx lived through were forgotten just at the moment when the time for the next great proletarian revolutions had arrived.

. . . The multiplicity of interpretations to which the Commune has been subjected and the multiplicity of interests which construed it in their favor, show that it was a thoroughly expansive political form, while all previous forms of government had been emphatically repressive. Its true secret was this. It was essentially *a working-class government*, the result of the struggle of the producing against the appropriating class, the political form, at last discovered, by which the economic emancipation of labor could be achieved.

Except on this last condition, the Communal organization would have been an impossibility and a delusion. . . .

The utopians busied themselves with "discovering" political forms under which the socialist transformation of society was to take place. The anarchists waived the question of political forms altogether. The opportunists of present-day Social Democracy accepted the bourgeois political forms of the parliamentary democratic state as the limit which should not be overstepped. They battered their foreheads praying before this "sacred image" and denounced as anarchism all desire to *smash* these forms.

Marx deduced from the whole history of socialism and the political struggle that the state was bound to disappear, and that the transitional form of its disappearance (the transition from state to non-state) would be the "proletariat organized as the ruling class." But Marx did not set out to *discover* the political *forms* of this future stage. He limited himself to observing precisely French history, to analyzing it, and to drawing the conclusion to which the year 1851 had led, *viz.*, that matters were moving towards the *smashing* of the bourgeois state machine.

And when the mass revolutionary movement of the proletariat burst forth, Marx, in spite of the failure of that movement, in spite of its short life and its patent weakness, began to study what forms it had *discovered*.

The Commune is the form "at last discovered" by the proletarian revolution, under which the economic emancipation of labor can take place.

The Commune is the first attempt of a proletarian revolution *to smash* the bourgeois state machine; and it is the political form "at last discovered," by which the smashed state machine can and must be *replaced*.

We shall see further on that the Russian revolutions of 1905 and 1917, in different circumstances and under different conditions, continue the work of the Commune and confirm Marx's brilliant historical analysis.

IV. CONTINUATION. SUPPLEMENTARY EXPLANATIONS BY ENGELS

Marx gave the fundamentals regarding the significance of the experience of the Commune. Engels returned to the same subject repeatedly and explained Marx's analysis and conclusions, sometimes elucidating *other* aspects of the question with such power and vividness that it is necessary to deal with his explanations separately.

1. "THE HOUSING QUESTION"

In his work, *The Housing Question* (1872), Engels already took into account the experience of the Commune and dealt several times with the tasks of the revolution in relation to the state. It is interesting to note that the treatment of this concrete subject clearly revealed, on the one hand, points of similarity between the proletarian state and the present state—such as give grounds for speaking of the state in both cases—and, on the other hand, points of difference between them, or the transition to the destruction of the state.

How is the housing question to be solved, then? In present-day society just as any other social question is solved: by the gradual economic adjustment of supply and demand, a solution which continually reproduces the question itself and therefore provides no solution. How a social revolution would solve this question not only depends on the particular circumstances in each case, but is also connected with much more far-reaching questions, one of the most fundamental of which is the abolition of the antithesis between town and country. As it is not our task to create utopian systems for the arrangement of the future society, it would be more than idle to go into the question here. But one thing is certain: there are already in existence sufficient buildings for dwellings in the big towns to aid immediately any real "housing *shortage*," given rational utilization of them. This can naturally only take place by the expropriation of the present owners, that is, by quartering in their houses homeless workers or workers excessively overcrowded in their present apartments. As soon as the proletariat has conquered political power such a measure dictated in the public interest will be just as easy to carry out as are other expropriations and billetings by the existing state. (German edition, 1887, p. 22.)

The change in the form of the state power is not examined here, but only the content of its activity. Expropriations and billetings take place by order even of the present state. From the formal point of view the proletarian state will also "order" the occupation of apartments and expropriation of homes. But it is clear that the old executive apparatus, the bureaucracy, which is connected with the bourgeoisie, would simply be unfit to carry out the orders of the proletarian state.

. . . It must be pointed out that the actual seizure of all the instruments of labor, the seizure of industry as a whole by the working people, is the exact opposite of the Proudhonist "redemption." Under the latter, the individual worker becomes the owner of the dwelling, the peasant farm, the instruments of labor. Under the former, the "working people" remain the collective owners of the houses, factories and instruments of labor, and will hardly permit their use, at least during the transition period, by individuals or associations without compensation for the cost. Just as the abolition of property in land is not the abolition of ground rent but its transfer, although in a modified form, to society. The actual seizure of all the instruments of labor by the working people, therefore, does not at all exclude the retention of the rent relation. (p. 68.)

We shall discuss the question touched upon in this passage, namely, the economic basis for the withering away of the state, in the next chapter. Engels expresses himself most cautiously, saying that the proletarian state would "hardly" permit the use of apartments without payment, "at least during the transition period." The letting of apartments that belong to the whole people, to individual families presupposes the collection of rent, a certain amount of control, and the employment of some standard in allotting the apartments. All this calls for a certain form of state, but it does not at all call for a special military and bureaucratic apparatus, with officials occupying especially privileged positions. The transition to a state of affairs when it will be possible to supply dwellings rent-free is connected with the complete "withering away" of the state.

Speaking of the conversion of the Blanquists to the principles of Marxism after the Commune and under the influence of its experience, Engels, in passing, formulates these principles as follows:

. . . The necessity of political action by the proletariat and of its dictatorship as the transition to the abolition of classes and with them of the state. . . . (p. 55.)

Addicts to hair-splitting criticism or bourgeois "exterminators of Marxism" will perhaps see a contradiction between this *recognition* of the "abolition of the state" and repudiation of this formula as an anarchist one in the above-quoted passage from *Anti-Dühring*. It would not be surprising if the opportunists stamped Engels, too, as an "anarchist," for now the practice of accusing the internationalists of anarchism is becoming more and more widespread among the social-chauvinists.

Marxism has always taught that with the abolition of classes the state will also be abolished. The well-known passage on the "withering away of the state" in *Anti-Dühring* accuses the anarchists not simply of being in favor of the abolition of the state, but of preaching that the state can be abolished "overnight."

In view of the fact that the now prevailing "Social Democratic" doctrine completely distorts the relation of Marxism to anarchism on the question of the abolition of the state, it will be particularly useful to recall a certain controversy in which Marx and Engels came out against the anarchists.

2. CONTROVERSY WITH THE ANARCHISTS

This controversy took place in 1873. Marx and Engels contributed articles against the Proudhonists, "autonomists" or "anti-authoritarians" to an Italian Socialist annual, and it was not until 1913 that these articles appeared in German in *Neue Zeit*.

". . . If the political struggle of the working class assumes revolutionary forms," wrote Marx, ridiculing the anarchists for their repudiation of politics, "if the workers set up their revolutionary dictatorship in place of the dictatorship of the bourgeoisie, they commit the terrible crime of violating principles, for in order to satisfy their wretched, vulgar, everyday needs, in order to crush the resistance of the bourgeoisie, they give the state a revolutionary and transient form, instead of laying down their arms and abolishing the state. . . ." (*Neue Zeit*, Vol. XXXII, 1, 1913-14, p. 40.)

It was solely against this kind of "abolition" of the state that Marx fought in refuting the anarchists! He did not at all combat the view that the state would disappear when classes disappeared, or that it would be abolished when classes were abolished. He opposed the proposition that the workers should renounce the use of arms, of organized violence, *that is, the state,* which is to serve to "crush the resistance of the bourgeoisie."

To prevent the true meaning of his struggle against anarchism from being distorted, Marx purposely emphasized the "revolutionary and *transient* form" of the state which the proletariat needs. The proletariat needs the state only temporarily. We do not at all disagree with the anarchists on the question of the abolition of the state as the *aim*. We maintain that, to achieve this aim, we must temporarily make use of the instruments, resources and methods of the state power *against* the exploiters, just as the temporary dictatorship of the oppressed class is necessary for the abolition of classes. Marx chooses the sharpest and clearest way of stating his case against the anarchists: after overthrowing the yoke of the capitalists, should the workers "lay down their arms," or use them against the capitalists in order to crush their resistance? But what is the systematic use of arms by one class against another class, if not a "transient form" of state?

Let every Social Democrat ask himself: is *that* the way he has been treating the question of the state in controversy with the anarchists? Is *that* the way it has been treated by the vast majority of the official Socialist parties of the Second International?

Engels expounds the same ideas in much greater detail and still more popularly. First of all he ridicules the muddled ideas of the Proudhonists, who called themselves "anti-authoritarians," *i.e.*, repudiated every form of authority, every form of subordination, every form of power. Take a factory, a railway, a ship on the high seas, said Engels—is it not clear that not one of these complex technical establishments, based on the employment of machinery and the planned co-operation of many people, could function without a certain amount of subordination and, consequently, without a certain amount of authority or power?

. . . When I submit arguments like these to the most rabid anti-authoritarians the only answer they can give me is the following: "Ah! That's true, but here it is not a case of authority which we confer on our delegates, *but of a particular assignment!*" These gentlemen think that when they have changed the names of things they have changed the things themselves. . . .

Having thus shown that authority and autonomy are relative terms, that the sphere of their application changes with the various phases of social development, that it is absurd to take them as absolutes, and adding that the sphere of the application of machinery and large-scale production is constantly expanding, Engels passes from the general discussion of authority to the question of the state:

". . . If the autonomists," he wrote, "confined themselves to saying that the social organization of the future would restrict authority solely to the limits within which the conditions of production render it inevitable, we could understand each other. But they are blind to all facts that make authority necessary, and they passionately fight the word.

"Why do the anti-authoritarians not confine themselves to crying out against political authority, against the state? All socialists are agreed that the political state, and with it political authority, will disappear as a result of the coming social revolution, that is, that public functions will lose their political character and be transformed into simple administrative functions, watching over the interests of society. But the anti-authoritarians demand that the authoritarian political state be abolished at one stroke, even before the social conditions that gave birth to it have been destroyed. They demand that the first act of the social revolution shall be the abolition of authority.

"Have these gentlemen ever seen a revolution? A revolution is certainly the most authoritarian thing there is. It is the act whereby one part of the population imposes its will upon the other part by means of rifles, bayonets and cannon, that is, by extreme authoritarian means. And if the victorious party does not want to have fought in vain, it must maintain this rule by means of the terror which its arms inspire in the reactionaries. Would the Paris Commune have lasted longer than a single day if it had not made use of this authority of the armed people against the bourgeois? Should we not, on the contrary, reproach it for not having used it freely enough? Therefore, either one of two things: either the anti-authoritarians don't know what they are talking about, in which case they are creating nothing but confusion; or they do know, and in that case they are betraying the movement of the proletariat. In either case they serve the reaction." (p. 39.)

This argument touches upon questions which must be examined in connection with the subject of the relation between politics and economics during the withering away of the state. (This subject is dealt with in the next chapter.) These questions concern the transformation of public functions from political into administrative, and the "political state." This last term, one particularly liable to cause misunderstanding, indicates the process of the withering away of the state: at a certain stage of this process the state which is withering away can be called a nonpolitical state.

Again, the most remarkable thing in this argument of Engels is the way he states the case against the anarchists. Social Democrats, claiming to be disciples of Engels, have argued against the anarchists millions of times since 1873, but they have *not* argued as Marxists can and should. The anarchist idea of the abolition of the state is muddled and *nonrevolutionary*—that is how Engels put it. It is precisely the revolution in its rise and development, with its specific tasks in relation to violence, authority, power, and the state, that the anarchists do not wish to see.

The usual criticism of anarchism by present-day Social Democrats has boiled down to the purest philistine banality: "We recognize the state, whereas the anarchists do not!"

Naturally, such banality cannot but repel workers who are even somewhat intelligent and revolutionary. What Engels says is different. He emphasizes the fact that all socialists recognize that the state will disappear as a result of the socialist revolution. He then deals concretely with the question of the revolution—the very question which, as a rule, the Social Democrats, because of their opportunism, evade and leave, so to speak, exclusively for the anarchists "to work out." And, when dealing with this question, Engels takes the bull by the horns: should not the Commune have made *more* use of the *revolutionary* power of the *state,* that is, of the proletariat armed and organized as the ruling class?

Prevailing official Social Democracy usually dismissed the question of the concrete tasks of the proletariat in the revolution either with a philistine sneer, or, at best, with the sophistic evasion: "wait and see." And the anarchists were thus justified in saying about such Social Democracy that it was betraying its task of giving the workers a revolutionary education. Engels draws upon the experience of the last proletarian revolution precisely for the purpose of making a most concrete study of what the proletariat should do in relation to both the banks and the state and how they should do it.

3. LETTER TO BEBEL

One of the most remarkable observations on the state, if not the most remarkable, in the works of Marx and Engels is contained in the following passages in Engels' letter to Bebel dated March 18-28, 1875. This letter, we may observe parenthetically, was first published, as far as we know, by Bebel in the second volume of his memoirs (*Aus meinem Leben*), which appeared in 1911, *i.e.,* thirty-six years after the letter had been written and mailed.

Engels wrote to Bebel criticizing that same draft of the Gotha Program which Marx also criticized in his famous letter to Bracke. Referring particularly to the question of the state, Engels said:

. . . The free people's state is transformed into the free state. Taken in its grammatical sense, a free state is one where the state is free in relation to its citizens, hence a state with a despotic government. All the chatter about the state should be dropped, especially since the Commune, which was no longer a state in the proper sense of the word. The "people's state" has been thrown in our faces by the anarchists to the point of disgust, although even Marx's book against Proudhon and later the *Communist Manifesto* specifically declare that with the introduction of the socialist order of society the state will dissolve of itself *(sich auflöst)* and disappear. Since the state is only a transitional institution which is used in the struggle, in the revolution, to hold down one's adversaries by force, it is pure nonsense to talk of a free people's state. So long as the proletariat still *uses* the state, it does not use it in the interests of freedom but in order to hold down its adversaries, and as soon as it becomes possible to speak of freedom the state as such ceases to exist. We would therefore propose to replace *state* everywhere by the word "commune" [*obshchina*] *(Gemeinwesen)*, a good old German word which can very well convey the meaning of the French word *"commune."* (pp. 321-22 of the German original.)

It should be borne in mind that this letter refers to the party program which Marx criticized in a letter dated only a few weeks later than the above (Marx's letter is dated May 5, 1875), and that at the time Engels was living with Marx in London. Consequently, when he says "we" in the last sentence, Engels undoubtedly, in his own as well as in Marx's name, suggests to the leader of the German workers' party that the word "state" *be struck out of the program* and replaced by the word "commune."

What a howl about "anarchism" would be raised by the leading lights of present-day "Marxism," which has been falsified for the convenience of the opportunists, if such a rectification of the program were suggested to them!

Let them howl. This will earn them the praises of the bourgeoisie.

And we shall go on with our work. In revising the program of our Party we must unfailingly take the advice of Engels and Marx into consideration in order to come nearer the truth, to restore Marxism by purging it of distortions, to guide the struggle of the working class for its emancipation more correctly. Certainly no one opposed to the advice of Engels and Marx will be found among the Bolsheviks. The only difficulty that may, perhaps, arise will be in regard to terminology. In German there are two words meaning "community," of which Engels used the one which does *not* denote a single community, but their totality, a system of communities. In Russian there is no such word, and perhaps we may have to choose the French word "commune," although this also has its drawbacks.

"The Commune was no longer a state in the proper sense of the word"—from the theoretical point of view this is the most important statement Engels makes. After what has been said above, this statement is perfectly clear. The Commune *was ceasing* to be a state in so far as it had to suppress, not the majority of the population, but a minority (the exploiters). It had smashed the bourgeois state machine, and in place of a *special* repressive force, the population itself came on the scene. All this was a departure from the state in the proper sense of the word. And had the Commune become firmly established, all traces of the state in it would have "withered away" of themselves. It would not have been necessary for it to "abolish" the institutions of the state: they would have ceased to function to the extent that they ceased to have anything to do.

"The 'people's state' has been thrown in our faces by the anarchists." In saying this, Engels above all has in mind Bakunin and his attacks on the German Social Democrats. Engels admits that these attacks were justified *in so far* as the "people's state" was as much an absurdity and as much a departure from socialism as the "free people's state." Engels tried to put the struggle of the German Social Democrats against the anarchists on the right track, to make this struggle correct in principle, to purge it of opportunist prejudices concerning the "state." Alas! Engels' letter was pigeonholed for thirty-six years. We shall see further on that, even after this letter was published, Kautsky obstinately repeated what in essence were the very mistakes against which Engels had warned.

Bebel replied to Engels in a letter, dated September 21, 1875, in which he wrote among other things, that he "fully agreed" with Engels' criticism of the draft program, and that he had reproached Liebknecht for his readiness to make concessions (p. 334 of the German edition of Bebel's *Memoirs*, Vol. II). But if we take Bebel's pamphlet, *Our Aims*, we find there views on the state that are absolutely wrong.

The state must be transformed from one based on *class rule* into a *people's state*. (*Unsere Ziele*, German edition, 1886, p. 14.)

This was printed in the *ninth* (the ninth!) edition of Bebel's pamphlet! It is not surprising that so persistently repeated opportunist views on the state were absorbed by German Social Democracy, especially as Engels' revolutionary interpretations had been safely pigeonholed, and all the conditions of life had long since "weaned" the Social Democrats from revolution!

4. Criticism of the Draft of the Erfurt Program

In examining the Marxian teaching on the state, the criticism of the draft of the Erfurt Program,[11] sent by Engels to Kautsky on June 29, 1891, and published only ten years later in *Neue Zeit*, cannot be ignored; for it is precisely the *opportunist* views of Social Democracy on questions of *state* structure that this criticism is mainly concerned with.

We shall note in passing that Engels also makes an exceedingly valuable observation on questions of economics, which shows how attentively and thoughtfully he watched the various changes occurring in modern capitalism, and how for this reason he was able to foresee to a certain extent the tasks of our present, the imperialist, epoch. Here is the observation. Referring to the word "planlessness" (*Planlosigkeit*) used in the draft program, as characteristic of capitalism, Engels writes:

. . . When we pass from joint-stock companies to trusts which assume control over, and monopolize, whole branches of industry, it is not only private production that ceases, but also planlessness. (*Neue Zeit*, Vol. XX, 1, 1901-1902, p. 8.)

Here we have what is most essential in the theoretical appraisal of the latest phase of capitalism, *i.e.*, imperialism; namely, that capitalism becomes monopoly *capitalism*. The latter must be emphasized because of the extremely widespread erroneous bourgeois-reformist assertion that monopoly capitalism or state-monopoly capitalism is *no longer* capitalism, that it can already be termed "state socialism," or something of the sort. The trusts, of course, never provided, do not now provide, and cannot provide complete planning. And however much they do plan, however much the capitalist magnates calculate in advance the volume of production on a national and even on an international scale, and however much they systematically regulate it, we still remain under *capitalism*—capitalism in its new stage, it is true, but still, undoubtedly, capitalism. The "proximity" of *such* capitalism to socialism should serve the genuine representatives of the proletariat as an argument proving the proximity, facility, feasibility and urgency of the socialist revolution, and not at all as an argument in favor of tolerating the repudiation of such a revolution and the efforts to make capitalism look more attractive, an occupation in which all the reformists are engaged.

But let us return to the question of the state. In this letter Engels makes three particularly valuable suggestions: first, concerning the republic; second, concerning the connection between the national question and the structure of state; and, third, concerning local self-government.

As to the republic, Engels made this the center of gravity in his criticism of the draft of the Erfurt Program. And when we recall what importance the Erfurt Program acquired for the whole of international Social Democracy, that it became the model for the whole of the Second International, we may state without exaggeration that Engels here criticized the opportunism of the whole Second International.

"The political demands of the draft," Engels writes, "have one great fault. What actually ought to be said *is not there*." (Engels' italics.)

And, later on, he makes it clear that the German constitution is but a copy of the highly reactionary constitution of 1850; that the Reichstag is only, as Wilhelm Liebknecht put it, "the fig leaf of absolutism"; and that to wish "to transform all the instruments of labor into public property" on the basis of a constitution which legalizes the existence of petty states and the federation of petty German states is an "obvious absurdity."

"To mention this subject is dangerous, however," Engels adds, knowing full well that it was impossible legally to include in the program the demand for a republic in Germany. But Engels does not rest content with just this obvious consideration which satisfies "everybody." He continues: "And yet somehow or other the thing has got to be attacked. How necessary this is is shown precisely at the present time by the inroads which opportunism is making in a large section of the Social Democratic press. Fearing a renewal of the Anti-Socialist Law[12] or recalling various premature utterances made during the reign of that law, they now want the Party to find the present legal order in Germany adequate for realizing all the demands of the Party by peaceful means. . . ."

Engels particularly stresses the fundamental fact that the German Social Democrats were prompted by fear of a renewal of the Anti-Socialist Law, and without hesitation calls this opportunism. He declares that precisely because there was no republic and no freedom in Germany, the dreams of a "peaceful" path were absolutely absurd. Engels is sufficiently careful not to tie his hands. He admits that in republican or very free countries "one can conceive" (only "conceive"!) of a peaceful development towards socialism, but in Germany, he repeats,

. . . in Germany, where the government is almost omnipotent and the Reichstag and all other representative bodies have no real power, to proclaim such a thing in Germany—and moreover when there is no need to do so—is to remove the fig leaf from absolutism, and become oneself a screen for its nakedness. . . .

The great majority of the official leaders of the German Social Democratic Party, who pigeonholed these observations, have indeed proved to be a screen for absolutism.

. . . Ultimately such a policy can only lead one's own party astray. They put general, abstract political questions into the foreground, thus concealing the immediate concrete questions, the questions which become the order of the day with the first great events, the first political crisis. What can result from this except that at the decisive moment the Party is suddenly left helpless, that unclarity and disunity on the most decisive issues reign in it because these issues have never been discussed? . . .

This forgetting of the great, essential considerations for the momentary interests of the day, this struggling and striving for the success of the moment without consideration for the later consequences, this sacrifice of the future of the movement for its present may be the result of "honest" motivations; but it is and remains opportunism, and "honest" opportunism is perhaps the most dangerous of all. . . .

If one thing is certain it is that our Party and the working class can only come to power in the form of a democratic republic. This is actually the specific form for the dictatorship of the proletariat, as the Great French Revolution has already shown. . . .

Engels repeats here in a particularly striking form the fundamental idea which runs like a red thread through all of Marx's works; namely, that the democratic republic is the nearest approach to the dictatorship of the proletariat.

For such a republic—without in the least abolishing the rule
of capital, and, therefore, the oppression of the masses and
the class struggle—inevitably leads to such an extension, development, unfolding and intensification of this struggle that,
as soon as there arises the possibility of satisfying the fundamental interests of the oppressed masses, this possibility
is realized inevitably and solely through the dictatorship of
the proletariat, through the leadership of those masses by
the proletariat. These, too, are "forgotten words" of Marxism
for the whole of the Second International, and the fact that
they have been forgotten was demonstrated with particular
vividness by the history of the Menshevik Party during the
first half year of the Russian Revolution of 1917.

On the subject of a federal republic, in connection with
the national composition of the population, Engels wrote:

What should take the place of present-day Germany? (with its
reactionary monarchical constitution and its equally reactionary
division into petty states, a division which perpetuates all the
specific features of "Prussianism" instead of dissolving them in
Germany as a whole). In my view, the proletariat can only use the
form of the single, indivisible republic. In the gigantic territory of
the United States a federal republic is still, on the whole, a necessity, although in the Eastern states it is already becoming a
hindrance. It would be a step forward in England, where the two
islands are peopled by four nations and where, in spite of a
single Parliament, three different systems of legislation exist side
by side even today. In little Switzerland, a federal republic has
long been a hindrance, tolerable only because Switzerland is content to be a purely passive member of the European state system.
For Germany, federalization on the Swiss model would be an
enormous step backward. Two points distinguish a federated state
from a completely unified state: first, that each separate state
forming part of the federation has its own civil and criminal legislative and judicial system, and, second, that together with a
popular chamber there is also a federal chamber in which each
canton, large and small, votes as such. In Germany the federal
state is the transitional stage to the completely unified state, and
the "revolution from above" of 1866 and 1870 must not be
reversed but supplemented by a "movement from below."

Far from displaying indifference in regard to the forms
of state, Engels, on the contrary, tried to analyze the transitional forms with the utmost thoroughness in order to establish, in accordance with the concrete, historical, specific

features of each separate case, *from what and into what* the given transitional form is passing.

Approaching the matter from the point of view of the proletariat and the proletarian revolution Engels, like Marx, upheld democratic centralism, the republic—one and indivisible. He regarded the federal republic either as an exception and a hindrance to development, or as a transitional form from a monarchy to a centralized republic, as a "step forward" under certain special conditions. And among these special conditions, the national question comes to the front.

Although mercilessly criticizing the reactionary nature of small states and efforts to obscure it by raising the national question in certain concrete cases, Engels, like Marx, never betrayed a trace of a desire to brush aside the national question—a desire of which the Dutch and Polish Marxists are often guilty, as a result of their perfectly justified opposition to the narrow philistine nationalism of "their" little states.

Even in regard to England, where geographical conditions, a common language and the history of many centuries would seem to have "put an end" to the national question in the separate small divisions of England—even in regard to that country, Engels reckoned with the patent fact that the national question was not yet a thing of the past, and recognized in consequence that the establishment of a federal republic would be a "step forward." Of course, there is not the slightest hint here of Engels abandoning his criticism of the shortcomings of a federal republic or his most determined propaganda and struggle for a unified and centralized democratic republic.

But Engels did not at all understand democratic centralism in the bureaucratic sense in which this term is used by bourgeois and petty-bourgeois ideologists, the anarchists among the latter. His idea of centralism did not in the least preclude a broad local self-government that would combine voluntary defense of the unity of the state by the "communes" and districts with complete abolition of all bureaucracy and all "ordering" from above. Enlarging on the program views of Marxism on the state, Engels wrote:

. . . So, then, a unitary republic—but not in the sense of the present French Republic, which is nothing but the Empire established in 1798 without the Emperor. From 1792 to 1798 each Department of France, each commune (*Gemeinde*), enjoyed complete self-government on the American model, and this is what we too must have. How self-government is to be organized and how we can manage without a bureaucracy has been shown to us by America and the first French Republic, and is being shown even today by Canada, Australia and the other English colonies. And a provincial and local self-government of this type is far freer than, for instance, Swiss federalism under which, it is true, the canton is very independent in relation to the Union (*i.e.*, the federated state as a whole), but is also independent in relation to the district and the commune. The cantonal governments appoint the district governors (*Bezirksstatthalter*) and prefects—a feature which is unknown in English-speaking countries and which we shall have to abolish here just as resolutely in the future, along with the Prussian *Landräte* and *Regierungsräte* (commissioners, district police chiefs, governors, and in general all officials appointed from above). Accordingly, Engels proposes the following wording for the self-government clause in the program: "Complete self-government for the provinces, districts and communes through officials elected by universal suffrage. The abolition of all local and provincial authorities appointed by the state."

I have already had occasion to note in *Pravda*[13] (No. 68, May 28, 1917), which was suppressed by the government of Kerensky and other "socialist" ministers—how on this point (of course, not by any means on this point alone) our pseudo-socialist representatives of pseudo-revolutionary pseudo democracy have made absolutely scandalous departures *from democracy*. Naturally, people who have bound themselves by a "coalition" with the imperialist bourgeoisie have remained deaf to this criticism.

It is extremely important to note that Engels, armed with facts, disproves by a most precise example the prejudice which is very widespread, particularly among petty-bourgeois democrats, that a federal republic necessarily means a greater amount of feedom than a centralized republic. This is not true. It is disproved by the facts cited by Engels regarding the centralized French Republic of 1792-1798 and the federal Swiss Republic. The really democratic centralized republic gave *more* freedom than the federal republic. In other words, the *greatest* amount of local, provincial and other freedom known in history was accorded by a *centralized* and not by a federal republic.

Insufficient attention has been and is being paid in our Party propaganda and agitation to this fact, as, indeed, to the whole question of the federal and the centralized republic and local self-government.

5. The 1891 Preface to Marx's "The Civil War in France"

In his preface to the third edition of *The Civil War in France* (this preface is dated March 18, 1891, and was orig-inally published in the *Neue Zeit*), Engels, in addition to some interesting incidental remarks on questions connected with the attitude towards the state, gives a remarkably vivid summary of the lessons of the Commune. This summary, rendered more profound by the entire experience of the twenty years that separated the author from the Commune and directed particularly against the "superstitious belief in the state" so widespread in Germany, may justly be called the *last word* of Marxism on the question under consideration.

"In France," Engels observes, "the workers emerged with arms after every revolution. Therefore, the disarming of the workers was the first commandment for the bourgeois, who were at the helm of the state. Hence, after every revolution won by the workers there is a new struggle, ending with the defeat of the workers. . . ."

This summary of the experience of bourgeois revolutions is as concise as it is expressive. The essence of the matter —also, by the way, on the question of the state (*has the op-pressed class arms?*)—is here remarkably well grasped. It is precisely this essence of the matter which is most often ig-nored both by professors, who are influenced by bourgeois ideology, and by petty-bourgeois democrats. In the Russian Revolution of 1917, the honor (Cavaignac honor) of blab-bing this secret of bourgeois revolutions fell to the "Men-shevik," "also-Marxist," Tsereteli. In his "historic" speech of June 11, Tsereteli blurted out that the bourgeoisie was de-termined to disarm the Petrograd workers—presenting, of course, this decision as his own, and as a matter of necessity for the "state" in general!

Tsereteli's historic speech of June 11 will, of course, serve every historian of the Revolution of 1917 as one of the most striking illustrations of how the Socialist-Revolutionary and Menshevik bloc, led by Mr. Tsereteli, deserted to the bour-geoisie *against* the revolutionary proletariat.

Another incidental remark of Engels', also connected with the question of the state, deals with religion. It is well known that German Social Democracy, as it decayed and became more and more opportunist, slipped more and more frequently into the philistine misinterpretation of the celebrated formula: "Religion is to be proclaimed a private matter." That is, this formula was interpreted to mean that religion was a private matter *even for the party* of the revolutionary proletariat!! It was against this utter betrayal of the revolutionary program of the proletariat that Engels vigorously protested. In 1891 he saw only the feeblest beginnings of opportunism in his party, and, therefore, he expressed himself extremely cautiously:

As almost only workers, or recognized representatives of the workers, sat in the Commune, its decisions bore a decidedly proletarian character. Either these decisions decreed reforms which the republican bourgeoisie had failed to pass solely out of cowardice, but which provided a necessary basis for the free activity of the working class—such as the realization of the principle that *in relation to the state*, religion is a purely private matter—or the Commune promulgated decrees which were in the direct interest of the working class and in part cut deeply into the old order of society. . . .

Engels deliberately underlined the words "in relation to the state" as a straight thrust at the German opportunism, which had declared religion to be a private matter *in relation to the party*, thus degrading the party of the revolutionary proletariat to the level of the most vulgar "free-thinking" philistinism, which is prepared to allow a nondenominational status, but which renounces the *party* struggle against the opium of religion which stupefies the people.

The future historian of German Social Democracy, in tracing the root causes of its shameful bankruptcy in 1914, will find a good amount of interesting material on this question, beginning with the evasive declarations in the articles of the party's ideological leader Kautsky, which open wide the door to opportunism, and ending with the attitude of the party towards the "Los-von-Kirche-Bewegung" (the "leave-the-church" movement) in 1913.

But let us see how, twenty years after the Commune, Engels summed up its lessons for the fighting proletariat. Here are the lessons to which Engels attached prime importance:

. . . It was precisely the oppressing power of the former centralized government, army, political police, bureaucracy, which

Napoleon had created in 1798 and which since then had been taken over by every new government as a welcome instrument and used against its opponents—it was precisely this power which was to fall everywhere, just as it had already fallen in Paris.

From the very outset the Commune was compelled to recognize that the working class, once come to power, could not go on managing with the old state machine; that in order not to lose again the supremacy it had only just won, this working class must, on the one hand, do away with all the old repressive machinery previously used against it, and, on the other, safeguard itself against its own deputies and officials, by declaring them all, without exception, subject to recall at any moment. . . .

Engels emphasizes again and again that not only under a monarchy, but *also in the democratic republic* the state remains a state, *i.e.*, it retains its fundamental characteristic feature of transforming the officials, the "servants of society," its organs, into the *masters* of society.

. . . Against this transformation of the state and the organs of the state from servants of society into masters of society—an inevitable transformation in all previous states—the Commune made use of two infallible means. In the first place, it filled all posts—administrative, judicial and educational—by election on the basis of universal suffrage of all concerned, subject to the right of recall at any time by the same electors. And, in the second place, all officials, high or low, were paid only the wages received by other workers. The highest salary paid by the Commune to anyone was 6,000 francs.[14] In this way an effective barrier to place-hunting and careerism was set up, even apart from the additional binding mandates to delegates in representative bodies which were introduced by the Commune. . . .

Engels here approaches the interesting boundary line at which consistent democracy, on the one hand, is *transformed* into socialism and, on the other, *demands* socialism. For, in order to abolish the state, the functions of the civil service must be converted into the simple operations of control and accounting that are within the capacity and ability of the vast majority of the population, and, subsequently, of every single individual. And in order to abolish careerism completely it must be made *impossible* for "honorable" though profitless posts in the public service to be used as a springboard to highly lucrative posts in banks or joint-stock companies, as *constantly* happens in all the freest capitalist countries.

But Engels did not make the mistake some Marxists make when, for example, they deal with the question of the right of nations to self-determination, and argue that this is impossible under capitalism and will be superfluous under socialism. Such a seemingly clever but actually incorrect statement might be made in regard to *any* democratic institution, including moderate salaries for officials; because fully consistent democracy is impossible under capitalism, and under socialism all democracy *withers away*.

It is a sophistry like the old joke as to whether a man will become bald if he loses one more hair.

To develop democracy *to the utmost*, to seek out the *forms* for this development, to test them *by practice*, and so forth—all this is one of the constituent tasks of the struggle for the social revolution. Taken separately, no kind of democracy will bring socialism. But in actual life democracy will never be "taken separately": it will be "taken together" with other things, exert its influence on economic life, promote *its* transformation, and in its turn be influenced by economic development, and so on. Such are the dialectics of living history.

Engels continues:

. . . This shattering (*Sprengung*) of the former state power and its replacement by a new and truly democratic one is described in detail in the third section of *The Civil War*. But it was necessary to dwell briefly here once more on some of its features, because in Germany particularly the superstitious belief in the state has been carried over from philosophy into the general consciousness of the bourgeoisie and even of many workers. According to the philosophical conception, the state is the "realization of the idea," or the Kingdom of God on earth, translated into philosophical terms, the sphere in which eternal truth and justice is or should be realized. And from this follows a superstitious reverence for the state and everything connected with it, a reverence which takes root all the more readily since people are accustomed from childhood to imagine that the affairs and interests common to the whole of society could not be looked after otherwise than as they have been looked after in the past, that is, through the state and its lucratively positioned officials. People think they have taken quite an extraordinarily bold step forward when they have rid themselves of belief in hereditary monarchy and swear by the democratic republic. In reality, however, the state is nothing but a machine for the oppression of one class by another, in the democratic republic no less than in the monarchy. At best the state is an evil inherited by the proletariat after its victorious struggle for class supremacy, and the victorious proletariat, just like the Commune, cannot avoid cutting off at once its worst sides, until such time as a generation reared in new, free social conditions is able to throw the entire lumber of the state on the scrap heap.

Engels warned the Germans not to forget the fundamentals of socialism on the question of the state in general when the time came for substituting a republic for the monarchy. His warnings now read like a veritable lesson to the Tseretelis and Chernovs, who in their "coalition" practice here revealed a superstitious belief in, and a superstitious reverence for, the state!

Two more remarks. 1. The fact that Engels said that in a democratic republic, "no less" than in a monarchy, the state remains a "machine for the oppression of one class by another" by no means signifies that the *form* of oppression is a matter of indifference to the proletariat, as some anarchists "teach." A wider, freer and more open *form* of the class struggle and of class oppression enormously assists the proletariat in its struggle for the abolition of classes in general.

2. Why will only a new generation be able to throw the entire lumber of the state on the scrap heap? This question is bound up with that of overcoming democracy, with which we shall deal now.

6. Engels on the Overcoming of Democracy

Engels had occasion to express his views on this subject in connection with the question of the *scientific* inaccuracy of the term "Social Democrat."

In a preface to an edition of articles he wrote in the seventies on various subjects, mainly on "international" questions (*Internationales aus dem Volksstaat*), dated January 3, 1894, *i.e.*, written a year and a half before his death, Engels wrote that in all his articles he used the word "Communist," and *not* "Social Democrat," because at that time the Proudhonists in France and the Lassalleans in Germany called themselves Social Democrats.

". . . For Marx and me," continues Engels, "it was therefore absolutely impossible to use such an elastic term to characterize our special point of view. Today things are different, and the word ("Social Democrat") may perhaps pass (*mag passieren*), however inexact (*unpassend*—unsuitable) it still is for a party whose economic program is not merely socialist in general, but specifically communist, and whose ultimate political aim is to overcome the whole state and, consequently, democracy as well. The names of *real* (Engels' italics) political parties, however, are never wholly appropriate; the party develops, while the name stays."

The dialectician Engels remains true to dialectics to the end of his days. Marx and I, he says, had a splendid, scientifically exact name for the party, but there was no real party, *i.e.*, no mass proletarian party. Now (at the end of the nineteenth century) there is a real party, but its name is scientifically inexact. Never mind, it will "pass," if only the party *develops*, if only the scientific inexactness of its name is not hidden from it and does not hinder its development in the right direction!

Perhaps some wit would console us Bolsheviks in the manner of Engels: we have a real party, it is developing splendidly; even such a meaningless and ugly term as "Bolshevik" will "pass," although it expresses nothing whatever but the purely accidental fact that at the Brussels-London Congress of 1903 [15] we were in the majority. . . . Perhaps, now that the persecution of our Party by republicans and "revolutionary" petty-bourgeois democracy in July and August has earned the name "Bolshevik" such a universal respect, now that, in addition, this persecution attests to the tremendous historical progress our Party has made in its *real* development, perhaps now even I might hesitate to insist on the suggestion I made in April to change the name of our Party. Perhaps I would propose a "compromise" to my comrades, *viz.*, to call ourselves the Communist Party, but to retain the word "Bolsheviks" in brackets. . . .

But the question of the name of the Party is incomparably less important than the question of the attitude of the revolutionary proletariat to the state.

In the usual arguments about the state, the mistake is constantly made against which Engels uttered his warning and which we have in passing indicated above; namely, it is constantly forgotten that the abolition of the state means also the abolition of democracy: the withering away of the state means the withering away of democracy.

At first sight this assertion seems exceedingly strange and incomprehensible. Indeed, someone may even begin to fear that we are expecting the advent of an order of society in which the principle of the subordination of the minority to the majority will not be observed—for democracy means the recognition of just this principle.

No, democracy is *not* identical with the subordination of the minority to the majority. Democracy is a *state* which recognizes the subordination of the minority to the majority, *i.e.*, an organization for the systematic use of *violence* by one class against the other, by one section of the population against another.

We set ourselves the ultimate aim of abolishing the state, *i.e.*, all organized and systematic violence, all use of violence against man in general. We do not expect the advent of an order of society in which the principle of the subordination of the minority to the majority will not be observed. But in striving for socialism we are convinced that it will develop into communism and, hence, that the need for violence against people in general, the *subordination* of one man to another, one section of the population to another, will vanish altogether since people will *become accustomed* to observing the elementary conditions of social life *without violence* and *without subordination*.

In order to emphasize this element of habit, Engels speaks of a new *generation*, "reared in new and free social conditions," which "will be able to throw on the scrap heap the entire lumber of the state"—every kind of state, including the democratic-republican state.

In order to explain this it is necessary to examine the question of the economic basis for the withering away of the state.

V. THE ECONOMIC BASIS FOR THE WITHERING AWAY OF THE STATE

Marx explains this question most thoroughly in his *Critique of the Gotha Program* (letter to Bracke, May 5, 1875, which was not published until 1891 when it was printed in *Neue Zeit*, IX, 1, and which has appeared in Russian in a special edition). The polemical part of this remarkable work, which contains a criticism of Lassalleanism, has, so to speak, overshadowed its positive part, the analysis of the connection between the development of communism and the withering away of the state.

1. PRESENTATION OF THE QUESTION BY MARX

From a superficial comparison of Marx's letter to Bracke of May 5, 1875, with Engels' letter to Bebel of March 28, 1875, which we examined above, it might appear that Marx was much more of a "champion of the state" than Engels, and that the difference of opinion between the two writers on the question of the state was very considerable.

Engels suggested to Bebel that all the chatter about the state be dropped altogether; that the word "state" be eliminated from the program altogether and the word "community" substituted for it. Engels even declared that the Commune was no longer a state in the proper sense of the word. Yet Marx even spoke of the "future state in communist society," *i.e.*, as though he recognized the need for the state even under communism.

But such a view would be fundamentally wrong. A closer examination shows that Marx's and Engels' views on the state and its withering away were completely identical, and that Marx's expression quoted above refers precisely to this state in the process of *withering away*.

Clearly there can be no question of defining the exact moment of the *future* "withering away"—the more so since it will obviously be a lengthy process. The apparent difference between Marx and Engels is due to the fact that they dealt with different subjects and pursued different aims. Engels set out to show Bebel graphically, sharply and in broad outline the utter absurdity of the current prejudices concerning the state (shared to no small degree by Lassalle). Marx only touched upon *this* question in passing, being interested in another subject, *viz.*, the *development* of communist society.

The whole theory of Marx is the application of the theory of development—in its most consistent, complete, considered and pithy form—to modern capitalism. Naturally, Marx was faced with the problem of applying this theory both to the *forthcoming* collapse of capitalism and to the *future* development of *future* communism.

On the basis of what *data*, then, can the question of the future development of future communism be dealt with?

On the basis of the fact that *it has its origin* in capitalism, that it develops historically from capitalism, that it is the result of the action of a social force to which capitalism *gave*

birth. There is no trace of an attempt on Marx's part to con-
jure up a utopia, to make idle guesses about what cannot be
known. Marx treats the question of communism in the same
way as a naturalist would treat the question of the development, say, of a new biological variety, once he knew that
such and such was its origin and such and such the definite
direction in which it was changing.

Marx, first of all, brushes aside the confusion that the
Gotha Program brings to the question of the relation between
state and society. He writes:

. . . Present-day society is capitalist society, which exists in all
civilized countries, more or less free from medieval admixture,
more or less modified by the special historical development of each
country, more or less developed. On the other hand, the "present-
day state" changes with a country's frontier. It is completely different in the Prusso-German Empire from what it is in Switzerland;
it is completely different in England from what it is in the United
States. The "present-day state" is, therefore, a fiction.

Nevertheless, the different states of the different civilized countries, in spite of their manifold diversity of form, all have this in
common, that they are based on modern bourgeois society, more
or less capitalistically developed. They have, therefore, also certain
essential features in common. In this sense it is possible to speak
of the "present-day state," in contrast with that of the future,
when its present root, bourgeois society, will have died off.

The question then arises: what transformation will the state
undergo in communist society? In other words, what social functions will then remain in existence that are analogous to the
present functions of the state? This question can only be answered
scientifically, and one does not get a flea-hop nearer to a solution
by a thousandfold combination of the word "people" with the
word "state". . . .

Having thus ridiculed all talk about a "people's state,"
Marx formulates the question and warns us, as it were, that
a scientific answer to it can be secured only by using firmly established scientific data.

The first fact that has been established with complete exactitude by the whole theory of development, by science as
a whole—a fact that was forgotten by the utopians and is
forgotten by present-day opportunists, fearful of the socialist
revolution—is that, historically, there must undoubtedly be a
special stage or a special phase of *transition* from capitalism
to communism.

2. THE TRANSITION FROM CAPITALISM TO COMMUNISM

Marx continues:

. . . Between capitalist and communist society lies the period of the revolutionary transformation of the one into the other. There corresponds to this also a political transition period in which the state can be nothing but *the revolutionary dictatorship of the proletariat.* . . .

Marx bases this conclusion on an analysis of the role played by the proletariat in modern capitalist society, on data concerning the development of this society, and on the irreconcilability of the antagonistic interests of the proletariat and the bourgeoisie.

Previously the question was put in this way: in order to achieve its emancipation, the proletariat must overthrow the bourgeoisie, win political power and establish its revolutionary dictatorship.

Now the question is put somewhat differently: the transition from capitalist society—which is developing towards communism—to a communist society is impossible without a "political transition period," and the state in this period can only be the revolutionary dictatorship of the proletariat.

What, then, is the relation of this dictatorship to democracy?

We have seen that the *Communist Manifesto* simply places side by side the two concepts: "to raise the proletariat to the position of the ruling class" and "to win the battle of democracy." On the basis of all that has been said above, it is possible to determine more precisely how democracy changes in the transition from capitalism to communism.

In capitalist society, providing it develops under the most favorable conditions, we have a more or less complete democracy in the democratic republic. But this democracy is always hemmed in by the narrow limits set by capitalist exploitation and, consequently, always remains, in essence, a democracy for the minority, only for the propertied classes, only for the rich. Freedom in capitalist society always remains about the same as it was in the ancient Greek republics: freedom for the slaveowners. Owing to the conditions of capitalist exploitation the modern wage slaves are so crushed by want and poverty that "they cannot be bothered with democracy," "they cannot be bothered with politics." In the ordinary peaceful course of events the majority of the population is debarred from participation in public and political life.

The correctness of this statement is perhaps most clearly confirmed by Germany, precisely because in that country constitutional legality steadily endured for a remarkably long time (1871-1914), and during this period Social Democracy in Germany was able to achieve far more than in other countries in the way of "utilizing legality," organizing a larger proportion of the workers into a political party than anywhere else in the world.

What is this largest proportion of politically conscious and active wage slaves that has so far been observed in capitalist society? One million members of the Social Democratic Party—out of fifteen million wage-workers! Three million organized in trade unions—out of fifteen million!

Democracy for an insignificant minority, democracy for the rich—that is the democracy of capitalist society. If we look more closely into the machinery of capitalist democracy, we shall see everywhere, in the "petty"—supposedly petty—details of the suffrage (residential qualification, exclusion of women, etc.), in the technique of the representative institutions, in the actual obstacles to the right of assembly (public buildings are not for "beggars"!), in the purely capitalist organization of the daily press, etc., etc.—we shall see restriction after restriction upon democracy. These restrictions, exceptions, exclusions, obstacles for the poor, seem slight, especially in the eyes of one who has never known want himself and has never been in close contact with the oppressed classes in their mass life (and nine tenths, if not ninety-nine hundredths, of the bourgeois publicists and politicians are of this category). But in their sum total these restrictions exclude and squeeze out the poor from politics, from active participation in democracy.

Marx grasped this *essence* of capitalist democracy splendidly, when, in analyzing the experience of the Commune, he said that the oppressed are allowed once every few years to decide which particular representatives of the oppressing class shall represent and repress them in parliament!

But from this capitalist democracy—that is inevitably narrow, stealthily pushes aside the poor, and is therefore hypocritical and false to the core—forward development does not proceed simply, directly and smoothly towards "greater and greater democracy," as the liberal professors and petty-bourgeois opportunists would have us believe. No, forward development, *i.e.*, towards communism, proceeds through the dictatorship of the proletariat. It cannot be otherwise, for the *resistance* of the capitalist exploiters cannot be *broken* by anyone else or in any other way.

And the dictatorship of the proletariat, *i.e.*, the organization of the vanguard of the oppressed as the ruling class for the purpose of suppressing the oppressors, cannot result merely in an expansion of democracy. *Simultaneously* with an immense expansion of democracy, which *for the first time*, becomes democracy for the poor, democracy for the people, and not democracy for the moneybags, the dictatorship of the proletariat imposes a series of restrictions on the freedom of the oppressors, the exploiters, the capitalists. We must suppress them in order to free humanity from wage slavery. Their resistance must be crushed by force; and it is clear that where there is suppression, where there is violence, there is no freedom and no democracy.

Engels expressed this splendidly in his letter to Bebel when he said, as the reader will remember, that "the proletariat uses the state not in the interests of freedom but in order to hold down its adversaries, and as soon as it becomes possible to speak of freedom the state as such ceases to exist."

Democracy for the vast majority of the people and suppression by force, *i.e.*, exclusion from democracy, of the exploiters and oppressors of the people—this is the change democracy undergoes during the *transition* from capitalism to communism.

Only in communist society, when the resistance of the capitalists has been completely crushed, when the capitalists have disappeared, when there are no classes (*i.e.*, when there is no difference between the members of society as regards their relation to the social means of production), *only* then "the state . . . ceases to exist," and it *"becomes possible to speak of freedom."* Only then will there become possible and be realized a truly complete democracy, democracy without any restrictions whatever. And only then will democracy begin to *wither away*, owing to the simple fact that, freed from capitalist slavery, from the untold horrors, savagery, absurdities and infamies of capitalist exploitation, people will gradually *become accustomed* to observing the elementary rules of social intercourse that have been known for centuries and repeated for thousands of years in all copybook maxims. They will become accustomed to observing them without force, without compulsion, without subordination, *without the special apparatus* for compulsion which is called the state.

The expression "the state *withers away*" is very well chosen, for it indicates both the gradual and the spontaneous nature of the process. Only habit can, and undoubtedly will, have such an effect; for we see around us on millions of occasions how readily people become accustomed to observing the necessary rules of social intercourse when there is no exploitation, when there is nothing that arouses indignation, nothing that evokes protest and revolt and creates the need for *suppression.*

Thus, in capitalist society we have a democracy that is curtailed, wretched, false; a democracy only for the rich, for the minority. The dictatorship of the proletariat, the period of transition to communism, will for the first time create democracy for the people, for the majority, along with the necessary suppression of the minority—the exploiters. Communism alone is capable of giving really complete democracy, and the more complete it is the more quickly will it become unnecessary and wither away of itself.

In other words, under capitalism we have the state in the proper sense of the word, that is, a special machine for the suppression of one class by another, and, what is more, of the majority by the minority. Naturally, to be successful, such an undertaking as the systematic suppression of the exploited majority by the exploiting minority calls for the utmost ferocity and savagery in the work of suppressing; it calls for seas of blood through which mankind has to wade in slavery, serfdom and wage labor.

Furthermore, during the *transition* from capitalism to communism suppression is *still* necessary; but it is now the suppression of the exploiting minority by the exploited majority. A special apparatus, a special machine for suppression, the "state," is *still* necessary. But this is now a transitional state and no longer a state in the proper sense of the word; for the suppression of the minority of exploiters by the majority of *yesterday's* wage slaves is comparatively so easy, simple and natural a task that it will entail far less bloodshed than the suppression of the risings of slaves, serfs or wage laborers, and it will cost mankind far less. Moreover, it is compatible with the extension of democracy to such an overwhelming majority of the population that the need for a *special machine* of suppression will begin to disappear. The exploiters are naturally unable to suppress the people without a highly complex machine for performing this task: but *the people* can suppress the exploiters with even a very simple "machine," almost without a "machine," without a special apparatus, by the simple *organization of the armed masses* (such as the Soviets of Workers' and Soldiers' Deputies, [16] we may note, anticipating somewhat).

Finally, only communism makes the state absolutely unnecessary, for there is *nobody* to be suppressed—"nobody" in the sense of a *class*, in the sense of a systematic struggle against a definite section of the population. We are not utopians and do not in the least deny the possibility and inevitability of excesses on the part of *individual persons* or the need to suppress *such* excesses. But, in the first place, no special machine, no special apparatus of suppression is needed for this: this will be done by the armed people itself, as simply and as readily as any crowd of civilized people, even in modern society, interferes to stop a scuffle or to prevent a woman from being assaulted. And, secondly, we know that the fundamental social cause of excesses, involving violations of the basic rules of social intercourse, is the exploitation of the masses, their want and their poverty. With the removal of this chief cause, excesses will inevitably begin to "*wither away*." We do not know how quickly and in what succession, but we know that they will wither away. With their withering away the state will also *wither away*.

Without indulging in utopias, Marx defined more fully what can be defined *now* regarding this future; namely, the difference between the lower and higher phases (levels, stages) of communist society.

3. THE FIRST PHASE OF COMMUNIST SOCIETY

In the *Critique of the Gotha Program*, Marx goes into detail to disprove Lassalle's idea that under socialism the worker will receive the "undiminished" or "full product of his labor." Marx shows that from the whole of the social labor of society there must be deducted a reserve fund, a fund for the expansion of production, for the replacement of the "wear and tear" of machinery, and so on. In addition, from the means of consumption there must be deducted a fund for the expenses of administration, schools, hospitals, homes for the aged, and so on.

Instead of Lassalle's hazy, obscure, general phrase ("the full product of his labor to the worker") Marx makes a sober estimate of exactly how socialist society will have to manage its economy. Marx proceeds to make a *concrete* analysis of the conditions of life of a society in which there will be no capitalism, and says:

What we have to deal with here (in analyzing the program of the workers' party) is not a communist society that has *developed* on its own foundations, but, on the contrary, that has just *emerged* from capitalist society and that is thus in every respect, economically, morally and intellectually, still stamped with the birthmarks of the old society from whose womb it emerges.

And it is this communist society—a society which has just emerged into the light of day out of the womb of capitalism and which, in every respect, bears the birthmarks of the old society—that Marx terms the "first," or lower phase of communist society.

The means of production are no longer the private property of individuals. The means of production belong to the whole of society. Every member of society, performing a certain part of the socially necessary work, receives a certificate from society to the effect that he has done such and such an amount of work. With this certificate he receives from the public store of consumers' goods a corresponding quantity of products. After a deduction is made of the amount of labor which goes to the public fund, every worker, therefore, receives from society as much as he has given to it.

"Equality" apparently reigns supreme.

But when Lassalle, having in view such a social order (usually called socialism, but termed by Marx the first phase of communism), says that this is "equitable distribution," that this is "the equal right of all members of society to an equal product of labor," Lassalle is mistaken and Marx exposes his error.

"Equal right," says Marx, we indeed have here; but it is *still* a "bourgeois right," which, like every right, *presupposes inequality*. Every right is an application of an *equal* measure to *different* people who in fact are not alike, are not equal to one another. That is why "equal right" is really a violation of equality and an injustice. Indeed, every man, having performed as much social labor as another, receives an equal share of the social product (after the above-mentioned deductions).

But people are not alike: one is strong, another is weak; one is married, another is not; one has more children, another has less, and so on. And the conclusion Marx draws is:

. . . with an equal performance of labor and, hence, an equal share in the social consumption fund, one will in fact receive more than another, one will be richer than another, and so on. To avoid all these defects, right instead of being equal would have to be unequal. . . .

Consequently, the first phase of communism cannot yet produce justice and equality: differences, and unjust differences, in wealth will still exist, but the *exploitation* of man by man will have become impossible, because it will be impossible to seize the *means of production,* the factories, machines, land, etc., as private property. While smashing Lassalle's petty-bourgeois, confused phrases about "equality" and "justice" *in general,* Marx shows the *course of development* of communist society, which is *compelled* to abolish at first *only* the "injustice" of the means of production having been seized by individuals, and which is *unable* at once to eliminate the other injustice, which consists in the distribution of articles of consumption "according to the amount of labor performed" (and not according to needs).

The vulgar economists, including the bourgeois professors and "our" Tugan among them, constantly reproach the socialists with forgetting the inequality of people and with "dreaming" of eliminating this inequality. Such a reproach, as we see, only proves the extreme ignorance of the bourgeois ideologists.

Marx not only most scrupulously takes account of the inevitable inequality of men, but he also takes into account the fact that the mere conversion of the means of production into the common property of the whole of society (commonly called "socialism") *does not remove* the defects of distribution and the inequality of "bourgeois right," which *continues to prevail* as long as products are divided "according to the amount of labor performed." Continuing, Marx says:

. . . But these defects are inevitable in the first phase of communist society, when it has just emerged after prolonged birth pangs from capitalist society. Right can never be higher than the economic structure of society and its cultural development conditioned thereby. . . .

And so, in the first phase of communist society (usually called socialism) "bourgeois right" is *not* abolished in its entirety, but only in part, only in proportion to the economic revolution so far attained, *i.e.,* only in respect of the means of production. "Bourgeois right" recognizes them as the private property of individuals. Socialism converts them into *common* property. *To that extent*—and to that extent alone—"bourgeois right" disappears.

However, it continues to exist as far as its other part is concerned: it continues to exist as a regulator (determining factor) in the distribution of products and the allotment of labor among the members of society. The socialist principle: "He who does not work, neither shall he eat," is *already* realized. The other socialist principle: "An equal amount of products for an equal amount of labor," is also *already* realized. But this is not yet communism, and it does not yet abolish "bourgeois right," which gives to unequal individuals, in return for unequal (really unequal) amounts of labor, equal amounts of products.

This is a "defect," says Marx, but it is unavoidable in the first phase of communism; for if we are not to indulge in utopianism, we must not think that having overthrown capitalism people will at once learn to work for society *without any standard of right;* and indeed the abolition of capitalism *does not immediately create* the economic premises for *such* a change.

And there is no other standard than that of "bourgeois right." To this extent, therefore, there still remains the need for a state, which, while safeguarding the public ownership of the means of production, would safeguard equality in labor and equality in the distribution of products.

The state withers away in so far as there are no longer any capitalists; there are no longer any classes, therefore, to be suppressed.

But the state has not yet completely withered away, since there still remains the safeguarding of "bourgeois right," which sanctifies actual inequality. For the state to wither away completely complete communism is necessary.

4. THE HIGHER PHASE OF COMMUNIST SOCIETY

Marx continues:

. . . In the higher phase of communist society, after the enslaving subordination of the individual to the division of labor and, therewith, also the antithesis between mental and physical labor, has vanished; after labor has become not only a means of life but life's prime need; after the productive forces have increased together with the advance of the individual's all-round development, and all the springs of co-operative wealth flow abundantly —only then can the narrow horizon of bourgeois right be crossed completely and society inscribe on its banners: "From each according to his ability, to each according to his needs!"

Only now can we appreciate to the full the correctness of Engels' remarks in which he mercilessly ridiculed the absurdity of combining the words "freedom" and "state." So long as the state exists there is no freedom. When there will be freedom, there will be no state.

The economic basis for the complete withering away of the state is that high stage of development of communism when the antithesis between mental and physical labor disappears, when there disappears consequently one of the principal sources of modern *social* inequality—a source, moreover, which cannot on any account be removed immediately by the mere conversion of the means of production into public property, by the mere expropriation of the capitalists.

This expropriation will create *the possibility* of an enormous development of the productive forces. And when we see how incredibly capitalism is already *retarding* this development, when we see how much progress could be achieved on the basis of the level of technique now already attained, we are entitled to say with the fullest confidence that the expropriation of the capitalists will inevitably result in an enormous development of the productive forces of human society. But how rapidly this development will proceed, how soon it will reach the point of breaking away from the division of labor, of doing away with the antithesis between mental and physical labor, of transforming labor into "the prime necessity of life"—we do not and *cannot* know.

That is why we are entitled to speak only of the inevitable

withering away of the state, emphasizing the protracted nature of this process and its dependence upon the rapidity of development of the *higher phase* of communism, and leaving completely open the question of the time required for, or the concrete forms of, the withering away, because there is *no* material for answering these questions.

It will become possible for the state to wither away completely when society adopts the rule: "From each according to his ability, to each according to his needs," *i.e.*, when people have become so accustomed to observing the fundamental rules of social intercourse and when their labor becomes so productive that they will voluntarily work *according to their ability*. "The narrow horizon of bourgeois right," which compels one to calculate with the coldheartedness of a Shylock whether one has not worked half an hour more than somebody else, whether one is not getting less pay than somebody else—this narrow horizon will then be crossed. There will then be no need for society to regulate the quantity of products to be received by each: each will take freely "according to his needs."

From the bourgeois point of view, it is easy to declare that such a social order is "sheer utopia" and to sneer at the socialists for promising everyone the right to receive from society, without any control over the labor of the individual citizen, any quantity of truffles, automobiles, pianos, etc. Even to this day, most bourgeois "savants" confine themselves to sneering in this way, thereby displaying both their ignorance and their mercenary defense of capitalism.

Ignorance—for it has never entered the head of any socialist to "promise" that the higher phase of the development of communism will arrive; whereas the great socialists, in *foreseeing* that it will arrive presuppose not the present productivity of labor *and not the present* ordinary run of people, who, like the seminary students in Pomyalovsky's stories, are capable of damaging the stocks of public wealth "just for fun" and of demanding the impossible.

Until the "higher" phase of communism arrives, the socialists demand the *strictest* control by society *and by the state* of the measure of labor and the measure of consumption; but this control must *start* with the expropriation of the capitalists and with the establishment of workers' control over the capitalists, and it must be exercised not by a state of bureaucrats, but by a state of *armed workers*.

The mercenary defense of capitalism by the bourgeois

ideologists (and their hangers-on, like the Tseretelis, Chernovs and Co.) consists precisely in that they *substitute* controversies and discussions about the distant future for the vital and burning question of *present-day* politics, *viz.*, the expropriation of the capitalists, the conversion of *all* citizens into workers and employees of *one* huge "syndicate"— the whole state—and the complete subordination of the entire work of this syndicate to a genuinely democratic state, to *the state of the Soviets of Workers' and Soldiers' Deputies.*

Actually, when a learned professor, followed by the philistine, who, in turn, is followed by the Tseretelis and Chernovs, talks about unreasonable utopias, the demagogic promises of the Bolsheviks, and the impossibility of "introducing" socialism, it is the higher stage or phase of communism they have in mind, which no one has ever promised or even thought to "introduce," because it generally cannot be "introduced."

And this brings us to the question of the scientific difference between socialism and communism, which Engels touched on in his above-quoted argument about the incorrectness of the name "Social Democrat." Politically the difference between the first, or lower, and the higher phase of communism will in time, probably, be tremendous; but it would be ridiculous to take cognizance of this difference now, under capitalism, and only individual anarchists, perhaps, could invest it with primary importance (if there still remain people among the anarchists who have learned nothing from the "Plekhanovite" conversion of the Kropotkins, the Graveses, the Cornelissens and other "stars" of anarchism into social-chauvinists or "anarcho-trenchists," as Ge, one of the few anarchists who have still preserved a sense of honor and a conscience, has put it).

But the scientific difference between socialism and communism is clear. What is usually called socialism was termed by Marx the "first" or lower phase of communist society. In so far as the means of production become *common* property, the word "communism" is also applicable here, providing we do not forget that this is *not* complete communism. The great significance of Marx's explanations is that here, too, he consistently applies materialist dialectics, the theory of development, regarding communism as something which develops *out of* capitalism. Instead of scholastically invented, "concocted" definitions and fruitless dis-

putes about words (what is socialism? what is communism?),
Marx gives an analysis of what might be called the stages
of the economic ripeness of communism.

In its first phase, or first stage, communism *cannot* as yet
be fully ripe economically and entirely free from traditions
or remnants of capitalism. Hence, the interesting phenomenon that communism in its first phase retains "the
narrow horizon of *bourgeois* right." Of course, bourgeois
right in regard to the distribution of articles of *consumption*
inevitably presupposes the existence of the *bourgeois state,*
for right is nothing without an apparatus capable of *enforcing* the observance of the standards of right.

It follows that under communism there remains for a time
not only bourgeois right, but even the bourgeois state without the bourgeoisie!

This may sound like a paradox or simply a dialectical co-
nundrum, of which Marxism is often accused by people who
do not take the slightest trouble to study its extraordinarily
profound content.

But as a matter of fact, remnants of the old surviving in
the new confront us in life at every step, both in nature and
in society. And Marx did not arbitrarily insert a scrap of
"bourgeois" right into communism, but indicated what is
economically and politically inevitable in a society emerging *out of the womb* of capitalism.

Democracy is of enormous importance to the working
class in its struggle against the capitalists for its emancipation. But democracy is by no means a boundary not to be
crossed: it is only one of the stages on the road from feudalism to capitalism and from capitalism to communism.

Democracy means equality. The great significance of the
proletariat's struggle for equality and of equality as a slogan
will be clear if we correctly interpret it as meaning the abolition of *classes*. But democracy means only *formal* equality.
And as soon as equality is achieved for all members of society *in relation* to ownership of the means of production,
that is, equality of labor and equality of wages, humanity
will inevitably be confronted with the question of advancing
farther, from formal equality to actual equality, *i.e.*, to the
realization of the rule, "from each according to his ability,
to each according to his needs." By what stages, by means of
what practical measures humanity will proceed to this supreme aim—we do not and cannot know. But it is important
to realize how infinitely mendacious is the ordinary bour-

geois conception of socialism as something lifeless, petrified, fixed once for all, whereas in reality *only* under socialism will there begin in all spheres of public and personal
life a rapid, genuine, really mass forward movement, embracing first the *majority* and then the whole of the population.

Democracy is a form of the state, one of its varieties. Consequently, like every state, it represents the organized, systematic use of violence against persons. But it also signifies
the formal recognition of the equality of citizens, the equal
right of all to determine the structure of the state and to
administer it. This, in turn, results in the fact that, at a certain stage in the development of democracy, it first welds
together the class that wages a revolutionary struggle against
capitalism—the proletariat, and enables it to crush, to smash
to bits, to wipe off the face of the earth the bourgeois, even
the republican bourgeois, the state machine, the standing
army, the police and the bureaucracy, and to substitute for
them a *more* democratic state machine, but a state machine
nevertheless, in the shape of the armed masses of workers
who develop into a militia in which the entire population
takes part.

Here "quantity turns into quality": *such* a degree of democracy involves leaving the boundaries of bourgeois society and beginning its socialist reconstruction. If really *all*
take part in the administration of the state, capitalism cannot retain its hold. And the development of capitalism itself
creates, in turn, the *premises* that *enable* "all" to take part
in the administration of the state. Some of these premises
are universal literacy, which has already been achieved in
a number of the most advanced capitalist countries, and the
"training and disciplining" of millions of workers by the
huge, complex, socialized apparatus of the postal service,
railways, big factories, large-scale commerce, banking, etc.,
etc.

Given these *economic* premises it is quite possible, after
the overthrow of the capitalists and the bureaucrats, to proceed immediately, overnight, to replace them in the *control*
of production and distribution, in the work of *keeping account* of labor and products by the armed workers, by the
whole of the armed population. (The question of control
and accounting should not be confused with the question of
the scientifically trained staff of engineers, agronomists and
so on. These gentlemen, working today in obedience to the

wishes of the capitalists, will work even better tomorrow in obedience to the wishes of the armed workers.)

Accounting and control—that is the *main* thing required for "arranging" the smooth working, the correct functioning of the *first phase* of communist society. *All* citizens are transformed here into hired employees of the state, which consists of the armed workers. *All* citizens become employees and workers of a *single* nationwide state "syndicate." All that is required is that they should work equally, do their proper share of work, and get equally paid. The accounting and control necessary for this have been *simplified* by capitalism to the extreme and reduced to the extraordinarily simple operations—which any literate person who knows arithmetic can perform—of supervising, recording, and issuing appropriate receipts.[17]

When the *majority* of the people begin independently and everywhere to keep such accounts and maintain such control over the capitalists (now converted into employees) and over the gentry intellectuals who preserve their capitalist habits, this control will really become universal, general, popular. And there will be no way of getting away from it; there will be "nowhere to go."

The whole of society will have become a single office and a single factory, with equality of labor and equality of pay.

But this "factory" discipline, which the proletariat, after defeating the capitalists and overthrowing the exploiters, will extend to the whole of society, is by no means our ideal, or our ultimate goal. It is but a necessary *step* for the purpose of thoroughly purging society of all the infamies and abominations of capitalist exploitation *and for further* progress.

From the moment all members of society, or even only the vast majority, have learned to administer the state *themselves,* have taken this work into their own hands, have "arranged" control over the insignificant minority of capitalists, the gentry who wish to preserve their capitalist habits and the workers who have been profoundly corrupted by capitalism—from this moment the need for government of any kind begins to disappear altogether. The more complete the democracy, the nearer the moment approaches when it becomes unnecessary. The more democratic the "state," consisting of the armed workers and "no longer a state in the proper sense of the word," the more rapidly does *every form* of state begin to wither away.

For when *all* have learned to administer and actually do administer independently social production, independently keep accounts and exercise control over the idlers, gentle-folk, swindlers and other such "guardians of capitalist tra-ditions," the escape from this popular accounting and con-trol will inevitably become so incredibly difficult, such a rare exception, and will probably be accompanied by such swift and severe punishment (for the armed workers are practical men and not sentimental intellectuals, and they will scarcely allow anyone to trifle with them), that the *necessity* of observing the simple, fundamental rules of hu-man intercourse will very soon become a *habit*.

And then the door will be wide open for the transition from the first phase of communist society to its higher phase, and with it, to the complete withering away of the state.

VI. THE VULGARIZATION OF MARXISM BY THE OPPORTUNISTS

The question of the relation of the state to the social rev-olution and the social revolution to the state, like the ques-tion of revolution generally, troubled the leading theoreti-cians and publicists of the Second International (1889-1914) very little. But the most characteristic thing about the gradual growth of opportunism, which led to the collapse of the Second International in 1914, is the fact that even when these people actually came right up against this ques-tion they *tried to evade* it or else failed to notice it.

In general, it may be said that *evasiveness* regarding the question of the relation of the proletarian revolution to the state—an evasiveness which was to the advantage of op-portunism and fostered it—resulted in the *distortion* of Marxism and its complete vulgarization.

To characterize this lamentable process, if only briefly, we shall take the most prominent theoreticians of Marxism: Plekhanov and Kautsky.

1. Plekhanov's Controversy with the Anarchists

Plekhanov wrote a special pamphlet on the relation of anarchism to socialism, entitled *Anarchism and Socialism* and published in German in 1894.

In treating this subject, Plekhanov contrived completely

to ignore the most urgent, burning, and politically most essential issue in the struggle against anarchism, *viz.*, the relation of the revolution to the state and the question of the state in general! Two sections of his pamphlet stand out: one of them is historical and literary and contains valuable material on the history of the ideas of Stirner, Proudhon and others; the other is philistine and contains a clumsy dissertation on the theme that an anarchist cannot be distinguished from a bandit.

A most amusing combination of subjects and most characteristic of Plekhanov's whole activity on the eve of the revolution and during the revolutionary period in Russia. Indeed, in the years 1905 to 1917, Plekhanov revealed himself as a semi-doctrinaire and semi-philistine who, in politics, trailed in the wake of the bourgeoisie.

We have seen how, in their controversy with the anarchists, Marx and Engels with the utmost thoroughness explained their views on the relation of revolution to the state. In 1891, in his foreword to Marx's *Critique of the Gotha Program*, Engels wrote that "we"—that is, Engels and Marx —"were at that time, hardly two years after the Hague Congress of the (First) International,[18] engaged in the most violent struggle against Bakunin and his anarchists."

The anarchists had tried to claim the Paris Commune as their "own," so to say, as a corroboration of their doctrine; and they utterly failed to understand its lessons and Marx's analysis of these lessons. Anarchism has failed to give anything even approximating a true solution of the concrete political problems: must the old state machine be *smashed?* and *what* should be put in its place?

But to speak of "anarchism and socialism" while completely evading the question of the state *and failing to take note* of the whole development of Marxism before and after the Commune, meant inevitably to slip into opportunism. For what opportunism needs most of all is that the two questions just mentioned should *not* be raised at all. That *in itself* is a victory for opportunism.

2. KAUTSKY'S CONTROVERSY WITH THE OPPORTUNISTS

Undoubtedly an immeasurably larger number of Kautsky's works have been translated into Russian than into any other language. It is not without reason that some German

Social Democrats say in jest that Kautsky is read more in
Russia than in Germany. (Let us say, parenthetically, that
there is a far deeper historical significance in this jest than
those who first made it suspect: by advancing in 1905 an
extraordinarily great and unprecedented demand for the
best works of the best Social Democratic literature in the
world, and by receiving translations and editions of these
works in quantities unheard of in other countries, the Russian workers transplanted, so to speak, at an accelerated
pace the enormous experience of a neighboring, more advanced country to the young soil of our proletarian movement.)

Besides his popularization of Marxism, Kautsky is particularly known in our country for his controversy with the
opportunists, with Bernstein at their head. But one fact is
almost unknown, one which cannot be overlooked if we set
ourselves the task of investigating how Kautsky drifted into
the morass of unbelievably disgraceful confusion and defense of social-chauvinism during the supreme crisis of
1914-1915. This fact is the following: shortly before he
came out against the most prominent representatives of opportunism in France (Millerand and Jaurès) and in Germany
(Bernstein), Kautsky gave evidence of very considerable
vacillation. The Marxist journal, *Zarya*,[19] which was published in Stuttgart in 1901-1902 and which advocated revolutionary proletarian views, was forced to *enter into
controversy* with Kautsky, to characterize as "elastic" the
half-hearted, evasive resolution, conciliatory towards the opportunists, that he proposed at the International Socialist
Congress in Paris in 1900.[20] Kautsky's letters published in
Germany reveal no less hesitancy on his part before he took
the field against Bernstein.

Of immeasurably greater significance, however, is the fact
that in his very controversy with the opportunists, his formulation of the question, and his manner of treating it, we
can now observe, as we investigate the *history* of Kautsky's
latest betrayal of Marxism, his systematic gravitation towards opportunism precisely on the question of the state.

Let us take Kautsky's first important work against opportunism, his *Bernstein and the Social Democratic Program*.
Kautsky refutes Bernstein in detail, but here is something
characteristic.

Bernstein, in his *Premises of Socialism*, of Herostratean
fame, accuses Marxism of *"Blanquism"* (an accusation since

repeated thousands of times by the opportunists and liberal bourgeois in Russia against the representatives of revolutionary Marxism, the Bolsheviks). In this connection Bernstein dwells particularly on Marx's *The Civil War in France*, and tries, quite unsuccessfully, as we have seen, to identify Marx's views on the lessons of the Commune with those of Proudhon. Bernstein pays particular attention to the conclusion which Marx emphasized in his 1872 preface to the *Communist Manifesto*, *viz.*, that "the working class cannot simply lay hold of the ready-made state machinery and wield it for its own purpose."

This statement "pleased" Bernstein so much that he repeated it no less than three times in his book—interpreting it in the most distorted, opportunist sense.

As we have seen, Marx meant that the working class must *smash, break, shatter* (*Sprengung*—explosion, the expression used by Engels) the entire state machine. But according to Bernstein it would appear as though Marx in these words warned the working class *against* excessive revolutionary zeal when seizing power.

A cruder and more hideous distortion of Marx's idea cannot be imagined.

How, then, did Kautsky proceed in his most detailed refutation of Bernsteinism?

He refrained from analyzing the utter distortion of Marxism by opportunism on this point. He cited the above-quoted passage from Engels' introduction to Marx's *Civil War* and said that according to Marx the working class cannot *simply* lay hold of the *ready-made* state machine, but that, generally speaking, it *can* lay hold of it—and that was all. Not a word does Kautsky utter about the fact that Bernstein attributed to Marx the *very opposite* of Marx's real views, the fact that since 1852 Marx had formulated the task of the proletarian revolution as being to "smash" the state machine.

The result was that the most essential difference between Marxism and opportunism on the subject of the tasks of the proletarian revolution was slurred over by Kautsky!

"We can safely leave the solution of the problem of the proletarian dictatorship to the future," said Kautsky, writing "*against*" Bernstein. (p. 172, German edition.)

This is not a polemic *against* Bernstein, but, in essence, a *concession* to him, a surrender to opportunism; for at present

the opportunists ask nothing better than to "safely lea\
the future" all fundamental questions of the tasks of ᴜ
proletarian revolution.

From 1852 to 1891, for forty years, Marx and Engels
taught the proletariat that it must smash the state machine.
Yet, in 1899, Kautsky, confronted with the complete betrayal of Marxism by the opportunists on this point, fraudulently
substituted for the question of whether it is necessary to
smash this machine the question of the concrete forms in
which it is to be smashed, and then sought refuge behind
the "indisputable" (and barren) philistine truth that concrete forms cannot be known in advance!!

A gulf separates Marx and Kautsky as regards their attitudes towards the proletarian party's task of preparing the
working class for revolution.

Let us take the next, more mature, work by Kautsky, which
was also, to a considerable extent, devoted to a refutation of
opportunist errors. This is his pamphlet, *The Social Revolution.* In this pamphlet the author chose as his special theme
the question of "the proletarian revolution" and "the proletarian regime." He gave much in it that was exceedingly
valuable, but as for the question of the state, he *avoided* it.
Throughout the pamphlet the author speaks of winning state
power—and no more; that is, he chooses a formula which
makes a concession to the opportunists, inasmuch as it *admits*
the possibility of seizing power *without* destroying the state
machine. The very thing which Marx, in 1872, declared to
be "obsolete" in the program of the *Communist Manifesto
is revived* by Kautsky in 1902!

A special paragraph in the pamphlet is devoted to "the
forms and the weapons of the social revolution." Here Kautsky speaks of the mass political strike, civil war, and the "instruments of power of the modern large state, such as the
bureaucracy and the army"; but not a word does he say
about what the Commune had already taught the workers.
Evidently, it was not without reason that Engels issued a
warning particularly to the German socialists against "superstitious reverence" for the state.

In his treatment of the question, Kautsky states that the
victorious proletariat "will carry out the democratic program," and he goes on to formulate its clauses. But not a
word does he say about the new material provided by the
year 1871 on the subject of the supersession of bourgeois de-

mocracy by proletarian democracy. Kautsky disposes of the
question by uttering such "solid" banalities as:

Still, it goes without saying that we shall not achieve supremacy
under the present conditions. Revolution itself presupposes a long
and intensive struggle, which, as it proceeds, will change our
present political and social structure.

Undoubtedly, this "goes without saying," just as does the
truth that horses eat oats, or that the Volga flows into the
Caspian Sea. Only it is a pity that an empty and bombastic
phrase about "intensive" struggle is used as a means of
avoiding a question of vital interest to the revolutionary
proletariat; namely, what expresses the "intensity" of *its* revolution in relation to the state, in relation to democracy, as distinct from previous, nonproletarian revolutions?

By avoiding this question, Kautsky *in practice* makes a
concession to opportunism on this most essential point, although *in words* he declares stern war against it, emphasizes the importance of the "idea of revolution" (how much
is this "idea" worth when one is afraid to teach the workers
the concrete lessons of revolution?), says, "revolutionary
idealism before everything else," and announces that the
English workers are now "hardly more than petty bourgeois."

"The most varied forms of enterprises—bureaucratic (??), trade
unionist, co-operative, private . . . can exist side by side in socialist
society," Kautsky writes. ". . . There are enterprises which cannot
do without a bureaucratic (??) organization, for example, the
railways. Here the democratic organization may take the following
shape: the workers elect delegates who form a sort of parliament,
which draws up the working regulations and supervises the management of the bureaucratic apparatus. The management of other
enterprises may be transferred to the trade unions, and still others
may become co-operative enterprises." (pp. 148 and 115, Russian
translation, published in Geneva, 1903.)

This reasoning is erroneous; it is a step backward compared with the explanations Marx and Engels gave in the
seventies, using the lessons of the Commune as an example.

As far as the supposedly necessary "bureaucratic" organization is concerned, there is no difference whatever between
railways and any other enterprise in large-scale machine
industry, any factory, large store, or large-scale capitalist agricultural enterprise. The technique of all such enter-

prises makes absolutely imperative the strictest discipline, the utmost precision on the part of everyone in carrying out his allotted task, otherwise the whole enterprise may come to a stop, or the machinery or finished product may be damaged. In all such enterprises the workers will, of course, "elect delegates who will form *a sort of parliament.*"

But the whole point is that this "sort of parliament" will *not* be a parliament in the sense in which we understand bourgeois-parliamentary institutions. The whole point is that this "sort of parliament" will *not* merely "draw up the working regulations and supervise the management of the bureaucratic apparatus," as imagined by Kautsky, whose ideas do not go beyond the bounds of bourgeois parliamentarism. In socialist society the "sort of parliament" consisting of workers' deputies will, of course, "draw up the working regulations and supervise the management" of the "apparatus" —*but* this apparatus will *not* be "bureaucratic." The workers, having conquered political power, will smash the old bureaucratic apparatus, shatter it to its very foundations, destroy it to the very roots. And they will replace it by a new one, consisting of the very same workers and office employees, *against* whose transformation into bureaucrats the measures will at once be taken which were specified in detail by Marx and Engels: 1) not only election, but also recall at any time; 2) pay not exceeding that of a workman; 3) immediate introduction of control and supervision by *all*, so that *all* shall become "bureaucrats" for a time and that, therefore, *nobody* may be able to become a "bureaucrat."

Kautsky has not reflected at all on Marx's words: "The Commune was a working, not a parliamentary body, legislative and executive at the same time."

Kautsky has not understood at all the difference between bourgeois parliamentarism, which combines democracy (*not for the people*) with bureaucracy (*against the people*), and proletarian democracy, which will take immediate steps to cut bureaucracy down to the roots, and which will be able to carry out these measures to the end, to the complete abolition of bureaucracy, to the introduction of complete democracy for the people.

Kautsky here displays the same old "superstitious reverence" for the state, and "superstitious belief" in bureaucracy.

Let us now pass on to the last and best of Kautsky's works against the opportunists, his pamphlet *The Road to*

Power (which, I believe, has not been translated into Russian, for it was published at the time when the reaction was at its height here, in 1909). This pamphlet marks a considerable step forward, inasmuch as it does not deal with the revolutionary program in general, as in the pamphlet of 1899 against Bernstein, or with the tasks of the social revolution irrespective of the time of its occurrence, as in the 1902 pamphlet, *The Social Revolution*. It deals with the concrete conditions which compel us to recognize that the "era of revolutions" is *approaching*.

The author definitely points to the intensification of class antagonisms in general and to imperialism, which plays a particularly important part in this connection. After the "revolutionary period of 1789-1871" in Western Europe, he says, a similar period began in the East in 1905. A world war is approaching with menacing rapidity. "The proletariat can no longer talk of premature revolution." "We have entered a revolutionary period." The "revolutionary era is beginning."

These declarations are perfectly clear. This pamphlet of Kautsky's should serve as a measure of comparison between what German Social Democracy *promised to be* before the imperialist war and how low it—Kautsky himself included— fell when the war broke out. "The present situation," Kautsky wrote in the pamphlet we are examining, "is fraught with the danger that we (*i.e.*, German Social Democracy) may easily appear to be more moderate than we really are." It turned out that in reality the German Social Democratic Party was much more moderate and opportunist than it appeared to be!

The more characteristic is it, therefore, that although Kautsky so definitely declared that the era of revolutions had already begun, in the pamphlet which he himself said was devoted precisely to an analysis of the "*political* revolution," he again completely avoided the question of the state.

These evasions of the question, these omissions and equivocations, inevitably led in their sum total to that complete transition to opportunism with which we shall now have to deal.

German Social Democracy, in the person of Kautsky, seems to have declared: I adhere to revolutionary views (1899); I recognize, in particular, the inevitability of the social revolution of the proletariat (1902); I recognize the

advent of a new era of revolutions (1909). Still, I am going
back on what Marx said as early as 1852 now that the
question of the tasks of the proletarian revolution in relation
to the state is being raised (1912).

It was precisely in this direct form that the question was
put in Kautsky's controversy with Pannekoek.

3. KAUTSKY'S CONTROVERSY WITH PANNEKOEK

In opposing Kautsky, Pannekoek came forward as one of
the representatives of the "left radical" trend which counted
in its ranks Rosa Luxemburg, Karl Radek and others. Advocating revolutionary tactics, they were united in the conviction that Kautsky was going over to the position of the
"center," which wavered in an unprincipled manner between Marxism and opportunism. The correctness of this
view was fully confirmed by the war, when this "centrist"
(wrongly called Marxist) trend, or "Kautskyism," revealed
itself in all its repulsive wretchedness.

In an article touching on the question of the state, entitled "Mass Action and Revolution" (*Neue Zeit*, 1912, Vol.
XXX, 2), Pannekoek described Kautsky's position as "passive
radicalism," as "a theory of inactive expectancy." "Kautsky
refuses to see the process of revolution," wrote Pannekoek
(p. 616). In presenting the matter in this way, Pannekoek
approached the subject which interests us, namely, the tasks
of the proletarian revolution in relation to the state.

"The struggle of the proletariat," he wrote, "is not merely a
struggle against the bourgeoisie *for* state power, but a struggle
against state power. . . . The content of the proletarian revolution
is the destruction and dissolution (*Auflösung*) of the instruments
of state power by the instruments of proletarian power. . . . The
struggle will cease only when, as a result of it, the state organization is utterly destroyed. The organization of the majority will
have demonstrated its superiority by destroying the organization of
the ruling minority." (p. 548.)

The formulation in which Pannekoek presented his ideas
suffers from serious defects, but its meaning is clear nonetheless; and it is interesting to note *how* Kautsky combated
it.

"Up to now," he wrote, "the difference between the Social Democrats and the anarchists has been that the former wished to

conquer state power, while the latter wished to destroy it. Pannekoek wants to do both." (p. 724.)

Although Pannekoek's exposition lacks precision and concreteness—not to speak of other shortcomings of his article which have no bearing on the present subject—Kautsky seized precisely on the point of *principle* raised by Pannekoek; and *on this fundamental* point of *principle* Kautsky completely abandoned the Marxian position and went over wholly to opportunism. His definition of the difference between the Social Democrats and the anarchists is absolutely wrong, and he utterly vulgarizes and distorts Marxism.

The difference between the Marxists and the anarchists is this: (1) The former, while aiming at the complete abolition of the state, recognize that this aim can only be achieved after classes have been abolished by the socialist revolution, as the result of the establishment of socialism, which leads to the withering away of the state. The latter want to abolish the state completely overnight, failing to understand the conditions under which the state can be abolished. (2) The former recognize that after the proletariat has conquered political power it must utterly destroy the old state machine and substitute for it a new one consisting of an organization of the armed workers on the model of the Commune. The latter, while insisting on the destruction of the state machine, have absolutely no clear idea of *what* the proletariat will put in its place and *how* it will use its revolutionary power: the anarchists even deny that the revolutionary proletariat should use the state power: they deny its revolutionary dictatorship. (3) The former demand that the proletariat be prepared for revolution by utilizing the present state. The anarchists reject this.

In this controversy it is not Kautsky but Pannekoek who represents Marxism, for it was Marx who taught that the proletariat cannot simply conquer state power in the sense that the old state apparatus passes into new hands, but must smash, break this apparatus and replace it by a new one.

Kautsky abandons Marxism for the camp of the opportunists, for this destruction of the state machine, which is utterly unacceptable to the opportunists, completely disappears from his argument, and he leaves a loophole for them in that "conquest" may be interpreted as a simple acquisition of a majority.

To cover up his distortion of Marxism, Kautsky behaves like a textman: he puts forward a "quotation" from Marx himself. In 1850 Marx wrote that "a resolute centralization of power in the hands of the state authority" was necessary; and Kautsky triumphantly asks: does Pannekoek want to destroy "centralism"?

This is simply a trick, similar to Bernstein's identification of the views of Marxism and Proudhonism on the subject of federalism as against centralism.

Kautsky's "quotation" is neither here nor there. Centralism is possible with both the old and the new state machine. If the workers voluntarily unite their armed forces, this will be centralism, but it will be based on the "complete destruction" of the centralized state apparatus—the standing army, the police and the bureaucracy. Kautsky acts like an outright swindler when he ignores the perfectly well-known arguments of Marx and Engels on the Commune and plucks out a quotation which has nothing to do with the case.

". . . Perhaps Pannekoek," Kautsky continues, "wants to abolish the state functions of the officials? But we do not get along without officials even in the party and the trade unions, much less in the state administration. Our program does not demand the abolition of state officials, but that they be elected by the people. . . . We are discussing here not the form the administrative apparatus of the 'future state' will assume, but whether our political struggle abolishes (literally dissolves—*auflöst*) the state power *before we have captured it* (Kautsky's italics). Which ministry with its officials could be abolished?" Then follows an enumeration of the ministries of education, justice, finance and war. "No, not one of the present ministries will be removed by our political struggle against the government. . . . I repeat, in order to avoid misunderstanding: we are not discussing here the form the 'future state' will be given by victorious Social Democracy, but how the present state is changed by our opposition." (p. 725.)

This is an obvious trick. Pannekoek raised the question of *revolution*. Both the title of his article and the passages quoted above clearly indicate this. In skipping to the question of "opposition" Kautsky replaces the revolutionary by the opportunist point of view. The conclusion to be drawn from his argument is this: at present we are an opposition; what we shall be *after* we have captured power, that we shall see. *Revolution has vanished!* And that is exactly what the opportunists wanted.

What is at issue is neither opposition nor political struggle

in general, but *revolution*. Revolution consists in the proletariat *destroying* the "administrative apparatus" and the *entire* state machine, replacing it with a new one, consisting
of the armed workers. Kautsky displays a "superstitious reverence" for "ministries"; but why can they not be replaced,
say, by committees of specialists, working under sovereign,
all-powerful Soviets of Workers' and Soldiers' Deputies?

The point is not at all whether the "ministries" will remain, or whether "committees of specialists" or some other
institutions will be set up; that is quite unimportant. The
point is whether the old state machine (bound by thousands of threads to the bourgeoisie and permeated through
and through with routine and inertia) shall remain, or be
destroyed and replaced by a *new* one. Revolution consists
not in the new class commanding, governing with the aid of
the *old* state machine, but in the class *smashing* this machine and commanding, governing with the aid of a *new*
machine. Kautsky slurs over this *basic* idea of Marxism or
completely fails to understand it.

His question about officials clearly shows that he does not
understand the lessons of the Commune or the teachings of
Marx. "We do not get along without officials even in the
party and the trade unions. . . ."

We do not get along without officials *under capitalism,*
under *the rule of the bourgeoisie.* The proletariat is oppressed; the toiling masses are enslaved by capitalism. Under capitalism democracy is restricted, cramped, curtailed,
mutilated by all the conditions of wage slavery, and by
the poverty and misery of the masses. This and this alone
is the reason why the functionaries of our political organizations and trade unions are corrupted—or, more precisely,
tend to be corrupted—by the conditions of capitalism and betray a tendency to become bureaucrats, *i.e.,* privileged persons divorced from the masses and standing *above* the
masses.

That is the *essence* of bureaucracy; and until the capitalists have been expropriated and the bourgeoisie overthrown, *even* proletarian functionaries will inevitably be
"bureaucratized" to a certain extent.

According to Kautsky, since elected functionaries will remain under socialism, officials will remain, bureaucracy will
remain! This is exactly where he is wrong. It was precisely
the example of the Commune that Marx used to show that
under socialism functionaries will cease to be "bureaucrats,"

to be "officials." They will cease to be so *in proportion as,* in addition to the principle of election of officials, the principle of recall at any time is *also* introduced, *and* as salaries are reduced to the level of the wages of the average worker, *and,* too, as parliamentary institutions are replaced by "working bodies, legislative and executive at the same time."

In essence, the whole of Kautsky's argument against Pannekoek, and particularly the former's wonderful point that we do not get along without officials even in our party and trade-union organizations, is merely a repetition of Bernstein's old "arguments" against Marxism in general. In his renegade book, *The Premises of Socialism,* Bernstein combats the ideas of "primitive" democracy, combats what he calls "doctrinaire democracy": imperative mandates, unpaid officials, impotent central representative bodies, etc. To prove that this "primitive democracy" is unsound, Bernstein refers to the experience of the British trade unions, as interpreted by the Webbs. He contends that seventy years of development in allegedly "absolute freedom," (p. 137, German edition), convinced the trade unions that primitive democracy was useless, and they replaced it with ordinary democracy, *i.e.,* parliamentarism combined with bureaucracy.

As a matter of fact the trade unions did not develop in "absolute freedom" *but in absolute capitalist slavery,* under which, it goes without saying, "one cannot avoid" a number of concessions to the prevailing evil, violence, falsehood, and exclusion of the poor from the affairs of the "higher" administration. Under socialism much of "primitive" democracy will inevitably be revived, since, for the first time in the history of civilized society, the *mass* of the population will rise to the level of taking an *independent* part, not only in voting and elections, *but also in the everyday administration of affairs.* Under socialism *all* will govern in turn and will soon become accustomed to no one governing.

Marx's critico-analytical genius perceived in the practical measures of the Commune the *turning point,* which the opportunists fear and do not want to recognize because of their cowardice, because they do not want to break irrevocably with the bourgeoisie, and which the anarchists do not want to perceive, either because they are in a hurry or because they do not understand at all the conditions of great social changes. "We must not even think of destroying the old state machine; how can we get along without ministries and officials?" argues the opportunist, who is completely saturated with philistinism, and who, at bottom, not only does not believe in revolution, in the creative power of revolution, but lives in mortal dread of it (like our Mensheviks and Socialist-Revolutionaries).

"We must think *only* of destroying the old state machine; it is no use probing into the *concrete* lessons of earlier proletarian revolutions and analyzing *what* to put in the place of what has been destroyed, and *how*"—argues the anarchist (the best of the anarchists, of course, and not those who, following Kropotkin and Co., trail in the wake of the bourgeoisie). Consequently, the tactics of the anarchist become the tactics of *despair* instead of a ruthlessly bold revolutionary effort to solve concrete problems while taking into account the practical conditions of the mass movement.

Marx teaches us to avoid both errors. He teaches us to act with supreme boldness in destroying the entire old state machine, and at the same time he teaches us to put the question concretely: the Commune was able in the space of a few weeks to *start* building a *new,* proletarian state machine by introducing such-and-such measures to secure wider democracy and to uproot bureaucracy. Let us learn revolutionary boldness from the Communards; let us see in their practical measures the *outline* of urgently practical and immediately possible measures, and then, *pursuing this road,* we shall achieve the complete destruction of bureaucracy.

The possibility of this destruction is guaranteed by the fact that socialism will shorten the working day, raise the *masses* to a new life, create such conditions for the *majority* of the population as will enable *everybody,* without exception, to perform "state functions," and this will lead to the *complete withering away* of every form of state in general.

". . . The object of the mass strike," Kautsky continues, "can never be to *destroy* the state power, but only to wring concessions from the government on some particular question, or to replace a hostile government by one that would be more yielding (*entgegenkommende*) to the proletariat. . . . But never, under any conditions, can it" (that is, the proletarian victory of a hostile government) "lead to the *destruction* of the state power: it can lead only to a certain *shifting* (*Verschiebung*) of the relation of force *within the state power.* . . . The aim of our political struggle remains, as hitherto, the conquest of state power by winning a majority in parliament and by converting parliament into the master of the government." (pp. 726, 727, 732.)

This is nothing but the purest and the most vulgar opportunism: repudiating revolution in deeds, while accepting it in word. Kautsky's thoughts go no further than a "government . . . that would be more yielding to the proletariat"—a step backward to philistinism compared with 1847, when the *Communist Manifesto* proclaimed "the organization of the proletariat as the ruling class."

Kautsky will achieve his beloved "unity" with the Scheidemanns, Plekhanovs and Vanderveldes, all of whom agree to fight for a government "that would be more yielding to the proletariat."

But we shall break with these traitors to socialism, and we shall fight for the complete destruction of the old state machine, in order that the armed proletariat itself *shall become the government*. These are "two vastly different things."

Kautsky will enjoy the pleasant company of the Legiens and Davids, Plekhanovs, Potresovs, Tseretelis and Chernovs, who are quite willing to work for the "shifting of the relation of forces within the state power," for "winning a majority in parliament," and converting parliament into the "master of the government"—a most worthy object, which is wholly acceptable to the opportunists and which keeps everything within the bounds of the bourgeois parliamentary republic.

But we shall break with the opportunists; and the entire class-conscious proletariat will be with us in the fight—not to "shift the relation of forces," but to *overthrow the bourgeoisie, to destroy* bourgeois parliamentarism, to achieve a democratic republic on the model of the Commune or a republic of Soviets of Workers' and Soldiers' Deputies, to achieve the revolutionary dictatorship of the proletariat.

* * *

To the right of Kautsky in international socialism, there are trends such as the *Socialist Monthly* [21] in Germany (Legien, David, Kolb and many others, including the Scandinavians Stauning and Branting); the followers of Jaurès and Vandervelde in France and Belgium; Turati, Trèves and other representatives of the Right wing of the Italian Party; the Fabians and "Independents" (the Independent Labor Party [22] which, in fact, has always been dependent on the Liberals) in England, and the like. All these gentlemen, who play a tremendous, very often a predominant role in the parliamentary work and the press of the party, repudiate outright the dictatorship of the proletariat and pursue a policy of unconcealed opportunism. In the eyes of these gentlemen, the "dictatorship" of the proletariat "contradicts" democracy!! There is really no essential difference between them and the petty-bourgeois democrats.

Taking this circumstance into consideration, we are justified in drawing the conclusion that the Second International, in the case of the overwhelming majority of its official representatives, has completely sunk into opportunism. The experience of the Commune has been not only forgotten, but distorted. Far from inculcating in the workers' minds the idea that the time is nearing when they must take action, smash the old state machine, replace it by a new one, and in this way make their political rule the foundation for the socialist reconstruction of society, they have actually preached to the masses the very opposite and have depicted the "conquest of power" in a way that has left thousands of loopholes for opportunism.

The distortion and suppression of the question concerning the relation of the proletarian revolution to the state could not but play an immense role at a time when states, possessing a military apparatus expanded as a consequence of imperialist rivalry, have turned into military monsters which are exterminating millions of people in order to settle the issue as to whether England or Germany—this or that finance capital—is to rule the world.[23]

III.
STALIN AND INDUSTRIALIZATION

Among the main characteristics that identify the Stalin years, the following are perhaps the most significant: a monolithic Party rule that ultimately reflected the will of Stalin himself; rapid industrialization and rural collectivization; police terror and forced labor camps; the "great retreat" in social and economic spheres involving a revival of class inequalities, traditional Russian family and educational institutions, and Russian nationalism; and the shift from Marxist determinism to individualistic "voluntarism" in official ideology. With few exceptions, these attributes of Stalinist Russia ultimately derive from the Leninist heritage and are either directly or indirectly related to the premature Marxist revolution in an underdeveloped rural economy.

The basic link joining Stalin to the Leninist heritage is the Party. Lenin demanded full-time professional revolutionaries as disciplined and obedient to central direction as military troops. Stalin's rise in the Party was a consequence of his success in meeting these requirements. Following the Revolution, Lenin's Party directed Russia in the same way that the Party's full-time "apparatus" attempted to guide the less ideologically enlightened workers in the labor movement before the revolution. Consequently, whoever controlled the Party controlled Russia. In the early years of Soviet power, Stalin was one of the least prominent of the Party leaders. His posts seemed unimpressive and they seldom brought him the public attention and fame that went to such leaders as Trotsky, Bukharin, Zinoviev and Kamenev. While these brilliant intellectuals made exciting speeches and represented Russia to the outside world, Stalin remained behind the scenes in such obscure offices as the Nationalities Commissariat and the Workers' and Peasants' Inspectorate. Since this sort of work gave him good experience with the growing Party bureaucracy and since his very lack of prominence made him appear little threat to the other leaders, Stalin was given the position of General Secretary of the Party. In the hands of one Krestinsky, this job had been a completely subordinate and routine affair that seemed politically harmless and that, in any case, held little attraction for other leading Bolsheviks.

If Russia after the Revolution had become a political democracy where public opinion was important for the success or failure of political leaders, the speeches and fame of men like Trotsky and Bukharin would have brought them to power. But Lenin had bequeathed a closed system based on a monopolistic and monolithic Party dictatorship. As General Secretary of the Party, responsible for appointing, assigning and supervising Party personnel, Stalin was gradually able to gain control of the Party membership. The members might be inwardly thrilled by the speeches of Trotsky or Zinoviev, but their careers depended on their support of Stalin.

Stalin thus came to power through an instrument that was a direct consequence of Lenin's premature socialist movement and revolution: the centralized Party dictatorship. Having won complete power by the end of the 1920's, Stalin was in a position to give expression to the second theme that associates Stalin with the Leninist heritage: he could now begin the industrialization of Russia that Lenin had been forced to postpone in 1921 but that had always been for all Russian Marxists the indispensable prerequisite for a socialist society. After eight years of NEP the Russian economy had become stabilized, the factories that had closed down during the Civil War were back in operation, the petty-bourgeois shopkeepers were providing sufficient consumers' goods to stimulate peasant production for urban, industrial and export markets. It was time to move on. Merely to attain the prerevolutionary industrial levels, as the Russian economy did by 1929, was hardly a sufficient economic basis for socialism. Moreover, some non-Marxist western economists argue that there were specific economic reasons compelling Russia at the end of the 1920's to abandon the method of gradual economic development and undertake massive increases in industrial production. Those arguing this interpretation conclude that rapid industrialization and the Five Year Plans associated with it were as much a consequence of economic conditions as they were a reflection of Marxist ideology or of the traditional Russian nationalistic desire to catch up with the West.

In any case, that such industrialization was undertaken at

all simply indicates once more that Lenin's revolution occurred too soon, that, unwilling to wait for bourgeois capitalism to develop the Russian economy as Marxism had predicted, the Bolsheviks were forced to undertake the painful
task themselves. Since no socialist revolution in an industrialized western nation had occurred and since the Bolsheviks
were fearful of economic dependency on capitalist countries, they were forced to undertake what they called "primitive socialist accumulation," that is, a policy of forcing the
mass laboring population to pay for industrial development
precisely as the Marxists said the capitalists had done in the
West in the period of "primitive capitalist accumulation."
Machinery had to be imported, a growing urban labor force
had to be fed and industrial raw materials had to be supplied. The peasants, in turn, had to provide the State with
vast amounts of agricultural products. In the 1920's, far less
agricultural production was needed, and this relatively
limited amount was produced and sold by the peasants because they wanted the consumers' goods made available
during the NEP retreat. Under the Five Year Plans, however, not only was the need immensely greater, but the factories, resources and labor had to be used for building heavy
industry, "capital goods," and could not be spared for consumers' goods. In other words, the peasants must furnish
much more to the State, but they could expect far less in
return. There was one way of solving this problem: the
forced collectivization of agriculture. All the produce would
now accumulate in State granaries and storehouses, and the
government could simply take what it needed, leaving to the
collective peasants what it considered politically necessary.

Forced industrialization with its deprivation of consumers' goods and its particularly extreme exploitation of the
peasantry contributed in its turn to many of the other features of Stalinist Russia. The forced labor camps were filled
with peasants unwilling to accept collectivization, petty-
bourgeois "nepmen" of the 1920's and intellectuals and political leaders who opposed the whole oppressive enterprise.
Stalin once said to Churchill that the war against the peasantry during collectivization was more difficult than the war
against Nazi Germany. Once again the Party was in a veritable
civil war and in order to win, its troops had to preserve iron
discipline. Since Stalin feared that the various Party factions he had defeated on his way to power during the twenties might use the crisis against him, they and any other

Party members suspected of opposing his policies must be liquidated. The nightmare of the mid-thirties with its grotesque trials and confessions, the ubiquitous fear and terror and its ever-expanding forced labor camps can be attributed to many causes including Stalin's own irrational motivations, the various petty intrigues and ambitions especially within the ranks of the Party and the secret police, and the dangers implicit in the rise of Hitler to power in Germany. Nevertheless, it seems clear that the entire dreadful situation is closely related to the general theory and practice of Marxism-Leninism—the absolute conviction in the scientific validity of Party policies, the demand for monolithic Party discipline especially during times of crisis and, above all, the consequences of taking power in an economically underdeveloped country.

It has often been pointed out that Stalin's "great retreat" in the area of social institutions is also associated with the requirements of industrialization. The 1920's are marked by a radical campaign against authority in the family, the school and virtually every other area where direction and leadership is the norm. It is also a decade of persistent efforts toward greater wage equality. After Stalin assumed control of the State and society, these efforts were replaced by an official support for the traditional family and school system and for the familiar differences in income, all of which, many sociologists today argue, are the natural concomitants of a society undergoing industrialization.

But what of the totalitarian features of Stalinist Russia? Is Stalin's effort to control and mold the individual from the cradle to the grave, to fashion a "new Soviet man" also associated with the Lenin heritage?

Lenin, in common with many other socialists, envisioned a finer type of human being whose unselfish, socially conscious motivations and relationships would sharply distinguish the socialist community from what the Marxists considered the selfishly individualistic, competitive economy and the crudely materialistic culture of capitalism. Moreover, as we have seen, Lenin doubted that the laboring masses, the ordinary individuals, were capable of developing this higher socialist consciousness by themselves, without the guidance of the socialist elite, the Party.

Although when Lenin expressed these views he was mainly concerned with mobilizing forces for a socialist revolution, it is obvious that such intellectual elitism had a much wider relevance. A Russian Marxist might justify this elitism on the grounds that the political backwardness of the Russian masses merely reflected the absence of the economic conditions necessary for fostering a truly socialist consciousness. But the experience of the working class in the West seemed to indicate that as economic conditions improved, the working class became more and more bourgeois and even less likely to behave in a selfless socialist fashion. Would not the guiding and educational role of the Party remain and even increase in this situation? In addition, was it not perfectly in keeping with the scientism, rationalism and social-engineering principles contained in the Marxist world view to utilize all available social institutions for this purpose? In fact, considering Lenin's suspicion of the "spontaneous" labor movement and his ardent rejection of western and Russian revisionism, one might argue that even if Russia had attained high levels of capitalist production before the Bolshevik Revolution, a system of totalitarian controls might have been undertaken in order to eradicate bourgeois attitudes and keep them from reappearing.

There are three other themes in Stalin's policies that are closely associated with Leninism. These are Stalin's "socialism in one country" program, his promotion of Russian nationalism, and his shift from Marxist determinism to "voluntarism." With regard to the first, when Lenin signed the treaty of Brest-Litovsk taking Russia out of the First World War and thereby undermined chances of a German socialist revolution, and when, realizing that there would be no such revolution in the West for a long time to come, he announced the New Economic Policy and the principles of a monolithic Party, Lenin was already saying in effect that Russia would either preserve and build upon its revolution independently or not at all. This reorientation from the program of world revolution (which regarded the Russian Revolution primarily as the spark for a socialist revolution in an advanced western country) to a program of building socialism in Russia without outside help was itself one cause for the intense nationalism and chauvinism that later characterized Stalin's reign. There were, of course, other and more important reasons for this revival of Russian nationalism. There was, above all, the need to rally the support of an essentially hostile population in order to meet the challenge of Nazi Germany. A loud and broad appeal to Russian national pride was one way of mitigating somewhat the intense hostility felt by the Russian people toward the Party during these years of industrialization, collectivization, forced labor camps and police terror.

In the realm of official ideology, Stalin is most famous for his remarkably daring emphasis on the "voluntarism" in Marxism at the expense of Marxist historical determinism. In virtually every area of life and thought a stress on individual will, action and responsibility took the place of the traditional Marxist concern with impersonal forces and with gradually evolving economic patterns and conditions that were believed to determine human behavior. At the end of the 1920's an important controversy occurred in the Party on the whole question of Marxist determinism. Bukharin ardently defended determinism, arguing that when Marxists organized a revolution they did so as an expression of prevailing economic conditions. Socialism, he insisted, came not as a result of individual will, but rather as a natural and inevitable outgrowth of capitalism. But what, then, of Lenin's Bolshevik Revolution? Lenin himself had insisted that "revolutions grow out of crises and turning points of history which mature objectively (independent of the will of a party or a class)." Other Marxists were not so sure. One of the earliest doubters was the Hungarian Marxist George Lukacs who stressed the role of power in revolution and, in fact, considered revolution as an expression of man's liberation from the realm of necessity that, according to Engels, would occur when socialism replaced capitalism. If one waited for the "immanent laws of economic development" to bring forth socialism, then it would never emerge, he argued.

In 1929, Stalin began to adopt this view in opposition to Bukharin, the leader of the "right" faction, the last remaining group standing between him and complete control of the Party. From this time on, the focus everywhere turned from environmental conditions to individual action and responsibility. In the writing of history, the orthodox Marxist view which emphasized mass movements, class relations and the ineluctable flow of economic history was replaced by a history of heroes that stressed above all the contributions of the great Russian Tsars. In psychology the importance of environmental conditioning gave way to personal choice and responsibility. In literature, this tendency found expression in the "positive hero," the Stalin-type man of boundless courage and will power, the activist, the builder, the leader in all walks of life. In the field of law, individual guilt and responsibility replaced a system of justice that was based on class origin of the accused and that considered civil law itself a bourgeois institution soon to wither away in the socialist society.

There are a number of reasons for this seemingly abrupt and radical change. In a country ruled by an elite party that was primarily concerned with fulfilling extravagant economic plans, it was necessary to emphasize constantly the personal responsibility of each individual in this great enterprise, to hold out examples in the press, speeches and literature of "heroes of labor" who faithfully met their obligations, and to punish those who failed to do so without tolerating extenuating circumstances involving "objective conditions."

The most important reason for this shift, however, is related to Lenin's political heritage. Throughout the Stalin era, Lenin's achievement in organizing the Revolution was extolled and Stalin's self-acclamation as a great leader, guide, and paternal protector attained its well-known insane proportions. Against the background of Lenin's "populist" seizure of power the significance of these eulogies of revolutionary leaders seems clear. It represents the theoretical justification of Lenin's Bolshevik Revolution as well as Stalin's own titanic efforts to achieve the industrialized economy that should have been attained before the Revolution. The actions of both Lenin and Stalin implied a complete reversal of the Marxist relationship between the political "superstructure" and the economic "substructure." Since a political revolution had succeeded before the economic conditions were ripe for socialism, the victorious Party, as Plekhanov had predicted, was forced to "retain the power it [had] seized in its own hands and on its own initiative undertake the organization of socialist production." In frank recognition of this doctrinal change Stalin wrote as early as 1926, that

the bourgeois revolution usually begins when there already exist more or less finished forms of the capitalist order, forms which have grown and ripened within the womb of feudal society prior to open revolution; whereas the proletarian revolution begins when finished forms of the socialist order are either absent or almost completely absent.

The main task of the bourgeois revolution consists in seizing power and making it conform to the already existing bourgeois economy, whereas the main task of the proletarian revolution

consists in seizing power in order to build up a new, socialist
economy.

The bourgeois revolution is usually consummated with the
seizure of power, whereas in the proletarian revolution the
seizure of power is only the beginning, and power is used as a
lever for transforming the old economy and organizing the new
one. . . .

After completing the first phases of industrialization and
collectivization, he was even more candid about the primacy of political power over economic processes:

In a period of eight to ten years we effected a transition in the
agriculture of our country from the bourgeois, individual-peasant
system to the socialist, collective-farm system. . . . But this revolution did not take place by means of an explosion, that is, by
the overthrow of the existing government power and the creation of a new power, but by a gradual transition from the old
bourgeois system in the countryside to a new system. And it
was possible to do that because it was a revolution from above,
because the revolution was accomplished on the initiative of the
existing power. . . .

In the following work by Stalin, *The Foundations of
Leninism,* the reader will find a comprehensive survey of
the principle themes in "orthodox" Stalinism. The selection
was originally presented as a series of lectures and published
in *Pravda* in April and May 1924. Notwithstanding the early
date of this work, it remained throughout the Stalin years
one of the standard, popular guides in indoctrinating official views on virtually all national and international issues.

Joseph Stalin

THE FOUNDATIONS OF LENINISM

The foundations of Leninism is a big subject. To exhaust it a whole volume would be required. Indeed, a number of volumes would be required. Naturally, therefore, my lectures cannot be an exhaustive exposition of Leninism; at best they can only offer a concise synopsis of the foundations of Leninism. Nevertheless, I consider it useful to give this synopsis, in order to lay down some basic points of departure necessary for the successful study of Leninism.

Expounding the foundations of Leninism still does not mean expounding the basis of Lenin's world outlook. Lenin's world outlook and the foundations of Leninism are not identical in scope. Lenin was a Marxist, and Marxism is, of course, the basis of his world outlook. But from this it does not at all follow that an exposition of Leninism ought to begin with an exposition of the foundations of Marxism. To expound Leninism means to expound the distinctive and new in the works of Lenin that Lenin contributed to the general treasury of Marxism and that is naturally connected with his name. Only in this sense will I speak in my lectures of the foundations of Leninism.

And so, what is Leninism?

Some say that Leninism is the application of Marxism to the conditions that are peculiar to the situation in Russia. This definition contains some truth, but not the whole truth by any means. Lenin, indeed, applied Marxism to Russian conditions, and applied it in a masterly way. But if Leninism were only the application of Marxism to the conditions that are peculiar to Russia it would be a purely national and only a national, a purely Russian and only a Russian, phenomenon. We know, however, that Leninism is not merely a Russian, but an international phenomenon rooted in the whole of international development. That is why I think this definition suffers from one-sidedness.

Others say that Leninism is the revival of the revolutionary elements of Marxism of the forties of the nineteenth century, as distinct from the Marxism of subsequent years, when, it is alleged, it became moderate, nonrevolutionary. If we disregard this foolish and vulgar division of the teachings of Marx into two parts, revolutionary and moderate, we must admit that even this totally inadequate and unsatisfactory definition contains a particle of truth. This particle of truth is that Lenin did indeed restore the revolutionary content of Marxism, which had been suppressed by the opportunists of the Second International. Still, that is but a particle of the truth. The whole truth about Leninism is that Leninism not only restored Marxism, but also took a step forward, developing Marxism further under the new conditions of capitalism and of the class struggle of the proletariat.

What, then, in the last analysis, is Leninism?

Leninism is Marxism in the era of imperialism and proletarian revolution. To be more exact, Leninism is the theory and tactics of the proletarian revolution in general and the theory and tactics of the dictatorship of the proletariat in particular. Marx and Engels pursued their activities in the prerevolutionary period (we have the proletarian revolution in mind), when developed imperialism did not yet exist, in the period of the proletarians' preparation for revolution, in the period when the proletarian revolution was not yet an immediate practical inevitability. But Lenin, the disciple of Marx and Engels, pursued his activities in the period of developed imperialism, in the period of the unfolding proletarian revolution, when the proletarian revolution had already triumphed in one country, had smashed bourgeois democracy and had ushered in the era of proletarian democracy, the era of the Soviets.

That is why Leninism is the further development of Marxism.

It is usual to point to the exceptionally militant and exceptionally revolutionary character of Leninism. This is quite correct. But this specific feature of Leninism is due to two causes: firstly, to the fact that Leninism emerged from the proletarian revolution, the imprint of which it cannot but bear; secondly, to the fact that it grew and became strong in clashes with the opportunism of the Second International, the fight against which was and remains an essential preliminary condition for a successful fight against capitalism. It must not be forgotten that between Marx and Engels, on the one hand, and Lenin, on the other, there lies a whole pe-

riod of undivided domination of Second International opportunism, and the ruthless struggle against this opportunism
could not but constitute one of the most important tasks of
Leninism.

I. THE HISTORICAL ROOTS OF LENINISM

Leninism grew up and took shape under the conditions
of imperialism, when the contradictions of capitalism had
reached an extreme point, when the proletarian revolution
had become an immediate practical question, when the former period of preparing the working class for revolution had
arrived at and passed into the new period, that of direct assault on capitalism.

Lenin called imperialism "moribund capitalism." Why?
Because imperialism carries the contradictions of capitalism
to their last bounds, to the extreme limit, beyond which
revolution begins. Of these contradictions, there are three
which must be regarded as the most important.

The *first contradiction* is the contradiction between labor
and capital. Imperialism is the omnipotence of the monopolist
trusts and syndicates, of the banks and the financial oligarchy, in the industrial countries. In the fight against this
omnipotence, the customary methods of the working class—
trade unions and co-operatives, parliamentary parties and
the parliamentary struggle—have proved to be totally inadequate. Either place yourself at the mercy of capital, eke out
a wretched existence as of old and sink lower and lower, or
adopt a new weapon—this is the alternative imperialism puts
before the vast masses of the proletariat. Imperialism leads
the working class to revolution.

The *second contradiction* is the contradiction among the
various financial groups and imperialist powers in their struggle for sources of raw materials, for foreign territory. Imperialism is the export of capital to the sources of raw materials,
the frenzied struggle for monopolist possession of these
sources, the struggle for a redivision of the already divided
world, a struggle waged with particular fury by new financial groups and powers seeking a "place in the sun" against
the old groups and powers, which cling tenaciously to what
they have seized. This frenzied struggle among the various
groups of capitalists is notable in that it includes as an in-

evitable element imperialist wars, wars for the annexation of foreign territories. This circumstance, in its turn, is notable in that it leads to the mutual weakening of the imperialists, to the weakening of the position of capitalism in general, to the acceleration of the advent of the proletarian revolution, and to the practical necessity of this revolution.

The *third contradiction* is the contradiction between the handful of ruling, "civilized" nations and the hundreds of millions of the colonial and dependent peoples of the world. Imperialism is the most barefaced exploitation and the most inhuman oppression of hundreds of millions of people inhabiting vast colonies and dependent countries. The purpose of this exploitation and this oppression is to squeeze out superprofits. But in exploiting these countries imperialism is compelled to build there railways, factories and mills, industrial and commercial centers. The appearance of a class of proletarians, the emergence of a native intelligentsia, the awakening of national consciousness, the growth of the liberation movement—such are the inevitable results of this "policy." The growth of the revolutionary movement in all colonies and dependent countries without exception clearly testifies to this fact. This circumstance is of importance for the proletariat inasmuch as it radically undermines the position of capitalism by converting the colonies and dependent countries from reserves of imperialism into reserves of the proletarian revolution.

Such, in general, are the principal contradictions of imperialism which have converted the old, "flourishing" capitalism into a moribund capitalism.

The significance of the imperialist war which broke out ten years ago lies, among other things, in the fact that it gathered all these contradictions into a single knot and threw them on the scales, thereby accelerating and facilitating the revolutionary battles of the proletariat.

In other words, imperialism not only made the revolution a practical inevitability; it also created favorable conditions for a direct assault on the citadels of capitalism.

Such was the international situation which gave birth to Leninism.

Some may say: this is all very well, but what has it to do with Russia, which was not and could not have been a classical land of imperialism? What has it to do with Lenin, who worked primarily in Russia and for Russia? Why did Russia, of all countries, become the home of Leninism, the birthplace of the theory and tactics of the proletarian revolution?

Because Russia was the focal point of all these contradictions of imperialism.

Because Russia, more than any other country, was pregnant with revolution, and she alone, therefore, was in a position to solve those contradictions in a revolutionary way.

To begin with, Tsarist Russia was the home of every kind of oppression—capitalist, colonial and militarist—in its most inhuman and barbarous form. Who does not know that in Russia the omnipotence of capital was combined with the despotism of tsarism, the aggressiveness of Russian nationalism with tsarism's role of executioner in regard to the non-Russian peoples, the exploitation of entire regions—Turkey, Persia, China—with the seizure of these regions by tsarism, with wars of conquest? Lenin was right in saying that tsarism was "military-feudal imperialism." Tsarism was the concentration of the worst features of imperialism, many times intensified.

To proceed. Tsarist Russia was a major reserve of Western imperialism, not only in the sense that it gave free entry to foreign capital, which controlled such basic branches of Russia's national economy as the fuel and metallurgical industries, but also in the sense that it could supply the Western imperialists with millions of soldiers. Remember the Russian army, fourteen million strong, which shed its blood on the imperialist fronts to safeguard the fantastic profits of the British and French capitalists.

Further, tsarism was not only the watchdog of imperialism in the east of Europe, but, in addition, it was the agent of Western imperialism for squeezing out of the population hundreds of millions by way of interest on loans obtained in Paris and London, Berlin and Brussels.

Finally, tsarism was a most faithful ally of Western imperialism in the partition of Turkey, Persia, China, etc. Who does not know that the imperialist war was waged by tsarism in alliance with the imperialists of the Entente, and that Russia was an essential element in that war?

That is why the interests of tsarism and Western imperialism were interwoven and ultimately became merged in a single skein of imperialist interests.

Could Western imperialism resign itself to the loss of such a powerful support in the East and such a rich reservoir of manpower and resources as old, tsarist, bourgeois Russia was without exerting all its strength to wage a life-and-death struggle against the revolution in Russia, with the object of defending and preserving tsarism? Of course not.

But from this it follows that whoever wanted to strike at tsarism necessarily raised his hand against imperialism, whoever rose against tsarism had to rise against imperialism as well; for whoever was bent on overthrowing tsarism had to overthrow imperialism too, if he really intended not merely to defeat tsarism, but to make a clean sweep of it. Thus the revolution against tsarism verged on and had to pass into a revolution against imperialism, into a proletarian revolution.

Meanwhile, in Russia a tremendous popular revolution was rising, headed by the most revolutionary proletariat in the world, which possessed so important an ally as the revolutionary peasantry of Russia. Does it need proof that such a revolution could not stop halfway, that in the event of success it was bound to advance further and raise the banner of revolt against imperialism?

That is why Russia was bound to become the focal point of the contradictions of imperialism, not only in the sense that it was in Russia that these contradictions were revealed most plainly, in view of their particularly repulsive and particularly intolerable character, and not only because Russia was a highly important prop of Western imperialism, connecting Western finance capital with the colonies in the East, but also because Russia was the only country in which there existed a real force capable of resolving the contradictions of imperialism in a revolutionary way.

From this it follows, however, that the revolution in Russia could not but become a proletarian revolution, that from its very inception it could not but assume an international character, and that, therefore, it could not but shake the very foundations of world imperialism.

Under these circumstances, could the Russian Communists confine their work within the narrow national bounds of the Russian revolution? Of course not. On the contrary, the whole situation, both internal (the profound revolutionary crisis) and external (the war), impelled them to go beyond these bounds in their work, to transfer the struggle to the international arena, to expose the ulcers of imperialism, to prove that the collapse of capitalism was inevitable, to smash social-chauvinism and social-pacifism, and, finally, to overthrow capitalism in their own country and to forge a new fighting weapon for the proletariat—the theory and tactics of the proletarian revolution—in order to facilitate the task of overthrowing capitalism for the proletarians of all countries. Nor could the Russian Communists act otherwise, for only by this path was it possible to count on certain changes in the international situation which could safeguard Russia against the restoration of the bourgeois order.

That is why Russia became the home of Leninism, and why Lenin, the leader of the Russian Communists, became its creator.

The same thing, approximately, "happened" in the case of Russia and Lenin as in the case of Germany and Marx and Engels in the forties of the last century. Germany at that time was pregnant with bourgeois revolution just like Russia at the beginning of the twentieth century. Marx wrote at that time in the *Communist Manifesto*:

> The Communists turn their attention chiefly to Germany, because that country is on the eve of a bourgeois revolution that is bound to be carried out under more advanced conditions of European civilization, and with a much more developed proletariat than that of England in the seventeenth century. The bourgeois revolution in Germany, consequently, may be but the immediate prelude to the proletarian revolution.

In other words, the center of the revolutionary movement was shifting to Germany.

There can hardly be any doubt that it was this very circumstance, noted by Marx in the above-quoted passage, that served as the probable reason why it was precisely Germany that became the birthplace of scientific socialism and why the leaders of the German proletariat, Marx and Engels, became its creators.

The same, only to a still greater degree, must be said of Russia at the beginning of the twentieth century. Russia was then on the eve of a bourgeois revolution. She had to accomplish this revolution at a time when conditions in Europe were more advanced, and do so with a proletariat that was more developed than that of Germany in the forties of the nineteenth century (let alone Britain and France). Moreover, all the evidence indicated that this revolution was bound to serve as a ferment and as a prelude to the proletarian revolution.

We cannot regard it as accidental that as early as 1902, when the Russian revolution had only just begun, Lenin wrote the prophetic words in his pamphlet *What Is to Be Done?*:

> History has now confronted us (*i.e.*, the Russian Marxists—J. S.) with an immediate task which is the *most revolutionary* of all the *immediate* tasks that confront the proletariat of any country.
>
> . . . The fulfillment of this task, the destruction of the most powerful bulwark, not only of European, but also (it may now be said) of Asiatic reaction, would make the Russian proletariat the vanguard of the international revolutionary proletariat. (See Vol. IV, p. 382.)

In other words, the center of the revolutionary movement was bound to shift to Russia.

As we know, the course of the revolution in Russia has more than vindicated Lenin's prediction.

Is it surprising, after all this, that a country which has accomplished such a revolution and possesses such a proletariat should have been the birthplace of the theory and tactics of the proletarian revolution?

Is it surprising that Lenin, the leader of Russia's proletariat, became also the creator of this theory and tactics and the leader of the international proletariat?

II. METHOD

I have already said that between Marx and Engels, on the one hand, and Lenin, on the other, there lies a whole period of domination of Second International opportunism. For the sake of exactitude I must add that it is not the formal domination of opportunism I have in mind, but only its actual domination. Formally, the Second International was headed by "faithful" Marxists, by the "orthodox"—Kautsky and others. Actually, however, the main work of the Second International followed the line of opportunism. The opportunists adapted themselves to the bourgeoisie because of their adaptive, petty-bourgeois nature; the "orthodox," in their turn, adapted themselves to the opportunists in order to "preserve unity" with them, in the interests of "peace within the party." Thus the link between the policy of the bourgeoisie and the policy of the "orthodox" was closed, and, as a result, opportunism reigned supreme.

This was the period of the relatively peaceful development of capitalism, the prewar period, so to speak, when the catastrophic contradictions of imperialism had not yet become so glaringly evident, when workers' economic strikes and trade unions were developing more or less "normally," when election campaigns and parliamentary groups yielded "dizzying" successes, when legal forms of struggle were lauded to the skies, and when it was thought that capitalism would be "killed" by legal means—in short, when the parties of the Second International grew fat and had no inclination to think seriously about revolution, about the dictatorship of the proletariat, about the revolutionary education of the masses.

Instead of an integral revolutionary theory, there were contradictory theoretical postulates and fragments of theory, which were divorced from the actual revolutionary struggle of the masses and had been turned into threadbare dogmas. For the sake of appearances, Marx's theory was mentioned, of course, but only to rob it of its living, revolutionary spirit.

Instead of a revolutionary policy, there was flabby philistinism and sordid political bargaining, parliamentary diplomacy and parliamentary scheming. For the sake of appearances, of course, "revolutionary" resolutions and slogans were adopted, but only to be pigeonholed.

Instead of the party being trained and taught correct revolutionary tactics on the basis of its own mistakes, there was a studied evasion of vexing questions, which were glossed over and veiled. For the sake of appearances, of course, there was no objection to talking about vexing questions, but only in order to wind up with some sort of "elastic" resolution.

Such was the physiognomy of the Second International, its method of work, its arsenal.

Meanwhile, a new period of imperialist wars and revolutionary battles of the proletariat was approaching. The old methods of fighting were proving obviously inadequate and impotent before the omnipotence of finance capital.

It became necessary to overhaul the entire activity of the Second International, its entire method of work, and to drive out all philistinism, narrow-mindedness, political scheming, renegade activities, social-chauvinism and social-pacifism. It became necessary to examine the entire arsenal of the Second International, to throw out all that was rusty and antiquated, to forge new types of weapons. Without this preliminary work it was useless embarking upon war against capitalism. Without this work the proletariat ran the risk of finding itself inadequately armed, or even completely unarmed, in the future revolutionary battles.

The honor of bringing about this general overhauling and general cleansing of the Augean stables of the Second International fell to Leninism.

Such were the conditions under which the method of Leninism was born and hammered out.

What are the requirements of this method?

Firstly, the *testing* of the theoretical dogmas of the Second International in the crucible of the revolutionary struggle of the masses, in the crucible of living practice—that is to say, the restoration of the broken unity between theory and practice, the healing of the rift between them; for only in this way can a truly proletarian party armed with revolutionary theory be created.

Secondly, the *testing* of the policy of the parties of the Second International, not by their slogans and resolutions (which cannot be trusted), but by their deeds, by their actions; for only in this way can the confidence of the proletarian masses be won and deserved.

Thirdly, the *reorganization* of all Party work on new revolutionary lines, with a view to training and preparing the masses for the revolutionary struggle; for only in this way can the masses be prepared for the proletarian revolution.

Fourthly, *self-criticism* within the proletarian parties, their education and training on the basis of their own mistakes: for only in this way can genuine cadres and genuine leaders of the Party be trained.

Such is the basis and substance of the method of Leninism.

How was this method applied in practice?

The opportunists of the Second International have a number of theoretical dogmas to which they always revert as their starting point. Let us take a few of these.

First dogma: concerning the conditions for the seizure of power by the proletariat. The opportunists assert that the proletariat cannot and ought not to take power unless it constitutes a majority in the country. No proofs are brought forward, for there are no proofs, either theoretical or practical, that can bear out this absurd thesis. Let us assume that this is so, Lenin replies to the gentlemen of the Second International. Well, suppose a historical situation has

arisen (a war, an agrarian crisis, etc.) in which the proletariat, constituting a minority of the population, has an opportunity to rally around itself the vast majority of the laboring masses; why should it not take power then? Why
should the proletariat not take advantage of a favorable international and internal situation to pierce the front of capital and hasten the general denouement? Did not Marx say
as far back as the fifties of the last century that things
could go "splendidly" with the proletarian revolution in
Germany were it possible to back it by, so to speak, a "second edition of the Peasant War"? Is it not a generally known
fact that in those days the number of proletarians in Germany was relatively smaller than, for example, in Russia
in 1917? Has not the practical experience of the Russian
proletarian revolution shown that this favorite dogma of the
heroes of the Second International is devoid of all vital
significance for the proletariat? Is it not clear that the
practical experience of the revolutionary struggle of the
masses refutes and smashes this obsolete dogma?

Second dogma: the proletariat cannot retain power if it
lacks an adequate number of trained cultural and administrative cadres capable of organizing the administration of the
country; these cadres must first be trained under capitalist
conditions, and only then can power be taken. Let us assume
that this is so, replies Lenin. But why not turn it this way:
first take power, create favorable conditions for the development of the proletariat, and then proceed with seven-league
strides to raise the cultural level of the laboring masses
and train numerous cadres of leaders and administrators from
among the workers? Has not Russian experience shown that
cadres of leaders recruited from the ranks of the workers
develop a hundred times more rapidly and effectually under
the rule of the proletariat than under the rule of capital?
Is it not clear that the practical experience of the revolutionary struggle of the masses ruthlessly smashes this theoretical dogma of the opportunists too?

Third dogma: the proletariat cannot accept the method
of the *political* general strike because it is unsound in
theory (see Engels' criticism) and dangerous in practice
(it may disturb the normal course of economic life in the
country, it may deplete the coffers of the trade unions);
it cannot serve as a substitute for parliamentary forms of
struggle, which are the principal form of the class struggle
of the proletariat. Very well, reply the Leninists. But, firstly,

Engels did not criticize every kind of general strike. He only criticized a certain kind of general strike, namely, the *economic* general strike advocated by the anarchists *in place of* the political struggle of the proletariat. What has this to do with the method of the *political* general strike? Secondly, where and by whom has it ever been proved that the parliamentary form of struggle is the principal form of struggle of the proletariat? Does not the history of the revolutionary movement show that the parliamentary struggle is only an auxiliary school for organizing the extraparliamentary struggle of the proletariat, that under capitalism the fundamental problems of the working-class movement are solved by force, by the direct struggle of the proletarian masses, their general strike, their uprising? Thirdly, who suggested that the method of the political general strike be substituted for the parliamentary struggle? Where and when have the supporters of the political general strike sought to substitute extraparliamentary forms of struggle for parliamentary forms? Fourthly, has not the revolution in Russia shown that the *political* general strike is a highly important school for the proletarian revolution and an indispensable means of mobilizing and organizing the vast masses of the proletariat on the eve of storming the citadels of capitalism? Why then the philistine lamentations over the disturbance of the normal course of economic life and over the coffers of the trade unions? Is it not clear that the practical experience of the revolutionary struggle smashes this dogma of the opportunists too?

And so on and so forth.

That is why Lenin said that "revolutionary theory is not a dogma," that it "assumes final shape only in close connection with the practical activity of a truly mass and truly revolutionary movement" (*"Left-Wing" Communism*); for theory must serve practice, for "theory must answer the questions raised by practice" (*What the "Friends of the People" Are*), for it must be tested by practical results.

As to the political slogans and the political resolutions of the parties of the Second International, it is sufficient to recall the history of the slogan "war against war" to realize how utterly false and utterly rotten are the political practices of these parties, which use pompous revolutionary slogans and resolutions to cloak their antirevolutionary deeds. We all remember the pompous demonstration of the Second International at the Basle Congress, at which it threatened the imperialists with all the horrors of insurrection if they should dare to start a war, and with the menacing slogan "war against war." But who does not remember that some time after, on the very eve of the war, the Basle resolution was pigeonholed and the workers were given a new slogan—to exterminate each other for the glory of their capitalist fatherlands? Is it not clear that revolutionary slogans and resolutions are not worth a cent unless backed by deeds? One need only contrast the Leninist policy of transforming the imperialist war into civil war with the treacherous policy of the Second International during the war to understand the utter baseness of the opportunist politicians and the full grandeur of the method of Leninism.

I cannot refrain from quoting at this point a passage from Lenin's book *The Proletarian Revolution and the Renegade Kautsky,* in which Lenin severely castigates an opportunist attempt by the leader of the Second International, K. Kautsky, to judge parties not by their deeds, but by their paper slogans and documents:

Kautsky is pursuing a typically petty-bourgeois, philistine policy by imagining . . . that *putting forward a slogan* alters the situation. The entire history of bourgeois democracy refutes this illusion; the bourgeois democrats have always advanced and still advance all sorts of "slogans" in order to deceive the people. The point is to *test* their sincerity, to compare their words with their *deeds,* not to be satisfied with idealistic or charlatan *phrases,* but to get down to *class reality.* (See Vol. XXIII, p. 377.)

There is no need to mention the fear the parties of the Second International have of self-criticism, their habit of concealing their mistakes, of glossing over vexing questions, of covering up their shortcomings by a deceptive show of well-being which blunts living thought and prevents the Party from deriving revolutionary training from its own mistakes—a habit which was ridiculed and pilloried by Lenin. Here is what Lenin wrote about self-criticism in proletarian parties in his pamphlet *"Left-Wing" Communism*:

The attitude of a political party towards its own mistakes is one of the most important and surest ways of judging how earnest the party is and how it *in practice* fulfills its obligations towards its *class* and the laboring *masses.* Frankly admitting a mistake, ascertaining the reasons for it, analyzing the circumstances which gave rise to it, and thoroughly discussing the means of correcting it—that is the earmark of a serious party; that is the way it should perform its duties, that is the way it should educate and train the *class*, and then the *masses*. (See Vol. XXV, p. 200.)

Some say that the exposure of its own mistakes and self-criticism are dangerous for the Party because they may be used by the enemy against the party of the proletariat. Lenin regarded such objections as trivial and entirely wrong. Here is what he wrote on this subject as far back as 1904, in his pamphlet *One Step Forward*, when our Party was still weak and small:

They (*i.e.*, the opponents of the Marxists—*J. S.*) gloat and smirk over our controversies; and, of course, they will try to pick isolated passages from my pamphlet, which deals with the defects and shortcomings of our Party, and use them for their own ends. The Russian Social Democrats are already steeled enough in battle not to be perturbed by these pinpricks and to continue, in spite of them, their work of self-criticism and ruthless exposure of their own shortcomings, which will unquestionably and inevitably be overcome as the working-class movement grows. (See Vol. VI, p. 161.)

Such, in general, are the characteristic features of the method of Leninism.

What is contained in Lenin's method was in the main already contained in the teachings of Marx, which, according to Marx himself, were "in essence critical and revolutionary." It is precisely this critical and revolutionary spirit that pervades Lenin's method from beginning to end. But it would be wrong to suppose that Lenin's method is merely the restoration of the method of Marx. As a matter of fact, Lenin's method is not only the restoration, but also the concretization and further development of the critical and revolutionary method of Marx, of his materialist dialectics.

III. THEORY

From this theme I take three topics:
a) the significance of theory for the proletarian movement;
b) criticism of the "theory" of spontaneity;
c) the theory of the proletarian revolution.

1) *The significance of theory.* Some think that Leninism is the precedence of practice over theory in the sense that its main point is the translation of Marxist theses into deeds, their "execution"; as for theory, it is alleged that Leninism is rather unconcerned about it. We know that Plekhanov time and again chaffed Lenin about his "unconcern" for theory, and particularly for philosophy. We also know that theory is not held in great favor by many present-day Leninist practical workers, particularly in view of the immense amount of practical work imposed upon them by the situation. I must declare that this more than odd opinion about Lenin and Leninism is quite wrong and bears no relation whatever to the truth and that the attempt of practical workers to brush theory aside runs counter to the whole spirit of Leninism and is fraught with serious dangers to the work.

Theory is the experience of the working-class movement in all countries taken in its general aspect. Of course, theory becomes purposeless if it is not connected with revolutionary practice, just as practice gropes in the dark if its path is not illumined by revolutionary theory. But theory can become a tremendous force in the working-class movement if it is built up in indissoluble connection with revolutionary practice; for theory, and theory alone, can give the movement confidence, the power of orientation, and an understanding of the inner relation of surrounding events; for it, and it alone, can help practice to realize not only how and in which direction classes are moving at the present time, but also how and in which direction they will move in the near future. None other than Lenin said and repeated scores of times the well-known thesis that:

Without a revolutionary theory there can be no revolutionary movement.[1] (See Vol. IV, p. 380.)

Lenin, better than anyone else, understood the great importance of theory, particularly for a party such as ours, in view of the role of vanguard fighter of the international proletariat which has fallen to its lot, and in view of the complicated internal and international situation in which it finds itself. Foreseeing this special role of our Party as far back as 1902, he thought it necessary even then to point out that:

*The role of vanguard fighter can be fulfilled only by a party
that is guided by the most advanced theory.* (See Vol. IV, p.
380.)

It scarcely needs proof that now, when Lenin's prediction
about the role of our Party has come true, this thesis of
Lenin's acquires special force and special importance.

Perhaps the most striking expression of the great importance which Lenin attached to theory is the fact that none
other than Lenin undertook the very serious task of generalizing, on the basis of materialist philosophy, the most
important achievements of science from the time of Engels
down to his own time, as well as of subjecting to comprehensive criticism the antimaterialistic trends among
Marxists. Engels said that "materialism must assume a new
aspect with every new great discovery." It is well known
that none other than Lenin accomplished this task for his
own time in his remarkable work *Materialism and Empirio-
Criticism.* It is well known that Plekhanov, who loved to
chaff Lenin about his "unconcern" for philosophy, did not
even dare to make a serious attempt to undertake such a
task.

2) *Criticism of the "theory" of spontaneity, or the role of
the vanguard in the movement.* The "theory" of spontaneity
is a theory of opportunism, a theory of worshiping the
spontaneity of the labor movement, a theory which actually
repudiates the leading role of the vanguard of the working
class, the party of the working class.

The theory of worshiping spontaneity is decidedly opposed to the revolutionary character of the working-class
movement; it is opposed to the movement taking the line of
struggle against the foundations of capitalism; it is in favor
of the movement proceeding exclusively along the line of
"realizable" demands, of demands "acceptable" to capitalism; it is wholly in favor of the "line of least resistance."
The theory of spontaneity is the ideology of trade unionism.

The theory of worshiping spontaneity is decidedly opposed to giving the spontaneous movement a politically con-
cious, planned character. It is opposed to the Party marching
at the head of the working class, to the Party raising the
masses to the level of political consciousness, to the Party
leading the movement. It is in favor of the politically conscious elements of the movement not hindering the movement from taking its own course; it is in favor of the Party

only heeding the spontaneous movement and dragging at the tail of it. The theory of spontaneity is the theory of belittling the role of the conscious element in the movement, the ideology of "tailism" (*khvostism*); the logical basis of *all* opportunism.

In practice this theory, which appeared on the scene even before the first revolution [2] in Russia, led its adherents, the so-called "Economists," to deny the need for an independent workers' party in Russia, to oppose the revolutionary struggle of the working class for the overthrow of tsarism, to preach a purely trade-unionist policy in the movement, and, in general, to surrender the labor movement to the hegemony of the liberal bourgeoisie.

The fight of the old *Iskra* [3] and the brilliant criticism of the theory of "tailism" in Lenin's pamphlet *What Is to Be Done?* not only smashed so-called "Economism," but also created the theoretical foundations for a truly revolutionary movement of the Russian working class.

Without this fight it would have been quite useless even to think of creating an independent workers' party in Russia and of its playing a leading part in the revolution.

But the theory of worshiping spontaneity is not an exclusively Russian phenomenon. It is extremely widespread— in a somewhat different form, it is true—in all the parties of the Second International, without exception. I have in mind the so-called "productive forces" theory as debased by the leaders of the Second International, which justifies everything and conciliates everybody, which records facts and explains them after everyone has become sick and tired of them, and, having recorded them, rests content. Marx said that the materialist theory could not confine itself to explaining the world, that it must also change it. But Kautsky and Co. are not concerned with this; they prefer to rest content with the first part of Marx's formula.

Here is one of the numerous examples of the application of this "theory." It is said that before the imperialist war the parties of the Second International threatened to declare "war against war" if the imperialists should start a war. It is said that on the very eve of the war these parties pigeonholed the "war against war" slogan and applied an opposite one, *viz.*, "war for the imperialist fatherland." It is said that as a result of this change of slogans millions of workers were sent to their death. But it would be a mistake to think that there were some people to blame for this, that someone was unfaithful to the working class or betrayed it. Not at all! Everything happened as it should have happened. Firstly, because the International, it seems, is "an instrument of peace," and not of war. Secondly, because, in view of the "level of the productive forces" which then prevailed, nothing else could be done. The "productive forces" are "to blame." That is the precise explanation vouchsafed to "us" by Mr. Kautsky's "theory of the productive forces." And whoever does not believe in that "theory" is not a Marxist. The role of the parties? Their importance for the movement? But what can a party do against so decisive a factor as the "level of the productive forces"? . . .

One could cite a host of similar examples of the falsification of Marxism.

It scarcely needs proof that this spurious "Marxism," designed to hide the nakedness of opportunism, is merely a European variety of the same theory of "tailism" which Lenin fought even before the first Russian revolution.

It scarcely needs proof that the demolition of this theoretical falsification is a preliminary condition for the creation of truly revolutionary parties in the West.

3) *The theory of the proletarian revolution.* Lenin's theory of the proletarian revolution proceeds from three fundamental theses.

First thesis: The domination of finance capital in the advanced capitalist countries; the issue of stocks and bonds as one of the principal operations of finance capital; the export of capital to the sources of raw materials, which is one of the foundations of imperialism; the omnipotence of a financial oligarchy, which is the result of the domination of finance capital—all this reveals the grossly parasitic character of monopolist capitalism, makes the yoke of the capitalist trusts and syndicates a hundred times more burdensome, intensifies the indignation of the working class against the foundations of capitalism, and leads the masses to proletarian revolution as their only salvation. (See Lenin, *Imperialism.*)

Hence the first conclusion: intensification of the revolutionary crisis within the capitalist countries and growth of explosive elements on the internal, proletarian front in the "metropolises."

Second thesis: The increase in the export of capital to the colonies and dependent countries; the expansion of "spheres of influence" and colonial possessions until they cover the whole globe; the transformation of capitalism into a *world system* of financial enslavement and colonial oppression of the vast majority of the population of the world by a handful of "advanced" countries—all this has, on the one hand, converted the separate national economies and national territories into links in a single chain called world economy, and, on the other hand, split the population of the globe into two camps: a handful of "advanced" capitalist countries which exploit and oppress vast colonies and dependencies, and the huge majority consisting of colonial and dependent countries which are compelled to wage a struggle for liberation from the imperialist yoke. (See *Imperialism*.)

Hence the second conclusion: intensification of the revolutionary crisis in the colonial countries and growth of the elements of revolt against imperialism on the external, colonial front.

Third thesis. The monopolistic possession of "spheres of influence" and colonies; the uneven development of the capitalist countries, leading to a frenzied struggle for the redivision of the world between the countries which have already seized territories and those claiming their "share"; imperialist wars as the only means of restoring the disturbed "equilibrium"—all this leads to the intensification of the struggle on the third front, the intercapitalist front, which weakens imperialism and facilitates the union of the first two fronts against imperialism, the front of the revolutionary proletariat and the front of colonial emancipation. (See *Imperialism*.)

Hence the third conclusion: that under imperialism wars cannot be averted, and that a coalition between the proletarian revolution in Europe and the colonial revolution in the East in a united world front of revolution against the world front of imperialism is inevitable.

Lenin combines all these conclusions into one general conclusion that *"imperialism is the eve of the socialist revolution."*[4] (See Vol. XIX, p. 71.)

The very approach to the question of the proletarian revolution, of the character of the revolution, its scope and its depth, of the pattern of the revolution in general, changes accordingly.

Formerly, the analysis of the prerequisites for the proletarian revolution was usually approached from the point of view of the economic state of individual countries. Now, this approach is no longer adequate. Now the matter must be approached from the point of view of the economic state of all or the majority of countries, from the point of view of the state of the world economy; for individual countries and individual national economies have ceased to be self-sufficient units and have become links in a single chain called world economy; for the old "cultured" capitalism has evolved into imperialism, and imperialism is a world system of financial enslavement and colonial oppression of the vast majority of the population of the world by a handful of "advanced" countries.

Formerly it was the accepted thing to speak of the existence or absence of objective conditions for the proletarian revolution in individual countries, or, to be more precise, in one or another developed country. Now this point of view is no longer adequate. Now we must speak of the existence of objective conditions for revolution in the entire system of the world imperialist economy as an integral whole. Moreover, the existence within this system of some countries that are not sufficiently developed industrially cannot serve as an insuperable obstacle to the revolution, *if* the system as a whole or, more correctly, *since* the system as a whole is already ripe for revolution.

Formerly it was the accepted thing to speak of the proletarian revolution in one or another developed country as of a separate and self-sufficient entity opposing a separate national front of capital as its antipode. Now, this point of view is no longer adequate. Now we must speak of the world proletarian revolution; for the separate national fronts of capital have become links in a single chain called the world front of imperialism, which must be opposed by a common front of the revolutionary movement in all countries.

Formerly the proletarian revolution was regarded exclusively as the result of the internal development of a given country. Now, this point of view is no longer adequate. Now the proletarian revolution must be regarded primarily as the result of the development of the contradictions within the world system of imperialism, as the result of the breaking of the chain of the world imperialist front in one country or another.

Where will the revolution begin? Where, in what country, can the front of capital be pierced first?

Where industry is more developed, where the proletariat constitutes the majority, where there is more culture, where there is more democracy—that was the reply usually given formerly.

No, objects the Leninist theory of revolution, *not neces-sarily where industry is more developed*, and so forth. The front of capital will be pierced where the chain of imperialism is weakest, for the proletarian revolution is the result of the breaking of the chain of the world imperialist front at its weakest link; and it may turn out that the country which has started the revolution, which has made a breach in the front of capital, is less developed in a capitalist sense than other, more developed, countries, which have, however, remained within the framework of capitalism.

In 1917 the chain of the imperialist world front proved to be weaker in Russia than in the other countries. It was there that the chain broke and provided an outlet for the proletarian revolution. Why? Because in Russia a great popular revolution was unfolding, and at its head marched the revolutionary proletariat, which had such an important ally as the vast mass of the peasantry, oppressed and exploited by the land-lords. Because the revolution there was opposed by such a hideous representative of imperialism as tsarism, which lacked all moral prestige and was deservedly hated by the whole population. The chain proved to be weaker in Russia, although Russia was less developed in a capitalist sense than, say, France or Germany, Britain or America.

Where will the chain break in the near future? Again, where it is weakest. It is not precluded that the chain may break, say, in India. Why? Because that country has a young, militant, revolutionary proletariat, which has such an ally as the national liberation movement—an undoubtedly powerful and undoubtedly important ally. Because there the revolution is confronted by such a well-known foe as foreign imperial-ism, which has no moral credit and is deservedly hated by all the oppressed and exploited masses of India.

It is also quite possible that the chain will break in Ger-many. Why? Because the factors which are operating, say, in India are beginning to operate in Germany as well; but, of course, the enormous difference in the level of development between India and Germany cannot but stamp its imprint on the progress and outcome of a revolution in Germany.

That is why Lenin said that:

The West-European capitalist countries will consummate their development towards socialism . . . not by the even "maturing" of socialism in them, but by the exploitation of some countries by others, by the exploitation of the first of the countries to be vanquished in the imperialist war combined with the exploitation of the whole of the East. On the other hand, precisely as a result of the first imperialist war, the East has definitely come into revolutionary movement, has been definitely drawn into the general maelstrom of the world revolutionary movement. (See Vol. XXVII, pp. 415-16.)

Briefly: the chain of the imperialist front must, as a rule, break where the links are weaker and, at all events, not necessarily where capitalism is more developed, where there is such and such a percentage of proletarians and such and such a percentage of peasants, and so on.

That is why in deciding the question of proletarian revolution statistical estimates of the percentage of the proletarian population in a given country lose the exceptional importance so eagerly attached to them by the doctrinaires of the Second International, who have not understood imperialism and who fear revolution like the plague.

To proceed. The heroes of the Second International asserted (and continue to assert) that between the bourgeois-democratic revolution and the proletarian revolution there is a chasm, or at any rate a Chinese Wall, separating one from the other by a more or less protracted interval of time, during which the bourgeoisie having come into power, develops capitalism, while the proletariat accumulates strength and prepares for the "decisive struggle" against capitalism. This interval is usually calculated to extend over many decades, if not longer. It scarcely needs proof that this Chinese Wall "theory" is totally devoid of scientific meaning under the conditions of imperialism, that it is and can only be a means of concealing and camouflaging the counterrevolutionary aspirations of the bourgeoisie. It scarcely needs proof that under the conditions of imperialism, fraught as it is with collisions and wars, under the conditions of the "eve of the socialist revolution," when "flourishing" capitalism becomes "moribund" capitalism (Lenin) and the revolutionary movement is growing in all countries of the world; when imperialism is allying itself with all reactionary forces without exception, down to and including tsarism and serfdom, thus making imperative the coalition of all revolutionary forces, from the proletarian movement of the West to the national liberation movement of the East; when the overthrow of the survivals of the regime of feudal serfdom becomes impossible without a revolutionary struggle against imperialism—

it scarcely needs proof that the bourgeois-democratic revolution, in a more or less developed country, must under such circumstances verge upon the proletarian revolution, that the former must pass into the latter. The history of the revolution in Russia has provided palpable proof that this thesis is correct and incontrovertible. It was not without reason that Lenin, as far back as 1905, on the eve of the first Russian revolution, in his pamphlet *Two Tactics* depicted the bourgeois-democratic revolution and the socialist revolution as two links in the same chain, as a single and integral picture of the sweep of the Russian revolution:

The proletariat must carry to completion the democratic revolution, by allying to itself the mass of the peasantry in order to crush by force the resistance of the autocracy and to paralyze the instability of the bourgeoisie. The proletariat must accomplish the socialist revolution, by allying to itself the mass of the semiproletarian elements of the population in order to crush by force the resistance of the bourgeoisie and to paralyze the instability of the peasantry and the petty bourgeoisie. Such are the tasks of the proletariat, which the new *Iskra*-ists present so narrowly in all their arguments and resolutions about the sweep of the revolution. (See Lenin, Vol. VIII, p. 96.)

There is no need to mention other, later works of Lenin's, in which the idea of the bourgeois revolution passing into the proletarian revolution stands out in greater relief than in *Two Tactics* as one of the cornerstones of the Leninist theory of revolution.

Some comrades believe, it seems, that Lenin arrived at this idea only in 1916, that up to that time he had thought that the revolution in Russia would remain within the bourgeois framework, that power, consequently, would pass from the hands of the organ of the dictatorship of the proletariat and peasantry into the hands of the bourgeoisie and not of the proletariat. It is said that this assertion has even penetrated into our communist press. I must say that this assertion is absolutely wrong, that it is totally at variance with the facts.

I might refer to Lenin's well-known speech at the Third Congress of the Party (1905), in which he defined the dictatorship of the proletariat and peasantry, *i.e.,* the victory of the democratic revolution, not as the "organization of 'order'" but as the "organization of war." (See Vol. VII, p. 264.)

Further, I might refer to Lenin's well-known article "On a Provisional Government" (1905), where, outlining the prospects of the unfolding Russian revolution, he assigns to the Party the task of "ensuring that the Russian revolution is not a movement of a few months, but a movement of many years, that it leads, not merely to slight concessions on the part of the powers that be, but to the complete overthrow of those powers." Enlarging further on these prospects and linking them with the revolution in Europe, he goes on here to say:

And if we succeed in doing that, then . . . then the revolutionary conflagration will spread all over Europe. The European worker, languishing under bourgeois reaction, will rise in his turn and will show us "how it is done." Then the revolutionary wave in Europe will sweep back again into Russia and will convert an epoch of a few revolutionary years into an epoch of several revolutionary decades. . . . (*Ibid.*, p. 191.)

I might further refer to a well-known article by Lenin published in November 1915, in which he writes:

The proletariat is fighting, and will fight valiantly, for the conquest of power, for a republic, for the confiscation of the land . . . for the participation of the "*non*proletarian masses of the people" in the liberation of *bourgeois* Russia from *military-feudal* "imperialism" (=tsarism). And the proletariat will *immediately* [5] take advantage of this liberation of bourgeois Russia from tsarism, from the agrarian power of the landlords, not to aid the rich peasants in their struggle against the rural worker, but to bring about the socialist revolution in alliance with the proletarians of Europe. (See Vol. XVIII, p. 318.)

Finally, I might refer to the well-known passage in Lenin's pamphlet *The Proletarian Revolution and the Renegade Kautsky,* where, referring to the above-quoted passage in *Two Tactics* on the sweep of the Russian revolution, he arrives at the following conclusion:

Things turned out just as we said they would. The course taken by the revolution confirmed the correctness of our reasoning. *First,* with the "whole" of the peasantry against the monarchy, against the landlords, against the medieval regime (and to that extent the revolution remains bourgeois, bourgeois-democratic). *Then,* with the poor peasants, with the semiproletarians, with all the exploited, *against capitalism,* including the rural rich, the kulaks, the profiteers, and to that extent the revolution becomes a *socialist* one. To attempt to raise an artificial Chinese Wall between the first and second, to separate them by anything else *than* the degree of preparedness of the proletariat and the degree of its unity with the poor peasants, means monstrously to distort Marxism, to vulgarize it, to replace it by liberalism. (See Vol. XXIII, p. 391.)

That is sufficient, I think.

Very well, we may be told; but if that is the case, why did Lenin combat the idea of "permanent (uninterrupted) revolution"? [6]

Because Lenin proposed that the revolutionary capacities of the peasantry be "exhausted" and that the fullest use be made of their revolutionary energy for the complete liquidation of tsarism and for the transition to the proletarian revolution, whereas the adherents of "permanent revolution" did not understand the important role of the peasantry in the Russian revolution, underestimated the strength of the revolutionary energy of the peasantry, underestimated the strength and ability of the Russian proletariat to lead the peasantry, and thereby hampered the work of emancipating the peasantry from the influence of the bourgeoisie, the work of rallying the peasantry around the proletariat.

Because Lenin proposed that the revolution *be crowned* with the transfer of power to the proletariat, whereas the adherents of "permanent" revolution wanted *to begin* at once with the establishment of the power of the proletariat, failing to realize that in so doing they were closing their eyes to such a "minor detail" as the survivals of serfdom and were leaving out of account so important a force as the Russian peasantry, failing to understand that such a policy could only retard the winning of the peasantry over to the side of the proletariat.

Consequently, Lenin fought the adherents of "permanent" revolution, not over the question of uninterruptedness, for Lenin himself maintained the point of view of uninterrupted revolution, but because they underestimated the role of the peasantry, which is an enormous reserve of the proletariat, because they failed to understand the idea of the hegemony of the proletariat.

The idea of "permanent" revolution should not be regarded as a new idea. It was first advanced by Marx at the end of the forties in his well-known *Address* to the *Communist League* (1850). It is from this document that our "permanentists" took the idea of uninterrupted revolution. It should be noted that in taking it from Marx our "permanentists" altered it somewhat, and in altering it "spoilt" it and made it unfit for practical use. The experienced hand of Lenin was needed to rectify this mistake, to take Marx's idea of uninterrupted revolution in its pure form and make it a cornerstone of his theory of revolution.

Here is what Marx says in his *Address* about uninterrupted (permanent) revolution, after enumerating a number of revolutionary-democratic demands which he calls upon the Communists to win:

> While the democratic petty bourgeoisie wish to bring the revolution to a conclusion as quickly as possible, and with the achievement of as many of the above demands as possible, it is our interest and our task to make the revolution permanent, until all the more or less propertied classes have been forced out of their position of dominance, until the proletariat has conquered state power, and the association of proletarians, not only in one country but in all the dominant countries of the world, has advanced so far that competition among the proletarians of these countries has ceased and that at least the decisive productive forces are concentrated in the hands of the proletarians.

In other words:

a) Marx did not at all propose *to begin* the revolution in the Germany of the fifties with the immediate establishment of proletarian power—*contrary* to the plans of our Russian "permanentists."

b) Marx proposed only that the revolution *be crowned* with the establishment of proletarian state power, by hurling, step by step, one section of the bourgeoisie after another from the heights of power, in order, after the attainment of power by the proletariat, to kindle the fire of revolution in every country. And everything that Lenin taught and carried out in the course of our revolution in pursuit of his theory of the proletarian revolution under the conditions of imperialism was *fully in line* with that proposition.

It follows, then, that our Russian "permanentists" have not only underestimated the role of the peasantry in the Russian revolution and the importance of the idea of the hegemony of the proletariat, but have altered (for the worse) Marx's idea of "permanent" revolution and made it unfit for practical use.

That is why Lenin ridiculed the theory of our "permanent-ists," calling it "original" and "fine," and accusing them of refusing to "think why, for ten whole years, life has passed by this fine theory." (Lenin's article was written in 1915, ten years after the appearance of the theory of the "per-manentists" in Russia. See Vol. XVIII, p. 317.)

That is why Lenin regarded this theory as a semi-Men-shevik theory and said that it "borrows from the Bolsheviks their call for a resolute revolutionary struggle by the prole-tariat and the conquest of political power by the latter, and from the Mensheviks the 'repudiation' of the role of the peasantry." (See Lenin's article "Two Lines of the Revolu-tion," *ibid.*)

This, then, is Lenin's idea of the bourgeois-democratic revolution passing into the proletarian revolution, of utiliz-ing the bourgeois revolution for the "immediate" transition to the proletarian revolution.

To proceed. Formerly, the victory of the revolution in one country was considered impossible, on the assumption that it would require the combined action of the proletarians of all or at least of a majority of the advanced countries to achieve victory over the bourgeoisie. Now this point of view no longer fits the facts. Now we must proceed from the pos-sibility of such a victory, for the uneven and spasmodic character of the development of the various capitalist coun-tries under the conditions of imperialism, the development within imperialism of catastrophic contradictions leading to inevitable wars, the growth of the revolutionary movement in all countries of the world—all this leads, not only to the possibility, but also to the necessity of the victory of the proletariat in individual countries. The history of the revolu-tion in Russia is direct proof of this. At the same time, how-ever, it must be borne in mind that the overthrow of the bourgeoisie can be successfully accomplished only when certain absolutely necessary conditions exist, in the absence of which one could not even think of the proletariat taking power.

Here is what Lenin says about these conditions in his pamphlet *"Left-Wing" Communism*:

The fundamental law of revolution, which has been confirmed by all revolutions and, particularly, by all three Russian revo-lutions in the twentieth century, is as follows: it is not enough for revolution that the exploited and oppressed masses should understand the impossibility of living in the old way and demand changes; it is essential for revolution that the exploiters should not be able to live and rule in the old way. Only when the *"lower classes" do not want* the old way, and when the "upper classes" *cannot carry on in the old way*—only then can revolution triumph. This truth may be expressed in other words: *revolution is impossible without a nation-wide crisis (affecting both the exploited and the exploiters)*.[7] It follows that for revolution it is essential, first, that a majority of the workers (or at least a majority of the class-conscious, thinking, politically active workers) should fully understand that revolution is necessary and be ready to sacrifice their lives for it; secondly, that the ruling classes should be ready to sacrifice their lives for it; finally, that the ruling classes should be passing through a governmental crisis, which draws even the most backward masses into politics . . . weakens the government and makes it possible for the revolutionaries to overthrow it rapidly. (See Vol. XXV, p. 222.)

But the overthrow of the power of the bourgeoisie and establishment of the power of the proletariat in one country does not yet mean that the complete victory of socialism has been ensured. After consolidating its power and leading the peasantry in its wake, the proletariat of the victorious country can and must build a socialist society. But does this mean that it will thereby achieve the complete and final victory of socialism, *i.e.*, does it mean that with the forces of only one country it can finally consolidate socialism and fully guarantee that country against intervention and, consequently, also against restoration? No, it does not. For this the victory of the revolution in at least several countries is needed. Therefore, the development and support of revolution in other countries is an essential task of the victorious revolution. Therefore, the revolution which has been victorious in one country must regard itself not as a self-sufficient entity, but as an aid, as a means for hastening the victory of the proletariat in other countries.

Lenin expressed this thought succinctly when he said that the task of the victorious revolution is to do "the utmost possible in one country *for* the development, support and awakening of the revolution *in all countries*." (See Vol. XXIII, p. 385.)

These, in general, are the characteristic features of Lenin's theory of proletarian revolution.

IV. THE DICTATORSHIP OF THE PROLETARIAT

From this theme I take three fundamental topics:

a) the dictatorship of the proletariat as the instrument of the proletarian revolution;

b) the dictatorship of the proletariat as the rule of the proletariat over the bourgeoisie;

c) Soviet power as the state form of the dictatorship of the proletariat.

1) *The dictatorship of the proletariat as the instrument of the proletarian revolution.* The question of the proletarian dictatorship is above all a question of the main content of the proletarian revolution. The proletarian revolution, its movement, its scope and its achievements, acquire flesh and blood only through the dictatorship of the proletariat. The dictatorship of the proletariat is the instrument of the proletarian revolution, its organ, its most important mainstay, brought into being for the purpose of, firstly, crushing the resistance of the overthrown exploiters and consolidating the achievements of the proletarian revolution, and, secondly, carrying the proletarian revolution to its completion, carrying the revolution to the complete victory of socialism. The revolution can defeat the bourgeoisie, can overthrow its power, even without the dictatorship of the proletariat. But the revolution will be unable to crush the resistance of the bourgeoisie, to maintain its victory, and to push forward to the final victory of socialism unless, at a certain stage in its development, it creates a special organ in the form of the dictatorship of the proletariat as its principal mainstay.

"The fundamental question of every revolution is the question of power." (Lenin.) Does this mean that all that is required is to assume power, to seize it? No, it does not. The seizure of power is only the beginning. For many reasons, the bourgeoisie that is overthrown in one country remains for a long time stronger than the proletariat which has overthrown it. Therefore, the whole point is to retain power, to consolidate it, to make it invincible. What is needed to attain this? To attain this it is necessary to carry out at least three main tasks that confront the dictatorship of the proletariat "the day after" victory:

a) to break the resistance of the landlords and capitalists

who have been overthrown and expropriated by the revolution, to liquidate every attempt on their part to restore the power of capital;

b) to organize construction in such a way as to rally all the working people around the proletariat, and to carry on this work along the lines of preparing for the elimination, the abolition of classes;

c) to arm the revolution, to organize the army of the revolution for the struggle against foreign enemies, for the struggle against imperialism.

The dictatorship of the proletariat is needed to carry out, to fulfil these tasks.

"The transition from capitalism to communism," says Lenin, "represents an entire historical epoch. Until this epoch has terminated, the exploiters inevitably cherish the hope of restoration, and this *hope* is converted into *attempts* at restoration. And after their first serious defeat, the overthrown exploiters—who had not expected their overthrow, never believed it possible, never conceded the thought of it—throw themselves with energy grown tenfold, with furious passion and hatred grown a hundredfold, into the battle for the recovery of the 'paradise' of which they have been deprived, on behalf of their families, who had been leading such a sweet and easy life and whom now the 'common herd' is condeming to ruin and destitution (or to 'common' labor . . .). In the train of the capitalist exploiters follow the broad masses of the petty bourgeoisie, with regard to whom decades of historical experience of all countries testify that they vacillate and hesitate, one day marching behind the proletariat and the next day taking fright at the difficulties of the revolution, and that they become panic-stricken at the first defeat or semidefeat of the workers, grow nervous, rush about, snivel, and run from one camp into the other." (See Vol. XXIII, p. 355.)

The bourgeoisie has its grounds for making attempts at restoration, because for a long time after its overthrow it remains stronger than the proletariat which has overthrown it.

"If the exploiters are defeated in one country only," says Lenin, "and this, of course, is the typical case, since a simultaneous revolution in a number of countries is a rare exception, they *still* remain *stronger* than the exploited." (*Ibid.*, p. 354.)

Wherein lies the strength of the overthrown bourgeoisie?

Firstly, "in the strength of international capital, in the strength and durability of the international connections of the bourgeoisie." (See Vol. XXV, p. 173.)

Secondly, in the fact that "for a long time after the revolution the exploiters inevitably retain a number of great practical advantages: they still have money (it is impossible to abolish money all at once): and some movable property—often fairly considerable; they still have various connections, habits of organization and management, knowledge of all the 'secrets' (customs, methods, means and possibilities) of management, superior education, close connections with the higher technical personnel (who live and think like the bourgeoisie), incomparably greater experience in the art of war (this is very important), and so on, and so forth." (See Vol. XXIII, p. 354.)

Thirdly, "in the *force of habit*, in the strength of *small production*. For, unfortunately, small production is still very, very widespread in the world, and small production *engenders* capitalism and the bourgeoisie continuously, daily, hourly, spontaneously, and on a mass scale" . . . for "the abolition of classes means not only driving out the landlords and capitalists—that we accomplished with comparative ease—it also means *abolishing the small commodity producers*, and they *cannot be driven out*, or crushed: we *must live in harmony* with them, they can (and must) be remolded and re-educated and only by very prolonged, slow, and cautious organizational work." (See Vol. XXV, pp. 173 and 189.)

That is why Lenin says:

The dictatorship of the proletariat is a most determined and most ruthless war waged by the new class against a *more powerful* enemy, the bourgeoisie, whose resistance is increased *tenfold* by its overthrow. . . .

The dictatorship of the proletariat is a stubborn struggle—bloody and bloodless, violent and peaceful, military and economic, educational and administrative—against the forces and traditions of the old society. (*Ibid.*, pp. 173 and 190.)

It is scarcely necessary to prove that there is not the slightest possibility of carrying out these tasks in a short period, of accomplishing all this in a few years. Therefore, the dictatorship of the proletariat, the transition from capitalism to communism, must not be regarded as a fleeting period of "superrevolutionary" acts and decrees, but as an entire historical era, replete with civil wars and external conflicts, with persistent organizational work and economic construction, with advances and retreats, victories and defeats. This historical era is needed not only to create the economic and cultural prerequisites for the complete victory of socialism, but also to enable the proletariat, firstly, to educate itself and become steeled as a force capable of governing the country, and, secondly, to re-educate and remold the petty-bourgeois strata along such lines as will assure the organization of socialist production.

"You will have to go through fifteen, twenty, fifty years of civil wars and international conflicts," Marx said to the workers, "not only to change existing conditions, but also to change yourselves and to make yourselves capable of wielding political power." (See K. Marx and F. Engels, *Works,* Vol. VIII, p. 506.)

Continuing and developing Marx's idea still further, Lenin wrote that:

"It will be necesary under the dictatorship of the proletariat to re-educate millions of peasants and small proprietors, hundreds of thousands of office employees, officials and bourgeois intellectuals, to subordinate them all to the proletarian state and to proletarian leadership, to overcome their bourgeois habits and traditions;" just as we must "in a protracted struggle waged on the basis of the dictatorship of the proletariat . . . re-educate . . . the proletarians themselves, who do not abandon their petty-bourgeois prejudices at one stroke, by a miracle, at the bidding of the Virgin Mary, at the bidding of a slogan, resolution or decree, but only in the course of a long and difficult mass struggle against mass petty-bourgeois influences." (See Vol. XXV, pp. 248 and 247.)

2) *The dictatorship of the proletariat as the rule of the proletariat over the bourgeoisie.* From the foregoing it is evident that the dictatorship of the proletariat is not a mere change of personalities in the government, a change of the "cabinet," etc., leaving the old economic and political order intact. The Mensheviks and opportunists of all countries, who fear dictatorship like fire and in their fright substitute the concept "conquest of power" for the concept dictatorship, usually reduce the "conquest of power" to a change of the "cabinet," to the accession to power of a new ministry made up of people like Scheidemann and Noske, MacDonald and Henderson. It is hardly necessary to explain that these and similar cabinet changes have nothing in common with

the dictatorship of the proletariat, with the conquest of real power by the real proletariat. With the MacDonalds and Scheidemanns in power, while the old bourgeois order is allowed to remain, their so-called governments cannot be anything else than an apparatus serving the bourgeoisie, a screen to conceal the ulcers of imperialism, a weapon in the hands of the bourgeoisie against the revolutionary movement of the oppressed and exploited masses. Capital needs such governments as a screen when it finds it inconvenient, unprofitable, difficult to oppress and exploit the masses without the aid of a screen. Of course, the appearance of such governments is a symptom that "over there" (*i.e.*, in the capitalist camp), "at the Shipka Pass"[8] all is not quiet. Nevertheless, governments of this kind inevitably remain governments of capital in disguise. The government of a MacDonald or a Scheidemann is as far removed from the conquest of power by the proletariat as heaven from the earth. The dictatorship of the proletariat is not a change of government, but a new state, with new organs of power, both central and local: it is the state of the proletariat, which has arisen on the ruins of the old state, the state of the bourgeoisie.

The dictatorship of the proletariat arises not on the basis of the bourgeois order, but in the process of its breakdown, after the overthrow of the bourgeoisie, in the process of the expropriation of the landlords and capitalists, in the process of the socialization of the principal instruments and means of production, in the process of violent proletarian revolution. The dictatorship of the proletariat is a revolutionary power based on the use of force against the bourgeoisie.

The state is a machine in the hands of the ruling class for suppressing the resistance of its class enemies. *In this respect* the dictatorship of the proletariat does not differ essentially from the dictatorship of any other class, for the proletarian state is a machine for the suppression of the bourgeoisie. But there is one *substantial* difference. This difference consists in the fact that all hitherto existing class states have been dictatorships of an exploiting minority over the exploited majority, whereas the dictatorship of the proletariat is the dictatorship of the exploited majority over the exploiting minority.

Briefly: *the dictatorship of the proletariat is the rule—unrestricted by law and based on force—of the proletariat over*

*the bourgeoisie, a rule enjoying the sympathy and support
of the laboring and exploited masses.* (Lenin, *The State and
Revolution.*)

From this follow two main conclusions:

First conclusion: The dictatorship of the proletariat cannot be "complete" democracy, democracy for *all,* for the rich
as well as for the poor; the dictatorship of the proletariat
"must be a state that is democratic *in a new way* (*for* [9] the
proletarians and the nonpropertied in general) and dictatorial *in a new way* (*against* [10] the bourgeoisie)." (See Vol.
XXI, p. 393.) The talk of Kautsky and Co. about universal
equality, about "pure" democracy, about "perfect" democracy, and the like, is a bourgeois disguise of the indubitable
fact that equality between exploited and exploiters is impossible. The theory of "pure" democracy is the theory of the
upper stratum of the working class, which has been broken in
and is being fed by the imperialist robbers. It was brought
into being for the purpose of concealing the ulcers of capitalism, of embellishing imperialism and lending it moral
strength in the struggle against the exploited masses. Under
capitalism there are no real "liberties" for the exploited, nor
can there be, if for no other reason than that the premises,
printing plants, paper supplies, etc., indispensable for the
enjoyment of "liberties" are the privilege of the exploiters.
Under capitalism the exploited masses do not, nor can they
ever, really participate in governing the country, if for no
other reason than that, even under the most democratic regime, under conditions of capitalism, governments are not
set up by the people but by the Rothschilds and Stinneses,
the Rockefellers and Morgans. Democracy under capitalism
is *capitalist* democracy, the democracy of the exploiting minority, based on the restriction of the rights of the exploited
majority and directed against this majority. Only under the
proletarian dictatorship are real liberties for the exploited
and real participation of the proletarians and peasants in
governing the country possible. Under the dictatorship of
the proletariat, democracy is *proletarian* democracy, the democracy of the exploited majority, based on the restriction
of the rights of the exploiting minority and directed against
this minority.

Second conclusion: The dictatorship of the proletariat cannot arise as the result of the peaceful development of bourgeois society and of bourgeois democracy; it can arise only

as the result of smashing the bourgeois state machine, the bourgeois army, the bourgeois bureaucratic apparatus, the bourgeois police.

"The working class cannot simply lay hold of the ready-made state machinery, and wield it for its own purposes," say Marx and Engels in a preface to the *Communist Manifesto*—The task of the proletarian revolution is ". . . no longer, as before, to transfer the bureaucratic-military machine from one hand to another, *but to smash* it . . .—this is the preliminary condition for every real people's revolution on the continent," says Marx in his letter to Kugelmann in 1871.

Marx's qualifying phrase about the continent gave the opportunists and Mensheviks of all countries a pretext for clamoring that Marx had thus conceded the possibility of the peaceful evolution of bourgeois democracy into a proletarian democracy, at least in certain countries outside the European continent (Britain, America). Marx did in fact concede that possibility, and he had good grounds for conceding it in regard to Britain and America in the seventies of the last century, when monopoly capitalism and imperialism did not yet exist, and when these countries, owing to the particular conditions of their development, had as yet no developed militarism and bureaucracy. That was the situation before the appearance of developed imperialism. But later, after thirty or forty years, when the situation in these countries had radically changed, when imperialism had developed and had embraced all capitalist countries without exception, when militarism and bureaucracy also had appeared in Britain and America, when the particular conditions for peaceful development in Britain and America had disappeared—then the qualification in regard to these countries necessarily could no longer hold good.

"Today," said Lenin, "in 1917, in the epoch of the first great imperialist war, this qualification made by Marx is no longer valid. Both Britain and America, the biggest and the last representatives—in the whole world—of Anglo-Saxon 'liberty' in the sense that they had no militarism and bureaucracy, have completely sunk into the all-European filthy, bloody morass of bureaucratic-military institutions which subordinate everything to themselves and trample everything underfoot. Today, in both Britain and America, 'the preliminary condition for every real people's revolution' is the *smashing*, the *destruction* of the 'ready-made state machinery' (perfected in those countries, between 1914 and 1917, up to the 'European,' general imperialist standard)." (See Vol. XXI, p. 395.)

In other words, the law of violent proletarian revolution, the law of the smashing of the bourgeois state machine as a preliminary condition for such a revolution, is an inevitable law of the revolutionary movement in the imperialist countries of the world.

Of course, in the remote future, if the proletariat is victorious in the principal capitalist countries, and if the present capitalist encirclement is replaced by a socialist encirclement, a "peaceful" path of development is quite possible for certain capitalist countries, whose capitalists, in view of the "unfavorable" international situation, will consider it expedient "voluntarily" to make substantial concessions to the proletariat. But this supposition applys only to a remote and possible future. With regard to the immediate future, there is no ground whatsoever for this supposition.

Therefore, Lenin is right in saying:

The proletarian revolution is impossible without the forcible destruction of the bourgeois state machine and the substitution for it of a *new one*. (See Vol. XXIII, p. 342.)

3) *Soviet power as the state form of the dictatorship of the proletariat.* The victory of the dictatorship of the proletariat signifies the suppression of the bourgeoisie, the smashing of the bourgeois state machine, and the substitution of proletarian democracy for bourgeois democracy. That is clear. But by means of what organizations can this colossal work be carried out? The old forms of organization of the proletariat, which grew up on the basis of bourgeois parliamentarism, are inadequate for this work—of that there can hardly be any doubt. What, then, are the new forms of organization of the proletariat that are capable of serving as the gravediggers of the bourgeois state machine, that are capable not only of smashing this machine, not only of substituting proletarian democracy for bourgeois democracy, but also of becoming the foundation of the proletarian state power?

This new form of organization of the proletariat is the Soviets.

Wherein lies the strength of the Soviets as compared with the old forms of organization?

In the fact that the Soviets are the most comprehensive mass organizations of the proletariat, for they and they alone embrace all workers without exception.

In the fact that the Soviets are the *only* mass organizations which unite all the oppressed and exploited, workers and peasants, soldiers and sailors, and in which the vanguard of the masses, the proletariat, can, for this reason, most easily and most completely exercise its political leadership of the mass struggle.

In the fact that the Soviets are the *most powerful organs* of the revolutionary struggle of the masses, the political actions of the masses, the uprising of the masses—organs capable of breaking the omnipotence of finance capital and its political appendages.

In the fact that the Soviets are the *immediate* organizations of the masses themselves, *i.e., the most democratic* and therefore the most authoritative organizations of the masses, which facilitate to the utmost their participation in the construction of the new state and in its administration, and which bring into full play the revolutionary energy, initiative and creative abilities of the masses in the struggle for the destruction of the old order, in the struggle for the new, proletarian order.

Soviet power is the union and constitution of the local Soviets into one common state organization, into the state organization of the proletariat as the vanguard of the oppressed and exploited masses and as the ruling class—their union in the Republic of Soviets.

The essence of Soviet power consists in the fact that these most comprehensive and most revolutionary mass organizations of precisely those classes that were oppressed by the capitalists and landlords are now the "*permanent and sole* basis of the whole power of the state, of the whole state apparatus"; that "precisely those masses which even in the most democratic bourgeois republics," while being equal in law, "have in fact been prevented by thousands of tricks and devices from taking part in political life and from enjoying democratic rights and liberties, and now drawn unfailingly into *constant* and, moreover, *decisive*" participation in the democratic administration of the state." [11] (See Lenin, Vol. XXIV, p. 13.)

That is why Soviet power is a *new form* of state organization, different in principle from the old bourgeois-democratic and parliamentary form, a *new type* of state, adapted not to the task of exploiting and oppressing the laboring masses, but to the task of completely emancipating them from all oppression and exploitation, the task facing the dictatorship of the proletariat.

Lenin is right in saying that with the appearance of Soviet power "the era of bourgeois-democratic parliamentarism has drawn to a close and a new chapter in world history—the era of proletarian dictatorship—has been opened."

Wherein lie the characteristic features of Soviet power?

In the fact that Soviet power is the most comprehensive and most democratic of all state organizations possible while classes continue to exist; for, being the arena of the bond and collaboration between the workers and the exploited peasants in their struggle against the exploiters, and basing itself in its work on this bond and on this collaboration, Soviet power is thus the power of the majority of the population over the minority, it is the state of the majority, the expression of its dictatorship.

In the fact that Soviet power is the most international of all state organizations in class society; for, by destroying every kind of national oppression and resting on the collaboration of the laboring masses of various nationalities, it facilitates the unification of these masses into a single state union.

In the fact that Soviet power, by its very structure, facilitates the task of leading the oppressed and exploited masses, the task of the vanguard of these masses—the proletariat, as the most united and most politically conscious core of the Soviets.

"The experience of all revolutions and of all movements of the oppressed classes, the experience of the world socialist movement teaches us," says Lenin, "that the proletariat alone is able to unite and lead the scattered and backward strata of the laboring and exploited population." (See Vol. XXIV, p. 14.) The point is that the structure of Soviet power facilitates the practical application of the lessons drawn from this experience.

In the fact that Soviet power, by combining legislative and executive power in a single state organization and replacing territorial electoral constituencies by industrial units, factories and mills, thereby directly links the workers and the laboring masses in general with the apparatus of state administration, teaches them how to govern the country.

In the fact that Soviet power alone is capable of releasing

the army from its subordination to bourgeois command and converting it from an instrument for oppressing the people, which it is under the bourgeois order, into an instrument for liberating the people from the yoke of the bourgeoisie, both native and foreign.

In the fact that "the Soviet organization of the state alone is capable of immediately and effectively smashing and finally destroying the old, *i.e.*, the bourgeois, bureaucratic and judicial apparatus." (*Ibid.*)

In the fact that the Soviet form of state alone, by drawing the mass organizations of the laborers and exploited into constant and unrestricted participation in state administration, is capable of preparing the ground for the withering away of the state, which is one of the basic elements of the future stateless communist society.

The Republic of Soviets is thus the political form, so long sought and finally discovered, within the framework of which the economic emancipation of the proletariat, the complete victory of socialism, must be accomplished.

The Paris Commune was the embryo of this form. Soviet power is its development and culmination.

That is why Lenin says:

> The Republic of Soviets of Workers', Soldiers', and Peasants' Deputies is not merely the form of a higher type of democratic institution . . . but the *only* [12] form capable of ensuring the most painless transition to socialism. (See Vol. XXII, p. 131.)

V. THE PEASANT QUESTION

From this theme I take four topics:

a) the presentation of the question;

b) the peasantry during the bourgeois-democratic revolution;

c) the peasantry during the proletarian revolution;

d) the peasantry after the consolidation of Soviet power.

1) *The presentation of the question.* Some think that the fundamental thing in Leninism is the peasant question, that the point of departure of Leninism is the question of the peasantry, its role and its relative importance. This is absolutely wrong. The fundamental question of Leninism, its point of departure, is not the peasant question, but the

question of the dictatorship of the proletariat, the conditions under which it can be achieved and the conditions under which it can be consolidated. The peasant question, as the question of the ally of the proletariat in its struggle for power, is a derivative question.

This circumstance, however, does not in the least deprive the peasant question of the serious and vital importance it unquestionably has for the proletarian revolution. It is known that the serious study of the peasant question in the ranks of Russian Marxists began precisely on the eve of the first revolution (1905), when the question of overthrowing tsarism and realizing the hégemony of the proletariat confronted the Party in all its magnitude, and when the question of the ally of the proletariat in the impending bourgeois revolution became of vital importance. It is also known that the peasant question in Russia assumed a still more urgent character during the proletarian revolution, when the question of the dictatorship of the proletariat, of achieving and maintaining it, led to the question of allies for the proletariat in the impending proletarian revolution. And this was natural. Those who are marching towards and preparing to assume power cannot but be interested in the question of who are their real allies.

In this sense the peasant question is part of the general question of the dictatorship of the proletariat, and as such it is one of the most vital problems of Leninism.

The attitude of indifference and sometimes even of outright antagonism displayed by the parties of the Second International towards the peasant question is to be explained not only by the specific conditions of development in the West. It is to be explained primarily by the fact that these parties do not believe in the proletarian dictatorship, that they fear revolution and have no intention of leading the proletariat to power. And those who are afraid of revolution, who do not intend to lead the proletarians to power, cannot be interested in the question of allies for the proletariat in the revolution —to them the question of allies is one of indifference, of no immediate significance. The ironical attitude of the heroes of the Second International towards the peasant question is regarded by them as a sign of good breeding, a sign of "true" Marxism. As a matter of fact, there is not a grain of Marxism in this, for indifference towards so important a question as the peasant question on the eve of the proletarian revolution is the reverse side of the repudiation of the dictatorship of the proletariat; it is an unmistakable sign of downright betrayal of Marxism.

The question is as follows: Are the revolutionary potentialities latent in the peasantry by virtue of certain conditions of its existence *already exhausted*, or not; and if not, *is there any hope, any basis*, for utilizing these potentialities *for* the proletarian revolution, for transforming the peasantry, the exploited majority of it, from the reserve of the bourgeoisie which it was during the bourgeois revolutions in the West and still is even now, into a reserve of the proletariat, into its ally?

Leninism replies to this question in the affirmative, *i.e.*, it recognizes the existence of revolutionary capacities in the ranks of the majority of the peasantry and the possibility of using these in the interests of the proletarian dictatorship.

The history of the three revolutions in Russia fully corroborates the conclusions of Leninism on this score.

Hence the practical conclusion that the laboring masses of the peasantry must be supported in their struggle against bondage and exploitation, in their struggle for deliverance from oppression and poverty. This does not mean, of course, that the proletariat must support *every* peasant movement. What we have in mind here is support for a movement or struggle of the peasantry which, directly or indirectly, facilitates the emancipation movement of the proletariat, which, in one way or another, brings grist to the mill of the proletarian revolution, and which helps to transform the peasantry into a reserve and ally of the working class.

2) *The peasantry during the bourgeois-democratic revolution.* This period extends from the first Russian revolution (1905) to the second revolution (February 1917), inclusive. The characteristic feature of this period is the emancipation of the peasantry from the influence of the liberal bourgeoisie, the peasantry's exodus from the Cadets,[13] its shift to the side of the proletariat, to the Bolshevik Party. The history of this period is the history of the struggle between the Cadets (the liberal bourgeoisie) and the Bolsheviks (the proletariat) for the peasantry. The outcome of this struggle was decided by the Duma[14] period, for the period of the four Dumas served as an object lesson to the peasantry. This lesson brought home to the peasantry the fact that they would receive neither land nor liberty at the hands of the Cadets, that the tsar was wholly in favor of the landlords, that the Cadets were supporting the tsar, and that the only force they could rely on

for assistance was the urban workers, the proletariat. The imperialist war merely confirmed the lessons of the Duma period and completed the peasantry's exodus from the bourgeoisie, completed the isolation of the liberal bourgeoisie; for the years of the war revealed the utter futility, the utter deceptiveness of all hopes of obtaining peace from the tsar and his bourgeois allies. Without the object lessons of the Duma period, the hegemony of the proletariat would have been impossible.

That is how the alliance between the workers and the peasants in the bourgeois-democratic revolution took shape. That is how the hegemony (leadership) of the proletariat in the common struggle for the overthrow of tsarism took shape—the hegemony which led to the February Revolution of 1917.

As is well known, the bourgeois revolutions in the West (Britain, France, Germany, Austria) took a different road. There, hegemony in the revolution belonged not to the proletariat, which by reason of its weakness did not and could not represent an independent political force, but to the liberal bourgeoisie. There the peasantry obtained its emancipation from the system of serfdom, not at the hands of the proletariat, which was numerically weak and unorganized, but at the hands of the bourgeoisie. There the peasantry marched against the old order side by side with the liberal bourgeoisie. There the peasantry acted as the reserve of the bourgeoisie. There, consequently, the revolution led to an enormous increase in the political weight of the bourgeoisie.

In Russia, on the contrary, the bourgeois revolution produced quite opposite results. The revolution in Russia led not to the strengthening, but to the weakening of the bourgeoisie as a political force, not to an increase in its political reserves, but to the loss of its main reserve, to the loss of the peasantry. The bourgeois revolution in Russia brought to the forefront not the liberal bourgeoisie, but the revolutionary proletariat, by rallying around the latter the millions of the peasantry.

Incidentally, this explains why the bourgeois revolution in Russia passed into a proletarian revolution in a comparatively short space of time. The hegemony of the proletariat was the embryo of, and the transitional stage to, the dictatorship of the proletariat.

How is this peculiar phenomenon of the Russian revolution, which has no precedent in the history of the bourgeois revolutions of the West, to be explained? Whence this peculiarity?

It is to be explained by the fact that the bourgeois revolution unfolded in Russia under more advanced conditions of class struggle than in the West; that the Russian proletariat had at that time already become an independent political force, whereas the liberal bourgeoisie, frightened by the revolutionary spirit of the proletariat, lost all semblance of revolutionary spirit (especially after the lessons of 1905) and turned towards an alliance with the tsar and the landlords against the revolution, against the workers and peasants.

We should bear in mind the following circumstances, which determined the peculiar character of the Russian bourgeois revolution.

a) The unprecedented concentration of Russian industry on the eve of the revolution. It is known, for instance, that in Russia 54 percent of all the workers were employed in enterprises employing over 500 workers each, whereas in so highly developed a country as North America no more than 33 percent of all the workers were employed in such enterprises. It scarcely needs proof that this circumstance alone, in view of the existence of a revolutionary party like the party of the Bolsheviks, transformed the working class of Russia into an immense force in the political life of the country.

b) The hideous forms of exploitation in the factories, coupled with the intolerable police regime of the tsarist henchmen—a circumstance which transformed every important strike of the workers into an imposing political action and steeled the working class into a thoroughly revolutionary force.

c) The political flabbiness of the Russian bourgeoisie, who after the Revolution of 1905 turned to servility to tsarism and downright counterrevolution—a fact to be explained not only by the revolutionary spirit of the Russian proletariat, which flung the Russian bourgeoisie into the embrace of tsarism, but also by the direct dependence of this bourgeoisie upon government contracts.

d) The existence in the countryside of the most hideous and most intolerable survivals of serfdom, coupled with the unlimited power of the landlords—a circumstance which threw the peasantry into the embrace of the revolution.

e) Tsarism, which stifled everything that was alive and intensified through its tyranny the oppression of the capitalist and the landlord—a circumstance which united the struggle of the workers and peasants into a single torrent of revolution.

f) The imperialist war, which fused all these contradictions in the political life of Russia into a profoundly revolutionary crisis and lent the revolution tremendous striking force.

To whom could the peasants turn under these circumstances? From whom could they seek support against the unlimited power of the landlords, against the tyranny of the tsar, against the devastating war which was ruining them? From the liberal bourgeoisie? But it was an enemy, as the long years of experience of all four Dumas had proved. From the Socialist-Revolutionaries? The Socialist-Revolutionaries were "better" than the Cadets, of course, and their program was "suitable," almost a peasant program; but what could the Socialist-Revolutionaries offer, considering that they thought of relying only on the peasants and were weak in the towns, from which the enemy primarily drew its forces? Where was the new force which would stop at nothing either in town or country, which would boldly march in the front ranks to fight the tsar and the landlords, which would help the peasants to free themselves from bondage, from land hunger, from oppression, from war? Was there such a force in Russia at all? Yes, there was. It was the Russian proletariat, which had shown its strength, its ability to fight to the end, its boldness and revolutionary spirit as far back as 1905.

At any rate, there was no other such force, and none could be found anywhere.

That is why the peasantry, when it turned its back on the Cadets and attached itself to the Socialist-Revolutionaries, at the same time came to realize the necessity of submitting to the leadership of such a courageous leader of the revolution as the Russian proletariat.

Such were the circumstances which determined the peculiar character of the Russian bourgeois revolution.

3) *The peasantry during the proletarian revolution.* This period extends from the February Revolution of 1917 to the October Revolution of 1917. This period is comparatively short, eight months in all; but from the point of view of the political enlightenment and revolutionary training of the masses these eight months can safely be put on a par with whole decades of ordinary constitutional development, for

they were eight months of *revolution*. The characteristic feature of this period was the further revolutionization of the peasantry, its disillusionment with the Socialist-Revolutionaries, the peasantry's exodus from the Socialist-Revolutionaries, its new *turn* towards a *direct rally* around the proletariat as the only consistently revolutionary force, capable of leading the country to peace. The history of this period in the history of the struggle between the Socialist-Revolutionaries (petty-bourgeois democracy) and the Bolsheviks (proletarian democracy) for the peasantry, to win over the majority of the peasantry. The outcome of this struggle was decided by the coalition period, the Kerensky [15] period, the refusal of the Socialist-Revolutionaries and the Mensheviks to confiscate the landlords' land, the fight of the Socialist-Revolutionaries and Mensheviks to continue the war, the June offensive at the front, the introduction of capital punishment for soldiers, the Kornilov revolt.

Whereas before, in the preceding period, the basic question of the revolution had been the overthrow of the tsar and of the power of the landlords, now, in the period following the February Revolution, when there was no longer any tsar and when the interminable war had exhausted the economy of the country and utterly ruined the peasantry, the question of liquidating the war became the main problem of the revolution. The center of gravity had manifestly shifted from purely internal questions to the main question—the war. "End the war," "Let's get out of the war"—such was the general outcry of the war-weary nation and primarily of the peasantry.

But in order to get out of the war it was necessary to overthrow the Provisional Government, it was necessary to overthrow the power of the bourgeoisie, it was necessary to overthrow the power of the Socialist-Revolutionaries and Mensheviks, for they, and they alone, were dragging out the war to a "victorious finish." There was no practical way of getting out of the war except by overthrowing the bourgeoisie.

This was a new revolution, a proletarian revolution, for it ousted from power the last group of the imperialist bourgeoisie, its extreme left wing, the Socialist-Revolutionary Party and the Mensheviks, in order to set up a new, proletarian power, the power of the Soviets, in order to put in power the party of the revolutionary proletariat, the Bolshevik Party, the party of revolutionary struggle against the imperialist war and for a democratic peace. The majority of the peasantry supported the struggle of the workers for peace, for the power of the Soviets.

There was no other way out for the peasantry. There could be no other way out.

Thus, the Kerensky period was a great object lesson for the toiling masses of the peasantry, for it showed clearly that with the Socialist-Revolutionaries and Mensheviks in power the country would not extricate itself from the war, and the peasants would never get either land or liberty; that the Mensheviks and Socialist-Revolutionaries differed from the Cadets only in their sweet talk and false promises, while they actually pursued the same imperialist, Cadet policy; that the only power that could lead the country along the proper road was the power of the Soviets. The further prolongation of the war merely confirmed the truth of this lesson, spurred on the revolution, and drove millions of peasants and soldiers to *rally directly* around the proletarian revolution. The isolation of the Socialist-Revolutionaries and Mensheviks became an incontrovertible fact. Without the object lessons of the coalition period the dictatorship of the proletariat would have been impossible.

Such were the circumstances which facilitated the process of the bourgeois revolution passing into the proletarian revolution.

That is how the dictatorship of the proletariat took shape in Russia.

4) *The peasantry after the consolidation of Soviet power.* Whereas before, in the first period of the revolution, the main objective was the overthrow of tsarism, and later, after the February Revolution, the primary objective was to get out of the imperialist war by overthrowing the bourgeoisie, now, after the liquidation of the civil war and the consolidation of Soviet power, questions of economic construction came to the forefront. Strengthen and develop the nationalized industry; for this purpose link industry with peasant economy through state-regulated trade; replace the surplus-appropriation system by the tax in kind so as, by gradually lowering the tax in kind, to arrive later at a system of exchanging products of industry for products of peasant farming; revive trade and develop the co-operatives, drawing into them the vast masses of the peasantry—this is how Lenin outlined the immediate tasks of economic construction on the way to building the foundations of a socialist economy.

It is said that this task may prove beyond the strength of a peasant country like Russia. Some skeptics even say that it is simply utopian, unfeasible, for the peasantry is a peasantry —it consists of small producers, and therefore cannot be of use in organizing the foundations of socialist production.

But the skeptics are mistaken, for they fail to take into account certain circumstances which in the present case are of decisive significance. Let us examine the most important of these.

Firstly. The peasantry in the Soviet Union must not be confused with the peasantry in the West. A peasantry that has been schooled in three revolutions, that fought against the tsar and the power of the bourgeoisie side by side with the proletariat and under the leadership of the proletariat, a peasantry that has received land and peace at the hands of the proletarian revolution and by reason of this has become the reserve of the proletariat—such a peasantry cannot but be different from a peasantry which during the bourgeois revolution fought under the leadership of the liberal bourgeoisie, which received land at the hands of that bourgeoisie, and in view of this became the reserve of the bourgeoisie. It scarcely needs proof that the Soviet peasantry, which has learnt to appreciate its political friendship and political collaboration with the proletariat and which owes its freedom to this friendship and collaboration, cannot but represent exceptionally favorable material for economic collaboration with the proletariat.

Engels said that "the conquest of political power by the socialist party has become a matter of the not too distant future," that "in order to conquer political power this party must first go from the towns to the country, must become a power in the countryside." (See Engels, *The Peasant Question,* 1922 ed.) He wrote this in the nineties of the last century, having in mind the Western peasantry. Does it need proof that the Russian Communists, after accomplishing an enormous amount of work in this field in the course of three revolutions, have already succeeded in gaining in the countryside an influence and backing the like of which is beyond even the dreams of our Western comrades? How can it be denied that this circumstance must decidedly facilitate the organization of economic collaboration between the working class and the peasantry of Russia?

The skeptics maintain that the small peasants are a factor that is incompatible with socialist construction. But listen to what Engels says about the small peasants of the West:

> We are decidedly on the side of the small peasant. We shall do everything at all permissible to make his lot more bearable, to facilitate his transition to the co-operative should he decide to make this transition and even to enable him to remain on his small holding for a protracted length of time to think the matter over, should he still be unable to bring himself to this decision. We do this not only because we consider it possible that the small peasant who does his own work may come over to our side, but also in the direct interest of the Party. The greater the number of peasants whom we can save from being actually hurled down into the proletariat, whom we can win to our side while they are still peasants, the more quickly and easily the social transformation will be accomplished. It would be useless for us to delay this transformation until capitalist production has developed everywhere to its utmost consequences, until the last small handicraftsman and the last small peasant have fallen victim to capitalist large-scale production. The material sacrifices to be made for this purpose in the interest of the peasants and to be defrayed out of public funds may seem, from the point of view of capitalist economy, as money thrown away, but it is nevertheless an excellent investment because it will effect a per-haps tenfold saving in the cost of the social reorganization in general. In this sense we can, therefore, afford to be very gener-ous with the peasants. (*Ibid.*)

That is what Engels said, having in mind the Western peasantry. But is it not clear that what Engels said can nowhere be realized so easily and so completely as in the land of the dictatorship of the proletariat? Is it not clear that only in Soviet Russia is it possible at once and to the fullest extent for "the small peasant who does his own work" to come over to our side, for the "material sacrifices" neces-sary for this to be made, and for the necessary "generosity towards the peasants" to be displayed? Is it not clear that these and similar measures for the benefit of the peasantry are already being carried out in Russia? How can it be denied that this circumstance, in its turn, must facilitate and ad-vance the work of economic construction in the land of the Soviets?

Secondly. Agriculture in Russia must not be confused with agriculture in the West. There, agriculture is developing along the ordinary lines of capitalism, under conditions of pro-found differentiation among the peasantry, with large landed estates and private capitalist latifundia at one extreme and pauperism, destitution and wage slavery at the other. Owing to this, disintegration and decay are quite natural there. Not so in Russia. Here agriculture cannot develop along such a path, if for no other reason than that the existence of Soviet power and the nationalization of the principal instruments and means of production preclude such a development. In Russia the development of agriculture must proceed along a different path, along the path of organizing millions of small and middle peasants in co-operatives, along the path of developing in the countryside a mass co-operative movement supported by the state by means of preferential credits. Lenin rightly pointed out in his articles on co-operation that the development of agriculture in our country must proceed along a new path, along the path of drawing the majority of the peasants into socialist construction through the co-operatives, along the path of gradually introducing into agriculture the principles of collectivism, first in the sphere of marketing and later in the sphere of production of agricultural products.

Of extreme interest in this respect are several new phenomena observed in the countryside in connection with the work of the agricultural co-operatives. It is well known that new, large organizations have sprung up within the Agricultural Union (*Selskosoyuz*), in different branches of agriculture, such as production of flax, potatoes, butter, etc., which have a great future before them. Of these, the Flax Center, for instance, unites a whole network of peasant flax growers' associations. The Flax Center supplies the peasants with seeds and implements; then it buys all the flax produced by these peasants, disposes of it on the market on a large scale, guarantees the peasants a share in the profits, and in this way links peasant economy with state industry through the Agricultural Union. What shall we call this form of organization of production? In my opinion, it is the domestic system of large-scale state-socialist production in the sphere of agriculture. In speaking of the domestic system of state-socialist production I do so by analogy with the domestic system under capitalism, let us say, in the textile industry, where the handicraftsmen, receiving their raw material and tools from the capitalist and turning over to him the entire product of their labor, were actually semi-wage earners working in their own homes. This is one of numerous indices showing the path along which our agriculture must develop. There is no need to mention here similar indices in other branches of agriculture.

It scarcely needs proof that the vast majority of the peasantry will eagerly take this new path of development, rejecting the path of private capitalist latifundia and wage slavery, the path of destitution and ruin.

Here is what Lenin says about the path of development of our agriculture:

State power over all large-scale means of production, state power in the hands of the proletariat, the alliance of this proletariat with the many millions of small and very small peasants, the assured leadership of the peasantry by the proletariat, etc.—is not this all that is necessary for building a complete socialist society from the co-operatives, from the co-operatives alone, which we formerly looked down upon as huckstering organizations and which from a certain aspect we have the right to look down upon as such now, under NEP? This is not yet the building of socialist society, but it is all that is necessary and sufficient for this building. (See Vol. XXVII, p. 392.)

Further on, speaking of the necessity of giving financial and other assistance to the co-operatives, as a "new principle of organizing the population" and a new "social system" under the dictatorship of the proletariat, Lenin continues:

Every social system arises only with the financial assistance of a definite class. There is no need to mention the hundreds and hundreds of millions of rubles that the birth of "free" capitalism cost. Now we must realize, and apply in our practical work, the fact that the social system, to which we must now give more than usual assistance, is the co-operative system. But it must be assisted in the real sense of the word, *i.e.*, it will not be enough to interpret assistance to mean assistance for any kind of co-operative trade: by assistance we must mean assistance for co-operative trade in which *really large masses of the population really take part.*" (*Ibid.*, p. 393.)

What do all these facts prove?

That the skeptics are wrong.

That Leninism is right in regarding the masses of laboring peasants as the reserve of the proletariat.

That the proletariat in power can and must use this reserve in order to link industry with agriculture, to advance socialist construction, and to provide for the dictatorship of the proletariat that necessary foundation without which the transition to a socialist economy is impossible.

VI. THE NATIONAL QUESTION

From this theme I take two main topics:

a) the presentation of the question;

b) the liberation movement of the oppressed peoples and the proletarian revolution.

1) *The presentation of the question.* During the last two decades the national question has undergone a number of very important changes. The national question in the period of the Second International and the national question in the period of Leninism are far from being the same thing. They differ profoundly from each other, not only in their scope, but also in their intrinsic character.

Formerly, the national question was usually confined to a narrow circle of questions, concerning, primarily, "civilized" nationalities. The Irish, the Hungarians, the Poles, the Finns, the Serbs, and several other European nationalities—that was the circle of unequal peoples in whose destinies the leaders of the Second International were interested. The scores and hundreds of millions of Asiatic and African peoples who are suffering national oppression in its most savage and cruel form usually remained outside of their field of vision. They hesitated to put white and black, "civilized" and "uncivilized" on the same plane. Two or three meaningless, lukewarm resolutions, which carefully evaded the question of liberating the colonies—that was all the leaders of the Second International could boast. Now we can say that this duplicity and half-heartedness in dealing with the national question has been brought to an end. Leninism laid bare this crying incongruity, broke down the wall between whites and blacks, between Europeans and Asiatics, between the "civilized" and "uncivilized" slaves of imperialism, and thus linked the national question with the question of the colonies. The national question was thereby transformed from a particular and internal state problem into a general and international problem, into a world problem of emancipating the oppressed peoples in the dependent countries and colonies from the yoke of imperialism.

Formerly, the principle of self-determination of nations was usually misinterpreted and frequently narrowed down to the idea of the right of nations to autonomy. Certain leaders of the Second International even went so far as to turn the right of self-determination into the right of cultural autonomy, *i.e.*, the right of oppressed nations to have their own cultural institutions, leaving all political power in the hands of the ruling nation. As a consequence, the idea of self-determination stood in danger of being transformed from an instrument for combating annexations into an instrument for justifying them. Now we can say that this confusion has been cleared up. Leninism broadened the conception of self-determination, interpreting it as the right of the oppressed peoples of the dependent countries and colonies to complete secession, as the right of nations to independent existence as states. This precluded the possibility of justifying annexations by interpreting the right of self-determination as the right of autonomy. Thus, the principle of self-determination itself was transformed from an instrument for deceiving the masses, which it undoubtedly was in the hands of the social-chauvinists during the imperialist war, into an instrument for exposing all imperialist aspirations and chauvinist machinations, into an instrument for the political education of the masses in the spirit of internationalism.

Formerly, the question of the oppressed nations was usually regarded as a purely juridical question. Solemn proclamations about "national equality of rights," innumerable declarations about the "equality of nations"—that was the stock-in-trade of the parties of the Second International, which glossed over the fact that "equality of nations" under imperialism, where one group of nations (a minority) lives by exploiting another group of nations, is sheer mockery of the oppressed nations. Now we can say that this bourgeois-juridical point of view on the national question has been exposed. Leninism brought the national question down from the lofty heights of high-sounding declarations to solid ground, and declared that pronouncements about the "equality of nations" not backed by the direct support of the proletarian parties for the liberation struggle of the oppressed nations are meaningless and false. In this way the question of the oppressed nations became one of supporting the oppressed nations, of rendering real and continuous assistance to them in their stuggle against imperialism for real equality of nations, for their independent existence as states.

Formerly, the national question was regarded from a reformist point of view, as an independent question having no
connection with the general question of the power of capital, of the overthrow of imperialism, of the proletarian revolution. It was tacitly assumed that the victory of the proletariat in Europe was possible without a direct alliance with
the liberation movement in the colonies, that the national-
colonial question could be solved on the quiet, "of its own
accord," off the highway of the proletarian revolution, without a revolutionary struggle against imperialism. Now we
can say that this antirevolutionary point of view has been
exposed. Leninism has proved, and the imperialist war and
the revolution in Russia have confirmed, that the national
question can be solved only in connection with and on the
basis of the proletarian revolution, and that the road to victory of the revolution in the West lies through the revolutionary alliance with the liberation movement of the colonies
and dependent countries against imperialism. The national
question is a part of the general question of the proletarian
revolution, a part of the question of the dictatorship of the
proletariat.

The question is as follows: Are the revolutionary potentialities latent in the revolutionary liberation movement of
the oppressed countries *already exhausted*, or not; and if not,
is there any hope, any basis, for utilizing these potentialities
for the proletarian revolution, for transforming the dependent and colonial countries from a reserve of the imperialist
bourgeoisie into a reserve of the revolutionary proletariat,
into an ally of the latter?

Leninism replies to this question in the affirmative, *i.e.*,
it recognizes the existence of revolutionary capacities in the
national liberation movement of the oppressed countries,
and the possibility of using these for overthrowing the common enemy, for overthrowing imperialism. The mechanics
of the development of imperialism, the imperialist war, and
the revolution in Russia wholly confirm the conclusions of
Leninism on this score.

Hence the necessity for the proletariat of the "dominant"
nations to support—resolutely and actively to support—the
national liberation movement of the oppressed and dependent peoples.

This does not mean, of course, that the proletariat must
support *every* national movement, everywhere and always,
in every individual concrete case. It means that support must

be given to such national movements as tend to weaken, to overthrow imperialism, and not to strengthen and preserve it. Cases occur when the national movements in certain oppressed countries come into conflict with the interests of the development of the proletarian movement. In such cases support is, of course, entirely out of the question. The question of the rights of nations is not an isolated, self-sufficient question; it is a part of the general problem of the proletarian revolution, subordinate to the whole, and must be considered from the point of view of the whole. In the forties of the last century Marx supported the national movement of the Poles and Hungarians and was opposed to the national movement of the Czechs and the South Slavs. Why? Because the Czechs and the South Slavs were then "reactionary peoples," "Russian outposts" in Europe, outposts of absolutism; whereas the Poles and the Hungarians were "revolutionary peoples," fighting against absolutism. Because support of the national movement of the Czechs and the South Slavs was at that time equivalent to indirect support of tsarism, the most dangerous enemy of the revolutionary movement in Europe.

"The various demands of democracy," writes Lenin, "including self-determination, are not absolutes, but *small parts* of the general democratic (now: general socialist) *world* movement. In individual concrete cases, the part may contradict the whole; if so, it must be rejected." (See Vol. XIX, pp. 257-58.)

This is the position in regard to the question of particular national movements, of the possible reactionary character of these movements—if, of course, they are appraised not from the formal point of view, not from the point of view of abstract rights, but concretely, from the point of view of the interests of the revolutionary movement.

The same must be said of the revolutionary character of national movements in general. The unquestionably revolutionary character of the vast majority of national movements is as relative and peculiar as is the possible reactionary character of certain particular national movements. The revolutionary character of a national movement under the conditions of imperialist oppression does not necessarily presuppose the existence of proletarian elements in the movement, the existence of a revolutionary or a republican program of the movement, the existence of a democratic basis of the movement. The struggle that the Emir of Afghanistan is waging for the independence of Afghanistan is objectively a *revolutionary* struggle, despite the monarchist views of the Emir and his associates, for it weakens, disintegrates and undermines imperialism; whereas the struggle waged by such "desperate" democrats and "socialists," "revolutionaries" and republicans as, for example, Kerensky and Tsereteli, Renaudel and Scheidemann, Chernov and Dan, Henderson and Clynes, during the imperialist war was a *reactionary* struggle, for its result was the embellishment, the strengthening, the victory, of imperialism. For the same reasons, the struggle that the Egyptian merchants and bourgeois intellectuals are waging for the independence of Egypt is objectively a *revolutionary* struggle, despite the bourgeois origin and bourgeois title of the leaders of the Egyptian national movement, despite the fact that they are opposed to socialism; whereas the struggle that the British "Labor" Government is waging to preserve Egypt's dependent position is for the same reasons a *reactionary* struggle, despite the proletarian origin and the proletarian title of the members of that government, despite the fact that they are "for" socialism. There is no need to mention the national movement in other, larger, colonial and dependent countries, such as India and China, every step of which along the road to liberation, even if it runs counter to the demands of formal democracy, is a steam-hammer blow at imperialism, *i.e.*, an undoubtedly *revolutionary* step.

Lenin was right in saying that the national movement of the oppressed countries should be appraised not from the point of view of formal democracy, but from the point of view of the actual results, as shown by the general balance sheet of the struggle against imperialism, that is to say, "not in isolation, but on a world scale." (See Vol. XIX, p. 257.)

2) *The liberation movement of the oppressed peoples and the proletarian revolution.* In solving the national question Leninism proceeds from the following theses:

a) the world is divided into two camps: the camp of a handful of civilized nations, which possess finance capital and exploit the vast majority of the population of the globe, and the camp of the oppressed and exploited peoples in the colonies and dependent countries, which constitute that majority;

b) the colonies and the dependent countries, oppressed and exploited by finance capital, constitute a vast reserve and a very important source of strength for imperialism;

c) the revolutionary struggle of the oppressed peoples in the dependent and colonial countries against imperialism is the only road that leads to their emancipation from oppression and exploitation;

d) the most important colonial and dependent countries have already taken the path of the national liberation movement, which cannot but lead to the crisis of world capitalism;

e) the interests of the proletarian movement in the developed countries and those of the national liberation movement in the colonies call for the union of these two forms of the revolutionary movement into a common front against the common enemy, against imperialism;

f) the victory of the working class in the developed countries and the liberation of the oppressed peoples from the yoke of imperialism are impossible without the formation and the consolidation of a common revolutionary front;

g) the formation of a common revolutionary front is impossible unless the proletariat of the oppressor nations renders direct and determined support to the liberation movement of the oppressed peoples against the imperialism of its "own country," for "no nation can be free if it oppresses other nations" (Engels);

h) this support implies the upholding, defense and implementation of the slogan of the right of nations to secession, to independent existence as states;

i) unless this slogan is implemented, the union and collaboration of nations within a single world economic system, which is the material basis for the victory of world socialism, cannot be brought about;

j) this union can only be voluntary, arising on the basis of mutual confidence and fraternal relations among peoples.

Hence the two sides, the two tendencies in the national question: the tendency towards political emancipation from the shackles of imperialism and towards the formation of an independent national state—a tendency which arose as a consequence of imperialist oppression and colonial exploitation, and the tendency towards closer economic relations among nations, which arose as a result of the formation of a world market and a world economic system.

"Developing capitalism," says Lenin, "knows two historical tendencies in the national question. First: the awakening of national life and national movements, struggle against all national states. Second: development and ever-increasing frequency of all kinds of contact between nations, breakdown of national barriers, creation of an international unity of capital, economic life in general, politics, science, etc.

"Both tendencies are a universal law of capitalism. The first predominates at the beginning of its development; the second characterizes capitalism that is mature and moving towards its transformation into a socialist society." (See Vol. XVII, pp. 139-40.)

For imperialism these two tendencies represent irreconcilable contradictions; because imperialism cannot exist without exploiting colonies and forcibly retaining them within the framework of the "integral whole"; because imperialism can bring nations together only by means of annexations and colonial conquest, without which imperialism is, generally speaking, inconceivable.

For communism, on the contrary, these tendencies are but two sides of a single cause—the cause of the emancipation of the oppressed peoples from the yoke of imperialism; because communism knows that the union of peoples in a single world economic system is possible only on the basis of mutual confidence and voluntary agreement, and that the road to the formation of a voluntary union of peoples lies through the separation of the colonies from the "integral" imperialist "whole," through the transformation of the colonies into independent states.

Hence the necessity for a stubborn, continuous and determined struggle against the dominant-nation chauvinism of the "socialists" of the ruling nations (Britain, France, America, Italy, Japan, etc.), who do not want to fight their imperialist governments, who do not want to support the struggle of the oppressed peoples in "their" colonies for emancipation from oppression, for secession.

Without such a struggle one cannot even think of educating the working class of the ruling nations in the spirit of true internationalism, in the spirit of closer relations with the laboring masses of the dependent countries and colonies, in the spirit of real preparation for the proletarian revolution. The revolution would not have been victorious in Russia, and Kolchak and Denikin would not have been crushed, had not the Russian proletariat enjoyed the sympathy and support of the oppressed peoples of the former Russian Empire. But to win the sympathy and support of these peoples it had first of all to break the fetters of Russian imperialism and free these peoples from the yoke of national oppression.

Without this it would have been impossible to consolidate Soviet power, to implant real internationalism, and to create that remarkable organization for the collaboration of peoples which is called the Union of Soviet Socialist Republics and which is the living prototype of the future union of peoples in a single world economic system.

Hence the necessity of fighting against the national isolationism, narrowness and aloofness of the socialists in the oppressed countries, who do not want to rise above their national parochialism and who do not understand the connection between the liberation movement in their own countries and the proletarian movement in the ruling countries.

Without such a struggle it is inconceivable that the proletariat of the oppressed nations can maintain an independent policy and its class solidarity with the proletariat of the ruling countries in the fight for the overthrow of the common enemy, in the fight for the overthrow of imperialism.

Without such a struggle, internationalism would be impossible.

Such is the way in which the toiling masses of both the dominant and the oppressed nations must be educated in the spirit of revolutionary internationalism.

Here is what Lenin says about this twofold task of communism in educating the workers in the spirit of internationalism:

Can such education . . . be *concretely identical* in great, oppressing nations and in small, oppressed nations, in annexing nations and in annexed nations?

Obviously not. The way to the one goal—to complete equality, to the closest relations and the subsequent *amalgamation of all* nations—obviously proceeds here by different routes in each concrete case; in the same way, let us say, as the route to a point in the middle of a given page lies towards the left from one edge and towards the right from the opposite edge. If a Social Democrat belonging to a great, oppressing, annexing nation, while advocating the amalgamation of nations in general, were to forget even for one moment that "his" Nicholas II, "his" Wilhelm, George, Poincaré, etc., *also stands for amalgamation* with small nations (by means of annexations)—Nicholas

II being for "amalgamation" with Galicia, Wilhelm II for "amalgamation" with Belgium, etc.—such a Social Democrat would be a ridiculous doctrinaire in theory and an abettor of imperialism in practice.

The weight of emphasis in the internationalist education of the workers in the oppressing countries must necessarily consist in their advocating and upholding freedom of secession for oppressed countries. Without this there can be *no* internationalism. It is our right and duty to treat every Social Democrat of an oppressing nation who *fails* to conduct such propaganda as an imperialist and a scoundrel. This is an absolute demand, even if the *chance* of secession being possible and "feasible" before the introduction of socialism be only one in a thousand. . . .

On the other hand, a Social Democrat belonging to a small nation must emphasize in his agitation the *second* word of our general formula: "voluntary *union*" of nations. He may, without violating his duties as an internationalist, be in favor of *either* the political independence of his nation *or* its inclusion in a neighboring state X, Y, Z, etc. But in all cases he must fight *against* small-nation narrow-mindedness, isolationism and aloofness, he must fight for the recognition of the whole and the general, for the subordination of the interests of the particular to the interests of the general.

People who have not gone thoroughly into the question think there is a "contradiction" in Social Democrats of oppressing nations insisting on "freedom of *secession*," while Social Democrats of oppressed nations insist on "freedom of *union*." However, a little reflection will show that there is not, and cannot be, any other road to the goal, any *other* road leading from the *given* situation to internationalism and the amalgamation of nations. (See Vol. XIX, pp. 261-62.)

VII. STRATEGY AND TACTICS

From this theme I take six topics:

a) strategy and tactics as the science of leading the class struggle of the proletariat;

b) strategy and the stages of the revolution;

c) tactics and the flow and ebb of the movement;

d) strategic leadership;

e) tactical leadership;

f) reformism and revolutionism.

1) *Strategy and tactics as the science of leading the class struggle of the proletariat.* The period dominated by the Second International was mainly a period of the formation and

training of the proletarian political armies under conditions of more or less peaceful development. It was the period of parliamentarism as the predominant form of the class struggle. Questions of great class conflicts, of preparing the proletariat for revolutionary clashes, of the means for achieving the dictatorship of the proletariat, did not seem to be on the order of the day at that time. The task was confined to utilizing all means of legal development for the purpose of forming and training the proletarian armies, to utilizing parliamentarism in conformity with the conditions under which the status of the proletariat remained, and, as it seemed, had to remain, that of an opposition. It scarcely needs proof that in such a period and with such a conception of the tasks of the proletariat there could be neither an integral strategy nor any elaborated tactics. There were fragmentary and detached ideas about tactics and strategy, but no tactics or strategy as such.

The mortal sin of the Second International was not that it pursued at that time the tactics of utilizing parliamentary forms of struggle, but that it overestimated the importance of these forms, that it considered them virtually the only forms; and that when the period of open revolutionary battles set in and the question of extraparliamentary forms of struggle came to the fore, the parties of the Second International turned their backs on these new tasks, refused to shoulder them.

Only in the subsequent period, the period of direct action by the proletariat, the period of proletarian revolution, when the question of overthrowing the bourgeoisie became a question of immediate practical action, when the question of the reserves of the proletariat (strategy) became one of the most burning questions, when all forms of struggle and organization, parliamentary and extraparliamentary (tactics), had quite clearly manifested themselves—only in this period could any integral strategy and elaborated tactics for the struggle of the proletariat be worked out. It was precisely in this period that Lenin brought out into the light of day the brilliant ideas of Marx and Engels on tactics and strategy that had been suppressed by the opportunists of the Second International. But Lenin did not confine himself to restoring particular tactical propositions of Marx and Engels. He developed them further and supplemented them with new ideas and propositions, combining them all into a system of rules and guiding principles for the leadership of the class struggle of the proletariat. Lenin's pamphlets, such as *What Is To Be Done?*, *Two Tactics*, *Imperialism*, *The State and Revolution*, *The Proletarian Revolution and the Renegade Kautsky*, "*Left-Wing*" *Communism*, undoubtedly constitute priceless contributions to the general treasury of Marxism, to its revolutionary arsenal. The strategy and tactics of Leninism constitute the science of leading the revolutionary struggle of the proletariat.

2) *Strategy and the stages of the revolution.* Strategy is the determination of the direction of the main blow of the proletariat at a given stage of the revolution, the elaboration of a corresponding plan for the disposition of the revolutionary forces (main and secondary reserves), the fight to carry out this plan throughout the given stage of the revolution.

Our revolution had already passed through two stages, and after the October Revolution it entered a third one. Our strategy changed accordingly.

First stage. 1903 to February 1917. Objective: to overthrow tsarism and completely wipe out the survivals of medievalism. The main force of the revolution: the proletariat. Immediate reserves: the peasantry. Direction of the main blow: the isolation of the liberal-monarchist bourgeoisie, which was striving to win over the peasantry and liquidate the revolution by a *compromise* with tsarism. Plan for the disposition of forces: alliance of the working class with the peasantry. "The proletariat must carry to completion the democratic revolution, by allying to itself the mass of the peasantry in order to crush by force the resistance of the autocracy and to paralyze the instability of the bourgeoisie." (See Lenin, Vol. VIII, p. 96.)

Second stage. March 1917 to October 1917. Objective: to overthrow imperialism in Russia and to withdraw from the imperialist war. The main force of the revolution: the proletariat. Immediate reserves: the poor peasantry. The proletariat of neighboring countries as probable reserves. The protracted war and the crisis of imperialism as a favorable factor. Direction of the main blow: isolation of the petty-bourgeois democrats (Mensheviks and Socialist-Revolutionaries), who were striving to win over the toiling masses of the peasantry and to put an end to the revolution by a *compromise* with imperialism. Plan for the disposition of forces: alliance of the proletariat with the poor peasantry. "The proletariat must accomplish the socialist revolution, by allying to itself the mass of the semiproletarian elements of the population in order to crush by force the resistance of the bourgeoisie and to paralyze the instability of the peasantry and the petty bourgeoisie." (*Ibid.*)

Third stage. It began after the October Revolution. Objective: to consolidate the dictatorship of the proletariat in one country, using it as a base for the defeat of imperialism in all countries. The revolution spreads beyond the confines of one country; the epoch of world revolution has begun. The main forces of the revolution: the dictatorship of the proletariat in one country, the revolutionary movement of the proletariat in all countries. Main reserves: the semiproletarian and small-peasant masses in the developed countries, the liberation movement in the colonies and dependent countries. Direction of the main blow: isolation of the petty-bourgeois democrats, isolation of the parties of the Second International, which constitute the main support of the policy of *compromise* with imperialism. Plan for the disposition of forces: alliance of the proletarian revolution with the liberation movement in the colonies and the dependent countries.

Strategy deals with the main forces of the revolution and their reserves. It changes with the passing of the revolution from one stage to another, but remains basically unchanged throughout a given stage.

3) *Tactics and the flow and ebb of the movement.* Tactics are the determination of the line of conduct of the proletariat in the comparatively short period of the flow or ebb of the movement, the rise or decline of the revolution, the fight to carry out this line by replacing old forms of struggle and organization by new ones, old slogans by new ones, by combining these forms, etc. While the object of strategy is to win the war against tsarism, let us say, or against the bourgeoisie, to carry through the struggle against tsarism or against the bourgeoisie to its end, tactics pursue less important objects, for their aim is not the winning of the war as a whole, but the winning of some particular engagements or some particular battles, the carrying through successfully of some particular campaigns or actions corresponding to the concrete circumstances in the given period of a rise or decline of the revolution. Tactics are a part of strategy, subordinate to it and serving it.

Tactics change according to flow and ebb. While the strategic plan remained unchanged during the first stage of the revolution (1903 to February 1917), tactics changed several times during that period. In the period from 1903 to 1905 the Party pursued offensive tactics, for the tide of the revolution was rising, the movement was on the upgrade, and tactics had to proceed from this fact. Accordingly, the forms of struggle were revolutionary, corresponding to the requirements of the rising tide of the revolution. Local political strikes, political demonstrations, the general political strike, boycott of the Duma, uprising, militantly revolutionary slogans—such were the successive forms of struggle during that period. These changes in the forms of struggle were accompanied by corresponding changes in the forms of organization. Factory committees, revolutionary peasant committees, strike committees, Soviets of workers' deputies, a workers' party operating more or less openly—such were the forms of organization during that period.

In the period from 1907 to 1912 the Party was compelled to resort to tactics of retreat; for we then experienced a decline in the revolutionary movement, the ebb of the revolution, and tactics necessarily had to take this fact into consideration. The forms of struggle, as well as the forms of organization, changed accordingly. Instead of the boycott of the Duma—participation in the Duma; instead of open revolutionary actions outside the Duma—actions and work in the Duma; instead of general political strikes—partial economic strikes, or simply a lull in activities. Of course, the Party had to go underground during that period, while the revolutionary mass organizations were replaced by cultural, educational, co-operative, insurance and other legal organizations.

The same must be said of the second and third stages of the revolution, during which tactics changed dozens of times, whereas the strategic plans remained unchanged.

Tactics deal with the forms of struggle and the forms of organization of the proletariat, with their changes and combinations. During a given stage of the revolution tactics may change several times, depending on the flow or ebb, the rise or decline, of the revolution.

4) *Strategic leadership.* The reserves of the revolution are:

direct: a) the peasantry and in general the intermediate strata of the population within the country; b) the proletariat of neighboring countries; c) the revolutionary movement in the colonies and dependent countries; d) the conquests and gains of the dictatorship of the proletariat—part of which the proletariat may give up temporarily, while retaining superiority of forces, in order to buy off a powerful enemy and gain a respite; and

indirect: a) the contradictions and conflicts among the nonproletarian classes within the country, which can be utilized by the proletariat to weaken the enemy and to strengthen its own reserves; b) contradictions, conflicts and wars (the imperialist war, for instance) among the bourgeois states hostile to the proletarian state, which can be utilized by the proletariat in its offensive or in maneuvering in the event of a forced retreat.

There is no need to speak at length about the reserves of the first category, as their significance is clear to everyone. As for the reserves of the second category, whose significance is not always clear, it must be said that sometimes they are of prime importance for the progress of the revolution. One can hardly deny the enormous importance, for example, of the conflict between the petty-bourgeois democrats (Socialist-Revolutionaries) and the liberal monarchist bourgeoisie (the Cadets) during and after the first revolution, which undoubtedly played its part in freeing the peasantry from the influence of the bourgeoisie. Still less reason is there for denying the colossal importance of the fact that the principal groups of imperialists were engaged in a deadly war during the period of the October Revolution, when the imperialists, engrossed in war among themselves, were unable to concentrate their forces against the young Soviet power, and the proletariat, for this very reason, was able to get down to the work of organizing its forces and consolidating its power and to prepare the rout of Kolchak and Denikin. It must be presumed that now, when the contradictions among the imperialist groups are becoming more and more profound, and when a new war among them is becoming inevitable, reserves of this description will assume ever greater importance for the proletariat.

The task of strategic leadership is to make proper use of all these reserves for the achievement of the main object of the revolution at the given stage of its development.

What does making proper use of reserves mean?

It means fulfilling certain necessary conditions, of which the following must be regarded as the principal ones:

Firstly. The concentration of the main forces of the revolution at the enemy's most vulnerable spot at the decisive moment, when the revolution has already become ripe, when the offensive is going full-steam ahead, when insurrection is knocking at the door, and when bringing the reserves up to the vanguard is the decisive condition of success. The Party's strategy during the period from April to October 1917 can be taken as an example of this manner of utilizing reserves. Undoubtedly, the enemy's most vulnerable spot at that time was the war. Undoubtedly, it was on this question, as the fundamental one, that the Party rallied the broadest masses of the population around the proletarian vanguard. The Party's strategy during that period was, while training the vanguard for street action by means of manifestations and demonstrations, to bring the reserves up to the vanguard through the medium of the Soviets in the rear and the soldiers' committees at the front. The outcome of the revolution has shown that the reserves were properly utilized.

Here is what Lenin, paraphrasing the well-known theses of Marx and Engels on insurrection, says about this condition of strategically utilizing the forces of revolution:

1) Never *play* with insurrection, but, when beginning it, firmly realize that you must *go to the end*.

2) Concentrate a great *superiority of forces* at the decisive point, at the decisive moment, otherwise the enemy, who has the advantage of better preparation and organization, will destroy the insurgents.

3) Once the insurrection has begun, you must act with the greatest *determination*, and by all means, without fail, take the *offensive*. "The defensive is the death of an armed rising."

4) You must try to take the enemy by surprise and seize the moment when his forces are scattered.

5) You must strive for *daily* successes, even if small (one might say hourly, if it is the case of one town), and at all costs retain the *"moral ascendancy."* (See Vol. XXI, pp. 319-20.)

Secondly. The selection of the moment for the decisive blow, the moment for starting the insurrection, so timed as to coincide with the moment when the crisis has reached its climax, when the vanguard is prepared to fight to the end, the reserves are prepared to support the vanguard, and maximum consternation reigns in the ranks of the enemy.

The decisive battle, says Lenin, may be deemed to have fully matured *if* "(1) all the class forces hostile to us have become sufficiently weakened themselves in a struggle which is beyond their strength"; *if* "(2) all the vacillating, wavering, unstable, intermediate elements—the petty bourgeoisie, the petty-

bourgeois democrats as distinct from the bourgeoisie—have sufficiently exposed themselves in the eyes of the people, have sufficiently disgraced themselves through their practical bankruptcy";
if "(3) among the proletariat a mass sentiment in favor of supporting the most determined, supremely bold, revolutionary
action against the bourgeoisie has arisen and has begun to grow
vigorously. Then revolution is indeed ripe. Then, indeed, if we
have correctly gauged all the conditions indicated above . . .
and if we have chosen the moment rightly, is our victory
assured." (See Vol. XXV, p. 229.)

The manner in which the October uprising was carried out
may be taken as a model of such strategy.

Failure to observe this condition leads to a dangerous
error called "loss of tempo," when the Party lags behind the
movement or runs far ahead of it, courting the danger of failure. An example of such "loss of tempo," of how the moment for an uprising should not be chosen, may be seen in
the attempt made by a section of our comrades to begin
the uprising by arresting the Democratic Conference in
September 1917,[16] when wavering was still apparent in the
Soviets, when the armies at the front were still at the cross-
roads, when the reserves had not yet been brought up to
the vanguard.

Thirdly. Undeviating pursuit of the course adopted, no
matter what difficulties and complications are encountered
on the road towards the goal. This is necessary in order that
the vanguard not lose sight of the main goal of the struggle
and the masses not stray from the road while marching towards that goal and striving to rally around the vanguard.
Failure to observe this condition leads to a grave error, well
known to sailors as "losing one's bearings." As an example of
this "losing one's bearings" we may take the erroneous conduct of our Party when, immediately after the Democratic
Conference, it adopted a resolution to participate in the Preparliament.[17] For the moment the Party, as it were, forgot
that the Preparliament was an attempt of the bourgeoisie to
switch the country from the path of the Soviets to the
path of bourgeois parliamentarism, that the Party's participation in such a body might result in mixing everything up
and confusing the workers and peasants, who were waging a
revolutionary struggle under the slogan: "All Power to the
Soviets." This mistake was rectified by the withdrawal of
the Bolsheviks from the Preparliament.

Fourthly. Maneuvering the reserves with a view to effecting a proper retreat when the enemy is strong, when retreat is inevitable, when to accept battle forced upon us by the enemy is obviously disadvantageous, when, with the given relation of forces, retreat becomes the only way to escape a blow against the vanguard and retain the vanguard's reserves.

"The revolutionary parties," says Lenin, "must complete their education. They have learned to attack. Now they have to realize that this knowledge must be supplemented with the knowledge of how to retreat properly. They have to realize—and the revolutionary class is taught to realize it by its own bitter experience—that victory is impossible unless they have learned both how to attack and how to retreat properly." (See Vol. XXV, p. 177.)

The object of this strategy is to gain time, to disrupt the enemy, and to accumulate forces in order later to assume the offensive.

The signing of the Brest Peace [18] may be taken as a model of this strategy, for it enabled the Party to gain time, to take advantage of the conflicts in the camp of the imperialists, to disrupt the forces of the enemy, to retain the support of the peasantry, and to accumulate forces in preparation for the offensive against Kolchak and Denikin.

"In concluding a separate peace," said Lenin at that time, "we free ourselves as much *as is possible at the present moment* from both warring imperialist groups, we take advantage of their mutual enmity and warfare, which hinder them from making a deal against us, and for a certain period have our hands free to advance and to consolidate the socialist revolution." (See Vol. XXII, p. 198.)

"Now even the biggest fool," said Lenin three years after the Brest Peace, "can see that the 'Brest Peace' was a concession that strengthened us and broke up the forces of international imperialism." (See Vol. XXVII, p. 7.)

Such are the principal conditions which ensure correct strategic leadership.

5) *Tactical leadership.* Tactical leadership is a part of strategic leadership, subordinated to the tasks and the requirements of the latter. The task of tactical leadership is to master all forms of struggle and organization of the proletariat and to ensure that they are used properly so as to achieve, with the given relation of forces, the maximum results necessary to prepare for strategic success.

What is meant by making proper use of the forms of struggle and organization of the proletariat?

It means fulfilling certain necessary conditions, of which the following must be regarded as the principal ones:

Firstly. To put in the forefront precisely those forms of struggle and organization which are best suited to the conditions prevailing during the flow or ebb of the movement at a given moment, and which therefore can facilitate and ensure the bringing of the masses to revolutionary positions, the bringing of the millions to the revolutionary front, and their disposition at the revolutionary front.

The point here is not that the vanguard should realize the impossibility of preserving the old regime and the inevitability of its overthrow. The point is that the masses, the millions, should understand this inevitability and display their readiness to support the vanguard. But the masses can understand this only from their own experience. The task is to enable the vast masses to realize from their own experience the inevitability of the overthrow of the old regime, to promote such methods of struggle and forms of organization as will make it easier for the masses to realize from experience the correctness of the revolutionary slogans.

The vanguard would have become detached from the working class, and the working class would have lost contact with the masses, if the Party had not decided at the time to participate in the Duma, if it had not decided to concentrate its forces on work in the Duma and to develop a struggle on the basis of this work, in order to make it easier for the masses to realize from their own experience the futility of the Duma, the falsity of the promises of the Cadets, the impossibility of compromise with tsarism, and the inevitability of an alliance between the peasantry and the working class. Had the masses not gained their experience during the period of the Duma, the exposure of the Cadets and the hegemony of the proletariat would have been impossible.

The danger of the "Recall" tactics [19] was that they threatened to detach the vanguard from the millions of its reserves.

The Party would have become detached from the working class, and the working class would have lost its influence among the broad masses of the peasants and soldiers, if the proletariat had followed the "Left" Communists, who called for an uprising in April 1917, when the Mensheviks and Socialist-Revolutionaries had not yet exposed themselves as advocates of war and imperialism, when the masses had not yet realized from their own experience the falsity of the speeches of the Mensheviks and Socialist-Revolutionaries about peace, land and freedom. Had the masses not gained this experience during the Kerensky period, the Mensheviks and Socialist-Revolutionaries would not have been isolated and the dictatorship of the proletariat would have been impossible. Therefore, the tactics of "patiently explaining" the mistakes of the petty-bourgeois parties and of open struggle in the Soviets were the only correct tactics.

The danger of the tactics of the "Left" Communists was that they threatened to transform the Party from the leader of the proletarian revolution into a handful of futile conspirators with no ground to stand on.

"Victory cannot be won with the vanguard alone," says Lenin. "To throw the vanguard alone into the decisive battle, before the whole class, before the broad masses have taken up a position either of direct support of the vanguard, or at least of benevolent neutrality towards it . . . would be not merely folly, but a crime. And in order that actually the whole class, that actually the broad masses of the working people and those oppressed by capital may take up such a position, propaganda and agitation alone are not enough. For this the masses must have their own political experience. Such is the fundamental law of all great revolutions, now confirmed with astonishing force and vividness not only in Russia, but also in Germany. Not only the uncultured, often illiterate masses of Russia, but the highly cultured, entirely literate masses of Germany had to realize through their own painful experience the absolute impotence and spinelessness, the absolute helplessness and servility to the bourgeoisie, the utter vileness of the ruling knights of the Second International, the absolute inevitability of a dictatorship of the extreme reactionaries (Kornilov in Russia, Kapp and Co. in Germany) as the only alternative to a dictatorship of the proletariat, in order to turn resolutely towards communism." (See Vol. XXV, p. 228.)

Secondly. To locate at any given moment the particular link in the chain of processes which, if grasped, will enable us to keep hold of the whole chain and to prepare the conditions for achieving strategic success.

The point here is to single out from all the tasks confronting the Party the particular immediate task, the fulfillment of which constitutes the central point, and the accomplish-

ment of which ensures the successful fulfillment of the other
immediate tasks.

The importance of this thesis may be illustrated by two
examples, one of which could be taken from the remote past
(the period of the formation of the Party) and the other
from the immediate present (the period of NEP).

In the period of the formation of the Party, when the
innumerable circles and organizations had not yet been
linked together, when amateurishness and the parochial
outlook of the circles were corroding the Party from top to
bottom, when ideological confusion was the characteristic
feature of the internal life of the Party, the main link and
the main task in the chain of links and in the chain of
tasks then confronting the Party proved to be the establishment of an all-Russian illegal newspaper (*Iskra*). Why? Because, under the conditions then prevailing, only by means
of an all-Russian illegal newspaper was it possible to create
a solid core of the Party capable of uniting the innumerable
circles and organizations into one whole, to prepare the
conditions for ideological and tactical unity, and thus to build
the foundations for the formation of a real party.

During the period of transition from war to economic construction, when industry was vegetating in the grip of disruption and agriculture was suffering from a shortage of
urban manufactured goods, when the establishment of a
bond between state industry and peasant economy became
the fundamental condition for successful socialist construction—in that period it turned out that the main link in the
chain of processes, the main task among a number of tasks,
was to develop trade. Why? Because under the conditions of
NEP the bond between industry and peasant economy cannot be established except through trade; because under the
conditions of NEP production without sale is fatal for industry; because industry can be expanded only by the expansion
of sales as a result of developing trade; because only after
we have consolidated our position in the sphere of trade,
only after we have secured control of trade, only after we
have secured this link can there be any hope of linking
industry with the peasant market and successfully fulfilling
the other immediate tasks in order to create the conditions
for building the foundations of socialist economy.

"It is not enough to be a revolutionary and an adherent of
socialism or a Communist in general," says Lenin. "One must

be able at each particular moment to find the particular link in the chain which one must grasp with all one's might in order to keep hold of the whole chain and to prepare firmly for the transition to the next link." . . .

"At the present time . . . this link is the revival of internal *trade* under proper state regulation (direction). Trade—that is the 'link' in the historical chain of events, in the transitional forms of our socialist construction in 1921-1922, '*which we must grasp with all our might.*' . . ." (See Vol. XXVII, p. 82.)

Such are the principal conditions which ensure correct tactical leadership.

6) *Reformism and revolutionism.* What is the difference between revolutionary tactics and reformist tactics?

Some think that Leninism is opposed to reforms, opposed to compromises and to agreements in general. This is absolutely wrong. Bolsheviks know as well as anybody else that in a certain sense "every little helps," that under certain conditions reforms in general, and compromises and agreements in particular, are necessary and useful.

"To carry on a war for the overthrow of the international bourgeoisie," says Lenin, "a war which is a hundred times more difficult, protracted and complicated than the most stubborn of ordinary wars between states, and to refuse beforehand to maneuver, to utilize the conflict of interests (even though temporary) among one's enemies, to reject agreements and compromises with possible (even though temporary, unstable, vacillating and conditional) allies—is not this ridiculous in the extreme? Is it not as though, when making a difficult ascent of an unexplored and hitherto inaccessible mountain, we were to refuse beforehand ever to move in zigzags, ever to retrace our steps, ever to abandon the course once selected and to try others?" (See Vol. XXV, p. 210.)

Obviously, therefore, it is not a matter of reforms or of compromises and agreements, but of the use people make of reforms and agreements.

To a reformist, reforms are everything, while revolutionary work is something incidental, something just to talk about, mere eyewash. That is why reforms resulting from reformist tactics under the conditions of bourgeois rule are inevitably transformed into an instrument for strengthening that rule, an instrument for disintegrating the revolution.

To a revolutionary, on the contrary, the main thing is revolutionary work and not reforms; to him reforms are a by-product of the revolution. That is why reforms resulting from revolutionary tactics under the conditions of bourgeois rule are naturally transformed into an instrument for disintegrating that rule, into an instrument for strengthening the revolution, into a strongpoint for the further development of the revolutionary movement.

The revolutionary will accept a reform in order to use it as an aid in combining legal work with illegal work, in order to intensify, under its cover, the illegal work for the revolutionary preparation of the masses for the overthrow of the bourgeoisie.

That is the essence of making revolutionary use of reforms and agreements under the conditions of imperialism.

The reformist, on the contrary, will accept reforms in order to renounce all illegal work, to thwart the preparation of the masses for the revolution and to rest in the shade of "bestowed" reforms.

That is the essence of reformist tactics.

Such is the position in regard to reforms and agreements under the conditions of imperialism.

The situation changes somewhat, however, after the overthrow of imperialism, under the dictatorship of the proletariat. Under certain conditions, in a certain situation, the proletarian power may find itself compelled temporarily to leave the path of the revolutionary reconstruction of the existing order of things and to take the path of its gradual transformation, the "reformist path," as Lenin says in his well-known article "The Importance of Gold," the path of flanking movements, of reforms and concessions to the nonproletarian classes—in order to disintegrate these classes, to give the revolution a respite, to recuperate one's forces and prepare the conditions for a new offensive. It cannot be denied that in a sense this is a "reformist" path. But it must be borne in mind that there is a fundamental distinction here, which consists in the fact that, in this case, the reform emanates from the proletarian power, that it strengthens the proletarian power and procures for it a necessary respite, and that its purpose is to disintegrate, not the revolution, but the nonproletarian classes.

Under such conditions a reform is thus transformed into its opposite.

The proletarian power is able to adopt such a policy because, and only because, the scope of the revolution in the preceding period was great enough and therefore provided a sufficiently wide expanse within which to retreat, substituting for offensive tactics the tactics of temporary retreat, the tactics of flanking movements.

Thus, while formerly, under bourgeois rule, reforms were a by-product of revolution, now, under the dictatorship of the proletariat, the source of reforms is the revolutionary gains of the proletariat, the reserves accumulated in the hands of the proletariat and consisting of these gains.

"Only Marxism," says Lenin, "has precisely and correctly defined the relation of reforms to revolution. However, Marx was able to see this relation only from one aspect, namely, under the conditions preceding the first, even somewhat permanent and lasting victory of the proletariat, if only in a single country. Under those conditions, the basis of the proper relation was the following: reforms are a by-product of the revolutionary class struggle of the proletariat. . . . After the victory of the proletariat, if only in a single country, something new enters into the relation between reforms and revolution. In principle, it is the same as before, but a change in form takes place, which Marx himself could not foresee, but which can be appreciated only on the basis of the philosophy and politics of Marxism. . . . After the victory (while still remaining a 'by-product' on an international scale) they (i.e., reforms—J.S.) are, in addition, for the country in which victory has been achieved, a necessary and legitimate respite in those cases when, after the utmost exertion of effort, it becomes obvious that sufficient strength is lacking for the revolutionary accomplishment of this or that transition. Victory creates such a 'reserve of strength' that it is possible to hold out even in a forced retreat, to hold out both materially and morally." (See Vol. XXVII, pp. 84-85.)

VIII. THE PARTY

In the prerevolutionary period, the period of more or less peaceful development, when the parties of the Second International were the predominant force in the working-class movement and parliamentary forms of struggle were regarded as the principal forms—under these conditions the Party neither had nor could have had that great and decisive importance which it acquired afterwards, under conditions of open revolutionary clashes. Defending the Second International against attacks made upon it, Kautsky says that the parties of the Second International are an instrument of peace and not of war, and that for this very reason they were powerless to take any important steps during the war, during the period of revolutionary action by the proletariat. That is quite true. But what does it mean? It means that the parties of the Second International are unfit for the revolutionary struggle of the proletariat, that they are not militant parties of the proletariat, leading the workers to power, but election machines adapted for parliamentary elections and parliamentary struggle. This, in fact, explains why, in the days when the opportunists of the Second International were in the ascendancy, it was not the party, but the parliamentary group that was the chief political organization of the proletariat. It is well known that the party at that time was really an appendage and subsidiary of the parliamentary group. It scarcely needs proof that under such circumstances and with such a party at the helm there could be no question of preparing the proletariat for revolution.

But matters have changed radically with the dawn of the new period. The new period is one of open class collisions, of revolutionary action by the proletariat, of proletarian revolution, a period when forces are being directly mustered for the overthrow of imperialism and the seizure of power by the proletariat. In this period the proletariat is confronted with the new tasks of reorganizing all party work on new, revolutionary lines, educating the workers in the spirit of revolutionary struggle for power, preparing and moving up reserves, establishing an alliance with the proletarians of neighboring countries, establishing firm ties with the liberation movement in the colonies and dependent countries, etc., etc. To think that these new tasks can be performed by the old Social Democratic parties, brought up as they were in the peaceful conditions of parliamentarism, is to doom oneself to hopeless despair, to inevitable defeat. If, with such tasks to shoulder, the proletariat remained under the leadership of the old parties, it would be completely unarmed. It scarcely needs proof that the proletariat could not consent to such a state of affairs.

Hence the necessity for a new party, a militant party, a revolutionary party, one bold enough to lead the proletarians in the struggle for power, sufficiently experienced to find its bearings amidst the complex conditions of a revolutionary situation, and sufficiently flexible to steer clear of all submerged rocks in the path to its goal.

Without such a party it is useless even to think of overthrowing imperialism, of achieving the dictatorship of the proletariat.

This new party is the party of Leninism.

What are the specific features of this new party?

1) *The Party as the advanced detachment of the working class.* The Party must be, first of all, the *advanced* detachment of the working class. The Party must absorb all the best elements of the working class, their experience, their revolutionary spirit, their selfless devotion to the cause of the proletariat. But in order that it may really be the advanced detachment, the Party must be armed with revolutionary theory, with a knowledge of the laws of the movement, with a knowledge of the laws of revolution. Without this it will be incapable of directing the struggle of the proletariat, of leading the proletariat. The Party cannot be a real party if it limits itself to registering what the masses of the working class feel and think, if it drags at the tail of the spontaneous movement, if it is unable to overcome the inertia and the political indifference of the spontaneous movement, if it is unable to rise above the momentary interests of the proletariat, if it is unable to raise the masses to the level of understanding the class interests of the proletariat. The Party must stand at the head of the working class; it must see farther than the working class; it must lead the proletariat, and not drag at the tail of the spontaneous movement. The parties of the Second International, which preach "tailism," are vehicles of bourgeois policy, which condemns the proletariat to the role of a tool in the hands of the bourgeoisie. Only a party which adopts the standpoint of an advanced detachment of the proletariat and is able to raise the masses to the level of understanding the class interests of the proletariat—only such a party can divert the working class from the path of trade unionism and turn it into an independent political force.

The Party is the political leader of the working class.

I have already spoken about the difficulties of the struggle of the working class, about the complicated conditions of the struggle, and about strategy and tactics, reserves and maneuvering, and attack and retreat. These conditions are no less complicated, if not more so, than the conditions of war. Who can see clearly under these conditions, who can give correct guidance to the proletarian millions? No army at war can dispense with an experienced General Staff if it does not want to be doomed to defeat. Is it not clear that the proletariat can still less dispense with such a General Staff if it does not want to allow itself to be devoured by its mortal enemies? But where is this General Staff? Only the revolutionary party of the proletariat can serve as this General Staff. The working class without a revolutionary party is an army without a General Staff.

The Party is the General Staff of the proletariat.

But the Party cannot be only an *advanced* detachment. It must at the same time be a detachment of the *class*, part of the class, closely bound up with it by all the fibers of its being. The distinction between the advanced detachment and the rest of the working class, between Party members and non-Party people, cannot disappear until classes disappear: it will exist as long as the ranks of the proletariat continue to be replenished with former members of other classes, as long as the working class as a whole is not in a position to rise to the level of the advanced detachment. But the Party would cease to be a party if this distinction developed into a gap, if the Party turned in on itself and became divorced from the non-Party masses. The Party cannot lead the class if it is not connected with the non-Party masses, if there is no bond between the Party and the non-Party masses, if these masses do not accept its leadership, if the Party does not enjoy moral and political credit among the masses.

Recently two hundred thousand new members from the ranks of the workers were admitted into our Party. The remarkable thing about this is the fact that these people did not so much join the Party themselves, as they were rather sent there by all the rest of the non-Party workers, who took an active part in the admission of the new members, and without whose approval no new member was accepted. This fact shows that the broad masses of non-Party workers regard our Party as *their* Party, as a Party *near* and *dear* to them, in whose expansion and consolidation they are vitally interested and to whose leadership they voluntarily entrust their destiny. It scarcely needs proof that without these intangible moral threads which connect the Party with the non-Party masses, the Party could not have become the decisive force of its class.

The Party is an inseparable part of the working class.

"We," says Lenin, "are the Party of a class; and, therefore, *almost the whole class* (and in times of war, in the period of civil war, the whole class) should act under the leadership of our Party, should adhere to our Party as closely as possible. But it would be Manilovism[20] and 'tailism' to think that at any time under capitalism almost the whole class, or the whole class, would be able to rise to the level of consciousness and activity of its advanced detachment, of its Social Democratic Party. No sensible Social Democrat has ever yet doubted that under capitalism even the trade union organizations (which are more primitive and more comprehensible to the undeveloped strata) are unable to embrace almost the whole, or the whole, working class. To forget the distinction between the advanced detachment and the whole of the masses which gravitate towards it, to forget the constant duty of the advanced detachment to *raise* ever wider strata to this most advanced level, means merely to deceive oneself, to shut one's eyes to the immensity of our tasks, and to narrow down these tasks." (See Vol. VI, pp. 205-06.)

2) *The Party as the organized detachment of the working class.* The Party is not only the *advanced* detachment of the working class. If it desires really to direct the struggle of the class it must at the same time be the *organized* detachment of its class. The Party's tasks under the conditions of capitalism are immense and extremely varied. The Party must direct the struggle of the proletariat under exceptionally difficult conditions of internal and external development: it must lead the proletariat in the offensive when the situation calls for an offensive; it must lead the proletariat so as to escape the blow of a powerful enemy when the situation calls for retreat; it must imbue the millions of unorganized non-Party workers with the spirit of discipline and system in the struggle, with the spirit of organization and endurance. But the Party can fulfill these tasks only if it is itself the embodiment of discipline and organization, if it is itself the *organized* detachment of the proletariat. Without these conditions there can be no question of the Party really leading the vast masses of the proletariat.

The Party is the organized detachment of the working class.

The conception of the Party as an organized whole is embodied in Lenin's well-known formulation of the first paragraph of our Party Rules, in which the Party is regarded as the *sum total* of its organizations, and the Party member as a member of one of the organizations of the Party. The Mensheviks, who objected to this formulation as early as 1903, proposed to substitute for it a "system" of self-enrollment in the Party, a "system" of conferring the "title" of Party member upon every "professor" and "high-school student," upon every "sympathizer" and "striker," who supported the Party in one way or another, but who did not join and did not want to join any one of the Party organizations. It scarcely needs proof that had this singular "system" become entrenched in our Party it would inevitably have led to our Party becoming inundated with professors and high-school students and to its degeneration into a loose, amorphous, disorganized "formation," losing itself in a sea of "sympathizers," obliterating the dividing line between the Party and the class, and upsetting the Party's task of raising the unorganized masses to the level of the advanced detachment. Needless to say, under such an opportunist "system" our Party would have been unable to fulfill the role of the organizing core of the working class in the course of our revolution.

"From the point of view of Comrade Martov," says Lenin, "the border line of the Party remains quite indefinite, for 'every striker' may 'proclaim himself a Party member.' What is the use of this vagueness? A wide extension of the 'title.' Its harm is that it introduces a *disorganizing* idea: the confusion of class and Party." (See Vol. VI, p. 211.)

But the Party is not merely the *sum total* of Party organizations. The Party is at the same time a single *system* of these organizations, their formal union into a single whole, with higher and lower leading bodies, with subordination of the minority to the majority, with practical decisions binding on all members of the Party. Without these conditions the Party cannot be a single organized whole capable of exercising systematic and organized leadership of the working-class struggle.

"*Formerly,*" says Lenin, "our Party was not a formally organized whole, but only the sum of separate groups, and therefore no other relations except those of ideological influence were possible between these groups. *Now* we have become an organized Party, and this implies the establishment of authority, the transformation of the power of ideas into the power of authority, the subordination of lower Party bodies to higher Party bodies." (See Vol. VI, p. 291.)

The principle of the minority submitting to the majority, the principle of directing Party work from a center, not infrequently gives rise to attacks on the part of wavering elements, to accusations of "bureaucracy," "formalism," etc. It scarcely needs proof that systematic work by the Party as one whole and directing of the struggle of the working class would be impossible without putting these principles into effect. Leninism in questions of organization is the unswerving application of these principles. Lenin terms the fight against these principles "Russian nihilism" and "aristocratic anarchism," which deserves to be ridiculed and swept aside.

Here is what Lenin says about these wavering elements in his book *One Step Forward*:

This aristocratic anarchism is particularly characteristic of the Russian nihilist. He thinks of the Party organization as a monstrous "factory." He regards the subordination of the part to the whole and of the minority to the majority as "serfdom" . . . ; division of labor under the direction of a center evokes from him a tragicomical outcry against people being transformed into "wheels and cogs" . . . ; mention of Party organizational rules calls forth a contemptuous grimace and the disdainful . . . remark that one could very well dispense with rules altogether.

It is clear, I think, that the cries about this celebrated bureaucracy are just a screen for dissatisfaction with the personal composition of the central bodies, a fig leaf. . . . You are a bureaucrat because you were appointed by the congress not by my will, but against it; you are a formalist because you rely on the formal decisions of the congress, and not on my consent; you are acting in a grossly mechanical way because you plead the "mechanical" majority at the Party Congress and pay no heed to my wish to be co-opted; you are an autocrat because you refuse to hand over the power to the old gang.[21] (See Vol. VI, pp. 310, 287.)

3) *The Party as the highest form of class organization of the proletariat*. The Party is the organized detachment of the working class. But the Party is not the only organization of the working class. The proletariat has also a number of other organizations, without which it cannot wage a successful struggle against capital: trade unions, co-operatives, factory organizations, parliamentary groups, non-Party women's associations, the press, cultural and educational organizations, youth leagues, revolutionary fighting organizations (in times of open revolutionary action), Soviets of deputies as the form of state organization (if the proletariat is in power), etc. The overwhelming majority of these organizations are non-Party, and only some of them adhere directly to the Party, or constitute offshoots of it. All these organizations, under certain

conditions, are absolutely necessary for the working class, for without them it would be impossible to consolidate the class positions of the proletariat in the diverse spheres of struggle; for without them it would be impossible to steel the proletariat as the force whose mission it is to replace the bourgeois order by the socialist order. But how can single leadership be exercised with such an abundance of organizations? What guarantee is there that this multiplicity of organizations will not lead to divergency in leadership? It may be said that each of these organizations carries on its work in its own special field, and that therefore these organizations cannot hinder one another. That, of course, is true. But it is also true that all these organizations should work in one direction for they serve *one* class, the class of the proletarians. The question then arises: who is to determine the line, the general direction, along which the work of all these organizations is to be conducted? Where is the central organization which is not only able, because it has the necessary experience, to work out such a general line, but, in addition, is in a position, because it has sufficient authority, to induce all these organizations to carry out this line, so as to attain unity of leadership and to make hitches impossible?

That organization is the Party of the proletariat.

The Party possesses all the necessary qualifications for this because, in the first place, it is the rallying center of the finest elements in the working class, who have direct connections with the non-Party organizations of the proletariat and very frequently lead them; because, secondly, the Party, as the rallying center of the finest members of the working class, is the best school for training leaders of the working class, capable of directing every form of organization of their class; because, thirdly, the Party, as the best school for training leaders of the working class, is, by reason of its experience and authority, the only organization capable of centralizing the leadership of the struggle of the proletariat, thus transforming each and every non-Party organization of the working class into an auxiliary body and transmission belt linking the Party with the class.

The Party is the highest form of class organization of the proletariat.

This does not mean, of course, that non-Party organizations, trade unions, co-operatives, etc., should be officially subordinated to the Party leadership. It only means that the members of the Party who belong to these organizations and are doubtlessly influential in them should do all they can to persuade these non-Party organizations to draw nearer to the Party of the proletariat in their work and voluntarily accept its political leadership.

That is why Lenin says that the Party is "the *highest* form of proletarian class association," whose political leadership must extend to every other form of organization of the proletariat. (See Vol. XXV, p. 194.)

That is why the opportunist theory of the "independence" and "neutrality" of the non-Party organizations, which breeds *independent* members of parliament and journalists *isolated* from the Party, *narrow-minded* trade union leaders and *philistine* co-operative officials, is wholly incompatible with the theory and practice of Leninism.

4) *The Party as an instrument of the dictatorship of the proletariat.* The Party is the highest form of organization of the proletariat. The Party is the principal guiding force within the proletarian class and among the organizations of that class. But it does not by any means follow from this that the Party can be regarded as an end in itself, as a self-sufficient force. The Party is not only the highest form of class association of the proletarians; it is at the same time an *instrument* in the hands of the proletariat *for* achieving the dictatorship, when that has not yet been achieved, and *for* consolidating and expanding the dictatorship, when it has already been achieved. The Party could not have risen so high in importance and could not have exerted its influence over all other forms of organization of the proletariat, if the latter had not been confronted with the question of power, if the conditions of imperialism, the inevitability of wars, and the existence of a crisis had not demanded the concentration of all the forces of the proletariat at one point, the gathering of all the threads of the revolutionary movement in one spot in order to overthrow the bourgeoisie and to achieve the dictatorship of the proletariat. The proletariat needs the Party first of all as its General Staff, which it must have for the successful seizure of power. It scarcely needs proof that without a party capable of rallying around itself the mass organizations of the proletariat and centralizing the leadership of the entire movement during the progress of the struggle, the proletariat in Russia could not have established its revolutionary dictatorship.

But the proletariat needs the Party not only to achieve the dictatorship; it needs it still more to maintain the dictatorship, to consolidate and expand it in order to achieve the complete victory of socialism.

"Certainly, almost everyone now realizes," says Lenin, "that the Bolsheviks could not have maintained themselves in power for two and a half months, let alone two and a half years, without the strictest, truly iron discipline in our Party, and without the fullest and unreserved support of the latter by the whole mass of the working class, that is, by all its thinking, honest, self-sacrificing and influential elements, capable of leading or of carrying with them the backward strata." (See Vol. XXV, p. 173.)

Now, what does to "maintain" and "expand" the dictatorship mean? It means imbuing the millions of proletarians with the spirit of discipline and organization; it means creating among the proletarian masses a cementing force and a bulwark against the corrosive influences of the petty-bourgeois elements and petty-bourgeois habits; it means strengthening the organizational work of the proletarians in re-educating and remolding the petty-bourgeois strata; it means helping the masses of the proletarians to educate themselves as a force capable of abolishing classes and of preparing the conditions for the organization of socialist production. But it is impossible to accomplish all this without a party which is strong by reason of its solidarity and discipline. •

"The dictatorship of the proletariat," says Lenin, "is a stubborn struggle—bloody and bloodless, violent and peaceful, military and economic, educational and administrative—against the forces and traditions of the old society. The force of habit of millions and tens of millions is a most terrible force. Without an iron party tempered in the struggle, without a party enjoying the confidence of all who are honest in the given class, without a party capable of watching and influencing the mood of the masses, it is impossible to conduct such a struggle successfully." (See Vol. XXV, p. 190.)

The proletariat needs the Party *for* the purpose of achieving and maintaining the dictatorship. The Party is an instrument of the dictatorship of the proletariat.

But from this it follows that when classes disappear and the dictatorship of the proletariat withers away, the Party also will wither away.

5) *The Party as the unity of will, unity incompatible with the existence of factions.* The achievement and maintenance

of the dictatorship of the proletariat is impossible without a party which is strong by reason of its solidarity and iron discipline. But iron discipline in the Party is inconceivable without unity of will, without complete and absolute unity of action on the part of all members of the Party. This does not mean, of course, that the possibility of conflicts of opinion within the Party is thereby precluded. On the contrary, iron discipline does not preclude but presupposes criticism and conflict of opinion within the Party. Least of all does it mean that discipline must be "blind." On the contrary, iron discipline does not preclude but presupposes conscious and voluntary submission, for only conscious discipline can be truly iron discipline. But after a conflict of opinion has been closed, after criticism has been exhausted and a decision has been arrived at, unity of will and unity of action of all Party members are the necessary conditions without which neither Party unity nor iron discipline in the Party is conceivable.

"In the present epoch of acute civil war," says Lenin, "the Communist Party will be able to perform its duty only if it is organized in the most centralized manner, if iron discipline bordering on military discipline prevails in it, and if its Party center is a powerful and authoritative organ, wielding wide powers and enjoying the universal confidence of the members of the Party." (See Vol. XXV, pp. 282-83.)

This is the position in regard to discipline in the Party in the period of struggle preceding the achievement of the dictatorship.

The same, but to an even greater degree, must be said about discipline in the Party after the dictatorship has been achieved.

"Whoever," says Lenin, "weakens in the least the iron discipline of the party of the proletariat (especially during the time of its dictatorship) actually aids the bourgeoisie against the proletariat." (See Vol. XXV, p. 190.)

But from this it follows that the existence of factions is compatible neither with the Party's unity nor with its iron discipline. It scarcely needs proof that the existence of factions leads to the existence of a number of centers, and the existence of a number of centers means the absence of one common center in the Party, the breaking up of unity of will, the weakening and disintegration of discipline, the weakening and disintegration of the dictatorship. Of course, the parties of the Second International, which are fighting against the dictatorship of the proletariat and have no desire to lead the proletarians to power, can afford such liberalism as freedom of factions, for they have no need at all for iron discipline. But the parties of the Communist International, whose activities are conditioned by the task of achieving and consolidating the dictatorship of the proletariat, cannot afford to be "liberal" or to permit freedom of factions.

The Party represents unity of will, which precludes all factionalism and division of authority in the Party.

Hence Lenin's warning about the "danger of factionalism from the point of view of Party unity and of achieving the unity of will of the vanguard of the proletariat as the fundamental condition for the success of the dictatorship of the proletariat," which is embodied in the special resolution of the Tenth Congress of our Party "On Party Unity."

Hence Lenin's demand for the "complete elimination of all factionalism" and the "immediate dissolution of all groups, without exception, that have been formed on the basis of various platforms," on pain of "unconditional and immediate expulsion from the Party." (See the resolution "On Party Unity.")

6) *The Party becomes strong by purging itself of opportunist elements.* The source of factionalism in the Party is its opportunist elements. The proletariat is not an isolated class. It is constantly replenished by the influx of peasants, petty bourgeois and intellectuals proletarianized by the development of capitalism. At the same time the upper stratum of the proletariat, principally trade union leaders and members of parliament who are fed by the bourgeoisie out of the superprofits extracted from the colonies, is undergoing a process of decay. "This stratum of bourgeoisified workers, or the 'labor aristocracy,'" says Lenin, "who are quite philistine in their mode of life, in the size of their earnings and in their entire outlook, is the principal prop of the Second International, and, in our days, the principal *social* (not military) *prop of the bourgeoisie.* For they are real *agents of the bourgeoisie in the working-class* movement, the labor lieutenants of the capitalist class . . . , real channels of reformism and chauvinism." (See Vol. XIX, p. 77.)

In one way or another, all these petty-bourgeois groups penetrate into the Party and introduce into it the spirit of indecision and opportunism, the spirit of demoralization and uncertainty. It is they, principally, that constitute the source of factionalism and disintegration, the source of disorganization and disruption of the Party from within. To fight imperialism with such "allies" in one's rear means to put oneself in the position of being caught between two fires, from the front and from the rear. Therefore, ruthless struggle against such elements, their expulsion from the Party, is a prerequisite for the successful struggle against imperialism.

The theory of "defeating" opportunist elements by ideological struggle within the Party, the theory of "overcoming" these elements within the confines of a single party, is a rotten and dangerous theory, which threatens to condemn the Party to paralysis and chronic infirmity, threatens to make the Party a prey to opportunism, threatens to leave the proletariat without a revolutionary party, threatens to deprive the proletariat of its main weapon in the fight against imperialism. Our Party could not have emerged onto the broad highway, it could not have seized power and organized the dictatorship of the proletariat, it could not have emerged victorious from the civil war, if it had had within its ranks people like Martov and Dan, Potresov and Axelrod. Our Party succeeded in achieving internal unity and unexampled cohesion of its ranks primarily because it was able in good time to purge itself of the opportunist pollution, because it was able to rid its ranks of the Liquidators and Mensheviks. Proletarian parties develop and become strong by purging themselves of opportunists and reformists, social-imperialists and social-chauvinists, social-patriots and social-pacifists.

The Party becomes strong by purging itself of opportunist elements.

"With reformists, Mensheviks, in our ranks," says Lenin, "it is *impossible* to be victorious in the proletarian revolution, it is *impossible* to defend it. That is obvious in principle, and it has been strikingly confirmed by the experience of both Russia and Hungary. . . . In Russia, difficult situations have arisen *many times*, when the Soviet regime would *most certainly* have been overthrown had Mensheviks, reformists and petty-bourgeois democrats remained in our Party. . . . In Italy, where, as is generally admitted, decisive battles betwen the proletariat and the bourgeoisie for the possession of state power are imminent—at such a moment it is not only absolutely necessary to remove the Mensheviks, reformists, the Turatists from the Party, but it may even be useful to remove excellent Communists who are liable to waver, and who reveal a tendency to waver towards "unity" with the reformists, to remove them from all responsible posts. . . . On the eve of a revolution, and at a moment when a most fierce struggle is being waged for its victory, the slightest wavering in the ranks of the Party may *wreck everything*, frustrate the revolution, wrest the power from the hands of the proletariat; because this power is not yet consolidated, and because the attack against it is still very strong. The desertion of wavering leaders at such a time does not weaken, but strengthens the Party, the working-class movement and the revolution." (See Vol. XXV, pp. 462, 463, 464.)

IX. STYLE IN WORK

I am not referring to literary style. What I have in mind is style in work, that specific and peculiar feature in the practice of Leninism which creates the special type of Leninist worker. Leninism is a school of theory and practice which trains a special type of Party and state worker, creates a special Leninist style in work.

What are the characteristic features of this style? What are its peculiarities?

It has two specific features:

a) Russian revolutionary sweep and

b) American efficiency.

The style of Leninism consists in combining these two specific features in Party and state work.

Russian revolutionary sweep is an antidote to inertia, routine, conservatism, mental stagnation and slavish submission to ancient traditions. Russian revolutionary sweep is the life-giving force which stimulates thought, impels things forward, breaks the past and opens up perspectives. Without it no progress is possible.

But Russian revolutionary sweep has every chance of degenerating in practice into empty "revolutionary" Manilovism if it is not combined with American efficiency in work. Examples of this degeneration are only too numerous. Who does not know the disease of "revolutionary" scheme concocting and "revolutionary" plan drafting, which springs from the belief in the power of decrees to arrange everything and remake everything? A Russian writer, I. Ehrenburg, in his story *The Percomman* (*The Perfect Communist Man*), has portrayed the type of a "Bolshevik" afflicted with this disease, who set himself the task of finding a formula for the ideally

perfect man and . . . became "submerged" in this "work."
The story contains a great exaggeration, but it certainly gives
a correct likeness of the disease. But no one, I think, has
so ruthlessly and bitterly ridiculed those afflicted with this
disease as Lenin. Lenin stigmatized this morbid belief in
concocting schemes and in turning out decrees as "communist swagger."

"Communist swagger," says Lenin, "means that a man, who is
a member of the Communist Party, and who has not yet been
purged from it, imagines that he can solve all his problems by
issuing communist decrees." (See Vol. XXVII, pp. 50-51.)

Lenin usually contrasted hollow "revolutionary" phrasemongering with plain everyday work, thus emphasizing that
"revolutionary" scheme concocting is repugnant to the spirit
and the letter of true Leninism.

"Fewer pompous phrases, more plain *everyday* work . . . "
says Lenin.
"Less political fireworks and more attention to the simplest but
most vital . . . facts of communist construction. . . ." (See
Vol. XXIV, pp. 343 and 335.)

American efficiency is, in contrast, an antidote to "revolutionary" Manilovism and fantastic scheme concocting.
American efficiency is that indomitable force which neither
knows nor recognizes obstacles; which with its businesslike
perseverance brushes aside all obstacles; which continues at
a task once started until it is finished, even if it is a minor
task; and without which serious constructive work is inconceivable.
But American efficiency has every chance of degenerating
into narrow and purposeless practicality if it is not combined
with Russian revolutionary sweep. Who has not heard of that
disease of narrow empiricism and purposeless practicality
which has not infrequently caused certain "Bolsheviks" to
degenerate and to abandon the cause of the revolution? We
find a reflection of this peculiar disease in a story by B. Pilnyak, entitled *The Naked Year,* which depicts types of Russian "Bolsheviks" of strong will and practical determination
who "function" very "energetically," but without vision, without knowing "what it is all about," and who, therefore,
stray from the path of revolutionary work. No one has ridiculed this disease of practicality so incisively as Lenin. He

branded it as "narrow-minded empiricism" and "brainless practicality." He usually contrasted it with vital revolutionary work and with the necessity of having a revolutionary perspective in all our daily activities, thus emphasizing that this purposeless practicality is as repugnant to true Leninism as "revolutionary" scheme concocting.

The combination of Russian revolutionary sweep with American efficiency is the essence of Leninism in Party and state work.

This combination alone produces the finished type of Leninist worker, the style of Leninism in work.

IV.

THE SOVIET BLOC AFTER STALIN:
THE NEW REVISIONISTS

It is a frequent occurrence in Russian history for periods of extreme reaction and tension to be followed by periods of relaxation. At the beginning of the nineteenth century the oppressive rule of Tsar Paul gave way to the remarkably liberal early years in the reign of Paul's son, Alexander I. The "Great Reforms" of Alexander II, in the 1860's, followed the profoundly conservative, militaristic despotism of Nicholas I and the distress and humiliation experienced during the Crimean War. The tensions and dislocations caused by industrialization and by the Russo-Japanese War at the turn of the century were largely responsible for the establishment of the first parliamentary limitations on autocracy in Russian history together with a general "thaw" in social, economic and cultural life. During the First World War, the extraordinarily short-sighted, reactionary policies of Nicholas II resulted in the overthrow of Tsarism in February 1917 and the formation of a liberal Provisional Government which was to have led to a fully democratic republic on the model of those existing in Western Europe. Finally, the crises of revolution and civil war, with all their accompanying sacrifices, forced Lenin in 1921 to announce the NEP retreat that lasted until 1929.

Against this background, it would have been surprising if at some point following the death of Stalin the intense suffering caused by his tyranny and by the tragic losses and deprivations endured during the Second World War had not been balanced by a period of liberalization. If there is anything unusual here it is that Stalin himself did not move in this direction after the war. Placing the post-Stalin "thaw" in its historical context in no way diminishes its significance, however. Even a cursory survey of the principal reforms achieved during most of the brief, prerevolutionary thaws shows that they either remained integral parts of a gradually evolving West European civilization or, if abolished by a subsequent reaction, served as symbols for later progress in this liberal direction. Since the end of 1956, when the remarkably frank "thaw" statements became associated with open political rebellion in Hungary and Poland against Soviet domination, there has been, in fact, a persistent and intense effort by the Soviet Party and its satellite representatives to repress this "revisionism." As a result, the radical publications that will be reviewed in this chapter have been driven, in large part, underground. Still, the writers who gained fame in these early "thaw" years continue to write, and in spite of the Party's campaign against revisionism, it continues to reappear in a way that would have been inconceivable during the Stalin years. Because of this tenacity, there are many today who believe that institutions and attitudes have emerged, in part as a result of Stalin's policies, that may prove strong enough to defend at least the main concessions granted since Stalin's death and perhaps even to foster additional liberalism.

The themes of the post-Stalin period were determined by those of the preceding Stalin years. Since ubiquitous and unrelieved police terror was the principal source of despair under Stalin, after Stalin's death in 1953 it became the first focus of attack. The last act of Stalinist terror, the so-called "doctors' plot," was dismissed as a police fabrication, the officials of the Ministry of State Security (the MVD) were criticized for having "forgotten they are servants of the people and guardians of Soviet legality" and for having "fabricated provocations against honest Soviet people and outstanding leaders of Soviet science." Two months later, Beria, the head of the MVD, was arrested along with other leaders of the secret-police empire. In December of that year, it was announced that they had been found guilty and shot. For several years thereafter other members of the police were purged, former victims of the Stalin terror were "rehabilitated," the MVD was put under the supervision of the Chief Procurator's Office, and the dreaded forced labor camps were either closed or significantly liberalized. Phrases like "the rights of the citizen," "socialist legality," and "civil rights" were often heard and read during these first years following Stalin's death, indicating that Party leaders were fully aware of the effects of Stalin's terror and the attitude of the Russian public toward it.

Still more dramatic, however, was the extensive campaign undertaken by the Party to sever its links with the Stalinist terror by openly and persistently attacking Stalin himself. In the dispute that raged in the Party when Lenin first publicized his strongly centralized leadership program, Trotsky had predicted that as a result of such a program "the organization of the Party takes the place of the Party itself; the Central Committee takes the place of the organization; and, finally, the dictator takes the place of the Central Committee." One of the most significant developments in the post-Stalin period is the tendency to move one step back in this evolution—from single dictatorship (the "cult of the personality") to rule by the central committee ("collective leadership"). At the Twentieth Party Congress in February 1956 and during the following spring the Party's attack against Stalin's terror and arbitrary despotism reached incredible proportions. The most dramatic point came when, at a closed session of the February Congress, Khrushchev delivered his famous "secret speech." Some idea of the content and character of this astounding statement can be gained from the following excerpts:

Stalin originated the concept "enemy of the people." This term automatically rendered it unnecessary that the ideological errors of a man or men engaged in a controversy be proven; this term made possible the usage of the most cruel repression, violating all norms of revolutionary legality, against anyone who in any way disagreed with Stalin, against those were only suspected of hostile intent, against those who had bad reputations. This concept "enemy of the people" actually eliminated the possibility of any kind of ideological fight or the making of one's views known on this or that issue, even those of a practical character. In the main, and in actuality, the only proof of guilt used, against all norms of current legal science, was the "confession" of the accused himself; and, as subsequent probing proved, "confessions" were acquired through physical pressures against the accused.

Arbitrary behavior by one person encouraged and permitted arbitrariness in others. Mass arrests and deportations of many thousands of people, execution without trial and without normal investigation created conditions of insecurity, fear and even desperation.

. . . It became apparent that many party, Soviet and economic activists, who were branded in 1937-1938 as "enemies," were actually never enemies, spies, wreckers, etc., but were always honest Communists; they were only so stigmatized and, often, no longer able to bear barbaric tortures, they charged themselves (at the order of the investigative judges-falsifiers) with all kinds of grave and unlikely crimes.

It was determined that of the 139 members and candidates of the party's Central Committee who were elected at the 17th Congress, 98 persons, *i.e.*, 70 percent were arrested and shot (mostly in 1937-1938).

Mass arrests of party, Soviet, economic and military workers caused tremendous harm to our country and to the cause of socialist advancement.

Mass repressions had a negative influence on the moral-political condition of the Party, created a situation of uncertainty, contributed to the spreading of unhealthy suspicion, and sowed distrust among Communists. All sorts of slanderers and careerists were active.

. . . And how is it possible that a person confesses to crimes which he has not committed? Only in one way—because of application of physical methods of pressuring him, tortures, bringing him to a state of unconsciousness, deprivation of his judgment, taking away of his human dignity. In this manner were "confessions" acquired.

. . . One of the most characteristic examples of Stalin's self-glorification and his lack of even elementary modesty is the edition of his Short Biography, which was published in 1948. This book is an expression of the most dissolute flattery, an example of making a man into a godhead, of transforming him into an infallible sage, "the greatest leader, sublime strategist of all times and nations."

Although it would require far too much space to show the impact of such remarks throughout the Soviet bloc, the effect can be seen in the following statement taken from a speech made by the Polish Party chief, Gomulka, in October 1956:

The 20th CPSU Congress stimulated a turn in the political life of the country. . . . People began to straighten their backs. Silent, enslaved minds began to shake off the poison of mendacity, falsehood and hypocrisy. The rigid clichés, previously predominant on Party platforms and at public meetings, as well as in the press, began to give place to creative, living words. In Poland, too, tragedy occurred when innocent people were sent to their deaths. Many others, including Communists, were imprisoned, often for many years, despite their innocence. Many people were submitted to bestial tortures. Terror and demoralization were widespread. On the soil of the cult of the individual, phenomena arose which violated and even nullified the most profound meaning of the people's power.

Besides attacking both Stalin and his system of universal terror, the Party showed its awareness of the sources of popular hostility by promising and actually working toward important improvements in living standards. Without shifting the main economic emphasis from investment in heavy industry, in military and scientific development, and in politically motivated foreign loans, the Party devoted a larger amount of the nation's resources to the production of consumers' goods. Moreover, to achieve these and other goals, political as well as economic, the Party, under the leadership of Khrushchev, introduced a number of changes in the economy: management of the economy was greatly decentralized, agricultural equipment was distributed among the collectives rather than controlled by the more centralized machine-tractor stations; and both the peasantry and the urban workers were granted important concessions in their general working conditions.

In some ways the most important aspect of the thaw has been the partial dismantling of the "iron curtain" that Stalin had erected between his realm and the outside world. The cultural exchange program brings Russians to the West and, together with the vast extension of tourism, brings westerners to Russia. There has been a liberalization in the range of western films and literature allowed into Russia and in the number of visiting professionals in the arts and sciences. No one who has visited Russia would exaggerate any of this: it is as difficult to find a noncommunist western newspaper in Russia as it is to find a Soviet citizen traveling apart from a group in the West; and one could hardly doubt either the absence of freedom as one knows it in the West or the prevalence of living conditions far lower than those characteristic of western societies. Still, when compared with conditions under Stalin, the gains are as obvious as they are welcomed by the Russian people.

There are a variety of interpretations offered as explanation for the thaw. Those who recall the number of similar retreats in Russian history and who emphasize both the force of the basic commitment to world communism and the power of Soviet totalitarianism, tend to believe that the post-Stalin thaw is a temporary, tactical move. It will continue, according to this interpretation, only until the Party once again completely establishes itself in power and, above all, until the intraparty conflict gives way to a dictatorship as unlimited as was Stalin's.

Others argue that what we are witnessing is Russia's coming of age economically, culturally and, perhaps, even politically. While much of "Stalinism" can be attributed to Stalin's own personality as well as to the Marxist-Leninist world view, a significant part in this intensely exploitative period was played by the needs of "primitive socialist accumulation," the needs of creating the urban-industrial base that should have been there long before the socialist revolution took place. Now this industrialization is nearing completion and the very existence of an urban-industrial society created by Stalin's exploitation may have removed some of the conditions necessary for the continuance of such exploitation. For one thing, the requirements of modern economic development, involving as they do more refined research, production and administrative abilities, are becoming increasingly inconsistent with Stalinist methods. As the Polish Premier Cyrankiewicz said in 1956:

Passivity, wherever it exists, is exercising a most negative influence on the productive apparatus. There is only one way of . . . overcoming passivity—the further consistent democratization of our life. . . . We cannot achieve this through methods of ordering about, of pressure, of compulsion. . . .

But those who see something permanent in the "thaw," argue that it is motivated by conditions more fundamental than the need of promoting new attitudes necessary for further economic expansion. They argue that the Russian population as a whole, and particularly the upper classes who hold the well-paid positions in the party, economy, and army and in the academic, literary, artistic and scientific professions, will simply not tolerate a revival of Stalinism. Moreover, the more urbanized and educated the society becomes, the more the upper social strata change from the self-sacrificing idealists of the Revolution to a status-conscious, privileged ruling class. In short, the more "bourgeois" they become. The party is thus caught in a most uncomfortable contradiction: to compete with the West, Russia must ever more rapidly advance in virtually all areas that have characterized western civilization—massive consumers' goods as well as rapid development of heavy industries, education on the highest levels as well as general literacy for propaganda purposes. Yet, every step in these directions brings the atti-

tudes and desires of the population closer to those prevalent
in the bourgeois urban societies of the West.

Marxism is here revenging itself against Lenin and the
Bolsheviks for having so completely ignored its doctrines in
1917. Impatient for power and concluding from "revisionism"
in the West that a "bourgeois" Russia would never create
conditions for a socialist revolution, Lenin took advantage
of the war crisis and conquered the State. Having won power
in an economically underdeveloped rural economy he was
forced to do what Plekhanov had predicted: he and his
Party after him had to do what the bourgeoisie should have
done for them—build an urban-industrial economy. Now, over
half a century since Lenin carried through his voluntaristic,
un-Marxist revolution, it is becoming painfully clear to the
remaining idealists in the Party that what the Bolsheviks have
created at such immense cost is a society possessing the
negative sides of the western urban, materialistic society
without its positive features. The persistent campaigns against
antisocial behavior, "parasitism," corruption, hooliganism,
and feathering one's own nest at the expense of the
State; the patently "bourgeois" lives of the well-placed officials, scientists, managers and the like; and the ever more
obvious desire among these segments of the population to
travel freely to the West and to enjoy the material and
cultural fruits of western civilization—all these are clear sign-
posts marking the road traveled by contemporary Russian
society. Looking back from today's Russia to the Revolution
of 1917 and its Marxist-socialist goals, it now seems clear
that the Bolsheviks have been fated to play the role of the
class they displaced, the bourgeois capitalists. Moreover, the
extremely low levels of economic production in prerevolutionary Russia, the heritage of Tsarist autocracy, the Marxist-
Leninist world view, and Stalin's irrationalism all combined
to make the Bolshevik "state capitalism" incomparably more
oppressive and exploitative then its western counterparts.

From the point of view of this survey, the most important
events of Khrushchev's "reign" thus far are his efforts to
counteract somehow these powerful tendencies gradually
transforming Russia into a bourgeois society. There are two
main lines of attack against these threatening processes: the
strengthening of institutions that are supposed to foster socialist attitudes and a new emphasis on the role of the Party as a
moral guide. In an effort to develop the institution that has

long been considered of primary importance in nurturing "the new Soviet man," the Party has undertaken an elaborate boarding-school program that is supposed to bring virtually all Soviet children under the constant guidance of professionals who are instructed to replace the individualistic attitudes fostered in the traditional family by a selfless socialist consciousness. In order to check the growing class differentiation, efforts are being made to narrow the range of incomes, to reduce the privileges of the Soviet upper classes, to rescind earlier permission supporting private home construction, and, finally, to impose on students who will fill the ranks of the elite some training in manual labor either in the factory or on the collective farm. In addition to these measures, the Party is making full use of such organizations as the "comradely courts" and the "volunteer civilian militia" and such laws as those against "parasitism" in order to bring all sorts of psychological, social and physical pressure to bear on those displaying antisocialist behavior—*i.e.*, "aping the West."

Regarding the role of the Party, we are witnessing the beginning of the third stage of its history. Under Lenin, a disciplined, monolithic party emerged as a result of Lenin's desire to take power even though the proper conditions for a socialist revolution or socialist society were lacking. The Party under Stalin was used to create these conditions: an industrial-urban economy that the bourgeoisie should have created before the socialist revolution. The result of this massive undertaking has been the establishment of what is rapidly becoming a fairly ordinary bourgeois, philistine society. The Party under Khrushchev and his successors, therefore, is being assigned the task of trying to make a bourgeois society produce socialist citizens.

In an interview with a correspondent from the *London Times*, Khrushchev summarized this new, and apparently permanent, Party responsibility.

The Party has stronger foundations than the state organs. It arose and exists not as a result of obligations of a legal order. Its development was called for by circumstances derived from political concepts, and mankind will always be in need of moral factors.

The State, representing the instrument of force, is still destined to wither away under communism, but not the Party. As one author in the party journal *Kommunist* wrote in 1958, the Party will use "no other methods but those of

This passion for honesty after decades of forced deception is one of the principal characteristics of Soviet society in the post-Stalin years. It is well summarized in the following excerpt from a poem by a leading "thaw" poet, Evtushenko:

t twenty, I've looked over everything again—
What I said but shouldn't have said,
What I didn't say but should have said.

another contribution to *Literary Moscow*, a short story enled "Levers," shows the Stalinist deception at work by conasting the honest comments exchanged at a Party meeting fore the meeting started with the dogmatic, doctrinaire tements made during the meeting. The outburst against alinist lies was even greater in the satellites. In April 1956, letter appeared in the Polish *Nowa Kultura* denouncing e entire Stalinist oppression in Poland in terms as forceful anything published in the West. The attack, not at all usual in 1956-1957, focused particular attention on the osed dishonesty:

s in architecture, lies in literature, lies in plastics. Were there at that time any intelligent people? There were, but they to be silent, those people, in order not to be subversive. . . . what were we supposed to do? What were we actually doing his "Stalinist" period? That which we were told to do. We ted; we clapped; we went to parades and meetings where idance was taken.

losely associated with this reaction against dishonesty fe and art, against, in other words, the demands of arian, socialist realism, is a rejection of the dehumanized, otyped "positive hero" of the Stalinist period in favor ore creditable, living characters. Lust, ambition, greed, ration, despair, loneliness, pessimism and the like are back where they belong. The so-called steam-shovel oach to literature that subordinated interest in human is to interest in various economic, political and miligoals is widely rejected now, even by Party officials. e has been a revival of lyric poetry, love stories and e human interest tales concerning ordinary human ons, desires and follies. Along with this is a new interest stern literature and art and, even more significant, a to learn as much as possible about prerevolutionary

persuasion, no other sanctions except moral censure and the force of public opinion; and this sanction is a truly communist one; it will be retained under communism." It would be impossible here to discuss the variety of tasks assigned the Party now and presumably forever, but as the following quotations from the party press indicate, they go considerably beyond either the Leninist effort to mobilize for revolution and civil war or the Stalinist task of mobilizing for industrialization, collectivization, police terror and international war.

We conduct political, cultural and educational work primarily in enterprises and institutions; that is, at places of work. But man does not work 24 hours a day. He spends a greater part of his time at home where he rests, studies and amuses himself. Can we be indifferent to the manner in which he conducts his way of life? The Central Committee of the CPSU has instructed the party organizations to evince more solicitude for political and cultural-enlightenment work during the workers' days of rest and holidays. On such days they are to arrange meetings with leading workers in the scientific field as well as in literature and the arts, and with production innovators; to organize walks in the squares, parks and market places; to arrange sports competitions, collective excursions of workers and employees with the participation of leading workers, and so on.

The Party is at war with the bourgeois tendencies in Russia and in the satellites. But, to a large extent the members of the Party belong to the very class, the privileged elite, who most often manifest bourgeois tendencies. It was one thing to turn a Party of former peasants, workers and idealistic intellectuals against the remnants of the prerevolutionary middle and upper classes. It is quite another to command a Party filled with representatives of the comfortable Soviet elite to oppose tendencies that they themselves demonstrate and that more and more are coming to characterize the privileged classes as a whole.

In order to organize an army of absolutely loyal, subservient bureaucrats, Stalin worked out an effective balance between the "carrot" of materialistic privileges and the "stick" of terror. Many believe that before Stalin's death it had become quite clear even to Stalin that if one result of this system was security for himself, another was a stagnant, routinized, class-stratified society and economy, controlled by an elite unwilling to show initiative or to make even the simplest decisions for fear of recrimination. According to this view, before his death Stalin had planned another great purge as a means of replacing this ossified ruling class by new blood from below, young men and women whose spirits had not been crushed by Stalinist despotism and who could be spurred on by promised material rewards. Stalin's death stopped the purge, and the bureaucracy remains, still in possession of its privileges and still displaying its self-centered materialistic philistinism and stultifying bureaucratism.

The character of this status-conscious, conservative ruling class is the subject of much of the "thaw" literature, both in the Soviet Union and in the East European satellites. The most famous criticism and certainly one of the most significant is *The New Class* written by Milovan Djilas, at one time second ranking member of the Yugoslav Communist Party. It is included in the collecton both because it represents an extremely perceptive analysis of the social and political system ultimately created by Leninism and Stalinism and because it represents one of the principal lines of attack against this system on the part of thoughtful and courageous Communists who have been disillusioned by it.

The difficult problem involved in using an organization filled with self-seeking careerism and complacency as a weapon against these same "bourgeois" characteristics in society as a whole is intensified manyfold because of the character of one segment of the Soviet Party élite—the intelligentsia. To appreciate this, however, one must keep continually in mind the official function of Soviet intellectuals, so different from that of their western counterparts. They are organically integrated into the life of the society and assigned one of its most vital functions. Recruited and trained to serve on one or another cultural "front," they are charged with instilling a well-defined and functionally indispensable set of goals, justifications, and criteria for judgment that sanction the rule of the Party and mobilize the nation to realize purposes established by the Party. They are given, in short, the task of providing legitimacy for the Party and its aims in a system that has no other institutionalized process for legitimizing power.

The attitudes of the intellectuals are becoming ever more inconsistent with this task. Consider, for example, the whole question of socialist realism. The socialist-realist writers and artists are supposed to portray an inspiring future socialist

"reality" and to present it in a way immediately comm to the mass public. Toward these ends, they have with oversimplified, stereotyped literary and pictoria that lack the ambiguities and complexities of real pec more important, they have exemplified in their subordination of personal, human interests and s to the purposes of society as a whole. All of this explicitly or implicitly rejected by the emerging of the Soviet intellectuals.

The despair felt by the economically succe painter, the socialist-realist Vladimir Pukhov in I burg's *Thaw*, and his open and persistent envy known, poor, garret-artist Saburov who painte and passionately, concerned only with creativity– whole theme in brief. In a famous eulogy ¢ Ehrenburg expressed other aspects of this conce esty in the arts:

Above all else, the lesson of Stendhal is for me al truthfulness of his books. . . . He hated ¢ servility. . . . The perversion of the soul by coerc bribery and threats was the major and, perhaps, th theme of Stendhal's novels. . . . No matter how analysis of society, no matter how subject any si to general processes, the world of the novel is dis osophical generalizations, government plans, and . . . There was neither nationalistic swagger in for foreign ways of life.

"There is nothing more harmful to art th make all theaters alike and to limit artisti the famous actor Cherkasov wrote in *Pravd* poser Khachaturian, appealing for freedom cized the "wrong practice of interfering wit creative process by officials in music institut be a writer so characterless that he needs t write?" asked Ehrenburg. In what is usual most significant single publication of the er II of *Literary Moscow*, a contributing attacked the Stalinist controls in the thought. Blind faith and dogma replace¢ artistic creativity, he argued; criticism b artists were relegated to the roles of illu of odes."

Russian literature long condemned as antisocial and decadent by the Party.

If the urge toward honesty has led to a new emphasis on the true-to-life individual, this new attention to the individual is associated with another and even more important concern among many of today's Soviet and East European intellectuals. Existing individuals have not only become important for the intellectual in his capacity as writer and artist, they have also become a focus for his ethical judgment. There is a critically important interrelationship here. The socialist-realist author molded his material around the scaffolding of historical determinism that both dehumanized the individual as an object in art and sanctioned his sacrifice as an object in society and in historical development. The current thaw sentiments reflect a radical change at each point in this pattern. In place of politicized, utilitarian art, there is a call for free creativity; in place of stereotyped abstract characters, there are more well-rounded, living beings; in place of the willingness to sacrifice the individual in the name of society, science and history, there is an insistence on his inviolability in the name of absolute moral values.

One of the finest expressions of this new attitude toward historical determinism and its relationship to traditional ethics was published by a young Polish philosopher, Laszek Kolakowski, a student of early modern European philosophy and a member of the faculty of the University of Warsaw. An essay from his work, *Responsibility and History*, has been selected for this collection.

One might be less encouraged by these developments were they associated with a passing phase, a temporary, aberrational situation conditioned, say, by the post-Stalin power crisis in the Soviet Union and its satellites. However, there are a number of reasons that suggest not only the permanence, but the intensification of these tendencies.

As Soviet society matures, the Soviet intellectual is more and more recruited from the privileged families which are able to provide their young with good educational opportunities and bring them into contact with traditional European and nineteenth-century Russian culture. The aspiring intellectual is thoroughly familiar with the finest productions of this cultural tradition. He cannot help but regard them as the models for good art and literature. Consequently, he cannot but experience tension and frustration when he is forced to violate his own artistic sensitivities by creating the mediocre potboilers that Party policy requires. Both the continued expansion of Soviet education and the continued formation of the familiar class society are predictable tendencies, notwithstanding the Party's recent intensive efforts to check the latter process.

Not only are the artists and the writers themselves attracted by western themes and styles, but the educated Soviet and East European citizens appear to be no less eager for this advance from the mediocrity of socialist realism. Since this educated public forms the dominant social, economic and political leadership, the westernism of the intelligentsia finds increasingly powerful support. We are witnessing the emergence of a social phenomenon similar to that occurring in France during the Enlightenment, when the aristocratic *salon* patronized the *philosophe* whose every word was a blow against the aristocracy and the *ancien régime* that nurtured it.

In the minds of Soviet bloc intellectuals, the cultural polarization between East and West is likely to remain, but they will tend increasingly to consider Russia part of the broad western tradition and to see Communist Chinese socialist realism as an expression of a culturally inferior East. In fact, judging from, on the one hand, the intense desire of Russian youth to visit the West and their increasing attraction to various forms of western culture and, on the other hand, the almost total lack of interest among Soviet citizens to tour the East and the frequent derogatory references to Chinese socialist-realist art and literature, this cultural pattern is already more an actuality than a prophecy.

The willingness to indulge in unorthodox artistic and literary expression is obviously linked to the risks involved. Consequently, the political liberalization contributes significantly to the conditions fostering westernizing tendencies. This touches an issue that is among those most ardently debated by western students of Soviet affairs. The "optimists" feel that the liberalization will advance slowly, or, in any case, that it is very unlikely that conditions will return to what they were under Stalin. If, in fact, political restrictions are further relaxed, or even if the situation in this respect remains stable, it is probable that more and more of the young intellectuals will find the attractions of creative

freedom worth the political and career risks. This tendency
is further promoted by another characteristic of the thaw
By ending mass terror and thus allowing individuals to express their views more freely, the post-Stalin Party has undermined the atomization of Soviet society that had been one of
the most important props of the Stalinist despotism. Under
Stalin it was virtually impossible to know the attitudes of
any but one's most intimate friends and members of one's
family; and even then one could never be sure. Universal
terror meant universal mistrust. The flood of criticism openly
and courageously expressed during the years since Stalin's
death showed each critic that there were indeed many who
shared his views and were willing to express them. Besides
fostering a sense of strength in numbers, this experience led
to the formation of all sorts of small intellectual circles where
students, painters, writers and those simply interested in such
matters gathered to discuss intellectual problems and to display and criticize unofficial works of art and literature.

Related to the preceding point is the prospect for a continuation and expansion of cultural contacts with the West.
As things are now, westernism is promoted by visitors from
the West, Soviet delegations touring the West, the admission into Russia of western art, music and literature, both
in the original and in translation, and the implicit sanction
given such communication by the "coexistence" campaign.
It should be kept in mind also that Yugoslavia and such
satellites as Poland and Czechoslovakia are important inter-
mediaries for western cultural influence. Whether this contact will continue, expand, decrease or end is impossible
to predict. However, it is likely that the appetite for things
western whetted by earlier contacts, particularly among
the dominant classes in Russia, will support the continuation
of these contacts.

Finally, and perhaps most important, there are excellent
prospects for a revival in the Soviet Union and Eastern
Europe of the intellectual's traditional role—*l'homme révolté.*
One of the most significant features of Soviet society has been
the absence of the social critic in the country where, before
the revolution, social criticism was the most extensive and
passionate in Europe. In addition to the tendencies mentioned above, there is another reason why one might predict
a sharp increase in social criticism in Communist Europe.
Brought up on high ideals of self-sacrifice, brotherhood, so-

cial service, heroic honesty and even stoic asceticism, the
Soviet youth find themselves in a society dominated by
hypocrisy, materialistic egoism and incessant intrigues that
flagrantly violate these norms. For many, a sense of extreme
alienation results from this contrast. Time and again visitors
to the Soviet Union as well as articles in the Soviet press
report this alienation, expressed in such things as excessive
drinking, a preoccupation with sex, thrills and petty crimes,
and a general empty, aimless amoralism.

Those familiar with the course of Russian intellectual
and social history in the nineteenth century will recognize
this mood as that characterizing the "hero of our time," the
"Byronic" or "superfluous" man filled with bitterness and
frustration. At a later stage in the evolution of the nineteenth-century Russian intelligentsia, this frustration became
the fuel of brilliant social criticism. It is quite possible that
a similar process will evolve in Soviet Russia and Eastern
Europe. The analogy is particularly close, since the alienated
youth of both periods are offspring of the privileged families.
Furthermore, in both periods traditional western values
play a vital role in fostering opposition to prevailing in-
justices.

In order for these values to become operative, it is necessary for the intelligentsia to abandon the dialectical historicism that sanctions the sacrifice of the living individual
for some future goal. As we have seen, this process is now
under way. It is also already clear from the thaw literature
that many young intellectuals have begun to sense deeply
the vast gap separating them and their class from the common people of the factory and, especially, of the collective
farm, and that they feel particular resentment towards the
comfortable, privileged officials who often display a virtually
feudal aloofness from the feelings and burdens of the lower
classes. Among young Communists this resentment sometimes takes the form of a neo-Leninism or neo-Bolshevism,
a desire to return to what these young party members believe to have been the early revolutionary ideals of the
Bolshevik Party. It is in this group within the Party that
the old-guard bureaucrats often find their most severe critics.

Certainly the Stalinist class "carrot" works to recruit an
administrative, economic and scientific elite. But we in the
West have not given sufficient attention to the response of
those who, conscious of the costs of this carrot, find it re-

pulsive fare. As Djilas' *New Class* and Kolakowski's *Responsibility and History* dramatically demonstrate, it takes but the smallest shift of attitude to turn the entire powerful battery of Marxist social, economic and ethical judgments against the very system that devotes so much of its resources to inculcating these judgments. Moreover, since the Communist ideals are more radical and uncompromising than were those of eighteenth- and nineteenth-century reformers, and since the evils of Soviet totalitarianism are even greater than those of the prerevolutionary autocracy, the contrast between the ideal and the real for the privileged and "conscience-stricken" Soviet youth may become even sharper and more intolerable than it was for their nineteenth-century predecessors.

The final selection in this chapter, the new draft proposal of the Soviet Communist Party, represents the official response to these post-Stalin developments. Published at the end of July 1961, and referred to by such phrases as "the Khrushchev Doctrine" and "the New Communist Manifesto," it is unquestionably the most important official document published in Russia since Stalin's death. It is also the clearest statement of Khrushchev's policies and aims yet published and, as such, is a direct and open challenge to the non-Communist world. At both the 18th Party Congress of 1939 and the 19th Congress of 1952 a new party program was promised. None appeared, however, and the following document thus represents the first complete revision of the party program since 1919, when Lenin presented a program to replace the original, 1898 statement of party aims.

Taken as a whole, the program seems strikingly moderate and even "revisionist" in character. In sharp contrast to the prospects placed before the Chinese people, who are repeatedly told that they must suffer further deprivations as the price of progress, the Soviet citizens are promised continual improvements in living standards, the rapid acquisition of typically western, "bourgeois" services and comforts, and a variety of free benefits that by 1980 will supposedly bring Russia to the very threshold of true communism. Similarly, whereas Chinese Communists persistently stress the bitter conflicts that divide the Communist and non-Communist worlds, the Soviet leaders here no less emphatically stress the possibilities of "peaceful coexistence."

Perhaps the most dramatic expression of this apparent

moderation, however, concerns the Communist Party both in Russia and in the non-Communist countries. Provision is herein made for the mandatory turnover by election of the Communist Party leadership. For the Communist Parties outside of Russia, the program not only acknowledges the possibility of a Communist victory by free election rather than by revolution, but also discusses co-operation with business groups and the achievement of socialism by means of buying-out the private owners. Finally, as indications of the prevailing moderation, there is no mention of Stalin in the document, and while East European communist achievements are given considerable attention, the Chinese Communists are granted only eleven words, and nothing is said about the commune, which the Chinese consider their main theoretical and practical contribution to communist developments.

The reader will soon see that this moderation and "revisionism" is balanced by a different and far harsher outlook. Alongside the promise of rapid advances in consumer goods, for example, there are heavy industry goals so extravagant that their achievement would seem to preclude almost any increase in light industry. If the goal for steel is to be met, the Soviet economy will have to increase steel production at an annual rate of some 9,000,000 tons, far more than the recent annual increases of about 5,000,000 tons. At a reception in Moscow on May 20, 1961, Khrushchev stated: "Now we consider our heavy industry as built. So we are not going to give it priority. Light industry and heavy industry will develop at the same pace." The goals for steel and electric power presented in the draft program are hardly consistent with this attitude. The reader will note a similar inconsistency in the area of international relations: how is "peaceful coexistence" to be preserved when the Soviet leaders continue to announce their full support for what they call "wars of liberation" but what they know the West regards as simply further steps in Soviet expansion? Finally, how effective can the proposed "democratic" innovations be, considering what is said about the future role of the Communist Party in Soviet affairs, the rejection of "factionalism," and the "exceptions" to be made in the turnover of party and government officials.

These are but a few of the inconsistencies that characterize the document and that together reflect the dualism that continues to run through Communist Party theory and practice. To appreciate further the extent and the significance of this dualism it would be of most value for the reader to compare the new program with the selections contained in the following section on the Chinese Communist Party.

Milovan Djilas

"THE NEW CLASS"

Laszek Kolakowski

THE CONSPIRACY OF
IVORY TOWER INTELLECTUALS

THE NEW PROGRAM
OF THE COMMUNIST PARTY
OF THE SOVIET UNION

Milovan Djilas
"THE NEW CLASS"

1.

Everything happened differently in the U.S.S.R. and other communist countries from what the leaders—even such prominent ones as Lenin, Stalin, Trotsky, and Bukharin—anticipated. They expected that the state would rapidly wither away, that democracy would be strengthened. The reverse happened. They expected a rapid improvement in the standard of living—there has been scarcely any change in this respect and, in the subjugated East European countries, the standard has even declined. In every instance, the standard of living has failed to rise in proportion to the rate of industrialization, which was much more rapid. It was believed that the differences between cities and villages, between intellectual and physical labor, would slowly disappear; instead these differences have increased. Communist anticipations in other areas—including their expectations for developments in the noncommunist world—have also failed to materialize.

The greatest illusion was that industrialization and collectivization in the U.S.S.R., and destruction of capitalist ownership, would result in a classless society. In 1936, when the new Constitution was promulgated, Stalin announced that the "exploiting class" had ceased to exist. The capitalist and other classes of ancient origin had in fact been destroyed, but a new class, previously unknown to history, had been formed.

It is understandable that this class, like those before it, should believe that the establishment of its power would result in happiness and freedom for all men. The only difference between this and other classes was that it treated the delay in the realization of its illusions more crudely. It thus affirmed that its power was more complete than the power of any other class before in history, and its class illusions and prejudices were proportionally greater.

This new class, the bureaucracy, or more accurately the

319

political bureaucracy, has all the characteristics of earlier ones as well as some new characteristics of its own. Its origin had its special characteristics also, even though in essence it was similar to the beginnings of other classes.

Other classes, too, obtained their strength and power by the revolutionary path, destroying the political, social, and other orders they met in their way. However, almost without exception, these classes attained power *after* new economic patterns had taken shape in the old society. The case was the reverse with the new class in the communist systems. It did not come to power to *complete* a new economic order but to *establish* its own and, in so doing, to establish its power over society.

In earlier epochs the coming to power of some class, some part of a class, or of some party, was the final event resulting from its formation and its development. The reverse was true in the U.S.S.R. There the new class was definitely formed after it attained power. Its consciousness had to develop before its economic and physical powers, because the class had not taken root in the life of the nation. This class viewed its role in relation to the world from an idealistic point of view. Its practical possibilities were not diminished by this. In spite of its illusions, it represented an objective tendency toward industrialization. Its practical bent emanated from this tendency. The promise of an ideal world increased the faith in the ranks of the new class and sowed illusions among the masses. At the same time it inspired gigantic physical undertakings.

Because this new class had not been formed as a part of the economic and social life before it came to power, it could only be created in an organization of a special type, distinguished by a special discipline based on identical philosophic and ideological views of its members. A unity of belief and iron discipline was necessary to overcome its weaknesses.

The roots of the new class were implanted in a special party, of the Bolshevik type. Lenin was right in his view that his party was an exception in the history of human society, although he did not suspect that it would be the beginning of a new class.

To be more precise, the initiators of the new class are not found in the party of the Bolshevik type as a whole but in that stratum of professional revolutionaries who made up its core even before it attained power. It was not by accident that Lenin asserted after the failure of the 1905 revolution that only professional revolutionaries—men whose sole profession was revolutionary work—could build a new party of the Bolshevik type. It was still less accidental that even Stalin, the future creator of a new class, was the most outstanding example of such a professional revolutionary. The new ruling class has been gradually developing from this very narrow stratum of revolutionaries. These revolutionaries composed its core for a long period. Trotsky noted that in prerevolutionary professional revolutionaries was the origin of the future Stalinist bureaucrats. What he did not detect was the beginning of a new class of owners and exploiters.

This is not to say that the new party and the new class are identical. The party, however, is the core of that class, and its base. It is very difficult, perhaps impossible, to define the limits of the new class and to identify its members. The new class may be said to be made up of those who have special privileges and economic preference because of the administrative monopoly they hold.

Since administration is unavoidable in society, necessary administrative functions may be coexistent with parasitic functions in the same person. Not every member of the party is a member of the new class, any more than every artisan or member of a middle-class party is a bourgeois.

In loose terms, as the new class becomes stronger and attains a more perceptible physiognomy, the role of the party diminishes. The core and the basis of the new class is created in the party and at its top, as well as in the state political organs. The once live, compact party, full of initiative, is disappearing to become transformed into the traditional oligarchy of the new class, irresistibly drawing into its ranks those who aspire to join the new class and repressing those who have any ideals.

The party makes the class, but the class grows as a result and uses the party as a basis. The class grows stronger, while the party grows weaker; this is the inescapable fate of every Communist party in power.

If it were not materially interested in production or if it did not have within itself the potentialities for the creation of a new class, no party could act in so morally and ideologically foolhardy a fashion, let alone stay in power for long. Stalin declared, after the end of the First Five-Year Plan: "If we had not created the apparatus, we would have failed!"

He should have substituted "new class" for the word "apparatus," and everything would have been clearer.

It seems unusual that a political party could be the beginning of a new class. Parties are generally the product of classes and strata which have become intellectually and economically strong. However, if one grasps the actual conditions in prerevolutionary Russia and in other countries in which communism prevailed over national forces, it will be clear that a party of this type is the product of specific opportunities and that there is nothing unusual or accidental in this being so. Although the roots of Bolshevism reach far back into Russian history, the party is partly the product of the unique pattern of international relationships in which Russia found itself at the end of the nineteenth and the beginning of the twentieth century. Russia was no longer able to live in the modern world as an absolute monarchy, and Russia's capitalism was too weak and too dependent on the interests of foreign powers to make it possible to have an industrial revolution. This revolution could only be implemented by a new class, or by a change in the social order. As yet, there was no such class.

In history, it is not important who implements a process, it is only important that the process be implemented. Such was the case in Russia and other countries in which communist revolutions took place. The revolution created forces, leaders, organizations, and ideas which were necessary to it. The new class came into existence for objective reasons, and by the wish, wits, and action of its leaders.

2.

The social origin of the new class lies in the proletariat just as the aristocracy arose in a peasant society, and the bourgeoisie in a commercial and artisans' society. There are exceptions, depending on national conditions, but the proletariat in economically underdeveloped countries, being backward, constitutes the raw material from which the new class arises.

There are other reasons why the new class always acts as the champion of the working class. The new class is anticapitalistic and, consequently, logically dependent upon the working strata. The new class is supported by the proletarian struggle and the traditional faith of the proletariat in a socialist, communist society where there is no brutal exploitation. It is vitally important for the new class to assure a normal flow of production, hence it cannot ever lose its connection with the proletariat. Most important of all, the new class cannot achieve industrialization and consolidate its power without the help of the working class. On the other hand, the working class sees in expanded industry the salvation from its poverty and despair. Over a long period of time, the interests, ideas, faith, and hope of the new class, and of parts of the working class and of the poor peasants, coincide and unite. Such mergers have occurred in the past among other widely different classes. Did not the bourgeoisie represent the peasantry in the struggle against the feudal lords?

The movement of the new class toward power comes as a result of the efforts of the proletariat and the poor. These are the masses upon which the party or the new class must lean and with which its interests are most closely allied. This is true until the new class finally establishes its power and authority. Over and above this, the new class is interested in the proletariat and the poor only to the extent necessary for developing production and for maintaining in subjugation the most aggressive and rebellious social forces.

The monopoly which the new class establishes in the name of the working class over the whole of society is, primarily, a monopoly over the working class itself. This monopoly is first intellectual, over the so-called *avant-garde* proletariat, and then over the whole proletariat. This is the biggest deception the class must accomplish, but it shows that the power and interests of the new class lie primarily in industry. Without industry the new class cannot consolidate its position or authority.

Former sons of the working class are the most steadfast members of the new class. It has always been the fate of slaves to provide for their masters the most clever and gifted representatives. In this case a new exploiting and governing class is born from the exploited class.

3.

When communist systems are being critically analyzed, it is considered that their fundamental distinction lies in the fact that a bureaucracy, organized in a special stratum, rules over the people. This is generally true. However, a more detailed analysis will show that only a special stratum of bureaucrats, those who are not administrative officials, make up the core of the governing bureaucracy, or, in my terminology, of the new class. This is actually a party or political bureaucracy. Other officials are only the apparatus under the control of the new class; the apparatus may be clumsy and slow but, no matter what, it must exist in every socialist society. It is sociologically possible to draw the borderline between the different types of officials, but in practice they are practically indistinguishable. This is true not only because the communist system by its very nature is bureaucratic, but because communists handle the various important administrative functions. In addition, the stratum of political bureaucrats cannot enjoy their privileges if they do not give crumbs from their tables to other bureaucratic categories.

It is important to note the fundamental differences between the political bureaucracies mentioned here and those which arise with every centralization in modern economy —especially centralizations that lead to collective forms of ownership such as monopolies, companies, and state ownership. The number of white-collar workers is constantly increasing in capitalistic monopolies, and also in nationalized industries in the West. In *Human Relations in Administration*,[1] R. Dubin says that state functionaries in the economy are being transformed into a special stratum of society.

. . . Functionaries have the sense of a common destiny for all those who work together. They share the same interests, especially since there is relatively little competition insofar as promotion is in terms of seniority. In-group aggression is thus minimized and this arrangement is therefore conceived to be positively functional for the bureaucracy. However, the esprit de corps and informal social organization which typically develops in such situations often leads the personnel to defend their entrenched interests rather than to assist their clientele and elected higher officials.

While such functionaries have much in common with communist bureaucrats, especially as regards "esprit de corps," they are not identical. Although state and other bureaucrats in noncommunist systems form a special stratum, they do not exercise authority as the communists do. Bureaucrats in a noncommunist state have political masters, usually elected, or owners over them, while communists have neither masters nor owners over them. The bureaucrats in a noncommunist state are officials in modern capitalist economy, while the communists are something different and new: a new class.

As in other owning classes, the proof that it is a special class lies in its ownership and its special relations to other classes. In the same way, the class to which a member belongs is indicated by the material and other privileges which ownership brings to him.

As defined by Roman law, property constitutes the use, enjoyment, and disposition of material goods. The communist political bureaucracy uses, enjoys, and disposes of nationalized property.

If we assume that membership in this bureaucracy or new owning class is predicated on the use of privileges inherent in ownership—in this instance nationalized material goods —then membership in the new party class, or political bureaucracy, is reflected in a larger income in material goods and privileges than society should normally grant for such functions. In practice, the ownership privilege of the new class manifests itself as an exclusive right, as a party monopoly, for the political bureaucracy to distribute the national income, to set wages, direct economic development, and dispose of nationalized and other property. This is the way it appears to the ordinary man who considers the communist functionary as being very rich and as a man who does not have to work.

The ownership of private property has, for many reasons, proved to be unfavorable for the establishment of the new class's authority. Besides, the destruction of private ownership was necessary for the economic transformation of nations. The new class obtains its power, privileges, ideology, and its customs from one specific form of ownership—collective ownership—which the class administers and distributes in the name of the nation and society.

The new class maintains that ownership derives from a designated social relationship. This is the relationship between the monopolists of administration, who constitute a narrow and closed stratum, and the mass of producers (farmers, workers, and intelligentsia) who have no rights. But that is not all, since the communist bureaucracy also has complete monopolistic control over material assets.

Every substantive change in the social relationship between those who monopolize administration and those who work is inevitably reflected in the ownership relationship.

Social and political relations and ownership—the totalitarianism of government and the monopoly of ownership—are being more fully brought into accord in communism than in any other political system.

To divest communists of their ownership rights would be to abolish them as a class. To compel them to relinquish their other social powers, so that workers may participate in sharing the profits of their work—which capitalists have had to permit as a result of strikes and parliamentary action—would mean that communists were being deprived of their monopoly over property, ideology, and government. This would be the beginning of democracy and freedom in communism, the end of communist monopolism and totalitarianism. Until this happens, there can be no indication that important, fundamental changes are taking place in communist systems, at least not in the eyes of men who think seriously about social progress.

The ownership privileges of the new class and membership in that class are the privileges of *administration*. This privilege extends from state administration and the administration of economic enterprises to that of sports and humanitarian organizations. Political, party, or so-called "general leadership" is executed by the core. This position of leadership carries privileges with it. In his *Staline au pouvoir*, published in Paris in 1951, Orlov states that the average pay of a worker in the U.S.S.R. in 1935 was 1,800 rubles annually, while the pay and allowances of the secretary of a rayon committee amounted to 45,000 rubles annually. The situation has changed since then for both workers and party functionaries, but the essence remains the same. Other authors have arrived at the same conclusions. Discrepancies between the pay of workers and party functionaries are extreme; this could not be hidden from persons visiting the U.S.S.R. or other communist countries in the past few years.

Other systems, too, have their professional politicians. One can think well or ill of them, but they must exist. Society cannot live without a state or a government, and therefore it cannot live without those who fight for it.

However, there are fundamental differences between professional politicians in other systems and in the communist system. In extreme cases, politicians in other systems use the government to secure privileges for themselves and their cohorts, or to favor the economic interests of one social stratum or another. The situation is different with the communist system where the power and the government are identical with the use, enjoyment, and disposition of almost all the nation's goods. He who grabs power grabs privileges and indirectly grabs property. Consequently, in communism, power or politics as a profession is the ideal of those who have the desire or the prospect of living as parasites at the expense of others.

Membership in the Communist Party before the Revolution meant sacrifice. Being a professional revolutionary was one of the highest honors. Now that the party has consolidated its power, party membership means that one belongs to a privileged class. And at the core of the party are the all-powerful exploiters and masters.

For a long time the communist revolution and the communist system have been concealing their real nature. The emergence of the new class has been concealed under socialist phraseology and, more important, under the new collective forms of property ownership. The so-called socialist ownership is a disguise for the real ownership by the political bureaucracy. And in the beginning this bureaucracy was in a hurry to complete industrialization, and hid its class composition under that guise.

4.

The development of modern communism, and the emergence of the new class, is evident in the character and roles of those who inspired it.

The leaders and their methods, from Marx to Khrushchev, have been varied and changing. It never occurred to Marx to prevent others from voicing their ideas. Lenin tolerated free discussion in his party and did not think that party forums, let alone the party head, should regulate the expression of "proper" or "improper" ideas. Stalin abolished every type of intraparty discussion, and made the expression of ideology solely the right of the central forum—or of himself. Other communist movements were different. For instance, Marx's International Workers' Union (the so-called First International) was not Marxist in ideology, but a union of varied groups which adopted only the resolutions on which its members agreed. Lenin's party was an *avant-garde* group combining an internal revolutionary morality and ideological monolithic structure with democracy of a kind. Under Stalin the party became a mass of ideologically disinterested men, who got their ideas from above, but were wholehearted and unanimous in the defense of a system that assured them unquestionable privileges. Marx actually never created a party; Lenin destroyed all parties except his own, including the Socialist Party. Stalin relegated even the Bolshevik Party to second rank, transforming its core into the core of the new class, and transforming the party into a privileged impersonal and colorless group.

Marx created a system of the roles of classes, and of class war in society, even though he did not discover them, and he saw that mankind is mostly made up of members of discernible classes, although he was only restating Terence's Stoic philosophy: *"Humani nihil a me alienum puto."* Lenin viewed men as sharing ideas rather than as being members of discernible classes. Stalin saw in men only obedient subjects or enemies. Marx died a poor emigrant in London, but was valued by learned men and valued in the movement; Lenin died as the leader of one of the greatest revolutions, but died as a dictator about whom a cult had already begun to form; when Stalin died, he had already transformed himself into a god.

These changes in personalities are only the reflection of changes which had already taken place and were the very soul of the communist movement.

Although he did not realize it, Lenin started the organization of the new class. He established the party along Bolshevik lines and developed the theories of its unique and leading role in the building of a new society. This is but one aspect of his many-sided and gigantic work; it is the aspect which came about from his actions rather than his wishes. It is also the aspect which led the new class to revere him.

The real and direct originator of the new class, however, was Stalin. He was a man of quick reflexes and a tendency to coarse humor, not very educated nor a good speaker. But he was a relentless dogmatician and a great administrator, a Georgian who knew better than anyone else whither the new powers of Greater Russia were taking her. He created the new class by the use of the most barbaric means, not even sparing the class itself. It was inevitable that the new class which placed him at the top would later submit to his unbridled and brutal nature. He was the true leader of that class as long as the class was building itself up, and attaining power.

The new class was born in the revolutionary struggle in the Communist Party, but was developed in the industrial revolution. Without the revolution, without industry, the class's position would not have been secure and its power would have been limited.

While the country was being industrialized, Stalin began to introduce considerable variations in wages, at the same time allowing the development toward various privileges to proceed. He thought that industrialization would come to nothing if the new class were not made materially interested in the process, by acquisition of some property for itself. Without industrialization the new class would find it difficult to hold its position, for it would have neither historical justification nor the material resources for its continued existence.

The increase in the membership of the party, or of the bureaucracy, was closely connected with this. In 1927, on the eve of industrialization, the Soviet Communist Party had 887,233 members. In 1934, at the end of the First Five Year Plan, the membership had increased to 1,874,488. This was a phenomenon obviously connected with industrialization: the prospects for the new class and privileges for its members were improving. What is more, the privileges and the class were expanding more rapidly than industrialization itself. It is difficult to cite any statistics on this point, but the conclusion is self-evident for anyone who bears in mind that the standard of living has not kept pace with industrial production, while the new class actually seized the lion's share of the economic and other progress earned by the sacrifices and efforts of the masses.

The establishment of the new class did not proceed smoothly. It encountered bitter opposition from existing classes and from those revolutionaries who could not reconcile reality with the ideals of their struggle. In the U.S.S.R. the opposition of revolutionaries was most evident in the Trotsky-Stalin conflict. The conflict between Trotsky and Stalin, or between oppositionists in the party and Stalin, as well as the conflict between the regime and the peasantry, became more intense as industrialization advanced and the power and authority of the new class increased.

Trotsky, an excellent speaker, brilliant stylist, and skilled polemicist, a man cultured and of excellent intelligence, was deficient in only one quality: a sense of reality. He wanted to be a revolutionary in a period when life imposed the commonplace. He wished to revive a revolutionary party which was being transformed into something completely different, into a new class unconcerned with great ideals and interested only in the everyday pleasures of life. He expected action from a mass already tired by war, hunger, and death, at a time when the new class already strongly held the reins and had begun to experience the sweetness of privilege. Trotsky's fireworks lit up the distant heavens; but he could not rekindle fires in weary men. He sharply noted the sorry aspect of the new phenomena but he did not grasp their meaning. In addition, he had never been a Bolshevik. This was his vice and his virtue. Attacking the party bureaucracy in the name of the revolution, he attacked the cult of the party and, although he was not conscious of it, the new class.

Stalin looked neither far ahead nor far behind. He had seated himself at the head of the new power which was being born—the new class, the political bureaucracy, and bureaucratism—and became its leader and organizer. He did not preach—he made decisions. He too promised a shining future, but one which bureaucracy could visualize as being real because its life was improving from day to day and its position was being strengthened. He spoke without ardor and color, but the new class was better able to understand this kind of realistic language. Trotsky wished to extend the revolution to Europe; Stalin was not opposed to the idea but this hazardous undertaking did not prevent him from worrying about Mother Russia or, specifically, about ways of strengthening the new system and increasing the power and reputation of the Russian state. Trotsky was a man of the revolution of the past; Stalin was a man of today and, thus, of the future.

In Stalin's victory Trotsky saw the Thermidorian reaction against the revolution, actually the bureaucratic corruption of the Soviet government and the revolutionary cause. Consequently, he understood and was deeply hurt by the amorality of Stalin's methods. Trotsky was the first, although he was not aware of it, who in the attempt to save the communist movement discovered the essence of contemporary communism. But he was not capable of seeing it through to the end. He supposed that this was only a momentary cropping up of bureaucracy, corrupting the party and the revolution, and concluded that the solution was in a change at the top, in a "palace revolution." When a palace revolution actually took place after Stalin's death, it could be seen that the essence had not changed; something deeper and more lasting was involved. The Soviet Thermidor of Stalin had not only led to the installation of a government more despotic than the previous one, but also to the installation of a class. This was the continuation of the other side of the coin, the violence of the revolution which had given birth and strength to the new class.

Stalin could, with equal if not greater right, refer to Lenin and all the revolution, just as Trotsky did. For Stalin was the lawful although wicked offspring of Lenin and the revolution.

History has no previous record of a personality like Lenin who, by his versatility and persistence, developed one of the greatest revolutions known to men. It also has no record of a personality like Stalin, who took on the enormous task of strengthening, in terms of power and property, a new class born out of one of the greatest revolutions in one of the largest of the world's countries.

Behind Lenin, who was all passion and thought, stands the dull, gray figure of Joseph Stalin, the symbol of the difficult, cruel, and unscrupulous ascent of the new class to its final power.

After Lenin and Stalin came what had to come; namely, mediocrity in the form of collective leadership. And also there came the apparently sincere, kind-hearted, nonintellectual "man of the people"—Nikita Khrushchev. The new class no longer needs the revolutionaries or dogmatists it once required; it is satisfied with simple personalities, such as Khrushchev, Malenkov, Bulganin, and Shepilov, whose every word reflects the average man. The new class itself is tired of dogmatic purges and training sessions. It would like to live quietly. It must protect itself even from its own authorized leader now that it has been adequately strengthened. Stalin remained the same as he was when the class was weak, when cruel measures were necessary against even those in its own ranks who threatened to deviate. Today this is all unnecessary. Without relinquishing anything it created under Stalin's leadership, the new class appears to be renouncing his authority for the past few years. But it is not really renouncing that authority—only Stalin's methods which, according to Khrushchev, hurt "good communists."

Lenin's revolutionary epoch was replaced by Stalin's epoch, in which authority and ownership, and industrialization, were strengthened so that the much-desired peaceful and good life of the new class could begin. Lenin's *revolutionary* communism was replaced by Stalin's *dogmatic* communism, which in turn was replaced by *nondogmatic* communism, a so-called collective leadership or a group of oligarchs.

These are the three phases of development of the new class in the U.S.S.R. or of Russian communism (or of every other type of communism in one manner or another).

The fate of Yugoslav communism was to unify these three phases in the single personality of Tito, along with national and personal characteristics. Tito is a great revolutionary, but without original ideas; he has attained personal power, but without Stalin's distrustfulness and dogmatism. Like Khrushchev, Tito is a representative of the people, that is, of the middle-party strata. The road which Yugoslav communism has traveled—attaining a revolution, copying Stalinism, then renouncing Stalinism and seeking its own form—is seen most fully in the personality of Tito. Yugoslav communism has been more consistent than other parties in preserving the substance of communism, yet never renouncing any form which could be of value to it.

The three phases in the development of the new class— Lenin, Stalin, and "collective leadership"—are not completely divorced from each other, in substance or in ideas.

Lenin too was a dogmatist, and Stalin too was a revolutionary, just as collective leadership will resort to dogmatism and to revolutionary methods when necessary. What is more, the nondogmatism of the collective leadership is applied only to itself, to the heads of the new class. On the other hand, the people must be all the more persistently "educated" in the spirit of the dogma, or of Marxism-Leninism. By relaxing its dogmatic severity and exclusiveness, the new class, becoming strengthened economically, has prospects of attaining greater flexibility.

The heroic era of communism is past. The epoch of its great leaders has ended. The epoch of practical men has set in. The new class has been created. It is at the height of its power and wealth, but it is without new ideas. It has nothing more to tell the people. The only thing that remains is for it to justify itself.

5.

It would not be important to establish the fact that in contemporary communism a new owning and exploiting class is involved and not merely a temporary dictatorship and an arbitrary bureaucracy, if some anti-Stalinist communists including Trotsky as well as some Social Democrats had not depicted the ruling stratum as a passing bureaucratic phenomenon because of which this new ideal, classless society, still in its swaddling clothes, must suffer, just as bourgeois society had had to suffer under Cromwell's and Napoleon's despotism.

But the new class is really a new class, with a special composition and special power. By any scientific definition of a class, even the Marxist definition by which some classes are lower than others according to their specific position in production, we conclude that, in the U.S.S.R. and other communist countries, a new class of owners and exploiters is in existence. The specific characteristic of this new class is its collective ownership. Communist theoreticians affirm, and some even believe, that communism has arrived at collective ownership.

Collective ownership in various forms has existed in all earlier societies. All ancient Eastern despotisms were based on the pre-eminence of the state's or the king's property. In ancient Egypt after the fifteenth century B.C., arable land passed to private ownership. Before that time only homes and surrounding buildings had been privately owned. State land was handed over for cultivation while state officials administered the land and collected taxes on it. Canals and installations, as well as the most important works, were also state-owned. The state owned everything until it lost its independence in the first century of our era.

This helps to explain the deification of the Pharaohs of Egypt and of the emperors, which one encounters in all the ancient Eastern despotisms. Such ownership also explains the undertaking of gigantic tasks, such as the construction of temples, tombs, and castles of emperors, of canals, roads, and fortifications.

The Roman state treated newly conquered land as state land and owned considerable numbers of slaves. The medieval Church also had collective property.

Capitalism by its very nature was an enemy of collective ownership until the establishment of shareholders' organizations. Capitalism continued to be an enemy of collective ownership, even though it could not do anything against new encroachments by collective ownership and the enlargement of its area of operations.

The communists did not invent collective ownership as such, but invented its all-encompassing character, more widely extended than in earlier epochs, even more extensive than in Pharaoh's Egypt. That is all that the communists did.

The ownership of the new class, as well as its character, was formed over a period of time and was subjected to constant change during the process. At first, only a small part of the nation felt the need for all economic powers to be placed in the hands of a political party for the purpose of aiding the industrial transformation. The party, acting as the *avant-garde* of the proletariat and as the "most enlightened power of socialism," pressed for this centralization which could be attained only by a change in ownership. The change was made in fact and in form through nationalization first of large enterprises and then of smaller ones. The abolition of private ownership was a prerequisite for industrialization, and for the beginning of the new class. However, without their special role as administrators over society and as distributors of property, the communists could not transform themselves into a new class, nor could a new class be formed and permanently established. Gradually material goods were nationalized, but in fact, through its right to use, enjoy, and distribute these goods, they became the property of a discernible stratum of the party and the bureaucracy gathered around it.

In view of the significance of ownership for its power— and also of the fruits of ownership—the party bureaucracy cannot renounce the extension of its ownership even over small-scale production facilities. Because of its totalitarianism and monopolism, the new class finds itself unavoidably at war with everything which it does not administer or handle, and must deliberately aspire to destroy or conquer it.

Stalin said, on the eve of collectivization, that the question of "who will do what to whom" had been raised, even though the Soviet government was not meeting serious opposition from a politically and economically disunited peasantry. The new class felt insecure as long as there were any other owners except itself. It could not risk sabotage in food supplies or in agricultural raw materials. This was the direct reason for the attack on the peasantry. However, there was a second reason, a class reason: the peasants could be dangerous to the new class in an unstable situation. The new class therefore had to subordinate the peasantry to itself economically and administratively; this was done through the kolkhozes and machine-tractor stations, which required an increase proportionate to the size of the new class in the villages themselves. As a result, bureaucracy mushroomed in the villages too.

The fact that the seizure of property from other classes, especially from small owners, led to decreases in production and to chaos in the economy was of no consequence to the new class. Most important for the new class, as for every owner in history, was the attainment and consolidation of ownership. The class profited from the new property it had acquired even though the nation lost thereby. The collectivization of peasant holdings, which was economically unjustified, was unavoidable if the new class was to be securely installed in its power and its ownership.

Reliable statistics are not available, but all evidence confirms that yields per acre in the U.S.S.R. have not been increased over the yields in Czarist Russia, and that the number of livestock still does not approach the prerevolutionary figure.

The losses in agricultural yields and in livestock can be calculated, but the losses in manpower, in the millions of peasants who were thrown into labor camps, are incalculable. Collectivization was a frightful and devastating war which resembled an insane undertaking—except for the fact that it was profitable for the new class by assuring its authority.

By various methods, such as nationalization, compulsory co-operation, high taxes, and price inequalities, private ownership was destroyed and transformed into collective ownership. The establishment of the ownership of the new class was evidenced in the changes in the psychology, the way of life, and the material position of its members, depending on the position they held on the hierarchical ladder. Country homes, the best housing, furniture, and similar things were acquired; special quarters and exclusive rest homes were established for the highest bureaucracy, for the elite of the new class. The party secretary and the chief of the secret police in some places not only became the highest authorities but obtained the best housing, automobiles, and similar evidence of privilege. Those beneath them were eligible for comparable privileges, depending upon their position in the hierarchy. The state budgets, "gifts," and the construction and reconstruction executed for the needs of the state and its representatives became the everlasting and inexhaustible sources of benefits to the political bureaucracy.

Only in cases where the new class was not capable of maintaining the ownership it had usurped, or in cases where such ownership was exorbitantly expensive or politically dangerous, were concessions made to other strata, or were other forms of ownership devised. For example, collectivization was abandoned in Yugoslavia because the peasants were resisting it and because the steady decrease in production resulting from collectivization held a latent danger for the regime. However, the new class never renounced the right in such cases to seize ownership again or to collectivize. The new class cannot renounce this right, for if it did, it would no longer be totalitarian and monopolistic.

No bureaucracy alone could be so stubborn in its purposes and aims. Only those engaged in new forms of ownership, who tread the road to new forms of production, are capable of being so persistent.

Marx foresaw that after its victory the proletariat would be exposed to danger from the deposed classes and from its own bureaucracy. When the communists, especially those in Yugoslavia, criticize Stalin's administration and bureaucratic methods, they generally refer to what Marx anticipated. However, what is happening in communism today has little connection with Marx and certainly no connection with this anticipation. Marx was thinking of the danger resulting from the growth of a parasitic bureaucracy, which is so prevalent in contemporary communism. Of course, it never occurred to him to include in that category today's communist strong men who control material assets for their own narrow caste's interests rather than for the bureaucracy as a whole. In this case, too, Marx serves as a good excuse for the communists, whether the excessive appetites of various strata of the new class or inefficient administration is under criticism.

Contemporary communism is not only a party of a certain type, or a bureaucracy which has sprung from monopolistic ownership and excessive state interference in the economy. More than anything else, the essential aspect of contemporary communism is the new class of owners and exploiters.

6.

No class is established by deliberate design, even though its ascent is accompanied by an organized and conscious struggle. This holds true for the new class in communism, but it also embodies some special characteristics. Since the hold of the new class on economic life and on the social structure was fairly precarious, and since it was fated to arise within a specific party, it required the highest possible degree of organization, as well as a consistent effort to present a united, balanced, class-conscious front. This is why the new class is better organized and more highly class-conscious than any class in recorded history.

This proposition is true only if it is taken relatively; consciousness and organizational structure being taken in relation to the outside world and to other classes, powers, and social forces. No other class in history has been as cohesive and single-minded in defending itself and in controlling that which it holds—collective and monopolistic ownership and totalitarian authority.

On the other hand, the new class is also the most deluded and least conscious of itself. Every private capitalist or feudal lord was conscious of the fact that he belonged to a special discernible social category. He usually believed that this category was destined to make the human race happy, and that without this category chaos and general ruin would ensue. A communist member of the new class also believes that, without his party, society would regress and founder. But he is not conscious of the fact that he belongs to a new ownership class, for he does not consider himself an owner and does not take into account the special privileges he enjoys. He thinks that he belongs to a group with prescribed ideas, aims, attitudes, and roles. That is all he sees. He cannot see that at the same time he belongs to a special social category: the *ownership* class.

Collective ownership, which acts to solidify the class, at the same time makes it unconscious of its class substance, and each one of the collective owners is deluded in that he thinks he uniquely belongs to a movement which would abolish classes in society.

A comparison of other characteristics of the new class with those of the other ownership classes reveals many similarities and many differences. The new class is voracious and insatiable, just as the bourgeoisie was. But it does not have the virtues of frugality and economy that the bourgeoisie had. The new class is as exclusive as the aristocracy but without aristocracy's refinement and proud chivalry.

The new class also has advantages over other classes. Because it is more compact it is better prepared for greater sacrifices and heroic exploits. The individual is completely and totally subordinated to the whole; at least, the prevailing ideal calls for such subordination even when he is out seeking to better himself. The new class is strong enough to carry out material and other ventures that no other class was ever able to do. Since it possesses the nation's goods, the new class is in a position to devote itself religiously to the aims it has set and to direct all the forces of the people to the furtherance of these aims.

The new ownership is not the same as the political government, but is created and aided by that government. The use, enjoyment, and distribution of property is the privilege of the party and the party's top men.

Party members feel that authority, that control over property, brings with it the privileges of this world. Consequently, unscrupulous ambition, duplicity, toadyism, and jealousy inevitably must increase. Careerism and an ever-expanding bureaucracy are the incurable diseases of communism. Because the communists have transformed themselves into owners, and because the road to power and to material privileges is open only through "devotion" to the party—to the class, to "socialism"—unscrupulous ambition must become one of the main ways of life and one of the main methods for the development of communism.

In noncommunist systems, the phenomena of careerism and unscrupulous ambition are a sign that it is profitable to be a bureaucrat, or that owners have become parasites, so that the administration of property is left in the hands of employees. In communism, careerism and unscrupulous ambition testify to the fact that there is an irresistible drive toward ownership and the privileges that accompany the administration of material goods and men.

Membership in other ownership classes is not identical

with the ownership of particular property. This is still less the case in the communist system inasmuch as ownership is collective. To be an owner or a joint owner in the communist system means that one enters the ranks of the ruling political bureaucracy and nothing else.

In the new class, just as in other classes, some individuals constantly fall by the wayside while others go up the ladder. In private-ownership classes an individual left his property to his descendants. In the new class no one inherits anything except the aspiration to raise himself to a higher rung of the ladder. The new class is actually being created from the lowest and broadest strata of the people, and is in constant motion. Although it is sociologically possible to prescribe who belongs to the new class, it is difficult to do so; for the new class melts into and spills over into the people, into other lower classes, and is constantly changing.

The road to the top is theoretically open to all, just as every one of Napoleon's soldiers carried a marshal's baton in his knapsack. The only thing that is required to get on the road is sincere and complete loyalty to the party or to the new class. Open at the bottom, the new class becomes increasingly and relentlessly narrower at the top. Not only is the desire necessary for the climb; also necessary is the ability to understand and develop doctrines, firmness in struggles against antagonists, exceptional dexterity and cleverness in intraparty struggles, and talent in strengthening the class. Many present themselves, but few are chosen. Although more open in some respects than other classes, the new class is also more exclusive than other classes. Since one of the new class's most important features is monopoly of authority, this exclusiveness is strengthened by bureaucratic hierarchical prejudices.

Nowhere, at any time, has the road been as wide open to the devoted and the loyal as it is in the communist system. But the ascent to the heights has never at any time been so difficult or required so much sacrifice and so many victims. On the one hand, communism is open and kind to all; on the other hand, it is exclusive and intolerant even of its own adherents.

7.

The fact that there is a new ownership class in communist countries does not explain everything, but it is the most important key to understanding the changes which are periodically taking place in these countries, especially in the U.S.S.R.

It goes without saying that every such change in each separate communist country and in the communist system as a whole must be examined separately, in order to determine the extent and significance of the change in the specific circumstances. To do this, however, the system should be understood as a whole to the fullest extent possible.

In connection with current changes in the U.S.S.R. it will be profitable to point out in passing what is occurring in the kolkhozes. The establishment of kolkhozes and the Soviet government policy toward them illustrates clearly the exploiting nature of the new class.

Stalin did not and Khrushchev does not consider kolkhozes as a "logical socialistic" form of ownership. In practice this means that the new class has not succeeded in completely taking over the management of the villages. Through the kolkhozes and the use of the compulsory crop-purchase system, the new class has succeeded in making vassals of the peasants and grabbing a lion's share of the peasants' income, but the new class has not become the only power of the land. Stalin was completely aware of this. Before his death, in *Economic Problems of Socialism in the U.S.S.R.*, Stalin foresaw that the kolkhozes should become state property, which is to say that the bureaucracy should become the real owner. Criticizing Stalin for his excess use of purges, Khrushchev did not however renounce Stalin's views on property in kolkhozes. The appointment by the new regime of 30,000 party workers, mostly to be presidents of kolkhozes, was only one of the measures in line with Stalin's policy.

Just as under Stalin, the new regime, in executing its so-called liberalization policy, is extending the "socialist" ownership of the new class. Decentralization in the economy does not mean a change in ownership, but only gives greater rights to the lower strata of the bureaucracy or of the new class. If the so-called liberalization and decentralization meant anything else, that would be manifest in the political right of at least part of the people to exercise some influence in the management of material goods. At least, the people would have the right to criticize the arbitrariness of the oligarchy. This would lead to the creation of a new political movement, even though it were only a loyal opposition. However, this is not even mentioned, just as democracy in the party is not mentioned. Liberalization and decentralization are in force only for communists; first for the oligarchy, the leaders of the new class; and second, for those in the lower echelons. This is the new method, inevitable under changing conditions, for the further strengthening and consolidation of monopolistic ownership and totalitarian authority of the new class.

The fact that there is a new owning, monopolistic, and totalitarian class in communist countries calls for the following conclusion: All changes initiated by the communist chiefs are dictated first of all by the interests and aspirations of the new class, which, like every social group, lives and reacts, defends itself and advances, with the aim of increasing its power. This does not mean, however, that such changes may not be important for the rest of the people as well. Although the innovations introduced by the new class have not yet materially altered the communist system, they must not be underestimated. It is necessary to gain insight into the substance of these changes in order to determine their range and significance.

The communist regime, in common with others, must take into account the mood and movement of the masses. Because of the exclusiveness of the Communist Party and the absence of free public opinion in its ranks, the regime cannot discern the real status of the masses. However, their dissatisfaction does penetrate the consciousness of the top leaders. In spite of its totalitarian management, the new class is not immune to every type of opposition.

Once in power, the communists have no difficulty in settling their accounts with the bourgeoisie and large-estate owners. The historical development is hostile to them and their property and it is easy to arouse the masses against them. Seizing property from the bourgeoisie and the large-estate owners is quite easy; difficulties arise when seizure of small properties is involved. Having acquired power in the course of earlier expropriations, the communists can do even this. Relations are rapidly clarified: there are no more old classes and old owners, society is "classless," or on the road to being so, and men have started to live in a new manner.

Under such conditions, demands to return to the old pre-revolutionary relations seem unrealistic, if not ridiculous. Material and social bases no longer exist for the maintenance of such relations. The communists meet such demands as if they were jests.

The new class is most sensitive to demands on the part of the people for a special kind of freedom, not for freedom in general or political freedom. It is especially sensitive to demands for freedom of thought and criticism, within the limits of present conditions and within the limits of "socialism"; not for demands for a return to previous social and ownership relations. This sensitivity originates from the class's special position.

The new class instinctively feels that national goods are, in fact, its property, and that even the terms "socialist," "social," and "state" property denote a general legal fiction. The new class also thinks that any breach of its totalitarian authority might imperil its ownership. Consequently, the new class opposes *any* type of freedom, ostensibly for the purpose of preserving "socialist" ownership. Criticism of the new class's monopolistic administration of property generates the fear of a possible loss of power. The new class is sensitive to these criticisms and demands depending on the extent to which they expose the manner in which it rules and holds power.

This is an important contradiction. Property is legally considered social and national property. But, in actuality, a single group manages it in its own interest. The discrepancy between legal and actual conditions continuously results in obscure and abnormal social and economic relationships. It also means that the words of the leading group do not correspond to its actions; and that all actions result in strengthening its property holdings and its political position.

This contradiction cannot be resolved without jeopardizing the class's position. Other ruling, property-owning classes could not resolve this contradiction either, unless forcefully deprived of monopoly of power and ownership. Wherever there has been a higher degree of freedom for society as a whole, the ruling classes have been forced, in one way or another, to renounce monopoly of ownership. The reverse is true also: wherever monopoly of ownership has been impossible, freedom, to some degree, has become inevitable.

In communism, power and ownership are almost always in the same hands, but this fact is concealed under a legal guise. In classical capitalism, the worker had equality with the capitalist before the law, even though the worker was being exploited and the capitalist was doing the exploiting. In communism, legally, all are equal with respect to material goods. The formal owner is the nation. In reality, because of monopolistic administration, only the narrowest stratum of administrators enjoys the rights of ownership.

Every real demand for freedom in communism, the kind of demand that hits at the substance of communism, boils down to a demand for bringing material and property relations into accord with what the law provides.

A demand for freedom—based on the position that capital goods produced by the nation can be managed more efficiently by society than by private monopoly or a private owner, and consequently should actually be in the hands or under control of society exercised through its freely elected representatives—would force the new class either to make concessions to other forces, or to take off the mask and admit its ruling and exploiting characteristics. The type of ownership and exploitation which the new class creates by using its authority and its administrative privileges is such that even the class itself must deny it. Does not the new class emphasize that it uses its authority and administrative functions in the name of the nation as a whole to preserve national property?

This makes the legal position of the new class uncertain and is also the source of the new class's biggest internal difficulties. The contradiction discloses the disharmony between words and actions: While promising to abolish social differences, it must always increase them by acquiring the products of the nation's workshops and granting privileges to its adherents. It must proclaim loudly its dogma that it is fulfilling its historical mission of "final" liberation of mankind from every misery and calamity while it acts in exactly the opposite way.

The contradiction between the new class's real ownership position and its legal position can furnish the basic reason for criticism. This contradiction has within it the ability not only to incite others but also to corrode the class's own ranks, since privileges are actually being enjoyed by only a few. This contradiction, when intensified, holds prospects of real changes in the communist system, whether the ruling class is in favor of the change or not. The fact that this contradiction is so obvious has been the reason for the changes made by the new class, especially in so-called liberalization and decentralization.

Forced to withdraw and surrender to individual strata, the new class aims at concealing this contradiction and strengthening its own position. Since ownership and authority continue intact, all measures taken by the new class— even those democratically inspired—show a tendency toward strengthening the management of the political bureaucracy. The system turns democratic measures into positive methods for consolidating the position of the ruling classes. Slavery in ancient times in the East inevitably permeated all of society's activities and components, including the family. In the same way, the monopolism and totalitarianism of the ruling class in the communist system are imposed on all the aspects of social life, even though the political heads are not aiming at this.

Yugoslavia's so-called workers' management and autonomy, conceived at the time of the struggle against Soviet imperialism as a far-reaching democratic measure to deprive the party of the monopoly of administration, has been increasingly relegated to one of the areas of party work. Thus, it is hardly possible to change the present system. The aim of creating a new democracy through this type of administration will not be achieved. Besides, freedom cannot be extended to the largest piece of the pie. Workers' management has not brought about a sharing in profits by those who produce, either on a national level or in local enterprises. This type of administration has increasingly turned into a safe type for the regime. Through various taxes and other means, the regime has appropriated even the share of the profits which the workers believed would be given to them. Only crumbs from the tables and illusions have been left to the workers. Without universal freedom not even workers' management can become free. Clearly, in an unfree society nobody can freely decide anything. The givers have somehow obtained the most value from the gift of freedom they supposedly handed the workers.

This does not mean that the new class cannot make concessions to the people, even though it only considers its own interests. Workers' management, or decentralization, is a concession to the masses. Circumstances may drive the new class, no matter how monopolistic and totalitarian it may be, to retreat before the masses. In 1948, when the conflict broke out between Yugoslavia and the U.S.S.R., the Yugoslav leaders were forced to carry out certain reforms. But they stopped the process and even reversed it, as soon as they felt that they were in jeopardy. Something similar happened recently in other East European countries.

In defending its authority, the ruling class must execute reforms every time it becomes obvious to the people that the class is treating national property as its own. Such reforms are not proclaimed as being what they really are, but rather as part of the "further development of socialism" and "socialist democracy." The ground work for reforms is laid when the discrepancy mentioned above becomes public. From the historical point of view the new class is forced to fortify its authority and ownership constantly, even though it is running away from the truth. It must constantly demonstrate how it is successfully creating a society of happy people, all of whom enjoy equal rights and have been freed of every type of exploitation. The new class cannot avoid falling continuously into profound internal contradictions; for in spite of its historical origin it is not able to make its ownership lawful, and it cannot renounce ownership without undermining itself. Consequently, it is forced to try to justify its increasing authority, invoking abstract and unreal purposes.

This is a class whose power over men is the most complete known to history. For this reason it is a class with very limited views, views which are shaky because they are based on falsehoods. Closely knit, isolated, and in complete authority, the new class must unrealistically evaluate its own role and that of the people around it.

Having achieved industrialization, the new class can now do nothing more than strengthen its brute force and pillage the people. It ceases to create. Its spiritual heritage is overtaken by darkness.

While the revolution can be considered an epochal accomplishment of the new class, its methods of rule fill some of the most shameful pages in history. Men will marvel at the grandiose ventures it accomplished and will be ashamed of the means it used.

When the new class leaves the historical scene—and this

must happen—there will be less sorrow over its passing than there was for any other class before it. Smothering everything except what suited its ego, it has condemned itself to failure and shameful ruin.

Laszek Kolakowski

THE CONSPIRACY OF
IVORY TOWER INTELLECTUALS

"Philosophy cannot produce its own subject matter; that always lies in present or past history. We construe philosophy badly, when we construe it, if that past contains experiences which we are unable to repeat. We are able to pronounce reliable judgment only on that which lies immediately before us. . . .

"People's behavior should not be derived from their philosophy; rather their philosophy should be derived from their behavior. Their history does not follow from their way of thinking, but their thinking follows from their history."

Despite appearances Karl Marx did not write these wise words. They were formulated a good half-century before his time by Friedrich Heinrich Jacobi, a writer who, on many counts, as a matter of fact, might awaken justified antipathies. Nonetheless, he made this penetrating observation, which is worth remembering when undertaking any philosophical or moral critiques. In particular, it is useful to contemplate this quotation before inaugurating criticism of any way of thought which might be characterized as programmatic *cessation of action*, programmatic political *detachment*, and ostentatious nonengagement of the individual in the onerous transformations of his contemporary world. Specifically, we pose the question: what human actions can give birth to a philosophy which negates action, if such a philosophy exists at all?

We do not ask this question as the result of abstract metaphysical inspiration, but because of current political experiences which have provided an unexpected opportunity to consider the problem of the social engagement of human individuals, of the obstacles in the way of that engagement, and the philosophy which is to explain these obstacles, or morally justify human impotence in the face of the excessive resistance of these obstacles. These are also the specific problems of decent men when they ask themselves the extent to which they are willing to be engaged in not altogether decent situations, and yet the largest part of their earthly existence consists of just such situations.

A case in point of the problem of social nonengagement is that of the intellectuals, or thoroughgoing and absolute intellectuals, whose appearance in contemporary life, if we are to believe certain allegations, constitutes the major threat to the Polish state and the most venomous factor of disintegration working, with impunity still, against the universal march of the nation toward a bright and magnificent future. Poland is threatened by a great conspiracy of sentimental intellectuals, a terrible conspiracy of pale esthetes based on the loftiness of great morality.

And now what is an intellectual in the eyes of his antagonists: a perfidious creature full of hypocrisy, knowing very well that as long as man lives he cannot avoid participation in contemporary conflicts, and yet, in spite of this, he pretends that he has accomplished just such a miracle of nonparticipation. In the disguise of a guardian of the great, all-human values, concealing hypocrisy and cowardice, the intellectual really wants to save his purely personal and private values, which are of no concern to anyone other than himself. Cosmic humbug that he is, he would like to walk through the bloody marshes of history in the spotless shoes of private virtue, and when he cannot do that, he pretends that he transcends the muck of the times and lifts his ethereal body on the wings of eternal values into a realm of spiritual freedom from which he can look on the world with the eyes of a merciless judge. Thus, the intellectual wants to reserve for himself the right of moral judgment of social reality without any responsibility for the course of social events. But only superficially and only in the consciousness of those he manages to deceive with his alleged castle in the air does the intellectual avoid engagement in history. In reality, he is immersed in its sticky ooze up to his neck, and acts on it with his slogans. He calls on mankind to cease action because a decent man cannot become personally involved in settling the dirty accounts of history. Actually, cessation of action is also action, though purely negative, because it consciously leaves the field to the forces of social regression. Social nature will not tolerate a vacuum and therefore the apparent holes made in it by the work of intellectuals are immediately filled by the brutal aggression of reaction. The Intellectual not only acts this way, but he knows the results of his actions as well; therefore, he is not an ignoramus but a hypocrite, not a philosopher with clean hands, but an active aid to reactionary forces.

And what is an Anti-intellectual in his own eyes? A person who recognizes the inevitability of choice which, whether we like it or not, we must make in the face of the world's great conflicts. He engages himself consciously because he does not wish to be engaged unwittingly, and so involved against his will in one of the conflicting forces. He also knows that in political strife any third force is only an illusion or a deceit, and that it is possible to attack only from one position. An Anti-intellectual maintains that he understands the moral side of political life, but he does not wish to use the obsession of clean hands as a pretext for escape from the battlefield. He therefore, collaborates with history in order to accelerate its course, not in order to satisfy his own highbrow conscience. He scorns the moralists' narcissism because it is contrary to a morality based on responsibility. If history works by brutal means, then he is consciously willing to accept its assumptions, not because of his private views, but because it is impossible to reject them. Thus, he is a *realist;* he sees the world from the viewpoint of *existence,* as distinguished from the intellectual who sees it from the viewpoint of *things as they should be; i.e.,* a fiction created by himself and imposed, without success, on reality.

The compromise of the Intellectual becomes wholly obvious in this conflict as the defeat of things as they should be when confronted with the world of reality.

Nonetheless, the problem is not quite so simple. Discussions of "intellectualism" have for years been conducted in a fog of adjectives, those most suggestive and deceptive parts of language. We deal with a field in which each position easily builds suggestive façades of words, which show that the discussion endeavors to avoid clear-cut and uniform questions, and is rhetorical rather than rational.

What then does an authentic Intellectual in the "classical" sense (*i.e.,* in the terms of Julien Benda) think of himself? and what does he think of his antagonist? The intellectual believes that he has no intention of making his position subservient to purely personal values. On the contrary, his main concern is not to let himself be carried away by group, class or national interests which are inevitably in conflict with those values common to all mankind, and characteristic of man as such rather than of man as a member of a particular group. The decadence of man begins whenever his most human quality—rational perception—becomes depraved in the service of mythology, blind emotion, and national hatreds. The human individual actively engaged in great political struggles can never afford an intellectual perspective from which he would be able to see the limitations of his own camp, the irrationality of those undertakings in which he himself participates. An active struggle uses up not only nervous energy, it also absorbs the human mind and involves its potentialities to such a degree that mankind is inevitably relegated to an animal level. To save what is most precious in man—his capacity for rational thought—is possible only by determined resistance against all the temptations of relativism, by perpetuating at all costs the fortress of indestructible values. If no one is left who, among the great conflicts, preserves objective and sober judgment, mankind will exterminate itself more effectively than could be accomplished by cosmic catastrophe.

"You say," the Intellectual says to his opponent, the Revolutionary, "that at a certain historical moment, the interests of the working class become wholly identified with the interests of all mankind, and not only preserve universal human values, but are the only force capable of preserving those values. But what proofs do you have for this other than vague historiosophical speculation? What right do I have, in the name of such speculative dialectics about the future, to renounce the best values of human life in the present? Moreover, history thus far does not confirm your optimism. On the contrary, it shows that special interests, as you understand them, are often realized by overriding eternal human values. And here are examples. . . . The first, the second the thousandth. . . . If you represent a specific historical reality, on what basis do you ask me to affirm it morally merely because it is a reality? I will not support any form of historical reality solely because somebody persuades me that it is inevitable, even if I believe in its inevitability, for which, by the way, I have no evidence. If crime is the law of history, then does my awareness of this law suffice to make me a criminal? Why should that be so? You do not permit me to measure your actions with the measuring rod of absolute values because, in your opinion, such values do not exist and are figments of the imagination. On the other hand, you yourselves talk about universal human values which must therefore be absolute; thus, silently you introduce a vague and equivocal axiomatic absolutism into your doctrine, only to destroy it immediately with equally equivocal historical relativism. And you come to me with this baggage demanding that I renounce immediately the best of everything created by human culture because your eschatology promises to return it to me intact after some indefinite period of time. Therefore, you demand for your philosophy of history, and your own history, an unlimited moral credit, though at every step both are unmasked as bankrupt.

"You, who rashly agree to give up everything to the Moloch of the present in the unjustified hope that it will be returned in the future, do not represent a philosophy of responsibility. He who really wishes to bear responsibility for the treasures produced and discovered by human history will defend them at all costs, even at the cost of separating himself from the chaos of current strife if those values can only be preserved outside of the battlefield."

"But it is noteworthy," the Anti-intellectual remarks at this juncture, "that you know how to save these eternal values only together with your own skin. It's also strange that, questioning my historical evidence, you ignore the direction in which the other side of history aims, whose evidence leaves no doubts. There, books are stacked in flaming pyres. What did you do to save them? Do you think it is enough if you yourself learn them by heart? There, bowels are torn out of bodies and faces trampled on by jackboots. What did you do to prevent that? Do you think you can accomplish anything with your sermons about universal love preached to fully armed soldiers, that you can extinguish fire by parroting the Ten Commandments?"

The Intellectual answers:

"Sinai has burning pyres on both sides. Shall I count them to recognize your moral superiority? That would be an insignificant victory indeed. You constantly tell me that the threat to human freedom is so great that to conquer it, it is worth giving up freedom. Over and over again, you din into my ears Saint-Just's motto: 'There is no freedom for the enemies of freedom.' To some extent I am willing to recognize that. But I must know who determines the division of men into enemies and defenders of freedom. There is always someone who counts himself in one of the camps, someone who in a trial is simultaneously one of the contending parties, judge, prosecutor, and policeman, all in one. The engagement to which I am constantly forced must, therefore, be based on absolute confidence in that man, in his present and future intentions; that is, I must have an absolute confidence in him which I hardly have in myself. On what basis could I afford an act of such complete confidence towards men who, in a conflict in which they are one of the litigants, simultaneously want to be the judges? They deny the eternal and most elementary principle of justice; they deny that the controversy between themselves and their enemies should be resolved by anyone but themselves. Still, a judge, if he is justly to pronounce one side right, must be impartial before he comes to court; he fulfills his function properly only when he uses the same measuring rod of abstract justice for both contestants. You refuse me this right, however, maintaining that first I must be on your side in order to judge justly; in short, I can only judge when I have previously taken one side in the trial.

"True, you have a separate theory to justify this abhorrent practice, namely the theory of the nonexistence of a third force in a society rent by class antagonisms; a theory according to which the office of judge, as defined by contemporary jurisprudence, is entirely untenable. You consider this theory obvious and ask me to recognize it. With that, you add that by rejecting this theory, by the very wish to judge the controversy, I automatically place myself in the camp of your opponents. In other words, if I recognize the possibility that a third force exists, I am immediately classified as an enemy, and as such morally deprived of the right to judge your arguments, because then I have already taken one side in the trial. I can avoid this only if I accept the theory that a third force is impossible, and so accept your viewpoint. I can judge and understand you only by being one of you.

"Aren't you aware of how you use the same arguments Soren Kierkegaard used in defense of Christianity, maintaining that to understand Christianity you must first accept it? Your statement is identical. To appreciate your position, it is necessary first to accept your arguments. You must be aware that this is a demand quite unacceptable to any rationalist in the world, because rationalism consists, among other things, in refraining from making a choice until the separate arguments have been weighed. Moreover, your premise requires me to accept your arguments without granting me the right to investigate them, a manifestation of the total irrationalism against which I am warned by the entire history of European culture. I do not deny that with such methods you may win followers, but remember that you never can win them by intellectual means. Your position is completely impervious to rational thought because *a priori* it rejects all criticism as acts inherently hostile to you, and as such, consciously or unconsciously, coming from the opposition camp. Your theory that no third force exists is thus programmatically irrational and indigestible to sensible human beings.

"And if you say that I protect these eternal cultural values which you ridicule, together with my own skin, and if for this reason you wish to unmask me before my audience as a narcissistic idealist, my answer is: I have no intention of becoming a scoundrel merely to demonstrate that I don't care about being considered a decent man."

The Revolutionary, in turn, replies: "Your own defense is your indictment."

"I am not defending myself," the Intellectual interrupts. "Why must the world for you inevitably consist of accused and prosecutor?"

"I did not create that world," the Anti-intellectual continues. "But one should be able to face its horrors rather than bewail them. You accuse us revolutionaries of splitting reality into two sides and demanding engagement on only one side. This is just as foolish as accusing meteorologists of creating hail and tornados. The history of mankind is proof of our arguments. The secondary proof is the *de facto* effectiveness of our social actions undertaken on the basis of this interpretation of conditions."

"History proves everything previously injected into it by the historian," the Intellectual replies. "You approach history with a ready-made scheme and at the end of your studies announce triumphantly that the scheme has actually emerged from your analysis, ignoring the fact that you yourselves imposed it on history to begin with. And the practical effectiveness of your world view has not yet been proved. How far any movement is really historically effective can only be seen *post hoc,* when the era is over. By maintaining that, for the first time in history, you are free of the limitations imposed on man's perspective by being time-bound, you are the victims of the very same confusion which you have rightly pointed out in your predecessors."

The Anti-intellectual laughs mockingly: *"In qua mensura mensi fueritis, remetietur vobis.* You want to show that we only boast of our freedom from historical limitations while you yourselves are really free of them. After all, it is you who maintain that you have the world of eternal values in hand, transcending history and free of its pressures. We, on the contrary, have a clear awareness of the relativity of values. Moreover, we are the only ones who have really mastered the ability to think historically, which permits us to analyze present history in the making."

"I know," the Intellectual responds, "that you *state* the general principle of historicism, but I don't see you use it. I would scarcely accuse you of this and of inconsistency generally, if you accepted the possibility of an alternate assumption which I accept: the recognition of values which can under no circumstances be destroyed, and the negation of which is evil under any conditions. But you act differently. Your relativism is masked by appearances of fictitious immutability. Basically, you have values which change daily and are daily pronounced final. This is the worst form of relativism because it denies both historical thinking, the value of which I do not deny, and the immutable and eternal human achievements. It is a strange cult that calls for monotheism but which daily changes the god which is the object of its worship.

"You must notice that we are conducting an unusual discussion. It is almost the precise counterpart of that fictitious dialogue between Lavoisier and Carnot as recorded by Romain Rolland. A certain naïveté easily discernible in that drama does not obscure the analogy. Carnot demands the sacrifice of the present to the future. Lavoisier replies that to sacrifice truth, self-respect, and eternal human values for the future is to sacrifice the future. I cannot disagree with him. Without sharing your faith, as optimistic as it is hollow, concerning the predictability of future events, I never know what future results will ensue from our present actions. I do not, therefore, agree that great moral and intellectual values should be sacrificed on the altar of objectives whose future is so uncertain. On the other hand, I know the contrary to be true, that measures used of necessity leave their mark on the ultimate result."

"You succumb to the deceptive pictures the liberal politicians always paint of the revolutionary movement in order to discredit it," the Anti-intellectual comments. "We are not building an eschatology in which the present is left behind to be destroyed. The present takes immediate advantage of the revolution and as a result the revolution can be forced not to exploit all its possibilities, and to renounce some of them in favor of results in the future. And all the measures used which make you so indignant are always defenses against greater evils. Remember, in politics, the choice between two evils is far more common than choice between absolute good and absolute evil. This is a premise in life created by neither of us."

"I'll never believe," the Intellectual says, "that the moral and intellectual life of mankind should conform to the laws of economic investment, that one should expect better results tomorrow by saving today, using lies to prepare the triumph of truth, and exploiting crime to pave the way for nobility. I know that often it is necessary to choose between two evils, but when both possibilities are largely evil, I will do everything in my power to refrain from choice. In so doing I also make a choice, if only the choice of man's right to evaluate the situation in which he finds himself. And that it not such a small thing."

"Nevertheless, to return to your example, history proved Carnot right."

"I do not see that."

"In that case, the condition of continuing our discussion must be to reinterpret all of world history, something we cannot do, especially if the choice concerning the completion of the task must be made immediately."

"Now you're talking to the point. If we must take a stand today on some current changes, we cannot wait for the uncertain conclusions of historiosophical discussions, which may remain unresolved for a hundred years. Our choice will therefore be best if it is determined by what small particles of certainty we possess. Enduring moral values, developed throughout the history of man up to this moment, are the surest supports we have if reality requires of us a choice which ultimately is of a moral nature. In any event, these

values are more worthy of confidence than any historiosophical explanation. And ultimately this is why I maintain my
position."

"Whatever happens?"

"Whatever happens."

This dialogue has gone on for decades. We leave it unresolved because we do not wish to take part in it; it is not
only unsolved but insoluble. The dialogue is a conflict in
which the bullets are intended to collide, but actually follow different trajectories because the common assumptions
indispensable to any discussion do not exist. We wish to lift
the discussion to a plane where the arguments of both
sides will be partly accepted; the opposing sides will not as a
result be removed, but the positions themselves will change.

To do this, it is necessary to describe the intellectual's
profile as seen from the outside; that is, seen as the product
of the situation in which the intellectual finds himself. For
the intellectual imagines that he has liberated himself from
history by basing himself on eternal values; in reality, however, his position is one he is forced to adopt by his situation. The intellectual is a humanist burdened with the tradition of humanism which he doesn't want to give up, and
which he would in all conscience have to surrender if he
joined any of the large camps which, as a result of their
conflicts, determine the course of world history. Voluntarily,
the intellectual detaches himself from history and renounces
social action because every social action requires him to pass
through that customs office of political realism which deprives him of all those values he holds most dear.

When condemnation of intellectualism begins, it is proof
that social conditions have arisen which favor its spread.
As is well known, whenever a specific moral norm, positive
or negative, comes to life in the social consciousness, it
testifies to the existence of conditions which favor its being
crushed because it arises as a barrier to some real tendency
in the society. If the commandment "Thou shalt not steal"
becomes vital in a society, it means that the society has
created the need to steal on a large scale. When attacks
on intellectuals are made, intellectualism apparently has
found conditions suitable for development in the society. But
a comment that intellectualism is mere petty-bourgeois
escapism is only the confession of a stubborn fighter who
wants to say that he has contempt for escapism. The state-

ment does not explain what social conditions favor the appearance of escapist attitudes. Saying that these are situations in which revolution is imminent, or actually in progress, is false, because revolutionary moments contain very few escapist tendencies. On the contrary, everything indicates that these are postrevolutionary situations; therefore, situations in which revolution is least probable, but at the same time when polarization of political forces is sharpest, and the possibilities of political choice take the form of a single alternative, both parts of which are for some reason unacceptable. Intellectualism is the defeat of political choice which ends in an escape from becoming engaged, an escape which camouflages itself as a defense of supra-historical values, while in fact it merely finds it impossible to discover values in existing history.

I bring up the problem of the single choice as one of the most important questions in the political life of our times, a question which most adequately sums up the great experience of the Stalinist era and the major left-wing traditions which grew out of that experience.

Most of the political and intellectual effort of recent times, whose results and effectiveness cannot presently be gauged, aim at an ideological renaissance of the revolutionary left wing, and can generally be characterized as an attempt to break the traditional Stalinist *blackmail of a single choice* in political life. Stalinism's permanent method aimed essentially at creating a situation in which every criticism of Stalinism objectively constituted automatic relegation to the camp of reaction, an automatic declaration of solidarity with capitalist imperialism. Stalinism frustrated any social criticism and constantly tried to attribute it to counter-revolutionary attitudes. Because of this, the objects of fiercest and most brutal attacks were always the leftist forces closest to the ideas of Communism. No one was the object of such lethal hatred or such terrible police and political persecution as the independent left wing, or any Communist or communizing movement critical of Stalinist practice and dogma. The Social Democratic right wing was placed in the political category; Trotskyism and Titoism were remanded to the category of fighting foreign espionage. From time to time the press could publish statements by bourgeois politicians, but this was unthinkable for activists of the non-Stalinist left.

It would be naïve to wonder about this practice, for it

seems to be a phenomenon easily understood and explained. For centuries death by fire was reserved for heretics rather than for pagans; and the proscribed books on the Catholic Church's *Index* are rarely those of non-Catholics. That special, merciless hatred which almost every organization with a political ideology bestows on its heretics, dissidents, apostles or renegades, a hatred surpassing a hundredfold the most violent revulsion felt toward the recognized enemy, is in reality an understandable product of all such social conditions, though not only of such conditions, in which a specific political or religious organization, originally intended by its authors only as a means to an end, becomes *an end in itself*. We say, "not only of such conditions," bearing in mind the notoriously obvious fact that the chief danger for every fighting group, especially a minority group, lies in the elements of internal subversion disintegrating its unity and militancy. External pressure, within certain limits, is an incentive for group consolidation, but internal centers of disintegration always constitute a threat of death.

The phenomenon we are discussing here cannot be explained simply as the natural self-defense of political organisms against an invasion of foreign bodies. It is not immunization against disease-bearing organisms which is a manifestation of social regression, but an attempt at creating as tight a protective shell as possible against any tendencies capable of bringing about gradual changes. The essential characteristic of any social structure given the name "sect" is the unrelenting vigilance concerning the extremely precise determination of its own boundaries; a ceaseless control to assure exact and unequivocal differentiations between itself and the whole outside world. These differentiations vary in nature—they are ideological, organizational, ritual, traditional—and the greater their number, specificity and variety, the more they indicate the progressive ossification of the sect; the more apparent it becomes that the social organism increasingly ceases to live as a result of natural assimilation and exchange of matter with the environment, and remains alive through miraculous self-reproduction, unknown in nature, and feeding on its own substance; the more it concentrates its activities on itself and the more its external activities are determined by its need for self-preservation.

The sect must continue to show great care to keep the lines dividing it from the environment from becoming blurred. The sect is a structure for which species reproduction is impossible, and therefore self-preservation is its only reason for existence. It can increase its weight, but it can neither develop nor conceive. Care for the prolongation of its individual life becomes its exclusive concern; the phenomenon of creation is organically impossible for it. Every creation, therefore, imposes the necessity of going outside of the sect and breaking its boundaries.

Thus, the phenomenon of sectarianism in political life, manifest, among other things, in that extreme care for the precise boundaries of the organization, constitutes evidence of the double process taking place within it. It testifies to the senescent changes and the loss of creative potential, and thus testifies that the political organization has become an end in itself, succumbed to alienation from the social tasks which gave birth to it, and formulated its own aim as its self-preservation. Sectarianism is not an individual's error; it is a social symptom of approaching death. Under these conditions, political suspicion, absurd and pathological in appearance, becomes an understandable phenomenon, social and not individual. It is comparable to that brutal egoism sometimes encountered in old age, which vaguely realizes that nature has turned against it. It is the frantic self-defense of a social structure against which the tide of history is turning. When police come to be the only regulator of social life, it becomes the knife of cruelty applied to an organism which has lost the capacity for natural self-defense, it then becomes an artificial response to symptoms prognosticating annihilation, and gives rise to the picture of an organism which cannot count on pity because pity is an attribute only of human individuals: it is unknown in history or in nature.

The metaphor above, whose biological inadequacy will I hope be forgiven by naturalists, is only an attempt at a symbolic presentation of one of the characteristic forms of action discernible in the development of the political phenomenon called, more or less properly, Stalinism. Irrespective of its dimensions, Stalinism is a way of life of a political sect. A Stalinist-type party is one which has ceased to treat itself as a means but has become an end in itself, making its existence independent of the social forces which once created it. Within its ranks, there grows an exclusive organized stratum, the Party apparatus, dominating the whole, which constitutes the outward manifestation of this process. When in the life of the Party, the apparatus is the only active element, the existence of separate interests of the apparatus is evidence of the different interests within the Party. Stalinism, in the life of Communist Parties, is not based on the fact that they are so badly organized as to prevent control of the apparatus by the Party masses; it is based on the fact that the social function of the Party renders impossible a change in this type of organization.

By surrounding itself with an impenetrable ideological and ritualistic crust, Stalinism as a political movement not only determines its own course, but all the rest of social reality is also determined by its relationship to Stalinism. Within the boundaries it arbitrarily sets up between itself and the rest of the world there are no connecting passages, no intermediate stages. Stalinism stubbornly aims to have all that remains outside its boundaries considered insignificant and unessential. The only division of social importance is that resulting from the existence of Stalinism as a camp. The world is divided into the saved and damned, into the City of God and the city of the devil, between which the boundaries are clearer than between a mountaintop and a valley. This boundary line divides every field of life; every fact, thought or fragment which constitutes the substance of social life is eternally branded as belonging to one realm or the other. Between them, the tribe of Abel and the tribe of Cain divide ideas, tools, social relations, morality, art, science, tradition, and even more, private emotions and tastes; in fact, almost all of nature itself.

Between the two kingdoms there are neither neutral nor mixed areas: one can only be absorbed by one of them. Because of this, Stalinism demanded either total acceptance or total rejection and was surprisingly successful in imposing that pattern on the world. Every new ritual and confirmed truth had to be accepted on the threat of complete exclusion from the community of the saved. Questioning the primacy of Yablokov over Edison was tantamount to questioning the dictatorship of the proletariat. This tie was *real*, not imaginary; more precisely, great effort was made to make it real, to make it a social fact. Stalinism peopled its world with thousands of constantly new idols, each of whom demanded worship under threat of falling into complete atheism: it insisted that there really is no difference between disbelief in the miracles of St. Expeditus and complete godlessness. Partisanship becomes so much a characteristic of every fragment of the world that, from time to time, even the forces of nature seem to participate in it. For many years, in the Stalinist press, natural calamities seemed to be the monopoly of capitalist countries and the impression was given that these calamities were the results of the political system.

We recall this picture not in order to ridicule its peculiarities of caricature, a thing easily done, but solely to understand the essential characteristic of the Stalinist era, which was the imposition on human reality of a program of single choice in all spheres of social life. This program was not only an official myth: it actually worked. Stalinism defined its enemies by defining itself. The mechanics of its existence served permanently to consolidate its enemies, because it threw a layer of permanent darkness over them in which all differences were eased. Among other things, this is one reason why the Stalinist party is organically incapable of acquiring allies, why in politics it is doomed to chronic incapacity in creating a popular front.

A popular front can be created effectively only under conditions of compromise; that is, on the assumption that there are divergences of opinion and action in some fields, and recognized agreement in others currently considered essential. However, the Stalinist interpretation of a popular front is based not on compromise but on total control. Those who would be admitted to it must accept the assumptions of Stalinism on essential problems, and on the remaining problems can have no assumptions whatsoever. The only concession the Stalinist party will agree to is the right it grants its allies to remain silent on purely secondary issues, but under no circumstances do they have the right to divergent opinions. For example, there is no possibility of an alliance with the anticolonial forces against colonialism if these forces do not, at the least, refrain from expressing an opinion on the Moscow trials. At best, an ally has the right to be silent on certain issues, in which case he can earn the distinguished reputation of being an immature and inconsistent ally, but an ally nonetheless. But woe to him if he raises his voice in criticism on any question. He will be rejected absolutely and put in the enemy camp. Doubting the legality of Bukharin's trial is tantamount to creating a police state on the blood of the workers and peasants.

Despite appearances, this single-choice world view was a great strength of the Stalinist system. We say despite appearances, because appearances would lead us to believe that the systematic extermination of potential allies and the demand that others accept one's own assumptions only in their absolute form is the best way to commit suicide. In reality, however, this depends on the social function of the organization. An aging sect can only with difficulty afford allies if the task of self-preservation dominates its consciousness and imposes on it the fearful obsession of losing its own boundaries. The more the sect becomes an end in itself, the greater the predominance of the tasks which are intended to perpetuate its own existence and to restore its vitality, and the more it is bound to consider even the most fragmentary criticism a threat to its very foundations. The entire external world becomes an enemy, not simply because some one's taste imposes on it such a view of reality, but because the objective situation imposes it. Every "otherness" is an enemy because the sect has lost the capacity for progressive evolution; hence, all changes can only constitute a threat of disintegration.

Of course, Stalinism contained in its arsenal the slogan of "unity" repeated in an atmosphere of constant indignation. The way of thought connected with the Stalinist system is idealist in nature: the constant repetition of the unity slogan was necessary for many reasons, but when it turns out that as a result, real unity remains no less distant and fictitious than before, the ideologists of Stalinism can do nothing else but complain of extreme human ingratitude and accuse their allies of ill will. "We do everything to bring about the unity of the labor movement—namely, we repeat the slogan of unity; the thing fails—which makes it apparent that the opposition stubbornly perseveres in hating progress."

This is the way a Stalinist ideologist imagines the world to be. He is unable to take into consideration social conditions of which he himself is a part, and which make the actual unity of the labor movement an unattainable ideal. He must, therefore, look for these conditions in the realm of the spirit, in the spitefulness of his opponents, in their ignorance or ill will, or best of all, in their dishonest intentions and subversive plans. Such a position is natural because the Stalinist ideologist does not admit the possibility that he could ever be justly criticized on any issue, and he is unable to undertake a revision of any of his premises, which after all have a sacred character. To his way of thinking, unity consists of the ally's voluntary relinquishing of all principles of action incompatible with his own principles. Nevertheless, his indignant astonishment that his own cries strike a void is sincere, because his imagination is so shaped that it precludes in advance any form of intellectual criticism.

In the seventeenth century the problem of the unity of Christianity was very much alive in the various religious movements. The supporters of that position, which used to be called the Irenic Movement, fabricated a fantastic utopia by maintaining that it would be possible to determine those basic assumptions of dogma which are common to all Christian religions, and out of them to shape some universal *confessio fidei*, impoverished in content but morally effective, which would put an end to the divisions of the Christian world and to religious wars. This concept, connected with the ideas of Lord Herbert of Cherbury, found many adherents. It was propagated by the Dutch Anabaptists and Socinians; many of the prominent French *libertines* fought for it; and Leibnitz was one of its most zealous propagators. The idea even had a following among contemporary rulers: it was discussed in the court of the Prussian King and in some localities, temples common to all Christian religions were established; even King Wladyslaw IV was deeply interested in the problem of unifying the churches.

The common basis on which the foundations of Christian unity might be laid was often formulated. In the name of the Roman Catholic Church this matter was discussed by the great Bossuet, who explained that he, of course, supported the plan, and unification should be effected as follows: the Protestants, recognizing the error of their ways, should be converted to the true faith and recognize the authority of the Pope. He stressed, naturally enough, that the Catholic Church would not relinquish any of its doctrine. This position was not cynical and is quite understandable. If Bossuet were asked why he refused to renounce any premises of Roman Catholic doctrine for the sake of unity, he would undoubtedly have answered: "After all, this is the true doctrine, not any other. To relinquish any of its postulates would be to betray the truth." The Church aims at unity with Protestants and is ready for it immediately, provided that the Protestants are converted to Roman Catholicism. There is no reason for making the personal stupidity of this energetic Bishop responsible for this way of thought. His way of thought was neither unique, nor was it even really thought; it was the natural reaction of a political organization against proposals which would doom its individuality. The main task of the Roman Church is to preserve that individuality because, as a political organization, it has its own differentiated interests, and naturally had no intention of committing suicide in order to end religious wars or contribute to peace on earth.

Clearly, every political organization for which self-preservation is an end in itself must act in the same way. It can understand unity only in terms of converting its partner. The Stalinist party cannot have allies, just as the Roman Church cannot surround itself with "allied" sects differing "slightly" in dogma. For instance, one would not recognize transubstantiation; a second would reject the resurrection of bodies; and the third, the dogma of the Trinity. Try to suggest to a Catholic Bishop that he overlook these "slight" doctrinal differences, and ask him to recognize a common doctrinal platform in the remaining matters as the foundation for unity! For a faithful Catholic the difference between an Anabaptist and an atheist becomes almost insignificant compared to the gap which separates both from orthodoxy. There is no salvation outside the Church and the world is not divided into a large number of views from which it is possible to form a continuous series from orthodox Catholics to atheists: rather, the world is divided into orthodox Catholics and all the others. The dualist, truly Manichean vision of human reality is the unavoidable form of sectarian thought and therefore it is senseless to condemn it morally. *Naturalia non sunt turpia.*

The extent to which this world picture corresponds to reality is now determined by the physical power of the sect. Stalinism was a powerful sect, and the genius of hypocrisy was on its side. It shaped a reality whose fundamental divisions were close to its own projections; that is, a reality in which criticism of Stalinism was forced to display great vigilance, if it were to avoid transforming itself into an apology for capitalism, towards which it was constantly pushed. The forces of reaction were powerful; the forces of the independent left were insignificant. Stalinist dissidents easily became renegades because there was no serious social force which could retain their criticism within the range of socialist thought.

Being a renegade is not an imaginary state. Renegades from the revolutionary movement are those ex-revolutionaries who actually, and not merely in the opinion of their former comrades, switch to positions of the political right, although it is true that everything had been done to pave the road for them. Doriot was a renegade. Arthur Koestler is a renegade, not in the least because he is the author of *Darkness at Noon*, a novel which beyond any doubt has a place in the history of contemporary culture, but because of his activities in recent years. Pierre Hervé is on the road towards becoming a renegade, and not because he published *La Révolution et les Fétiches*, a shy and weak criticism of several Stalinist premises, but because he subsequently displayed his readiness to ally himself with an authentic reaction as the lesser evil compared with Stalinism. That he was forced on this road is irrelevant to this point of view: it only confirms the above-mentioned effectiveness of the political practice of Stalinism. The renegades from Communism are those—so numerous—persons who, breaking with Stalinism, begin to see in it the only danger to the world, and are willing in their struggle against it to make common cause with anybody: with colonialists, with the aggressive counterrevolution, with the most extreme right wing. Succumbing to the obsession of their anti-Communist mission, they begin to treat fascism as a specter invented by Stalinists. For them anti-Stalinism becomes sufficient basis for agreement with any former opponent. Silently, they accept the Stalinist vision of reality and the theory of the nonexistence of a third force, and in so doing become an illustration of its rightness. They fall victim to the blackmail of the single choice, and abandoning one camp, voluntarily join the other. The renegades constitute a great Stalinist triumph. They are an argument which constantly speaks in its favor, for the transformation of dissidents into renegades, which can be seen in a thousand examples, is the *de facto* result of Stalinism. The effectiveness of its actions are manifest in the fact that Stalinism had no allies, that the forces of the independent left which refused to be totally absorbed, or pushed beyond the barrier into the counterrevolution, were so small and remained alive with such difficulty.

By exploiting this situation, sanctioning it with the metaphysics of the two camps and the theory of the inevitable polarization of social life, Stalinism imposed upon the consciousness of the left the fatalism of choosing between heaven and hell, and paralyzed criticism by treating it as the automatic ticket to the camp of reaction. Those who thought this a choice between two forms of hell were, as a result, not considered enemies of both, but as sympathizers with the opposition's hell.

There is no greater danger for the development of the socialist movement in its present phase than to allow a repeated intensification of the political polarization that leads to the circumstances of a single alternative. That premise is the point of departure for all considerations which are to give meaning to the notion of "political realism" in actual politics. The disappearance of socialist social criticism, determined by whatever factors, would inevitably result in the fact that all criticism would be forced to authentically counterrevolutionary positions, and taken over by the obscurantist and clerical social forces which tend toward restoration of capitalism.

Thus, apart from the choice of being a renegade on the one hand, and a loyalist opportunist on the other, the intellectual's viewpoint would be the only third possibility, indicating however, a resignation from an active role in political life and capitulation in the face of the existing political alternatives. The more the intellectuals' attitude becomes the object of attack, the more the attack becomes testimony of the objective development of events towards that political polarization described above. An attempt to break down the program of single choice in political life, as has been mentioned, would be the shortest way to contribute to a renaissance of the revolutionary movement, and to undo the work of its long-lasting compromise. The death of these tendencies would be tantamount to liquidation of all forces, however weak, which can nonetheless prevent the transformation of democratic criticism into a counterrevolutionary force, and which can therefore prevent a situation in which any economic demands of the working class become acts of sabotage; any voice of political criticism, a voice of solidarity with Western imperialism; any discussion of the limits of social freedoms, the consequences of clerical inspiration; any economic criticism, the triumph of shopkeepers and speculators.

The possibility of socialist criticism is an indispensable condition for effectively overcoming counterrevolutionary criticism. The absence of such a possibility is identical with the inevitable outgrowth of administrative and repressive action as a method of rule, inevitable because it does not depend on intention, but results from the objective develop-

ment of political life; that is, a phenomenon contrary to socialist construction.

Unfavorable economic conditions greatly multiply this
danger because they intensify the difference between the legitimate demands of the working class and the capacities
of the state, which is its employer, and thus find expression
in the deeper contradictions between the conscience of the
masses and the political organization of the state and its representatives. It is also known that the power of capitalism in
Poland is great, while the social amnesia, which we may
regret but which is in practice incurable, presents that capitalism to the people in an adequate form, not in the form of
Polish capitalism prior to 1939—a dwarfish capitalism, technically backward, obscurantist and clerical in culture, fascist
in politics—but as it appears today in the form of West Germany's standard of living, the democratic system of Great
Britain, and the technical level of the United States. The
observation that English democracy is practically attainable
only after one has had more than ten decades of English
history is unquestionably right, but it is an equally unquestionable fact that it is virtually impossible to persuade public opinion of that truth. To convince the masses that it is
impossible to transfer Poland to the British Isles is an undertaking almost as difficult as actually transferring Poland to
the British Isles. Overcoming the attractive force of capitalism by historical information is hopeless because this attraction is not the simple result of ignorance of past history, but
the result of the effective passage of current history. The attractive force of capitalism's *de facto* existence and evidence
can effectively be countered only by the *de facto* existence
and evidence of socialism.

If Polish history crushed capitalism in a country delayed
in its development and ruined by war, the socialist movement of that country bears not only the burden of that monstrous task, the race to equal the technical development of
the capitalist world, but also the equally heavy burden of
the necessity to break the continued and inevitable inertia of
social consciousness towards capitalism. The antinomy of the
Polish social situation consists, among other things, in the
fact that this inertia of consciousness cannot be overcome by
any direct influence, but only indirectly by making daily life
socialist and attractive simultaneously. But this very same
inertia makes that task difficult. Thus, both difficulties rein-

force each other, and apart from economic changes directly felt by the working people of the country, can be counteracted only by the power of repression and the power of socialist consciousness. Since the power of socialist consciousness is, on a large scale, directly proportional to the range of permissible socialist criticism, and the latter inversely proportional to the range of *de facto* counterrevolutionary criticism, the reserves of social reaction increase when the effective possibilities for socialist and democratic criticism weaken. As a result, the necessity, not merely the intention, to use force and repression increases and there is a rise in the importance repression must have in the system of government. For this reason, pressure aimed at paralyzing socialist criticism must involve repressive measures against a large mass of people, because it causes any criticism to become the tool of political backwardness, and is espoused only in its defense.

History seems to teach us that in the life of one generation the comedies of national unity last for weeks, while the tragedies of national controversy fill the rest of the generation's life. There is no more important task for Poland than to work to make the largest possible part of these controversies take place on the socialist scene. This is also the positive program of socialist criticism which wants to be critical from conviction and socialist by conviction, and which is attracted by the temptation to abstain from speaking up when circumstances confront it with the neccesity of choice between opportunism or joining the ranks of renegades. This abstaining from choice is the fate of the intellectual and can then be explained (which doesn't mean morally justified) by the objective conditions of the political world. Intellectualism is an act of capitulation; however, we are not concerned with recording that truth but rather with investigating the reality in which the concept of capitulation may take on the dimensions of a social force. Contemporary intellectualism, as an ideology of abstaining from choice, is the result of confronting two social facts: the consciousness of the ideological anti-Stalinist left, and reality which denies this consciousness the possibility of practical realization in social life.

Because of this, intellectualism does not permit itself to be disarmed by the slogan of "political realism" alone. What is the meaning of that slogan? Deprived of more detailed commentary, it is also deprived of any matter-of-fact meaning, and becomes an ordinary militant slogan, one of the thousand ideological missiles political polemists fling at each other not in order to understand their problems but to achieve tactical superiority: in daily political practice, the notion of "realism" does not throw the smallest ray of light on reality, it is exclusively an instrument of invective. The spokesmen of realism want to convince their public that they utilize this term to describe the attitude of those men who simply "take reality into account," do not pursue chimeras, do not build castles in the air, do not belabor the sun with a stick, etc. In other words, they wish to persuade themselves and others that everything else they say within the confines of their political program can easily be deduced from the most trivial principle of taking the facts into account. On the other hand, the opposition, the builders of imaginary utopian edifices, deeply scorn reality and consider it easily shaped by their imaginations; therefore, they are simply visionaries with a rich imagination, and thus social evildoers and myth producers.

In reality, the matter is not so simple. If the alleged utopians were only a group of visionaries weaving a perfect world out of the threads of their fantasies, no one would take the trouble to criticize them. If criticism of utopian doctrines becomes, or is considered, an important social problem, it shows that utopian doctrine itself is a serious fact in social consciousness, and also therefore an important component of the social situation in which the spokesmen of realism, thusly interpreted, act and want to act. In such a case the campaign against utopianism in no way resembles the criticism which Engels directed against Fourier; this is not criticism of the social ineffectiveness of utopian thought, but of its effectiveness, which in the opinion of its critics is harmful and undesirable because it hampers the only political efforts which are possible in the given situation.

Because of this, the conflict centered on the subject of political realism is intellectually barren and transforms itself into a demonstration of empty slogans if it does not discuss the real limits of applying the concept of realism, whose usefulness no one questions, if it is not a discussion about concrete social needs, about which are concrete, which merely utopian, and if utopian, to what extent. Otherwise, the discussion is limited to listing platitudes about realism, which

are universally applicable, and therefore serve only to cam-
ouflage the existing differences. We remember that gener-
alized slogans can be used to justify anything.[2]

However, we are not presently raising the question of the
concrete limits of the applicability of the concept of political
realism. We are satisfied with expressing our own refusal to
discuss the subject, "Should reality be taken into account or
not?" And we consider the controversy when thus formulated to be fictitious. Whenever we receive the answer to the
proposition, "The laws of nature cannot be broken," instead
of proof that this proposition is contrary to some verified definite law of nature, we know we are talking to a critic who
is indifferent to reason and argument. This is analogous to
meeting an accusation that one's spelling is incorrect with
the sole justification: the rules of spelling exist. Thus, without debating the problem of whether reality should or
should not be taken into account, we want to consider another question: will it be possible to formulate a general
principle of regulating the mutual relationship between our
knowledge of historical necessities and our moral convic-
tions? between the world of being and the world of values?
between reality and morality? We formulate the discussion
preliminaries in order to stop the pitiable controversies in
which one side announces, with the air of making a discovery, that it is necessary to take reality into account, and the
other assures it with zeal that it never intended to question
that commandment.

THE NEW PROGRAM OF THE
COMMUNIST PARTY OF THE SOVIET UNION

INTRODUCTION

The great October Socialist Revolution ushered in a new era in the history of mankind, the era of the downfall of capitalism and the establishment of communism. Socialism has triumphed in the Soviet Union and has achieved decisive victories in the people's democracies; socialism has become a cause of practical significance to hundreds of millions of people, and the bearer of the revolutionary movement of the working class throughout the world.

More than 100 years ago Karl Marx and Frederick Engels, the great teachers of the proletariat, wrote in the "Communist Manifesto": "A specter is haunting Europe, the specter of communism." The courageous and selfless struggle of the proletariat of all countries brought mankind nearer to communism. First, dozens and hundreds of people, then thousands and millions, inspired by the ideals of communism, stormed the old world. The Paris Commune, the October Revolution, the Socialist revolution in China and in a number of European and Asian countries are the major historical stages in the heroic battle fought by the international working class for the victory of communism. A tremendously long road, a road drenched in the blood of fighters for the happiness of the people, a road of glorious victories and temporary reverses, had to be traversed before communism, which had once seemed a mere specter, became the great force of modern times, a type of society that is being built up over vast areas of the globe.

In the early twentieth century the center of the international revolutionary movement shifted to Russia. Russia's heroic working class, led by the Bolshevik party headed by Vladimir Ilyich Lenin, became its vanguard. The Communist party inspired and led the socialist revolution; it was the organizer and leader of the first workers' and peasants' state in history. The brilliant genius of Lenin, whose name will live forever, illumines mankind's road to communism.

On entering the arena of political struggle, the Leninist

Communist party raised high the banner of revolutionary Marxism over the whole world. Marxism-Leninism became a powerful ideological weapon for the revolutionary transformation of society. At every stage of historical progress, the party, taking guidance from the theory of Marx-Engels-Lenin, accomplished the tasks scientifically formulated in its programs.

In adopting its first program at its Second Congress in 1903 the Bolshevik party called on the working class and all working people of Russia to fight for the overthrow of the Czarist autocracy and then of the bourgeois-landlord system and for the establishment of the dictatorship of the proletariat. In February 1917, the Czarist regime was swept away. In October 1917, the proletarian revolution abolished the capitalist system so hated by the people. A Socialist country came into being for the first time in history. The creation of a new world began.

The first program of the party had been carried out.

Adopting its second program at the Eighth Congress in 1919, the party promulgated the task of building a Socialist society. Treading on unexplored ground and overcoming difficulties and hardships, the Soviet people under the leadership of the Communist party put into practice the plan for Socialist construction drawn up by Lenin. Socialism triumphed in the Soviet Union completely and finally.

The second program of the party has likewise been carried out.

The gigantic revolutionary exploits accomplished by the Soviet people roused and inspired the masses in all countries and continents. A mighty unifying thunderstorm marking the springtime of mankind is raging over the earth. The Socialist revolution in European and Asian countries has resulted in the establishment of the world Socialist system. A powerful wave of national liberation revolutions is sweeping away the colonial system of imperialism.

One-third of mankind is building a new life under the banner of scientific communism. The first contingents of the working class to shake off obsolete oppression are facilitating victory for fresh contingents of their class brothers. The Socialist world is expanding; the capitalist world is shrinking. Socialism will inevitably succeed capitalism everywhere. Such is the objective law of social development. Imperialism is powerless to check the irresistible process of emancipation.

Our effort, whose main content is the transition from

capitalism to socialism, is an effort and struggle between the two opposing social systems, an effort of Socialist and national liberation revolutions, of the breakdown of imperialism and the abolition of the colonial system, an effort of the transition of more and more people to the Socialist path, of the triumph of socialism and communism on a world-wide scale. The central factor of the present effort is the international working class and its main creation, the world Socialist system.

Today the Communist party of the Soviet Union (C.P. S.U.) is adopting its third program, a program for the building of Communist society. The new program is a constructive generalization of the experience of Socialist construction, it takes account of the revolutionary movement throughout the world and, giving expression to the collective opinion of the party, defines the main tasks and principal stages of Communist construction.

The supreme goal of the party is to build a Communist society on whose banner will be inscribed: "From each according to his ability, to each according to his needs." The party's motto, "Everything in the name of man, for the benefit of man," will be put into effect in full.

The Communist party of the Soviet Union, true to proletariat internationalism, always follows the militant slogan, "Workers of all countries, unite!" The party regards Communist construction in the U.S.S.R. as the Soviet people's great internationalist task, in keeping with the interests of the world Socialist system as a whole, and with the interests of the international proletariat and all mankind.

Communism accomplishes the historic mission of delivering all men from social inequality, from every form of oppression and exploitation, from the horrors of war, and proclaims peace, labor, freedom, equality and happiness for all peoples of the earth.

I. THE TRANSITION FROM CAPITALISM TO COMMUNISM IS THE ROAD OF HUMAN PROGRESS

1. THE HISTORICAL NECESSITY OF THE TRANSITION FROM CAPITALISM TO SOCIALISM

The epoch-making turn of mankind from capitalism to socialism, initiated by the October Revolution, is a natural result of the development of society. Marxism-Leninism discovered the objective laws of social development and revealed the contradictions inherent in capitalism, the inevitability of their bringing about a revolutionary explosion and of the transition of society to communism.

Capitalism is the last exploiting system. Having developed its productive forces to an enormous extent, it became a tremendous obstacle to social progress. Capitalism alone is responsible for the fact that the twentieth century, a century of colossal growth of the productive forces and of great scientific progress, has not yet put an end to the poverty of hundreds of millions of people, has not provided an abundance of material and spiritual values for all men on earth. The growing conflict between productive forces and production relations imperatively demands that mankind should break the decayed capitalist shell, release the powerful productive forces created by man and use them for the good of society as a whole.

Whatever the specific character of the rise and development of capitalism in any country, that system has everywhere common features and objective laws.

The development of world capitalism and of the revolutionary struggle of the working class has fully confirmed the correctness of the Marxist-Leninist analysis of capitalism and its highest stage, imperialism, given in the first and second programs of the party. The basic propositions of this analysis are also given in the present program.

Under capitalism, the basic and decisive means of production belong to the numerically small capitalist class, while the vast majority of the population consists of proletarians and semi-proletarians, who own no means of production and are therefore compelled to sell their labor-power and by their labor create profits and riches for the ruling classes of society. The bourgeois state, whatever its form, is an instrument of the domination of labor by capital.

The development of large-scale capitalist production—production for profit, for the appropriation of surplus value—leads to the elimination of small independent producers, makes them wholly dependent on capital. Capitalism extensively exploits female and child labor. The economic laws of its development necessarily give rise to a huge reserve army of unemployed, which is constantly replenished by ruined peasants and urban petty bourgeoisie. The exploitation of the working people is continuously increasing, social inequality is becoming more and more marked, the gulf between the haves and have-nots is widening, and the sufferings and privations of the millions are growing worse.

Capitalism, by concentrating millions of workers in its factories, socializing the process of labor, imparts a social character to production; nevertheless it is the capitalists who appropriate the fruits of labor. This fundamental contradiction of capitalism—the contradiction between the social character of production and the private-capitalist form of appropriation—manifests itself in production anarchy and in the fact that the purchasing power of society falls short of the expansion of production and leads periodically to destructive economic crises. Crises and periods of industrial stagnation, in turn, are still more ruinous to small producers, increase the dependence of wage-labor on capital and lead more rapidly to a relative, and sometimes an absolute, deterioration of the condition of the working class.

The growth and development of the contradictions of bourgeois society are accompanied by the growing discontent of the working people and the exploited masses with the capitalist system, by an increase in the number of proletarians and their greater unity, and by a sharpening of their class struggle against the exploiters. At the same time there is an accelerated creation of the material conditions that make possible the replacement of capitalist by Communist production relations, that is, the accomplishment of the social revolution which is the aim of the Communist party, the politically conscious exponent of the class movement of the proletariat.

The working class, which is the most consistent revolutionary class, is the chief motive force of the revolutionary transformation of the world. In the course of class struggles it becomes organized, sets up its trade unions and political parties, and wages an economic, political and theoretical struggle against capitalism. In fulfilling its historic mission as the revolutionary remaker of the old society and creator of a new system, the working class has become the exponent, not only of its own class interests, but of the interests of all working people. It is the natural leader of all forces fighting against capitalism.

The dictatorship of the proletariat and the leadership of the Marxist-Leninist party are indispensable conditions for the triumph of the Socialist revolution and the building of socialism.

The process of concentration and centralization of capital, while destroying free competition, led in the early twentieth century to the establishment of powerful capitalist monopoly associations—syndicates, cartels and trusts—which acquired decisive importance in the economy, to the merging of bank capital and immensely concentrated industrial capital, and to intensive export of capital. The trusts, which encompassed entire groups of capitalist powers, began the economic division of a world already divided territorially among the wealthiest countries. Capitalism has entered its final stage, the stage of monopoly capitalism, of imperialism.

The period of a more or less smooth spread of capitalism all over the globe gave way to spasmodic, cataclysmic development causing an unprecedented growth and aggravation of all the contradictions of capitalism—economic, political, class and national. The imperialist powers' struggle for markets, for spheres of capital investment, for raw materials and labor, and for world domination became more intense than ever. In an epoch of the undivided rule of imperialism, that struggle necessarily led to devastating wars.

Imperialism is decaying and moribund capitalism; it is the eve of the Socialist revolution. The world capitalist system as a whole is ripe for the social revolution of the proletariat.

The exceedingly high degree of development of world capitalism in general; the replacement of free competition by state-monopoly capitalism; the establishment, by banks as well as associations of capitalists, of machinery for the social regulation of the production and the distribution of products; the growing cost of living and the oppression of the working class by the syndicates, which are due to the growth of capitalist monopolies; the enslavement of the working class by the imperalist state, and the growing difficulty of the economic and political struggle of the proletariat; and the horrors, hardships and ruination brought about by imperialist war have all made inevitable the downfall of capitalism and the transition to a higher type of social economy.

The revolutionary defeat of imperialism does not take place all over the world simultaneously. The uneven character of the economic and political development of the capitalist countries under imperialism leads to revolutions occurring at different periods in different countries.

V. I. Lenin developed the theory of the Socialist revolution in new historical conditions, elaborated the theory of the possibility of socialism triumphing first in one capitalist country taken singly.

Russia was the weakest link in the imperialist system and the focal point of all its contradictions. On the other hand, she had all the conditions necessary for the victory of socialism. Her working class was the most revolutionary and best organized in the world and had considerable experience of class struggle. It was led by a Marxist-Leninist party armed with an advanced, revolutionary theory and steeled in class battles.

The Bolshevik party brought together in one revolutionary torrent the struggle of the working class for socialism, the country-wide peace movement, the peasants' struggle for land, and the national-liberation movement of the oppressed peoples of Russia, and directed these forces to the overthrow of capitalism.

2. THE HISTORIC SIGNIFICANCE OF THE OCTOBER REVOLUTION AND OF THE VICTORY OF SOCIALISM IN THE U.S.S.R.

The great October Revolution breached the imperialist front in Russia, one of the world's largest countries, firmly established the dictatorship of the proletariat and created a new type of state—the Soviet state—and a new type of democracy—democracy for the working people.

Workers' and peasants' power, born of the revolution, took Russia out of the bloodbath of the imperialist war, saved her from the national catastrophe to which the exploiting classes had doomed her, and delivered her peoples from the danger of enslavement by foreign capital.

The October Revolution undermined the economic basis of a system of exploitation and social injustice. Soviet power nationalized industry, the railways, banks and the land. It abolished landed proprietorship and fulfilled the peasants' age-long dream of land.

The October Revolution smashed the chains of national oppression; it proclaimed and put into effect the right of nations to self-determination, up to and including the right to secede. The revolution completely abolished the social-estate and class privileges of the exploiters. For the first time in history, it emancipated women and granted them the same rights as men.

The Socialist revolution in Russia shook the entire structure of world capitalism to its very foundations; the world split into two opposing systems.

For the first time there emerged in the international arena a state which put forward the great slogan of peace and began carrying through new principles in relations between peoples and countries. Mankind acquired a reliable bulwark in its struggle against wars of conquest, for peace and the security of the peoples.

The October Revolution led the country on to the road of socialism. The path which the Soviet people were to traverse was an unexplored and arduous one. The reactionary forces of the old world did all they could to strangle the Soviet state at its birth. The young Soviet Republic had to cope with intervention and civil war, economic blockade and disruption, conspiracies, sabotage, subversion, terrorism and numerous other trials. Socialist construction was rendered incredibly difficult by the socio-economic, technical and cultural backwardness of the country.

The victorious workers and peasants lacked knowledge of state administration and the experience necessary for the construction of a new society. The difficulties of Socialist construction were greatly increased by the fact that for almost thirty years the U. S. S. R. was the world's only Socialist state, and was subjected to incisive attacks by the hostile capitalist environment. The class struggle in the period of transition from capitalism to socialism was therefore acute.

The enemies of Leninism maintained that Russia was not mature enough for a Socialist revolution, that it was impossible to build socialism in one country. But the enemies of Leninism were put to shame.

A wise, discerning policy, the greatest stanchness, organization and deep faith in their own strength and in the strength of the people were required of the party and the working class. It was necessary to steer the right course in Socialist construction and insure the victory of socialism, despite the highly complicated international situation and a relatively weak industrial basis, in a country whose economy had been badly ravaged by war and where small-commodity production was overwhelmingly predominant.

The party proved equal to that historic task. Under the leadership of Lenin it worked out a plan for the radical transformation of the country, for the construction of socialism. On the basis of a thorough scientific analysis, Lenin elaborated the policy of the proletarian state for the entire period of transition from capitalism to socialism. He evolved the New Economic Policy (N. E. P.), designed to bring about the victory of socialism. The main elements of the Lenin plan for the building of a Socialist society were industrialization of the country, agricultural cooperation, and the cultural revolution.

The party upheld that plan in an acute struggle against skeptics and capitulators, against the Trotskyists, Right opportunists, nationalist-deviators and other hostile groups. It rallied the whole of the Soviet people to put Lenin's program into practice.

The point at issue at the time was: either perish or forge full steam ahead and overtake the capitalist countries economically.

The Soviet state had first of all to solve the problem of industrialization. In a historically brief period, without outside help, the Soviet Union built up a large-scale modern industry. By the time it had fulfilled three five-year plans (1928-1941) the Soviet Union had become a mighty industrial power that had achieved complete economic independence from the capitalist countries. Its defense capacity had increased immeasurably. The industrialization of the U. S. S. R. was a great exploit performed by the working class and the people as a whole, for they spared no effort or means, and consciously made sacrifices to lift the country out of its backward state.

The destiny of socialism in a country like the U. S. S. R. largely depended on the solution of a most difficult problem, namely, the transition from a small-scale, dispersed peasant economy to Socialist cooperation. Led by the party, aided and fully supported by the working class, the peasantry took the road to socialism. Millions of small individual farms went into voluntary association to form collective farms. A large number of Soviet state farms and machine and tractor stations were established. The introduction in the Soviet countryside of large-scale Socialist farming meant a far-reaching revolution in economic relation, in the entire way of life of the peasantry. Collectivization forever delivered the countryside from kulak bondage, from class differentiation, ruin and poverty. The real solution of the eternal peasant question was provided by the Lenin cooperative plan.

To build socialism it was necessary to raise the cultural level of the people; that task too was accomplished. A cultural revolution was carried out in the country. It freed the working people from spiritual slavery and ignorance and gave them access to the cultural values accumulated by mankind. The country, the bulk of whose population had been illiterate, made breath-taking progress in science and culture.

Socialism, which Marx and Engels scientifically predicted as inevitable and the plan for the construction of which was mapped out by Lenin, has become a reality in the Soviet Union.

Socialism has done away forever with the supremacy of private ownership of the means of production, that source of the division of society into antagonistic classes. Socialist ownership of the means of production has become the solid economic foundation of society. Unlimited opportunities have been afforded for the development of the productive forces.

Socialism has solved a great social problem—it has abolished the exploiting classes and the causes engendering the exploitation of man by man. There are now two friendly classes in the U. S. S. R.—the working class and the peasantry. And these classes, furthermore, have changed. The common character of the two forms of Socialist property has brought the working class and the collective-farm peasantry close together; it has strengthened their alliance and made their friendship indestructible.

A new intelligentsia, coming from the people and devoted to socialism, has emerged. The one-time antithesis between town and countryside, between labor by hand and by brain, has been abolished. The common vital interests of the workers, peasants and intellectuals have furnished a basis for the indestructible socio-political and ideological unity of the Soviet people.

The Socialist principle "From each according to his abilities, to each according to his work" has been put into effect in the Soviet Union. This principle insures that the members of society have a material interest in the fruits of their labor; it makes it possible to harmonize personal and social interests in the most effective way and serves as a powerful stimulus for increasing productivity of labor, developing the economy and raising the people's standard of living.

The awareness that they work for themselves and their society and not for exploiters inspires the working people with labor enthusiasm; it encourages their effort for in-

novation, their creative initiative and mass Socialist emulation. Socialism is creative effort by the working masses. The
growing activity of the people in the building of a new life
is a law of the Socialist epoch.

The aim of socialism is to meet the growing material and
cultural requirements of the people ever more fully by continuously developing and improving social production.

The entire life of Socialist society is based on the principle of broad democracy. Working people take an active
part, through the Soviets, trade unions and other mass organizations, in managing the affairs of the state and in solving
problems of economic and cultural advancement. Socialist
democracy includes both political freedoms—freedom of
speech, of the press and of assembly, the right to elect and
to be elected, and also social rights—the right to work, to rest
and leisure, to education, to material security in old age and
in case of illness or disability; equality of citizens of all
races and nationalities; equal rights for women and men in
all spheres of political, economic and cultural activity. Socialist democracy, unlike bourgeois democracy, does not merely proclaim the rights of the people, but makes it really possible for the people to exercise them. Soviet society insures
the real liberty of the individual. The highest manifestation
of this liberty is man's emancipation from exploitation, which
is what primarily constitutes genuine social justice.

Socialism has created conditions for the rapid progress of
science. The achievements of Soviet science clearly show the
superiority of the Socialist system and testify to the unlimited
possibilities of scientific progress and to the growing role
of science under socialism. It is only logical that the country
of victorious socialism should have ushered in the era of the
utilization of atomic energy for peaceful purposes, and that it
should have blazed a trail into outer space. The man-made
satellites of the earth and the sun, powerful space rockets
and interplanetary space ships, atomic power stations and
the first triumphal orbiting of the globe, accomplished by a
Soviet citizen, which are a source of pride to all mankind,
have become symbols of the creative energy of ascendant
communism.

The solution of the national question is one of the greatest
achievements of socialism. This question is of especial importance to a country like the Soviet Union, inhabited by more
than a hundred nations and nationalities. Socialist society
has not only guaranteed the political equality of nations, but

has also abolished the economic and cultural backwardness inherited from the old system. With reciprocal fraternal assistance, primarily from the great Russian people, all the Soviet non-Russian republics have set up their own modern industries, trained their own national working class and intelligentsia and developed a culture that is national in form and Socialist in content.

Many nations which in the past were backward have achieved socialism, by-passing the capitalist stage of development. The union and consolidation of equal peoples on a voluntary basis in a single multi-national state—the Union of Soviet Socialist Republics—their close cooperation in state, economic and cultural development, their fraternal friendship and a flourishing economy and culture constitute the most important result of the Leninist nationalities policy.

The Soviet people were destined by history to start on a new road, to blaze a new path of social development. This required special efforts of them, a continuous quest for forms and methods of building the new society which had to be tested in the crucible of practice. For nearly two out of little more than four decades, the Soviet people were compelled to devote their energies to the repulsion of invasions by the imperialist powers and to post-war economic rehabilitation. The Soviet system was put to a particularly severe test during the Great Patriotic War, the most trying war in history. By winning that war, the Soviet people proved that there are no forces in the world capable of stopping the progress of Socialist society.

What are the principal lessons to be learned from the experience of the Soviet people?

Soviet experience has shown that the peoples are able to achieve socialism only as a result of the Socialist revolution and the dictatorship of the proletariat. Despite certain specific features due precisely to the historical conditions of Socialist construction in the Soviet Union, then in a hostile capitalistic encirclement, this experience has fully confirmed the fundamental principles of Socialist revolution and Socialist construction, principles which are of universal significance.

Soviet experience has shown that socialism alone can put an end to the exploitation of man by man, production anarchy, economic crises, unemployment and the poverty of the people, and insure planned, continuous and rapid development of the economy and steady improvement of the people's standard of living.

Soviet experience has shown that the working class can fulfill its historical mission as the builder of a new society only in a sound alliance with the nonproletarian working masses, primarily the peasantry.

Soviet experience has shown that the victory of the Socialist revolution alone provides all possibilities and conditions for the abolition of all national oppression, for the voluntary union of free and equal nations and nationalities in a single state.

Soviet experience has shown that the Socialist state is the main instrument for the Socialist transformation of society. The state organizes and unites the masses, exercises planned leadership of economic and cultural construction, and safeguards the revolutionary gains of the people.

Soviet experience has shown that socialism and peace are inseparable. The might of socialism serves peace. The Soviet Union saved mankind from Fascist enslavement. The Soviet state, which champions peace and implements the Leninist principle of peaceful coexistence, is a mighty barrier to imperialist aggression.

Soviet experience has fully borne out the Marxist-Leninist theory that the Communist party plays a decisive role in the formation and development of Socialist society. Only a party that steadfastly pursues a class, proletarian policy, and is equipped with progressive, revolutionary theory, only a party solidly united and closely linked with the masses, can organize the people and lead them to the victory of Socialism.

Soviet experience has shown that fidelity to the principles of Marxism-Leninism, of proletarian internationalism, their firm and unswerving implementation, and defense of those principles against opportunists and all other enemies, are imperative conditions for the victory of socialism.

The world's greatest revolution and the Socialist reorganization of society, which has attained unprecedented heights in its development and prosperity, have confirmed in practice the historical truth of Leninism and have delivered a crushing blow to social-reformist ideology.

As a result of the devoted labor of the Soviet people and the theoretical and practical activities of the Communist party of the Soviet Union, there exists in the world a Socialist society that is a reality and a science of Socialist construction that has been tested in practice. The highroad to Socialism has been paved. Many peoples are already marching along it, and it will be taken sooner or later by all peoples.

3. THE WORLD SOCIALIST SYSTEM

The Soviet Union is not pursuing the tasks of Communist construction alone but in fraternal community with the other Socialist countries.

The defeat of German fascism and Japanese militarism in World War II, in which the Soviet Union played a decisive part, created favorable conditions for the overthrow of capitalist and landlord rule by the peoples in a number of European and Asian countries. The peoples of Albania, Bulgaria, China, Czechoslovakia, the Democratic Republic of Vietnam, the German Democratic Republic, Hungary, the Korean People's Democratic Republic, Poland and Rumania, and still earlier the people of the Mongolian People's Republic, adopted the path of Socialist construction and, together with the Soviet Union, formed the Socialist camp. Yugoslavia likewise took the Socialist path. But the Yugoslav leaders by their revisionist policy contraposed Yugoslavia to the Socialist camp and the international Communist movement, thus threatening the loss of the revolutionary gains of the Yugoslav people.

The Socialist revolutions in Europe and Asia dealt imperialism a further powerful blow. The victory of the revolution in China was of special importance. The revolutions in European and Asian countries are the biggest event in world history since October, 1917.

A new form of political organization of society, people's democracy, a variety of the dictatorship of the proletariat, emerged. It reflected the distinctive development of Socialist revolution at a time when imperialism had lost strength and the balance of forces had tilted in favor of socialism. It also reflected the distinctive historical and national features of the countries concerned.

There emerged a world Socialist system, a social, economic and political community of free sovereign peoples pursuing the Socialist and Communist path, united by common interests and goals and the close bonds of international Socialist solidarity.

In the people's democracies Socialist production relations are dominant and the socio-economic possibility of capitalist restoration has been eliminated. The successes of these countries have conclusively proved that true progress in all lands, irrespective of the level of their economic development, their area and population, is feasible only under socialism.

The combined forces of the Socialist camp guarantee each Socialist country against encroachments of imperialist reaction. The consolidation of the Socialist countries in a single camp, its increasing unity and steadily growing strength, ensure the complete victory of socialism within the framework of the system as a whole.

The countries of the Socialist system have accumulated considerable collective experience in the remodeling of the lives of hundreds of millions of people and have contributed many new and specific features to the forms of political and economic organization of society. This experience is a most valuable asset to the international revolutionary movement.

It has been borne out in practice and recognized by all Marxist-Leninist parties that the processes of Socialist revolution and construction are founded on a number of basic objective laws applicable to all countries entering upon the Socialist path.

The world Socialist system is a new type of economic and political relationship between countries. The Socialist countries have the same type of economic basis—social ownership of means of production; the same type of political system—rule of the people with the working class at their head; a common ideology—Marxism-Leninism; common interests in the defense of their revolutionary gains and national independence from encroachments by the imperialist camp; and a great common goal—communism. This socio-economic and political community of purpose is the objective groundwork for lasting and friendly intergovernmental relations within the Socialist camp. The distinctive features of the relations existing between the countries of the Socialist community are complete equality, respect for independence and sovereignty and fraternal mutual assistance. In the Socialist camp or, which is the same thing, in the world community of Socialist countries, none have, nor can have, any special rights or privileges.

The experience of the world Socialist system has confirmed the need for the closest unity of countries that fall away from capitalism, for their united effort in the building of socialism and communism. The line of Socialist construction in isolation, detached from the world community of Socialist countries, is theoretically untenable because it conflicts with the objective laws governing the development of Socialist society. It is harmful economically because it causes waste of social labor, retards the rates of growth of production and makes the country dependent upon the capitalist world. It is reactionary and politically dangerous because it does not unite, but divides the peoples in face of the united front of imperialist forces, because it nourishes bourgeois-nationalist tendencies and may ultimately lead to the loss of the Socialist gains.

As they combine their effort in the building of a new society, the Socialist states give active support to and extend their political, economic and cultural cooperation with countries that have cast off colonial rule. They maintain—and are prepared to maintain—broad mutually advantageous trade relations and cultural contacts with the capitalist countries.

The development of the world Socialist system and of the world capitalist system is governed by diametrically opposed laws. The world capitalist system emerged and developed in fierce struggle between the countries composing it, through the subjection and exploitation of the weaker countries by the strong, through the enslavement of hundreds of millions of people and the reduction of entire continents to the status of colonial appendages of the imperialist metropolitan countries. The formation and development of the world Socialist system, on the other hand, proceeds on the basis of sovereignty and free will and in conformity with the fundamental interests of the working people of all the countries of that system.

Whereas the world capitalist system is governed by the law of uneven economic and political development that leads to conflicts between countries, the world Socialist system is governed by opposite laws, which ensure the rapid, steady and balanced growth of the economies of all the countries belonging to that system. Growth of production in a country belonging to the capitalist world deepens the contradiction between countries and intensifies competitive rivalries. The development of each Socialist country, on the other hand, promotes the general progress and consolidation of the world Socialist system as a whole. The economy of world capitalism develops at a slow rate, and goes through crises and upheavals. Typical of the economy of world socialism, on the other hand, are high and stable rates of growth and the common unintermittent economic progress of all Socialist countries.

All the Socialist countries make their contribution to the building and development of the world Socialist system and the consolidation of its might. The existence of the Soviet Union greatly facilitates and accelerates the building of socialism in the people's democracies. The Marxist-Leninist parties and the peoples of the Socialist countries proceed from the fact that the successes of the world Socialist system as a whole depend on the contribution and effort made by each country, and therefore consider the greatest possible development of the productive forces of their country an internationalist duty.

The cooperation of the Socialist countries enables each country to use its resources and develop its productive forces to the full and in the most rational manner. A new type of international division of labor is taking shape in the process of the economic, scientific and technical cooperation of the Socialist countries, the coordination of their economic plans, the specialization and combination of production.

The establishment of the Union of Soviet Socialist Republics and, later, of the world Socialist system, is the commencement of the historical process of an all-round association of peoples. With the disappearance of class antagonisms in the fraternal family of socialist countries, national antagonisms also disappear. The rapid cultural progress of the peoples of the Socialist community is attended by a progressive mutual enrichment of the national cultures, and an active moulding of the internationalist features typical of man in Socialist society.

The experience of the peoples of the world Socialist community has confirmed that their fraternal unity and cooperation conform to the supreme national interests of each country. The strengthening of the unity of the world Socialist system on the basis of proletarian internationalism is an imperative condition for the further progress of all its member countries.

The world Socialist system has to cope with certain difficulties, deriving chiefly from the fact that most of the countries in that system had a medium or even low level of economic development in the past, and also from the fact that world reaction is doing its utmost to impede the building of socialism.

The experience of the Soviet Union and the people's democracies has confirmed the accuracy of Lenin's thesis that the class struggle does not disappear in the period of the building of socialism. The general development of the class struggle within the Socialist countries in conditions of successful Socialist construction leads to consolidation of the position of the Socialist forces and weakens the resistance of the remnants of the hostile classes. But this development does not follow a straight line. Changes in the domestic or external situation may cause the class struggle to intensify in specific periods. This calls for constant vigilance in order to frustrate in good time the designs of hostile forces within and without, who persist in their attempts to undermine people's power and sow strife in the fraternal community of Socialist countries.

Nationalism is the chief political and ideological weapon used by international reaction and the remnants of the domestic reactionary forces against the unity of the Socialist countries. Nationalist sentiments and national narrow-mindedness do not disappear automatically with the establishment of the Socialist system. Nationalist prejudice and survivals of former national strife are a province in which resistance to social progress may be most protracted and stubborn, bitter and insidious.

The Communists consider it their prime duty to educate working people in a spirit of internationalism, Socialist patriotism and intolerance of all possible manifestations of nationalism and chauvinism. Nationalism is harmful to the common interests of the Socialist community and, above all, the people of the country where it obtains, since isolation from the Socialist camp holds up that country's development, deprives it of the advantages deriving from the world Socialist system and encourages the imperialist powers to make the most of the nationalist tendencies for their own ends. Nationalism can gain the upper hand only where it is not consistently combated.

The Marxist-Leninist internationalist policy and determined efforts to wipe out the survivals of bourgeois nationalism and chauvinism are an important condition for the further consolidation of the Socialist community. Yet while they oppose nationalism and national egoism, Communists always show utmost consideration for the national feelings of the masses.

The world Socialist system is advancing steadfastly toward decisive victory in its economic competition with capitalism. It will shortly surpass the world capitalist system in aggregate industrial and agricultural production. Its influence on the course of social development in the interests of peace, democracy and socialism is growing more and more.

The magnificent edifice of the new world being built by the heroic labors of the free peoples on vast areas of Europe and Asia is a prototype of new society, of the future of all mankind.

4. CRISIS OF WORLD CAPITALISM

Imperialism has entered the period of decline and collapse. The inexorable process of decay has seized capitalism from top to bottom—its economic and political system, its politics and ideology. Imperialism has forever lost its power over the bulk of mankind. The main content, main trend and main features of the historical development of mankind are being determined by the world Socialist system, by the forces fighting against imperialism, for the Socialist reorganization of society.

World War I and the October Revolution ushered in the general crisis of capitalism. The second stage of this crisis developed at the time of World War II and the Socialist revolutions in a number of European and Asian countries. World capitalism has now entered a new, third stage of that crisis, the principal feature of which is that its development was not due to a world war.

The breakaway from capitalism of more and more countries; the weakening of imperialist positions in the economic competition with socialism; the breakup of the imperialist colonial system; the intensification of imperialist contradictions with the development of state-monopoly capitalism and the growth of militarism; the mounting internal instability and decay of capitalist economy evidenced by the increasing inability of capitalism to make full use of the productive forces (low rates of production growth, periodic crises, continuous underloading of production plant, and chronic unemployment); the mounting struggle between labor and capital; an acute intensification of contradictions within the world capitalist economy; and unprecedented growth of political reaction in all spheres, rejection of bourgeois freedoms and establishment of Fascist and despotic regimes in a number of countries, and the profound crisis of bourgeois policy and ideology—all these are manifestations of the general crisis of capitalism.

In the imperialist stage state-monopoly capitalism comes to

the fore. The emergence and growth of monopolies leads to the direct intervention of the state, in the interests of the financial oligarchy, in the process of capitalist reproduction. It is in the interests of the financial oligarchy that the bourgeois state institutes various types of regulation and resorts to the nationalization of some branches of the economy. World wars, economic crises, militarism and political upheavals have accelerated the development of monopoly capitalism into state-monopoly capitalism.

The oppression of finance capital keeps growing. Giant monopolies controlling the bulk of social production dominate the life of the nation. A handful of millionaires and multimillionaires wield arbitrary power over the entire wealth of the capitalist world and make the life of entire nations mere small change in their selfish deals. The financial oligarchy is getting fabulously rich.

The state is becoming a committee for the management of the affairs of the monopoly bourgeoisie. The bureaucratization of the economy is rising steeply. State-monopoly capitalism combines the strength of the monopolies and that of the state into a single mechanism whose purpose is to enrich the monopolies, suppress the working-class movement and the national-liberation struggle, save the capitalist system and launch aggressive wars.

The proponents of social-democratism and revisionism are making out state-monopoly capitalism to be socialism. The facts give the lie to this contention. State-monopoly capitalism does not change the nature of imperialism. Far from altering the position of the principal classes in the system of social production, it widens the rift between labor and capital, between the majority of the nation and the monopolies.

Attempts at state regulation of the capitalist economy cannot eliminate competition and anarchy of production, cannot insure the planned development of the economy on a nationwide scale because capitalist ownership and exploitation of wage-labor remain the basis of production. The bourgeois theories of "crisis-free" and "planned" capitalism have been laid in the dust by the development of contemporary capitalist economy. The dialectics of state-monopoly capitalism is such that instead of shoring up the capitalist system, as the bourgeoisie expects, it aggravates the contradictions of capitalism and undermines its foundations. State-monopoly capitalism is the fullest material preparation for socialism.

The new phenomena in imperialist development corroborate the accuracy of Lenin's conclusions on the principal objective laws of capitalism in its final stage and on its increasing decay. Yet this decay does not signify complete stagnation, a palsy of its productive forces, and does not rule out growth of capitalist economy at particular times and in particular countries.

All in all, capitalism is increasingly impeding the development of the contemporary productive forces. Mankind is entering the period of a great scientific and technical revolution bound up with the conquest of nuclear energy, space exploration, the development of chemistry, automation and other major achievements of science and engineering. But the relations of production under capitalism are much too narrow for a scientific and technical revolution. Socialism alone is capable of effecting it and of applying its fruits in the interests of society.

Technical progress under the rule of monopoly capital is turning against the working class. By using new forms, the monopolies intensify the exploitation of the working class. Capitalist automation is robbing the worker of his daily bread. Unemployment is rising, the living standard is dropping. Technical progress is continuously throwing more sections of small producers overboard. Imperialism is using technical progress chiefly for military purposes. It is turning the achievements of human genius against humanity. As long as imperialism exists, mankind cannot feel secure about its future.

Modern capitalism has made the market problem extremely acute. Imperialism is incapable of solving it, because lag of effective demand behind growth of production is one of its objective laws. Moreover, it retards the industrial development of the under-developed countries. The world capitalist market is shrinking relative to the more rapidly expanding production capacity. It is partitioned by countless customs barriers and restrictive fences and split into exclusive currency and finance zones. An acute competitive struggle for markets, spheres of investment and sources of raw materials is under way in the imperialist camp. It is becoming doubly acute since the territorial sphere of capitalist domination has been greatly narrowed.

Monopoly capital has, in the final analysis, doomed bourgeois society to low rates of production growth that in some countries barely keep ahead of the growth of population. A considerable part of the production plant stands idle, while millions of unemployed wait at the factory gates. Farm production is artificially restricted, although millions are underfed in the world. People suffer want in material goods, but imperialism is squandering them on war preparations.

Abolition of the capitalist system in a large group of countries and the strengthening of the world Socialist system, the disintegration of the colonial system and the collapse of old empires, the commencing break-up of the colonial economic structure in the newly free countries and the expanding economic connections between the latter and the Socialist world —all these factors intensify the crisis of the world capitalist economy.

State-monopoly capitalism stimulates militarism to an unheard-of degree. The imperialist countries maintain immense armed forces even in peacetime. Military expenditures devour an ever-growing portion of the state budgets. The imperialist countries are turning into militarist states run by the army and the police. Militarization pervades the life of bourgeois society.

While enriching some groups of the monopoly bourgeoisie, militarism leads to the exhaustion of nations, to the ruin of the peoples languishing under an excessive tax burden, mounting inflation and a high cost of living. Within the lifetime of one generation imperialism plunged mankind into the abyss of two destructive world wars. In the First World War the imperialists annihilated ten million and crippled twenty million people. The Second World War claimed nearly fifty million human lives. In the course of these wars entire countries were ravaged, thousands of towns and villages were demolished and the fruits of the labor of many generations were destroyed. The new war being hatched by the imperialists threatens mankind with unprecedented human losses and destruction. Even the preparations for it bring suffering and privation to millions of people.

The progress achieved in the development of the productive forces and the socialization of labor is being usurped by the contemporary capitalist state in the interest of the monopolies.

The monopoly bourgeoisie has become a useless growth on the social organism, one unneeded in production. The industries are run by hired managers, engineers and technicians. The monopolists lead a parasitical life and with their menials consume a substantial portion of the national income created by the toil of proletarians and peasants.

Fear of revolution, the successes of the Socialist countries and the pressure of the working-class movement compel the bourgeoisie to make partial concessions with respect to wages, labor conditions and social security. But more often than not mounting prices and inflation reduce these concessions to nought. Wages lag behind the daily material and cultural requirement of the worker and his family, which grow as society develops.

Even the relatively high standard of living in the small group of capitalistically developed countries rests upon the poverty of the Asian, African and Latin-American peoples, upon non-equivalent exchange, discrimination of female labor, brutal oppression of Negroes and immigrant workers, and also upon the intensified exploitation of the working people in those countries.

The bourgeois myth of "full employment" has proved to be sheer mockery, for the working class is suffering continuously from mass unemployment and insecurity. In spite of some successes in the economic struggle, the condition of the working class in the capitalist world is, on the whole, deteriorating.

The development of capitalism has dissipated the legend of the stability of small peasant farming once and for all. The monopolies have seized dominant positions in agriculture as well. Millions of farmers and peasants are being driven off the land, and their farms are being brought under the hammer. Small farms survive at the price of appalling hardships, excessive labor and the peasants' underconsumption. The peasantry is groaning under the burden of mounting taxes and debts. Agrarian crises are bringing ever greater ruin to the countryside. Unspeakable want and poverty fall to the lot of the peasantry in the colonial and dependent countries; it suffers the dual oppression of the landlords and the monopoly bourgeoisie.

The monopolies are also ruining small urban properties. Handicrafts are going under. Small-scale industrial and commercial enterprises are fully dependent upon the monopolies.

Life has fully confirmed the Marxist thesis of increasing proletarization in capitalist society. The expropriated masses have no other prospect of acquiring property than the revolutionary establishment of the social ownership of means of production, that is, making them the property of the whole people.

The uneven development of capitalism alters the balance of forces between countries and makes the contradictions between them more acute. The economic and with it the political and military center of imperialism has shifted from Europe to the United States. United States monopoly capital, gorged on war profits and the arms race, has seized the main sources of raw materials, the markets and the spheres of investment, has built up a covert colonial empire and become the biggest international exploiter. Taking cover behind spurious professions of freedom and democracy, United States imperialism is in effect performing the function of world gendarme, supporting reactionary dictatorial regimes and decayed monarchies, opposing democratic, revolutionary changes and launching aggressions against peoples fighting for independence.

The United States monopoly bourgeoisie is the mainstay of international reaction. It has assumed the role of "savior" of capitalism. The United States financial tycoons are engineering a "holy alliance" of imperialists and founding aggressive military blocs. American troops and war bases are stationed at the most important points of the capitalist world.

But the facts reveal the utter incongruity of the United States imperialist claims to world domination. Imperialism has proved incapable of stemming the Socialist and national-liberation revolutions. The hopes which American imperialism pinned on its atomic-weapons monopoly fell through. The United States monopolies have not been able to retain their share in the economy of the capitalist world, although they are still its chief economic, financial and military force. The United States, the strongest capitalist power, is past its zenith and has entered the stage of decline. Imperialist countries such as Great Britain, France, Germany and Japan have also lost their former power.

The basic contradiction of the contemporary world, that between socialism and imperialism, does not eliminate the deep contradictions rending the capitalist world. The aggressive military blocs founded under the aegis of the United States of America are time and again faced with crises. The international state-monopoly organizations springing up under the motto of "integration," the mitigation of the market problem, are in reality new forms of the redivision of the world capitalist market and are becoming seats of acute strain and conflict.

The contradictions between the principal imperialist powers are growing deeper. The economic rehabilitation of the imperialist countries defeated in the Second World War leads to the revival of the old and the emergence of new knots of imperialist rivalry and conflict. The Anglo-American, Franco-American, Franco-German, American-German, Anglo-German, Japanese-American and other contradictions are becoming especially acute. Fresh contradictions will inevitably arise and grow in the imperialist camp.

The American monopolies and their British and French allies are openly assisting the resurgence of West German imperialism which is cynically advocating aggressive aims of revenge and preparing a war against the Socialist countries and other European states. A dangerous center of aggression, imperiling the peace and security of all peoples is being revived in the heart of Europe. In the Far East the American monopolies are reviving Japanese militarism, another dangerous hotbed of war threatening the peoples of Asia and, above all, the Socialist countries.

The interests of the small group of imperialist powers are incompatible with the interests of the other countries, the interests of all peoples. Deep-rooted antagonism divides the imperialist countries from the countries that have won national independence and those that are fighting for liberation.

Contemporary capitalism is inimical to the vital interests and progressive aspirations of all mankind. Capitalism with its exploitation of man by man, with its chauvinist and racist ideology, with its moral degradation, its rampage of profiteering, corruption and crime is defiling society, the family, and man.

The bourgeois system came into being with the alluring slogans of liberty, equality, fraternity. But the bourgeoisie made use of these slogans merely to elbow out the feudal gentry and to assume power. Instead of equality a new gaping abyss of social and economic inequality appeared. Not fraternity but ferocious class struggle reigns in bourgeois society.

Monopoly capital is revealing its reactionary, anti-democratic substance more and more strikingly. It does not tolerate even the former bourgeois-democratic freedoms, although it proclaims them for its demagogic ends. In the current stage of historical development it is getting harder for the bourgeoisie to propagate, as heretofore, slogans of equality and liberty. The upswing of the international labor movement restricts the maneuvers of finance capital. Finance capital can no longer squash revolutionary sentiments and cope with the inexorably growing anti-imperialist movement by means of the old slogans and by bribing the labor bureaucracy.

Having taken full possession of the principal material values, monopoly capital refuses to share political power with anyone. It has established a dictatorship, the dictatorship of the minority over the majority, the dictatorship of the capitalist monopolies over society.

The ideologists of imperialism hide the dictatorship of monopoly capital behind specious slogans of freedom and democracy. They declare the imperialist powers to be countries of the "free world" and represent the ruling bourgeois circles as opponents of all dictatorship. In reality, however, freedom in the imperialist world signifies nothing but freedom to exploit the working class, the working people, not only at home, but in all the other countries that fall under the iron heel of the monopolies.

The bourgeoisie gives extensive publicity to the allegedly democratic nature of its election laws, singing special praise to its multi-party system and the possibility of nominating many candidates. In reality, however, the monopolists deprive the masses of the opportunity to express their will and elect genuine champions of their interests. Being in control of such potent means as capital, the press, radio, cinema, television and also of their henchmen in the trade unions and other mass organizations, they mislead the masses, imposing their own candidates upon the electorate. The different bourgeois parties are usually no more than different factions of the ruling bourgeoisie.

The dictatorship of the bourgeoisie also grossly violates the will of the electorate. Whenever the bourgeoisie sees that the working people are likely to use their constitutional rights to elect a considerable number of the champions of their interests to the legislative organs, it brazenly alters the election system and arbitrarily limits the number of working people's representatives in Parliament.

The financial oligarchy resorts to the establishment of Fascist regimes, banking on the army, police and gendarmerie as a last refuge from the people's wrath, particularly when the masses try to make use even of their democratic rights, albeit curtailed, to uphold their interests and end the all-pervading power of the monopolies. Although the vicious German and Italian fascism has crashed, Fascist regimes still survive in some countries and fascism is being revived in new forms in others.

Thus, the world imperialist system is rent by deep-rooted and acute contradictions. The antagonism of labor and capital, the contradictions between the people and the monopolies, growing militarism, the breakup of the colonial system, contradictions between the imperialist countries, conflicts and contradictions between the young national states and the old colonial powers, and—most important of all—the precipitous growth of world socialism, are sapping and destroying imperialism, leading to its weakening and collapse.

Not even nuclear weapons can protect the monopoly bourgeoisie from the unalterable course of historical development. Mankind has learned the true face of capitalism. Hundreds of millions of people see that capitalism is a system of economic chaos and periodical crises, chronic unemployment, mass poverty and indiscriminate waste of productive forces, a system fraught with the danger of war. Mankind does not want to, and will not, tolerate the historically outdated capitalist system.

5. THE INTERNATIONAL REVOLUTIONARY MOVEMENT OF THE WORKING CLASS

The international revolutionary movement of the working class has achieved epoch-making victories. Its chief gain is the world Socialist system. The example of victorious socialism has a revolutionizing effect on the minds of the working people of the capitalist world; it inspires them to fight against imperialism and greatly facilitates their struggle.

Social forces that are to ensure the victory of socialism are taking shape, multiplying and becoming steeled in the womb of capitalist society. A new contingent of the world proletariat—the young working-class movement of the newly-free, dependent and colonial countries of Asia, Africa and Latin America—has entered the world arena. Marxist-Leninist parties have arisen and matured. They are becoming a universally recognized national force enjoying ever greater prestige and followed by large sections of the working people.

The international revolutionary movement has accumulated vast experience in the struggle against imperialism and its placement in the ranks of the working class. It has become more mature ideologically and possesses great organized might and a militantly dynamic spirit. The trade union movement, which unites vast masses of working people, is playing an increasing role.

The capitalist countries are continuously shaken by class battles. Militant actions of the working class in defense of its economic and political interests are growing in number. The working class and all working people have frequently imperiled the class rule of the bourgeoisie. In an effort to maintain its power, the finance oligarchy, in addition to methods of suppression, uses diverse ways of deceiving and corrupting the working class and its organizations, and of splitting the trade union movement on a national and international scale.

It bribes the top stratum of trade unions, cooperatives and other organizations and swells the labor bureaucracy, to which it allots lucrative positions in industry, the municipal bodies and the government apparatus. Anti-Communist and anti-labor legislation, the banning of Communist parties, wholesale dismissal of Communists and other progressive workers, blacklisting in industry, government employee loyalty screening, police reprisals against the democratic press, and the suppression of strikes by military force have all become routine methods of action for the governments of the imperialist bourgeoisie in their efforts to preserve their dictatorship.

The reactionary forces in individual capitalist countries can no longer cope with the growing forces of democracy and socialism. Struggle and competition between the capitalist states do not preclude, however, a certain unity among them in the face of the increasing strength of socialism and the working-class movement. The imperialists form reactionary alliances; they enter into mutual agreements and set up military blocs and bases spearheaded not only against the Socialist countries, but also against the revolutionary working-class and national-liberation movement. The reactionary bourgeoisie in a number of European states have in peacetime opened the doors of their countries to foreign troops.

The bourgeoisie seeks to draw definite lessons from the October Revolution and the victories of socialism. It is using new methods to cover up the ulcers and vices of the capitalist system. Although all these methods render the activities of the revolutionary forces in the capitalist countries more difficult, they cannot reduce the contradictions between labor and capital.

The world situation today is more favorable to the working-class movement. The achievements of the U. S. S. R. and the world Socialist system as a whole, the deepening crisis of world capitalism, the growing influence of the Communist parties among the masses, and the ideological breakdown of reformism have brought about a substantial change in the conditions of class struggle that is to the advantage of the working people. Even in those countries where reformism still holds strong positions, appreciable shifts to the Left are taking place in the working-class movement.

In the new historical situation, the working class of many countries can, even before capitalism is overthrown, compel the bourgeoisie to carry out measures that transcend ordinary reforms and are of vital importance to the working class and the progress of its struggle for socialism, as well as to the majority of the nation. By uniting large sections of the working people, the working class can make ruling circles cease preparations for a new world war, renounce the idea of starting local wars, and use the economy for peaceful purposes; it can beat back the offensive of Fascist reaction and bring about the implementation of a national program for peace, independence, democratic rights and a certain improvement of the living standard of the people.

The capitalist monopolies are the chief enemy of the working class. They are also the chief enemy of the peasants, handicraftsmen and other small urban proprietors, of most office workers, intellectuals and small capitalists, and even of a section of the middle capitalists.

The working class directs its main blow against the capitalist monopolies. All the main sections of a nation have a vital interest in abolishing the unlimited power of the monopolies. This makes it possible to unite all the democratic movements opposing the oppression of the finance oligarchy in a mighty anti-monopoly torrent.

The proletariat advances a political program for combating the power of the monopolies with due regard to the present as well as the future interests of its allies. It advocates broad nationalization on terms most favorable to the people, control by parliament, the trade unions and other democratic representative bodies over the nationalized industries and over the entire economic activity of the state. It backs the peasants' demands for radical land reforms and works for the realization of the slogan "The land to those who till it."

The proletariat, together with other sections of the people, wages a resolute struggle for broad democracy. It mobilizes the masses for effective action against the policy of the finance oligarchy, which strives to abolish democratic freedoms, restrict the power of Parliament, revise the constitution with the aim of establishing the personal power of monopoly puppets, and to go over from the parliamentary system to some variety of fascism.

It is in this struggle that the alliance of the working class and all working people is shaped. The working class unites the peasantry, its chief ally, to combat the survivals of feudalism and monopoly domination. Large sections of the office workers and a considerable section of the intelligentsia, whom capitalism reduces to the status of proletarians and who realize the need of changes in the social sphere, become allies of the working class.

General democratic struggles against the monopolies do not delay the Socialist revolution but bring it nearer. The struggle for democracy is a component of the struggle for socialism. The broader the democratic movement, the higher becomes the level of the political consciousness of the masses and the more clearly they see that only socialism clears for them the way to genuine freedom and well-being. In the course of this struggle, Right-Socialist, reformist illusions are dispelled and a political army of the Socialist revolution is brought into being.

Socialist revolutions, anti-imperialist national-liberation revolutions, people's democratic revolutions, broad peasant movements, popular struggles to overthrow Fascist and other despotic regimes, and general democratic movements against national oppression—all these merge in a single revolutionary process undermining and destroying capitalism.

The proletarian revolution in a country, being part of the world Socialist revolution, is accomplished by the working class of that country and the masses of its people. The revolution is not made to order. It cannot be imposed on the people from without. It results from the profound internal and international contradictions of capitalism. The victorious proletariat cannot impose any "felicity" on another people without thereby undermining its own victory.

Together with the other Marxist-Leninist parties, the Communist party of the Soviet Union regards it as its internationalist duty to call on the peoples of all countries to rally, muster all their internal forces, take vigorous action, and drawing on the might of the world Socialist system, forestall or firmly repel imperialist interference in the affairs of the people of any country risen in revolt and thereby prevent imperialist export of counter-revolution.

It will be easier to prevent export of counter-revolution if the working people, defending the national sovereignty of their country, work to bring about the abolition of foreign military bases on their territory and to make their country dissociate itself from aggressive military blocs.

Communists have never held that the road to revolution lies necessarily through wars between countries. Socialist revolution is not necessarily connected with war. Although both world wars, which were started by the imperialists, culminated in Socialist revolutions, revolutions are quite feasible without war. The great objectives of the working class can be realized without world war. Today the conditions for this are more favorable than ever.

The working class and its vanguard—the Marxist-Leninist parties—prefer to achieve the transfer of power from the bourgeoisie to the proletariat by peaceful means, without civil war. Realization of this possibility would meet the interests of the working class and the people as a whole, it would accord with the national interests of the country.

The working class, supported by the majority of the people and firmly repelling opportunist elements incapable of renouncing the policy of compromise with the capitalists and landlords, can defeat the reactionary, anti-popular forces, win a solid majority in parliament, transform it from a tool serving the class interests of the bourgeoisie into an instrument serving the working people, launch a broad mass struggle outside Parliament, smash the resistance of the reactionary forces and provide the necessary conditions for a peaceful socialist revolution. This can be done only by extending and continuously developing the class struggle of the workers and peasants and the middle strata of the urban population against big monopoly capital and reaction, for far-reaching social reforms, for peace and socialism.

Where the exploiting classes resort to violence against the people, the possibility of a non-peaceful transition to socialism should be borne in mind. Leninism maintains, and historical experience confirms, that the ruling classes do not yield power of their own free will. Hence, the degree of bitterness of the class struggle and the forms it takes will depend not so much on the proletariat as on the strength of the reactionary groups' resistance to the will of the over-whelming majority of the people, and on the use of force by these groups at a particular stage of the struggle for so-cialism. In each particular country the actual applicability of one method of transition to socialism or the other depends on concrete historical conditions.

It may well be that as the forces of socialism grow, the working-class movement gains strength and the positions of capitalism are weakened, there will arise in certain countries a situation in which it will be preferable for the bourgeoisie, as Marx and Lenin foresaw it, to agree to the means of pro-duction being purchased from it and for the proletariat to "pay off" the bourgeoisie.

The success of the struggle which the working class wages for the victory of the revolution will depend on how well the working class and its party master the use of all forms of struggle—peaceful and non-peaceful, parliamentary and extra-parliamentary—and how well they are prepared to re-place one form of struggle by another as quickly and unex-pectedly as possible.

While the principal law-governed processes of the So-cialist revolution are common to all countries, the diversity of the national peculiarities and traditions that have arisen in the course of history creates specific conditions for the revolutionary process and for the variety of forms and rates of the proletariat's advent to power. This predetermines the possibility and necessity, in a number of countries, of transi-tion stages in the struggle for the dictatorship of the pro-letariat, and a variety of forms of political organization of the society building socialism. But whatever the form in which the transition from capitalism to socialism is effected, that transition can come about only through revolution. How-ever varied the forms of a new, people's state power in the period of Socialist construction their essence will be the same—dictatorship of the proletariat, which represents gen-uine democracy, democracy for the working people.

A bourgeois republic, however democratic, however hal-lowed by slogans purporting to express the will of the people or nation as a whole, or an extra-class will, inevitably re-mains in practice—owing to the existence of private capitalist ownership of the means of production—a dictatorship of the bourgeoisie, a machine for the exploitation and suppression of the vast majority of the working people by a handful of capitalists. In contrast to the bourgeoisie, which conceals the class character of the state, the working class does not deny the class character of states.

The dictatorship of the proletariat is a dictatorship of the overwhelming majority over the minority; it is directed against the exploiters, against the oppression of peoples and nations, and is aimed at abolishing all exploitation of man by man. The dictatorship of the proletariat expresses not only the interests of the working class, but also those of all working people; its chief content is not violence but creation, the building of a new, classless society, and the defense of its gains against the enemies of socialism.

Overcoming the split in its ranks is an important condition for the working class to fulfill its historic mission. No bastion of imperialism can withstand a closely knit working class that exercises unity of action. The Communist parties favor cooperation with the Social-Democratic parties not only in the struggle for peace, for better living conditions for the working people and for the preservation and extension of their democratic rights and freedoms, but also in the struggle to win power and build a Socialist society.

At the same time Communists criticize the ideological positions and Right-opportunist practice of social-democracy and expose the Right Social-Democratic leaders, who have sided openly with the bourgeoisie and renounced the traditional Socialist demands of the working class.

The Communist parties are the vanguard of the world revolutionary movement. They have demonstrated the vitality of Marxism-Leninism and their ability not only to propagate the great ideals of scientific communism, but also to put them into practice. Today the international Communist movement is so powerful that the combined forces of reaction cannot crush it.

The Communist movement grows and becomes steeled as it fights against various opportunist trends. Revisionism, Right opportunism, which is a reflection of bourgeois influence, is the chief danger within the Communist movement today. The revisionists, who mask their renunciation of Marxism with talk about the necessity of taking account of the latest developments in society and the class struggle, in effect play the role of peddlers of bourgeois-reformist ideology within the Communist movement. They seek to rob Marxism-Leninism of its revolutionary spirit, to undermine the faith which the working class and all working people have in the Socialist cause, to disarm and disorganize them in their struggle against imperialism. The revisionists deny the historical necessity of the Socialist revolution and of the dictatorship of the proletariat, deny the leading role of the Marxist-Leninist party, undermine the foundations of proletarian internationalism, and drift to nationalism. The ideology of revisionism is most fully embodied in the program of the League of Communists of Yugoslavia.

Another danger is dogmatism and sectarianism, which cannot be reconciled with a creative development of revolutionary theory, lead to the dissociation and isolation of Communists from the masses of the working people, doom them to passive expectation or incite them to Leftist adventurist actions in the revolutionary struggle, and hinder a correct appraisal of the changing situation and the use of new opportunities for the benefit of the working class and all democratic forces. Dogmatism and sectarianism, unless steadfastly combated, can also become the chief danger at a particular stage of the development of individual parties.

The Communist party of the Soviet Union holds that an uncompromising struggle against revisionism, dogmatism and sectarianism, against all departures from Leninism, is a necessary condition for the further strengthening of the unity of the world Communist movement and for the consolidation of the Socialist camp.

The Communist parties are independent and they shape their policies with due regard to the specific conditions prevailing in their own countries. They base relations between themselves on equality and the principles of proletarian internationalism. They coordinate their actions, consciously and of their own free will, as components of a single international army of labor. The Communist party of the Soviet Union, like the other Communist parties, regards it as its internationalist duty to abide by the appraisals and conclusions which the fraternal parties have reached jointly concerning their common tasks in the struggle against imperialism, for peace, democracy and socialism, and by the declaration and the statement adopted by the Communist parties at their international meetings.

Vigorous defense of the unity of the world Communist movement in line with the principles of Marxism-Leninism and proletarian internationalism, and the prevention of any action likely to disrupt that unity are an essential condition for victory in the struggle for national independence, democracy and peace, for the successful accomplishment of the tasks of the socialist revolution, for the construction of socialism and communism.

The C.P.S.U. will continue to strengthen the unity and cohesion of the ranks of the great army of Communists of all countries.

6. THE NATIONAL-LIBERATION MOVEMENT

The world is experiencing a period of stormy national-liberation revolutions. Imperialism suppressed the national independence and freedom of the majority of the peoples and put the fetters of brutal colonial slavery on them, but the rise of socialism marks the advent of the era of emancipation of the oppressed peoples. A powerful wave of national-liberation revolutions is sweeping away the colonial system and undermining the foundations of imperialism. Young sovereign states have arisen, or are arising, in one-time colonies or semi-colonies. Their peoples have entered a new period of development. They have emerged as makers of a new life and as active participants in world politics, as a revolutionary force destroying imperialism.

But the struggle is not yet over. The peoples who are throwing off the shackles of colonialism have attained different levels of freedom. Many of them, having established national states, are striving for economic sovereignty and durable political independence. The peoples of those formally independent countries that in reality depend on foreign monopolies politically and economically are rising to fight against imperialism and reactionary pro-imperialist regimes. The peoples who have not yet cast off the chains of colonial slavery are conducting a heroic struggle against their foreign enslavers.

The young sovereign states do not belong either to the system of imperialist states or to the system of Socialist states. But the overwhelming majority of them have not yet broken free from world capitalist economy even though they occupy a special place in it. They constitute that part of the world which is still being exploited by the capitalist monopolies. As long as they have not put an end to their economic dependence on imperialism, they will be playing the role of a "world countryside," and will remain objects of semi-colonial exploitation.

The existence of the world Socialist system and the weakening of imperialism offer the peoples of the newly free countries the prospect of a national renascence, of ending agelong backwardness and poverty, and achieving economic independence.

The interests of a nation call for the elimination of the remnants of colonialism, the eradication of imperialist rule, the ousting of foreign monopolies, the foundation of a national industry, the abolition of the feudal system and its survivals, the implementation of radical land reforms with the participation of the entire peasantry and in its interests, the pursuit of an independent foreign policy of peace, the democratization of the life of society and the strengthening of political independence. The solution of national problems is in the best interest of all patriotic and progressive forces of the nation. That is the basis on which the latter can be unified.

Foreign capital will retreat only before a broad union of patriotic democratic forces pursuing an anti-imperialist policy. The pillars of feudalism will crumble only under the impact of a general democratic movement. None but far-reaching agrarian reforms and a broad peasant movement can sweep away those remnants of medievalism that fetter the development of the productive forces, and solve the food problem that stares the peoples of Asia, Africa and Latin America so starkly in the face. Political independence can be made secure only by a nation that has won democratic rights and freedoms and is taking an active part in governing the state.

A consistent struggle against imperialism is a paramount condition for the solution of national tasks. Imperialism seeks to retain one-time colonies and semi-colonies within the system of capitalist economy and perpetuate their underprivileged position in it. United States imperialism is the chief bulwark of modern colonialism.

The imperialists are using new methods and new forms to maintain colonial exploitation of the peoples. They have recourse to whatever means they can (colonial wars, military blocs, conspiracies, terrorism, subversion, economic pressure, bribery) to control the newly free countries and to reduce the independence they have won to mere form or to deprive them of that independence. Under the guise of "aid," they are trying to retain their old positions in those countries and capture new ones, to extend their social basis, lure the national bourgeoisie to their side, implant military despotic regimes and put obedient puppets in power. Using the poisoned weapon of national and tribal strife, the imperialists seek to split the ranks of the national-liberation movement; reactionary groups of the local exploiting classes play the role of allies of imperialism.

Imperialism thus remains the chief enemy, and the chief obstacle to the solution of the national problems facing the young sovereign states and all dependent countries.

A national-liberation revolution does not end with the winning of political independence. Independence will be unstable and will become fictitious unless the revolution brings about radical changes in the social and economic spheres and solves the pressing problems of national rebirth.

The working class is the most consistent fighter for the consummation of the revolution, for national interests and social progress. As industry develops, its ranks will swell and its role on the socio-political scene will increase. The alliance of the working class and the peasantry is the fundamental condition for the success of the struggle to carry out far-reaching democratic changes and achieve economic and social progress. This alliance must form the core of a broad national front.

The extent to which the national bourgeoisie will take part in the anti-imperialist and anti-feudal struggle will depend in considerable measure on the solidity of the alliance of the working class and the peasantry. The national front also embraces the urban petty bourgeoisie and the democratic intelligentsia.

In many countries, the liberation movement of the peoples that have awakened proceeds under the flag of nationalism. Marxists-Leninists draw a distinction between the nationalism of the oppressed nations and that of the oppressor nations. The nationalism of an oppressed nation contains a general democratic element directed against oppression, and Communists support it because they consider it historically justified at a given stage. That element finds expression in the striving of the oppressed peoples to free themselves from imperialist oppression, to gain national independence and bring about a national renascence. But the nationalism of an oppressed nation has yet another aspect, one expressing the ideology and interests of the reactionary exploiting top stratum.

The national bourgeoisie is dual in character. In modern conditions the national bourgeoisie in those colonial, one-time colonial and dependent countries where it is not connected with the imperialist circles is objectively interested in accomplishing the basic tasks of an anti-imperialist and anti-feudal revolution. Its progressive role and its ability to participate in the solution of pressing national problems are, therefore, not yet spent.

But as the contradictions between the working people and the propertied classes grow and the class struggle inside the country becomes more aggravated, the national bourgeoisie shows an increasing inclination to compromise with imperialism and domestic reaction.

The development of the countries which have won their freedom may be a complex multi-stage process. By virtue of varying historical and socio-economic conditions in the newly free countries, the revolutionary initiative of the masses will impart distinctive features to the forms and rates of their social progress.

One of the basic issues confronting these peoples is, which road of development the countries that have freed themselves from colonial tyranny are to take, whether the capitalist road or the noncapitalist.

What can capitalism bring them?

Capitalism is the road of suffering for the people.

It will not insure rapid economic progress nor eliminate poverty; social inequality will increase. The capitalist development of the countryside will ruin the peasantry still more. The workers will be fated either to engage in back-breaking labor to enrich the capitalists, or to swell the ranks of the disinherited army of the unemployed. The petty bourgeoisie will be crushed in competition with big capital. The benefits of culture and education will remain out of reach of the people. The intelligentsia will be compelled to trade its talent.

What can socialism bring the peoples?

Socialism is the road to freedom and happiness for the peoples. It insures rapid economic and cultural progress. It transforms a backward country into an industrial country within the lifetime of one generation and not in the course of centuries. Planned Socialist economy is an economy of progress and prosperity by its very nature. Abolition of the exploitation of man by man does away with social inequality. Unemployment disappears completely. Socialism provides all peasants with land, helps them to develop farming, combines their labor efforts in voluntary cooperatives and puts modern agricultural machinery and agronomy at their disposal. Peasant labor becomes more productive and the land is made more fertile. Socialism provides a high material and cultural standard of living for the working class and all working people. Socialism lifts the people out of darkness and ignorance and gives them access to modern culture. The intelligentsia is offered ample opportunities for creative effort for the benefit of the people.

It is for the peoples themselves to decide which road they are to choose. In view of the present balance of the world forces and the actual feasibility of powerful support on the part of the world Socialist system, the peoples of the former colonies can decide this question in their own interest. Their choice will depend on the balance of the class forces. The noncapitalist road of development is insured by the struggle of the working class and the masses of the people, by the general democratic movement, and meets the interests of the absolute majority of the nation. This road will require concessions from the bourgeoisie, but those will be concessions on behalf of the nation. All sections of the population can find application for their energies, if they follow the noncapitalist road of development.

Establishing and developing national democracies opens vast prospects for the peoples of the underdeveloped countries. The political basis of a national democracy is a bloc of all the progressive, patriotic forces fighting to win complete national independence and broad democracy, and to consummate the anti-imperialist, anti-feudal, democratic revolution.

A steady growth of the class and national consciousness of the masses is a characteristic of the present stage of social development. The imperialists persist in distorting the idea of national sovereignty, trying to rob it of its main content and to use it as a means of fomenting national egoism, implanting a spirit of national exclusiveness and increasing national antagonisms.

The democratic forces establish the idea of national sovereignty in the name of equality for the peoples, of their mutual trust, friendship and assistance and of closer relations between them, in the name of social progress. The idea of national sovereignty in its democratic sense becomes more and more firmly established; it acquires increasing significance and becomes an important factor in the progressive development of society.

The Communist parties are steadfastly carrying on an active struggle to consummate the anti-imperialist, anti-feudal, democratic revolution, to establish a state of national democracy and achieve social progress. The Communists' aims are in keeping with the supreme interests of the nation. The attempts of reactionary circles to disrupt the national front under the guise of anti-communism, and their persecution of Communists lead to the weakening of the national liberation movement and run counter to the national interests of the peoples; they threaten the loss of the gains achieved.

The national states become ever more active as an independent force on the world scene; objectively, this force is in the main a progressive, revolutionary and anti-imperialist force. The countries and peoples that are now free from colonial oppression are to play a prominent part in the prevention of a new world war—the focal problem of today. The time is past when imperialism could freely use the manpower and material resources of those countries in its predatory wars. The time has come when the peoples of those countries, breaking the resistance of the reactionary circles connected with the colonialists and overcoming the vacillation of the national bourgeoisie can put their resources at the service of universal security and become a new bulwark of peace. This is what their own fundamental interests and the interests of all peoples demand.

The joining of the efforts of the newly-free peoples and of the peoples of the Socialist countries in the struggle against the war danger is a major factor for world peace. This mighty front, which expresses the will and strength of two-thirds of mankind, can force the imperialist aggressors into retreat.

The Socialist countries are sincere and true friends of peoples fighting for their liberation and of those that have freed themselves from imperialist tyranny and render them all-around support. They stand for the abolition of all forms of colonial oppression and vigorously promote the strengthening of the sovereignty of the states rising on the ruins of colonial empires.

The C. P. S. U. considers fraternal alliance with the peo-

ples who have thrown off colonial or semi-colonial tyranny
to be a cornerstone of its international policy. This alliance
is based on the common vital interests of world socialism
and the world national-liberation movement. The C. P. S. U.
regards it as its internationalist duty to assist the peoples
who have set out to win and strengthen their national independence, all peoples who are fighting for the complete abolition of the colonial system.

7. The Struggle Against Bourgeois
and Reformist Ideology

A grim struggle is going on between two ideologies—Communist and bourgeois—in the world today. This struggle is a
reflection, in the spiritual life of mankind, of the historic
process of transition from capitalism to socialism.

The new historic epoch has brought the revolutionary
world outlook of the proletariat a genuine triumph. Marxism-
Leninism has gripped the minds of progressive mankind.

Bourgeois doctrines and schools have failed in the test of
history. They have been and still are unable to furnish scientific answers to the questions posed by life. The bourgeoisie is no longer in a position to put forward ideas that will
induce the masses to follow it. Bourgeois ideology is experiencing a grave crisis.

A revolutionary change in the minds of vast human masses
is a long and complex process. The more victories the world
Socialist system achieves, the deeper the crisis of world capitalism and the sharper the class struggle, the more important becomes the role of Marxist-Leninist ideas in unifying
and mobilizing the masses to fight for communism. The ideological struggle is a most important element of the class
struggle of the proletariat.

Imperialist reaction mobilizes every possible means to exert
ideological influence on the masses as it attempts to deni-
grate communism and its noble ideas and to defend capitalism. The chief ideological and political weapon of imperialism is anti-communism, which consists mainly in slandering
the Socialist system and distorting the policy and objectives
of the Communist parties and Marxist-Leninist theory.

Under cover of anti-communism, imperialist reaction per-
secutes and hounds all that is progressive and revolutionary;
it seeks to split the ranks of the working people and to par-

alyze the proletarians' will to fight. Rallied to this black banner today are all the enemies of social progress: the finance
oligarchy and the military, the Fascists and reactionary
clericals, the colonialists and landlords and all the ideological and political vehicles of imperialist reaction. Anti-communism is a reflection of the extreme decadence of bourgeois ideology.

The defenders of the bourgeois system, seeking to keep
the masses in spiritual bondage, invent new "theories" designed to mask the exploiting character of the bourgeois system and to embellish capitalism. They assert that modern
capitalism has changed its nature, and that it has become
"people's capitalism" in which property is "diffused" and
capital becomes "democratic," that classes and class contradictions are disappearing, that "incomes are being equalized" and economic crises are being eliminated.

In reality, however, the development of modern capitalism
confirms the accuracy of the Marxist-Leninist theory of the
growing contradictions and antagonisms in capitalist society
and of the aggravation of the class struggle within it.

The advocates of the bourgeois state call it a "welfare
state." They propagate the illusion that the capitalist state
opposes monopolies and can achieve social harmony and
universal well-being. But the masses see from their own experience that the bourgeois state is an obedient tool of the
monopolies and that the vaunted "welfare" is welfare for
the magnates of finance capital, but suffering and torture
for hundreds of millions of working men.

The "theoreticians" of anti-communism describe modern
imperialism as "the free world." In reality the "free world"
is a world of exploitation and lack of rights, a world where
human dignity and national honor are trampled underfoot,
a world of obscurantism and political reaction, of rabid militarism and bloody reprisals against the working people.

The monopolies are reviving Fascist ideology—the ideology
of extreme chauvinism and racism. Fascism in power is an
open terroristic dictatorship of the most reactionary, most
chauvinistic and most imperialist elements of finance capital.
Fascism begins everywhere and always with vicious anti-
communism to isolate and rout the parties of the working
class, to split the forces of the proletariat and defeat them
piecemeal, and then to do away with all the other democratic parties and organizations and turn the people into the
blind tool of the policy of the capitalist monopolies.

Fascism strikes first of all at the Communist parties since they are the most consistent, stanch and incorruptible defenders of the interests of the working class and all working people.

Inperialist reaction makes extensive use of chauvinism to incite nationalist conflicts, persecute entire nationalities and national groups (anti-Semitism, racial discrimination against Negroes and the peoples of the under-developed countries), blunt the class consciousness of the working people and divert the proletariat and its allies from the class struggle.

Clericalism is acquiring ever greater importance in the political and ideological arsenal of imperialism. The clericals do not confine themselves to using the Church and its ramified machinery. They now have their own big political parties which in many capitalist countries are in power. They set up their own trade-union, youth, women's and other organizations and split the ranks of the working class and all working people. The monopolies lavishly subsidize clerical parties and organizations, which exploit the religious sentiments of the working people and their superstitions and prejudices.

Bourgeois ideology assumes a variety of forms and uses the most diverse methods and means of deceiving the working people. But they all amount to the same—defense of the declining capitalist system. The ideas running through the political and economic theories of the modern bourgeoisie, through its philosophy and sociology, through its ethics and aesthetics, substantiate monopoly domination, justify exploitation, defame social property and collectivism, glorify militarism and war, whitewash colonialism and racism, and foment enmity and hatred among the peoples.

Anti-communism is becoming the main instrument of reaction in its struggle against the democratic forces of Asia, Africa and Latin America. It is the meeting ground of imperialist ideology and the ideology of the feudal, pro-imperialist elements and the reactionary groups of the bourgeoisie of the countries which have gained their freedom from colonial tyranny.

The anti-popular circles of those countries seek to tone down the general democratic content of nationalism, to play up its reactionary aspect, to push aside the democratic forces of the nation, to prevent social progress, and to hinder the spread of scientific socialism.

At the same time they advance theories of "socialism of the national type," propagate socio-philosophical doctrines that are, as a rule, so many variations of the petty-bourgeois illusion of socialism, an illusion which rules out the class struggle. These theories mislead the people, hamper the development of the national-liberation movement and imperil its gains.

National-democratic, anti-imperialist ideas are becoming widespread in the countries which have liberated themselves from colonial oppression. The Communists and other proponents of these ideas patiently explain to the masses the untenability of the illusion that it is possible to insure national independence and social progress without an active struggle against imperialism and internal reaction. They come out actively against chauvinism and other manifestations of reactionary ideology, which justify despotic regimes and the suppression of democracy. At the same time the Communists act as exponents of the Socialist ideology, rallying the masses under the banner of scientific socialism.

The ideological struggle of the imperialist bourgeoisie is spearheaded primarily against the working class and its Marxist-Leninist parties. Social-democratism in the working-class movement and revisionism in the Communist movement reflect the bourgeois influence on the working class.

The contemporary Right-wing Social-Democrats are the most important ideological and political prop of the bourgeoisie within the working-class movement. They eclectically combine old opportunist ideas with the "latest" bourgeois theories. The Right wing of Social-Democracy has completely broken with Marxism and contraposed so-called democratic socialism to scientific socialism. Its adherents deny the existence of antagonistic classes and the class struggle in bourgeois society; they forcefully deny the necessity of the proletarian revolution and oppose the abolition of the private ownership of the means of production. They assert that capitalism is being "transformed" into socialism.

The Right-wing Socialists began by advocating social reforms in place of the Socialist revolution and went as far as to defend state-monopoly capitalism. In the past they impressed on the minds of the proletariat that their differences with revolutionary Marxism bore not so much on the ultimate goal of the working-class movement as on the ways of achieving it.

Now they openly renounce socialism. Formerly the Right-wing Socialists refused to recognize the class struggle to the point of recognizing the dictatorship of the proletariat. Today they deny, not only the existence of the class struggle in bourgeois society, but also the very existence of antagonistic classes.

Historical experience has shown the bankruptcy of both the ideology and the policy of Social-Democracy. Even when reformist parties come to power they limit themselves to partial reforms that do not affect the rule of the monopoly bourgeoisie. Anti-communism has brought social reformism to an ideological and political impasse. This is one of the main reasons for the crisis of Social-Democracy.

Marxism-Leninism is winning more and more victories. It is winning them because it expresses the vital interests of the working class, of the vast majority of mankind, which seeks peace, freedom and progress, and because it expresses the ideology of the new society succeeding capitalism.

8. Peaceful Coexistence and the Struggle for World Peace

The C.P.S.U. considers that the chief aim of its foreign-policy activity is to provide peaceful conditions for the building of a Communist society in the U.S.S.R. and developing the world Socialist system and together with the other peace-loving peoples to deliver mankind from a world war of extermination.

The C.P.S.U. maintains that forces capable of preserving and promoting world peace have arisen and are growing in the world. It is becoming possible to establish essentially new relations between states.

Imperialism knows no relations between states other than those of domination and subordination, of oppression of the weak by the strong. It bases international relations on dictation and intimidation, on violence and arbitrary rule. It regards wars of aggression as a natural means of settling international issues. For the imperialist countries, diplomacy has been, and remains, a tool for imposing their will upon other nations and preparing wars. At the time of the undivided rule of imperialism the issue of war and peace was settled by the finance and industrial oligarchy in the utmost secrecy from the peoples.

Socialism, in contrast to imperialism, advances a new type of international relations. The foreign policy of the Socialist countries, which is based on the principle of peace, the equality and self-determination of nations, and respect for the independence and sovereignty of all countries, as well as the fair, humane method of Socialist diplomacy, is exerting a growing influence on the world situation. At a time when imperialism no longer plays a dominant role in international relations while the Socialist system is playing an increasing role, and when the influence of the countries that have won national independence and of the masses of the people in the capitalist countries has grown very considerably, it is becoming possible for the new principles advanced by socialism to gain the upper hand over the principles of aggressive imperialist policy.

For the first time in history, a situation has arisen in which not only the big states, but also the small ones, the countries which have chosen independent development, and all the states which want peace, are in a position, irrespective of their strength, to pursue an independent foreign policy.

The issue of war and peace is the principal issue of today. Imperialism is the only source of the war danger. The imperialist camp is making preparations for the worst crime against mankind—a world thermonuclear war that can bring unprecedented destruction to entire countries and wipe out entire nations. The problem of war and peace has become a life-and-death problem for hundreds of millions of people.

The peoples must concentrate their efforts on curbing the imperialists in good time and preventing them from making use of lethal weapons. The important thing is to ward off a thermonuclear war, not to let it break out. This can be done by the present generation.

The consolidation of the Soviet state and the formation of the world Socialist system were historic steps towards the realization of mankind's age-old dream of banishing wars from the life of society. In the Socialist part of the world there are no classes or social groups interested in starting a war. Socialism, outstripping capitalism in a number of important branches of science and technology, has supplied the peace-loving peoples with powerful material means of curbing imperialist aggression.

Capitalism established its rule with fire and sword, but socialism does not require war to spread its ideals. Its weapon is its superiority over the old system in social organization, political system, economy, the improvement of the standard of living and spiritual culture.

The Socialist system is a natural center of attraction for

the peace-loving forces of the globe. The principles of its foreign policy are gaining ever greater international recognition and support. A vast peace zone has taken shape on earth. In addition to the Socialist countries, it includes a large group of non-Socialist countries that for various reasons are not interested in starting a war. The emergence of those countries in the arena of world politics has substantially altered the balance of forces in favor of peace.

There is a growing number of countries that adhere to a policy of neutrality and strive to safeguard themselves against the hazards of participation in military blocs.

In the new historical epoch the masses have a far greater opportunity of actively influencing the settlement of international issues. The peoples are taking the solution of the problem of war and peace into their own hands more and more vigorously. The anti-war movement of the masses, which takes various forms, is a major factor in the struggle for peace. The international working class, the most uncompromising and most consistent fighter against imperialist war, is the great organizing force in this struggle of the people as a whole.

It is possible to avert a world war by the combined efforts of the mighty Socialist camp, the peace-loving non-Socialist countries, the international working class and all the forces championing peace. The growing superiority of the Socialist forces over the forces of imperialism, of the forces of peace over those of war, will make it actually possible to banish world war from the life of society even before the complete victory of socialism on earth, with capitalism surviving in a part of the world. The victory of socialism throughout the world will do away completely with the social and national causes of all wars. To abolish war and establish everlasting peace on earth is a historical mission of communism.

General and complete disarmament under strict international control is a radical way of guaranteeing a durable peace. Imperialism has imposed an unprecedented burden of armaments on the people. Socialism sees its duty towards mankind in delivering it from this absurd waste of national wealth. The solution of this problem would have historical significance for mankind. By an active and determined effort the peoples can and must force the imperialists into disarmament.

Socialism has offered mankind the only reasonable principle of maintaining relations between states at a time when the world is divided into two systems—the principle of the peaceful coexistence of states with different social systems, put forward by Lenin.

Peaceful coexistence of the Socialist and capitalist countries is an objective necessity for the development of human society. War cannot and must not serve as a means of settling international disputes. Peaceful coexistence or disastrous war—such is the alternative offered by history. Should the imperialist aggressors nevertheless venture to start a new world war, the peoples will no longer tolerate a system which drags them into devastating wars. They will sweep imperialism away and bury it.

Peaceful coexistence implies renunciation of war as a means of settling international disputes, and their solution by negotiation; equality, mutual understanding and trust between countries; consideration of mutual interests; non-interference in internal affairs; recognition of the right of every people to solve all the problems of their country by themselves; strict respect for the sovereignty and territorial integrity of all countries; promotion of economic and cultural cooperation on the basis of complete equality and mutual benefit.

Peaceful coexistence serves as a basis for the peaceful competition between socialism and capitalism on an international scale and constitutes a specific form of class struggle between them. As they consistently pursue the policy of peaceful coexistence, the Socialist countries are steadily strengthening the positions of the world Socialist system in its competition with capitalism. Peaceful coexistence affords more favorable opportunities for the struggle of the working class in the capitalist countries and facilitates the struggle of the peoples of the colonial and dependent countries for their liberation.

Support for the principle of peaceful coexistence is also in keeping with the interests of that section of the bourgeoisie which realizes that a thermonuclear war would not spare the ruling classes of capitalist society either. The policy of peaceful coexistence is in accord with the vital interests of all mankind, except the big monopoly magnates and the militarists.

The Soviet Union has consistently pursued, and will continue to pursue, the policy of peaceful coexistence of states with different social systems.

The Communist party of the Soviet Union advances the following tasks in the field of international relations:

To use, together with the other Socialist countries, peaceful states and peoples every means of preventing war and providing conditions for the complete elimination of war from the life of society;

To pursue a policy of establishing sound international relations, and work for the disbandment of all military blocs opposing each other, the discontinuance of the "cold war" and the propaganda of enmity and hatred among the nations, and the abolition of all air, naval, rocket and other military bases on foreign territory;

To work for general and complete disarmament under strict international control;

To strengthen relations of fraternal friendship and close cooperation with the countries of Asia, Africa and Latin America which are fighting to attain or consolidate national independence, with all peoples and states that advocate the preservation of peace;

To pursue an active and consistent policy of improving and developing relations with all capitalist countries, including the United States of America, Great Britain, France, the Federal Republic of Germany, Japan, Italy, and other countries, with a view to safeguarding peace;

To contribute in every way to the militant solidarity of all contingents and organizations of the international working class, which oppose the imperialist policy of war;

Steadfastly to pursue a policy of consolidating all the forces fighting against war. All the organizations and parties that strive to avert war, the neutralist and pacifist movements and the bourgeois circles that advocate peace and normal relations between countries will meet with understanding and support on the part of the Soviet Union;

To pursue a policy of developing international co-operation in the fields of trade, cultural relations, science and technology;

To be highly vigilant with regard to the aggressive circles, which are intent on violating peace; to expose, in good time, the initiators of military adventures; to take all necessary steps to safeguard the security and inviolability of our Socialist country and the Socialist camp as a whole.

The C.P.S.U. and the Soviet people as a whole will continue to oppose all wars of conquest, including wars be-

tween capitalist countries, and local wars aimed at strangling
people's emancipation movements, and consider it their duty
to support the sacred struggle of the oppressed peoples and
their just anti-imperialist wars of liberation.

The Communist party of the Soviet Union will hold high
the banner of peace and friendship among the nations.

II. THE TASKS OF THE COMMUNIST PARTY OF THE SOVIET UNION IN BUILDING A COMMUNIST SOCIETY

Communism—The Bright Future of all Mankind

The building of a Communist society has become an immediate practical task for the Soviet people. The gradual
development of socialism into communism is an objective
law, it has been prepared by the development of Soviet
Socialist society throughout the preceding period.

What is communism?

Communism is a classless social system with one form of
public ownership of the means of production and full social
equality of all members of society; under it, the all-round
development of people will be accompanied by the growth of
the productive forces through continuous progress in science
and technology, all sources of public wealth will gush forth
abundantly, and the great principle, "From each according
to his ability, to each according to his needs," will be implemented. Communism is a highly organized society of free,
socially conscious working people in which public self-government will be established, in which labor for the good of
society will become the prime and vital requirement of everyone, a necessity recognized by one and all, and the
ability of each person will be employed to the greatest
benefit of the people.

A high degree of Communist consciousness, industry,
discipline and devotion to the public interest are qualities
typifying the man of Communist society.

Communism insures the continuous development of social production and high labor productivity through rapid
scientific and technological progress; it equips man with the
best and most powerful machines, greatly increases his
power over nature and enables him to control its elemental
forces to an ever greater extent. The social economy reaches

the highest stage of planned organization, and the most effective and rational use is made of the material wealth and labor reserves to meet the growing requirements of the members of society.

Under communism, the classes, and the socio-economic and cultural distinctions, and differences in living conditions, between town and countryside disappear completely; the countryside rises to the level of the town in the development of the productive forces and the nature of work, the forms of production relations, living conditions and the well-being of the population. With the victory of communism mental and physical labor will merge organically in the production activity of people. The intelligentsia will no longer be a distinct social stratum, since workers by hand will have risen in cultural and technological standards to the level of workers by brain.

Thus, communism puts an end to the division of society into classes and social strata, whereas the whole history of mankind, with the exception of its primitive period, was one of class society in which division into opposing classes led to the exploitation of man by man, class struggle, and antagonisms between nations and states.

Under communism all people will have equal status in society, will stand in the same relation to the means of production, will enjoy equal conditions of work and distribution, and will actively participate in the management of public affairs. Harmonious relations will be established between the individual and society on the basis of the unity of public and personal interests. For all their diversity, the requirements of people will express the sound, reasonable requirements of perfectly developed persons.

The purpose of Communist production is to insure uninterrupted progress of society and to provide all its members with material and cultural benefits according to their growing needs, their individual requirements and tastes.

People's requirements will be satisfied from public sources. Articles of personal use will come into the full ownership of each member of society and will be at his disposal.

Communist society, which is based on highly organized production and advanced technology, alters the character of work, but it does not release the members of society from work. It will by no means be a society of anarchy, idleness and inactivity. Everyone will participate in social labor and thereby insure the steady growth of the material and spirit-

ual wealth of society. Thanks to the changed character of
labor, its greater mechanization and the high degree of
consciousness of all members of society, the latter will work
willingly for the public benefit according to their own inclinations.

Communist production demands high standards of organization, precision and discipline, which are insured, not by
compulsion, but thanks to an understanding of public duty,
and are determined by the whole tenor of life in Communist society. Labor and discipline will not be a burden to
people, labor will no longer be a mere source of livelihood
—it will be a genuinely creative process and a source of
happiness.

Communism represents the highest form of organization
of public life. All production units and self-governing associations will be harmoniously interlinked by a common planned
economy and a uniform rhythm of social labor.

Under communism the nations will draw closer and closer
together in all spheres on the basis of a complete identity
of economic, political and spiritual interests of fraternal
friendship and co-operation.

Communism is the system under which the abilities and
talents of free man, his best moral qualities, blossom forth
and reveal themselves in full. Family relations will be completely freed from material considerations and will be
based solely on mutual love and friendship.

In defining the basic tasks to be accomplished in building
a Communist society, the party is guided by Lenin's great
formula: "Communism is Soviet power plus the electrification of the whole country."

The C.P.S.U., being a party of scientific communism, proposes and fulfills the tasks of Communist construction in step
with the preparation and maturing of the material and
spiritual prerequisites, considering that it would be wrong
to jump over necessary stages of development, and that it
would be equally wrong to halt at an achieved level and
thus check progress. The building of communism must be
carried out by successive stages.

In the current decade (1961-1970), the Soviet Union, in
creating the material and technical basis of communism,
will surpass the strongest and richest capitalist country, the
U.S.A., in production per head of population, the people's
standard of living and their cultural and technical standards

will improve substantially, everyone will live in easy circumstances, all collective and state farms will become highly productive and profitable enterprises, the demand of the Soviet people for well-appointed housing will, in the main, be satisfied, hard physical work will disappear, the U.S.S.R. will become the country with the shortest working day.

In the next decade (1971-1980) the material and technical basis of communism will be created and there will be an abundance of material and cultural benefits for the whole population, Soviet society will come close to a stage where it can introduce the principle of distribution according to needs, and there will be a gradual transition to one form of ownership—public ownership. Thus, a Communist society will, on the whole, be built in the U.S.S.R. The construction of Communist society will be fully completed in the subsequent period.

The majestic edifice of communism is being erected by the persevering effort of the Soviet people—the working class, the peasantry and the intelligentsia. The more successful their work, the closer the great goal—Communist society.

1. The Tasks of the Party in the Field of Economic Development and in the Creation and Promotion of the Material and Technical Basis of Communism

The main economic task of the party and the Soviet people is to create the material and technical basis of communism within two decades. This means the complete electrification of the country and the perfection on this basis of the techniques, technologies and organization of social production in industry and agriculture, the comprehensive mechanization of production operations and a growing degree of their automation, the widespread use of chemistry in the national economy, the vigorous development of new, economically effective branches of production, new types of power and new materials, the all-round and rational utilization of natural resources, the organic fusion of science and production, and rapid scientific and technical progress, a high cultural and technical level for the working people, substantial superiority over the more developed capitalist countries in productivity of labor, which constitutes a most important prerequisite for the victory of the Communist system.

As a result, the U.S.S.R. will possess productive forces of unparalleled might, it will surpass the technical level of the most developed countries and occupy first place in the world in per capita production. This will serve as a basis for the gradual transformation of Socialist social relations into Communist social relations and for a development of industry and agriculture that will make it possible to meet in abundance the requirements of society and all its members.

In contrast to capitalism, the planned Socialist system of economy combines accelerated technical progress with the full employment of all able-bodied citizens. Automation and comprehensive mechanization serve as a material basis for the gradual development of Socialist labor into Communist labor. Technical progress will require higher standards of production and a higher level of the vocational and general education of all workers. The new machinery developed will be used to improve radically the Soviet people's working conditions, and make them easier, to reduce the length of the working day, to improve living conditions, eliminate hard physical work and, subsequently, all unskilled labor.

The material and technical basis will develop and improve continuously together with the evolution of society towards the complete triumph of communism. The level of development of science and technology, and the degree of mechanization and automation of production operations, will steadily rise.

The creation of the material and technical basis of communism will call for huge investments. The task is to utilize these investments most rationally and economically, with the maximum effect and gain of time.

(1.) *The development of industry; its role in creating the productive forces of communism.*

The creation of the material and technical basis of communism, the task of making Soviet industry technologically the best and strongest in the world, calls for the further development of heavy industry. On this basis, all the other branches of the national economy—agriculture, the consumer goods industries, the building industry, transport and communications, as well as the branches directly concerned with services for the population—trade, public catering, health, housing and communal services—will be technically re-equipped.

A first-class heavy industry, the basis for the country's technical progress and economic might, has been built up in the Soviet Union. The C.P.S.U. will continue to devote unflagging attention to the growth of heavy industry, which insures the development of the country's productive forces and defense potential. In the new period of the Soviet Union's development, the growth and technological progress of heavy industry must insure the expansion of those branches of economy producing consumer goods to meet ever more fully the requirements of the people.

Thus, the main task of heavy industry is to meet the needs of the country's defense in full and to satisfy the daily requirements of the man of Soviet society better and more fully.

With these aims in view, the C.P.S.U. plans the following increases in total industrial output:

Within the current ten years, by approximately 150 per cent, exceeding the contemporary level of U.S. industrial output.

Within twenty years, by not less than 500 per cent, leaving the present over-all volume of U.S. industrial output far behind.

To achieve this, it is necessary to raise productivity of labor in industry by more than 100 per cent within ten years, and by 300 to 350 per cent within twenty years. In twenty years' time labor productivity in Soviet industry will exceed the present level of labor productivity in the U.S.A. by roughly 100 per cent, and considerably more in terms of per-hour output, due to the reduction of the working day in the U.S.S.R.

Such an intensive development of industry will call for major progressive changes in its structure. The role of new branches insuring the greatest technical progress will grow very considerably. The less effective fuels, types of power, raw and semi-manufactured materials will be increasingly superseded by highly effective ones, and their comprehensive use will increase greatly. The share of synthetic materials, metals and alloys with new properties will increase considerably. New types of automatic and electronic machinery, instruments and apparatus will be rapidly introduced on a large scale.

Electrification, which is the backbone of the economy of

Communist society, plays a key role in the development of all economic branches and in all modern technological progress.

It is therefore important to insure the priority development of electric power output. The plan for the electrification of the country provides for an almost threefold increase in the use of electricity to equip industrial labor within the present decade, a considerable expansion of industries with a high rate of power consumption through the supply of cheap power, and extensive electrification of transport, agriculture and the household in town and countryside. The electrification of the whole country will on the whole be completed in the course of the second decade.

The annual output of electricity must be brought up to 900,000-1,000,000 million killowatt-hours by the end of the first decade and to 2,700,000-3,000,000 million kwh by the end of the second decade. For this it will be necessary in the course of twenty years to increase accordingly the installed capacities of electric power plants and to build hundreds of thousands of kilometers of high-tension transmission and distribution lines throughout the country. A single power grid for the whole U. S. S. R. will be built and will have sufficient capacity reserves to transmit electric power from the eastern regions to the European part of the country. It will link up with the power grids of other Socialist countries.

As atomic energy becomes cheaper, the construction of atomic power stations will be expanded, especially in areas poor in other power sources, and the use of atomic energy for peaceful purposes in the national economy, in medicine and science will increase.

The further rapid expansion of the output of metals and fuels, the basis of modern industry, remains one of the major economic tasks. Within twenty years metallurgy will develop sufficiently to produce about 250,000,000 tons of steel a year. Steel output must cover the growing requirements of the national economy in accordance with the technological progress achieved in that period. The output of light, nonferrous and rare metals will grow very appreciably; the output of aluminum and its use in electrification, engineering, building and the household will considerably increase. A steady effort will be made to insure priority output of oil and gas which will be used increasingly as raw materials for the chemical industry. Oil output must meet the requirements of the national economy in full.

One of the most important tasks is the all-round development of the chemical industry, and the full use in all economic fields of the achievements of modern chemistry. This provides greater opportunities to increase the national wealth and the output of new, better and cheaper capital and consumer goods. Metal, wood and other building materials will be increasingly replaced by economical, durable, light synthetic materials. The output of mineral fertilizers and chemical weed and pest killers will rise sharply.

Of primary importance for the technical re-equipment of the entire national economy is the development of mechanical engineering, with special stress laid on the accelerated production of automated production lines and machines, automatic, telemechanic and electronic devices and precision instruments. The designing of highly efficient machines consuming less raw materials and power and leading to higher productivity will make rapid progress. The requirements of the national economy in all types of modern machinery, machine tools and instruments must be met in full.

The development of mechanical engineering in the first decade will serve as the basis for comprehensive mechanization in industry, agriculture, building, transport, loading and unloading operations and in the municipal economy. Comprehensive mechanization will exclude manual labor from both basic and auxiliary operations.

Within the twenty-year period the comprehensive automation of production will be effected on a large scale, with more and more shops and plants being fully automated. The introduction of highly efficient automatic control systems will be accelerated. Cybernetics, computers and control systems must be introduced on a large scale in industry, research, designing, planning, accounting, statistics and management.

The vast scope of capital construction calls for the rapid development and technological modernization of the building industry, a substantial increase in the output of better and cheaper building materials, the maximum acceleration of the rate and reduction of the cost of building through steady industrialization and the use of prefabricated elements.

The C. P. S. U. will concentrate its efforts on insuring a rapid increase in the output of consumer goods. The growing resources of industry must be used more and more to fully meet all the requirements of the Soviet people and to build and equip enterprises and establishments catering to the household and cultural needs of the population. Along with the accelerated development of all branches of the light and food industries, the share of consumer goods in the output of heavy industry will also increase. More electricity and gas will be supplied to the population.

The growth of the national economy will call for the accelerated development of all transport facilities. The most important tasks in the sphere of transport are: expansion of transport and road construction to meet in full the requirements of the national economy and the population in all types of traffic; further modernization of the railways and other transport systems; a considerable increase of the speed of rail, sea and river traffic; the coordinated development of all types of transport as integral parts of a single transport network. The share of pipe transport will increase.

A single deep-water system will link the main inland waterways of the European part of the U. S. S. R.

A ramified network of modern roads will be built throughout the country. The automobile fleet will increase sufficiently to fully meet freight and passenger traffic requirements; car hire centers will be organized on a large scale. Air transport will become a means of mass passenger traffic extending to all parts of the country.

Up-to-date jet engineering will develop rapidly, above all in air transport, as well as in space exploration.

All means of communication (post, radio and television, telephone and telegraph) will be further developed. All regions of the country will have reliable telephone and radio communications and a link-up system of television stations.

Full-scale Communist construction calls for a more rational geographic distribution of the industries, to save social labor and insure the comprehensive development of areas and the specialization of their industries, do away with the overpopulation of big cities, facilitate the elimination of substantial distinctions between town and countryside, and further even out the economic levels of different parts of the country.

To gain time, priority will be given to developing easily exploited natural resources that provide the greatest economic effect.

The industry in the areas to the east of the Urals, where

there are immense natural riches, raw material and power resources, will expand greatly.

The following must be achieved within the next twenty years: in Siberia and Kazakhstan—the creation of new large power bases using deposits of cheap coal or the waterpower resources of the Angara and Yenisei Rivers, the organization of big centers of power-consuming industries and the completion, in Siberia, of the country's third metallurgical base, the development of new rich ore and coal deposits, and the construction of a number of new large machine-building centers; in areas along the Volga, in the Urals, North Caucasus and Central Asia—the rapid development of the power, oil, gas and chemical industries and the development of ore deposits. The Soviet people will be able to carry out daring plans to change the courses of some northern rivers and regulate their discharge for the purpose of utilizing vast quantities of water for the irrigation of arid areas.

The economy in the European part of the U. S. S. R., which contains the bulk of the population and where there are great opportunities for increased industrial output, will make further substantial progress.

The maximum acceleration of scientific and engineering progress is a major national task which calls for daily effort to reduce the time spent on designing new machinery and introducing it in industry. It is necessary to promote in every way the initiative of economic councils, enterprises, social organizations, scientists, engineers, designers, workers and collective farmers in creating and applying technical improvements. Of utmost importance is the material and moral stimulation of mass invention and rationalization movement, of enterprises, shops, teams and innovators who master the production of new machinery and utilize them skillfully.

The party will do everything to enhance the role of science in the building of Communist society, it will encourage research to discover new possibilities for the development of the productive forces, and the rapid and extensive application of the latest scientific and technical achievements, a decisive advancement in experimental work, including research directly at enterprises, and the efficient organization of scientific and technical information and of the whole system of studying and disseminating progressive Soviet and foreign methods. Science will itself in full measure become a productive force.

The constant improvement in the technology of all industries and production branches is a requisite for industrial development. Technological progress will facilitate the substantial intensification and acceleration of production operations without putting undue strain on the worker, and will achieve the highest degree of precision, the standardization of mass-produced items and the maximum use of production lines. Machining will be supplemented and, when necessary, replaced by chemical methods, the technological use of electricity, electro-chemistry, electric heat treatment, etc., radioelectronics, semiconductors and ultrasound will occupy a more important place in production techniques. The construction of new, technically up-to-date enterprises will proceed side by side with the reconstruction of those now in existence and the replacement and modernization of their equipment.

The development of the specialization and cooperation of enterprises is a most important condition for technical progress and the rational organization of social labor. Articles of similar type should be manufactured mainly at large specialized plants.

New techniques and the reduction of the working day call for better organization of work. Technical progress and better production organization must be fully utilized to increase labor productivity and reduce production costs at every enterprise. This implies a higher rate of increase in labor productivity as compared with remuneration, better rate-fixing, prevention of loss of working time, and operation on a profitable basis at all stages of production.

Most important will be the task of systematically improving the qualifications of those working in industry and other branches of the economy in connection with technical progress. The planned training, instruction and rational employment of those released from various jobs and transferred to other jobs due to mechanization and automation are essential.

Existing enterprises will be improved and developed into enterprises of Communist society. Typical of this process will be new machinery, high standards of production organization and efficiency through increased automation of production operations and the introduction of automation into control, an improvement of the cultural and technical standards of the workers, the increasing fusion of physical and mental labor and the growing proportion of engineers and technicians in industry, the expansion of research, and closer links between enterprises and research institutes, promotion of the emulation movement, the application of achievements of science and the best forms of labor organization and best methods of raising labor productivity, the extensive participation of workers' collectives in the management of enterprises, and the spreading of Communist forms of labor.

(2.) *Development of agriculture and social relations in the countryside.*

Along with a powerful industry, a flourishing, versatile and highly productive agriculture is an imperative condition for the building of communism. The party organizes a great development of productive forces in agriculture, which will enable it to accomplish two basic, closely related tasks: (a.) To build up an abundance of high-quality food products for the population and of raw materials for industry, and (b.) to effect the gradual transition of social relations in the Soviet countryside to Communist relations and eliminate, in the main, the distinctions between town and country.

The chief means of achieving progress in agriculture and satisfying the growing needs of the country in farm produce are comprehensive mechanization and consistent intensification: high efficiency of crop farming and stock-breeding based on science and progressive experience in all kolkhozes [collectives] and state farms, a steep rise in the yielding capacity of all crops and greater output per hectare with the utmost economy of labor and funds. On this basis, it is necessary to achieve an unintermittent growth of agricultural production in keeping with the needs of society. Agriculture will approach the level of industry in technical equipment and the organization of production, farm labor will turn into a variety of industrial labor, and the dependence of agriculture upon the elements will decrease considerably, and ultimately drop to a minimum.

The development of virgin and disused land and establishment of new large-scale state farms, the reorganization of the machine-and-tractor stations, the sale of implements of production to the collective farms, and the enhancement of material incentives for agricultural workers—all constitute an important stage in the development of agriculture.

The further advance of the countryside to communism

will proceed through the development and improvement of the two forms of socialist farming—the kolkhozes and state farms.

The kolkhoz system is an integral part of Soviet Socialist society. It is a way charted by V. I. Lenin for the gradual transition of the peasantry to communism; it has stood the test of history and conforms to the distinctive features of the peasantry.

Kolkhoz farming accords in full with the level and needs of the development of modern productive forces in the countryside, and makes possible effective use of new machinery and the achievements of science, and rational employment of manpower. The kolkhoz blends the personal interests of the peasants with common, nationwide interests, blends individual with collective interest in the results of production, and offers extensive opportunities for raising the incomes and the well-being of peasants on the basis of growing labor productivity. It is essential to make the most of the possibilities and advantages of the kolkhoz system. By virtue of its organizational structure and its democratic groundwork, which will develop more and more, the kolkhoz is a social economic form which insures that production is run by the kolkhoz members themselves, that their creative initiative is enhanced and that they are educated in the Communist spirit. The kolkhoz is a school of communism for the peasantry.

Economic advancement of the kolkhoz system creates conditions for the gradual rapprochement and, in the long run, also for the merging of kolkhoz property and the property of the whole people into one Communist property.

The state farms, which are the leading Socialist agricultural enterprises, play an ever increasing role in the development of agriculture. The state farms must serve the kolkhozes as a model of progressive, scientifically managed, economically profitable social production, of high efficiency and labor productivity.

The C. P. S. U. proceeds from the fact that the further consolidation of the unbreakable alliance of the working class and the kolkhoz peasantry is of crucial political and socio-economic importance for the building of communism in the U. S. S. R.

A. BUILDING UP AN ABUNDANCE OF AGRICULTURAL PRODUCE.

In order fully to satisfy the requirements of the entire population and of the national economy in agricultural produce, the task is to increase the aggregate volume of agricultural production in ten years by about 150 per cent, and in twenty years of 250 per cent. Agricultural output must keep ahead of the growing demand. In the first decade the Soviet Union will outstrip the United States in output of the key agricultural products per head of population.

Accelerated growth of grain production is the chief link in the further development of all agriculture and a basis for the rapid growth of stock-breeding. The aggregate grain crops will more than double in twenty years, and their yielding capacity will double. The output of wheat, maize, cereal and leguminous crops will increase substantially.

Livestock breeding will develop at a rapid rate. The output of animal products will rise: meat about threefold in the first ten years and nearly fourfold in twenty years, and milk more than double in the first decade and nearly threefold in twenty years. The planned increase in the output of animal products will be achieved by increasing the cattle and poultry population, improving stock and productivity, and building up reliable fodder resources, chiefly maize, sugar beet, fodder beans and other crops.

Productivity of labor in agriculture will rise not less than 150 per cent in ten years, and five-to-six-fold in twenty years. The rapid rise of the productivity of farm labor—at a higher rate than in industry—will serve to eliminate the lag of agriculture behind industry and will turn it into a highly developed branch of the economy of Communist society.

The further mechanization of agriculture, introduction of comprehensive mechanization and use of automated devices and highly efficient and economical machinery adapted to the conditions of each zone, will be the basis for the growth of productivity of farm labor. The party considers rapid electrification of agriculture one of the most important tasks. All state farms and kolkhozes will be supplied electric power for production and domestic purposes from the state power grid, and also from power stations built in the countryside.

The technical re-equipment of agriculture must combine with the most progressive forms and methods of the organization of labor and production and the maximum improvement of the cultural and technical education of farm workers. Qualified workers with special agricultural training and proficient in the use of new machinery will increasingly predominate in the kolkhozes and state farms.

To insure high, stable, steadily increasing harvests, to deliver agriculture from the baneful effects of the elements, especially droughts, to steeply raise land fertility, and to rapidly advance livestock breeding, it is necessary:

To introduce in all parts of the country scientific systems of land cultivation and animal husbandry in keeping with local conditions and the specialization of each farm, insuring the most effective use of the land and the most economically expedient combination of branches, the best structure of crop acreage with the substitution of high-yielding and valuable crops for crops of little value and those giving low yields, to insure that every kolkhoz and state farm masters the most advanced methods of crop farming with the application of efficient crop rotation and the sowing of high-grade seeds only, to build up reliable fodder resources in all districts and to introduce the foremost stock-breeding techniques in kolkhozes and state farm.

To effect a scientifically expedient disposition of agriculture by natural-economic zones and districts, and a more thorough and stable specialization of agriculture with priority given to the type of farm product where the best conditions for it exist and the greatest saving in outlay is achieved.

To effect a consistent introduction of chemicals in all branches of agriculture, to meet all its needs in mineral fertilizers and chemical means of combating weeds, blights, diseases and plant and animal pests, and to insure the best use of local fertilizers in all kolkhozes.

To apply broadly biological achievements and microbiology, which is assuming ever greater importance, to improve soil fertility, to carry through a far-flung irrigation program, to irrigate and water millions of hectares of land in the arid areas and improve existing irrigated farming, to expand field-protective afforestation, building of water reservoirs, irrigation of pastures and melioration of overmoist land, and to combat, systematically, the water and wind erosion of soil.

The party will promote the development of agricultural science, focus the creative efforts of scientists on the key problems of agricultural progress, and work for the practical application and extensive introduction of the achievements of science and progressive production experience in crop farming and stock-breeding. Research institutions and experimental stations must become important links in agricultural management, and scientists and specialists must become the direct organizers of farm production. Each region or group of regions of the same zonal type should have agricultural research centers, with their own large-scale farms and up-to-date material, and technical resources, to work out recommendations for state farms and kolkhozes applicable to the given district. Agricultural research and educational establishments must be chiefly located in rural areas and be directly associated with farm production, so that students may learn while working and work while learning.

B. THE KOLKHOZES AND STATE FARMS ON THE ROAD TO COMMUNISM; REMOLDING SOCIAL RELATIONS IN THE COUNTRYSIDE.

The economic basis for the development of kolkhozes and state farms lies in the continuous growth and best use of their productive forces, improvement of the organization of production and methods of management, steady rise of labor productivity and strict observance of the principle: higher payment for good work, for better results. On this basis the kolkhozes and state farms will become to an increasing degree enterprises of the Communist type by virtue of their production relations, character of labor, and the living and cultural standard of their personnel.

The policy of the Socialist state in relation to the kolkhozes is based on blending country-wide interests with the material interest of the kolkhozes and their members in the results of their labor. The state will promote the growth of the productive forces of the kolkhoz system and the economic advancement of all kolkhozes. Concurrently, the kolkhoz peasantry must also contribute more widely to the building of Communist society.

The state will insure the full satisfaction of the needs of the kolkhozes in modern machinery, chemicals and other means of production, will train new hundreds of thousands of skilled farm workers, and will considerably increase capital investments in the countryside, in addition to the greater investments by the kolkhozes themselves. The amount of manufactured goods made available to the kolkhoz villages will increase greatly.

Strict observance of their contracted commitments to the

state by the kolkhozes and their members is an irrevocable principle of their participation in the development of the national economy.

The system of state purchasing must be concentrated on increasing the amount and improving the quality of the agricultural products bought on the basis of an all-round advancement of kolkhoz farming. It is essential to coordinate the planning of state purchases and the productions plans of the kolkhozes, with utmost consideration for the interests of agricultural production, its correct disposition and specialization.

The policy in the sphere of the state purchasing prices of agricultural produce and selling prices of means of production for the countryside must take account of the interests of extended reproduction in both industry and agriculture and of the need to accumulate funds in the kolkhozes. It is essential that the level of state purchasing prices encourage the kolkhozes to raise labor productivity and reduce production expenses, since greater farm output and lower production costs are the basis of greater incomes for the kolkhozes.

The proper ratio of accumulation and consumption in the distribution of incomes is a prerequisite of successful kolkhoz development. The kolkhozes cannot develop without continuously extending their commonly owned assets for production, insurance, cultural and community needs. At the same time, it must be a standing rule for every kolkhoz to raise its members' incomes from collective farming and to enhance their living standard as labor productivity rises.

Great importance attaches to improved methods of ratesetting and labor remuneration at kolkhozes, supplementary forms of payment for labor, and other incentives to obtain better production figures. Increasingly equal economic conditions must be provided that will improve the incomes of kolkhozes existing under unequal natural-economic conditions in different zones, and also within the zones, in order to put into effect more consistently the principle of equal pay for equal work on a scale embracing the entire kolkhoz system. Farming on all kolkhozes must be conducted in accordance with a strict principle of profitability.

In its organizational work and economic policy, the party will strive to overcome the lag of the economically weak kolkhozes and to turn all kolkhozes into economically strong, high-income farms in the course of the next few years. The party sets the task of continuously improving and educating kolkhoz personnel, of insuring the further extension of kolkhoz democracy and promoting the principle of collectivism in management.

As the kolkhozes develop, their basic production assets will expand, and modern technical means will become dominant.

The economic advancement of the kolkhozes will make it possible to perfect kolkhoz internal relations: to raise the degree to which production is socialized, to bring the rate setting, organization and payment of labor closer to the level and the forms employed at state enterprises and effect a transition to a guaranteed monthly wage, to develop community services more broadly (public catering, kindergartens and nurseries, and other services, etc.).

At a certain point the collective production at kolkhozes will achieve a level at which it will fully satisfy members' requirements. On this basis, supplementary individual farming will gradually become economically unnecessary. When collective production at the kolkhozes is able to replace in full that of the supplementary individual plot of the kolkhoz members, when the collective farmers see for themselves that their supplementary individual farming is unprofitable, they will give it up of their own accord.

As the productive forces increase, inter-kolkhoz production ties will develop and the socialization of production will transcend the limits of individual kolkhozes. The building, jointly by several kolkhozes, of enterprises and cultural and other welfare institutions, state-kolkhoz power stations and enterprises for the primary processing, storage and transportation of farm products, for various types of building, the manufacture of building materials, etc., should be encouraged. As the commonly-owned assets increase, the kolkhozes will participate more and more in establishing enterprises and cultural and other welfare institutions for general public use, boarding schools, clubs, hospitals and holiday homes. All these developments, which must proceed on a voluntary basis and when the necessary economic conditions are available, will gradually impart to kolkhoz-cooperative property the nature of public property.

The state farms have a long way to travel in their development—to attain high rates of growth of labor productivity, to steadily reduce production costs and raise farm efficiency. This calls for the economically expedient specialization of state farms. Their role in supplying food to the urban population will grow. They must become mechanized and well-organized first-class factories of grain, cotton, meat, milk, wool, vegetables, fruit and other products, and must develop seed farming and pure-strain animal husbandry to the utmost.

The material and technical basis of the state farms will be extended and improved, and the living and cultural conditions at the state farms will approach those in towns. State farm management should follow a more and more democratic pattern which will allot a greater role to the personnel, and to general meetings and production conferences in deciding production, cultural and other community issues.

As the kolkhozes and state farms develop, their production ties with each other and with local industrial enterprises will grow stronger. The practice of jointly organizing various enterprises will expand. This will insure a fuller and more balanced use of manpower and production resources throughout the year, raise the productivity of social labor and enhance the living and cultural standards of the population. Agrarian-industrial associations will gradually emerge wherever economically expedient, in which, given appropriate specialization and cooperation of agricultural and industrial enterprises, agriculture will combine organically with the industrial processing of its produce.

As production in kolkhozes and state farms develops and social relations within them advance, agriculture rises to a higher level, affording the possibility of transition to Communist forms of production and distribution. The kolkhozes will draw level in economic conditions with the nationally-owned agricultural enterprises. They will turn into highly developed mechanized farms. By virtue of high labor productivity all kolkhozes will become economically powerful. Kolkhoz members will be adequately provided and their requirements fully satisfied out of collective-farm production. They will have the services of catering establishments, bakeries, laundries, kindergartens and nurseries, clubs, libraries, and sports grounds. The payment of labor will be the same as at nationally-owned enterprises and they will be provided all forms of social security (pensions, holidays, etc.) out of kolkhoz and state funds.

Gradually, the kolkhoz villages will grow into amalgamated urban communities with modern housing facilities, public amenities and services, and cultural and medical institutions. The rural population will ultimately draw level with the urban population in cultural and living conditions.

Elimination of socio-economic and cultural distinctions between town and country and differences in their living conditions will be one of the greatest gains of Communist construction.

(3.) *Management of the national economy and planning.*

The building of the material and technical basis of communism calls for a continuous improvement in economic management. Chief emphasis at all levels of planning and economic management must be laid on the most rational and effective use of the material, labor and financial resources and natural wealth and on the elimination of excessive expenditures. The immutable law of economic development is to achieve in the interests of society the highest results at the lowest cost.

Planning must at all levels concentrate on the rapid development and introduction of new techniques. It is essential that progressive scientifically expedient standards for the use of means of production be strictly observed in all sectors of the national economy.

The party attaches prime importance to the more effective investment of capital, the choice of the most profitable and economical trends in capital construction, achievement everywhere of the maximum growth of output per invested ruble, and reduction of the time lapse between investment and return. It is necessary continuously to improve the structure of capital investments and to expand that portion of them which is spent on equipment, machinery, and machine tools.

Continuous improvement of the quality of output is an imperative factor of economic development. The quality of goods produced by Soviet enterprises must be considerably higher than that of the best capitalist enterprises. For this purpose, it is necessary to apply a broad set of measures, including public control, and to enhance the role of quality indexes in planning, in the assessment of the work of enterprises and in socialist emulation.

Communist construction presupposes the maximum development of democratic principles of management coupled with a strengthening and improvement of centralized economic management by the state. The economic independence and the rights of local organs and enterprises will continue to expand within the framework of the single national economic plan. Plans and recommendations made at lower levels, beginning with enterprises, must play an increasing role in planning.

Centralized planning should chiefly concentrate on working out and ensuring the fulfillment of the key targets of the economic plans with the greatest consideration paid to recommendations made at lower levels; on coordinating and dove-tailing plans drawn up locally; on spreading scientific and technical achievements and advanced production experience; on enforcing a single state policy in the spheres of technical progress, capital investment, distribution of production, payment of labor, prices, and finance, and a unified system of accounting and statistics.

It is essential that the national economy develop on a strictly proportionate basis, that economic disproportions are prevented in good time, ensuring sufficient economic reserves as a condition for stable high rates of economic development, uninterrupted operation of enterprises and continuous improvement of the people's well-being.

The growing scale of the national economy, the rapid development of science and technology call for an improvement of the scientific level of planning, accounting, statistics, and industrial designing. A better scientific, technical and economic basis for the plans will insure their greater stability, which also presupposes timely correction and amendment of plans in the course of their fulfillment. Planning must be continuous, and the annual and long-term plans must be organically integrated.

Firm and consistent discipline, day-to-day control, and determined elimination of elements of parochialism and of a narrow departmental approach in economic affairs are necessary conditions for successful Communist construction.

There must be a further expansion of the role and responsibility of local bodies in economic management. The transfer of a number of functions of economic management by the all-union bodies to those of the republics, by republican bodies to those of the regions and by regional bodies to those of the districts should be continued. It is necessary to improve the work of the economic councils as the most viable form of management in industry and building that conforms to the present level of the productive forces. The improvement of the work of economic councils within the economic administration areas will also be accompanied by greater coordination of the work of other economic bodies, in order better to organize the planned comprehensive economic development of such major economic areas as the Urals, the Volga area, Siberia, Transcaucasia, the Baltic area, Central Asia, etc.

Extension of operative independence and of the initiative of enterprises on the basis of the state-plan targets is essential in order to mobilize untapped resources and make more effective use of capital investments, production facilities and finances. It is necessary for enterprises to play a substantially greater part in introducing the latest machinery.

The selection, training and promotion of people to head enterprises and kolkhozes, those who organize and manage production, are of decisive importance in economic management. The sphere of material production is the main sphere in the life of society; the most capable people must, therefore, be given leading posts in the sphere of production.

The direct and most active participation of trade unions in elaborating and realizing economic plans, in matters concerning the labor of factory and office workers, in setting up organs of economic administration and of management of enterprises, must be extended more and more at top level and locally. The role of the collectives of factory and office workers in matters concerning the work of enterprises must be enhanced.

In the process of Communist construction economic management will make use of material and moral incentives for high production figures. Proper combination of material and moral labor incentives is a great creative factor in the struggle for Communism. In the course of the advance to Communism the importance of moral labor incentives, public recognition of achieved results and the sense of responsibility of each for the common cause will become continuously greater.

The entire system of planning and assessing the work of central and local organizations, enterprises and collective farms must stimulate their interest in higher plan targets and the maximum dissemination of progressive production experience. Initiative and successes in finding and using new ways of improving the quantitative and qualitative indexes of production should be specially encouraged.

There must be a continuous improvement in rate setting, the system of labor payments and bonuses, in the financial control over the quantity and quality of work, in the elimination of leveling and the stimulation of collective forms of incentives raising the interest of each employee in the high efficiency of the enterprise as a whole.

It is necessary in Communist construction to make full use of commodity-money relations in keeping with their new substance in the Socialist period. In this, such instruments of economic development as cost accounting, money, price, production cost, profit, trade, credit and finance play a big part. When the transition to a one Communist form of people's property and the Communist system of distribution is completed, commodity-money relations will become economically outdated and will wither away.

The important role of the budget in distributing the social product and national income will prevail throughout the period of full-scale Communist construction. There will be a further strengthening of the monetary and credit system, a consolidation of Soviet currency, a steady rise of the rate of exchange of the ruble by virtue of its growing purchasing power, and a strengthening of the role of the ruble in the international arena.

It is necessary to promote profitable operation of enterprises, to work for lower production costs and higher profitability. The price system should be continuously improved in conformity with the tasks of Communist construction, technical progress, growth of production and consumption, and the reduction of production expenditures. Prices must to a growing extent, reflect the socially-necessary outlays of labor, insure return of production and circulation expenditures and a certain profit for each normally operating enterprise. Systematic, economically justified price reductions based on growth of labor productivity and reduction of production costs, are the main trend of the price policy in the period of Communist construction.

Soviet society possesses immense national assets. For this reason, the role of accounting and control over the maintenance and proper use of the national wealth increases. Thrift, good use of every ruble belonging to the people, competent utilization of funds, the continuous improvement of planning and methods of management, improvement of organization and conscious discipline, and development of the initiative of the people are powerful means of accelerating the advance of Soviet society to communism.

2. THE TASKS OF THE PARTY IN IMPROVING
THE LIVING STANDARDS OF THE PEOPLE

The heroic labor of the Soviet people has produced a powerful and versatile economy. There is now every possibility to improve rapidly the living standards of the entire population—the workers, peasants, and intellectuals. The C.P.S.U. sets the historically important task of achieving in the Soviet Union a living standard higher than that of any of the captalist countries.

This task will be effected by: (A) Raising the individual payment of employees according to the quantity and quality of work, coupled with reduction of retail prices and abolition of taxes paid by the population, (B) Increase of the public funds distributed among members of society irrespective of the quantity and quality of their labor, that is, free of charge (education, medical treatment, pensions, maintenance of children at children's institutions, transition to cost-free use of public amenities, etc.).

The rise of the real incomes of the population will be outstripped by rapid increase in the amount of commodities and services, and by far-flung construction of dwellings and cultural and service buildings.

Soviet people will be more prosperous than people in the developed capitalist countries even if average incomes will be equal, because in the Soviet Union the national income is distributed fairly among the members of society and there are no parasitical classes as in the bourgeois countries who appropriate and squander immense wealth plundered from millions of working people.

The party acts upon Lenin's thesis that Communist construction must be based upon the principle of material incentive. In the coming twenty years payment according to one's work will remain the principal source for satisfying the material and cultural needs of the working people.

The disparity between high and comparatively low incomes must gradually shrink. Increasingly greater numbers of unskilled personnel will become skilled, and the diminishing difference in proficiency and labor productivity will be accompanied by a steady reduction of disparities in the level of pay. As the living standard of the entire population rises, low income levels will approach the higher, and the disparity between the incomes of peasants and workers, low-paid and high-paid personnel and the populations of different parts of the country, will gradually shrink.

At the same time, as the country advances towards communism, personal needs will be increasingly met out of public consumption funds, whose rate of growth will exceed the rate of growth of payments for labor. The transition to Communist distribution will be completed after the principle of distribution according to one's work will exhaust itself, that is, when there will be an abundance of material and cultural wealth and labor will become life's prime necessity for all members of society.

A. PROVISION OF A HIGH LEVEL OF INCOME AND CONSUMPTION FOR THE WHOLE POPULATION.

The national income of the U.S.S.R. in the next ten years will increase nearly 150 per cent, and about 400 per cent in twenty years. The real income per head of population will increase by more than 250 per cent in twenty years.

In the course of the coming ten years the real incomes of factory and office workers (including public funds) per employed person will, on the average, be almost doubled, and in twenty years will increase by approximately 200 to 250 per cent. The increase in the real incomes of factory, office and professional workers paid relatively lower wages will be brought to a level at which low-paid brackets throughout the country will be eliminated within ten years. The real incomes of factory and office workers receiving the minimum wages will be approximately trebled (including what they get from public funds) over this period.

By virtue of higher rates of growth of the labor productivity of collective farmers their real incomes will grow more rapidly than the incomes of factory workers, and will, on an average per employed person, more than double in the next ten years and increase more than fourfold in twenty years.

The wages of such numerically large sections of the Soviet intelligentsia as engineers and technicians, agronomists and stockbreeding experts, teachers, medical and cultural workers, will rise considerably.

As the incomes of the population grow, the general level of popular consumption will rise rapidly. The entire population will be able to satisfy to the full its need in high quality and varied foodstuffs. The share of animal products (meat, fats, dairy produce), fruit and high-grade vegetables in popular consumption will rise substantially in the near future. The demand of all sections of the population for high-quality consumer goods: attractive clothes, footwear and goods improving and adorning the daily life of Soviet people, such as comfortable modern furniture, up-to-date domestic goods, a wide range of goods for cultural purposes, etc., will be amply satisfied. Production of motor-cars for the population will be considerably extended.

Output of consumer goods must meet the growing consumer demand in full, and must conform to its changes. Timely output of goods in accordance with the varied demand of the population, with consideration for local, national and climatic conditions, is an imperative requirement for the consumer industries. Good shopping facilities will be arranged throughout the country, this being a necessary and important condition for the satisfaction of the growing requirements of the population.

The second decade will see an abundance of material and cultural benefits for the whole population, and material prerequisites will be created to complete the transition to the Communist principle of distribution according to need in the period to follow.

B. SOLUTION OF THE HOUSING PROBLEM AND IMPROVEMENT OF LIVING CONDITIONS.

The C.P.S.U. undertakes the task of solving the most acute problem in the improvement of the well-being of the Soviet people—the housing problem. As a result of the second decade, every family, including newly-weds, will have a comfortable flat conforming to the requirements of hygiene and cultured living. Peasant houses of the old type will, in the main, give place to new modern dwellings, or—wherever possible—they will be rebuilt and appropriately improved. In the course of the second decade housing will be gradually provided to all citizens rent free.

An extensive program of public-services construction and of improvements in all towns and workers' estates will be carried out in the coming period, which will involve completion of their electrification, the necessary gasification, provision of public-transport facilities and waterworks, and measures for the further improvement of sanitary conditions in towns and other populated localities, including tree planting, pond building and effective measures to combat air, soil and water pollution. Well-appointed small and middle-size towns will be increasingly developed, making for better and healthier living conditions.

Public-transport facilities (tramways, buses, trolley buses and subways) will become free in the course of the second decade, and at the end of it such public amenities as water, gas and heating will also be free.

C. REDUCTION OF WORKING HOURS AND THE FURTHER IMPROVEMENT OF WORKING CONDITIONS.

In the coming ten years the country will go over to a six-hour working day with one day off a week, or a thirty-four-to-thirty-six-hour working week with two days off, and in underground and harmful jobs to a five-hour working day or a thirty-hour, five-day working week.

By virtue of a corresponding rise in labor productivity, transition to a still shorter working week will be begun in the second decade.

The Soviet Union will thus have the world's shortest and, concurrently, the most productive and highest-paid working day. Working people will have much more leisure time, and this will add to their opportunities of improving their cultural and technical level.

The length of the annual paid holidays of working people will be increased together with the reduction of the working day. Gradually the minimum length of leave for all industrial, professional and office workers will increase to three weeks and subsequently to one month. Paid holidays will be gradually extended to kolkhoz members.

All-round measures to make working conditions healthier and lighter constitute an important task in improving the well-being of the people. Modern means of labor safety and hygiene designed to prevent occupational injuries and diseases will be introduced at all enterprises. Night shifts will be gradually abolished at enterprises, save those where round-the-clock operation is required by the production process or the need to service the population.

D. HEALTH SERVICES AND MEASURES FOR INCREASED LONGEVITY.

The Socialist state is the only state which undertakes to protect and continuously improve the health of the whole population. This is provided for by a system of socio-economic and medical measures. There will be an extensive program designed to prevent and sharply reduce diseases, wipe out mass infectious diseases and further increase longevity. The needs of the urban and rural population in all forms of highly-qualified medical services will be met in full. This calls for the extensive building of medical institutions, including hospitals and sanatoria, the equipment of all medical institutions with modern appliances, and regular medical check-ups for the entire population. Special emphasis must be laid on extending in town and country the network of mother-and-child health institutions (maternity homes, medical consultation centers, children's health homes and hospitals, forest schools, etc.)

In addition to the existing free medical services, accommodation of sick persons at sanatoria and the dispensing of medicines will become gratuitous. In order to afford the population an opportunity to rest in an out-of-town environment, holiday homes, boarding houses, country hotels and tourist camps will be built, where working people will be accommodated at a reasonable charge or, by way of a bonus, as well as at a discount or gratis.

The party considers it a most important task to ensure the education from early childhood of a sound young generation harmoniously developed physically and spiritually. This calls for utmost encouragement of all forms of mass sport and physical training, specifically at schools, and for drawing greater and greater sections of the population, particularly the youth, into sports.

E. IMPROVEMENT OF FAMILY CONDITIONS AND OF THE POSITION OF WOMEN. MAINTENANCE OF CHILDREN AND INCAPACITATED PEOPLE AT PUBLIC EXPENSE.

The remnants of the unequal position of women in domestic life must be totally eliminated. Social and living conditions must be provided to enable women to combine happy motherhood with increasingly active and creative participation in social labor and social activities, and in scientific and artistic pursuits. Women must be given relatively lighter and yet sufficiently well-paid jobs. Leave of absence from work during confinement will be of longer duration.

It is essential to provide conditions to reduce and lighten the domestic work of women, and later to make possible the replacement of domestic work by public forms of satisfying the daily needs of the family. Up-to-date inexpensive domestic machinery, appliances and electrical devices will be made extensively available for this purpose, the needs of the population in service establishments will be fully met in the next few years.

The extension of public catering, including canteens at enterprises, institutions and in big dwelling houses, until it meets the deamands of the population, calls for special attention. The service at catering establishments and the quality of catering must be radically improved, so that meals at public catering establishments should be tasty and nourishing and should cost the family less than meals cooked at home. Price reductions in public catering will keep ahead of price reductions for foodstuffs in the shops. By virtue of this public catering will be able to take precedence over home cooking within ten to fifteen years.

The transition to free public catering (midday meals) at enterprises and institutions, and for collective farmers at work will begin in the second decade.

A happy childhood for every child is one of the most important and noble aspects of Communist construction. The development of a ramified network of children's institutions will make it possible for more and more families, and in the second decade for every family, to keep children and adolescents free of charge at children's establishments if they so desire. State and community children's institutions will be able to accommodate the bulk of children under school age within the next few years.

In town and country there will be full and cost-free satisfaction of the need in kindergartens, playgrounds, nurseries, and young pioneer camps, the provision of mass boarding schools with free maintenance of children, free hot meals at all schools, introduction of extended school hours with free dinners for schoolchildren, and free issue of school uniforms and educational aids.

In keeping with the growth of the national income, the state, the trade unions and the kolkhozes will in the course of the twenty years gradually undertake maintenance of all citizens incapacitated through old age or some disability. Sickness and temporary disability grants and old-age pensions will be extended to kolkhoz members, old-age and disability pensions will be steadily raised. The number of comfortable homes for old people and invalids providing free accommodations for all applicants will be greatly increased in town and country.

By fulfilling the tasks set by the party for the improvement of the well-being of the people, the Soviet Union will make considerable headway towards the practical realization of the Communist principle of distribution according to need.

At the end of the twenty years public consumption funds will total about half of the aggregate real income of the population. This will make it possible to provide at public expense:

Free maintenance of children at children's institutions and boarding schools (if parents wish),

Maintenance of disabled people,

Free education at all educational establishments,

Free medical services for all citizens, including the supply of medicines and the treatment of sick persons at sanatoria,

Rent-free housing and, later, free public services, free public transport facilities,

Free use of some types of communal services,

Steady reduction of charges for, and, partially free use of holiday homes, boarding houses and tourist camps,

Increasingly broad provision of the population with benefits, privileges and scholarships (grants to unmarried mothers, scholarships for students),

Gradual introduction of free public catering (midday meals) at enterprises and institutions, and for kolkhoz farmers at work.

The Soviet state will thus demonstrate to the world a truly full satisfaction of all the growing material and cultural requirements of man. The living standard of Soviet people will improve all the faster, the faster the productive forces of the country develop and labor productivity grows, and the more broadly the creative energy of the Soviet people comes into play.

The set program can be fulfilled with success under conditions of peace. Complications in the international situation and the resultant necessity of increasing defense expenditures may hold up the fulfillment of the plans for raising the living standard of the people. An enduring normalization of international relations, reduction of military expenditures and, in particular, the realization of general and complete disarmament under an appropriate agreement between countries, would make it possible greatly to surpass the plans for raising the people's living standard.

The fulfillment of the grand program of improving the living standard of the Soviet people will have world-wide historic impact. The party calls on the Soviet people to work perseveringly, with inspiration. Every one of the working people of the Soviet Union must do his duty in the building of a Communist society and in the struggle to fulfill the program for the improvement of the people's living standard.

3. The Tasks of the Party in the Spheres of State Development and the Further Promotion of Socialist Democracy

The dictatorship of the proletariat, born of the Socialist revolution, has played an epoch-making role by insuring the victory of socialism in the U. S. S. R. In the course of Socialist construction, however, it underwent changes. After the exploiting classes had been abolished, the state function of suppressing their resistance ceased to exist. The chief functions of the Socialist state—economic and organizational, cultural and educational—have developed in full measure. The Socialist state has entered a new phase.

The state has begun to grow over into a nation-wide organization of the working people of Socialist society. Proletarian democracy is becoming more and more a Socialist democracy of the people as a whole. The working class is the only class in history that does not aim to perpetuate its power. Having brought about a complete and final victory of socialism—the first phase of communism—and the transition of society to the full-scale construction of communism, the dictatorship of the proletariat has fulfilled its historic mission and has ceased to be indispensable in the U. S. S. R. from the point of view of the tasks of internal development.

The state, which arose as a state of the dictatorship of the proletariat, has become a state of the entire people, an organ expressing the interests and will of the people as a whole. Since the working class is the foremost and best organized force of Soviet society, it plays a leading role also in the period of the full-scale construction of communism. The working class will have completed its function of leader of society after communism is built and classes disappear.

The party holds that the dictatorship of the working class will cease to be necessary before the state withers away. The state as an organization embracing the entire people will survive until the complete victory of communism.

Expressing the will of the people, it must organize the building up of the material and technical basis of communism, and the transformation of Socialist relations into Communist relations, must exercise control over the measure of work and rate of consumption, promote welfare, protect the rights and freedoms of Soviet citizens, Socialist law and order and Socialist property, instil in the people conscious discipline and a Communist attitude to labor, guarantee the defense and security of the country, promote fraternal cooperation with the Socialist countries, uphold world peace and maintain normal relations with all countries.

Vigorous extension and perfection of Socialist democracy, active participation of all citizens in the administration of the state, in the management of economic and cultural development, improvement of the Government apparatus, and increased control over its activity by the people constitute the main direction in which Socialist statehood develops in the period of the building of communism.

As Socialist democracy develops, the organs of state power will gradually be transformed into organs of public self-government. The Leninist principle of democratic centralism, which insures the proper combination of centralized leadership with the maximum encouragement of local initiative, the extension of the rights of the union republics and greater creative activity of the masses, will be promoted. It is essential to strengthen discipline, control the activities of all the elements of the administrative apparatus, check the execution of the decisions and laws of the Soviet state and heighten the responsibility of every official for the strict and timely implementation of these laws.

(1.) *The soviets and promotion of the democratic principles of government.*

The role of the soviets, which have become an all-inclusive organization of the people embodying their unity, will grow as Communist construction progresses. The soviets, which combine the features of a government body and a social organization, operate more and more like social organizations, with the masses participating in their work extensively and directly.

The party considers it essential to perfect the forms of popular representation and promote the democratic principles of the soviet electoral system.

In nominating candidates for election to the soviets, it is necessary to guarantee the widest and fullest discussion of the moral qualities and the activities of the candidates at meetings and in the press to insure the election of the worthiest and most authoritative of them.

To improve the work of the soviets and bring fresh forces into them, it is desirable that at least one-third of the total number of deputies to a soviet should be elected anew each time so that more hundreds of thousands and millions of working people may learn to govern the state.

The party considers systematic renewal of the leading bodies necessary to bring a wider range of able persons into them and rule out abuses of authority by individual Government officials. It is advisable to introduce the principle that the leading officials of the union, republican and local bodies should be elected to their offices, as a rule, for not more than three consecutive terms. In those cases when the personal gifts of the official in question are generally believed to make his further activity within a leading body useful and necessary, his re-election may be allowed. His election shall be considered valid, not if he wins with a simple majority, but if not less than three quarters of the votes are cast in his favor.

The party regards the perfection of the principles of Socialist democracy and their rigid observance as a most important task. It is necessary to develop more and more fully regular accountability of soviets and deputies to their constituents and the right of the electorate to recall ahead of term deputies who have not justified confidence placed in them, publicity and the free and full discussion of all the important questions of Government and of economic and cultural development at the meetings of soviets, regular accountability of executive Government bodies to meetings of soviets—from top to bottom, checking the work of these bodies and control over their activity, systematic discussion by the soviets of questions raised by deputies, criticism of shortcomings in the work of government, economic and other organizations.

Every deputy to a soviet must take an active part in Government affairs and carry on definite work. The role of the standing committees of the soviets will become greater. The standing committees of the Supreme Soviets must systematically control the activities of ministries, departments, and economic councils. They must actively contribute to the implementation of the decisions adopted by the respective Supreme Soviets. To improve the work of the legislative bodies and increase control over the executive bodies, deputies shall be periodically released from their official duties for full-time committee work.

An increasing number of questions which now come under the jurisdiction of the departments and sections of executive bodies must be gradually referred to the standing committees of the local soviets for decision.

The rights of the local Soviets of Working People's Deputies (local self-government) will be extended. Local soviets will make final decisions on all questions of local significance.

Special attention should be paid to the strengthening of the district bodies. As kolkhoz-cooperative and public property draws closer together, a single democratic body administering all enterprises, organizations and institutions at district level will gradually take shape.

The participation of social organizations and associations of the people in the legislative activity of the representative bodies of the Soviet state will be extended. The trade unions, the Komsomol and other mass organizations as represented by their all-union and republican bodies must be entitled to take legislative initiative, that is, to propose draft laws.

Discussion by the people of draft laws and other decisions of both national and local significance must become the rule. The most important draft laws should be put to a nation-wide referendum.

The C.P.S.U. attaches great importance to improving the work of the government apparatus, which is largely responsible for the proper utilization of all the resources of the country and the timely settlement of all questions relating to the cultural and every-day needs of the people. The Soviet Government apparatus must be simple, qualified, inexpensive, efficient and free of bureaucracy, formalism and red tape.

Constant state and public control is an important means of accomplishing this task. In keeping with Lenin's directions, permanent control bodies must function to combine state control with public inspection at the center and in the localities. The party regards inspection by people's control bodies as an effective means of drawing large sections of the people into the management of state affairs, and control over the strict observance of legality as a means of perfecting the government apparatus, eradicating bureaucracy and promptly realizing proposals made by the people.

The government apparatus of the Socialist states serves the people and is accountable to them. Negligence and abuse of power by an official must be resolutely combatted and the official concerned must be severely punished regardless of the position he holds. It is the duty of Soviet people to see to it that legality and law and order are rigidly enforced. They must not tolerate any abuses, and must combat them.

The party holds that democratic principles in administration must be developed further. The principle of electivity and accountability to representative bodies and to the electorate will be gradually extended to all the leading officials of government bodies.

An effort should be made to insure that the salaried government staffs are reduced, that ever larger sections of the people learn to take part in administration and that work on government staffs eventually ceases to constitute a profession.

While every executive must be held strictly and personally responsible for the job entrusted to him, it is necessary consistently to exercise the principle of collective leadership at all levels of the government and economic apparatus.

The broadest democracy must go hand in hand with unrelenting observance of comradely discipline by the working people, which it must promote through control from above and from below. The important thing in the activity of all government bodies is organizational work among the masses, proper selection, testing and appraisal of officials on the strength of their practical work, and control over the actual fulfillment of the assignments and decisions of the leading bodies.

The further promotion of Socialist law and order and the improvement of legal norms governing economic, organizational, cultural and educational work and contributing to the accomplishment of the tasks of Communist construction and to the all-round development of the individual are very important.

The transition to communism means the fullest extension of personal freedom and the rights of Soviet citizens. Socialism has granted the working people the broadest guaranteed rights and freedoms. Communism will bring the working people further great rights and opportunities.

The party calls for enforcing strict observance of Socialist legality, to eradicate all violations of law and order, abolish crime and remove all the causes of crime.

Justice in the U.S.S.R. is exercised in full conformity with the law. It is based on truly democratic lines: Election and accountability of the judges and people's assessors, the right to recall them before expiration of their term, the publicity of court proceedings, and the participation of prosecutors and lawyers appointed by social organizations in the work of courts with strict observance of legality and all the rules of judicial procedure. The democratic foundations of justice will be developed and improved with the bodies of investigation and inquest.

There should be no room for law-breakers and criminals in a society building communism. But as long as there are criminal offenses, it is necessary severely to punish those who commit crimes dangerous to society, violate the rules of the Socialist community and refuse to live by honest labor. Attention should be focused on crime prevention.

Higher standards of living and culture and greater social consciousness of the people will pave the way to the ultimate replacement of judicial punishment by measures of public influence and education. Under socialism, anyone who has strayed from the path of a working man can return to useful activity.

The whole system of government and social organizations educates the people in a spirit of voluntary and conscientious fulfillment of their duties and leads to a gradual fusion of rights and duties to form the integral rules of Communist society.

(2.) *The further heightening of the role of social organizations. The state and communism.*

The role of social organizations increases in the period of the full-scale construction of communism. The trade unions acquire particular importance as schools of administration and economic management, as schools of communism. The party will help the trade unions to take a growing share in economic management and to make the standing production conferences increasingly effective in improving the work of enterprises and exercising control over production. The trade unions shall:

Work constantly to increase the Communist consciousness of the masses, organize an emulation movement for Communist labor and help the people in learning to manage state and social affairs, take an active part in controlling the measure of labor and rate of consumption;

Encourage the activity of factory and office workers, enlisting their aid in the work for continuous technical progress, for higher productivity of labor, for the fulfillment and overfulfillment of state plans and assignments;

Work steadfastly for the improvement of the skill of factory and office workers and their working and living conditions, protect the material interests and rights of the working people;

Insure that housing and cultural development plans are fulfilled and that public catering, trade, social insurance and health resort services are improved;

Insure control over the spending of public consumption funds and over the work of all enterprises and institutions serving the people;

Improve cultural services and recreation facilities for the working people, encourage physical training and sports.

The Young Communist League, a voluntary social organization of the youth which helps the party to educate young people in a Communist spirit, enlist them in the practical job of building the new society and train a generation of harmoniously developed people who will live, work and manage public affairs under communism, will play a greater role. The party regards the youth as a great creative force in the Soviet people's struggle for communism.

The Y.C.L. must display greater initiative in all fields of activity, must encourage the activity and labor heroism of the youth. Y.C.L. organizations must concentrate on educating the youth in a spirit of utmost devotion to their people, the Communist party and country, the Communist cause, constant preparedness for labor for the good of the country and for overcoming all difficulties and improving the general education and technical knowledge of all young men and women.

It is the sacred duty of the Y.C.L. to prepare young people for the defense of their Socialist country, to educate them as selfless patriots capable of firmly repelling any enemy and also to educate the youth in a spirit of strict adherence to Communist moral principles and standards. Y.C.L. influence in the schools and Young Pioneer organizations must contribute actively to the moulding of a buoyant, industrious and physically and morally sound generation.

A greater role will be played by cooperatives—kolkhozes, consumers', housing and other cooperative organizations—as a form of drawing the masses into Communist construction, as media of Communist education and schools of public self-government.

Other social associations of the working people—scientific and scientific-technical societies, rationalisers' and inventors' organizations, associations of writers, artists and journalists, cultural-education organizations, and sports societies will likewise be developed.

The party regards it as a major task of the social organizations to promote labor emulation and Communist forms of labor in every possible way, to encourage the activity of working people in building a Communist society, to work for the improvement of the living conditions of the people. Social organizations should be induced to take a greater part in managing cultural and health institutions; within the next few years they should be entrusted with the management of theatres and concert halls, clubs, libraries and other state-controlled cultural-education establishments; they should be encouraged to play a greater part in promoting public order, particularly through the people's volunteer squads and comradely courts.

To extend the independent activities of social organizations, the party considers it necessary further to reduce their salaried staffs from top to bottom, to renew each public body by roughly as many as one-half of its members at the regular election and to consider it advisable for the leading functionaries of social organizations not to be elected, as a general rule, for more than two consecutive terms.

As Socialist statehood develops, it will gradually become public Communist self-government which will embrace the Soviets, trade unions, cooperatives and other mass organizations of the people. This process will represent a still greater development of democracy, ensuring the active participation of all members of society in the management of public affairs.

Public functions similar to those performed by the state today in the sphere of economic and cultural management will be preserved under communism and will be modified and perfected as society develops. But the character of the functions and the ways in which they are carried out will be different from those under socialism. The bodies in charge of planning, accounting, economic management and cultural advancement, now Government bodies, will lose their political character and will become organs of public self-government. Communist society will be a highly organized community of working men. Universally recognized rules of Communist conduct will be established whose observance will become an organic need and habit with everyone.

Historical development is bound to lead to the withering away of the state. To insure that the state withers away completely, it is necessary to provide both internal conditions —the building of a developed Communist society—and external conditions—the final settlement of the contradictions between capitalism and communism in the world arena in favor of communism.

(3.) *The strengthening of the armed forces and the defense potential of the Soviet Union.*

With the wholehearted support of the entire Soviet people, the C.P.S.U. steadfastly upholds and defends the gains of socialism and the cause of world peace, and works tirelessly to deliver mankind for all time from wars of aggression. The Leninist principle of peaceful coexistence has been, and remains, the general principle of the foreign policy of the Soviet state.

The Soviet Union perseveringly seeks to bring about the realization of the proposals for general and complete disarmament under strict international control. But the imperialist countries stubbornly refuse to accept these proposals, and feverishly build up their armed forces. They refuse to reconcile themselves to the existence of the world Socialist system, and openly proclaim their insane plans for the liquidation of the Soviet Union and the other Socialist states through war. This obliges the Communist party, the armed forces, the state security organs and all the peoples of the U.S.S.R. to be keenly vigilant with regard to the aggressive intrigues of the enemies of peace, always to protect peaceful labor, and to be constantly prepared to take up arms in defense of their country.

The party maintains that as long as imperialism survives, the threat of aggressive wars will remain. The C.P.S.U. regards the defense of the Socialist motherland, and the strengthening of the defense potential of the U.S.S.R., of the might of the Soviet armed forces, as a sacred duty of the party and the Soviet people as a whole, as a most important function of the Socialist state. The Soviet Union sees it as its internationalist duty to guarantee, together with the other Socialist countries, the reliable defense and security of the entire Socialist camp.

In terms of internal conditions, the Soviet Union needs no army. But since the danger of war coming from the imperialist camp persists, and since complete and general disarmament has not been achieved, the C.P.S.U. considers it necesssary to maintain the defensive power of the Soviet state and the combat preparedness of its armed forces at a level insuring the decisive and complete defeat of any enemy who dares to encroach upon the Soviet Union. The Soviet state will see to it that its armed forces are powerful; that they have the most up-to-date means of defending the country—atomic and thermonuclear weapons, rockets of every range, and that they keep all types of military equipment and all weapons up to standard.

The party educates the Communists and all Soviet people in the spirit of constant preparedness for the defense of their Socialist country, of love of their armed forces. Defense of the country, and service in the Soviet armed forces, is a lofty and honorable duty of Soviet citizens.

The C.P.S.U. is doing everything to insure that the Soviet armed forces are a well-knit and smoothly operating organism, that they have a high standard of organization and discipline, carry out in exemplary fashion the tasks assigned them by the party, the Government and the people, and are prepared at any moment to administer a crushing rebuff to imperialist aggressors. One-man leadership is a major principle of the organization of the Soviet armed forces.

The party will work indefatigably to train army and navy

officers and political personnel fully devoted to the Communist cause and recruited among the finest representatives of the Soviet people. It considers it necessary for the officer corps tirelessly to master Marxist-Leninist theory, to possess a high standard of military-technical training, meet all the requirements of modern military theory and practice, strengthen military discipline. All Soviet soldiers must be educated in the spirit of unqualified loyalty to the people, to the Communist cause, of readiness to spare no effort and, if necessary, to give their lives in the defense of their Socialist country.

Party leadership of the armed forces, and the increased role and influence of the party organizations in the army and navy are the bedrock of military development. The party works unremittingly to increase its organizing and guiding influence on the entire life and activity of the army, air force and navy, to rally the servicemen round the Communist party and the Soviet Government, to strengthen the unity of the armed forces and the people, and to educate the soldiers in the spirit of courage, bravery and heroism, of readiness at any moment to take up the defense of their Soviet country, which is building communism.

4. THE TASKS OF THE PARTY IN THE FIELD OF NATIONAL RELATIONS

Under socialism the nations flourish and their sovereignty grows stronger. The development of nations does not proceed along lines of strengthening national barriers, national narrowmindedness and egoism, as it does under capitalism, but along lines of their association, fraternal mutual assistance and friendship. The appearance of new industrial centers, the prospecting and development of mineral deposits, the virgin land development project and the growth of all modes of transport increase the mobility of the population and promote greater intercourse between the peoples of the Soviet Union.

People of many nationalities live together and work in harmony in the Soviet republics. The boundaries between the constituent republics of the U.S.S.R. are increasingly losing their former significance, since all the nations are equal, their life is based on a common Socialist foundation, the material and spiritual needs of every people are satisfied to the same extent, and they are all united in a single family by common vital interests and are advancing together to the common goal—communism.

Spiritual features deriving from the new type of social relations and embodying the finest traditions of the peoples of the U.S.S.R. have taken shape and are common to Soviet men and women of different nationalities.

Full-scale Communist construction constitutes a new stage in the development of national relations in the U.S.S.R. in which the nations will draw still closer together until complete unity is achieved. The building of the material and technical basis of communism leads to a still greater association of the Soviet peoples. The exchange of material and cultural wealth between nations becomes more and more intensive, and the contribution of each republic to the common cause of Communist construction increases.

Obliteration of distinctions between classes and the development of Communist social relations make for a greater social homogeneity of nations and contribute to the development of common Communist traits in their culture, morals and way of living, to a further strengthening of their mutual trust and friendship.

With the victory of communism in the U.S.S.R., the nations will draw still closer together, their economic and ideological unity will increase and the Communist traits common to their spiritual make-up will develop. However, the effacement of national distinctions, and especially of language distinctions, is a considerably longer process than the effacement of class distinctions.

The party approaches all questions of national relationships arising in the course of Communist construction from the standpoint of proletarian internationalism and firm pursuance of the Leninist national policy. The party neither ignores nor over-accentuates national characteristics.

The party sets the following tasks in the sphere of national relations:

A. To continue the all-round economic and cultural development of all the Soviet nations, insuring their increasingly closer fraternal cooperation, mutual aid, unity and affinity in all spheres of life, thus achieving the utmost strengthening of the Union of Soviet Socialist Republics; to make full use of, and advance the forms of, national statehood of the peoples of the U.S.S.R.;

B. In the economic sphere, it is necessary to pursue the

line of comprehensive development of the economies of the Soviet republics, effect a rational geographic location of production and a planned working of natural wealth, and promote Socialist division of labor among the republics, unifying and combining their economic efforts, and properly balancing the interests of the state as a whole and those of each Soviet republic.

The extension of the rights of the union republics in economic management having produced substantial positive results, such measures may also be carried out in the future, with due regard to the fact that the creation of the material and technical basis of communism will call for still greater interconnection and mutual assistance between the Soviet republics. The closer the intercourse between the nations and the greater the awareness of the country-wide tasks, the more successfully can manifestations of parochialism and national egoism be overcome.

In order to insure the successful accomplishment of the tasks of Communist construction and the coordination of economic activities, inter-republican economic organs may be set up in some zones, notably for such matters as irrigation, power grids, transport, etc.

The party will continue its policy of promoting the actual equality of all nations and nationalities with full consideration for their interests and devoting special attention to those areas of the country which are in need of more rapid development. Benefits growing in the course of Communist construction must be fairly distributed among all nations and nationalities;

C. To work for the further all-round development of the Socialist cultures of the peoples of the U.S.S.R., the big scale of Communist construction and the new victories of Communist ideology are enriching the cultures of the peoples of the U.S.S.R., which are Socialist in content and national in form. The ideological unity of the nations and nationalities is growing, and there is a rapprochement of their cultures. The historical experience of the development of Socialist nations shows that national forms do not ossify; they change, advance and draw closer together, shedding all outdated traits that contradict the new living conditions. An international culture common to all the Soviet nations is developing. The cultural treasures of each nation are increasingly augmented by works of international import.

Attaching decisive importance to the development of the Socialist content of the cultures of the peoples of the U.S.S.R., the party will promote their further mutual enrichment and rapprochement, the consolidation of their international basis, and thereby the formation of the future single world-wide culture of Communist society. While supporting the progressive traditions of each people, and making them the property of all Soviet people, the party will in all ways further new revolutionary traditions of the builders of communism common to all nations.

D. To continue promoting the free development of the languages of the peoples of the U.S.S.R. and the complete freedom of every citizen of the U.S.S.R. to speak, and to bring up and educate his children in any language, ruling out all privileges, restrictions or compulsions in the use of this or that language. By virtue of the fraternal friendship and mutual trust of peoples, national languages are developing on a basis of equality and mutual enrichment.

The voluntary study of Russian in addition to the native language is of positive significance, since it facilitates reciprocal exchanges of experience and access of every nation and nationality to the cultural gains of all the other peoples of the U.S.S.R., and to world culture. The Russian language has, in effect, become the common medium of intercourse and cooperation between all the peoples of the U.S.S.R.

E. To pursue consistently as heretofore the principles of internationalism in the field of national relations, to strengthen the friendship of peoples as one of the most important gains of socialism, to conduct a relentless struggle against manifestations and survivals of nationalism and chauvinism of all types, against trends of national narrow-mindedness and exclusiveness, idealization of the past and the veiling of social contradictions in the history of peoples, and against obsolete customs and habits. The growing scale of Communist construction calls for the continuous exchange of trained personnel among the nations. Manifestations of national aloofness in the education and employment of workers of different nationalities in the Soviet republics are impermissible. The liquidation of manifestations of nationalism is in the interests of all nations and nationalities of the U.S.S.R. Every Soviet republic can continue to flourish and strengthen only in the great family of fraternal Socialist nations of the U.S.S.R.

5. THE TASKS OF THE PARTY IN THE SPHERES OF IDEOLOGY, EDUCATION, INSTRUCTION, SCIENCE AND CULTURE

Soviet society has made great progress in the Socialist education of the masses, in the molding of active builders of socialism. But even after the Socialist system has triumphed, there persist in the minds and behavior of people survivals of capitalism, which hamper the progress of society.

In the struggle for the victory of communism, ideological work becomes an increasingly powerful factor. The higher the social consciousness of the members of society, the more fully and broadly their creative activities come into play in the building of the material and technical basis of communism, in the development of Communist forms of labor and new relations between people, and, consequently, the more rapidly and successfully the building of communism proceeds.

The party considers that the paramount task in the ideological field in the present period is to educate all working people in a spirit of ideological integrity and devotion to communism, and cultivate in them a Communist attitude to labor and the social economy, to eliminate completely the survivals of bourgeois views and morals, to insure the all-round, harmonious development of the individual, to create a truly rich spiritual culture. Special importance is attached by the party to the molding of the rising generation.

The molding of the new man is effected through his own active participation in Communist construction and the development of Communist principles in the economic and social spheres, under the influence of the educational work carried out by the party, the state, and various social organizations, work in which the press, radio, cinema and television play an important part. As Communist forms of social organization are created, devotion to Communist ideas will become stronger in life and work and in human relations, and people will develop the ability to enjoy the benefits of communism in a rational way. Joint planned labor by the members of society, their daily participation in the management of state and public affairs, and the development of Communist relations of comradely cooperation and mutual support recast the minds of people in a spirit of collectivism, industry and humanism.

Increased Communist consciousness of the people furthers the ideological and political unity of the workers, collective farmers and intellectuals and promotes their gradual fusion in the single collective of the working people of Communist society.

The party sets the following tasks:

(1.) *In the field of development of Communist consciousness.*

A. The Shaping of a Scientific World Outlook.

Under socialism and at a time when a Communist society is being built, when spontaneous economic development has given way to the conscious organization of production and social life as a whole, and when theory is daily translated into practice, the shaping of a scientific world outlook in all working people is of prime importance. The ideological basis of this world outlook is shaped as Marxism-Leninism, an integral and harmonious system of philosophical, economic and socio-political views. The party calls for the education of the population as a whole in the spirit of scientific communism and strives to insure that all working people master the ideas of Marxism-Leninism, that they fully understand the course and perspectives of world development, take a correct view of international and domestic events and consciously build their life on Communist lines. Communist ideas and Communist deeds should blend organically in the behavior of every person and in the activities of all collectives and organizations.

The theoretical elaboration and timely practical solution of new problems raised by life are essential to the successful advance of society to communism. Theory must continue to illumine the road of practice, and help detect and eliminate difficulties and contradictions hindering successful Communist construction. The party regards one of its most important duties to further elaborate Marxist-Leninist theory by studying and generalizing new phenomena in the life of Soviet society and the experience of the world revolutionary working-class and liberation movements, and creatively to combine the theory and the practice of Communist construction.

B. LABOR EDUCATION.

The party sees the development of a Communist attitude to labor in all members of society as its chief educational task. Labor for the benefit of society is the sacred duty of all. Any labor for society, whether physical or mental, is honorable and commands respect. Exemplary labor and outstanding management in the social economy should serve to educate all working people.

Everything required for life and human progress is created by labor. Hence everyone must take part in creating the means which are indispensable for his life and work and for the welfare of society. Anyone who received any benefits from society without doing his share of work would be a parasite living at the expense of others.

It is impossible for a man in Communist society not to work, for neither his social consciousness nor public opinion would permit it. Work according to one's ability will become a habit, a prime necessity of life, for every member of society.

C. THE AFFIRMATION OF COMMUNIST MORALITY.

In the course of transition to communism, the moral principles of society become increasingly important, the sphere of action of the moral factor expands and the importance of the administrative control of human relations diminishes accordingly. The party will encourage all forms of conscious civic self-discipline leading to the assertion and promotion of the basic rules of the Communist way of life.

The Communists reject the class morality of the exploiters; in contrast to the perverse, selfish views and morals of the old world, they promote Communist morality, which is the noblest and most just morality, for it expresses the interests and ideals of the whole of working mankind.

Communism makes the elementary standards of morality and justice, which were distorted or shamelessly flouted under the power of the exploiters, into inviolable rules for relations both between individuals and between peoples. Communist morality encompasses the fundamental norms of human morality which the masses of the people evolved in the course of millenniums as they fought against vice and social oppression. The revolutionary morality of the working class is of particular importance to the moral advancement of society. As Socialist and Communist construction progresses, Communist morality is enriched with new principles, a new content.

The party holds that the moral code of the builder of communism should comprise the following principles:

Devotion to the Communist cause, love of the Socialist motherland and of the other Socialist countries;

Conscientious labor for the good of society—he who does not work, neither shall he eat;

Concern on the part of everyone for the preservation and growth of public wealth;

A high sense of public duty, intolerance of actions harmful to the public interest;

Collectivism and comradely mutual assistance: one for all and all for one;

Humane relations and mutual respect between individuals —man is to man a friend, comrade and brother;

Honesty and truthfulness, moral purity, modesty and guilelessness in social and private life;

Mutual respect in the family, and concern for the upbringing of children;

An uncompromising attitude to injustice, parasitism, dishonesty and careerism;

Friendship and brotherhood among all peoples of the U.S.S.R., intolerance of national and racial hatred;

An uncompromising attitude to the enemies of communism, peace and the freedom of nations;

Fraternal solidarity with the working people of all countries, and with all peoples.

D. THE PROMOTION OF PROLETARIAN INTERNATIONALISM AND SOCIALIST PATRIOTISM.

The party will untiringly educate Soviet people in the spirit of proletarian internationalism and will vigorously promote the international solidarity of the working people. In fostering the Soviet people's love of their country, the party maintains that with the emergence of the world Socialist system the patriotism of the members of Socialist society is expressed in devotion and loyalty to their own country and to the entire comity of Socialist countries.

Socialist patriotism and Socialist internationalism necessarily imply proletarian solidarity with the working class and all working people of all countries. The party will continue perseveringly to combat the reactionary ideology of bourgeois nationalism, racism and cosmopolitanism.

E. ALL-ROUND AND HARMONIOUS DEVELOPMENT OF THE INDIVIDUAL.

In the period of transition to communism, there are greater opportunities of educating a new man, who will harmoniously combine spiritual wealth, moral purity and a perfect physique.

All-round development of the individual has been made possible by historic social gains—freedom from exploitation, unemployment and poverty, from discrimination on account of sex, origin, nationality or race. Every member of society is provided with equal opportunities for education and creative labor. Relations of dependence and inequality between people in public affairs and in family life disappear. The personal dignity of each citizen is protected by society. Each is guaranteed an equal and free choice of occupation and profession with due regard to the interests of society.

As less and less time is spent on material production, the individual is afforded ever greater opportunities to develop his abilities, gifts and talents in the fields of production, science, engineering, literature and the arts. People will increasingly devote their leisure to public pursuits, cultural intercourse, intellectual and physical development and artistic endeavor. Physical training and sports will become part and parcel of the everyday life of people.

F. ELIMINATION OF THE SURVIVALS OF CAPITALISM IN THE MINDS AND BEHAVIOR OF PEOPLE.

The party considers it an integral part of its Communist education work to combat manifestations of bourgeois ideology and morality, and the remnants of private-owner psychology, superstitions and prejudices.

The general public, public opinion, and extensive criticism and self-criticism must play a big role in combating survivals of the past and manifestations of individualism and selfishness.

Comradely censure of antisocial behavior will gradually become the principal means of doing away with manifestations of bourgeois views, customs and habits. The power of example in public affairs and in private life, in the performance of one's public duty, acquires tremendous educational significance.

The party uses ideological media to educate people in the spirit of a scientific materialist world conception, to overcome religious prejudices without insulting the sentiments of believers. It is necessary to explain patiently the untenability of religious beliefs, which were engendered in the past when people were overawed by the elemental forces and social oppression and did not know the real causes of natural and social phenomena. This can be done by making use of the achievements of modern science, which steadily solves the mysteries of the universe and extends man's power over nature, leaving no room for religious inventions about supernatural forces.

G. The Exposure of Bourgeois Ideology.

The peaceful coexistence of states with different social systems does not imply discontinuance of the ideological struggle. The Communist party will go on exposing the antipopular, reactionary nature of capitalism and all attempts to draw pretty pictures of the capitalist system. The party will steadfastly propagate the great advantages of socialism and communism over the declining capitalist system.

The party advances the scientific ideology of communism in contrast to reactionary bourgeois ideology. Communist ideology, which expresses the fundamental interests of the working class and all working people, teaches them to struggle, to live and work, for the happiness of all. It is the most humane ideology. Its ideals are to establish truly human relations between individuals and peoples, to deliver mankind from the threat of extermination, and bring about universal peace and a free, happy life for all men on earth.

(2) In the field of public education.

The transition to communism implies training that will make people Communist-minded and highly cultured, thus, fitting them for both physical and mental labor, for active work in various social, governmental, scientific and cultural spheres.

The system of public education is so organized as to insure that the instruction and education of the rising generation are closely bound up with life and productive labor, and that the adult population can combine work in the sphere of production with further training and education in keeping with their vocations and the requirements of society. Public education along these lines will make for the molding of harmoniously developed members of Communist society and for the solution of a cardinal social problem, namely, the elimination of substantial distinctions between mental and physical labor.

The main tasks in the field of instruction and education are:

A. THE INTRODUCTION OF UNIVERSAL COMPULSORY SECONDARY EDUCATION.

In the next decade compulsory secondary general and polytechnical eleven-year education is to be introduced for all children of school age, and education of eight classes for young people engaged in the national economy who have not had the appropriate schooling. In the subsequent decade everyone is to receive a complete secondary education. Universal secondary education is guaranteed by the development of general and polytechnical education along with the participation of school children in socially useful labor to the extent of their physical capacity, as well as by a considerate expansion of the network of evening schools, which provide a secondary education in off-work hours.

Secondary education must furnish a solid knowledge of the fundamentals of the basic sciences, an understanding of the principles of the Communist world outlook, and a labor and polytechnical training in accordance with the rising level of science and engineering, with due regard to the needs of society and to the abilities and inclinations of the students, as well as the moral, esthetic and physical education of a healthy rising generation.

In view of the rapid progress of science and engineering, the system of industrial and vocational training should be improved continuously, so that the production skills of those engaged in production may go hand in hand with their better general education in the social and natural sciences and with the acquisition of specialized knowledge of engineering, agronomy, medicine and other fields.

B. THE PUBLIC UPBRINGING OF CHILDREN OF PRE-SCHOOL AND SCHOOL AGE.

The Communist system of public education is based on the public upbringing of children. The educational influence which the family exerts on children must be brought into ever greater harmony with their public upbringing.

The growing number of pre-school institutions and boarding schools of different types will fully meet the requirements of all working people who wish to give their children of pre-school and school age a public upbringing.

The importance of the school, which is to cultivate love of labor and of knowledge in children and to raise the younger generation in the spirit of Communist consciousness and morality, will increase. An honorable and responsible role in this respect falls to teachers.

C. THE CREATION OF CONDITIONS FOR HIGH-STANDARD INSTRUCTION AND EDUCATION OF THE RISING GENERATION.

The party plans to carry out an extensive program for the construction of schools and cultural-education establishments to meet fully the needs of education and instruction. All schools will be housed in good buildings and will go over to a one-shift timetable. They will all have study workshops and chemical, physical and other laboratories, rural schools will also have their own farming plots, large factories will have production training shops for school children. The largest facilities—cinema, radio and television—will be widely used in schools.

For physical training and esthetic education, all schools and extra-scholastic establishments will have gymnasiums, sports grounds and facilities for the creative endeavor of children in music, painting, sculpture, etc. The network of sports schools, sports grounds, tourist camps, skiing centers, aquatic stations, swimming pools and other sports facilities will be expanded in town and countryside.

D. HIGHER AND SECONDARY SPECIALIZED EDUCATION.

In step with scientific and technical progress, higher and secondary specialized education, which must train highly skilled specialists with a broad theoretical and political background, will be expanded.

Shorter working hours and a considerable improvement in the standard of living of the entire population will provide everyone with an opportunity to receive a higher or secondary specialized education if he so desires. The number of higher and secondary specialized schools, evening correspondence schools in particular, as well as higher schools as factories, agricultural institutes on large state farms, people's universities, studios, conservatories, etc., must be increased in all areas of the country, with support from the factories and from the trade unions and other social organizations. The plan is to considerably increase every year the number of students at higher and secondary specialized schools. Specialized education will be afforded to tens of millions of people.

(3.) *In the field of science.*

Under the Socialist system of economy, scientific and technical progress enables man to employ the riches and forces of nature most effectively in the interests of the people, to discover new types of energy and to create new materials, to develop means of weather control, and to master outer space. Application of science in production becomes a decisive factor of rapid growth of the productive forces of society. Scientific progress and the introduction of scientific achievements into the economy will remain an object of special concern to the party.

Most important are the following tasks:

A. DEVELOPMENT OF THEORETICAL INVESTIGATIONS.

The further perspectives of scientific and technical progress depend in the present period primarily on the achievements of the key branches of natural science. A high level of development in mathematics, physics, chemistry and biology is a necessary condition for the advancement and the effectiveness of technical medical, agricultural and other sciences.

Theoretical investigations will be promoted to the utmost, primarily in such decisive fields of technical progress as electrification of the whole country, comprehensive mechanization and automation of production, the application of chemistry to the leading branches of the national economy, industrial uses of atomic energy, transport and communications. This applies to:

Studying the power and fuel balance of the country, finding the best ways and means of utilizing the natural sources of power, working out the scientific fundamentals of a single power grid, discovering new power sources and developing methods of direct conversion of thermal, nuclear, solar and chemical energy into electric power, and solving problems related to control of thermonuclear reactions:

Working out the theory and principles of designing new machines, automatic and telemechanical systems, intensively developing machines, automatic and telemechanical systems, intensively developing radioelectronics, elaborating the theoretical foundations of computing, control and information machines, and improving them technically;

Investigating chemical processes, working out new, more efficient technologies and creating inexpensive high-quality artificial and synthetic materials for all branches of the national economy: mechanical engineering, building, the manufacture of domestic goods and mineral fertilizers, and creating new preparations for use in medicine and agriculture;

Improving existing methods and devising new, more effective methods of prospecting minerals and making comprehensive use of natural wealth.

Big advances are to be made in the development of all the biological sciences in order successfully to solve medical problems and achieve further progress in agriculture. The main tasks to be solved by these sciences in the interests of mankind are: ascertainment of the nature of the phenomena of life, study and control of the vital processes, in particular, metabolism and heredity. Medicine must concentrate on discovering means of preventing and conquering cancer, virulent cardio-vascular and other dangerous diseases.

It is important to study and extensively use micro-organisms in the economy and public health, among other things for the production of foods and fodder, vitamins, antibiotics and enzymes, and for the development of new agricultural techniques.

Artificial earth satellites and spaceships have, by enabling man to penetrate into outer space, provided great opportunities of discovering new natural phenomena and laws, and investigating the planets and the sun.

In the age of rapid scientific progress, the elaboration of

the philosophical problems of modern natural science on the basis of dialectical materialism, the only scientific world outlook and method of cognition, becomes still more urgent.

There must be intensive development of research work in the social sciences, which constitute the scientific basis for the guidance of the development of society. Most important is experience gained in Communist construction, investigation of the key objective laws governing the economic, political and cultural progress of socialism and its development into communism, and elaboration of the problems of Communist education.

The task of economic science is to theoretically generalize new phenomena in the economic life of society, and to work out the national economic problems whose solution promotes successful Communist construction. Economists must concentrate on finding the most effective ways of utilizing material and labor resources in the economy, the best methods of planning and organizing industrial and agricultural production, and elaborating the principles of a rational distribution of the productive forces and of the technical and economic problems of Communist construction.

The investigation of the problems of world history and contemporary world development must disclose the law-governed process of mankind's advance toward communism, the change in the balance of forces in favor of socialism, the aggravation of the general crisis of capitalism, the breakup of the colonial system of imperialism and its consequences, and the upsurge of the national-liberation movement of the peoples.

It is important to study the historical experience of the Communist party and the Soviet people, the objective laws of development of the world socialist system and the world Communist and working-class movement.

The social sciences must continue to struggle with determination against bourgeois ideology, against Right Socialist theory and practice and against revisionism and dogmatism. They must uphold the purity of the principles of Marxism-Leninism.

B. Merger of Science and Production.

Close ties with the creative labor of the people and practical Communist construction are an earnest of a fruitful development of science.

In conformity with the demands of economic and cultural development, it is essential to extend and improve the network of research institutions, including those attached to the central bodies directing economic development and those attached to the economic councils, and the network of research laboratories and institutes at the major industrial plants and in farming areas, to develop research at higher educational establishments, to improve the geographical distribution of research institutions and higher educational establishments, and to insure the further development of science in all the union republics and major economic areas.

The research institutions must plan and coordinate their work in the most important trends of research in accordance with the plans of economic and cultural development. The role of the collective opinion of scientists in directing scientific work will increase. Free comradely discussions promoting the creative solution of pressing problems are an essential condition for scientific development:

The party will adopt measures to extend and improve and to enlist the most capable creative forces in scientific pursuits.

It is a point of honor for Soviet scientists to consolidate the advanced positions which Soviet science has won in major branches of knowledge and to take a leading place in world science in all the key fields.

(4.) In the field of cultural development, literature and art.

Cultural development during the full-scale construction of Communist society will constitute the closing stage of a great cultural revolution. At this stage, all the necessary ideological and cultural conditions will be created for the victory of communism.

The growth of the productive forces, progress in engineering and in the organization of production, increased social activity of the working people, development of the democratic principles of self-government, and a Communist reorganization of everyday life depend in very large measure on the cultural advancement of the population.

Communist culture, which will have absorbed and will develop all the best that has been created by world culture, will be a new, higher stage in the cultural progress of mankind. It will embody the versatility and richness of the spiritual life of society, and the lofty ideals and humanism of the new world. It will be the culture of a classless society, a culture of the entire people, of all mankind.

A. ALL-ROUND ADVANCEMENT OF THE CULTURAL LIFE OF SOCIETY.

In the period of transition to communism, creative effort in all fields of culture becomes particularly fruitful, becomes accessible to all members of society. Soviet literature, music, painting, cinema and theatre, and all the other arts, will attain higher standards in their ideological make-up and artistry. People's theatres, mass amateur art, technical invention and other forms of creative endeavor by the people will become widespread. The amateurs will produce new gifted writers, artists, musicians and actors. The development and enrichment of the arts are based on a combination of mass amateur endeavor and professional art.

The party will work unremittingly to insure that literature, art and culture flourish, that every individual is given full scope to apply his abilities, that the people are educated esthetically and develop a fine artistic taste and cultural habits.

To provide the material basis for cultural development on a grand scale:

Book publishing and the press will be vigorously developed, and the printing and paper industries will be expanded accordingly;

There will be more libraries, lecture halls and reading rooms, theatres, clubs, houses of culture, and cinemas;

The country-wide radio diffusion network will be completed, television stations covering all industrial and agricultural areas will be built;

People's universities, people's theatrical companies and other amateur cultural organizations will be widely developed.

A large network of scientific and technical laboratories and of art and cinema studios will be provided for the use of all who have the inclination and ability.

The party considers it necessary to distribute cultural institutions evenly throughout the country in order gradually to bring the cultural standard of the countryside level with that of the town and achieve rapid cultural progress in all the newly-developed areas.

High standards in urban development, in the architectural treatment and planning of towns and rural communities, industrial, cultural and service premises and dwellings acquire great importance. Art will inspire labor, adorn life and ennoble man.

B. ENHANCEMENT OF THE EDUCATIONAL ROLL OF LITERATURE AND ART.

Soviet literature and art, imbued with optimism and dynamic Communist ideas, are great factors in ideological education and cultivate in Soviet people the qualities of builders of a new world. They must be a source of happiness and inspiration to millions of people, must express their will, their sentiments and ideas, must enrich them ideologically and educate them morally.

The high-road of literature and art lies through the strengthening of links with the life of the people, through faithful and highly artistic depiction of the richness and versatility of Socialist reality, imspired and vivid portrayal of all that is new and genuinely Communist, and exposure of all that hinders the progress of society.

In the art of Socialist realism, which is based on the principles of partisanship and kinship with the people, bold pioneering in the artistic depiction of life goes hand in hand with the cultivation and development of the progressive traditions of world culture. Writers, artists, musicians, theatrical workers and film makers will have better opportunities of displaying creative initiative and skill, using manifold forms, styles and genres.

The Communist party shows solicitude for the proper development of literature and art and their ideological and artistic standards, helps social organizations and literary and art associations in their activities.

C. THE EXPANSION OF INTERNATIONAL CULTURAL RELATIONS.

The party considers it necessary to expand the Soviet Union's cultural relations with the countries of the Socialist system and with all other countries for the purpose of pooling scientific and cultural achievements and of bringing about mutual understanding and friendship among the peoples.

6. COMMUNIST CONSTRUCTION IN THE U.S.S.R. AND COOPERATION OF THE SOCIALIST COUNTRIES

The C.P.S.U. regards Communist construction in the Soviet Union as a component of the building of Communist society by the peoples of the entire world Socialist system.

The fact that Socialist revolutions took place at different times and that the economic and cultural levels of the countries concerned are dissimilar, predetermines the non-simultaneous completion of Socialist construction in those countries and their non-simultaneous entry into the period of the full-scale construction of communism. Nevertheless, the fact that the Socialist countries are developing as members of a single world Socialist system and utilizing the objective laws and advantages of this system enables them to reduce the time necessary for the construction of socialism and offers them the prospect of effecting the transition to communism more or less simultaneously, within one and the same historical epoch.

The first country to advance to communism facilitates and accelerates the advance of the entire world Socialist system to communism. In building communism, the peoples of the Soviet Union are breaking new roads for mankind, testing their correctness by their own experience, bringing out difficulties, finding ways and means of overcoming them, and selecting the best forms and methods of Communist construction.

Since the social forces—the working class, the cooperative peasantry and the people's intelligentsia—and the social forms of economy (enterprises based on the two forms of Socialist property) in the Soviet Union and in the other Socialist countries are of one type, there will be common basic objective laws for Communist construction in the U.S.S.R. and in those countries, with due allowance made for the historical and national peculiarities of each country.

The construction of communism in the U.S.S.R. promotes the interests of every country of the Socialist community, for it increases the economic might and defense potential of the world Socialist camp and provides progressively favorable opportunities for the U.S.S.R. to expand its economic and cultural cooperation with the other Socialist countries and render them assistance and support.

The C.P.S.U. maintains that the existing forms of economic relations between the Socialist countries—foreign trade, coordination of economic plans, and specialization and combination of production—will be developed and perfected more and more.

The Socialist system makes possible the abolition of the economic and cultural gap between countries—a legacy of capitalism—the more rapid development of the countries whose economy lagged behind under capitalism, the steady promotion of their economy and culture with the purpose of evening up the general level of development of the Socialist countries. This is insured by the advantages of the Socialist economic system and by equality in economic relations, by mutual assistance and the sharing of experience, specifically, by reciprocal exchanges of scientific and technological achievements, and by co-ordinated research, by the joint construction of industrial projects and by co-operation in the development of natural resources. All-round fraternal co-operation benefits every Socialist country and the world Socialist system as a whole.

It is in the best interest of Socialist and Communist construction that each Socialist country combine the effort to strengthen and develop its national economy with the effort to expand economic cooperation of the Socialist camp as a whole. The general economic levels of the Socialist countries must be raised and evened up primarily by every country fully using its internal resources and by improving the forms and methods of economic leadership, steadily applying the Leninist principles and methods of Socialist economic management, and making effective use of the advantages of the world Socialist system.

Material prerequisites for the construction of communism are created by the labor of the people of the country concerned and by its steadily growing contribution to the common cause—the consolidation of the Socialist system. This purpose is served by the application in Socialist construction of the law of planned, proportionate development; encouragement of the creative initiative and labor activity of the masses, continuous perfection of the system of the international division of labor through the co-ordination of national economic plans, specialization and combination of production within the world Socialist system on the basis of voluntary participation, mutual benefit and an over-all improvement of the level of science and engineering, the study of collective experience, the promotion of cooperation and fraternal mutual assistance, strict adherence to the principles of material incentive and the all-round promotion of moral stimuli to work for the good of society, control over the measure of labor and rate of consumption.

Socialism brings peoples and countries together. In the course of extensive co-operation in all economic, socio-political and cultural fields, the common economic basis of world socialism will be consolidated.

The objective laws of the world Socialist system, the growth of the productive forces of Socialist society, and the vital interests of the peoples of the Socialist countries predetermine an increasing affinity of the various national economies, and the eventual unification in a single world Communist economy that Lenin foresaw.

The C.P.S.U. and the Communist parties of the other Socialist countries consider their tasks to be:

In the political field, the utmost strengthening of the world Socialist system, promotion of fraternal relations with all the Socialist countries on lines of complete equality and voluntary co-operation, political consolidation of the countries of the Socialist community in a joint struggle for universal peace and for the complete triumph of communism;

In the economic field, expansion of trade between the Socialist countries, development of the Socialist international division of labor, increasing co-ordination of long-range economic plans among the Socialist countries envisaging a maximum saving of social labor and an accelerated development of the world Socialist economy, the promotion of scientific and technical co-operation;

In the cultural field, steady development of all forms of cultural co-operation and intercourse between the peoples of the Socialist countries, exchanges of cultural achievements, encouragement of joint creative effort by scientists, writers and artists, extensive measures to insure the mutual enrichment of national cultures and bring the mode of life and the spiritual cast of the Socialist nations closer together.

The C.P.S.U. and the Soviet people will do everything in their power to support all the peoples of the Socialist community in the construction of socialism and communism.

7. The Party in the Period of Full-Scale Communist Construction

As a result of the victory of socialism in the U.S.S.R. and the consolidation of the unity of Soviet society the Communist party of the working class has become the vanguard of the Soviet people, a party of the entire people, and extended its guiding influence to all spheres of social life. The party is the brain, the honor and the conscience of our epoch, of the Soviet people, which is effecting great revolutionary transformations. It looks keenly into the future and shows the people scientifically motivated roads along which to advance, arouses titanic energy in the masses and leads them to the accomplishment of great tasks.

The period of full-scale Communist construction is characterized by a further enhancement of the role and importance of the Communist party as the leading and guiding force of Soviet society.

Unlike all the preceding socio-economic formations, Communist society does not develop sporadically, but as a result of conscious and purposeful efforts of the masses led by the Marxist-Leninist party. The Communist party, which unites the foremost representatives of the working people and is closely connected with the masses, which enjoys unbounded authority among the people and understands the laws of social development, provides proper leadership in Communist construction as a whole, giving it an organized, planned and scientifically based character.

The enhancement of the role of the party in the life of Soviet society in the new stage of its development derives from:

The growing scope and complexity of the tasks of Communist construction, which call for a higher level of political and organizational leadership;

The growth of the creative activity of the masses and the participation of fresh millions of working people in the administration of state affairs and of production;

The further development of Socialist democracy, the enhancement of the role of social organizations, the extension of the rights of the union republics and local organizations;

The growing importance of the theory of scientific communism, of its creative development and propaganda, the necessity for improving the Communist education of the working people and for the struggle to overcome the survivals of the past in the minds of people.

There must be a new, higher stage in the development of the party itself and of its political, ideological and organizational work that is in conformity with the full-scale building of communism. The party will continuously improve the forms and methods of its work, so that its leadership of the masses, of the building of the material and technical basis of communism, of the development of society's spiritual life will keep pace with the growing requirements of the epoch of Communist construction.

Being the vanguard of the people building a Communist society, the party must also be in the van in internal party organization and serve as an example and model in developing the most advanced forms of public Communist self-government.

Undeviating observance of the Leninist standards of party life and the principle of collective leadership, enhancement of the responsibility of party organs and their personnel to the party rank and file, promotion of the activity and initiative of all Communists and of their participation in elaborating and realizing the policy of the party, and the development of criticism and self-criticism are a law of party life.

This is an imperative condition of the ideological and organizational strength of the party itself, of the greater unity and solidarity of party ranks, of an all-round development of inner-party democracy and an activization of this basis of all party forces, and of the strengthening of ties with the masses.

The cult of the individual and the violations of collectivism in leadership, of inner-party democracy and Socialist legality arising out of it are incompatible with the Leninist principles of party life. The cult of the individual belittles the role of the party and the masses and hampers the development of the ideological life of the party and the creative activity of the working people.

In order to effect the Leninist principle of collective leadership consistently, to insure a greater influx of fresh party forces into the leading party organs, to properly combine old and young cadres, and to rule out the possibility of an excessive concentration of power in the hands of individual officials and prevent cases of their getting beyond the control of the collective, the party considers it necessary to carry out the following measures:

A. To introduce in practice a regular renewal, in certain proportions, of the members of all elected party bodies—from primary organizations to the Central Committee, thus insuring continuity of leadership.

At all regular elections, not less than one-quarter of the members of the Central Committee of the C.P.S.U. and its Presidium shall be renewed. Presidium members shall, as a rule, be elected for not more than three successive terms. Particularly party workers may, by virtue of their generally recognized authority and high political, organizational and other abilities, be successively elected to the leading bodies for a longer period. In that case, the respective candidate is considered elected, provided not less than three-quarters of the votes are cast for him by secret ballot.

Members of the Central Committees of the Communist parties of union republics, of territorial and regional committees shall be renewed by not less than one-third at each regular election, and that of area, city and district committees, and the committees and bureaus of primary party organizations shall be renewed by one-half. Furthermore, members of the leading party bodies may be elected consecutively for not more than three years, and secretaries of the primary party organizations for not more than two consecutive terms.

A party organization may, in consideration of the political and professional qualities of a person, elect him to a leading body for a longer period. In that case a candidate is considered elected if not less than three-quarters of the Communists attending vote for him.

Party members not re-elected to a leading party body on the expiration of their term may be re-elected at subsequent elections.

A decision on removal from the Central Committee of the C.P.S.U. and other leading organs shall be adopted solely by secret ballot, and is valid when not less than two-thirds of the total membership of the body concerned vote in favor of the decision.

B. To extend the application of the elective principle and that of accountability in party organizations at all levels, including party organizations working under special conditions (army, navy).

C. To enhance the role of party meetings, conferences,

congresses and plenary meetings of party committees and other collective bodies. To provide favorable conditions for a free and businesslike discussion within the party of questions concerning its policy and practical activities, for comradely discussions of controversial or insufficiently clear matters.

D. To reduce steadily the salaried party staffs, enlisting Communists more extensively as nonsalaried workers doing volunteer work.

E. To develop criticism and self-criticism to the utmost as a tried and tested method of work and a means of disclosing and rectifying errors and shortcomings and the proper education of cadres.

In the period of full-scale Communist construction the role and responsibility of every party member will steadily increase. It is the duty of a Communist, in production, in social and personal life, to be a model in the struggle for the development and consolidation of Communist relations, and to observe the principles and norms of Communist morality. The C.P.S.U. will reinforce its ranks with the most politically conscious and active working people and keep pure and hold high the name of Communist.

The development of inner-party democracy must insure greater activity among Communists and enhance their responsibility for the realization of the noble Communist ideals. It will promote the cultivation in them of an inner, organic need to behave and act in all matters in full accordance with the principles of the party and its lofty aims.

The party will continue to strengthen the unity and solidarity of its ranks, and to maintain the purity of Marxism-Leninism. The party preserves such organizational guarantees as are provided by the rules of the C.P.S.U. against all manifestations of factionalism and group activity incompatible with Marxist-Leninist party principles. The unshakable ideological and organizational unity of the party is the most important source of its invincibility, a guarantee for the successful solution of the great tasks of Communist construction.

The people are the decisive force in the building of communism. The party exists for the people, and it is in serving the people that it sees the purpose of its activity. To further extend and deepen the ties between the party and the people is an imperative condition of success in the struggle for communism. The party considers it its duty always to consult the working people on the major questions of home and foreign policy, to make these questions an object of nationwide discussion, and to attract the more extensive participation of nonmembers in all its work. The more Socialist democracy develops, the broader and more versatile the work of the party among the working people must be, and the stronger will be its influence among the masses.

The party will in every way promote the extension and improvement of the work of the Soviets, the trade unions, the Y.C.L. and other mass organizations of working people, the development of the creative energy and initiative of the masses, and strengthen the unity and friendship of all the peoples of the U.S.S.R.

The C.P.S.U. is an integral part of the international Communist and working-class movement. The tried and tested Marxist-Leninist principles of proletarian internationalism will continue to be inviolable principles which the party will follow undeviatingly.

The Communist party of the Soviet Union will continue to strengthen the unity of the international Communist movement, to develop fraternal ties with all the Communist and workers' parties and to co-ordinate its actions with the efforts of all the contingents of the world Communist movement in the joint struggle against the danger of a new world war, for the interests of the working people, for peace, democracy and socialism.

Such is the program of work for Communist construction which the Communist party of the Soviet Union has mapped out.

The achievement of communism in the U.S.S.R. will be the greatest victory mankind has ever won throughout its long history. Every new step made toward the bright peaks of communism inspires the working masses in all countries, renders immense moral support to the struggle for the liberation of all peoples from social and national oppression, and brings closer the triumph of Marxism-Leninism on a worldwide scale.

When the Soviet people will enjoy the blessings of communism, new hundreds of millions of people on earth will say: "We are for communism." It is not through war with other countries, but by the example of a more perfect organization of society, by rapid progress in developing the productive forces, the creation of all conditions for the happiness and well-being of man, that the ideas of communism win the minds and hearts of the masses.

The forces of social progress will inevitably grow in all countries, and this will assist the builders of communism.

The party proceeds from the Marxist-Leninist proposition: the people are the maker of history, and communism is a creation of the people, of its energy and intelligence. The victory of communism depends on the people, and communism is built for the people. Every Soviet man brings the triumph of communism nearer by his labor. The successes of Communist construction spell abundance and happy life to all, and enhance the might, prestige and glory of the Soviet Union.

The party is confident that the Soviet people will accept the new program of the C.P.S.U. as their own vital cause, as the greatest purpose of their life and as a banner of nation-wide struggle for the building of communism. The party calls on all Communists, on the entire Soviet people—all working men and women, kolkhoz farmers and workers by brain—to apply their energies to the successful fulfillment of the historic tasks set forth in this program.

Under the tried and tested leadership of the Communist party, under the banner of Marxism-Leninism, the Soviet people have built socialism.

Under the leadership of the party, under the banner of Marxism-Leninism, the Soviet people will build Communist society.

The party solemnly proclaims: the present generation of Soviet people shall live under communism.

V.
CHINA AND ORTHODOX LENINISM

The features that distinguished the history of Marxism in Russia from its history in Western Europe emerge still more strikingly in the evolution of Chinese communism. The Chinese economy was even less developed than was the Russian and, for reasons discussed in the sections on Russian Marxism, it was even more necessary for impatient Marxist revolutionaries to form a monolithic party, to associate the revolution with the peasantry, and, once power was won, to force industrialization at the expense of the mass peasantry by means of a political and ideological totalitarianism.

The Chinese Communist Party acquired its monolithic character after its defeat in 1927 by the military faction of the Kuomintang under Chiang Kai-shek. By the time the party won power some twenty-two years later, it had already experienced the transition that had occurred in Russia from the party congress of 1903 until Stalin's conquest of the party in 1929, a transition from a party tolerating debate and inspiring idealistic enthusiasm to a monolithic, bureaucratic and essentially militaristic order. It was, in short, a completely "Stalinist" organization that came to power in China in 1949.

Associated with this development was the party's attitude toward the peasantry. Following the 1927 defeat the communists moved to the countryside, first to the Southeast, then, after the "long march" of 1934-1935, to the North. As a result of these resettlements, the party completely lost its links with the cities and became a mass peasant party led by a tightly organized group of intellectuals. It became, in other words, a "populist" party that had succeeded in winning a regional power base. This was, clearly, one step further than Lenin had taken in returning to revolutionary populist traditions. Whereas Lenin had called for an alliance with the peasantry because the proletariat was deficient in both number and socialist "consciousness," Mao Tse-tung had to put

487

his hopes entirely on the peasantry. The role of the party
elite was, therefore, correspondingly greater in China than in
Russia, since the tasks of tutoring the unenlightened masses
in Marxism and transforming the economy were far more
demanding. On the basis of his own modifications of
Marxism to suit similar conditions, Lenin was well aware
of the Marxist parties' dependency on the peasantry in economically underdeveloped countries. In 1920, for example,
he wrote that "it is the duty of the Communist parties, and
of those elements which are associated with them, to carry
on propaganda in favor of the idea of Peasants' Soviets, of
Toilers' Soviets everywhere, in backward countries and in
colonies. . . ." Reflecting the same judgment, the Comintern
stated in 1928 that in "the colonies where there is no proletariat, the overthrow of the domination of the imperialists
implies the establishment of the rule of people's (peasant)
Soviets."

The activities of this monolithic, ideologically disciplined
and pragmatically oriented party after it assumed power
can be divided into four phases: the period of consolidation,
1949-1952; the First Five-Year-Plan period, 1953-1957; the
years of the "great leap forward" and the establishment of
communes, 1958-1960; and the temporary retreat during the
famine years of 1960-1961. The principal tasks of the first
period were the distribution of land to the peasantry and the
restoration of industrial production to prewar levels. It resembled the decade between the Bolshevik Revolution and
the beginning of Stalinism.

The next period, that of the First Five Year Plan, indicates an interesting divergence from the Russian experience.
The industrialization and the concomitant exploitation of
the peasantry were considerably more moderate in China
than they had been in Russia. One reason for this relative
moderation was the absence of the dramatic purges, trials
and the like that had occurred in Russia during the corresponding phase. As mentioned above, the Chinese party
had already become a well-disciplined "Stalinist" dictatorship before power was won and, therefore, could avoid the
dreadful bloodbath that terrorized the party during Stalin's
industrialization and collectivization. Another reason lies in
the fact that at first, the establishment of peasant co-operatives in China involved less oppression and exploitation than
did Stalin's collectivization; and the nationalization of Chinese businesses was accompanied by less distress, since the

owners were often kept on as managers or even allowed to retain partial ownership. It was as though, having learned from the Russian experience, the Chinese party tried to reach a halfway mark between NEP and forced industrialization and attempted to avoid the extreme "class war" violence that pervaded the Five-Year-Plan period in Stalin's Russia.

In taking this relatively tolerant view of the "class enemy," the Chinese were not only expressing a realistic understanding of the needs of the economy; they were also revealing the fact that they had departed even more from Marxist determinism toward ideological voluntarism than had their Russian predecessors. No matter what a person's class origin, the Party seemed to believe, he could be molded into a socialist by the proper "thought reform." The "thought reform" program of the early fifties, the remarkable psychological manipulations often referred to as "brain-washing," the insistence on constant self-censorship aganst negative thoughts, and the ubiquitous reorientation study groups all illustrate this belief. The similarities between this process the Confucian attitudes and practices have often been noted, but whatever its origins, its implications are dramatically opposed to Marxist economic determinism. Finally, this non-class view is obviously associated with prevailing economic conditions: one could hardly make a proletarian origin a prerequisite for loyal socialist thinking in a country that lacked a mass proletariat.

In 1958, following the end of the First Five-Year-Plan period, the picture changed radically. The moderate approach was replaced by a radical program even more extreme than Stalin had dared undertake. It is difficult to find adequate explanation for this dramatic shift. Not even the tensions fostered by the Korean War had been enough to inspire the almost frenzied hysteria that accompanied the "great leap forward" and the establishment of the communes. Moreover, the change came just one year after Mao Tse-tung had issued his liberal appeal to "Let a Hundred Flowers Bloom," that is, to let all opinions be heard. There seems to be a direct link between the results of this liberalism and the new party extremism. The frank and often bitter criticism that burst forth in 1957 in response to the Party's liberal proclamations led, that summer, to a complete re-establishment of severe ideological controls and a new indoctrination campaign. Associated with this renewed discipline was the apparent success of the more extreme, full-time party "apparatus" against the more moderate party leaders who held positions in the government and the economy.

Perhaps even more significant as an explanation of the "great leap forward" program was the fact that Chinese industrialization seemed to have reached an impasse in 1956-1957. The moderate co-operative organization that had been established in the countryside was not providing sufficient agricultural products for export and for the new urban centers. The Chinese Communists seemed to have reached the crisis that the Russian party faced in 1929, and they responded in a similar way by announcing, at the Eighth Congress of May 1958, a vastly ambitious new economic program. The industrial goals were sharply raised above those that had just been established in January, when the Second Five Year Plan was published, and the formation of giant communes was begun.

"Twenty years concentrated into a day." "Three years of hard labor—ten thousand years of happy life." With such slogans as these China undertook its "great leap forward." Although the program of the commune was not officially announced until September of that year, 1958, the campaign to consolidate the previous co-operatives into massive communes began during the summer. A few months after Peking had announced the People's Commune program, some 740,000 recently organized peasant co-operatives had already been consolidated into 26,000 gigantic communes.

Each was to exist as an autonomous unit, utilizing to the fullest local resources and above all, local manpower. In addition to agricultural work, the peasants operated workshops and small-scale enterprises, established schools and institutions of higher learning and formed citizen army units. Communal barracks and dining halls were built for the adults and boarding schools for the children, in order to free their mothers for "useful" labor in the workshops and fields, or on the giant canal or bridge projects that employed tens of millions of peasant laborers. The inevitable strains and the opposition from the reluctant peasantry led to a temporary retreat in December 1958, particularly with respect to communal barracks and dining halls. But, the following year, the critics were attacked and the wisdom of the basic communal program re-emphasized. Optimistic forecasts of the results of the communes continued until the famine crisis of 1960-1961.

From the point of view of this survey of Marxism in underdeveloped economies, one of the most interesting aspects of the Chinese commune is its striking similarity to the plans of prerevolutionary Russian populists. They, too, felt that a socialist society could be built on the basis of rural communal institutions that incorporated industrial as well as agricultural activities. In this respect, therefore, the communal system represents one more retreat from Western Marxism to meet the needs of impatient Marxists in rural countries. Lenin had seized power in a rural country and, lacking the expected socialist revolution in the industrial West, was forced to plan for the industrialization of Russia. However, only after such an industrial base had been set could Lenin or any other Russian Marxist consider the prerequisites for socialism or communism attained. The Chinese now went much farther than this. Perhaps because of the fact that China was even less industrialized than Russia and that the road to a Marxist socialism was that much longer, they announced that the communal system together with massive socialist re-education would allow China to enter the stage of communism in the near future, even before China was properly industrialized. One can well imagine the indignation of the Russian Communists when they read that because of the commune the Chinese "people who are in their seventies and eighties, even those in their nineties, will live to see the attainment of Communism."

What was perhaps most embarrassing for the Russian Communists was the fact that, as we have seen in the preceding section, current Russian developments seem to support the Chinese argument: great achievements in industrialization within the framework of "socialist" ownership of the means of production were not in themselves enough to produce a socialist consciousness. In fact, even though Russia had reached incomparably higher levels of productivity, Khrushchev's persistent campaign for intensive indoctrination, his picture of the Party as a permanent moral guide, and his various other efforts to counter "bourgeois" tendencies were little different from the efforts of the Chinese.

It was only after forcing on Russia decades of vast suffering, that Stalin was able to announce in 1952 that Russia had at last reached the "transition phase from socialism to communism." What the Chinese were now saying was that because of the commune system and advanced techniques of socialist indoctrination they could not only avoid private-property capitalism, as Russia had done, but they could also pass directly to communism even before achieving an industrial society that Soviet Russia had struggled so long to attain. Here was the most radical modification of Marxism: It was not material abundance created by modern science and technology that brought socialism; on the contrary, this sort of progress alone seemed more likely to promote typically bourgeois attitudes. Socialism was to be created by actual social living in socialist institutions formed by the Party and by socialist thoughts indoctrinated by the Party.

To meet this daring challenge, the Russian Communists used all the arguments against radical impatience and antihistorical voluntarism that the prerevolutionary Mensheviks, Legal Marxists and Economists had hurled against Lenin. Many believe that when, at the Hungarian Party Congress in December 1959, Khrushchev warned Communist leaders that they must not "disregard objective conditions" he had Mao Tse-tung as well as the Hungarian Stalinist Rakosi in mind. He was more explicit earlier in the year, when he emphasized at the 21st Party Congress that the transition to communism is "a natural historic process which cannot be intentionally violated or bypassed." Those, he continued, who "prematurely" tried to introduce communist institutions would only harm the cause of communism. Besides referring to the failure of experiments with the commune in the early days of Soviet power, the Russians emphasized the indispensability of high levels of production as a basis for communism:

. . . since the communist principle of distribution presupposes inexhaustible sources of abundance, it would be the sheerest absurdity to begin applying this principle to the collective farm countryside, the most backward sector of the socialist economy. Therefore, transformation of the artel [the Russian collective farm] into a commune has been precluded in practice for an entirely indefinite period.

- But the Chinese held their ground, and again sounding like prerevolutionary Russian populists, they argued that they could advance their own way and without depending on the Russians. The Chinese were urged in their press to "triumph by [their] own unaided efforts," and the General Secretary of the Chinese Communist Party stated in a *Pravda* article published in October 1959, that "under all conditions the Chinese people have always carried on their struggle resolutely on their own."

Not satisfied with advancing the view that they would follow their own path and thereby enter the stage of communism before Russia and Eastern Europe, the Chinese went on to praise their leader Mao Tse-tung as the leading living theorist. "The yardstick by which to judge each individual as to whether or not he is a genuine Marxist," according to an official party journal, "is his comprehension of Mao Tse-tung's ideology." While even refusing at times to print Khrushchev's comments, the party press eulogized Mao Tse-tung as "the most outstanding contemporary revolutionist, statesman, and theoretician of Marxism-Leninism."

If the world comprised only Russia, Eastern Europe and China, Khrushchev might have preferred to ignore Chinese extreme statements and practices, especially considering Tito's reaction to Stalin's efforts to impose conformity. But the Russians could not do so, because Chinese policies powerfully affected Russia's own relations both with the West and with the economically underdeveloped areas of the world. There is an open conflict between Russia and China for leadership of the communist movement in Africa, Southeast Asia, Latin America and other regions with similar conditions and histories. For a variety of reasons, China is at least holding her own in this contest. The extremism of the Chinese, reflecting as it does economic conditions similar to those prevailing in the underdeveloped countries, seems to have a stronger appeal to the radical intelligentsia of these countries than does current Soviet moderation.

One can guess some of the reasons for this when one compares, for example, Russian and Chinese attitudes to the question of the revolutionary phases through which these countries are expected to pass on their way to socialism. Ironically ignoring their own Party's history, the Russian Communists insist that in the underdeveloped areas, the bourgeois nationalists and not the Communists must take the lead, and that the struggle must be directed for a long time not against domestic bourgeois elements, but against imperialism and remnants of feudalism. In reply, the Chinese use Leninist theory and practice and the experience of the Bolshevik Revolution itself to argue that because of special conditions in these areas just emerging from feudalism and colonialism, the bourgeoisie "cannot adopt a resolute, revolutionary line and can adopt only a wavering, conciliatory line." Consequently, not only will they never carry out a transition to socialism, but they will not be able "to fulfill thoroughly the task of the nationalist, democratic revolution. . . . In the final analysis, they can never escape from the control and bondage of imperialism." The only way of assuring a rapid and an uninterrupted transition through the various phases leading to socialism "is the firm grasping of hegemony in the democratic revolution [the bourgeois-nationalist phase] by the proletariat through the Communist Party."

Marxist socialism in both its Chinese and Russian forms appeals to the intellectuals of the underdeveloped countries for a variety of reasons, most of which have already been considered in the preceding commentaries. Above all, the socialistically organized economy and rapid industrialization represent magnificent instruments for achieving two cherished goals—the nationalistic aim of winning independence and prominence in a world heretofore dominated by the caucasian West and the humanitarian aim of replacing intolerable poverty by material welfare. For those familiar with the economic policies and the nationalistic goals of Peter the Great and Louis XIV, the political assumption underlying this program is hardly novel. In this respect, Marxism might well be considered the "mercantilism" of today's newly emerging nations. The radicalism of the Chinese and their urgent and uncompromising ëmphasis on a rapid and total economic transformation is becoming, for obvious reasons, increasingly more attractive than the relatively modest and cautious Russian approach to these processes. The Communist parties of most of the underdeveloped countries of the world are split, for example, on the issue of whether to support the Soviet Russian tactics of temporary alliance with the nationalist bourgeoisie, or the Chinese conviction that the local ˙Communists must strive to take full power whenever the opportunity is at hand. Perhaps remembering their own defeat at the hands of the Chinese "bourgeois" nationalists under Chiang Kai-shek, the Chinese are appalled at Khrushchev's moderate response to the policy of suppressing local Communists by "bourgeois nationalist" leaders in Egypt and Iraq. Furthermore, they see only opportunism and cowardly reformism in his appeal to the Communists in India, Indonesia and the newly emerging African nations to avoid "premature slogans of socialist transformation . . . where conditions for them have not yet matured." The appeal of Chinese attitudes and policies for the

Communist parties in these areas is obvious and understandably resented by the Russians.

As for the reasons behind the Russian position, at least one of these can be seen in the following statement made by the Italian Communist leader Palmiro Togliatti:

Our distinction between just and unjust wars still holds true. When it is a matter of defending freedom, national independence, or the cause of socialism, then such a war is just and people wage it willingly, to win. . . . But if we think of the possibility of complete destruction which concerns both sides, it becomes quite clear that other considerations must be added to the definition of the just character of a war. Let us imagine, in concrete terms, 20 or 30 nuclear explosions taking place in our country, which would be enough to effect complete destruction and turn everything into a desert. Would it really be possible to build socialism under such circumstances? We should be lying to the people if we were say that it is now possible to approach socialism with the help of war. . . . What changes have occurred at the present juncture that compel us to maintain that war not only should, but can, be avoided? The nature of war has changed and the relation of forces betwen socialism and imperialism has changed. Woe to the man who fails to understand the nature that war has acquired. He risks falling behind at least a generation in his thinking about war and peace. . . . Now . . . everything is ranged along a single line of the front—the line of death. Secondly, modern military means of mass destruction are such that their use may lead to the complete destruction of the centers of civilization. . . .

. . . We know that it would be a great mistake to expect or to hope that the capitalist system may be overthrown thanks to the intervention of the armed forces of the socialist countries. Revolutions cannot be exported or imposed by force of arms. Furthermore, considering the fact that today war would be conducted with the help of nuclear weapons, such a prospect would be truly catastrophic. Our country, for example, as a result of nuclear war, would be completely destroyed and for several generations would probably be unfit for life. What socialism could possibly be constructed under such conditions?

Russia is now a highly industrialized nation. In terms of productivity, if not distribution, she is very much a "have" nation. Moreover, not only has she gained much in wealth and power since the Second World War, but in her eyes the future seems ever more promising. Why risk all of this for one or another peripheral gain? As the author of a *Pravda* article published in August 1960 said: "Why create, why build, if you know in advance that the fruit of your labors will be destroyed by war?" On various occasions, Khrushchev has expressed similar sentiments, as the following quotations indicate:

Let us not approach the matter commercially and figure out the losses this or the other side would sustain. War would be a calamity for all the peoples of the world.

Imagine what will happen when bombs begin to explode over cities. These bombs will not distinguish between communists and noncommunists.

No, everything alive can be wiped out in the conflagration of nuclear explosions.

In the concluding selection of the book, the reader will see that the Chinese Communists take a different view of the relative gains and losses associated with a nuclear war. This official statement, *Long Live Leninism*, first appeared in *Red Flag* and, on April 26, 1960, was published in English translation by the *Peking Review*. The article provides an excellent survey of current Chinese views on a wide range of theoretical and practical issues. It would be most instructive to compare this document with the New Party Program of the Soviet Communist Party. Preceding this article, there are two essays by Mao Tse-tung. Both were originally published in 1937, and have become standard statements of Chinese Communist theory. In the first, *On Practice*, Mao Tse-tung criticizes the "dogmatists" in much the same way that he and other Chinese Party leaders are at present being criticized by the Russian Communists. The essay is also an interesting example of the persistent efforts of all Communist parties to avoid both "leftist adventurism" and "rightist opportunism."

Mao Tse-tung

ON PRACTICE—ON THE RELATION BETWEEN KNOWL-EDGE AND PRACTICE—BETWEEN KNOWING AND DOING

Mao Tse-tung

COMBAT LIBERALISM

LONG LIVE LENINISM!

Mao Tse-tung

ON PRACTICE

In the study of the problem of knowledge pre-Marxist materialism leaves man's social nature and historical development out of account. Hence it cannot explain the dependence of cognition upon social practice—its dependence upon production and class struggle.

First of all, a Marxist regards human productive activity as the most fundamental practice determining all other human activities. Cognitively man depends mainly upon his activity in material production for a gradual understanding of nature's phenomena, its characteristics, its laws, and its relation to himself; at the same time, through productive activity, man comes to understand gradually and in varying degrees certain human interrelations. None of such knowledge can be obtained apart from productive activity. In a classless society everyone in his capacity as one of its members works together with other members of society, comes into certain relations of production with them, and engages in production to solve the problem of man's material life. In various kinds of class societies, members of society from all classes come in different ways into certain relations of production with each other and engage in production to solve the same problem. This is the fundamental source of the development of human knowledge.

Productive activity is not the only form of man's social practice. There are various other forms—class struggle, political life, scientific and artistic activities. In short, man participates as a social being in every sphere of the actual life of society. Thus besides his cognition of things of material life, man comes to know in varying degrees the different kinds of human relations through his political and cultural life closely connected with his material life. Among these, class struggle in its various forms especially exerts a profound influence on the development of man's knowledge. In a class society everyone lives with a certain class status and all his thoughts are stamped with the seal of his class.

According to the Marxist, man's activity in social production develops step by step from a low stage to a high stage, and consequently man's knowledge, whether of nature or of society, also develops step by step from a low stage to a high stage, *viz.*, from the elementary to the advanced, and from the one-sided to the many-sided. For a very long period in human history, people were, as they could only be, limited to a phasic understanding of the history of society. This was due on the one hand to the constant distortion of it by the exploiting classes with their biased views, and on the other to the small scale of production which limited the breadth of view of the people. Not until the modern proletariat appeared along with greatly increased productive forces or big industry did man begin to have a comprehensive and historical understanding of the development of society and turn his knowledge of society into a science. This is none other than the science of Marxism.

According to the Marxist, man's social practice alone is the criterion of truth in his cognition of the external world, for in actuality human cognition becomes verified only when man arrives at the results predicted, through the process of social practice, *viz.*, through the processes of material production, of class struggle, and of scientific experiments. If anyone wants to be successful in his work or to achieve the anticipated results, he must make his ideas correspond to the laws of the external world; otherwise he will fail in practice. It is from failure that one derives lessons and corrects one's ideas so as to make them correspond to the laws of the external world. This is how one turns failure into success. This is exactly what is meant by failure being the mother of success, and by "a fall into the pit, a gain in your wit."

The epistemology of dialectical materialism raises practice to a position of primary importance. It regards human knowledge as being at no point separable from practice, refuting all the incorrect theories which deny the importance of practice or which separate knowledge from it. Thus Lenin said, "Practice is more important than (theoretical) knowledge, because it not only has the virtue of universality but also the virtue of direct reality."

Marxist philosophy, dialectical materialism, has two most outstanding characteristics. One is its class nature: it openly declares itself to be in the service of the proletariat. The other is its practicality: it emphasizes the dependence of theory on practice, practice being the foundation of theory which in turn serves practice. One's theory or cognition is judged to be true or untrue not by how it is subjectively felt to be, but by what objectively the result is in social practice. The criterion of truth can only be social practice. The viewpoint which emphasizes practice is primary and basic in the epistemology of dialectical materialism.

But how after all does human knowledge arise from practice and serve practice in turn? This will be clear after an examination of the developing process of cognition.

At first man sees in the process of practice only the phenomena of things, their individual aspects, and their external relations to each other. For instance, a number of outside people came to Yenan on an observation tour. On the first day or two, they saw the topography, the streets, and the houses of Yenan; met people; went to feasts, evening parties, and mass meetings; heard what was talked about; read what was written: these are the phenomena of things, their individual aspects, and their external relations. This is called the perceptual stage of knowledge, namely, the stage of sensation and imagery. It is also the first stage of knowledge, the stage in which these different things in Yenan affected the sense organs of the gentlemen of the observation commission, gave rise to sensations, and left many images in their brain together with a crude outline of their external relations. In this stage one cannot as yet form profound concepts or draw logical conclusions.

With the continuation of man's social practice, the sensations and images of a thing are repeated innumerable times in his practice and then a sudden change in the cognitive process takes place in his brain resulting in the formation of concepts. Concepts as such represent no longer the phenomena of things, their individual aspects, or their external relations. Through concepts man comes to grasp a thing in its entirety, its essence, and its internal relations. Conception is not only quantitatively but also qualitatively different from perception. Proceeding from concepts, we can employ the method of judgment and inference and arrive at logical conclusions. What is known as "knit your brows, and the idea comes to your mind" in the *Tale of the Three Kingdoms* or "let me think" in our workaday language refers to the employment of concepts in our brain to form judgments and draw inferences. This is the second stage of knowledge.

The gentlemen of the observation commission after having gathered various kinds of data and in addition reflected on them may come to the judgment: The policy of the National Anti-Japanese United Front pursued by the Communist Party is thorough, sincere, and honest. If these gentlemen themselves were sincerely in favor of unity for national salvation, then after having made the above judgment they could go a step further and conclude that "the National Anti-Japanese United Front can succeed." In the complete process of knowing a thing this stage of conception, judgment, and inference is more important than the first stage. It is the stage of rational knowledge.

The real task of cognition is to arrive at thought through perception, at a gradual understanding of the internal contradictions of objective things, their laws, the internal relations between this and that process, that is, at rational knowledge. To repeat, the reason why rational knowledge is different from perceptual knowledge is that perceptual knowledge is knowledge of a thing in its individual aspects, its appearance, and its external relations, whereas rational knowledge, marking a great step in advance, is knowledge of a thing in its entirety, its essence, and its internal relations. When one arrives at rational knowledge, one is able to reveal the internal contradictions of the surrounding world and thus grasp the development of that world by considering it in its entirety—the internal relations of and between all its aspects.

Before the advent of Marxism none had proposed a theory of knowledge that takes account of the developing process of cognition that is based on practice, that proceeds from the elementary to the advanced, and that is dialectically materialistic. Marxist materialism for the first time correctly solved this problem, pointing out both materialistically and dialectically the ever-deepening process of cognition, a process that turns perceptual knowledge into rational knowledge through the complex and regularly recurring practices of man as a social being in his production and class struggle. Lenin said: "The abstract concept of matter, of a law of nature, of economic value or any other scientific (*i.e.*, correct and basic, not false or superficial) abstraction reflects nature more deeply, truly, and fully." What characterizes respectively the two stages of the process of cognition, according to Marxism-Leninism, is that in the lower stage knowledge appears in perceptual form and in the higher stage in rational form; each of these two stages, however, constitutes a stage in one united process of cognition. Perceptual knowledge and rational knowledge are different in nature, but not separate from each other, being united on the basis of practice.

It is our practice that proves that things perceived are not readily understood, and that only things understood are more profoundly perceived. It proves that perception only solves the problem of how things appear, and that understanding answers the question as to what their essence is. Thus these problems cannot be solved at all apart from practice. If anybody wants to know something, he cannot do otherwise than to come into contact with that thing, that is, to live (practice) in its setting.

In a feudal society one cannot know beforehand the laws of capitalist society, because, capitalist society not yet having appeared, there cannot be any practice appropriate to it. Marxism can only be the product of capitalist society. In the age of the capitalism of free competition, Marx could not know concretely beforehand some of the special laws of the age of imperialism, because this age, the last stage of capitalism, had not yet arrived and there was no practice appropriate to it. Only Lenin and Stalin could shoulder this task.

Aside from their genius, what enabled Marx, Engels, Lenin, and Stalin to formulate their theories was mainly their personal participation in the practice of the class struggle and scientific experiments of their time. Without the latter condition no genius could succeed in such a task. "A scholar knows all that is happening in the world without going out of his door" was only an empty phrase in the technologically undeveloped times of old. Although this dictum could be true in the present age of technological development, yet real knowledge through direct acquaintance is only for all those in the world who are engaged in actual practice. Through practice these people obtain knowledge which, when put into the hands of the scholar through the communication of language and technical devices, enables him indirectly to know about "all that is happening in the world."

If one wants to know directly some things or some kinds of things one can do so only through personal participation in the practical struggle to change existing conditions, to change those things or those kinds of things. Only thus can one come into contact with the phenomena of those things or those kinds of things; and only thus can the essence of those things or those kinds of things be revealed and understood. This is actually the path to knowledge along which everyone travels. Only some people deliberately argue to the contrary to confuse and confound.

The most ridiculous persons in the world are those "know-it-alls" who pick up crumbs of knowledge piecemeal and proclaim themselves, each of them, "the number one of the world." This serves merely to show that they have not taken proper measure of themselves.

Knowledge is a matter of science, and there is no room for the slightest insincerity or conceit. What is required is decidedly the opposite, sincerity and modesty. If one wants to have knowledge one has to participate in the practice of changing existing conditions. If one wants to know the taste of a pear one has to transform the pear by eating it oneself. If one wants to know the composition and properties of atoms one has to perform physical and chemical experiments to change their original state. If one wants to know the theory and method of revolution, one has to participate in revolution.

All knowledge originates from direct experience. But no one can directly experience everything. As a matter of fact, most of our knowledge is of things indirectly experienced. All our knowledge of ancient times and foreign lands belongs to this category, but for the ancients and foreigners it is knowledge of things directly experienced. If this kind of knowledge of the ancients and foreigners from their direct experience conforms to the requirements of "scientific abstraction" mentioned by Lenin and reflects objective things scientifically, then it is reliable knowledge, otherwise it is not. Hence one's knowledge consists of two parts: knowledge of things directly experienced and knowledge of things indirectly experienced. And what is indirectly experienced by one is nevertheless dirctly experienced by others. Hence taken as a whole, any kind of knowledge is inseparable from direct experience.

All knowledge originates in man's perception of the external world through his sense organs. If one denies perception, denies direct experience, and denies personal participation in the practice of changing existing conditions, one is not a materialist. This is exactly where the "know-it-alls" are ridiculous. The Chinese have an old saying: "If one doesn't enter the tiger's den, one cannot obtain tiger cubs." This statement is as true of epistemology as of man's practice. Knowledge is impossible if separated from practice.

In order to understand the dialectical materialist conception of the process of cognition based upon and issuing from the practice of changing existing conditions—the process of cognition in its gradually deepening movement—let us take a few examples.

The knowledge of capitalist society the proletariat had in the first period of its practice, the period of machine-smashing and spontaneous struggle, was only perceptual knowledge. It was only a knowledge of the individual aspects and the external relations of the various phenomena of capitalism. At that time the proletariat was what is called a *class in itself*. But when this class reached the second period of its practice, the period of conscious, organized economic and political struggle, there emerged the ideology of Marxism as a result of the practice of this class, its experience of constant and continuous struggle and the scientific summary and integration of all these experiences by Marx and Engels. When this ideology was used to educate the proletariat and enabled it to understand the essence of capitalist society, the relation of exploitation between classes, and its own historic task, it transformed itself into a *class for itself*.

The Chinese people came to know imperialism in the same way. The first stage was one of perceptual knowledge of the appearance of things. It was marked with the indiscriminately antiforeign struggle of the T'aip'ing (1850-1864) [1] and the Boxer (1900) [2] revolutionary movements. It was only in the second stage that the Chinese people arrived at rational knowledge. They saw the internal and external contradictions of imperialism. They also saw the essence of the exploitation of China's broad masses by imperialism in alliance with the comprador and feudal classes. This kind of knowledge came to light only about the time of the May Fourth Movement of 1919.[3]

Let us look at war. If those who are to direct a war have no experience of it, they would not understand at first the deep underlying laws for conducting a particular war such as that of our Agrarian Revolution of the past ten years.[4] In the beginning they merely go through the experience of much fighting and many defeats, but subsequently from such experience (of victories and especially of defeats) they are able to understand the inner thread that runs through the whole of the fighting, namely, the laws of that particular war. They thus understand strategy and tactics and are able to direct the fighting with confidence. At such a time if an inexperienced man is appointed to take over the command, he still will not be able to understand the correct laws of war until he has also suffered defeats and gathered experiences from them.

Comrades who are not brave enough to accept an assignment are often heard to say: "I have no confidence." Why have they no confidence? Because they have no systematic understanding of the nature of the work nor the conditions under which it will be undertaken. Probably they have had little or even no contact with this kind of work and hence cannot know the underlying laws. After a close analysis of the nature and conditions of the work, they feel more confident and are willing to undertake it. If those people have gained experiences in this work after a period of time, and if they are not given to approaching things subjectively, one-sidedly, or superficially, but endeavor to understand them with an open mind, they are able to draw their own conclusions as to how they should proceed and their courage to undertake the task will be greatly enhanced. Those are bound to stumble who approach problems only subjectively, one-sidedly, superficially, who, upon reaching any place, start to issue orders or directives self-assuredly without considering their environment, without viewing things in their totality (their history and their present state as a whole), without coming into contact with the essence of things (their qualities and the internal relations between one thing and another).

It is thus seen that the first step in the process of cognition is to come into contact with the things of the external world; this belongs to the stage of perception. The second step is to synthesize the data of perception, to rearrange and reconstruct them; this belongs to the stage of conception, judgment, and inference. It is only when the perceptual data are abundant, not fragmentary or incomplete, and are in correspondence with reality, instead of being illusory, that they can serve as the basis for valid concepts, judgments, and inferences.

Here, two important points are to be emphasized. To repeat what has already been mentioned before, the first one is the dependence of rational knowledge upon perceptual knowledge. If one thinks that rational knowledge need not be derived from perceptual knowledge, one is an idealist. In the history of philosophy there were the so-called rationalists who admitted only the reality of reason, but not the

reality of experience, regarding reason alone as reliable
and perceptual experience as unreliable. The mistake of this
school consisted in turning things upside down. What is
rational is reliable precisely because it originates from the
senses, otherwise it would be like water without source or
trees without roots and become something unreliable and
self-engendered.

As to the sequence in the process of cognition, perceptual
experience comes first. We point out with special emphasis
the significance of social practice in the process of cognition
precisely because it is only through social practice that
human cognition comes to pass, that people begin to obtain
perceptual experience from the external world. There could
be no such thing as knowledge for a person who shuts his
eyes, stops his ears, and totally cuts himself off from the external world. Knowledge starts from experience—this is epistemological materialism.

The second point is that knowledge depends upon a
deepening process, upon developing from the perceptual into
the rational. This is epistemological dialectics. If anyone
thinks that knowledge may stop at the low stage of perception
and that perceptual knowledge alone is reliable, but not
rational knowledge, then one repeats the historical mistake
of empiricism. The mistake of such a theory is that it fails
to take into account the fact that although the data of perception are the reflection of certain realities of the external
world—I am not speaking of the idealist empiricism which
limits experience to the so-called introspection—yet these
data concern merely the aspects and appearances of things.
This kind of reflection is incomplete and it is not one of the
essence of things. To reflect a thing in its entirety, its essence,
and its underlying laws, it is necessary to ponder over the
wealth of data, to remodel and to reconstruct them so as to
form a system of concepts and theories by straining the
refined from the crude, sifting the true from the false, deriving the yet unascertained from the ascertained, and probing into the deep-seated from the superficial. To do all these,
it is necessary to leap from perceptual knowledge to rational
knowledge.

Knowledge after this kind of reconstruction is not emptier
or more unreliable; on the contrary, only what has been re-
constructed scientifically on the basis of practice in the process of cognition can, as Lenin said, reflect nature or objective
things more deeply, truly, fully. Vulgar plodders absorbed in

daily trifles do not know this. They bow down before experience and despise theory, hence they cannot have a comprehensive grasp of the entire objective process, lack a clear direction and a long perspective, but are self-satisfied with one instance of success, one ray of light. Were these persons to lead a revolution, they would direct it to a dead end.

Rational knowledge depends upon perceptual knowledge and perceptual knowledge has to develop into rational knowledge. This is the epistemology of dialectical materialism. Both rationalism and empiricism in philosophy fail to account for the dialectical and historical nature of knowledge, and although each represents an aspect of truth (here it is materialist, not idealist, rationalism and empiricism that are in question), yet both are invalid so far as concerns their respective epistemology as a whole. The dialectical materialist process of cognition from the perceptual to the rational applies to a minor process of cognition such as knowing one thing or one undertaking, as well as to a major one such as knowing a society or a revolution.

But at this point the process of cognition is not yet concluded. If we stop the discussion of the dialectical materialist process of cognition merely at rational knowledge, we have touched upon only half of the problem. And from the point of view of Marxist philosophy we have only touched upon the half that is not quite so important. What Marxist philosophy considers most important is not understanding the laws of the external world and thereby explaining it, but actively changing the world by applying the knowledge of objective laws. Theory is important from the viewpoint of Marxism; its importance is sufficiently shown in the statement Lenin made: "Without a revolutionary theory there can be no revolutionary movement." But when Marxism emphasizes theory, it does so precisely and only because it can guide our actions. If we had a correct theory, but merely prated about it, pigeonholed it, and refused to act accordingly, then that theory, however good, would be totally devoid of significance.

Cognition starts with practice and through practice it reaches the theoretical plane, and then it has to go back to practice. The active effect of cognition not only manifests itself in the active leap from perceptual knowledge to rational knowledge, but also, what is more important, manifests itself in that leap from rational knowledge to revolutionary practice. After having grasped the laws of the world we must redirect this knowledge to the practice of changing the world, to the practice of production, of revolutionary class struggle and national struggle as well as of scientific experiments. This is the process of testing and developing theory, the continuation of the entire process of cognition.

The problem whether theories correspond to objective realities is not entirely solved in the process of cognition from the perceptual to the rational as mentioned before: there it cannot be entirely solved. The only way to solve this problem completely is to redirect rational knowledge to social practice and apply theory to practice to see whether it can achieve preconceived results. This is the reason why many theories of natural science are regarded as truths not only at the time of their discovery by natural scientists, but also subsequently when they are verified by scientific practice. The reason why Marxism-Leninism is regarded as truth lies in the fact that it was not only scientifically formulated by Marx, Engels, Lenin, and Stalin, but also subsequently verified in the revolutionary practice of class struggle and national struggle. Dialectical materialism is a universal truth because no one in his practice can escape from the sphere of its applicability.

The history of human knowledge tells us that the truth of many theories is incomplete but that this incompleteness is remedied when put to the test of practice. Many theories are incorrect, but their mistakes are corrected when put to the test of practice. That is why practice is the criterion of truth and why the standpoint of practice is "first and fundamental in the theory of knowledge." Stalin very well said: "Theory becomes aimless if it is not connected with revolutionary practice, just as practice gropes in the dark if its path is not illumined by revolutionary theory."

When we get to this point, is the process of cognition completed? Our answer is yes and no. By the reflection of the objective process and the effects of their own capacity for activity, men as social beings engaged in the practice of changing a certain objective process in a certain stage of its development (irrespective of whether the practice is one of changing a natural process or one of changing a social process) are enabled to advance their knowledge from the perceptual to the rational, bringing forth ideas, theories, plans, or programs which on the whole correspond to the laws of that objective process. These are then put into practice in the said process. If they enable us to realize the preconceived aim, *viz.*, when these ideas, theories, plans, or programs are changed or on the whole changed into facts through practice in that objective process, then so far as this concrete process is concerned, the process of cognition is regarded as completed. For example, in the process of changing nature, the realization of an engineering plan, the verification of a scientific hypothesis, the manufacturing of a utensil or instrument, and the reaping of agricultural produce; and in the process of changing society, the victory of a strike or of a war, the materialization of an educational plan—these can all be regarded as the realization of a preconceived aim.

But generally speaking, in the practice of changing either nature or society, people's original ideas, theories, plans, or programs are hardly ever realized without any change whatever. This is because those who are engaged in changing existing conditions are limited in many ways. They are limited not only by the scientific and technological conditions, but also by the objective process itself, both in its development and in the degree to which it reveals its aspects and its essence. In such a situation, on account of unforeseen circumstances discovered in practice, our ideas, theories, plans, or programs are often partially and sometimes even entirely changed. That is to say, the original ideas, theories, plans, or programs may not correspond partially or entirely to reality and are partially or entirely incorrect. It often happens that failures are repeated several times before our cognition is corrected of its errors and made into knowledge that corresponds to the laws of the objective process so that subjective things can be transformed into objective things, *viz.*, preconceived results can be achieved in practice. But in any case, at such a point, the process of one's knowing a certain objective process in a certain stage of its development is regarded as completed.

But as the objective process advances from stage to stage, one's process of cognition is by no means completed. As any objective process, whether natural or social, advances and develops in consequence of its internal contradictions and conflicts, one's cognitive process should also advance and develop accordingly. In terms of social movement, not only must a truly revolutionary leader be adept at correcting his ideas, theories, plans, or programs when they are mistaken, as mentioned above, but he must also be adept at making himself and his fellow participants in the revolution advance and change their subjective cognition accordingly when a certain objective process has already advanced from one stage of development to another. That is to say, he must propose the new revolutionary tasks and program in such a way as to correspond to the new changes in the circumstances. The situation in a revolutionary period changes quickly. If the cognition of revolutionaries does not change quickly with it they cannot lead the revolution towards victory. However, people's ideas often fall behind actual events because man's knowledge is limited by many social conditions.

We are opposed to the die-hards in the revolutionary ranks. Their ideas do not advance with the changing objective circumstances and have manifested themselves historically in the form of right opportunism. These people do not see that the conflict of the contradictions has already pushed the objective process forward and their cognition still remains at the old stage. All die-hards have shown this characteristic in their ideas. Their ideas having departed from social practice, they cannot advance at the head of the chariot of social progress as its guide. All they do is to trail behind and grumble that it runs rather too fast. They attempt to halt the chariot and drag it back.

We are also opposed to the idle talk of the "left." The ideas of these "leftists" are far ahead of a given stage of development of the objective process. Some of them regard their hallucinations as the truth; others strain themselves to realize at present an ideal which can only be realized in the future. They have separated themselves from the practice of the majority of the people and the realities of their time and their ideas, when translated into action, reveal themselves in the form of adventurism.

Idealism and mechanistic materialism, opportunism and adventurism are all characterized by the separation of the subjective from the objective, the divorce of knowledge from practice. The epistemology of Marxism-Leninism characterized by its scientific social practice cannot but be strongly opposed to these incorrect ideologies. A Marxist recognizes that the development of the total process of the universe is absolute, whereas the development of each particular process in this total process is relative. Hence in the great river of absolute truth man's knowledge of a particular process in each given stage of development is only relatively true. Absolute truth is compounded of a sum-total of relative truths.

The development of the objective process is full of contradictions and conflicts, and so is the development of the process of man's cognition. All the dialectical movements of the external world can sooner or later find their reflection in man's knowledge. The process of coming into being, development, and elimination in social practice as well as in human knowledge is infinite. As the practice of changing objective existing conditions based upon certain ideas, theories, plans, or programs moves forward step by step, man's knowledge of objective reality also deepens step by step. The movement or change of the world of objective realities is never finished, hence man's recognition of truth through practice is also never complete. Marxism-Leninism has in no way put an end to the discovery of truths, but continues to blaze the path towards the recognition of truths through practice. Our conclusion is that we stand for the concrete and historical unity of the subjective and the objective, of theory and practice, and of knowledge and action; we are against any incorrect ideology, whether right or "left," that departs from the realities of history.

At the present stage of the development of society the responsibility of correctly understanding the world and of changing it has already fallen with the whole weight of history upon the shoulders of the proletariat and its political party. This process of the practice of changing the world on the basis of a scientific knowledge of it has already reached a historic moment both in China and in the whole world, a moment of such importance as the world has never witnessed before. This change is none other than the complete overturn of the world of darkness both in China and elsewhere and the transformation of it into a world of light that never existed before.

The struggle of the proletariat and revolutionary people in changing the world consists in achieving the following tasks: to reconstruct the external world; to reconstruct their own subjective world, *i.e.*, to remold their faculty of knowing; and to change the relations between the subjective and external worlds. Such a change has already been effected in one part of the globe, namely, the Soviet Union. The people there are still expediting this process of change. The people of China and the rest of the world are either passing, or will pass, through this kind of change.

What is meant by the external world which is to be changed includes the persons who are opposed to that change. To be remolded they will have to go through a stage of compulsion before they enter into a stage of remolding of their own accord. When the whole of mankind of its own accord remolds itself and changes the world, that will be the age of World Communism.

The discovery of truths through practice, and through practice the verification and the development of them; the active development of perceptual knowledge into rational knowledge, and, by means of rational knowledge, the active direction of revolutionary practice and the reconstruction of the subjective and the external world; practice, knowledge, more practice, more knowledge, and the repetition *ad infinitum* of this cyclic pattern, and with each cycle, the elevation of the content of practice and knowledge to a higher level: such is the whole epistemology of dialectical materialism, such is its theory of the unity of knowledge and action.

Mao Tse-tung
COMBAT LIBERALISM

We advocate an active ideological struggle, because it is the weapon for achieving solidarity within the Party and the revolutionary organizations and making them fit to fight. Every communist and revolutionary should take up this weapon.

But liberalism negates ideological struggle and advocates unprincipled peace, with the result that a decadent, philistine style in work has appeared and certain units and individuals in the Party and the revolutionary organizations have begun to degenerate politically.

Liberalism manifests itself in various ways.

Although the person concerned is clearly known to be in the wrong, yet because he is an old acquaintance, a fellow townsman, a schoolmate, a bosom friend, a beloved one, an old colleague or a former subordinate, one does not argue with him on the basis of principles but lets things slide in order to maintain peace and friendship. Or to touch lightly upon the matter without finding a thorough solution in order to maintain harmony all around. As a result, harm is done to the organization as well as to the individual concerned. This is the first type.

To indulge in irresponsible criticisms in private without making positive suggestions to the organization. To say nothing to people's faces, but to gossip behind their backs; or to say nothing at a meeting, but gossip after it. Not to care for the principle of collective life but only for unrestrained self-indulgence. This is the second type.

Things of no personal concern are put on the shelf; the less said the better about things that are clearly known to be wrong; to be cautious in order to save one's own skin, and anxious only to avoid reprimands. This is the third type.

To disobey orders and place personal opinions above everything. To demand special dispensation from the organization but to reject its discipline. This is the fourth type.

To engage in struggles and disputes against incorrect views not for the sake of solidarity, progress or improvement in work, but for the sake of making personal attacks, letting off steam, venting personal grievance or seeking revenge. This is the fifth type.

Not to dispute incorrect opinions on hearing them, and even not to report counterrevolutionary opinions on hearing them, but to bear with them calmly as if nothing had happened. This is the sixth type.

Not to engage in propaganda and agitation, make speeches or carry on investigations and inquiries among the masses, but to leave the masses alone, without any concern about their weal and woe; to forget that one is a communist and to behave as if a communist were just an ordinary person. This is the seventh type.

Not to feel indignant at actions detrimental to the interests of the masses, not to dissuade or to stop the person responsible for them or explain to him, but to allow him to continue. This is the eighth type.

To work half-heartedly without any definite plan or direction; to work perfunctorily and let things drift; "so long as I remain a bonze, I go on tolling the bell." This is the ninth type.

To regard oneself as having performed meritorious service in the revolution and to put on the airs of a veteran; to be incapable of doing great things, yet to disdain minor tasks; to be careless in work and slack in study. This is the tenth type.

To be aware of one's own mistakes yet to make no attempt to rectify them and adopt a liberal attitude towards oneself. This is the eleventh type.

We can name some more. But these eleven are the principal ones.

All these are manifestations of liberalism.

In revolutionary organizations liberalism is extremely harmful. It is a corrosive which disrupts unity, undermines solidarity, induces inactivity and creates dissension. It deprives the revolutionary ranks of compact organization and strict discipline, prevents the policies from being thoroughly carried out and divorces the organizations of the Party from the masses under their leadership. It is an extremely bad tendency.

Liberalism stems from the selfishness of the petty bourgeoisie which puts personal interests foremost and the interests of the revolution in the second place, thus giving rise to ideological, political and organizational liberalism.

Liberals look upon the principles of Marxism as abstract dogmas. They approve of Marxism but are not prepared to practice it or to practice it in full; they are not prepared to replace their own liberalism with Marxism. Such people have got Marxism, but they have also got liberalism: they talk Marxism but practise liberalism; they apply Marxism to others but liberalism to themselves. Both kinds of goods are in stock and either has its particular use. That is the way in which the mind of certain people works.

Liberalism is a manifestation of opportunism and fundamentally conflicts with Marxism. It is passive in character and objectively produces the effect of helping the enemy; thus the enemy welcomes its preservation in our midst. Such being its nature, there should be no place for it in the revolutionary ranks.

We must use the active spirit of Marxism to overcome the liberalism with its passivity. A communist should be frank, faithful and active, looking upon the interests of the revolution as his very life and subordinating his personal interests to those of the revolution; he should, always and everywhere, adhere to correct principles and wage a tireless struggle against all incorrect ideas and actions, so as to consolidate the collective life of the Party and strengthen the ties between the Party and the masses; and he should be more concerned about the Party and the masses than about the individual and more concerned about others than about himself. Only thus can he be considered a communist.

All loyal, honest, active and staunch communists must unite to oppose the liberal tendencies shown by certain people among us, and turn them in the right direction. This is one of the tasks on our ideological front.

LONG LIVE LENINISM!
from the *Peking Review*, April 1960

April 22 of this year is the ninetieth anniversary of the birth of Lenin.

1871, the year after Lenin's birth, saw the heroic uprising of the Paris Commune. The Paris Commune was a great, epoch-making revolution, the first dress rehearsal of universal significance in the proletariat's attempt to overthrow the capitalist system. When the Commune was on the verge of defeat as a result of the counterrevolutionary attack from Versailles, Marx said:

If the Commune should be destroyed, the struggle would only be postponed. The principles of the Commune are perpetual and indestructible; they will present themselves again and again until the working class is liberated. ("Speech on the Paris Commune," *Collected Works of Marx and Engels*, 1st Russ. ed., Vol. XIII, part 2, p. 655.)

What is the most important principle of the Commune? According to Marx, it is that the working class cannot simply take hold of the existing state machine, and use it for its own purposes. In other words, the proletariat should use revolutionary means to seize state power, smash the military and bureaucratic machine of the bourgeoisie and establish the proletarian dictatorship to replace the bourgeois dictatorship. Anyone familiar with the history of proletarian struggle knows that it is precisely this fundamental question which forms the dividing line between Marxists on the one hand and opportunists and revisionists on the other, and that after the death of Marx and Engels it was none other than Lenin who waged a thoroughly uncompromising struggle against the opportunists and revisionists in order to safeguard the principles of the Commune.

The cause in which the Paris Commune did not succeed finally triumphed 46 years later in the Great October Revolution under Lenin's direct leadership. The experience of the Russian Soviets was a continuation and development of the experience of the Paris Commune. The principles of the

Commune continually expounded by Marx and Engels and enriched by Lenin in the light of the new experience of the Russian revolution, became a living reality for the first time on one-sixth of the earth. Marx was perfectly correct in saying that the principles of the Commune are perpetual and indestructible.

In their attempt to strangle the new-born Soviet State, the imperialist jackals carried out armed intervention against it, in league with the Russian counterrevolutionary forces of that time. But the heroic Russian working class and the people of the various nationalities of the Soviet Union drove off the foreign bandits, wiped out the counterrevolutionary rebellion within the country and thus consolidated the world's first great Socialist Republic.

Under the banner of Lenin, under the banner of the October Revolution, a new world revolution began, with the proletarian revolution playing the leading role. A new era dawned in human history.

Through the October Revolution, the voice of Lenin quickly resounded throughout the world. The Chinese people's anti-imperialist, anti-feudal May 4 Movement in 1919, as Comrade Mao Tse-tung put it, "came into being at the call of the world revolution of that time, of the Russian Revolution and of Lenin." ("On New Democracy," *Selected Works of Mao Tse-tung*, Lawrence and Wishart, London, 1954, Vol. III, p. 146.)

Lenin's call is powerful because it is correct. Under the historical conditions of the imperialist era, Lenin revealed a series of irrefutable truths concerning the proletarian revolution and the proletarian dictatorship.

Lenin pointed out that the oligarchs of finance capital in a small number of capitalist powers, that is, imperialists, not only exploit the masses of people in their own countries, but oppress and plunder the whole world, turning most countries into their colonies and dependencies. Imperialist war is a continuation of imperialist policy. World wars are started by the imperialists because of their insatiable greed in struggling for world markets, sources of raw materials and fields for investment, and to redivide the world. So long as capitalist imperialism exists in the world, the sources and possibility of war will remain. The proletariat should guide the masses of people to an understanding of the sources of war and to struggle for peace and against imperialism.

Lenin asserted that imperialism is monopolistic, parasitic or decaying, moribund capitalism, that it is the final stage in the development of capitalism and therefore is the eve of the proletarian revolution. The emancipation of the proletariat can only be arrived at by the road of revolution, and certainly not by the road of reformism. The liberation movement of the proletariat in the capitalist countries should ally itself with the national liberation movements in the colonies and dependent countries; this alliance can smash the alliance of the imperialists with the feudal and comprador reactionary forces in the colonies and dependent countries, and will therefore inevitably put a final end to the imperialist system throughout the world.

In the light of the law of the uneven economic and political development of capitalism, Lenin came to the conclusion that, because capitalism developed extremely unevenly in different countries, socialism would achieve victory first in one or several countries but could not achieve victory simultaneously in all countries. Therefore, in spite of the victory of socialism in one or several countries, other capitalist countries will still exist, and this will give rise not only to friction but also to imperialist subversive activities against the socialist states. Hence the struggle will be protracted. The struggle between socialism and capitalism will embrace a whole historical epoch. The socialist countries should maintain constant vigilance against the danger of imperialist attack and do their best to guard against this danger.

The fundamental question of all revolutions is the question of state power. Lenin showed in a comprehensive and penetrating way that the fundamental question of the proletarian revolution is the proletarian dictatorship. The proletarian dictatorship, established by smashing the state machine of the bourgeois dictatorship by revolutionary means, is an alliance of a special type between the proletariat and the peasantry and all other working people; it is a continuation of the class struggle in another form under new conditions; it involves a persistent struggle, both sanguinary and bloodless, violent and peaceful, military and economic, educational and administrative, against the resistance of the exploiting classes, against foreign aggression and against the forces and traditions of the old society. Without the proletarian dictatorship, without its full mobilization of the working people on these fronts to wage these unavoidable struggles stubbornly and persistently, there can be no socialism, nor can there be any victory for socialism.

Lenin considered it of prime importance for the proletariat to establish its own genuinely revolutionary political party which completely breaks with opportunism, that is, a Communist Party, if the proletarian revolution is to be carried through and the proletarian dictatorship established and consolidated. This political party is armed with the theory of Marxist dialectical materialism and historical materialism. Its program is to organize the proletariat and all oppressed working people for class struggle, to set up proletarian rule and passing through socialism to reach the final goal of communism. This political party must identify itself with the masses and attach great importance to their creative initiative in the making of history; it must closely rely on the masses in revolution and must do the same in socialist and communist construction.

These truths were constantly set forth by Lenin before and after the October Revolution. The world reactionaries and philistines of the time thought these truths of Lenin terrifying. But we see these truths winning victory after victory in the practical life of the world.

In the forty years and more since the October Revolution, tremendous new changes have taken place in the world.

Through its great achievements in socialist and communist construction, the Soviet Union has transformed itself from an economically and technically very backward country in the days of imperial Russia into a first-rate world power with the most advanced technology. By its economic and technological leaps the Soviet Union has left the European capitalist countries far behind and left the United States behind, too, in technology.

The great victory of the antifascist war in which the Soviet Union was the main force broke the chain of imperialism in Central and Eastern Europe. The great victory of the Chinese people's revolution broke the chain of imperialism on the Chinese mainland. A new group of socialist countries was born. The whole socialist camp headed by the Soviet Union has one quarter of the earth's land space and over one third of the world's population. The socialist camp has now become an independent world economic system, standing opposite the capitalist world economic system. The gross industrial output value of the socialist countries now accounts for nearly 40 per cent of the world total, and it will not be long before it surpasses the gross industrial output value of all the capitalist countries put together.

The imperialist colonial system has disintegrated and is disintegrating further. The struggle naturally has its twists and turns, but on the whole the storm of the national liberation movement is sweeping over Asia, Africa and Latin America on a daily increasing scale. Things are developing towards their opposites: There the imperialists are going step by step from strength to weakness, while the people are going step by step from weakness to strength.

The relative stability of capitalism, which existed for a time after the First World War, ended long ago. With the formation of the socialist world economic system after the Second World War, the capitalist world market has greatly shrunk. The contradiction between the productive forces and production relations in capitalist society has become more acute. The periodic economic crises of capitalism no longer come as before once every ten years or so, but once almost every three or four years. Recently, some representatives of the U.S. bourgeoisie have admitted that the United States has suffered three "economic recessions" in ten years, and they now have premonitions of a new "economic recession" after just having pulled through the one in 1957-58. The shortening of the interval between capitalist economic crises is a new phenomenon. It is a further sign that the world capitalist system is drawing nearer and nearer to its inevitable doom.

The unevenness in the development of the capitalist countries is worse than ever before. The domain of the imperialists has shrunk more and more, so that they collide with one another. U.S. imperialism is constantly grabbing markets and spheres of influence away from the British, French and other imperialists. The imperialist countries headed by the United States have been expanding armaments and making war preparations for more than ten years, while West Germany and Japanese militarism, defeated in the Second World War, have risen again with the help of their former enemy—U.S. imperialism. The imperialists of these two countries have come out to join in the scramble for the capitalist world market, are now once again talking long and loudly about their "traditional friendship" and are engaging in new activities for a so-called "Bonn-Tokyo axis with

Washington as the starting point." West German imperialism is looking brazenly around for military bases abroad. This aggravates the bitter conflicts within imperialism and at the same time heightens the threat to the socialist camp and all peace-loving countries. The present situation is very much like that after the First World War when the U.S. and British imperialists fostered the resurgence of German militarism, and the outcome will again be their "picking up a rock only to drop it on their own feet." The U.S. imperialists' creation of world tension after the Second World War is a sign not of their strength but of their weakness and precisely reflects the unprecedented instability of the capitalist system.

The U.S. imperialists, in order to realize their ambition for world domination, not only carry out all kinds of premeditated sabotage and subversion against the socialist countries, but also, under the pretext of opposing "the communist menace," in their self-appointed role of world gendarme for suppressing the revolution in various countries, deploy their military bases all around the world, seize the intermediate areas and carry out military provocations. Like a rat running across the street while everyone shouts "Throw something at it!" the U.S. imperialists run into bumps and bruises everywhere and, contrary to their intentions, everywhere arouse a new upsurge of the people's revolutionary struggle. Now, they themselves are becoming aware that, in contrast with the growing prosperity of the socialist world headed by the Soviet Union, "the influence of the United States as a world power is declining." In them, one "can only see the decline and fall of ancient Rome."

The changes taking place in the world in the past forty years and more indicate that imperialism rots with every passing day while for socialism things are daily getting better. It is a great, new epoch that we are facing, and its main characteristic is that the forces of socialism have surpassed those of imperialism, that the forces of the awakening people of the world have surpassed those of reaction.

The present world situation has obviously undergone tremendous changes since Lenin's lifetime, but these changes have not proved the obsoleteness of Leninism; on the contrary, they have more and more clearly confirmed the truths revealed by Lenin and all the theories he advanced during the struggle to defend revolutionary Marxism and develop Marxism.

In the historical conditions of the epoch of imperialism and proletarian revolution, Lenin carried Marxism forward to a new stage and showed all the oppressed classes and people the path along which they could really shake off capitalist-imperialist enslavement and poverty. These forty years have been forty years of victory for Leninism in the world, forty years in which Leninism has found its way deeper into the hearts of the world's people. Leninism has not only won and will continue to win great victories in countries where the socialist system has been established, but is also constantly achieving new victories in the struggles of all oppressed peoples.

The victory of Leninism is acclaimed by the people of the whole world, and at the same time cannot but incur the enmity of the imperialists and all reactionaries. The imperialists, to weaken the influence of Leninism and paralyze the revolutionary will of the masses, launch the most barbarous and despicable attacks and slanders against Leninism, and, moreover, put up and utilize the vacillators and renegades within the workers' movement to distort and emasculate the teachings of Lenin. At the end of the nineteenth century when Marxism was putting various anti-Marxist trends to rout, spreading widely throughout the workers' movement and gaining a predominant position, the revisionists represented by Bernstein proposed to revise the teachings of Marx, in keeping with the needs of the bourgeoisie. Now, when Leninism is guiding the working class and all oppressed classes and nations of the world to great victories in the march against imperialism and all kinds of reactionaries, the modern revisionists represented by Tito propose to re-vise the teachings of Lenin (that is, modern Marxist teach-ings), in keeping with the needs of the imperialists. As pointed out in the Declaration of the meeting of representa-tives of the Communist and Workers' Parties of the socialist countries held in Moscow in November 1957, "The existence of bourgeois influence is an internal source of revisionism, while surrender to imperialist pressure is its external source." Old revisionism attempted to prove that Marxism was out-moded, while modern revisionism attempts to prove that Len-inism is outmoded. The Moscow Declaration said:

Modern revisionism seeks to smear the great teaching of Marx-ism-Leninism, declares that it is "outmoded" and alleges that it has lost its significance for social progress. The revisionists try to kill the revolutionary spirit of Marxism, to undermine faith in socialism among the working class and the working people in general.

This passage of the Declaration has put it correctly; such is exactly the situation.

Are the teachings of Marxism-Leninism now "outmoded"? Does the whole, integrated teaching of Lenin on imperialism, on proletarian revolution and proletarian dictatorship, on war and peace, and on the building of socialism and communism still retain its vigorous vitality? If it is still valid and does retain vigorous vitality, does this refer only to a certain portion of it or to the whole? We usually say that Leninism is Marxism in the epoch of imperialism and proletarian revolution, Marxism in the epoch of the victory of socialism and communism. Does this view remain correct? Can it be said that Lenin's original conclusions and our usual conception of Leninism have lost their validity and correctness, and that therefore we should turn back and accept those revisionist and opportunist conclusions which Lenin long ago smashed to smithereens and which have gone disgracefully bankrupt in actual life? These questions now confront us and must be answered. Marxist-Leninists must thoroughly expose the absurdities of the imperialists and modern revisionists on these questions, eradicate their influence among the masses, awaken those they have temporarily hoodwinked and further arouse the revolutionary will of the masses.

II.

The U.S. imperialists, open representatives of the bourgeoisie in many countries, the modern revisionists represented by the Tito clique, and the right-wing Social Democrats, in order to mislead the people of the world, do all they can to paint an utterly distorted picture of the contemporary world situation in an attempt to confirm their ravings on how "Marxism is outmoded," and "Leninism is outmoded too."

Tito's speech at the end of last year referred repeatedly to the so-called "new epoch" of the modern revisionists. He said, "Today the world has entered an epoch in which nations can relax and tranquilly devote themselves to their internal construction tasks." Then he added, "We have entered an epoch when new questions are on the agenda, not questions of war and peace but questions of co-operation, economic and otherwise, and when economic co-operation is concerned, there is also the question of economic competition." (From Tito's speech in Zagreb, December 12, 1959.) This renegade completely writes off the question of class contradictions and class struggle in the world, in an attempt to negate the consistent interpretation of Marxist-Leninists that our epoch is the epoch of imperialism and proletarian revolution, the epoch of the victory of socialism and communism.

But how do things really stand in the world?

Can the exploited and oppressed people in the imperialist countries "relax"? Can the peoples of all the colonies and semi-colonies still under imperialist oppression "relax"?

Has the armed intervention led by the U.S. imperialists in Asia, Africa and Latin America become "tranquil"? Is there "tranquillity" in our Taiwan [Formosa] Straits when the U.S. imperialists are still occupying our country's Taiwan? Is there "tranquillity" on the African continent when the people of Algeria and many other parts of Africa are subjected to armed repressions by the French, British and other imperialists? Is there any "tranquillity" in Latin America when the U.S. imperialists are trying to wreck the people's revolution in Cuba by means of bombing, assassination and subversion?

What kind of "construction" is meant in saying "(they) devote themselves to their internal construction tasks"? Everyone knows that there are different types of countries in the world today, and principally two types of countries with social systems fundamentally different in nature. One type belongs to the socialist world system, the other to the capitalist world system. Is Tito referring to the "internal construction tasks" of arms expansion which the imperialists are carrying out in order to oppress the peoples of their own countries and oppress the whole world? Or is it the "internal construction" carried out by socialism for the promotion of the people's happiness and in the pursuit of lasting world peace?

Is the question of war and peace no longer an issue? Is it that imperialism no longer exists, the system of exploitation no longer exists, and therefore the question of war no longer exists? Or is it that there can be no question of war even if imperialism and the system of exploitation are allowed to survive for ever? The fact is that since the Second World War there has been continuous and unbroken warfare. Do not the imperialist wars to suppress national liberation movements and the imperialist wars of armed intervention against revolutions in various countries count as wars? Even though these wars have not developed into world wars, still do not these local wars count as wars? Even though these wars were not fought with nuclear weapons, still do not wars using so-called conventional weapons count as wars? Does not the U.S. imperialists' allocation of nearly 60 per cent of the 1960 budget outlay to arms expansion and war preparations count as a bellicose policy on the part of U.S. imperialism? Will the revival of West German and Japanese militarisms not confront mankind with the danger of a new big war?

What kind of "co-operation" is meant? Is it "co-operation" of the proletariat with the bourgeoisie to protect capitalism? Is it "co-operation" of the colonial and semi-colonial peoples with the imperialists to protect colonialism? Is it "co-operation" of socialist countries with capitalist countries to protect the imperialist system in its oppression of the peoples in these countries and suppression of national liberation wars?

In a word, the assertions of the modern revisionists about their so-called "epoch" are so many challenges to Leninism on the foregoing issues. It is their aim to obliterate the contradiction between the masses of people and the monopoly capitalist class in the imperialist countries, the contradiction between the colonial and semi-colonial peoples and the imperialist aggressors, the contradiction between the socialist system and the imperialist system, and the contradiction between the peace-loving people of the world and the warlike imperialist bloc.

There have been different ways of describing the distinctions between different "epochs." Generally speaking, there is one way which is merely drivel, concocting and playing around with vague, ambiguous phrases to cover up the essence of the epoch. This is the old trick of the imperialists, the bourgeoisie and the revisionists in the workers' movement. Then there is another way, which is to make a concrete analysis of the concrete situation with regard to the over-all class contradictions and class struggle, putting forward strictly scientific definitions, and thus bringing the essence of the epoch thoroughly to light. This is the work of every serious Marxist.

On the features that distinguish an epoch, Lenin said:

. . . We are speaking here of big historical epochs; in every epoch there are, and there will be, separate, partial movements sometimes forward, at other times backwards; there are, and there will be, various deviations from the average type and average tempo of the movements.

We cannot know how fast and how successfully certain historical movements of the given epoch will develop. But we can and do know *which class* occupies a central position in this or that epoch and determines its main content, the main direction of its development, the main characteristics of the historical situation in the given epoch, etc.

Only on this basis, *i.e.*, by taking into consideration first and foremost the fundamental distinctive features of different "epochs" (and not of individual episodes in the history of different countries) can we correctly work out our tactics. . . . ("Under a False Flag," *Collected Works*, 4th Russ. ed., Vol. XXI, p. 125.)

An epoch, as referred to here by Lenin, presents the question of which class holds the central position in an epoch and determines its main content and main direction of development.

Faithful to Marx's dialectics, Lenin never for a single moment departed from the standpoint of analyzing class relations. He held that: "Marxism judges 'interests' by the class antagonisms and the class struggles which manifest themselves in millions of facts of everyday life." ("Collapse of the Second International," *Selected Works*, International Publishers, New York, 1943, Vol. V, p. 189.) He stated:

The method of Marx consists, first of all, in taking into consideration the *objective* content of the historical process at the given concrete moment, in the given concrete situation, in understanding first of all *which* class it is whose movement constitutes the mainspring of possible progress in this concrete situation. . . . ("Under a False Flag," *Collected Works*, 4th Russ. ed., Vol. XXI, p. 123.)

Lenin always demanded that we examine the concrete process of historical development on the basis of class analysis, instead of talking vaguely about "society in general" or "progress in general." We Marxists must not base proletarian policy merely on certain passing events or minute political changes, but on the over-all class contradictions and class struggle of a whole historical epoch. This is a basic theoretical position of Marxists. It was by taking a firm stand on this position that Lenin, in the new period of class changes, in the new historical period, came to the conclusion that the

hope of humanity lay entirely with the victory of the proletariat and that the proletariat must prepare itself to win
victory in this great revolutionary battle and establish a
proletarian dictatorship. After the October Revolution, at the
Seventh Congress of the Russian Communist Party (Bolsheviks) in 1918, Lenin stated:

We must begin with the general basis of the development of
commodity production, the transition to capitalism and the transformation of capitalism into imperialism. Thereby we shall be
theoretically taking up and consolidating a position from which
nobody can dislodge us. From this follows an equally inevitable
conclusion: the era of social revolution is beginning. ("Report
on Revising the Program and Name of the Party," *Selected
Works,* International Publishers, New York, 1943, Vol. VIII,
p. 317.)

This is Lenin's conclusion, a conclusion which up to the
present still requires deep consideration by all Marxists.

The formulation of revolutionary Marxists that ours is
the epoch of imperialism and proletarian revolution, the
epoch of the victory of socialism and communism is irrefutable, because it grasps with complete correctness the
basic features of our present great epoch. The formulation
that Leninism is the continuation and development of revolutionary Marxism in this great epoch and that it is the theory
and policy of proletarian revolution and proletarian dictatorship is also irrefutable, because it is precisely Leninism that
exposed the contradictions in our great epoch—the contradictions between the working class and monopoly capital,
the contradictions among the imperialist countries, the contradictions between the colonial and semi-colonial peoples
and imperialism, and the contradictions between the socialist countries, where the proletariat has triumphed, and
the imperialist countries. Leninism has, therefore, become our
banner of victory. Contrary, however, to this series of revolutionary Marxist formulation, in the so-called "new epoch" of
the Titos, there is actually no imperialism, no proletarian
revolution and, needless to say, no theory and policy of the
proletarian revolution and proletarian dictatorship. In short,
with them, the fundamental focal points of the class contradictions and class struggles of our epoch are nowhere to
be seen, the fundamental questions of Leninism are missing
and there is no Leninism.

The modern revisionists assert that in their so-called "new epoch," because of the progress of science and technology, the "old conceptions" of Marx and Lenin are no longer applicable. Tito made the following assertion: "We are not dogmatists, for Marx and Lenin did not predict the rocket on the moon, atomic bombs and the great technical progress." (From Tito's speech in Zagreb, December 12, 1959.) Not dogmatists, that's fine. Who wants them to be dogmatists? But one can oppose dogmatism to defend Marxism-Leninism or one can actually oppose Marxism-Leninism in the name of opposing dogmatism. The Titos belong to the latter category. On the question of what effect scientific and technological progress has on social development, there are people who hold incorrect views because they are not able to approach the question from the materialist viewpoint of history. This is understandable. But the modern revisionists, on the other hand, are deliberately creating confusion on this question in a vain attempt to make use of the progress in science and technology to throw Marxism-Leninism to the winds.

In the past few years, the achievements of the Soviet Union in science and technology have been foremost in the world. These Soviet achievements are products of the Great October Revolution. These outstanding achievements mark a new era in man's conquest of nature and at the same time play a very important role in defending world peace. But, in the new conditions brought about by the development of modern technology, has the ideological system of Marxism-Leninism been shaken, as Tito says, by the "rocket on the moon, atomic bombs and the great technical progress" which Marx and Lenin "did not predict"? Can it be said that the Marxist-Leninist world outlook, social-historical outlook, moral outlook and other basic concepts have therefore become what they call stale "dogmas" and that the law of class struggle henceforth no longer holds good?

Marx and Lenin did not live to the present day, and of course could not see certain specific details of technological progress in the present-day world. But what, after all, does the development of natural science and the advance of technology augur for the capitalist system? Marx and Lenin held that this could only augur a new social revolution, but could certainly not augur the fading away of social revolution.

We know that both Marx and Lenin rejoiced in the new discoveries and progress of natural science and technology in the conquest of nature. Engels said in his "Speech at the Graveside of Karl Marx":

Science was for Marx a historically dynamic, revolutionary force. However great the joy with which he welcomed a new discovery in some theoretical science whose practical application perhaps it was as yet quite impossible to envisage, he experienced quite another kind of joy when the discovery involved immediate revolutionary changes in industry, and in historical development in general. (*Selected Works of Marx & Engels,* Foreign Languages Publishing House, Moscow, 1955, Vol. II, p. 168.)

Engels added: "For Marx was before all else a revolutionist." Well said! Marx always regarded all new discoveries in the conquest of nature from the viewpoint of a proletarian revolutionist, not from the viewpoint of one who holds that the proletarian revolution will fade away.

Wilhelm Liebknecht wrote in his *Reminiscences of Marx:*

Marx made fun of the victorious European reaction which imagined that it had stifled the revolution and did not suspect that natural science was preparing a new revolution. King Steam, who had revolutionized the world in the previous century, was coming to the end of his reign and another incomparably greater revolutionary would take his place, the electric spark..
. . . The consequences are unpredictable. The economic revolution must be followed by a political one, for the latter is only the expression of the former.
In the manner in which Marx discussed this progress of science and mechanics, his conception of the world, and especially what has been termed the materialist conception of history, was so clearly expressed that certain doubts which I had hitherto still maintained melted away like snow in the sunshine of spring. (Wilhelm Liebknecht and Paul Lafargue's *Reminiscences of Marx,* Lawrence & Wishart, p. 15.)

This is how Marx felt the breath of revolution in the progress of science and technology. Marx held that the new progress of science and technology would lead to a social revolution to overthrow the capitalist system. To Marx, the progress of natural science and technology further strengthens the whole position of the Marxist world outlook and the materialist conception of history, and certainly does not shake it. The progress of natural science and technology further strengthens the position of the proletarian revolution, and of the oppressed nations in their fight against imperialism, and certainly does not weaken it.

Like Marx, Lenin also viewed technological progress in connection with the question of revolution in the social system. Thus Lenin held that:

The age of steam is the age of the bourgeoisie, the age of electricity is the age of socialism. ("Report on Work of All-Russia Central Executive Committee and People's Council," *Collected Works,* 4th Russ. ed., Vol. XXX, p. 310.)

Please note the contrast between the revolutionary spirit of Marx and Lenin and the modern revisionists' shameful attitude of betraying the revolution!

In class society, in the epoch of imperialism, Marxist-Leninists can only approach the question of the development and use of technology from the viewpoint of class analysis.

Inasmuch as the socialist system is progressive and represents the interests of the people, the socialist countries want to utilize such new techniques as atomic energy and rocketry to serve peaceful domestic construction and the conquest of nature. The more the socialist countries master such new techniques and the more rapidly they develop them, the better will they attain the aim of high-speed development of the social productive forces to meet the needs of the people, and the more will they strengthen the forces for checking imperialist war and increase the possibility of defending world peace. Therefore, for the welfare of their peoples and in the interest of peace for people the world over, the socialist countries should, wherever possible, master more and more of such new techniques serving the well-being of the people.

At the present time, the socialist Soviet Union clearly holds the upper hand in the development of new techniques. Everybody knows that the rocket that hit the moon was launched by the Soviet Union and not by the United States, the country where capitalism is most developed. This shows that only in the socialist countries can there be unlimited prospects for the large-scale development of new techniques.

On the contrary, inasmuch as the imperialist system is reactionary and against the people, the imperialist powers want to use such new techniques for military purposes of aggression against foreign countries, to intimidate the people within their own countries, to make weapons for human slaughter. To the imperialist powers, the emergence of such new techniques only means pushing to a new stage the contradiction between the development of the social productive forces and the capitalist relations of production. What this will bring about is not by any means the perpetuation of capitalism but the further rousing of the revolution of the people in those countries and the destruction of the old, criminal, cannibalistic system of capitalism.

The U.S. imperialists and their partners use weapons like atom bombs to threaten war and blackmail the whole world. They declare that anyone who does not submit to the domination of U.S. imperialism will be destroyed. The Tito clique echoes this line; it takes up the U.S. imperialist refrain to spread terror of atomic warfare among the masses. U.S. imperialist blackmail and the chiming in of the Tito clique can only temporarily dupe those who do not understand the real situation, but cannot cow the people who have awakened. Even those who for the time being do not understand the real situation will gradually come to understand it with the help of the advanced elements.

Marxist-Leninists have always maintained that in world history it is not technique but man, the masses of people, that determine the fate of mankind. There was a theory current for a time among some people in China before and during the War of Resistance to Japanese Aggression, which was known as the "weapons-mean-everything theory"; from this theory they concluded that since Japan's weapons were new and its techniques advanced while China's weapons were old and its techniques backward, "China would inevitably be subjugated." Comrade Mao Tse-tung in his work *On the Protracted War* published at that time refuted such nonsense. He made the following analysis: The Japanese imperialists' war of aggression against China was bound to fail because it was reactionary, unjust, and being unjust lacked popular support; the Chinese people's war of resistance against Japan would certainly win because it was progressive, just, and being just enjoyed abundant support. Comrade Mao Tse-tung pointed out that the most abundant source of strength in war lay in the masses, and that a people's army organized by awakened and united masses of people would be invincible throughout the world. This is a Marxist-Leninist thesis. And what was the outcome? The outcome was that the Marxist-Leninist thesis triumphed and the "theory of national subjugation" ended in defeat. During the Korean war after the Second World War, the triumph of the Korean and Chinese peoples over U.S. aggressors far superior in weapons and equipment again bore out this Marxist-Leninist thesis.

An awakened people will always find new ways to counteract a reactionary superiority in arms and win victory for themselves. This was so in past history, it is so at present, and it will still be so in the future. Because the socialist Soviet Union has gained supremacy in military techniques, the U.S. imperialists have lost their monopoly of atomic and nuclear weapons; at the same time, as a result of the awakening of the people the world over and the awakening of the people in the United States itself, there is now in the world the possibility of concluding an agreement for the banning of atomic and nuclear weapons. We are striving for the conclusion of such an agreement. Unlike the bellicose imperialists, the socialist countries and peace-loving people the world over actively and firmly stand for the banning and destruction of atomic and nuclear weapons. We are always struggling against imperialist war, for the banning of atomic and nuclear weapons and for the defense of world peace. The more broadly and profoundly this struggle is waged and the more fully and thoroughly exposed are the brutish faces of the bellicose U.S. and other imperialists, the more will we be able to isolate these imperialists before the people of the world, the greater will be the possibility of tying their hands and the better it will be for the cause of world peace. If, on the contrary, we lose our vigilance against the danger of the imperialists launching a war, do not work to arouse the people of all countries to rise up against imperialism but tie the hands of the people, then imperialism can prepare for war just as it pleases and the inevitable result will be an increase in the danger of the imperialists launching a war and, once war breaks out, the people may not be able quickly to adopt a correct attitude towards it because of complete lack of preparation or inadequate preparation, thus being unable to vigorously check the war. Of course, whether or not the imperialists will unleash a war is not determined by us; we are, after all, not chiefs-of-staff to the imperialists. As long as the people of all countries enhance their awareness and are fully prepared, with the socialist camp also mastering modern weapons, it is certain that if the U.S. or other imperialists refuse to reach an agreement on the banning of atomic and nuclear weapons and should dare to fly in the face of the will of all humanity by launching a war using atomic and nuclear weapons, the result will be the very speedy destruction of these monsters encircled by the peoples of the world, and the result will certainly not be the annihilation of mankind. We consistently oppose the launching of criminal wars by imperialism, because imperialist war would impose enormous sacrifices upon the peoples of various countries (including the peoples of the United States and other imperialist countries). But should the imperialists impose such sacrifices on the peoples of various countries, we believe that, just as the experience of the Russian revolution and the Chinese revolution shows, those sacrifices would be repaid. On the debris of a dead imperialism, the victorious people would create very swiftly a civilization thousands of times higher than the capitalist system and a truly beautiful future for themselves.

The conclusion can only be this: whichever way you look at it, none of the new techniques like atomic energy, rocketry and so on has changed, as alleged by the modern revisionists, the basic characteristics of the epoch of imperialism and proletarian revolution pointed out by Lenin. The capitalist-imperialist system absolutely will not crumble of itself. It will be overthrown by the proletarian revolution within the imperialist country concerned, and the national revolution in the colonies and semi-colonies. Contemporary technological progress cannot save the capitalist-imperialist system from its doom but only rings a new death knell for it.

III.

The modern revisionists, proceeding from their absurd arguments on the current world situation and from their absurd argument that the Marxist-Leninist theory of class analysis and class struggle is obsolete, attempt to totally overthrow the fundamental theories of Marxism-Leninism on a series of questions like violence, war, peaceful coexistence, etc.

There are also some people who are not revisionists, but well-intentioned persons who sincerely want to be Marxists, but get confused in the face of certain new historical phenomena and thus have some incorrect ideas. For example, some of them say that the failure of the U.S. imperialists' policy of atomic blackmail marks the end of violence. While thoroughly refuting the absurdities of the modern revisionists, we should also help these well-intentioned people to correct their erroneous ideas.

What is violence? Lenin had a lot to say on this question in his book *The State and Revolution.* The emergence and existence of the state is in itself a kind of violence. Lenin introduced the following elucidation by Engels:

... it (this public power) consists not merely of armed men, but of material appendages, prisons and coercive institutions of all kinds. . . . (*Selected Works,* International Publishers, New York, Vol. VII, p. 10.)

Lenin tells us that we must draw a distinction between two types of states different in nature, the state of bourgeois dictatorship and the state of proletarian dictatorship, and between two types of violence different in nature, counterrevolutionary violence and revolutionary violence; as long as there is counterrevolutionary violence, there is bound to be revolutionary violence to oppose it. It would be impossible to wipe out counterrevolutionary violence without revolutionary violence. The state in which the exploiting classes are in power is counterrevolutionary violence, a special force for suppressing the exploited classes in the interest of the exploiting classes. Both before the imperialists had atomic bombs and rocket weapons, and since they have had these new weapons, the imperialist state has always been a special force for suppressing the proletariat at home and the people of its colonies and semi-colonies abroad, has always been such an institution of violence; even if it is compelled not to use these new weapons, the imperialist state will of course still remain an imperialist institution of violence until it is overthrown and replaced by the people's state, the state of the dictatorship of the proletariat of that country.

Never since the dawn of history have there been such large-scale, such utterly vicious forces of violence as those of present-day capitalist imperialists. For the past ten years and more, the U.S. imperialists have, without any scruples, adopted means of persecution a hundred times more savage than before, trampling upon the outstanding sons of the country's working class, trampling upon the Negro people, trampling upon all progressives, and moreover, recklessly declaring that they intend to put the whole world under their rule of violence. They are continuously expanding their forces of violence, and at the same time the other imperialists also take part in the race to increase their forces of violence.

The bloated military build-up of the imperialist countries headed by the United States has appeared during the unprecedentedly grave general crisis of capitalism. The more frantically the imperialists carry the expansion of their military forces to a peak, the nearer they draw to their own doom. Now even some representatives of the U.S. imperialists have premonitions of the inevitable extinction of the capitalist system. But will the imperialists themselves put an end to their violence? Will those in power in the imperialist countries abandon of their own accord the violence they have set up just because imperialism is drawing near to its doom?

Can it be said that, compared with the past, the imperialists are no longer addicted to violence, or that there has been a lessening in the degree of their addiction?

Lenin answered such questions on several occasions long ago. He pointed out in his book *Imperialism, the Highest Stage of Capitalism*:

. . . for politically imperialism is in general a striving towards violence and reaction. (*Selected Works,* International Publishers, New York, Vol. V, p. 83.)

After the October Revolution, in his book *The Proletarian Revolution and the Renegade Kautsky* he made a special point of recounting history, comparing the differences between premonopoly capitalism and monopoly capitalism, *i.e.,* imperialism. He said:

Premonopoly capitalism, which reached its zenith in the seventies of the nineteenth century, was, by virtue of its fundamental *economic* traits (which were most typical in England and America) distinguished by its relative attachment to peace and freedom. Imperialism, *i.e.,* monopoly capitalism, which finally matured only in the twentieth century, is, by virtue of its fundamental *economic* traits, distinguished by the least attachment to peace and freedom, and by the greatest and universal development of militarism everywhere. (*Selected Works,* International Publishers, Vol. VII, pp. 125-126.)

Of course, these words of Lenin were uttered in the early period of the October Revolution, when the proletarian state was newly born, and its economic forces still young and weak, while with the lapse of forty years and more, the face of the Soviet state itself, and of the whole world has undergone a tremendous change, as we have already described. Then, are the foregoing pronouncements of Lenin obsolete, because the nature of imperialism has changed owing to the might of the Soviet Union, the might of the forces of socialism and the might of the forces of peace? Or, is it that imperialism, although its nature has not changed, will no longer resort to violence? Do these ideas conform to the real situation?

The socialist world system has obviously gained the upper hand in its struggle with the capitalist world system. This great historic fact has weakened the position of imperialist violence in the world. But will this fact cause the imperialists never again to oppress the people of their own country, never again engage in outward expansion and aggressive activities? Can it make the warlike circles of the imperialists "lay down the butcher knife" and "sell their knives and buy oxen"? Can it make the groups of munitions merchants in the imperialist countries change over to peaceful pursuits?

All these questions confront every serious Marxist-Leninist, and require deep consideration. It is obvious that whether these questions are viewed and handled correctly or incorrectly has a close bearing on the success or failure of the proletarian cause and the destiny of humanity.

War is the most acute form of expression of violence. One type is civil war, another is foreign war. Violence is not always expressed by war, its most acute form. In capitalist countries, bourgeois war is the continuation of the bourgeois policies of ordinary times, while bourgeois peace is the continuation of bourgeois wartime policy. The bourgeoisie are always switching back and forth between the two forms, war and peace, to carry on their rule over the people and their external struggle. In what they call peace time, the imperialists rely on armed force to deal with the oppressed classes and nations by such forms of violence as arrest, imprisonment, sentencing to hard labor, massacre and so forth, while at the same time, they also carry on preparations for using the most acute form of violence—war—to suppress the revolution of the people at home, to carry out plunder abroad, to overwhelm foreign competitors and to stamp out revolutions in other countries. Or, peace at home may exist side by side with war abroad.

In the initial period of the October Revolution, all the imperialist powers resorted to violence in the form of war against the Soviet Union, which was a continuation of their imperialist policies; in the Second World War, the German imperialists used violence in the form of large-scale war to attack the Soviet Union, which was a continuation of their imperialist policy. But on the other hand, the imperialists also establish diplomatic relations of peaceful coexistence with the Soviet Union in different periods, which is also, of course, a continuation of imperialist policy in another form under certain conditions.

True, some new questions have now arisen concerning peaceful coexistence. Confronted with the powerful Soviet Union and the powerful socialist camp, the imperialists must at any rate carefully consider whether they wouldn't hasten their own extinction, as Hitler did, or bring about the most serious consequences for the capitalist system itself, if they should attack the Soviet Union, attack the socialist countries.

"Peaceful Coexistence"—this is a new concept which arose only after socialist countries appeared in the world following the October Revolution. It is a new concept formed under circumstances Lenin had predicted before the October Revolution, when he said:

Socialism cannot achieve victory simultaneously in all countries. It will achieve victory first in one or several countries, while the others will remain bourgeois or pre-bourgeois for some time. ("The War Program of the Proletarian Revolution," *Selected Works,* F.L.P.H., Moscow, 1952, Vol. I, part 2, p. 571.)

This new concept is one advanced by Lenin after the great Soviet people overcame the armed imperialist intervention. As was pointed out above, at the outset the imperialists were not willing to coexist peacefully with the Soviet Union. The imperialists were compelled to "coexist" with the Soviet Union only after the war of intervention against the Soviet Union had failed, after there had been several years of actual trial of strength, after the Soviet state had planted its feet firmly on the ground, and after a certain balance of power had taken shape between the Soviet state and the imperialist countries. Lenin said in 1920:

We have won conditions for ourselves under which we can exist alongside the capitalist powers, which are now forced to enter into trade relations with us. ("Our Internal and External

Situation and the Party's Tasks," *Collected Works*, 4th Russ. ed., Vol. XXI, p. 384.)

It can be seen that the realization of peaceful coexistence for a certain period between the world's first socialist state and imperialism was won entirely through struggle. Before the Second World War, the 1920-1940 period prior to Germany's attack on the Soviet Union was a period of peaceful coexistence between imperialism and the Soviet Union. During all those twenty years, the Soviet Union kept faith with peaceful coexistence. However, in 1941, Hitler was no longer willing to coexist peacefully with the Soviet Union, the German imperialists perfidiously launched a savage attack on the Soviet Union. Owing to victory in the antifascist war, with the great Soviet Union as the main force, the world saw once again a situation of peaceful coexistence between the socialist and capitalist countries. Nevertheless, the imperialists have not given up their designs. The U.S. imperialists have set up networks of military bases and guided missile bases everywhere around the Soviet Union and the entire socialist camp. They are still occupying our territory Taiwan and continually carrying out military provocations against us in the Taiwan Straits. They carried out armed intervention in Korea, conducting a large-scale war against the Korean and Chinese peoples on Korean soil, which resulted in an armistice agreement only after their defeat—and up to now they are still interfering with the unification of the Korean people. They gave aid in weapons to the French imperialist occupation forces in their war against the Vietnamese people, and up to now they are still interfering with the unification of the Vietnamese people. They engineered the counterrevolutionary rebellion in Hungary, and up to now they are continually making all sorts of attempts at subversion in the East European and other socialist countries. The facts are still just as Lenin presented them to a U.S. correspondent in February 1920: on the question of peace, "there is no obstacle on our side. The obstacle is the imperialism of American (and all other) capitalists." (*Collected Works*, 4th Russ. ed., Vol. XXX, p. 340.)

The foreign policy of socialist countries can only be a policy of peace. The socialist system determines that we do not need war, absolutely would not start a war, and absolutely must not, should not and could not encroach one inch on the territory of a neighboring country. Ever since its founding, the People's Republic of China has adhered to a foreign policy of peace. Our country together with two neighboring countries, India and Burma, jointly initiated the well-known Five Principles of Peaceful Coexistence; and at the Bandung Conference of 1955, our country together with various countries of Asia and Africa adopted the ten principles of peaceful coexistence. The Communist Party and Government of our country have in the past few years consistently supported the activities for peace carried out by the Central Committee of the Communist Party and the Government of the Soviet Union headed by Comrade N.S. Khrushchev, considering that these activities on the part of the Communist Party and the Government of the Soviet Union have further demonstrated before the people of the world the firmness of the socialist countries' peaceful foreign policy as well as the need for the peoples to stop the imperialists from launching another world war and to strive for a lasting world peace.

The Declaration of the Moscow Conference of 1957 states:

The cause of peace is upheld by the powerful forces of our era: the invincible camp of socialist countries headed by the Soviet Union; the peace-loving countries of Asia and Africa taking an anti-imperialist stand and forming, together with the socialist countries, a broad peace zone; the international working class and above all its vanguard—the Communist Parties; the liberation movement of the peoples of the colonies and semi-colonies; the mass peace movement of the peoples; the peoples of the European countries who have proclaimed neutrality, the peoples of Latin America and the masses in the imperialist countries who themselves are firmly resisting plans for a new war. An alliance of these mighty forces could prevent war.

So long as there is a continuous development of these mighty forces, it is possible to maintain the situation of peaceful coexistence, or even to obtain some sort of official agreement on peaceful coexistence or to conclude an agreement on prohibition of atomic and nuclear weapons. That would be a fine thing in full accord with the aspirations of the peoples of the world. However, even under those circumstances, as long as the imperialist system still exists, the most acute form of violence, namely, war, has by no means ended in the world. The fact is not as described by the Yugoslav revisionists, who declare obsolete Lenin's definition that "war is the continuation of politics" ("Active Coexistence and Socialism," *Narod-*

na Armija, November 28, 1958), a definition which he repeatedly explained and upheld in combating opportunism.

We believe in the absolute correctness of Lenin's thinking: War is an inevitable outcome of systems of exploitation and the source of modern wars is the imperialist system. Until the imperialist system and the exploiting classes come to an end, wars of one kind or another will always occur. They may be wars among the imperialists for redivision of the world, or wars of aggression and anti-aggression between the imperialists and the oppressed nations, or civil wars of revolution and counterrevolution between the exploited and exploiting classes in the imperialist countries, or, of course, wars in which the imperialists attack the socialist countries and the socialist countries are forced to defend themselves. All these kinds of wars represent the continuation of the policies of definite classes. Marxist-Leninists absolutely must not sink into the mire of bourgeois pacifism, and can only appraise all these kinds of wars and thus draw conclusions for proletarian policy by adopting the method of concrete class analysis. As Lenin put it: "Theoretically, it would be quite wrong to forget that every war is but the continuation of politics by other means." ("The War Program of the Proletarian Revolution," *Selected Works*, F.L.P.H., Moscow, 1952, Vol. I, part 2, p. 572.)

To attain their aim of plunder and oppression, the imperialists always have two tactics: the tactics of war and the tactics of "peace"; therefore, the proletariat and the people of all countries must also use two tactics to counter the imperialists: the tactics of thoroughly exposing the imperialists' peace fraud and striving energetically for a genuine world peace, and the tactics of preparing for a just war to end the imperialist unjust war when and if the imperialists should unleash it.

In a word, in the interests of the people of the world, we must thoroughly shatter the falsehoods of the modern revisionists and uphold the Marxist-Leninist viewpoints on the questions of violence, war and peaceful coexistence.

The Yugoslav revisionists deny the inherent class character of violence and thereby obliterate the fundamental difference between revolutionary violence and counterrevolutionary violence; they deny the inherent class character of war and thereby obliterate the fundamental difference between just war and unjust war; they deny that imperialist war is a continuation of imperialist policy, deny the danger of the imperialists unleashing another big war, deny that it will be possible to do away with war only after doing away with the exploiting classes, and even shamelessly call the U.S. imperialist chieftain Eisenhower "the man who laid the cornerstone for eliminating the cold war and establishing lasting peace with peaceful competition between different political systems" ("Eisenhower Arrives in Rome," *Borba*, December 4, 1959); they deny that under the conditions of peaceful coexistence there are still complicated, acute struggles in the political, economic and ideological fields, and so on. All these arguments of the Yugoslav revisionists are aimed at poisoning the minds of the proletariat and the people of all countries, and are helpful to the imperialist policy of war.

IV.

Modern revisionists seek to confuse the peaceful foreign policy of the socialist countries with the domestic policies of the proletariat in the capitalist countries. They thus hold that peaceful coexistence of countries with differing social systems mean that capitalism can peacefully grow into socialism, that the proletariat in countries ruled by the bourgeoisie can renounce class struggle and enter into "peaceful co-operation" with the bourgeoisie and the imperialists, and that the proletariat and all the exploited classes should forget about the fact that they are living in a class society, and so on. All these views are also diametrically opposed to Marxism-Leninism. They are put forward in an attempt to protect imperialist rule and hold the proletariat and all the rest of the working people perpetually in capitalist enslavement.

Peaceful coexistence of nations and people's revolutions in various countries are in themselves two different things, not one and the same thing; two different concepts, not one; two different kinds of question, and not one and the same kind of question.

Peaceful coexistence refers to relations between nations; revolution means the overthrow of the oppressors as a class by the oppressed people within each country, while in the case of the colonial and semi-colonial countries, it is first and foremost a question of overthrowing alien oppressors, namely, the imperialists. Before the October Revolution the question of peaceful coexistence between socialist and capitalist countries simply did not exist in the world, as there were as yet no socialist countries; but there did exist at that time the questions of the proletarian revolution and the national revolution, as the peoples in various countries, in accordance with their own specific conditions, had long ago put revolutions of one kind or the other on the agenda of the day to determine the destinies of their countries.

We are Marxist-Leninists. We have always held that revolution is each nation's own affair. We have always maintained that the working class can only depend on itself for its emancipation, and that the emancipation of the people of any given country depends on their own awakening, and on the ripening of revolution in that country. Revolution can neither be exported nor imported. No one can prevent the people of a foreign country from carrying out a revolution, nor can one produce a revolution in a foreign country by using the method of "helping the rice shoots to grow by pulling them up."

Lenin put it well when he said in June 1918:

There are people who believe that the revolution can break out in a foreign country to order, by agreement. These people ar either mad or they are provocateurs. We have experienced two revolutions during the past twelve years. We know that revolutions cannot be made to order, or by agreement: they break out when tens of millions of people come to the conclusion that it is impossible to live in the old way any longer. ("The Fourth Conference of Trade Unions and Factory Committees of Moscow," *Selected Works*, International Publishers, New York, Vol. VII, p. 414.)

In addition to the experience of the Russian revolution, is not the experience of the Chinese revolution also one of the best proofs of this? The Chinese people, under the leadership of the Chinese Communist Party, have experienced several revolutions. The imperialists and all the reactionaries, like lunatics, have always asserted that our revolutions were made to order from abroad, or in accordance with foreign agreements. But people all over the world know that our revolutions were not imported from abroad, but were brought about because our people found it impossible to continue to live in the old China and because they wanted to create a new life of their own.

When a socialist country, in the face of imperialist aggression, is compelled to launch counterattacks in a defensive war, and goes beyond its own border to pursue and eliminate its enemies from abroad, as the Soviet Union did in the war against Hitler, is this justified? Certainly it is completely justified, absolutely necessary and entirely just. In accordance with the strict principles of communists, such operations by the socialist countries must be strictly limited to the time when the imperialists launch a war of aggression against them. Socialist countries never permit themselves to send, never should and never will send their troops across their borders unless they are subjected to aggression from a foreign enemy. Since the armed forces of the socialist countries fight for justice, when these forces have to go beyond their borders to counterattack a foreign enemy, it is only natural that they should exert an influence and have an effect wherever they go; but even then, the emergence of people's revolutions and the establishment of the socialist system in those places and countries where they go will still depend on the will of the masses of the people there.

The spread of revolutionary ideas knows no national boundaries. But these ideas will only yield revolutionary fruit in the hands of the masses of people themselves, under specific circumstances in a given country. This is so not only in the epoch of proletarian revolution, but also in the epoch of bourgeois revolution. The bourgeoisie of various countries at the time of their revolution took Rousseau's *Social Contract* as their gospel, while the revolutionary proletariat in various countries take as their gospels Marx's *Communist Manifesto* and *Capital* and Lenin's *Imperialism, the Highest Stage of Capitalism* and *The State and Revolution*. Times vary, the classes vary, the ideologies vary and the character of the revolutions varies. But no one can hold back a revolution in any country if there is a desire for that revolution and when the revolutionary crisis there has matured. In the end the socialist system will replace the capitalist system. This is an objective law independent of human will. No matter how hard the reactionaries may try to prevent the advance of the wheel of history, revolution will take place sooner or later and will surely triumph. The same applies to the replacement of one society by another throughout human history. The slave system was replaced by the feudal system which, in its turn, gave way to the capitalist system. These, too, follow laws independent of human will. These replacements were carried out through revolution.

That notorious old revisionist Bernstein once said, "Remember ancient Rome, there was a ruling class that did no work, but lived well, and as a result, this class weakened. Such a class must gradually hand over its power." That the slaveowners as a class weakened was a historical fact that Bernstein could not conceal, any more than the present U.S. imperialists can conceal the fact of their own steady decline. Yet Bernstein, shameless, self-styled "historian" that he was, chose to cover up the following basic facts of ancient Roman history: the slaveowners never "handed over power" of their own accord; their rule was overthrown by protracted, repeated, continuous slave revolutions.

Revolution means the use of revolutionary violence by the oppressed class, it means revolutionary war. This is true of the slave revolution; this is also true of the bourgeois revolution. Lenin has put it well:

History teaches us that no oppressed class ever achieved power, nor could achieve power, without going through a period of dictatorship, *i.e.*, the conquest of political power and suppression by force of the most desperate, frenzied resistance always offered by the exploiters. . . . The bourgeoisie . . . came to power in the advanced countries through a series of insurrections, civil wars, the suppression by force of kings, feudalists, slaveowners and their attempts at restoration. ("Theses on Bourgeois Democracy and Proletarian Dictatorship Presented to the First Congress of the Communist International," *Lenin Against Revisionism*, F.L.P.H., Moscow, 1959, p. 488.)

Why do things happen this way?

In answering this question, again we have to quote Lenin.

In the first place, as Lenin said: "No ruling class in the world ever gave way without a struggle." ("Speech at Workers' Conference of Presnia District," *Collected Works*, 4th Russ. ed., Vol. XXVIII, p. 338.)

Secondly, as Lenin explained: "The reactionary classes themselves are usually the first to resort to violence, to civil war; they are the first to 'place the bayonet on the agenda.'" ("Two Tactics of Social-Democracy in the Democratic Revolution," *Selected Works*, F.L.P.H., Moscow, Vol. I, part 2, p. 142.)

In the light of this how shall we conceive of the proletarian socialist revolution?

In order to answer this question we must quote Lenin again.

Let us read the following passage by him.

Not a single great revolution in history has ever been carried out without a civil war and no serious Marxist will believe it possible to make the transition from capitalism to socialism without a civil war. ("Prediction," *Collected Works*, 4th Russ. ed., Vol. XXVII, p. 457.)

These words of Lenin here explain the question very clearly.

And here is another quotation from Lenin:

If socialism had been born peacefully—but the capitalist gentlemen did not wish to let it be born thus. . . . Even if there had been no war the capitalist gentlemen would still have done all they could to prevent such a peaceful development. Great revolutions, even when they began peacefully, like the great French Revolution, have ended in desperate wars, which have been started by the counterrevolutionary bourgeoisie. ("First All-Russian Conference on Social Education," *Collected Works*, 4th Russ. ed., Vol. XXIX, p. 334.)

This is also very clearly put.

The Great October Revolution is the best material witness to the truth of these propositions of Lenin.

So is the Chinese revolution. No one will ever forget that it was only after twenty-two years of bitter civil war under the leadership of the Chinese Communist Party that the Chinese people and the Chinese proletariat won nationwide victory and captured state power.

The history of the proletarian revolution in the West after the First World War tells us: even when the capitalist gentlemen do not exercise direct, open control of state power, but rule through their lackeys—the treacherous Social Democrats, these despicable renegades will surely be ready at any time, in accordance with the dictates of the bourgeoisie, to cover up the violence of the bourgeois White Guards and plunge the proletarian revolutionary fighters into a blood bath. This is just the way it was in Germany at that time. Vanquished, the big German bourgeoisie handed over state power to the Social Democrats. The Social-Democratic government, on coming to power, immediately set about a bloody suppression of the German working class in January 1919. Let us recall how Karl Liebknecht and Rosa Luxemburg, whom Lenin called "the best representatives of the world proletarian International" and "the immortal leaders of the international socialist revolution," shed their blood as a result of the violence of the Social Democrats of the day. Let us also recall, in Lenin's words, "the vileness and shamelessness of these murders" (*A Letter to the Workers of Europe and America*, F.L.P.H., Moscow, 1954, p. 16) perpetrated by these renegades—these so-called "socialists" for the purpose of preserving the capitalist system and the interests of the bourgeoisie! Let us, in the light of bloody facts both of the historical past and of the modern capitalist world, examine all this nonsense about the "peaceful growth of capitalism into socialism" put out by the old revisionists and their modern counterparts.

Does it follow, then, that we Marxist-Leninists will refuse to adopt the policy of peaceful transition even when there exists the possibility of such peaceful development? No, decidedly not!

As we all know, Engels, one of the great founders of scientific communism, in the famous work *Principles of Communism* answered the question: "Can private property be eliminated by peaceful means?" He wrote:

One would wish that it could be thus, and communists, of course, would be the last to object to this. Communists know well that all plots are not only futile, but even pernicious. They know very well that revolutions cannot be thought up and made as one wishes and that revolutions have always and everywhere been the necessary result of existing conditions, which have absolutely not depended on the will and leadership of separate parties and whole classes. But at the same time, they see that the development of the proletariat in nearly all civilized countries is being violently suppressed and that in this way the opponents of the communists are working as hard as they can for the revolution. . . . ("Principles of Communism," *Collected Works of Marx and Engels*, 2nd Russ. ed., Vol. IV, p. 331.)

This was written over a hundred years ago, yet how fresh it is as we read it again!

We also know that for a time following the Russian February Revolution, in view of the specific conditions of the time, Lenin did adopt the policy of peaceful development of the revolution. He considered it "an extraordinarily rare opportunity in the history of revolutions" ("The Tasks of the Revolution," *Collected Works*, 4th Russ. ed. Vol. XXVI, p. 45) and grasped tight hold of it. The bourgeois Provisional Government and the White Guards, however, destroyed this possibility of peaceful development of the revolution and so drenched the streets of Petrograd in the blood of the workers and soldiers marching in a peaceful mass demonstration in July. Lenin, therefore, pointed out:

The peaceful course of development has been rendered impossible. A nonpeaceful and most painful course has begun. ("On Slogans," *Selected Works*, F.L.P.H., Moscow, Vol. II, part 1, p. 89.)

We know too that as the Chinese War of Resistance to Japanese Aggression came to an end, there was a widespread and ardent desire for peace in the country. Our Party then conducted peace negotiations with the Kuomintang, seeking to institute social and political reforms by peaceful means, and in 1946 an agreement on achieving peace throughout the country was reached with the Kuomintang. The reactionary Kuomintang clique, however, defying the will of the whole people, tore up this agreement and, with the support of the U.S. imperialists, launched a civil war on a nationwide scale, leaving the people with no option but to counter it with a revolutionary war. As we never relaxed our vigilance or gave up the people's armed forces even in our struggle for·peaceful reform but were fully prepared, the people were not cowed by the war, but those who launched the war were made to eat their own bitter fruit.

It would be in the best interests of the people if the proletariat could attain power and carry out the transition to socialism by peaceful means. It would be wrong not to make use of such a possibility when it occurs. Whenever an opportunity for "peaceful development of the revolution" presents itself communists must seize it, as Lenin did, so as to realize the aim of the socialist revolution. However, this sort of opportunity is always, in Lenin's words, "an extraordinarily rare opportunity in the history of revolutions." When in a given country a certain local political power is already surrounded by revolutionary forces or when in the world a certain capitalist country is already surrounded by socialism

—in such cases, there might be a greater possibility of opportunities for the peaceful development of the revolution. But even then, the peaceful development of the revolution should never be regarded as the only possibility and it is therefore necessary to be prepared at the same time for the other possibility, *i.e.*, nonpeaceful development of the revolution. For instance, after the liberation of the Chinese mainland, although certain areas ruled by slaveowners and serfowners were already surrounded by the absolutely predominant people's revolutionary forces, yet, as an old Chinese saying goes, "Cornered beasts will still fight," a handful of the most reactionary slaveowners and serf-owners still gave a last kick, rejecting peaceful reforms and launching armed rebellions. Only after these rebellions were quelled was it possible to carry out the reform of the social systems.

At a time when the imperialist countries and the imperialists are armed to the teeth as never before in order to protect their savage man-eating system, can it be said that the imperialists have become very "peaceable" towards the proletariat and the people at home and the oppressed nations abroad, as the modern revisionists claim, and that therefore, the "extraordinarily rare opportunity in the history of revolutions" that Lenin spoke about after the February Revolution, will become a normal state of affairs for the world proletariat and all the oppressed people, so that what Lenin referred to as a "rare opportunity" is easily available to the proletariat in the capitalist countries? We hold that these views are completely groundless.

Marxist-Leninists should never forget this truth: the armed forces of all ruling classes are used in the first place to oppress their people at home. Only on the basis of oppression of the people at home can the imperialists oppress other countries, launch aggression and wage unjust wars. In order to oppress their own people they need to maintain and strengthen their reactionary armed forces. Lenin once wrote in the course of the Russian revolution of 1905:

A standing army is used not so much against the external enemy as against the internal enemy. ("The Army and the Revolution," *Collected Works*, 4th Russ. ed., Vol. X, p. 38.)

Is this conclusion valid for all countries where the exploiting classes dominate, for capitalist countries? Can it be said that it was valid then but has become incorrect now? In our opinion, this truth remains irrefutable and the facts are confirming its correctness more and more. Strictly speaking, if the proletariat of any country fails to see this clearly it will not be able to find the way to liberation.

In *The State and Revolution* Lenin centered the problem of revolution on the smashing of the bourgeois state machine. Quoting the most important passages from Marx's *Civil War in France,* he wrote:

After the revolution of 1848-49, the state power became "the national war engine of capital against labor." (*Selected Works of Lenin,* F.L.P.H., Moscow, 1952, Vol. II, part 1, p. 240.)

The main machine of the bourgeois state power to wage an antilabor war is its standing army. Therefore, ". . . the first decree of the commune . . . was the suppression of the standing army, and the substitution for it of the armed people. . . ." (*ibid.,* Vol. II, part 1, p. 241.)

So this question, in the last analysis, must be treated in the light of the principles of the Paris Commune which, as Marx puts it, are perpetual and indestructible.

In the seventies of the nineteenth century Marx took Britain and the United States to be exceptions, holding that as far as these two countries were concerned there did exist the possibility of "peaceful" transition to socialism, because militarism and bureaucracy were at an early stage of development in these two countries. But in the era of imperialism, as Lenin put it, "this qualification made by Marx is no longer valid" for these two countries "have today completely sunk into the all-European filthy, bloody morass of bureaucratic-military institutions which subordinate everything to themselves and trample everything underfoot." ("The State and Revolution," *Selected Works,* F.L.P.H., Moscow, 1952, Vol. II, part 1, pp. 237-8.) This was one of the focal points of the debate Lenin had with the opportunists of the day. The opportunists represented by Kautsky distorted this "no longer valid" conclusion of Marx, in an attempt to oppose the proletarian revolution and proletarian dictatorship, that is, to oppose the revolutionary armed forces and armed revolution which are indispensable to the liberation of the proletariat. The reply Lenin gave to Kautsky was as follows:

The revolutionary dictatorship of the proletariat is violence against the bourgeoisie; and the necessity for such violence is *particularly* created, as Marx and Engels have repeatedly explained in detail, by the existence of *militarism and bureaucracy*. But it is precisely these institutions that were nonexistent in England and America in the seventies of the nineteenth century, when Marx made his observation (they *do* exist in England and in America *now*.) ("Proletarian Revolution and the Renegade Kautsky," *Selected Works,* International Publishers, New York, Vol. VII, p. 125.)

It can thus be seen that the proletariat is compelled to resort to the means of armed revolution. Marxists have always wanted to follow the peaceful way in the transition to socialism. As long as the peaceful way is there to adopt, Marxist-Leninists will never give it up. But it is precisely this way that the bourgeoisie seeks to block when it possesses a powerful, militaristic and bureaucratic machine of oppression.

The above quotation was written by Lenin in November 1918. How do things stand now? Is it that Lenin's words were historically valid, but are no longer so under present conditions, as the modern revisionists allege? Everybody can see that with hardly any exception the capitalist countries, particularly the few imperialist powers headed by the United States, are trying hard to strengthen their militaristic and bureaucratic machine of oppression, and especially their military machine.

The Declaration of the Moscow Meeting of the Representatives of the Communist and Workers' Parties of the Socialist Countries of November 1957 states:

Leninism teaches, and experience confirms, that the ruling classes never relinquish power voluntarily. In this case the bitterness and forms of the class struggle will depend not so much on the proletariat as on the resistance put up by the reactionary circles to the will of the overwhelming majority of the people, on these circles using force at one or another stage of the struggle for socialism.

This is a new summing up of the experience of the struggle of the international proletariat in the few decades since Lenin's death.

The question is not whether the proletariat is willing to carry out a peaceful transformation; it is rather whether the bourgeoisie will accept such a peaceful transformation. This is the only possible way in which followers of Lenin can approach this question.

So, contrary to the modern revisionists who seek to paralyze the revolutionary will of the people by empty talk about peaceful transition, Marxist-Leninists hold that the question of possible peaceful transition to socialism can be raised only in the light of the specific conditions in each country at a particular time. The proletariat must never allow itself to one-sidedly and groundlessly base its thinking, policy and its whole work on the calculation that the bourgeoisie is willing to accept peaceful transformation. It must, at the same time, prepare for alternatives: one for the peaceful development of the revolution and the other for the nonpeaceful development of the revolution. Whether the transition will be carried out through armed uprising or by peaceful means is a question that is fundamentally separate from that of peaceful coexistence between the socialist and capitalist countries; it is an internal affair of each country, one to be determined only by the relation of classes in that country in a given period, a matter to be decided only by the communists of that country themselves.

V.

After the October Revolution, in 1919, Lenin discussed the historical lessons to be drawn from the Second International. He said that the growth of the proletarian movement during the period of the Second International "was in breadth, at the cost of a temporary fall in the revolutionary level, a temporary increase in the strength of opportunism, which in the end led to the disgraceful collapse of this International." ("Third International and Its Place in History," *Selected Works*, F.L.P.H., Moscow, 1952, Vol. II, part 2, p. 199.)

What is opportunism? According to Lenin, "Opportunism consists in sacrificing fundamental interests in order to gain temporary, partial benefits." ("Speech at Conference of Activists of the Moscow Party Organization," *Collected Works*, 4th Russ. ed., Vol. XXXI, p. 412.)

And what does the fall in the revolutionary level mean? It means that the opportunists seek to lead the masses to focus their attention on their day-to-day, temporary and partial interests only, and forget their long-term, fundamental and over-all interests.

Marxist-Leninists hold that the question of parliamentary

struggle should be considered in the light of long-term fundamental and over-all interests.

Lenin told us about the limitations of parliamentary struggle, but he also warned communists against narrow-minded, sectarian errors. In his well-known work *Left-wing Communism, an Infantile Disorder* Lenin elucidated the experience of the Russian revolution, showing under what conditions a boycott of parliament is correct and under what other conditions it is incorrect. Lenin held that every proletarian party should make use of every possible opportunity to participate in necessary parliamentary struggles. It was fundamentally wrong and would only harm the cause of the revolutionary proletariat for a Communist Party member to engage only in empty talk about the revolution, while being unwilling to work perseveringly and painstakingly, and shunning necessary parliamentary struggles.

Lenin then criticized the mistakes of the communists in some European countries in refusing to participate in parliament. He said:

The childishness of those who "repudiate" participation in parliament consists precisely in the fact that they think it possible to "solve" the difficult problem of combating bourgeois-democratic influences *within* the working-class movement by such "simple," "easy," supposedly revolutionary methods, when in reality they are only running away from their own shadow, only closing their eyes to difficulties and only trying to brush them aside with mere words. (*Selected Works*, F.L.P.H., Moscow, 1952, Vol. II, part 2, p. 443.)

Why is it necessary to engage in parliamentary struggle? According to Lenin, it is for the purpose of combating bourgeois influences within the ranks of the working-class movement, or, as he pointed out elsewhere,

Precisely for the purpose of educating the backward strata of its own class, precisely for the purpose of awakening and enlightening the undeveloped, downtrodden, ignorant, rural *masses*. (*Selected Works*, F.L.P.H., Moscow, 1952, Vol. II, part 2, p. 383.)

In other words, it is to enhance the political and ideological level of the masses, to co-ordinate parliamentary struggle with revolutionary struggle, and not to lower our political and ideological standards and divorce parliamentary struggle from the revolutionary struggle.

Identify with the masses but no lowering of revolutionary standards—this is a fundamental principle which Lenin taught us to firmly adhere to in our proletarian struggle.

We should take part in parliamentary struggles, but have no illusions about the bourgeois parliamentary system. Why? Because so long as the militarist-bureaucrat state machine of the bourgeoisie remains intact, parliament is nothing but an adornment for the bourgeois dictatorship even if the working-class party commands a majority in parliament or becomes the biggest party in it. Moreover, so long as such a state machine remains intact, the bourgeoisie is fully able at any time, in accordance with the needs of its own interests, either to dissolve parliament when necessary, or to use various open and underhanded tricks to turn a working-class party which is the biggest party in parliament into a minority, or to reduce its seats in parliament, even when it has polled more votes in an election. It is, therefore, difficult to imagine that changes will take place in a bourgeois dictatorship itself as the result of votes in parliament and it is just as difficult to imagine that the proletariat can adopt measures in parliament for a peaceful transition to socialism just because it has won a certain number of votes in parliament. A series of experiences in the capitalist countries long ago proved this point fully and the experience in various European and Asian countries after the Second World War provide additional proof of it.

Lenin said: "The proletariat cannot be victorious unless it wins over to its side the majority of the population. But to limit or condition this to the gathering of a majority of votes at elections while the bourgeoisie remains dominant is the most utter stupidity or simply swindling the workers." ("Elections to the Constituent Assembly and the Dictatorship of the Proletariat," *Collected Works*, 4th Russ. ed., Vol. XXX, p. 243.) Modern revisionists hold that these words of Lenin are out of date. But living realities bear witness to the fact that these words of Lenin are still the best medicine, though bitter tasting, for proletarian revolutionaries in any country.

Lowering revolutionary standards means lowering the theoretical standards of Marxism-Leninism. It means lowering political struggles to the level of economic ones and restricting revolutionary struggles to within the limits of parliamentary struggles. It means bartering away principles for temporary benefits.

At the beginning of the twentieth century Lenin in *What Is to Be Done?* drew attention to the question that "the spread of Marxism was accompanied by a certain lowering of theoretical standards." Lenin cited Marx's opinion contained in a letter on "The Gotha Program" that we may enter into agreements to attain the practical aims of the movement, but we must never trade in principles and make "concessions" in theory. Afterwards, Lenin wrote the following words which by now are well known to almost all communists:

Without a revolutionary theory there can be no revolutionary movement. This cannot be insisted upon too strongly at a time when the fashionable preaching of opportunism is combined with absorption in the narrowest forms of practical activity. ("What Is to Be Done?" *Selected Works,* International Publishers, New York, Vol. II, p. 47.)

What an important revelation this is to revolutionary Marxists! It was precisely under the guidance of this thought —that the Bolshevik Party headed by the great Lenin must firmly uphold revolutionary Marxist theory—that the entire revolutionary movement in Russia gained victory in October 1917.

The Chinese Communist Party also gained experience in regard to the above-mentioned question on two occasions. The first was during the 1927 revolutionary period. At that time Chen Tu-hsiu's opportunism as shown over the policy towards the Communist Party's united front with the Kuomintang was a departure from the principles and stand which a Communist Party should uphold. He advocated that the Communist Party should in principle be reduced to the level of the Kuomintang. The result was defeat for the revolution. The second occasion was during the period of the War of Resistance to Japanese Aggression. The Central Committee of the Chinese Communist Party firmly upheld the Marxist-Leninist stand, exposed the differences in principle between the Communist Party and the Kuomintang in their attitudes towards the conduct of the war against Japan, and held that the Communist Party must never make concessions in principle on such attitudes. But the right opportunists represented by Wang Ming repeated the mistakes made by Chen Tu-hsiu ten years earlier and wanted to reduce the Commu-

nist Party in principle to the level of the Kuomintang. Therefore, our entire Party carried out a great debate with the
right opportunists throughout the Party. Comrade Mao Tse-
tung said:

. . . If Communists forget this point of principle, they will not
be able to guide the Anti-Japanese War correctly, they will be
powerless to overcome the Kuomintang's one-sidedness, and
they will lower themselves to a stand which is against their
principles and reduce the Communist Party to the level of the
Kuomintang. They will then commit a crime against the sacred
cause of the national revolutionary war and the defence of the
motherland. ("After the Fall of Shanghai and Taiyuan," *Selected
Works*, Lawrence & Wishart, London, Vol. II, pp. 105-6.)

It was precisely because the Central Committee of our
Party refused to make the slightest concessions on questions
of principle, and because it adopted a policy of both unity
and struggle in our Party's united front with the Kuomintang, that we were able to consolidate and expand the Party's
positions in the political and economic fields, consolidate and
expand the national revolutionary united front and, consequently, strengthen and expand the forces of the people in
the War of Resistance to Japanese Aggression. It also enabled us to smash the large-scale attacks launched by the
Chiang Kai-shek reactionaries after the conclusion of the War
of Resistance to Japanese Aggression and win nationwide victory in the great people's revolution.

Judging by the experience of the Chinese revolution, mistakes of right deviation are likely to occur in our Party when
the proletariat enters into political co-operation with the bourgeoisie, whereas mistakes of "left" deviation are likely to occur in our Party when these two classes break away from
each other politically. In the course of leading the Chinese
revolution, our Party has waged struggles against "left" adventurism on many occasions. The "left" adventurists were
unable to take a Marxist-Leninist viewpoint on the correct
handling of the complex class relations in China; they failed
to understand how to adopt different correct policies towards
different classes at different historical periods, but only followed the erroneous policy of struggle without unity. Had
this mistake of "left" adventurism not been overcome, it
would have been impossible for the Chinese revolution to
advance to victory.

In line with Lenin's viewpoint the proletariat in any country, if it wants to gain victory in the revolution, must have a genuinely Marxist-Leninist party which is skilled at integrating the universal truths of Marxism-Leninism with concrete revolutionary practice in its own country, correctly determining whom the revolution should be directed against at different periods, settling the question of organizing the main force and its allies and the question of whom it should rely on and unite with. The revolutionary proletarian party must rely closely on the masses of its own class and on the semi-proletariat in the rural areas, namely, the broad masses of poor peasants and establish the worker-peasant alliance led by the proletariat. Only then is it possible, on the basis of this alliance, to unite with all the social forces that can be united with and so establish the united front of the working people with all the non-working people that can be united with in accordance with specific conditions in the different countries at different periods. If it fails to do so, the proletariat will not be able to achieve its purpose of gaining victory in the revolution at different periods.

The modern revisionists and certain representatives of the bourgeoisie try to make people believe that it is possible to achieve socialism without a revolutionary party of the proletariat and without the series of correct policies of the revolutionary party of the proletariat mentioned above. This is sheer nonsense and pure deception. The *Communist Manifesto* by Marx and Engels pointed out that there were different kinds of "socialism"; there was petty-bourgeois "socialism," bourgeois "socialism," feudal "socialism," etc. Now, as a result of the victory of Marxism-Leninism and the decay of the capitalist system, more and more of the mass of the people in various countries are aspiring to socialism and a more motley variety of so-called "socialisms" have emerged from among the exploiting classes in certain countries. Just as Engels said, these so-called "socialists" also "wanted to eliminate social abuses through their various universal panaceas and all kinds of patchwork, without hurting capital and profit in the least." They "stood outside the labor movement and looked for support rather to the 'educated' classes." ("Preface to the German Edition of the Manifesto of the Communist Party," *Selected Works of Marx and Engels*, F.L.P.H., Moscow, 1958, Vol. I, p. 31.) They only put up the signboard of "socialism" but actually practice capitalism. In these circumstances it is extremely important to adhere firmly to the revolutionary principles of Marxism-Leninism and to wage an irreconcilable struggle against any tendency to lower the revolutionary standards, especially against revisionism and right opportunism.

In regard to the question of safeguarding world peace at the present time there are also certain people who declare that ideological disputes are no longer necessary, or that there is no longer any difference in principle between communists and social democrats. This is tantamount to lowering the ideological and political standards of communists to those of the bourgeoisie and social democrats. Those who make such statements have been influenced by modern revisionism and have departed from the stand of Marxism-Leninism.

The struggle for peace and the struggle for socialism are two different kinds of struggle. It is a mistake not to make a proper distinction between these two kinds of struggle. The social composition of those taking part in the peace movement is, of course, more complex; it also includes bourgeois pacifists. We communists stand right in the forefront in defending world peace, right in the forefront in opposing imperialist wars, in advocating peaceful coexistence and opposing nuclear weapons. In this movement we shall work together with many complex social groups and enter into necessary agreements for the attainment of peace. But at the same time we must uphold the principles of the working-class party and not lower our political and ideological standards and reduce ourselves to the level of the bourgeois pacifists in our struggle for peace. It is here that the question of alliance and criticism arises.

"Peace" in the mouths of modern revisionists is intended to whitewash the war preparations of the imperialists, to play again the tune of "ultra imperialism" of the old opportunists, which was long since refuted by Lenin, and to distort our communist policy concerning peaceful coexistence of countries with two different systems into elimination of the people's revolution in various countries. It was that old revisionist Bernstein who made this shameful and notorious statement: The movement is everything, the final aim is nothing. The modern revisionists have a similar statement: The peace movement is everything, the aim is nothing. Therefore, the "peace" they talk about is in practice limited to the "peace" which may be acceptable to the imperialists under certain historical conditions. It attempts to lower the revolutionary standards of the peoples of various countries and destroy their revolutionary will.

We communists are struggling in defense of world peace, for the realization of the policy of peaceful coexistence. At the same time we support the revolutionary wars of the oppressed nations against imperialism. We support the revolutionary wars of the oppressed people for their own liberation and social progress because all these revolutionary wars are just wars. Naturally, we must continue to explain to the masses Lenin's thesis concerning the capitalist-imperialist system as the source of modern war; we must continue to explain to the masses the Marxist-Leninist thesis on the replacement of capitalist imperialism by socialism and communism as the final goal of our struggle. We must not hide our principles before the masses.

VI.

We are living in a great new epoch in which the collapse of the imperialist system is being further accelerated, the victory of the people throughout the world and their awakening are constantly advancing.

The peoples of the various countries are now in a much more fortunate situation than ever before. In the forty-odd years since the October Revolution, one third of all mankind have freed themselves from oppression by capitalist imperialism and founded a number of socialist states where a life of lasting internal peace has really been established. They are exerting their influence on the future of all mankind and will greatly speed the day when universal, lasting peace will reign throughout the world.

Marching in the forefront of all the socialist countries and of the whole socialist camp is the great Soviet Union, the first socialist state created by the workers and peasants led by Lenin and their Communist Party. Lenin's ideals have been realized in the Soviet Union, socialism has long since been built and now, under the leadership of the Central Committee of the Communist Party of the Soviet Union and the Soviet Government headed by Comrade Khrushchev, a great period of the extensive building of communism is already beginning. The valiant and enormously talented Soviet workers, peasants and intellectuals have brought about a great, new labor upsurge in their struggle for the grand goal of building communism.

We, the Chinese Communists and the Chinese people, cheer every new achievement of the Soviet Union, the native land of Leninism.

The Chinese Communist Party, integrating the universal truths of Marxism-Leninism with the concrete practice of the Chinese revolution, has led the people of the entire country in winning great victories in the people's revolution, marching along the broad common road of socialist revolution and socialist construction charted by Lenin, carrying the socialist revolution to full completion and it has already begun to win great victories on the various fronts of socialist construction. The Central Committee of the Chinese Communist Party creatively set down for the Chinese people, in accordance with Lenin's principles and in the light of conditions in China, the correct principles of the general line for building socialism, the big leap forward and the people's communes, which have inspired the initiative and revolutionary spirit of the masses throughout the country and are thus day after day bringing about new changes in the face of our country.

Under our common banner of Leninism, the socialist countries in Eastern Europe and the other socialist countries in Asia have also attained progress by leaps and bounds in socialist construction.

Leninism is an ever-victorious banner. For the working people throughout the world, holding firm this great banner means taking hold of truth and opening up for themselves a road of continuous victory.

Lenin will always live in our hearts. And when modern revisionists endeavor to smear Leninism, the great banner of the international proletariat, our task is to defend Leninism.

All of us remember what Lenin wrote in his famous work *The State and Revolution* about what happened to the teachings of revolutionary thinkers and leaders in the past struggles of various oppressed classes for liberation. Lenin wrote that after the death of these revolutionary thinkers and leaders distortions ensued, "emasculating the essence of the revolutionary teaching, blunting its revolutionary edge and vulgarizing it." Lenin continued,

At the present time, the bourgeoisie and the opportunists within the working-class movement concur in this "doctoring" of

Marxism. They omit, obliterate and distort the revolutionary side of this teaching, its revolutionary soul. They push to the foreground and extol what is or seems acceptable to the bourgeoisie. ("The State and Revolution," *Selected Works*, F.L.P.H., Moscow, 1952, Vol. II, part 1, p. 202.)

Just so, at the present time we are again confronted by certain representatives of U.S. imperialism who once again assuming the pious mien of preachers, even declare that Marx was "a great thinker of the nineteenth century" and even acknowledge that what Marx predicted in the nineteenth century about the days of capitalism being numbered, "is well-grounded" and "correct"; but, these preachers continue, after the advent of the twentieth century, and especially in recent decades, Marxism has become incorrect, because capitalism has become a thing of the past and has ceased to exist, at least in the United States. After hearing such nonsense from these imperialist preachers, we cannot but feel that the modern revisionists are talking the same language as they do. But the modern revisionists do not stop at distorting the teachings of Marx, they go further to distort the teachings of Lenin, the great continuer of Marxism who carried Marxism forward.

The Declaration of the Moscow Meeting pointed out that "the main danger at present is revisionism, or, in other words, right-wing opportunism." Some say that this judgment of the Moscow Meeting no longer holds good under today's conditions. We hold this to be wrong. It makes the people overlook the importance of the struggle against the main danger —revisionism, and is very harmful to the revolutionary cause of the proletariat. Just as from the beginning of the seventies of the nineteenth century there was a period of "peaceful" development of capitalism during which the old revisionism of Bernstein was born, so under the present circumstances when the imperialists are compelled to accept peaceful coexistence and when there is a kind of "internal peace" in many capitalist countries, revisionist trends find it easy to grow and spread. Therefore, we must always maintain a high degree of vigilance against this main danger in the working-class movement.

As pupils of Lenin and as Leninists, we must utterly smash all attempts of the modern revisionists to distort and carve up the teachings of Lenin.

Leninism is the complete and integrated revolutionary teaching of the proletariat, it is a complete and integrated revolutionary world outlook which, following Marx and Engels, continues to express the thinking of the proletariat. This complete and integrated revolutionary teaching and revolutionary outlook must not be distorted or carved up. We hold the view that the attempts of the modern revisionists to distort and carve up Leninism are nothing but a manifestation of the last-ditch struggle of the imperialists facing their doom. In face of continuous victories in building communism in the Soviet Union, in face of continuous victories in building socialism in the socialist countries, in face of the constant strengthening of the unity of the socialist camp headed by the Soviet Union and of the steadfast and valiant struggles being waged by the increasingly awakened peoples of the world seeking to free themselves from the shackles of capitalist imperialism, the revisionist endeavors of Tito and his ilk are completely futile.

Long live great Leninism!

NOTES

I. *The Formation and Appeal of "Scientific Socialism"*

1. The "French Radicals" were nonsocialist republicans in the 1848 Revolution. They included Hippolyte Carnot, who became minister of education in the provisional government, and Pierre Marie, who became minister of public works. As minister of public works, it was Marie's responsibility to put into effect Louis Blanc's "social workshops." Instead of carrying through Blanc's proposals, he established the so-called "national workshops" with which, it is usually argued, he intended to discredit Blanc's socialist views. The abolition of the workshops, which had served to relieve unemployment, contributed to the Parisian insurrection of June.

2. [Engels] By bourgeoisie is meant the class of modern capitalists, owners of the means of social production and employers of wage-labor; by proletariat, the class of modern wage-laborers who, having no means of production of their own, are reduced to selling their labor power in order to live.

3. [Engels] That is, all *written* history. In 1837, the pre-history of society, the social organization existing previous to recorded history, was all but unknown. Since then Haxthausen discovered common ownership of land in Russia, Maurer proved it to be the social foundation from which all Teutonic races started in history and, by and by, village communities were found to be, or to have been, the primitive form of society everywhere from India to Ireland. The inner organization of this primitive communistic society was laid bare, in its typical form, by Morgan's crowning discovery of the true nature of the *gens* and its relation to the *tribe*. With the dissolution of these primeval communities, society begins to be differentiated into separate and finally antagonistic classes. I have attempted to retrace this process of dissolution in *The Origin of the Family, Private Property and the State*.

4. [Engels] Guild-master, that is, a full member of a guild, a master within, not a head of a guild.

5. The word "manufacture" is used by Engels to refer to pro-

duction carried on by laborers who, though gathered in a single building, operated by much the same manual labor as had their medieval artisan predecessors. This system, therefore, contrasts with the next stage of production, the "industrial" stage that utilizes machinery and steam power.

6. [Engels] "Commune" was the name taken in France by the nascent towns even before they had conquered from their feudal lords and masters local self-government and political rights as the "Third Estate." Generally speaking, for the economic development of the bourgeoisie, England is here taken as the typical country; for its political development, France.

7. The word in the German original is *Rentier*, meaning here the property-owner earning an income from investments.

8. In 1847, the year before the publication of the *Manifesto*, Parliament limited the work day to ten hours.

9. The Revolution of 1830 deposed the ultra-royalist monarch Charles X and replaced him by the more liberal Louis Philippe, who represented a younger branch of the Bourbon family, the Orleans branch.

10. [Engels] Not the English Restoration, 1660 to 1689, but the French Restoration, 1814 to 1830.

11. The Legitimists favored the elder branch of the Bourbon family deposed in the July (1830) Revolution. As indicated by Engels in this passage, they attempted to gain lower-class support by attacking Louis Philippe's economic policies which served the interests of the wealthy commercial and industrial bourgeoisie.

12. The "Young England" group comprised English Conservatives who sought the support of the working class, particularly in the cities, against the Liberals by advocating social and economic reforms. The most famous members of the group were Benjamin Disraeli and Thomas Carlyle.

13. [Engels] This applies chiefly to Germany where the landed aristocracy and squirearchy have large portions of their estates cultivated for their own account by stewards, and are, moreover, extensive beetroot-sugar manufacturers and distillers of potato spirits. The wealthier British aristocrats are, as yet, rather above that; but they, too, know how to make up for declining rents by lending their names to floaters of more or less shady joint-stock companies.

14. The most famous expressions of Christian Socialism occurred in England in the sixties when such men as Charles Kingsley persistently campaigned for social and economic reforms to be achieved by Christian love and sympathy rather than by violent class struggle and hatred. Similar views, to which reference is made here by Engels, appeared earlier on the Continent. The most prominent continental Christian Socialist was the Catholic priest Lamennais, whose Christian social-

ism clearly appears in his *Words of a Believer,* published in 1834.

15. The phrase "Practical Reason" refers here to Immanuel Kant's *Critique of Practical Reason.* As this section of the *Manifesto* indicates, Marx and Engels had little patience with the abstract philosophizing of the German "idealists."

16. The phrases in quotation marks are from the German philosopher Hegel. Besides suffering from the defects Marx and Engels saw in all German "idealist" philosophy, these Hegelian statements attract additional criticism because of their association with the philosophical socialism of the "True Socialists." Led by Karl Grün and Moses Hess, the "True Socialists" opposed violence, emphasized moral sentiment, and were essentially hostile to industrialism as such.

17. [Engels] Phalansteries were socialist colonies on the plan of Charles Fourier; Icaria was the name given by Cabet to his Utopia and, later on, to his American Communist colony.

18. The Chartist movement developed in England in the period 1838-1848. The success of the higher bourgeoisie in winning electoral franchise in 1832 stimulated among the working class a demand for similar political opportunities as a means of legislating necessary economic reforms, reforms that were felt to be particularly urgent because of the economic depression in these years. An improvement in economic conditions together with factional divisions in the movement led to its collapse.

19. The Parisian newspaper *La Réforme* was an influential voice of the republican revolutionaries in 1848. The reference here is to those associated with this journal.

20. In the middle of the century an organization called "Young America" was formed in New York State calling for the nationalization of land and maximum limits on farms of 160 acres.

21. [Engels] The party then represented in Parliament by Ledru-Rollin, in literature by Louis Blanc, in the daily press by the *Réforme.* The name of Social-Democracy signified, with these its inventors, a section of the Democratic or Republican party more or less tinged with socialism.

22. [Engels] This is the passage on the French Revolution: "Thought, the concept of law, all at once made itself felt, and against this the old scaffolding of wrong could make no stand. In this conception of law, therefore, a constitution has now been established, and henceforth everything must be based upon this. Since the sun had been in the firmament, and the planets circled round it, the sight had never been seen of man standing upon his head—*i.e.,* on the Idea—and building reality after this image. Anaxagoras first said that the Nous, reason, rules the world; but now, for the first time, had man come to recognize that the Idea must rule

the mental reality. And this was a magnificent sunrise. All thinking beings have participated in celebrating this holy day. A sublime emotion swayed men at that time, an enthusiasm of reason pervaded the world, as if now had come the reconciliation of Divine Principle with the world." (Hegel: *Philosophy of History*, 1840, p. 535.) Is it not high time to set the anti-socialist law in action against such teachings, subversive and to the common danger, by the late Professor Hegel?

23. The *Social Contract* was written by Jean Jacques Rousseau, a leading representative of the French eighteenth-century "Enlightenment." The book, published in 1762, contains the principal themes of Rousseau's political philosophy.

24. The Levellers were radical English Puritans active during the seventeenth-century English Revolution and led by John Lilburne. Among the goals that differentiated them from the more moderate revolutionaries, such as Cromwell, was their demand for universal manhood suffrage.

25. Engels here refers to the works of Thomas Moore, (sixteenth century) and Tommaso Campanella (seventeenth century).

26. After the execution of Jacobin leader Robespierre, the French Revolution began its retreat from the extreme "left" to the "right." The "Thermidorian Reaction," as this period is called, produced the four-year reign (1795-1799) of the Directory, a committee of revolutionary leaders formerly associated with Robespierre. Under the Directory, the principal gains of the Revolution won by the middle class were preserved, the extreme "socialist" factions were crushed, terror was largely ended and the enforced puritanism of the Jacobins gave way to a period of unrestrained libertinism.

27. [Engels] From "The Revolution in Mind and Practice," p. 21, a memorial addressed to all the "red republicans, communists and socialists of Europe," and sent to the provisional government of France, 1848, and also "to Queen Victoria and her responsible advisers."

28. [Engels] *l.c.*, p. 22.

29. The Alexandrian period extends from the third century B.C. to the seventh century A.D. Its name derives from Alexandria in Egypt, one of the most important centers of intellectual development and international trade at that time.

30. Engels refers here to his work, *The Mark*.

31. [Engels] *The Condition of the Working Class in England* (Sonnenschein & Co.), p. 84.

32. [Engels] I say "have to." For only when the means of production and distribution have actually outgrown the form of management by joint-stock companies, and when, therefore, taking them over by the state has become *economically* inevitable, only then—even if it is the state of today that

effects this—is there an economic advance, the attainment
of another step preliminary to the taking over of all productive forces by society itself. But of late, since Bismarck went
in for state ownership of industrial establishments, a kind
of spurious socialism has arisen, degenerating, now and
again, into something of flunkeyism, that without more ado
declares *all* state ownership, even of the Bismarckian sort,
to be socialistic. Certainly, if the taking over by the state
of the tobacco industry is socialistic, then Napoleon and
Metternich must be numbered among the founders of socialism. If the Belgian state, for quite ordinary political and
financial reasons, itself constructed its chief railway lines; if
Bismarck, not under any economic compulsion, took over for
the state the chief Prussian lines, simply to be the better
able to have them in hand in case of war, to bring up the
railway employees as voting cattle for the government, and
especially to create for himself a new source of income independently of parliamentary votes—this was, in no sense, a
socialistic measure, directly or indirectly, consciously or unconsciously. Otherwise, the Royal Maritime Company, the
Royal porcelain manufacture, and even the regimental tailor
shops of the Army would also be socialistic institutions, or
even, as was seriously proposed by a sly dog in Frederick
William III's reign, the taking over by the state of the
brothels.

33. [Engels] A few figures may serve to give an approximate
idea of the enormous expansive force of the modern means
of production, even under capitalist pressure. According to
Mr. Giffen, the total wealth of Great Britain and Ireland
amounted, in round numbers in 1814 to £2,200,000,000

1865 to £6,100,000,000

1875 to £8,500,000,000

As an instance of squandering the means of production and
products during a crisis, the total loss in the German iron
industry alone, in the crisis of 1873-78, was given at the
second German Industrial Congress (Berlin, February 21,
1878) as £22,750,000.

II. *Lenin and the Premature Socialist Revolution*

1. In 1875, the year after the collapse of the First International,
the two main factions of German socialism, the followers of
Ferdinand Lassalle and the Marxists, led by Wilhelm Liebknecht, met in Gotha, Germany, to outline a unity program.
The program was submitted to Marx, who was then living
in England. Marx attacked it bitterly for what he considered
its tone of compromise and moderation and its belief that
socialism could be won by peaceful campaigns for social

and economic reform. The *Critique of the Gotha Program*, published in 1875, was Marx's last major involvement in the affairs of the German party.

2. The "July Monarchy" was established after the 1830 Revolution deposed Charles X. From 1830 until his own overthrow in the Revolution of 1848, Louis Philippe reigned as "King of the French," instead of with the traditional title "King of France." During his reign, French imperial interests were advanced by the acquisition of Algiers, and France experienced a period of rapid economic progress, particularly to the advantage of the wealthiest bourgeoisie. His indifference to social and economic reforms for the lower classes and his opposition to middle-class demands for a wider electoral franchise contributed to his overthrow in 1848.

3. On February 27, 1917, the Russian Parliament, the Duma, defied the orders of the Tsar by continuing to meet, though unofficially, after he had prorogued it. At this essentially illegal meeting, the Duma elected a committee that, following the abdication of the Tsar on March 2, proclaimed the establishment of a Provisional Government. Significantly, on this same February 27, there was formed an organization that was to compete with the Provisional Government for ultimate revolutionary authority through the entire year, the Petrograd Soviet of Workers' Deputies, which, on March 2, became the Soviet of Workers' and Soldiers' Deputies.

4. The Black Hundreds is the name usually given the Union of the Russian People, formed in St. Petersburg in October 1905. It was an extreme nationalist organization that functioned through some 3,000 local committees and included in its membership lower-middle-class townspeople, minor government officials, and representatives of the clergy. While it is perhaps most notorious for its anti-Semitic outrages, its enemies included Finns, Poles and other minority nationalities in the Empire, and its primary political importance was its violent defense of the Autocracy against liberals and socialists of all varieties.

5. The term "Cadet" is a contraction of the party name Constitutional Democrats. Officially organized as a party in July 1905, the "Cadets" were to become the most important opposition party in the 1905 Revolution. Its membership included socialists and nonsocialist constitutionalists. In the elections for the First Duma, that sat from April to July 1906, it won 175 of the 524 seats, by far the most received by any of the 26 parties and 16 nationality groups represented in the Duma.

6. One of the major issues debated in 1917 was the election of a Constituent Assembly that would establish a legal government in place of the Provisional Government. Time required for preparing voting lists and related procedural

problems were the reasons given by the Provisional Government for delaying the elections. When the elections were finally held, in mid-November (a month after the Bolshevik victory), they gave an absolute majority of approximately 58% of the vote to the Social-Revolutionary Party, the main socialist opponent of Marxist Social Democrats and a party that had participated in and had come virtually to dominate the Provisional Government. The Bolsheviks received approximately 25% of the vote. For reasons that will be clear from *State and Revolution*, Lenin argued that "the republic of the Soviets is a higher form of democratic organization than the usual bourgeois republic with a Constituent Assembly." Consequently, the Assembly was allowed only a single meeting at which it elected as President Victor Chernov, a leader of the Social-Revolutionaries and a former Minister of Agriculture in the Provisional Government. The Assembly was disbanded by a Bolshevik military guard who ordered the meeting to end because "the guards were tired."

7. The main events of the revolution from mid-August involved the attempt of General Kornilov, the Commander-in-Chief of the army, to overthrow the Provisional Government, then under the control of the socialist Kerensky. Faced with this threat from the "right," Kerensky assumed dictatorial powers and, on August 27, turned for support to the Bolshevik Party. This represented a complete reversal of the repressive policy adopted by the Provisional Government since the armed workers' and soldiers' demonstrations in July, attributed to Bolshevik leadership. With this support from Kerensky, the Bolsheviks began to arm the workers, laying the basis for the Red Guards that were to contribute significantly to the Bolshevik victory in October.

8. *Die Neue Zeit* was a leading journal of the German Social Democrats published in Stuttgart from 1883 to 1923. Although in the years 1885-1895 it carried articles by Engels, the journal became identified with Bernstein revisionists from the end of the 1890's.

9. *Delo Naroda* (*The People's Cause*) was a daily newspaper published by the Social-Revolutionary Party in Petrograd from March 1917 until June 1918. It continued to appear sporadically and under various names until March 1919 when it was suppressed by the Bolshevik government.

10. The Girondists were the more moderate members of the Paris Commune during the French Revolution of 1789. Although they at first prevailed over the more radical, Jacobin members of the Commune and were able to control the Convention of 1792, the continuing and deepening revolutionary crises led to their defeat by the Jacobins and their expulsion from the Convention. In contrast to the predominantly Parisian Jaco-

bins, the Girondists tended to represent the more conservative provinces.

11. The Erfurt Program of the German Social Democratic Party was adopted in October 1891 to replace the Gotha Program of 1875. The main characteristic of the Erfurt Program was the elimination of most of the concessions made at Gotha to the followers of Lassalle and a return to more "orthodox" Marxian doctrines. Engels, who was a close observer of the Erfurt Congress, criticized the Program in his *On the Critique of the Social-Democratic Draft Program of 1891*. Although Bernstein, together with Kautsky, played a leading part in the preparation of the Program, he was soon to direct much of his revisionist attack against it.

12. The Anti-Socialist Laws were put through by Bismarck in response to the strengthening of the socialist movement resulting from the 1875 Gotha alliance discussed in earlier notes. The principal laws, adopted by the Reichstag in 1878, repressed the distribution of socialist literature, allowed the police to break up socialist meetings, and transferred cases involving socialists to police courts. The consequence of the measures was an increase in the number of parliamentary seats won by the socialists!

13. *Pravda (Truth)* was founded in April 1912 and was to become the main organ of the Bolshevik Party press. It was published daily in St. Petersburg with an average circulation, according to Soviet sources, of some 40,000 copies. As was the case with most radical opposition publications, *Pravda* suffered persistent repression and continually appeared under different names, always with the word *Pravda*, however. It finally ceased publication in July 1914, on the eve of the First World War, and did not reappear until March 5, 1917, three days after the abdication of Nicholas II.

14. [Lenin] Nominally about 2,400 rubles, and according to the present rate of exchange, about 6,000 rubles. Those Bolsheviks who propose that a salary of 9,000 rubles be paid to members of municipal councils, for instance, instead of a maximum salary of 6,000 rubles—quite an adequate sum—*for the whole state* are acting in an unpardonable way.

15. The 1903 Congress, the Second Congress of the Russian Social Democratic Party, was the Congress at which the Party divided into its Menshevik and Bolshevik factions. It was here that Lenin came to the fore as a major force in the Party, on a par with such venerable leaders as Plekhanov, who had set the foundations of Russian Marxism twenty years before. By skillful maneuvering before and during the Congress, Lenin was able to gain control of the main organizations of the Party. His victory was short-lived, however, for soon afterwards he found himself virtually alone.

16. As noted earlier, the title Soviet of Workers' and Soldiers'

Deputies was the new name given the Petrograd Soviet of Workers' Deputies that had been organized February 27, the same day that leaders of the former Duma began to take the steps that would soon lead to the Provisional Government. The Soviet comprised some of the more radical members of the Duma, a number of politically active workers, and various professionals—journalists, doctors, lawyers and the like. After the numbers attending meetings reached into the thousands, a system of representation for workers and soldiers was established. Although the Petrograd Soviet was the most important single council of this type, similar Soviets were organized throughout the country, and in June the First All-Russian Soviet Congress met, with representatives from the provincial Soviets. It soon became evident that the Soviets had more real political power than the Provisional Government, and Lenin's primary goal was to gain a majority for the Bolsheviks first in the Petrograd Soviet then in the All-Russian Soviet Congress.

17. [Lenin] When most of the functions of the state are reduced to such accounting and control by the workers themselves, it will cease to be a "political state" and the "public functions will lose their political character and become simple administrative functions" (cf. above, Chapter IV, §2, Engels' controversy with the anarchists).

18. The First International is the customary name given to the International Workingmen's Association organized in England in 1864 under the leadership of Karl Marx. Although it had little direct political effect, this first international organization of the working class was very instrumental in familiarizing workers with socialist doctrines and goals. The effectiveness of the International was diminished as a result of internal factional disputes. The most harmful were those that raged between the followers of Marx and the anarchist and syndicalist followers of the Russian anarchist revolutionary, Michael Bakunin. In large part as a consequence of this controversy between the Marxists and the anarcho-syndicalists, the International came to an end in 1874, meeting for the last time in Philadelphia.

19. *Zarya (Dawn)* was published in the years 1901-1902 by the émigré Russian Social Democrats. It was distinguished from other periodicals published by the Party by nature of its more theoretical and even "scholarly" approach, in contrast to the purely topical, agitational character of such publications as *Iskra (The Spark)*.

20. Reference here is to the Fifth Congress of the Second International meeting in Paris in September 1900.

21. The Socialist Monthly *(Sozialistische Monatshefte)* was one of the main organs of the German Social Democratic Party, appearing in the years 1897-1933. It was attacked by Lenin

for what he considered its "social-chauvinist" defense of
Germany during the First World War.

22. The Independent Labour Party was formed in 1893 with J.
Ramsay MacDonald included among the leaders. An independent socialist party, it was part of the Second International until 1919. Two years after it left the Second International, it joined the Labor and Socialist International (the
"2½ International") and still later returned to the revived
Second International.

23. The manuscript of *State and Revolution* ends with the following brief reference to a later section of the book that
Lenin was unable to complete because of the exigencies
of the revolution.

THE EXPERIENCE OF THE RUSSIAN REVOLUTIONS
OF 1905 AND 1917

The subject indicated in the title of this chapter is so vast
that volumes could and should be written about it. In the
present pamphlet we shall have to confine ourselves, naturally,
to the most important lessons provided by experience, those
touching directly upon the tasks of the proletariat in the revolution as they relate to state power.

III. *Stalin and Industrialization*

1. [Stalin] My italics.
2. The Revolution of 1905 that led to the establishment of the
first Russian Parliament, the Duma of 1906-1917.
3. The reference here is to the years 1900-1903, when Lenin
played the leading role on the editorial board of *Iskra*
(*The Spark*).
4. [Stalin] My italics.
5. [Stalin] My italics.
6. Among the main points distinguishing the views of Trotsky
(one of the originators of the "permanent revolution"
theory) from those of Lenin and Stalin in the years before
the Bolshevik Revolution was Trotsky's reluctance to associate the proletarian revolution with the mass peasantry.
7. [Stalin] My italics.
8. A pass through the Balkans in central Bulgaria, north of
which the Russians defeated the Turks in 1878.
9. [Stalin] My italics.
10. [Stalin] My italics.
11. [Stalin] All italics mine.
12. [Stalin] My italics.
13. The "Cadets" were the Constitutional Democrats, a party
of liberals including representatives of the urban professional
groups and the rural self-governing bodies, the *zemstva*.
The "Cadets" were the most influential and effective organ-

ization in the 1905 revolution and won the most seats in the First Duma.

14. The "Duma period" extended from April 1906 until the February 1917 Revolution, when a group of liberal Duma representatives assumed the leadership of the revolution, negotiated the abdication of Tsar Nicholas II, and established the Provisional Government. There were four Dumas during these years.

15. Alexander Kerensky, a member of the fourth and last Duma, was the only socialist to become a member of the first Provisional Government organized after the abdication of Tsar Nicholas II. After rising from Minister of Justice to Minister of War, he succeeded Prince Lvov as head of the cabinet in July. From this time until the Bolshevik Revolution in October, he dominated the official domestic and international policies of Russia.

16. The Democratic Conference was convoked by Kerensky in an attempt to consolidate support among the moderate left-wing groups represented by the co-operatives, the trade unions and the institutions of local government. He hoped by this conference to counteract the rapid rise in Bolshevik popularity following the "rightist" attempt of General Kornilov to overthrow the Kerensky government.

17. "Preparliament" is the name usually given to the Council of the Republic, which was called by Kerensky following the close of the September Democratic Conference and which was to form a link between the Provisional Government and the forthcoming Constituent Assembly. Lenin bitterly opposed the participation of the Bolsheviks in the Preparliament, but he was outvoted by the Bolshevik Party's central committee. The Bolshevik delegates, however, walked out after the first session. The Preparliament continued to meet until disbanded by the Bolsheviks after the October Revolution.

18. At Brest-Litovsk, in what is now White Russia, the Bolsheviks signed a humiliating and highly costly treaty with Germany on March 3, 1918. Realizing that the Bolsheviks must keep their promise and leave the war or risk the danger of being overthrown, Lenin was willing to give up Russian control of the Baltic states, Eastern Poland, Georgia and the Ukraine, as well as other territories, and pay to Germany a large indemnity. By the treaty, Russia also lost a large proportion of its richest agrarian and industrial territories.

19. Those Bolsheviks proposing the "otzovist" ("recall") or "boycott" tactics were against Bolshevik participation in the Third Duma. Lenin stood virtually alone in the party when, in 1907 and 1908, he rejected this policy as unrealistic, romantic "leftism."

20. The term comes from the name Manilov, a character in Gogol's *Dead Souls*, distinguished for his complacency, philistinism and futile daydreaming.

21. The "gang" here referred to is that of Axelrod, Martov, Potresov and others, who opposed Lenin's program at the Second Congress of the Russian Social Democratic Party in 1903.

IV. *The Soviet Bloc after Stalin: The New Revisionists*

1. [Djilas] New York, Prentice-Hall, 1951.

2. [Kolakowski] Some ten or twelve years ago, a lengthy discussion was current in Poland concerning socialist humanism as well as the relationship of morality to history. The arguments used at that time against intellectualism, utopianism, and the naïve preaching which was to take the place of historical analysis are today being revived unchanged, as if a circle of history were closed and returned to its beginning. These arguments, summarized briefly here in the dispute with the Intellectual, were often used at that time by this author in polemical conflicts. One of the participants in that discussion, writing under the pen name of Pawel Konrad, was at that time withdrawn from historical circulation, murdered by the missionaries of the great, historical justice. The participants in today's discussion should remember this when they return to those arguments of ten years ago and repeat them unchanged. They should remember, I say, how much it was possible, and therefore also will be possible, to justify and to sanctify things with the general phrase about historical necessity, about political realism, and about the situation of the single alternative to which the world, allegedly, is doomed.

V. *China and Orthodox Leninism*

1. The T'aip'ing Revolution of 1850-1864 was directed against the Manchu dynasty. The movement was led by the Chinese scholar Hung Hsiu-ch'üan and won such wide support that it succeeded in winning the eastern valley of the Yangtze river and capturing Nanking. Although the movement was defeated, in part as a result of British military support for the reigning Manchu, its effects significantly contributed to the Manchu's fall in 1912.

2. The Boxer movement represented an intensely antiforeign reaction against the rapid rise of western influence in China in the second half of the nineteenth century. With the

support of one faction of the royal family, the Boxers in 1899 began attacks against foreigners and Christian Chinese, and in 1900 occupied Peking. The rising was crushed by the combined forces of the British, French, Russian, American, German, and Japanese troops. As punishment for the rising, the Chinese were required to pay a large indemnity to the foreign powers and to allow the stationing of foreign troops in Peking.

3. The May Fourth Movement occurred in 1919, when, on this day, over 3,000 students and intellectuals rioted in opposition to the foreign policy of the Anfu government in Peking which was considered pro-Japanese. Since the demonstrations merged with labor strikes, the movement is often considered the beginning of the revolutions in the early 'twenties. The event has been considered by the Chinese communists both as an expression of the "bourgeois-democratic revolution" and as part of the "world revolution of the proletarian class."

4. 1927-1937.

support of one faction of the royal family, the forces of 1864 began attacks against foreigners and Chinese. China had in 1900 occupied Peking. The siege was crushed by the combined forces of the British, French, Russian, American, German, and Japanese troops. As punishment to the nation, the Chinese were required to pay a large indemnity to the foreign powers and to allow the stationing of foreign troops in Peking.

8. The May Fourth Movement occurred in 1919, when on this date over 3,000 students and intellectuals protested in opposition to the foreign policy of the Anti Government of Peking, which was considered anti-Japanese. Since the demonstrations merged with labor strikes, the expression of other conditions and the beginning of the revolution, in the early twenties, this event had been considered by the Chinese communists both as an expression of the "bourgeois democratic movement" and as part of the "world revolution of the proletarian class."

1927-1937

A SELECTED GLOSSARY OF NAMES

Avksentev, Nikolai (1878-1943), a leader in the Social Revolutionary Party. He became Minister of Internal Affairs in the Kerensky cabinet and chairman of the so-called "Preparliament" during the Provisional Government phase of the 1917 Revolution.

Axelrod, Pavel (1850-1928), a Marxist associate of Plekhanov. He joined Plekhanov in the transition from populism to Marxism during the early 1880's and was later one of the leading Menshevik opponents of Lenin's policies.

Babeuf, François (1760-1797), a socialist revolutionary during the French Revolution. In the "Directory" period, following the fall of Robespierre, he formed an organization calling for radical socialist legislation, and he later organized the Conspiracy of Equals in an effort to overthrow the Directory. He was arrested and executed.

Bastiat, Frédéric (1805-1850), a French economist, who helped formulate the theories of laissez faire, and who ardently defended free trade.

Bazarov, B. (pseudonym of B. Rudnev) (b. 1874), a member of the Bolshevik Party from 1904 and, after 1905, a Menshevik opponent of Lenin. He propagated the positivist views of Mach and Avenarius against the metaphysical and "idealistic" tendencies emerging among the Russian intelligentsia in this decade.

Bebel, August (1840-1913), a leader of the German Social Democrats and a member of the Reichstag.

Belyaev, Ivan (1810-1873), a Russian historian and professor at Moscow University. He was mainly concerned with the history of Russian law.

Belinsky, Vissarion (1810-1848), one of the founders of Russian radicalism. After passing through a number of stages in his intellectual development, he became a socialist at the end of his life. He is also considered a forerunner of "socialist realism" in literary criticism.

Benda, Julien (1876-1956), a French author and critic. He is famous both for his attack against the views of Bergson and for his belief, argued most forcefully in *The Treason of the Intellectuals*, that the intellectual must devote himself to the search for truth in spite of all consequences.

Bissolati, Leonida (1857-1920), an Italian socialist and editor of the party's main journals. He later left the original party and helped form a revisionist, moderate socialist party.

Bogdanov, A. (pseudonym of A. Malinovsky) (b. 1873), a Marxist philosopher and economist. At one time a close associate of Lenin and editor of Bolshevik party journals, he broke with Lenin over party tactics and philosophical views. He opposed Lenin's decision to participate in the Russian Duma and he accepted, against Lenin's bitter opposition, the "empiromonism" of Mach.

Bossuet, Jacques (1627-1704), Bishop of Meaux. He was the author of a number of works in the fields of religious history and theology and is usually considered the chief defender of the official French Catholic position against the secular rationalists, the Protestants, and the Jesuits.

Bracke, Wilhelm (1842-1880), a prominent German Social Democrat who, together with Bebel and Wilhelm Liebknecht, merged the Lassallean and Marxian principles in the party platform.

Branting, Hjalmar (1860-1925), a leader of the Swedish Social Democratic Labor Party and three times Premier of the Swedish government.

Breshkovskaya, Catherine (1844-1943), a Russian populist revolutionary. Often called the "grandmother of the Russian Revolution," she came from a wealthy noble family and paid for her revolutionary activities by some thirty years in prison and Siberian exile. She returned to Russia after the Bolshevik Revolution, but left soon afterwards because of her opposition to Bolshevik policies.

Bulgakov, Serge (1871-1944), a Russian philosopher and theologian. One of the earliest Russian Marxists, Bulgakov abandoned Marxism for philosophical idealism, then moved on to orthodox religion. He was a voluminous writer in various fields and a penetrating critic of Marxism.

Carnot, Lazare (1753-1823), the military expert of the French revolutionary army. After the death of Robespierre, Carnot became a member of the Directory, and, still later, served in Napoleon's government.

Cavaignac, Louis (1802-1857), a French general. He is most famous for leading the troops that crushed the rebellious Parisians during the "June Days" of the 1848 Revolution.

Chernov, Victor (1876-1952), one of the founders and leaders of the Russian Social Revolutionary Party. He became Minister of Agriculture in the Kerensky cabinet during the Provisional Government phase of the 1917 Revolution. Following the elections to the Constituent Assembly at the close of 1917, he was elected the first and only freely elected Russian president.

Chernyshevsky, Nikolai (1828-1889), a Russian revolutionary

and literary critic. Chernyshevsky was one of the acknowledged spokesmen of the radical revolutionaries of the 1860's, particularly the nihilists and populists. His extreme materialistic and positivistic theories contrasted sharply with the prevailing "idealistic" emphasis of the earlier intelligentsia.

Clynes, John (1869-1949), an English labor leader and politician. He became President of the National Union of General and Municipal Workers and a parliamentary representative for labor in the periods 1906-1931 and 1935-1945.

Cunow, Heinrich (1862-1936), an ethnographer and theoretician of the German Social Democratic Party. In his ethnographic studies, he concentrated on the history of primitive societies, and in his socialist writings he supported the revisionists.

Dan, Fedor (pseudonym of F. Gurvich) (b. 1871), a Russian Social Democrat, Menshevik. Dan joined the social-democratic movement in 1894 and was active on the socialists' journals. Although a Menshevik opponent of Lenin, he continued to live in Russia after the Bolshevik Revolution until his expulsion in 1922. He is known for his excellent studies of Russian Marxism.

Denikin, Anton (1872-1947), a Russian general. Denikin supported the Kornilov attempt to seize power from Kerensky during the period of the Provisional Government in 1917. After the Bolshevik Revolution, he led the "white" forces against the "reds" until he gave up his command to General Wrangel in 1920.

Doriot, Jacques (1888-1945?), a French communist and, later, fascist. Doriot was expelled from the French Communist Party for "Trotskyite" views, and almost immediately thereafter turned to fascism. He was an open supporter of Hitler and became a considerable power in France during the Nazi occupation. He escaped to Germany in 1944 and is believed to have been killed there in an air raid in 1945.

Dühring, Eugen (1833-1921), a German philosopher and economist. What prominence Dühring has today is probably due to Engels' bitter attack on him in *Anti-Dühring*. He advocated the preservation of capitalism, purged of its abuses as a result of a strong labor movement.

Ehrenburg, Ilya (b. 1891), a Soviet writer. Unlike most Soviet authors, Ehrenburg spent many years abroad (1921-1940) and continued to live an unusually cosmopolitan life, influenced by western culture, even during the Stalin years. He is most recently famous as the author of *The Thaw*, which reflects the general liberalization of Soviet attitudes after Stalin's death in 1953.

Feuerbach, Ludwig (1804-1872), a German philosopher. He is mainly known for the extreme materialist views he developed in reaction to his earlier Hegelian idealism. Religion became his main focus of attack. As mentioned in the first commentary, he exerted a strong influence on Marx.

Fourier, Charles (1772-1837), a French socialist. One of the so-called utopian socialists, Fourier looked forward to the establishment of ideal communities called "phalansteries," in which individuals would work according to their talent and interest, alternate occupations to escape boredom, and enjoy material abundance as a result of a carefully organized socialist economy.

Ge, Nikolai (1831-1894), a Russian painter, known for his realism.

Guesde, Jules (1845-1922), a French socialist. After his exile for participating in the Paris Commune, he became a Marxist and cooperated with Paul Lafargue in gaining a predominance for Marxism over other tendencies in French socialism.

Henderson, Arthur (1863-1935), a leader of the English Labour Party. Henderson was first elected to Parliament in 1903, then rose to successively higher posts in the government until he became foreign secretary in the second ministry of Ramsay MacDonald.

Herbert of Cherbury (1583-1648), an English philosopher, diplomat and poet. Lord Herbert is considered an early exponent of deism or "natural religion" that prevailed among the intellectuals of the English and French "enlightenment."

Hervé, Edouard (1835-1899), a prominent French publicist and defender of conservative and monarchical programs.

Hyndman, Henry (1842-1921), a founder and chairman of the English Labour Party. Although an early supporter of Marxism in England, he reorganized the Labour Party after many of its members left to join the Communist Party.

Jacobi, Friedrich (1743-1819), a German philosopher. Jacobi gave up a commercial career to devote himself to philosophical studies. In his publications, he criticized Kant and Spinoza for their efforts to separate the empirical world of causation and determinism from the world of morals and values, and he attempted to encompass both realms in a unified, rational system of cause and effect.

Jaurès, Jean (1859-1914), a French socialist. Jaurès was a consistent fighter for various social, economic and political causes. He tried, together with other revisionists, to reconcile Marx's materialism and determinism with traditional and neo-Kantian idealism, and to replace Marx's predictions of violent revolution with the goal of gradual, peaceful attainment of socialism. Because of his opposition to the extreme French nationalism that arose on the eve of the First World War, he was assassinated by a fanatic patriot in July 1914.

Kautsky, Karl (1854-1938), a leader of the German Social Democratic Party. Kautsky attempted to hold a middle ground between the revisionism of Bernstein and the Bolshevik views of Lenin and his German Communist followers. In addition to various works on socialist themes, Kautsky edited the German sources used in a famous four-volume study of the origins of the First World War.

Kerensky, Alexander (b. 1881), a Russian socialist and Premier of the 1917 Provisional Government. After serving as a representative in the Fourth Duma, Kerensky rose to prominence as a result of the February Revolution. He was the only socialist to accept a position in the liberal, "bourgeois" cabinet formed to hold power provisionally until the meeting of a Constituent Assembly. In July, he assumed the leadership of the cabinet, which by then included other socialists. Unable to solve the incredibly difficult economic, political and international problems facing the Provisional Government, he gradually lost support and was finally overthrown by the Bolsheviks on October 25, 1917.

Kierkegaard, Sören (1813-1855), a Danish philosopher. In addition to his works on the nature of knowledge, he wrote extensively on religious subjects and emphasized the "existential anxiety" that faces all mankind because of the radical gap between the real and the ideal.

Koestler, Arthur (b. 1905), novelist, essayist and social critic. Koestler began his career as a correspondent for the German press. From the time he reported the Spanish Civil War, he devoted himself to publishing and lecturing on a variety of political and social issues of contemporary urgency. He directed much of his criticism against all varieties of dictatorship, whether of the "right" or of the "left."

Kornilov, Lavr (1870-1918), a Russian general and leader of the armies opposing the Bolsheviks after the Revolution. Kornilov rose from Siberian peasant origins to become a general in the Tsarist Army. He supported the February Revolution, and advanced in rank until, under Kerensky, he became commander-in-chief. After experiencing the failure of an important offensive in June 1917, he attempted to overthrow the Kerensky government, which he blamed for the military failure because of its tolerance of leftist influences that undermined the discipline of the troops. He was killed in the civil war that followed the Bolshevik victory in October.

Kropotkin, Peter (1842-1921), a Russian geographer and anarchist. Of princely origins, Kropotkin first gained fame as a geographer, but he is best known to the world as the author of books preaching a decentralized, anarchistic socialism. Having spent most of his life abroad, he returned to Russia after the Revolution, in spite of his opposition to the Bolsheviks.

Kugelmann, Ludwig (1830-1902), a German socialist. A Hanoverian physician and a personal friend of Marx, Kugelmann was an active propagandist of Marx's theories from the 1840's.

He participated in the Revolution of 1848 and was a member of the First International. The correspondence between Marx and Kugelmann is of considerable value for students of Marxist thought.

Lassalle, Ferdinand (1825-1864), a leading German socialist. Next to Marx, Lassalle is probably the most famous nineteenth-century German socialist. Although it was partly under the influence of Marx's writings that he turned to socialism, his stress on the role of the State as an instrument for social reform differentiates him from Marx. His active participation in German political life laid the foundations for what was to become the German Social Democratic Party, but the differences between his views and Marx's continued to breed dissension in the party.

Lavoisier, Antoine (1743-1794), a French scientist. Lavoisier was instrumental in developing quantitative techniques in chemistry and in explaining the nature of combustion and the behavior of oxygen. In addition, he held a number of high academic and governmental posts in France and was deeply concerned with social and economic problems.

Legien, Carl (1861-1920), a German labor leader. Legien became chairman of the German Federation of Trade Unions and editor of the Federation's journal. On the eve of the First World War, he was among those socialists who supported Germany's war aims.

Liebknecht, Karl (1871-1919), a radical German socialist. Liebknecht opposed Germany's entry into the First World War, and, partly because of the party conflict caused by this issue, he helped form the extremist Spartacus Party, the basis of the later German Communist Party. He was arrested and killed as a result of an attempt by his party to overthrow the moderate socialist government that came to power in Germany after the war.

Luxemburg, Rosa (1870-1919), a leader of the radical wing of the German Social Democrats. With Karl Liebknecht, she helped organize the Spartacus Party and died with him as a result of the failure of the 1919 Spartacist rising. In spite of her radical views, she opposed Lenin's Bolshevik theories and tactics.

Mably, Gabriel (1709-1785), a French abbot and advocate of communism.

MacDonald, Ramsay (1866-1937), British Prime Minister and socialist leader. Rising from poverty, MacDonald advanced through the socialist and labor movements to become leader of the Labour Party and, in 1924, Prime Minister of the first Labour government in English history. After a second Prime Ministership, he joined a coalition government with the Conservatives, for which he was bitterly attacked by the majority of the Labour Party.

Mach, Ernst (1838-1916), an Austrian physicist and philosopher. Mach attempted to merge his knowledge of physics and psychology into a rigorous positivism that eliminated as sources of knowledge everything that could not be known by the senses.

Martov, Y. (pseudonym for Y. Tsederbaum) (1873-1923), a leading Russian Social Democrat, Menshevik. Martov was at first a close associate of Lenin, but at the Second Congress of the party in 1903 he opposed Lenin's policies and became one of the prominent leaders of the Mensheviks.

Mehring, Franz (1846-1919), a representative of the extreme left wing of the German Social Democratic movement. Besides participating in the Spartacist faction of the German socialists, Mehring was a literary critic and a historian of the Social Democratic movement.

Mikhailovsky, Nikolai (1842-1904), a populist literary critic and publicist. Mikhailovsky attained prominence as a penetrating critic, an advocate of moderate populist socialism and a pioneering Russian sociologist. He is regarded as the leading theorist of so-called "legal populism."

Millerand, Alexandre (1859-1943), a French moderate socialist. Millerand is famous in European socialist history as the first socialist to hold a ministerial position in a "bourgeois," liberal cabinet. In the early 1900's, he became premier and was elected president of the Republic. His political views gradually became more conservative and nationalistic.

Morelly, an eighteenth-century French abbot who outlined an idealist communist community. His utopia is characterized by an abundance of laws to keep the ideal society operating like a smoothly functioning machine. Little is known about him other than the fact that he is the author of *Le Code de la Nature,* from which most knowledge of his views derives.

Münzer, Thomas (c. 1490-1525), a leader of the German Anabaptists during the Reformation. Münzer represented the radical social and economic tendencies in the Reformation and agitated rebellion among the peasants and artisans. He was executed as punishment for this and for his seizure of a town, where he established a communist theocracy.

Noske, Gustav (1868-1946), a German Social Democrat. Noske was a "revisionist" Marxist. He supported Germany in the First World War and became War Minister in the postwar government. He helped organize the suppression of the "Spartacist rising."

Owen, Robert (1771-1858), an English manufacturer and "utopian" socialist. Together with Fourier and Saint-Simon, Owen is considered by Marxists as one of the main utopian socialists. While managing a successful textile factory, he organized a model, patriarchal, welfare community at New Lanark, Scotland. He also helped establish the co-operative movement and the trade union movement in England. In

America he attempted to achieve his social goals in a community formed at New Harmony, Indiana.

Pannekoek, Anton (b. 1873), a Dutch socialist and astronomer. He opposed the moderate tendencies in Dutch socialism and, in 1909, formed a separate Marxist party. A consistent supporter of Lenin, he joined the Comintern in 1919.

Pilnyak, Boris (pseudonym of Boris Vogau) (1894-1938?), a Soviet author. Pilnyak was particularly popular in Russia during the relaxed years of Lenin's New Economic Policy. He used unusual stylistic devices and merged a stark realism with complex psychological analysis. During the Stalin period he was exiled and probably executed.

Potresov, Aleksander (1869-1934), a Russian Social Democrat, Menshevik. One of Lenin's closest associates in the 1890's, Potresov later broke with Lenin and became a prominent Menshevik. He opposed the underground, conspiratorial character of the Russian party and condemned the Bolshevik Revolution of 1917.

Prugavin, Aleksander (b. 1850), an ethnographer and populist critic. Prugavin is famous for his research into the lives of the Russian religious sects. He was frequently criticized by both populists and Marxists for what they regarded as his oversimplified and idealized view of the Russian peasantry.

Radek, Karl (b. 1883), a Russian Social Democrat, Bolshevik. Radek was an active Social Democrat in Poland, Russia, and Germany from 1901. He joined Lenin in refusing to support any government during the First World War. He became a member of the Bolshevik Party in October 1917, the month of the Revolution. After the Revolution, he played an important role in Soviet international affairs. Radek was one of Stalin's purge victims.

Rodbertus, Karl (1805-1875), a German economist. Rodbertus was a moderate socialist who predicted a gradual, nonviolent development of society toward socialism.

Rolland, Romain (1866-1944), a French author. A prolific writer in such diverse fields as biography, musicology, drama, and the novel, he is best known in America for his ten-volume novel *Jean-Christophe*, written in the years 1904-1912. In addition to his literary activities, Rolland was a consistent supporter of liberal and socialist causes.

Saint-Just, Louis (1767-1794), a French Jacobin revolutionary. Saint-Just was one of Robespierre's most loyal supporters and an important organizer of the revolutionary armies. He was completely committed to Robespierre's goal of an ideal society based on puritanical virtues and to Robespierre's willingness to use terror as a means of attaining such a society.

Saint-Simon, Claude (1760-1825), a French "utopian" socialist. After participating in both the American and the French revolutions and gaining a fortune in business, Saint-Simon devoted himself to formulating and propagating socialist theories. His socialist program is distinguished by its emphasis on the role of science and industrial management in the ideally organized welfare society.

Skobelev, Mikhail (1843-1882), a Russian general. Skobelev is famous for his role in the Russo-Turkish War of 1877-1878.

Socinus and Socinianism. Laelius (1525-1562) and his nephew Faustus (1539-1604). The Socinuses developed reformist religious views, particularly with reference to the Trinity. They propagated their "Socinianism" in Poland and Switzerland.

Stirner, Max (pseudonym of Kaspar Schmidt) (1806-1856), a German philosopher and anarchist. Stirner was a "left" Hegelian who is most famous for his uncompromising philosophical justification of absolute individual freedom.

Struve, Peter (1870-1944), a Russian publicist, socialist and constitutional democrat. Struve was one of the early advocates of Marxism in Russia during the 1890's. At the turn of the century, he rejected Marxism for neo-Kantian idealism. His principal concern, even while a Marxist, was the constitutional movement in which he played a leading role.

Treves, Claudio (1868-1933), an Italian socialist. Treves was a revisionist Marxist and an ardent opponent of the Bolshevik Revolution and the European Communists.

Tsereteli, Irakly (b. 1882), a Georgian Social Democrat, Menshevik. Tsereteli supported the Provisional Government in 1917 against Lenin's call for its overthrow, and he held the position of Minister of Post and Telegraph in the Kerensky cabinet. During the civil war, he fought the Bolsheviks in Georgia. He left Russia in 1921.

Tugan (Tugan-Baranovsky), Mikhail (1865-1919), a Russian economist and socialist. In the 1890's Tugan-Baranovsky was a leading defender of Marxian economics and was one of the so-called "legal Marxists." He later rejected much of Marxism, particularly its materialism and its political extremism, although he remained a socialist. His reputation in the West is based largely on his theories of crises in capitalist economies.

Turati, Filippo (1857-1932), an Italian socialist. Turati was one of the founders of the Italian Socialist Party. He took a revisionist view of politics and was elected to the Italian parliament in 1896. He opposed the Bolshevik Revolution and the European Communists.

Vandervelde, Émile (1866-1938), a Belgian socialist and prominent political leader. In addition to holding a number of high government posts, Vandervelde was an important Marxist revisionist theoretician.

Vorontsov, Vasily (pseudonym, V. V.) (1847-1918), a Russian populist economist. One of the leading "legal populists," Vorontsov advocated a government-promoted socialism based on the peasant communal system. He was a persistent opponent of Russian Marxism and became a principal focus of attack by the Marxists.

Webb. Sidney (1859-1947) and Beatrice (1858-1943), English socialists and social historians. The Webbs were active participants in a variety of socialist and labor movements and were among the moderate "Fabian" socialists. They are also famous as authors of a series of scholarly works in English social, economic, and political history.

Weitling, Wilhelm (1808-1871), a radical socialist. A tailor by trade, Weitling traveled about preaching violent class war, terror, and the recruiting of criminals for revolutionary action.

Weydemeyer, Joseph (1818-1866), a German communist. Weydemeyer was a personal friend of Marx and persistent advocate of Marx's more radical views. In 1851, he emigrated to America.

Wladyslaw IV (1595-1648), King of Poland (1632-1648). Wladyslaw tried unsuccessfully to organize a strong monarchy and check the power of the Polish nobility in order to defend Poland against the Swedes, Russians, and Turks. His reign marks the beginning of Russian ascendancy over Poland in the Ukraine.

Yablochkov, Pavel (1847-1894), a Russian scientist. Yablochkov experimented with electric currents and devised innovations in electric lighting, transformers and condensers.

A SELECTED BIBLIOGRAPHY

ACZEL, TAMAS and TIBOR MERAY, *The Revolt of the Mind* (New York, 1959)

ADORATSKY, V., ed., *Selected Correspondence, Karl Marx and Frederick Engels* (New York, 1942)

—— *Dialectical Materialism* (New York, 1934)

ALEXANDER, ROBERT J., *Communism in Latin America* (New Brunswick, N.J., 1957)

ALMOND, GABRIEL, *The Appeals of Communism* (Princeton, N.J., 1954)

Anti-Stalinization Campaign and International Communism (Columbia University, New York, 1957)

ARMSTRONG, JOHN A., *The Soviet Bureaucratic Elite* (New York, 1959)

BASS, ROBERT and ELIZABETH MARBURY, eds., *The Soviet-Yugoslav Dispute* (London, 1948)

BAUER, RAYMOND A., *The New Man in Soviet Psychology* (Cambridge, Mass., 1959)

——, ALEX INKELES and CLYDE KLUCKHOHN, *How the Soviet System Works* (Cambridge, Mass., 1956)

——, *Nine Soviet Portraits* (New York, 1955)

——, and ALEX INKELES, *The Soviet Citizen* (Cambridge, Mass., 1956)

BECK, F. and W. GODIN, *Russian Purge and the Extraction of Confession* (New York, 1951)

BEER, MAX, *Fifty Years of International Socialism* (London, 1956)

——, *A History of British Socialism* (London, 1940)

BERDYAEV, NIKOLAI, *The Origin of Bolshevism* (Naperville, Illinois, 1955)

BERLAU, A. JOSEPH, *The German Social Democratic Party, 1914-1921* (New York, 1950)

BERLIN, ISAIAH, *Karl Marx* (Oxford, 1939, 1960)

BOBER, M. M., *Karl Marx's Interpretation of History* (New York, 1927)

BÖHM-BAWERK, EUGEN VON, *Karl Marx and the Close of His System* (New York, 1949)

BOORMAN, HOWARD, *et al.*, *The Moscow-Peking Axis: Strengths and Strains* (New York, 1957)

587

588   *Bibliography*

BORKENAU, FRANZ, *The Communist International* (London, 1938)

——, *European Communism* (New York, 1953)

BRANDT, CONRAD, *Stalin's Failure in China: 1924-1927* (Stanford U., Palo Alto, Calif., 1958)

BRZEZINSKI, ZBIGNIEW, *The Permanent Purge: Politics in Soviet Totalitarianism* (Cambridge, Mass., 1956)

——,*The Soviet Bloc* (Cambridge, Mass., 1960)

BUKHARIN, N., *Historical Materialism* (New York, 1924)

CANTRIL, HADLEY, *The Politics of Despair* (New York, 1958)

CAREW-HUNT, R. N., *The Theory and Practice of Communism* (London, 1950)

——, *Marxism: Past and Present* (New York, 1954)

CARR, E. H., *The Bolshevik Revolution,* (2 vols., New York, 1950-1954)

CHAMBERLIN, WILLIAM HENRY, *The Russian Revolution, 1917-1921* (2 vols., rev. ed., New York, 1952)

CHANG, S. H., *The Marxian Theory of the State* (Philadelphia, 1931)

CHAO, KUO-CHUN, *The Communist Movement in China* (Cambridge, Mass., 1950)

COLE, G. D. H., *Communism and Social-Democracy, 1914-1931* (London, 1959)

——,*What Marx Really Meant* (New York, 1934)

——, *A History of Socialist Thought* (4 vols., London, 1953-1958)

——, *British Working Class Politics, 1832-1914* (London, 1914)

COUNTS, G., *Country of the Blind* (Boston, 1949)

CROCE, BENEDETTO, *Historical Materialism and the Economics of Karl Marx* (English trans., New York, 1914)

DANIELS, ROBERT V., *The Conscience of The Revolution* (Cambridge, Mass., 1960)

DEUTSCHER, ISAAC, *Stalin: A Political Biography* (Fair Lawn, N.J., 1954)

——, *The Prophet Armed: Trotsky* (Oxford, 1954)

——, *The Prophet Unarmed* (New York, 1959)

DINERSTEIN, HERBERT, *Communism and the Russian Peasant* (Chicago, 1955)

DJILAS, MILOVAN, *Anatomy of a Moral* (New York, 1951)

EASTMAN, MAX, *Marxism: Is It a Science* (New York, 1940)

ENGELS, FRIEDRICH. The following works are available in English translation: *Germany: Revolution and Counterrevolution; Ludwig Feuerbach and the Outcome of Classical German Philosophy; Herr Eugen Dühring's Revolution in Science; Dialectics of Nature; The British Labor Movement; Origin of the Family, Private Property and State*

ERLICH, ALEXANDER, *The Soviet Industrialization Debate, 1924-1928* (Cambridge, Mass., 1960)

FAINSOD, MERLE, *How Russia Is Ruled* (Cambridge, Mass., 1953)

FISCHER, RUTH, *Stalin and German Communism* (Cambridge, Mass., 1948)

FITZGERALD, CHARLES, *Revolution in China* (New York, 1952)

FÜLOP-MILLER, RENÉ, *The Mind and Face of Bolshevism* (New York, 1928)

GAY, PETER, *The Dilemma of Democratic Socialism* (New York, 1952)

GIBIAN, GEORGE, *Soviet Literature During the Thaw: Interval of Freedom* (University of Minnesota, Minneapolis, 1960)

GRAY, ALEXANDER, *The Socialist Tradition* (New York, 1946)

GURIAN, WALDEMAR, *Bolshevism: Theory and Practice* (New York, 1932)

——, *Bolshevism: Introduction to Soviet Communism* (Notre Dame, South Bend, Ind., 1953)

——, *Rise and Decline of Marxism* (New York, 1938)

HAIMSON, LEOPOLD, *Russian Marxists and the Origins of Bolshevism* (Cambridge, Mass., 1955)

HILFERDING, R, *Böhm-Bawerk's Criticism of Marx* (English trans., Glasgow, n. d.)

HILLQUIT, M., *From Marx to Lenin* (New York, 1935)

HOOK, S., *From Hegel to Marx* (New York, 1935)

——, *The Hero in History* (New York, 1943)

——, *Towards the Understanding of Karl Marx* (New York, 1933)

——, *Reason, Social Myth and Democracy* (New York, 1940)

——, *The Ambiguous Legacy: Marx and the Marxists* (New York, 1955)

ISAACS, HAROLD, *The Tragedy of the Chinese Revolution* (Stanford U., Palo Alto, Calif., 1951)

JAURÈS, J., *Problems of Socialism* (English trans., New York, 1904)

KAUTSKY, JOHN, *Moscow and the Communist Party of India* (New York, 1956)

KAUTSKY, KARL, *The Economic Doctrines of Karl Marx* (English trans., London, 1925)

——, *Ethics and the Materialistic Conception of History* (English trans., Chicago, 1918)

——, *Bolshevism at a Deadlock* (English trans., New York, 1951)

——, *Communism vs. Social-Democracy* (English trans., New York, 1946)

KENNEDY, M. A., *A Short History of Communism in Asia* (London, 1957)

LAQUEUR, WALTER and GEORGE LICHTHEIM, eds., *The Soviet Cultural Scene* (New York, 1958)

——, *Communism and Nationalism in the Middle East* (New York, 1956)

LEITES, NATHAN and ELSA BERNAUT, *Ritual of Liquidation* (Chicago, 1954)

——, *A Study of Bolshevism* (Chicago, 1953)

LENIN, N., *Selected Works* (12 vols., English trans., Moscow and New York, 1935)

LENZ, J., *The Rise and Fall of the Second International* (New York, 1932)

LUXEMBURG, ROSA, *The Russian Revolution* (English trans., New York, 1940)

MACLANE, CHARLES, *Soviet Policy and the Chinese Communists* (New York, 1958)

MARCUSE, HERBERT, *Soviet Marxism* (New York, 1958)

——, *Reason and Revolution: Hegel and the Rise of Social Theory* (New York, 1955)

MARX, KARL. The following are among Marx's principal works that have been translated into English: *Capital; The German Ideology; The Poverty of Philosophy; Wage, Labor and Capital; The Class Struggles in France; The Eighteenth Brumaire of Louis Bonaparte; Civil War in France; Civil War in the United States; Revolution in Spain; Critique of the Gotha Program; Correspondence, 1846-1895* (letters by Marx and Engels); *Letters to Dr. Kugelmann; Economic and Philosophic Manuscripts of 1844*

MEHNERT, KLAUS, *Stalin versus Marx* (London, 1952)

MEHRING, F., *Karl Marx* (English trans., New York, 1936)

MENDEL, ARTHUR, *Dilemmas of Progress in Tsarist Russia: Legal Marxism and Legal Populism* (Cambridge, Mass., 1961)

MERAY, TIBOR, *Thirteen Days That Shook the Kremlin* (New York, 1959)

MEYER, ALFRED, *Leninism* (Cambridge, Mass., 1957)

——, *Marxism: The Unity of Theory and Practice* (Cambridge, Mass., 1954)

——, *Communism* (New York, 1960)

MILOSZ, C., *The Captive Mind* (New York, 1953)

MITRANY, D., *Marx Against the Peasant* (London, 1951)

MOORE, BARRINGTON, JR., *Soviet Politics* (Cambridge, Mass., 1950)

——, *Terror and Progress* (Cambridge, Mass., 1954)

MORAES, FRANK, *Report on Mao's China* (New York, 1953)

NAGY, IMRE, *On Communism; In Defense of the New Course* (New York, 1957)

NEAL, F. W., *Titoism in Action: Reforms in Yugoslavia, 1948-1954* (Berkeley, Calif., 1958)

NORTH, ROBERT C., *Moscow and the Chinese Communists* (Stanford U., Palo Alto, Calif., 1953)

PLAMENATZ, J., *German Marxism and Russian Communism* (New York, 1954)

PLEKHANOV, G. The following are among the principal works by Plekhanov that have been translated into English: *The Role of the Individual in History; Fundamental Problems of Marx-*

ism; On the Monistic View of History; Essays in the History of Materialism

POPPER, K. R., *The Open Society and Its Enemies* (2 vols., London, 1945)

ROBINSON, JOAN, *An Essay on Marxian Economics* (New York, 1952)

ROSENBERG, ARTHUR, *A History of Bolshevism from Marx to the First Five Years' Plan* (London, 1934)

———, *Democracy and Socialism* (New York, 1939)

ROSTOW, W. W. *et al., Prospects of Communist China* (New York, 1954)

ROY, M. N., *Revolution and Counterrevolution in China* (Calcutta, 1946)

RUSSELL, B., *The Theory and Practice of Bolshevism* (New York, 1920)

SCHAPIRO, LEONARD, *The Communist Party of the Soviet Union* (New York, 1960)

———, *The Origin of the Communist Autocracy* (Cambridge, Mass., 1955)

SCHUMPETER, JOSEPH, *Capitalism, Socialism and Democracy* (New York, 1943)

SCHWARTZ, BENJAMIN, *Chinese Communism and the Rise of Mao* (Cambridge, Mass., 1951)

SELZNICK, PHILIP, *The Operational Weapon* (New York, 1952)

SERGE, V., *Russia After Twenty Years* (English trans., New York, 1937)

SIMKHOVITCH, V., *Marxism versus Socialism* (New York, 1923)

SOUVARINE, BORIS, *Stalin* (English trans., New York, 1940)

STALIN, J. V., *Works* (9 vols., English trans., Moscow, 1953)

STEINER, H. A., *Chinese Communists in Action* (Los Angeles, 1953)

STILLMAN, EDMUND, ed., *Bitter Harvest* (New York, 1959)

SYROP, KONRAD, *Spring in October: The Polish Revolution of 1956* (London, 1957)

TANG, PETER, *Communist China Today* (New York, 1958)

TIMASHEFF, N. S., *The Great Retreat* (New York, 1946)

TOMASIC, D. A., *National Communism and Soviet Strategy* (Washington, D. C., 1957)

TREADGOLD, DONALD, *Lenin and His Rivals* (New York, 1955)

———, *Revolution Betrayed* (English trans., New York, 1937)

ULAM, ADAM, *Titoism and the Cominform* (Cambridge, Mass., 1952)

———, *The Unfinished Revolution* (New York, 1960)

WALKER, RICHARD, *China under Communism* (New Haven, Conn., 1955)

WETTER, GUSTAV, *Dialectical Materialism* (English trans., New York, 1959)

WHITING, ALLAN, *Soviet Policies in China, 1917-1924* (New York, 1954)

WILBUR, C. M., *Documents on Communism, Nationalism and Soviet Advisers in China, 1918-1927* (New York, 1956)

WOLFE, BERTRAM D., *Three Who Made a Revolution* (Boston, 1955)

ZINNER, PAUL ed., *National Communism and Popular Revolt in Eastern Europe* (New York, 1956)

ABOUT THE EDITOR

ARTHUR P. MENDEL, Professor of Russian History at the University of Michigan, is also the author of *Dilemmas of Progress in Tsarist Russia.* From 1953 to 1955, on two successive Fulbright scholarships, Dr. Mendel did research in Finland. The following year he was a member of the Russian Research Center at Harvard University. During the summer of 1960, he studied in Russia under a Social Science Research Council fellowship.

FREE!
Bantam Book Catalog

It lists over a thousand money-saving bestsellers originally priced from $3.75 to $15.00 —bestsellers that are yours now for as little as 50¢ to $2.25!

The catalog gives you a great opportunity to build your own private library at huge savings!

So don't delay any longer—send for your catalog TODAY! It's absolutely FREE!